9/11
SYNTHETIC
TERROR
MADE IN USA

9/11
SYNTHETIC
TERROR
MADE IN USA

Webster Griffin Tarpley

PROGRESSIVE PRESS
Progressive

2008

9/11 SYNTHETIC TERROR: MADE IN USA

© 2005-2007 by Webster Griffin Tarpley – All Rights Reserved

Published by Progressive Press, www.ProgressivePress.Com, PO Box 126, Joshua Tree, Calif. 92252.

Topics: US History; Oligarchy; Intelligence Agencies; the 9/11 Myth; Workings of State-Sponsored False-Flag Terrorism.

LCCN: 2006-283675. Library of Congress Subject Classification: September 11 Terrorist Attacks, 2001. War on Terrorism, 2001– Terrorism—Government policy—United States.

Fourth edition. Publication date: April 2007. ISBN 0-930852-37-0. EAN 978-0930852-375. Length: 240,000 words plus index, on 512 pages.

Sixth printing, July 2008. Printed in Malaysia.
First & second editions: ISBN 0-930852-31-1, LCCN 2005357439.

Art Credits: USS *Maine*, pg. 67, Guy Fawkes, p. 69, from author's collection; artists unknown. Charts on p. 72, Patsies & moles; p. 158, Bush-Nazi links; and p. 365, NeoCon family tree: Leah Tarpley. Icon flowchart, p. 77: concept J. Leonard; drawing Michael Keating. Plato's Cave, p. 346: original by Lilian Barac, © Progressive Press. Cover graphics: Abel Robinson. Faces on cover: Wolfowitz, Cheney, Atta, Blair, bin Laden and Rumsfeld. "Question 911 = ? ! !" logo: © John Leonard.

Photo Credits: p. 244, Row of explosive charges © Tito Harnisch, in Wisnewski *Operation 9/11: Angriff auf den Globus*; p. 245, Toppling tower: AP Wide World, from cover of *War on Freedom*; p. 247, Dustjacket of *Demolition,* © Black Dog & Leventhal; p. 249, "Where is the plane?" by Cpl. Jason Ingersoll USMC.

Photo ownership unknown: p. 138, Osama's double: from 911research.wtc7.net, as shown in *Waking up from Our Nightmare*; p. 244, Madrid hotel fire, from www.reopen911.org; Two women in the gash in North tower, explosion sequence of South tower, from *Painful Questions*; p. 245, Exploding tower from http://mouv4x8.club.fr; p. 246, WTC-7 collapse sequence, from *Painful Questions*; p. 248, "A bunker-busting Boeing?" from http://0911.site.voila.fr/index1.htm.

Indexed, edited, and typeset by Progressive Press in 11 pt. Times New Roman left-justified, for optimum value and ease of reading.

TABLE OF CONTENTS

TABLE OF ILLUSTRATIONS

For Leah and Chloe

E s'io al vero son timido amico,
Temo di perder vita tra coloro
Che questo tempo chiameranno antico.

– Il Paradiso, Canto XVII, 117-120

And if I'm a timid friend to truth,
I fear to lose life among those
who will call these times ancient.

- *The Divine Comedy*
of Dante Alighieri.

Preface

I was already familiar with Webster Tarpley's work from reading his unauthorized biography of Bush père, which appeared more than a dozen years ago. That is a work which I still consult regularly, even now. There are points which were made in that book which everyone repeats today. In my opinion, that biography will remain as a reference work; it is the best book on the subject.

I therefore expected that Tarpley's new book on 9/11 would have the same quality of precision. But I found that, in addition, Tarpley has created a totally new genre, a new avenue of inquiry into 9/11.

There have already been many books on 9/11. Paul Thompson has done a kind of exhaustive review on this subject. David Ray Griffin has pointed out the logical contradictions among the successive versions of the official story. Mike Ruppert has attempted to understand the context of these events.

But Tarpley has posed a new question: that of comparing the techniques used by the US intelligence agencies in creating 9/11 with the methods used by US intelligence in the past. Many people are going to copy what Tarpley has done.

That is why this book is so important. The inquiry initiated here needs to be carried further. Not everything found here will necessarily be confirmed, but Tarpley has opened up a new path. People will keep coming back to this book in order to ask new questions along this line of inquiry.

Thierry Meyssan

Président, Réseau Voltaire

Author of

9/11: The Big Lie

and *Pentagate*

Paris, February 15, 2005

PREFACE TO THE SECOND EDITION

"Why the thermonuclear mushroom cloud on the cover?" That question has come from a number of readers of this book, who probably expected to find the more usual photographs of the World Trade Center tragedy, or the explosions at the Pentagon which are seen on the covers of other 9/11 books. The mushroom cloud is there to signal that this book is concerned not only with what did happen on 9/11, but also with larger tragedies which came close to happening, but which ultimately did not occur. Among these was the threat of thermonuclear escalation among the great powers. Important material which has come to light during 2005, after the first edition of this book was published, provides decisive support for this avenue of inquiry, and to this new material we will turn presently.

But first, a note on methodology. This book argues the rogue network MIHOP ("made it happen on purpose") position. That is to say, it represents the analytical point of view which sees the events of September 11, 2001 as a deliberate provocation manufactured by an outlaw network of high officials infesting the military and security apparatus of the United States and Great Britain, a network ultimately dominated by Wall Street and City of London financiers. It is our contention that any other approach not only misrepresents what actually happened in the terror attacks, but also must tend to leave the public naïve and helpless when it comes to identifying the present and future threat of state-sponsored, false flag synthetic terrorism, and therefore preventing repeat performances of 9/11, including on a far larger scale.

What are the alternatives to MIHOP? There is of course the official version as codified in the Kean-Hamilton commission report of July 2004, notoriously a tissue of lies. A demagogic variation on this is the "official version and it serves you right" or "blowback" position, which accepts all the crucial elements of the official version – Bin Laden, Atta and the rest of the 19 hijackers, al Qaeda, the US intelligence failure, and so forth. But here the official version is endorsed with its moral signs inverted: the catastrophe of 9/11 is seen as just retribution by the victims of imperialism for the chronic crimes of the system. This is the thesis which, in understated form, underlies the approach of Noam Chomsky and Gore Vidal, as the first edition made clear. "Blowback" is dear to the hearts of a whole series of left gatekeepers, to the extent that they are willing to say anything at all about 9/11. This view has been embraced in the most grotesque form by the veteran *agent provocateur* Ward Churchill of the University of Colorado.

Churchill learned demolitions during his career in the Long Range Reconnaissance Patrols in Vietnam, and upon his return from the war became associated with the terrorist Weatherman faction, the group of police agents who systematically destroyed Students for a Democratic Society, the largest leftist membership organization in the US in the twentieth century. "Churchill briefly taught the Weathermen and Weatherwomen how to make bombs and how to fire weapons," we read in the *Denver Post* of January 18, 1987 (http://www.khow.com/img/

churchill-scan.html). Some of these Weathermen perished when they blew up a townhouse in Manhattan; they had not been well taught.

During the first few months of 2005, the Fox News *O'Reilly Factor* attempted to promote Churchill to the status of chief spokesman for the 9/11 truth movement by paying obsessive attention to his demagogic claims that the office workers who perished on 9/11 were war criminals in the service of imperialism. With this, the 9/11 truth movement was demonized in the eyes of millions. More important for our purposes here, Churchill also ranted that anyone who rejected the attribution of the crimes of 9/11 to Atta, Bin Laden, and al Qaeda was a racist who was really arguing that Arabs were genetically inferior and thus incapable of carrying out this complex and spectacular attack. Churchill is thus the leading contender for the Arlen Spector Award for the most imaginative defense of the official version so far recorded. Academics, in particular, seemed unable to see him for what he was. His posturing, which was given lavish attention by the corporate media, did more than anything else to discredit and disorient the 9/11 truth movement, precisely at a time when an advertising campaign by the political philanthropist Jimmy Walter was actually beginning to educate the public about how it had been hoodwinked.

Other commentators tentatively accept the 9/11 commission report, but hasten to add that they have unanswered questions. "Official version with unanswered questions" is the most nondescript of views, and it has not stood the test of time. Unanswered questions were a mark of courage in October 2001, and were still a healthy symptom in 2002. By 2004 this position had been rendered obsolete and untenable by the progress of research, and by 2005 it had come to embody a basic refusal to understand, whether out of fear or prejudice. But the "unanswered questions" gambit remained popular, perhaps because it was quite compatible with the continued receipt of foundation funding. On Judgment Day, when Gabriel blows his horn and the dead rise from their sepulchers, this contingent will still be parading their unanswered questions as an alibi for their political impotence and paralysis.

"Let it happen on purpose" (LIHOP) is a better analysis, although ultimately an inadequate one. LIHOP assumes that Bin Laden, al Qaeda, Atta, and company actually have at least a semi-independent existence and possess the will and the physical-technical capability to strike the United States in the ways seen on 9/11. But LIHOP also posits that the al Qaeda attack could not have been successful without the active cooperation of elements of the Pentagon and Bush administration who deliberately sabotaged US air defenses so as to allow the suicide pilots to reach their targets at the World Trade Center and Pentagon. The LIHOP view of things has been vociferously and voluminously defended by Mike Ruppert, whose book features the constant refrain borrowed from Delmart "Mike" Vreeland, "Let one happen. Stop the rest!" Nafeez Ahmed's first book also verged on LIHOP.

LIHOP is increasingly at war with masses of evidence. A more outré version of LIHOP admits that Atta and his cohorts were working for the CIA, but only as gun-runners and drug-runners, not terrorists. At a certain point, this view alleges, the drug-runners decided to revolt against their arrogant CIA masters by blowing up the World Trade Center and the Pentagon! But even this recondite scheme cannot address the absence of air defense for one hour and forty-five minutes, nor the controlled demolition which overtook the two trade towers.

In 2002 and 2003, LIHOP represented progress beyond the unanswered questions way station. But here too, as more new material has come to light, LIHOP has also become untenable, as I will try to show below. A Zogby poll commissioned by Jimmy Walter in August 2004 showed that almost 50% of New Yorkers believed that US officials knew in advance that 9/11 was going to happen – a reasonable approximation of LIHOP. The statement by MI-5 whistleblower David Shayler to a London gathering in early June 2005 – "I was LIHOP; I am MIHOP" – is therefore coherent with the increasingly successful quest for truth. Today the LIHOP position is increasingly unstable. Some devotees of LIHOP have a curious habit of reverting to a very tepid unanswered questions posture as soon as a microphone or television camera approaches.

David Ray Griffin's *New Pearl Harbor* exemplified what might be called Bush-Cheney MIHOP, although this must be qualified by Griffin's repeated caveat that he was not advancing an overall explanation for what happened on 9/11. The emphasis on Bush-Cheney as the possible masterminds of 9/11 is problematic, since the rogue network has demonstrably been around since the blowing up of the USS *Maine* more than a century ago – long before Bush and Cheney. In addition, we must ask if serious plotters would ever dream of assigning an important role to a moron, or to a man who has had multiple heart attacks, who has had a pacemaker installed and who is living on borrowed time. These objections apply to all allegations that assign Cheney an absolutely central role, including those of Mike Ruppert. The invisible government, in fact, will not necessarily be defeated if its puppets of the moment – Bush, Cheney, and company – are ousted. Griffin then turned to a detailed refutation of the Kean-Hamilton report, a task that could easily have been left to the unanswered questions people or even relegated as fiction to literary critics, as Griffin himself has suggested. We are left with Griffin's basically agnostic view, which means that we are effectively disarmed in the face of new threats of state-sponsored terrorism as they continued to emerge, especially during the second half of 2005.

Differences among these categories are worth stressing, even though they may be blurred. For example, a successful terrorist provocation generally has a LIHOP function built into it, since it typically is the job of the moles in the FBI and Justice Department to make sure that normal law enforcement does not interfere with the patsies and throw them into jail, thus stripping the operation of its indispensable scapegoats. But this is only one part of the terror deployment, and the presence of trained professionals who actually produce the results observed, which the patsies could never produce, suffices to validate a MIHOP analysis for the entire operation.

Some other commentators have, either consciously or unconsciously, advanced an outlook which might be called Mossad MIHOP. As I show in this book, it is a well-established fact that the Mossad meticulously observed every phase of the preparation and execution of 9/11. The Mossad is also known to be a very nefarious organization. But what is missing is convincing proof of a direct operative role for the Mossad in 9/11. So far not even limited subcontracting of specific 9/11 tasks by CIA to Mossad, a standard practice, has been established. Mossad MIHOP would appear to appeal to a chauvinistic mentality which implicitly believes that Americans would never do such a thing to their fellow Americans, so a foreign group, the Mossad, has to be blamed. This is dangerous nonsense, and those who profess it need to be reminded of the Operation Northwoods documents, which contemplate precisely the sort of killing of Americans by Americans they think is impossible. As far as I know, MI-6 MIHOP, another possible variant, has not been argued; here the evidence is greater, but still not enough. Therefore, my second edition still asserts on the cover that the 9/11 terror was: "Made In USA."

THE FIFTEEN DRILLS OF 9/11

Ruppert's *Crossing the Rubicon* is aware of five exercises related to 9/11 – Vigilant Warrior, Vigilant Guardian, Northern Vigilance, Tripod II, and the National Reconnaissance Office drill. The first printing of my book discusses these, plus Northern Guardian, Amalgam Virgo, and a local DC-area drill, for a total of eight. As of this writing, it has been established that there were as many as 15 drills either ongoing on 9/11 or directly related to the events of that day. This figure may be slightly higher or lower according to the counting criteria used.

911 WAR GAMES AND TERROR DRILLS	
Amalgam Virgo	Air defense against rogue state/terror cruise missiles, hijackings
Vigilant Guardian	Air defense against hijacking
Northern Guardian	Air defense
Vigilant Warrior	NORAD exercise
Northern Vigilance	NORAD deploys fighters to Alaska, northern Canada
Amalgam Warrior	Large live-fly air defense and air intercept, tracking surveillance
Global Guardian	Nuclear warfighting, "Armageddon"
Crown Vigilance	Air combat command exercise
Apollo Guardian	Large scale live-fly air defense and air intercept, tracking surveillance
National Reconnaissance Office (NRO)	Crashing planes into buildings

AWACS	AWACS over Florida, Washington DC
Fort Meyer, Virginia	Firemen (Pentagon), "aircraft crash refresher course" for firefighters
TRIPOD II, Manhattan	Response to biochemical attack
Timely Alert II	Emergency response to bomb attack

Ruppert focuses exclusively on the drills which crippled air defense, the ones we may call LIHOP drills. It is of course vital to know about these war games which moved fighter planes to northern Canada and Alaska, which introduced fake radar blips on the screens of military personnel, and which deployed civilian and military aircraft in the guise of hijacked airliners. This was one way the vaunted US air defense in the northeast corridor was paralyzed for about one hour and forty-five minutes. But even this argument has limits. Loyal military officers would have positioned their interceptor assets in the skies over Washington DC to prevent their recurrent nightmare, the decapitation of the national command authority by a lightning stroke. The fact that this was not done for so many minutes is irrefutable evidence that the commanders were not loyal. It does no good to argue that red-blooded US fighter pilots would never have obeyed a stand-down order when this is manifestly exactly what they did, for the critical hour and three quarters.

But there are additional 9/11 maneuvers which claim our attention. These are the MIHOP drills, which provided cover and operational capabilities for terror operations run through the official bureaucracy. The most obvious is the exercise that morning at the headquarters of the National Reconnaissance Office in Chantilly, Virginia involving the simulation of an airliner crashing into the NRO's headquarters tower. It involved, in other words, a plane crashing into a building. Given all we have learned about the intimate relationship between military drills and terrorist acts, it is clear that there is a strong *prima facie* case here that the NRO drill in question was in fact a control center or vehicle for crashing aircraft or other flying objects into the towers of the World Trade Center. This is no weird happenstance, but a crucial window on the entire operation.

Then there is the case of Amalgam Virgo, which did come up during the 9/11 commission hearings. Thanks to cooperativeresearch.org, we know that Amalgam Virgo 01 was run on June 1-2, 2001. It was "a multi-agency planning exercise sponsored by NORAD involving the hypothetical scenario of a cruise missile being launched by 'a rogue [government] or somebody' from a barge off the East Coast. Bin Laden is pictured on the cover of the proposal for the exercise. [American Forces Press Service, 6/4/02]" The exercise takes place at Tyndall Air Force Base in Florida. [Global Security, 4/14/02] Although the barge could have been located somewhere else, this looks very much like what happened at the Pentagon, since it is clear that no commercial airliner ever hit that building on 9/11. The 2002 edition of this exercise was set to include "two simultaneous commercial aircraft hijackings," with FBI agents impersonating the hijackers – another component which may have occurred in the real world on 9/11.

These are leading examples of what may be termed MIHOP drills, since they point towards the basic fact that the 9/11 terror operations were not just facilitated or allowed, but manufactured and produced, by activities taking place inside the US military-security bureaucracy, under the cover of theoretically legal and sanctioned drills.

As I showed in the original edition, the open secret about drills is that they often hide the real thing, as illustrated by the examples of Hilex 75 (a cover for possible nuclear confrontation with the Warsaw Pact) and Nine Lives 81 (a cover for the Hinckley hit on President Reagan). Another excellent example is Able Archer 83, a US nuclear weapons exercise which looked so realistic that Soviet leaders became concerned that it was a cover for a real sneak attack on their country with nuclear missiles. They put their own Strategic Rocket Troops and related units on highest alert, and the world found itself on the brink of an all-out nuclear exchange. (See *William M. Arkin*, Code Names (Hanover, NH: Steerforth Press, 2005, p. 245, and Benjamin B. Fischer, *A Cold War Conundrum,* History Staff, Center for the Study of Intelligence, Central Intelligence Agency, 1997, online at http://www.cia.gov/csi/monograph/coldwar/source.htm).

The principle directly at stake here is that state terrorists wishing to conduct an illegal terror operation often find it highly advantageous to conduit or bootleg that illegal operation through the government military/security bureaucracy with the help of an exercise or drill that closely resembles or mimics the illegal operation. Once the entire apparatus is set up, it is only necessary to make apparently small changes to have the exercise go live, and turn into a real hecatomb. If there is a gas dispersion drill announced in Manhattan, as there was in August 2005, it is merely necessary to replace the inert gas with a highly toxic one to go from drill to mass slaughter. A drill simulating a terror attack provides the greatest possible camouflage of the criminal intent of the perpetrators and allows the terror attack to occur through minor departures from the scenario script. All these drills try to be as realistic as possible. But the greatest realism is an actual terror attack. The fact that attempts at disruption, infiltration, harassment, and sabotage may be built in simply increases the opportunities available to the plotters, as do the varying levels of awareness of the participants, only a very few of whom need to know that a real terror attack is intended, or what the fate of certain patsies might be. To prevent new terror attacks from providing the pretexts for new wars, it is imperative that this mechanism be understood, but it cannot be understood in the unanswered questions, LIHOP, and agnostic frames of reference. That is why the apparent moderation of these theoretical points of view is so crippling and so dangerous.

Thanks to Arkin and cooperativeresearch.org, there is another 9/11 drill which can be given the special mention it deserves. My book more than any other stresses the thermonuclear war potentials unleashed on 9/11, and this emphasis is fully vindicated by this additional drill. In effect, the mushroom cloud on the cover was there for excellent reasons. The heart of the matter is Global Guardian, a nuclear warfighting or Armageddon exercise staged by STRATCOM on 9/11 from Offutt Air Force Base, where Brent Scowcroft and Warren Buffett were converging in what might have been the nucleus of a Committee of Public Safety set to govern in case Bush had to be ousted. Global Guardian involved land-based missiles, nuclear submarines, and B-52 and B-1 bombers loaded with live H-bombs at bases like Offutt (Nebraska), Barksdale (Louisiana), Minot (North Dakota) and Whiteman (Missouri). The first two became destinations for Bush that day. The Doomsday–Night-Watch–Looking Glass flying command posts were mobilized. Another crucial aspect is pointed out by cooperativeresearch. com:

> A 1998 Defense Department newsletter reported that for several years Stratcom had been incorporating a computer network attack (CNA) into Global Guardian. The attack involved Stratcom "red team" members and other organizations acting as enemy agents, and included attempts to penetrate the Command using the Internet and a "bad" insider who had access to a key command and control system. The attackers "war dialed" the phones to tie them up and sent faxes to numerous fax machines throughout the Command. They also claimed they were able to shut down Stratcom's systems. Reportedly, Stratcom planned to increase the level of computer network attack in future Global Guardian exercises. [IAnewsletter, 6/98]

Here is a portal through which the rogue network could have launched nuclear missiles without the help of Bush, as I argued in the original edition. The targets for such missiles could have been Arab or Islamic capitals, if Bush had refused to initiate the war of civilizations in conventional form by attacking Afghanistan. The target could also have been China, or Russia. We must never lose sight of the Bush-Putin telephone call on 9/11, which was the central diplomatic and strategic event of the day even though most 9/11 books do not even mention it. In that telephone call, Bush in effect delivered an ultimatum that the United States was determined to seize Afghanistan (where the Soviets had staged an invasion and a long war in response to a grab for power by Brzezinski in 1979), plus bases in former Soviet central Asia. What if Putin's response to Bush's ultimatum had been a more traditional defense of Mother Russia, coupled with a threat to incinerate New York if Bush dared to do any such thing? The rogue network had obviously thought of that eventuality in advance, and had evidently provided a back door through which they could direct a confrontation.

ABLE DANGER: 2.5 TERABYTES OF TREASON

Another important MIHOP issue emerges from these drills. Able Warrior, according to Arkin's listing, would seem to represent the big Special Forces (SOCOM) "anti-terror" defensive drill of each fiscal year. Keeping in mind the military bureaucracy's predilection for naming drills in binary pairs, we might speculate as to the meaning of a drill or activity known as Able Danger. The name would suggest that this might be the simulated attacker paired with the defensive Able Warrior. In other words, Able Danger might represent the case officers and terrorist controllers for a group of government-run terrorists (double agents, plus dupes, fanatics, and criminal energy types) used to play the roles of terrorists in the various anti-terror drills. Does the reader smell a fault?

Such suspicions materialized in August 2005 when Congressman Curt Weldon of Pennsylvania began holding press conferences about Able Danger, which turned out to be a co-production of the Special Forces command with the Defense Intelligence Agency. Weldon's main interest was in the report from a certain Col. Schaffer and a certain Navy Captain Philpott that Able Danger had been well aware of the presence of Mohamed Atta in the United States during the early months of 2000, long before the Kean-Hamilton commission said he had arrived. The Able Danger officers produced detailed accounts of how they told the 9/11 commission investigators all about this, only to see their testimony completely ignored. In a grotesque comedy of errors, Kean, Hamilton and their hack apparatus clumsily denied these allegations, then retracted the denial, then denied them again. The role of Philip Zelikow, the executive director of the 9/11 commission staff, was especially slimy, which should have come as no surprise to readers of this book. The first by-product of Congressman Weldon's maverick performance was thus to provide an absolutely water-tight case study in how, when dealing with highly material information, the 9/11 commission had suppressed evidence, obstructed justice, and deliberately and systematically lied. What else could one expect from Zelikow, the unfortunate Miss Rice's partner in a book venture?

But that was just the beginning. Weldon admitted that, in addition to observing and combating the supposed terrorists, one task of Able Danger had been to "manipulate" them. With this one word, the door was wide open to deploying terrorist counter-gangs and pseudo-gangs on the full Frank Kitson model for real live terror operations. Able Danger were indeed the terrorist controllers and case officers for Atta and the rest. This case was made harder to prove when Able Danger successfully destroyed its own database and records, to the tune of an estimated 2.5 terabytes of material – according to some experts, the approximate equivalent of one quarter of all the books and other records stored in the Library of Congress. Suddenly, all the reports of Atta and the others living on military bases, studying on military bases, and so forth began to fit into place.

During 2005, the hollow demagogy and hypocrisy of the phony US-UK war on terror emerged for all to see. Elias Achmadov, a Chechen butcher and terrorist, was living in Washington DC, not only openly, but enjoying a generous stipend from the US State Department, complete with an office, a secretary, a travel budget, and a public relations budget courtesy of the American taxpayer. The State Department pays terrorists – there was no longer any doubt, after Achmadov got his picture on the cover of the Washington Post weekly magazine. Then there was Luis Posada Carriles, a long-serving retainer of the Bush family, most recently attached to Jeb Bush's Florida gun-running and drug-running apparatus. Posada had blown up a Cuban airliner, killing upwards of 75 people.

Posada was living openly in the US for several months despite being a very illegal alien when the international heat from Cuba, Venezuela, and other states made this CIA terror asset too compromising to be allowed to roam free. He was accordingly detained, but not extradited to those who wanted to put him on trial.

SAS CAR BOMBERS IN BASRA

Even more dramatic were the terrorist counter-gang operations of the US and UK military in Iraq. In September 2005 two soldiers of the British Special Air Services (SAS) were arrested for sniping at civilians in Basra. These two, who were members of a super-elite unit called Special Reconnaissance Regiment, were driving around in a car bomb which they doubtless intended to set off near a Shiite school, hospital, or mosque. At this time, the US-UK terrorist counter-gang leader had declared war against all Shiites – a stance so outrageous for a supposed Iraqi fighter that it drew a reproof from MI-6's Zawahiri. When the Iraqi police arrested this pair, the British sent a column of tanks to break down the jail and extract them, lest they tell all. These two killer provocateurs were living proof that the US-UK occupation of Iraq was using terrorist counter-gangs and agents provocateurs in a bid to isolate and demonize the national resistance. These techniques had been refined by UK Colonel Frank Kitson in Kenya during the early 1950s Mau Mau era, as shown in Kitson's book on low intensity warfare. It was Kitson who had coined the immensely useful term counter-gang (or pseudogang). If you want to discredit a clandestine organization, then set up your own false-flag group under the same name, and have them commit unspeakable atrocities in the name of the target group. If the SAS-SRR car bomb had claimed its toll of Shiites, the usual Limbaugh-O'Reilly-Hannity-Savage chorus of fascist parrots would have been on the air the next day denouncing the Sunnis as a criminal race. We may assume that a large part of the beheadings and other spectacular atrocities coming out of Iraq were in fact perpetrated by US-UK-Mossad, acting through these obvious counter-gangs.

As I argued in the first edition of this book, there was acute danger of large-scale state-sponsored terrorist provocation, followed by a wider war in the Middle East or elsewhere during the months before the November 2004 US elections. The general outlines of this analysis were confirmed in a conversation with the author in the shadow of the Washington monument on September 25, 2005: Wayne Madsen reported that he had detected signs of intensive preparations in numerous US commands during that time frame, including especially on aircraft carriers.

May-July 2005 began a similar time of heightened risk of US aggression. In late July, an article by former CIA agent Philip Giraldi in *The American Conservative* signaled that the Cheney faction had ordered the Pentagon to prepare for the atomic bombing of Iran in the wake of a new 9/11 terror attack. It was clear that the Cheneyacs would not wait for a new 9/11 to happen, but would have it delivered on special order. In response to this, a group of activists around

the websites team8plus.org and total411.info, with help from my weekly broadcasts, began to look forward in time to identify terror drills and war games which
might lend themselves to use as war provocations.

This was an effort to put the MIHOP lessons learned from the study of 9/11
into action to shut down the terrorist controllers. The cover for the Kennedy
assassination was Operation Mongoose. The hit on Reagan in 1981 had been
conduited through Nine Lives, a presidential succession exercise. We have seen
the drills on 9/11. The London July 7, 2005 bombs (see www.waronfreedom.org/
777.html) were set up under Atlantic Blue, Topoff III, and Triple Play, plus help
from Visor Consultants. What would be the drill that would serve as the vehicle
for Cheney's desired war provocation?

Activists soon discovered Sudden Response 05, based on a 10-kiloton nuclear
explosion in the harbor of Charleston, South Carolina. The websites mentioned
raised such a hue and cry about this drill, forcing an article in the main local
newspaper trying to calm worried people down. The exposure worked well
enough to cause the drill to be shut down before its completion. This was
followed by a terror drill involving explosions in San Francisco Bay; a strange
blast in the financial district at the end of this drill sent a woman to the hospital in
critical condition. Then came Granite Shadow/Power Geyser in Washington DC,
with weapons of mass destruction and overtones of a military coup. All of these
exercises were made more sinister by the shift of the official US strategic nuclear
posture from deterrence and retaliation to global strike, meaning nuclear sneak
attack, under CONPLAN 8022-22.

The last months of 2005 were therefore a dangerous time. By some
calculations, this period was marked by the greatest density of war game and
terror drill activity since 9/11 itself. The vaguely reassuring Global Guardian was
replaced by the much more aggressive and threatening Global Storm, presumably
as a result of the shift to the global strike posture. Global Storm embraces
worldwide nuclear war using all arms. Occurring simultaneously with this were
Positive Response 06 (the drills go by fiscal years, and the US fiscal year begins
on October 1), a Joint Chiefs of Staff interoperability exercise. These were paired
with Global Lightning, Vigilant Shield, and Busy Night Seminars – a code name
for nuclear warfare. Scenarios at work here included a radiological dirty bomb
detonated in Mobile Bay, Alabama, by a country or terror network designated as
Purple, but identified with the DPRK (North Korea). North Korea was supposed
to launch long-range missiles at the US, with subsequent retaliation. The
Pentagon's primitive missile defense system was supposed to come into play. At
the same time, other drills saw the US intervening massively in Ukraine, eliciting
a Russian defensive response, thus precipitating all-out nuclear war.

Small wonder therefore that Russian President Putin had issued a blunt
warning of his own on August 17, 2005, admonishing Bush:

"I think that lowering the threshold for the use of nuclear arms is a
dangerous trend, because somebody may feel tempted to use nuclear

weapons... If that happens, the next step can be taken – more powerful nuclear arms can be used, which may lead to a nuclear conflict. This extremely dangerous trend is in the back of the mind of some politicians and military officials."

Persons of good will needed to scan the websites of the Pentagon, Homeland Security, the CIA, NATO, the British Defence Ministry, and similar organizations to identify drills and exercises that were likely to go live. These drills and war games needed to be denounced, exposed, and shut down. Activists of all types, from the anti-war to the neighborhood level, needed to join the growing movement to prevent the outrageous and illegal abuse of drills and exercises for purposes of terrorism, among other things by contributing to the drill monitoring set up by the Independent International Commission on 9/11 at websites like team8plus.org. This kind of aggressive and pre-emptive vigilance represents MIHOP in action. The purpose of such pre-emptive exposure and denunciation is not to gather kudos for how smart we are, but rather to identify, shut down, and dismantle the rogue network's illegal terror operations.

It was clearly essential that measures be taken to keep the fingers of Bush, Cheney, and the increasingly desperate neocon fascist madmen away from the nuclear button. During Watergate, when Nixon had called his infamous 1973 worldwide nuclear alert as a result of the October 1973 Middle East war, British Prime Minister Ted Heath had seen the entire stunt as a manufactured diversion from Nixon's Watergate troubles at home. As the Bush administration disintegrates, it is clear that conditions today are similar. On October 28, 2005, when special counsel Fitzgerald presented his indictment of the neocon fanatic Irv Lewis Libby, Bush simultaneously made a raving speech branding Iran and Syria as outlaw states with whom his patience was exhausted. Many cable networks showed Fitzgerald and Bush, along with Cheney, as parts of the same split screen. There it was: wag the dog, in real time. Kissinger and Haig, sociopaths though they were, had taken measures to supervise Nixon's access to the football, the briefcase containing the nuclear launch codes. In the last weeks of Watergate, Defense Secretary Schlesinger had issued a standing order to combat commanders telling them to ignore any and all orders by Nixon to launch attacks unless and until they were confirmed by himself or by Kissinger. In today's White House, there are no figures to look to who might impose similar restraint: quite the contrary. Faced with looming indictments of many of their clique, the neocons tended towards a mood of Götterdämmerung and apocalypse. The neocons would doubtless prefer a new world war to life behind bars; like the SS in Berlin during the last days, they would think nothing of letting the river water into the subway tunnels where their insufficiently martial fellow citizens were hiding.

The impeachment of Bush and of many others could hardly wait until 2007.

Gunpowder Day, November 5, 2005

Preface to the Third Edition
The 9/11 Issue: Key to Avoiding World War III

During October and November of 2005, there was great hope that the Scooter Libby indictment, new evidence of Bush's lies, the Katrina debacle, and the Safavian and Delay-Abramoff prosecutions, combined with the two thousandth officially conceded US battle death in Iraq and growing losses in Afghanistan, might bring about the collapse of the Bush regime. By the spring of 2006, it was clear that this perspective had been illusory. The Bush-Cheney-neocon regime could count on a base of public support amounting to 35-40% of the US population. By March of 2006 – after Cheney's shooting incident again pointed to his mental instability, alcohol abuse, and flagrant violation of the law – Bush was again bumping along at the lower edge of this range. But it would be foolhardy to expect that he would decline much below the 35% level, unless an important sea-change had occurred. The most obvious and efficient sea-change was by way of spectacular public revelations overthrowing the Kean-Hamilton-Zelikow official account, and establishing the criminal participation of US military/intelligence rogue networks in the crimes of 9/11.

Nothing but 9/11 truth could effectively erode and attrite the Bush-Cheney base. These 35-40% were persons of limited political horizon, gulled by the controlled corporate media brainwashing machine. They had accepted the terror demagogy, the Bush-Cheney regime's war on terror, and were simply scared out of their wits. Such hysterical fear presented an insuperable obstacle to arguments based on reason.

One is tempted to classify the 35-40% who support "pre-emptive war" as morally insane, or crazed by fear, but we must also remember that these gullible persons had been shamefully betrayed by the left liberal and radical liberal intelligentsia, the principal group in this society which might have been expected to take the lead in denouncing and rejecting the Bush regime's fantastic, racist, warmongering nightmare account of the events of 9/11 and the "war on terror" that was supposed to derive from them. Instead of loudly denouncing the official account, these liberals had prostrated themselves before it, even taking up the task of vilifying and ostracizing 9/11 skeptics and heretics.

The 35-40% were virtually impervious to arguments revolving around the criminal folly of the Afghan and Iraq wars, the suicidal insanity of a wider war with Iraq or Syria, and around such issues as Guantanamo, Abu Ghraib, torture, secret CIA prisons, illegal renditions, violations of the Geneva Convention, NSA wiretaps, and totalitarian police state measures in general. For the terrified 35-40%, any acts of genocide or aggression must necessarily appear as fully justified measures of self-defense, dictated by the hard necessities of a war on terror which had been imposed on the United States by treacherous killers from abroad. For Bush to fall substantially below 35%, and thus become vulnerable to the impeachment and criminal prosecutions which were so obviously his due, it was necessary to show parts of the 35% that the 9/11 attacks were provocations from inside the bowels of the Pentagon, CIA, NSA, and so forth, rather than from Bin Laden's myth-drenched cave in Afghanistan.

9/11 was the ultimate weapon against Bush; indeed, it was the only effective weapon – how ironic that it was the weapon which the hysterical left liberals categorically refused to take up. Here were persons who claimed they would do anything to stop the war in Iraq, anything to roll back the domestic police state. But address the truth about 9/11, where the absurdities of the official version cried out to heaven? Horrors! Never! – was the response of Noam Chomsky, Amy Goodman, Michael Moore, *The Nation* magazine, Greg Palast, and most of the broadcasters associated with Air America. From one plausible point of view, the left gatekeepers were, by their craven refusal to tackle 9/11, taking upon themselves a large measure of Afghan and Iraq (and Iran) war guilt, plus responsibility for totalitarianism on the home front.

What a wretched position was that of the gatekeepers! They were propounding the patent absurdity that, while Bush had been an inveterate liar all his life until September 11, 2001, he mysteriously began to tell the truth on that day – even if he relapsed into mendacity in the early days of January, 2002, before his "axis of evil" State of the Union speech. The left gatekeepers preened themselves on never believing Bush. If they were caught in public giving credence to Bush on any other issue – be it Iraq, the deficit, Katrina, Plamegate, prescription drug reform, or oil drilling in Alaska, they would have died of mortification and humiliation. But on 9/11, the biggest issue of them all, the fountainhead of all wars, the pretext for all police states, the true *caput horum et causa malorum* – they were eager not just to repeat Bush's lies, but to aid in crushing anyone who dared to contradict them.

Was there any doubt that the 9/11 Big Lie was the basis for the Bush regime, the Republican Party, and of all their crimes? If so, one had only to listen to Karl Rove in his early 2006 address to the winter meeting of the Republican National Committee, when this notorious scoundrel announced that "Republicans have a post-9/11 world view and many Democrats have a pre-9/11 world view." (*Washington Post*, January 21, 2006) It was clear from this that 9/11 would be the basis of the Republican campaign in 2006, just as it had been in 2002 and 2004. If even more documentation were needed to enlighten the gatekeepers, they could turn to hilarious variation on the same theme by Gary Trudeau in *Doonesbury*, including the strip published December 11, 2005, which went beyond Bush's use of 9/11 as a universal excuse to illustrate how 9/11 could be cited as a free pass to bail out clumsy shop clerks, football players having a bad day, and adulterous husbands caught in the act by their wives.

Just how big a favor the gatekeepers were doing Bush was demonstrated by the courageous observations of the famous actor Charlie Sheen, who was interviewed on the Alex Jones radio program on Monday, March 20, 2006. Alex Jones, the dean of conservative 9/11 critics, is a valiant fighter against the police state and the globaloney new world order, and I have been a strong supporter of his efforts since my first interview on his program on the day before Thanksgiving, 2001. In his talk with Jones, Sheen expressed his strong skepticism about the 19 hijackers, about the nature of the flying objects shown hitting the WTC towers, and about the fall of the buildings. He called for a neutral, international panel – virtually identical to the Independent International Truth Commission described elsewhere in this book. For Sheen, the 9/11 case was not closed.

His remarks were not delivered on prime time television, but on a daytime radio broadcast on a decidedly anti-regime network. Yet they were destined to knock the US controlled corporate media on their ear. Thanks to the Internet, Sheen's views went around the world. On Wednesday, March 22, Sheen's critique of the official version was the centerpiece of Showbiz Tonight on CNN Headline News Prime Time Live. The show's New York host, A.J. Hammer, told the audience that he had never swallowed the official story, and proceeded to give a full airing to what Sheen had said. A short segment showed me recalling that, according to a Zogby poll, 50% of New Yorkers were already LIHOP in the late summer of 2004. This was a tiny fraction of the 15 to 20 minutes I had recorded that day at the CNN Washington DC studio, and it was not one of my signature issues, but it was the first time that a 9/11 author of the full, political, invisible government, MIHOP school had appeared on CNN. Showbiz Tonight returned to the same themes on the following two evenings, and was set to continue the following week when it was stopped, after no spokesperson could be found to defend the official side. CNN's viewer poll showed 83% supporting Charlie Sheen. On Friday, March 24, I appeared on the Alex Jones radio program along with Charlie Sheen.

On that same Monday, March 20, *New York Magazine* hit the newsstands and the internet with an article ("The Ground Zero Grassy Knoll") on the 9/11 truth movement by Mark Jacobson, who had attended my lecture at St. Mark's in the Bowery Church on January 15, 2006, as well as the spirited dinner discussion with Nick Levis and Nico Haupt which followed. In this article, I had in effect the honor of being the keynote speaker for the 9/11 truth movement. Given the obvious limits imposed by the circumstances, Jacobson's article was a notable achievement. He showed people now in their fifties, sixties, and beyond that they needed to challenge the 9/11 cover-up in the same way that so many of them had rejected the Warren Commission on the Kennedy assassination. Jacobson provided a wealth of facts, more than enough to strike down the government story. He also helpfully listed a multitude of movement websites where skeptics could find out more. He quoted a 9/11 widow saying that the 9/11 truth movement cared more than the official commissioners. It was an article which served the cause of truth. *New York Magazine* wields considerable influence in the publishing, glitterati, communications, advertising, and financial elites of the city. When CNN called me for an interview later that week, they had learned I was an authority from *New York Magazine*.

The conservative Alex Jones and the liberals at *New York Magazine* had provided the best 9/11 reality check in many months. It showed that the obsolete ideological categories of left and right were meaningless husks when it came to the cardinal question of our time. Because I was the single 9/11 author involved in both the Charlie Sheen/Alex Jones and the *New York Magazine* developments, this book affirmed itself as never before in the weeks after March 20. In the Amazon sales rankings, it outclassed the Kean-Hamilton-Zelikow official version, as well as the Ruppert and D. R. Griffin studies. This book appeared to be challenging the 500 barrier in those rankings when Amazon ran out of copies on March 28, and production of this third edition has had to be accelerated accordingly. The political significance of all this is that the US 9/11 reading public is becoming more sophisticated and more radicalized, and is no longer content with the government's big lies, nor with a pale and diluted LIHOP, nor with an overall agnosticism about who did what to whom in the 9/11 big picture. Hypertechnical accounts, which focus on whether the murder weapon was an icepick, a hatpin, or an awl, rather than naming the murderer, also fall short. The public wants and deserves a comprehensive and consistent political MIHOP, and this is what I have done everything in my power to provide. My books stands as the only example of such MIHOP originally written in English; the great European studies by Meyssan, von Bülow, Wisnewski, and Blondet are each in their own way MIHOP from the word go.

Charlie Sheen had spoken as a patriotic citizen concerned about his country. Bloggers went wild, pro and con. The entire neocon faction responded by collective-ly falling on the ground in apoplectic rage and chewing whatever carpet chanced to be nearby. When Alan Colmes asked Sean Hannity what he thought of Charlie Sheen, Hannity vilified Sheen as a leftist. When Colmes responded that conser-vatives were actually taking the lead, Hannity stammered that the bereaved families were certainly offended. Colmes responded that the families had shown gratitude for the skeptics' quest for truth. For once the bully was silenced. The chronicles of neocon invective against Charlie Sheen are too long to be reproduced here. Jerry Doyle and many others took part. But other broadcasters gave space to opponents of the government's lies: Rachel Madow of Air America hosted Mark Jacobson, while Lionel dedicated a program to Victor Thorn's book on controlled demolition, and Colmes interviewed Phil Berg about the civil RICO suit against Bush-Cheney. Then, in the last days of March, political philanthropist Jimmy Walter and North Tower hero William Rodriguez, speaking from Caracas, told Alex Jones that Venezuelan President Hugo Chavez's government was considering the advisability of a 9/11 truth summit, and the hope here was that it would be along the lines of the Independent International Truth Commission.

The expected countermoves of the US-UK intelligence establishment were not long in coming. On Thursday, April 6, 9/11 agent provocateur Ward Churchill was given an excellent soapbox by the witch-hunting reactionaries of the Students for Academic Freedom in a debate with David Horowitz at George Washington University, with the self-styled Weatherman bomb expert playing the leftist. The next evening, Fox News darling Ward Churchill was given an endless segment to spout his lunatic rant about the 9/11 victims being "little Eichmanns." Hannity, who had been silenced by Charlie Sheen two weeks before, had a field day. Remember that Churchill is the most rabid defender of the official version, condemning skeptics as racists who don't think the Arabs are capable of such great things. If the US public could be convinced that Ward Churchill was the spokesman of the 9/11 truth move-ment, the official version would be invulnerable forever, no matter how many lies it contained. On March 30, in a related counter-move, Democratic Congresswoman Cynthia McKinney of Georgia, the elected official who had the highest national profile on 9/11 truth, was deliberately harassed by a member of the Capitol Hill police as she entered the Congress. The provocateur was presumably one of the Bull Connor clones who have been hired by the reactionary Republican House leadership over the past years. The media assault on Rep. McKinney was unprecedented. Still, the Charlie Sheen flap proved that the entire pompous castle of 9/11 lies was exceedingly vulnerable. Imagine what a few senators could do with 9/11! Truly 9/11 truth offered the greatest bang for the buck.

Behind all these events loomed the likelihood that a minority faction of the US-UK ruling elite, correctly judging that the Bush-Cheney regime was unhinged, deranged, off the deep end, living in a bubble, and divorced from reality, had decided to brandish the threat of a limited hangout on 9/11 to discipline these two, and get them to address the main ruling class concern: the death agony of the US dollar, made worse by the end of the yen carry trade, and by the Iran oil bourse. The mood of elite discontent was expressed by calls in the London *Financial Times* for the immediate ouster of Cheney and Rumsfeld, and by a drum-beat in the *Washington Post* for the replacement of Treasury Secretary Snow; this latter point showed where the greatest concern was. The conclusive evidence on this came in a *Vanity Fair* article by Al Gore, who noted that Bush "was warned on Aug. 6, 2001, of an attack by Al Qaeda. 'Bin Laden Determined to Strike in US,' said the intelligence community in a message so important that it was the headline of the President's daily briefing that day, five weeks before the attacks." Gore lambasted Bush for his inaction: "Didn't he see that clear warning?" asked the former Vice President. "Why were no questions asked, meetings called, evidence marshaled, clarifications sought?" This was the refurbished option of sinking Bush for his catatonic paralysis and non-feasance before 9/11, all well within the confines of the official version, an option developed in *Harper's Magazine* of October 2004, and later stressed by Kean-Hamilton commission member Bob Kerrey. 9/11 Truth sectarians would always grumble, but a limited hangout was always better than no hangout at all, primarily because of the chance that enterprising truth activists might push it beyond any limits.

A major attempt to shore up the collapsing 9/11 myth came with the Zacharias Moussaoui show trial in Alexandria, Virginia. This wretched man was a classic patsy, half double agent and half psychotic dupe, several levels of acumen below Lee Harvey Oswald, and a long-time denizen of the FBI-Able Danger patsy stable. Moussaoui had already saved the government's collapsing case against him once by pleading guilty, and for over three years his defense lawyers had argued that he was a part of a plot not related to 9/11. The government claimed that, if Moussaoui had spilled the beans, they would have mobilized to stop 9/11. If that had been the case, as I told KPFK Los Angeles on March 7, then the FBI's David Frasca should have been a capital defendant as well, since it was he who had sabotaged the Minneapolis warnings and the Phoenix memorandum, as described in this book. In fact, the FBI had all the facts it needed to roll up the patsy network, were it not for the pervasive moles. The FBI could have stopped 9/11, not because the Arab patsies were really going to fly the planes into the towers, but because if the patsies had all been in jail, they could not have been made the scapegoats. FBI agent Harry Samit of Minneapolis, a colleague of Colleen Rowley, accused the FBI bigwigs of "criminal negligence" and "careerism" for ignoring his seventy messages warning of Moussaoui & Co. But this is exactly what invisible government moles are supposed to do. Michael Rolince had been Frasca's boss at FBI headquarters, and he testified that he had never seen the critical August 18, 2001 warning from Minneapolis.

After severe prosecutorial misconduct in prepping witnesses, Moussaoui obligingly placed his neck in the noose by raving that he had indeed been a part of 9/11, since he and Richard Reid (the shoe bomber of December 2001!) had intended to commandeer a Boeing 747 and crash it into the White House. As shown in this book, Reid was a psychotic derelict even more impaired than Moussaoui, and the two of them could not have hijacked a pushcart. Both were products of the British intelligence School for Patsies maintained at Brixton and Finsbury mosques in London. Moussaoui was reportedly wearing an electric stun belt when he testified – to encourage his eloquence, no doubt. He dumped his defense lawyers, who tried to save him by proving that he was a "paranoid schizophrenic;" it was an accurate diagnosis. Moussaoui rated lifetime confinement in a prison for the criminally insane.

Other theses of this book have been supported by recent events. Why did Bush refuse to go to the FISA court to get wiretap warrants? The FISA judges, everyone knew, would put a wiretap on a ham sandwich, if asked by the government. Why did Bush not use them? Evidently because Bush's backers feared that any court supervision might disclose how the rogue networks infesting the government were running and directing ongoing terror activity, as in the case of the terror controllers of Able Danger. Bush's proposal to Blair on January 31, 2003 to paint a US plane in UN colors and fly it over Iraq in the hopes of getting it shot down was straight out of Operation Northwoods (Philippe Sands, *Lawless World*).

In the haggling over the Congressional 9/11 resolution, Bush first demanded authorization to use military force to "deter and pre-empt any future acts of terrorism or aggression against the United States," a declaration of war against the world which the Congress rejected. Just before the final passage, Bush demanded the go-ahead for "all necessary and appropriate force **in the United States** and against those nations, organizations or persons [the president] determines planned, authorized, committed or aided" the 9/11 attacks. This was also rejected, but the threatened use of force in this country clearly foreshadowed civil war. (Tom Daschle, "Power We Didn't Grant," *Washington Post*, Dec. 23, 2005) Since March 11, 2006 I have been discussing these issues with a series of distinguished guests on my program, World Crisis Radio, on www.RBNLive.com each Saturday from 4 to 6 PM eastern time.

As this book goes to press, the news is full of dire warnings of an imminent dollar disintegration, couched in such terms as "payment shock," "tsunami," "hurricane," "cataclysm," "systemic disruption," "disorderly adjustment," and "global financial collapse" coming from such figures as the head of the IMF, the Governor of the Bank of England, the European Union Finance Ministers, top officials of the Asian Development Bank and the US Office of Thrift Supervision, Danish pension fund managers and US bond salesmen. Equally prominent are the Strangelove threats of atomic bombing of Iran, or of a thermonuclear first strike against Russia and China, as ventilated in the March/April 2006 issue of *Foreign Affairs* by Lieber and Press – a stark reminder of why a mushroom cloud is displayed on the cover of this book. For those who oppose world economic breakdown crisis and thermonuclear war, 9/11 truth is the only road, and more urgent to travel than ever.

Webster Griffin Tarpley
Washington, DC
April 12, 2006

INTRODUCTION

> There exists a shadowy government with its own Air Force, its own Navy, its own fundraising mechanism, and the ability to pursue its own ideas of the national interest, free from all checks and balances, and free from the law itself.
> – Senator Daniel K. Inouye, during the Iran-Contra scandal.

This book would not have been possible without the efforts of the 9/11 truth movement, a true planetary cooperation by citizens of the world, which was called into being by the crimes of September 11, 2001 and the subsequent cover-up. I am indebted for many insights to numerous authors of print and Internet studies of 9/11; the extent of this indebtedness and the names of the individual researchers are acknowledged in the text and the bibliography. The 9/11 truth movement, its activists, organizers, filmmakers and demonstrators, have the immense historical merit of opposing those who have sought to incarcerate the intellectual life of the world in a grim new prison house of the human spirit, the monstrous 9/11 myth.

On September 7, 2001 I left Dulles Airport in northern Virginia on an Air France flight en route to Europe. 9/11 itself overtook me in Berlin. Because of the time difference, I learned of the terror attacks in the afternoon. I immediately concluded that the events of that day, because of their scope, complexity, and technical precision, could not have been possible without the massive complicity of a faction of the US political and military command structure. This was the "intelligence" that the US taxpayers were paying $40 billion a year for! not to mention 10 times that sum for "defense." It was also clear to me that the goal of this operation was a new world war on a vast scale – something along the lines of the Thirty Years' War of 1618-1648, which killed about a third of the population of central Europe. In the intentions of its planners, this new conflict was to be a population war, designed to exterminate large parts of the population of the developing sector, including the Arab and Muslim countries, and eventually China. It was the desperate bid of a bankrupt and declining power to re-assert world domination based on blackmail. It was a world-historical turn towards disaster.

On the evening of 9/11, I attended a memorial service at the Berliner Dom, the Berlin cathedral which had been destroyed by allied bombing during World War II, and which had lain in ruins through most of the communist era in East Berlin. I listened and approved as a leading prelate called for a peaceful response to the gigantic atrocity. This was the wisdom of Berlin, a city which had undergone not one, but scores of days of 3,000 dead during the world wars. This was the lesson of the twentieth century, which the neocons refuse to learn: the utter futility of war. A day later, I went to the Kaiser-Wilhelms-Gedächtnis-kirche, the Emperor William II memorial church on the Kurfürstendamm in what

Note: Arabic page numbering starts at p. 5 to remain consistent with first edition.

had been the western sector. This church had also been reduced to rubble by the Allied bombing. The remains had been kept as shell-scarred ruins, and a modern chapel was erected next to them during the early 1960s. And here prayer services were being held around the clock in response to the immense tragedy. Here I realized that it was my duty to do everything in my power to establish the truth of 9/11, and to tear down the absurd myth that was already being elaborated as the pretext for new world wars and incalculable human losses.

I issued my first challenge to the prevailing orthodoxy regarding 9/11 on October 26, 2001 at the Indiana Consortium of International Programs, which was held in the beautiful Hoosier countryside about fifty miles east of the Wabash River at Brown County State Park. Here I invited an audience of academics and scholars to think back to Vietnam as a time when the government, most professors, the media, and the pundits were all tragically wrong about virtually everything – facts in the case, diagnosis of the world situation, strategy, and tactics. We were now living through another such time, I argued. The invasion of Afghanistan, then under way, was as I argued not a military operation, but the systematic bribing of the CIA's old network of druglords and warlords, backed up with bombing and special forces as enforcers.

I gave an expanded, more detailed, and above all more radical version of this critique on January 20, 2002 at Hanover College, a picturesque Indiana campus set on the bluffs of the Ohio River overlooking wooded hills on the Kentucky side. This time the audience was larger, some 150 people in a packed lecture hall. Here I was able to build on the pioneering insights of French activist Thierry Meyssan and the Réseau Voltaire website, on former SPD German Technology Minister Andreas von Bülow's landmark interview to the Berlin *Tagespiegel* of January 13, 2002, and former German Chancellor Helmut Schmidt's incisive remark of December 10, 2001 to German N-TV that the activation of Article V of the North Atlantic Treaty on mutual assistance among the alliance members was illegitimate, since "proof had to be delivered that the Sept. 11 terror attacks came from abroad… that proof has still not been provided." (N-TV, Dec. 10) Three and a half years and many failed commissions and investigations later, it has still not been provided. My own understanding of the 9/11 events developed further through my participation as speaker and listener in the Lucerne, Switzerland conference of November 1-2, 2003, which was attended by Andreas von Bülow, Gerhard Wisnewski, Peter Dale Scott, Mike Ruppert, Nick Begich, and Thomas Meyer; in Carol Brouillet's San Francisco International Inquiry, Phase One of March 26-29, 2004; in the Toronto International Inquiry, Phase Two of May 25-31, 2004, organized by Barrie Zwicker, Ian Woods, and Michel Chossudovsky; and in the Manhattan Center conference of September 11, 2004 in New York City, organized by Nico Haupt and Nick Levis with the support of Jimmy Walter. I also derived encouragement and ideas from a manuscript on the collapse of air defense on 9/11 sent to me by my good friend Maurizio Blondet, a courageous Catholic journalist who writes for *Avvenire*, the Milan daily newspaper of the Italian Catholic Bishops' Conference.

At the conferences mentioned and others, I have advocated the creation of an **Independent International Truth Commission (IITC) on 9/11, in which a panel of distinguished international personalities, including statesmen, artists, philosophers, historians, scientists, and humanitarians would hear evidentiary briefs prepared by the leading experts in the 9/11 truth movement, for the purpose of rendering an authoritative finding on the veracity of the official version**. The approximate model for such proceedings would be the Russell-Sartre Tribunal of 1966-67; without wanting to endorse the philosophical views of its two leading personalities, it is clear that this was an effective forum in educating the intellectuals of the world against the Vietnam War, and could have a similar function in the age of the phony "war on terrorism." I have since benefited from the wise advice of Ralph Schoenman of KPFA in San Francisco, who was the general secretary of the Russell Tribunal. He and I belong to a very exclusive club, that of graduates of Princeton University who have made the critique of the current US oligarchy and ruling class into the central business of our lives. It is my hope that this book will add new momentum to the forces around the world that are converging on the IITC as an indispensable part of the effort for 9/11 truth, and thus for world peace and economic development, in the months and years ahead.

A key feature of this study is its approach to the roots of 9/11. I do not see 9/11 as an event growing exclusively or even primarily out of conditions in Afghanistan or the Middle East. Rather, I see 9/11 as the culmination of a decade-long crisis of economics, finance, politics, military affairs, and culture in the United States. In the broadest sense, 9/11 is the wages of a disastrous decade of economic globalization, and of the impoverishment and weakening of an entire society. 9/11 does not grow out of US strength, but represents a desperate flight forward in an attempt to mask US weakness. 9/11 fits within the tradition of NATO geopolitical or spheres-of-influence terrorism as it was practiced in Italy and West Germany during the years 1965 to 1993.

I reject the naïve or sociological explanation of terrorism, the assumption that misery, oppression, and desperation give rise to terrorist organizations which spontaneously express these underlying moods. But we live in an era in which political and social reality are incessantly manipulated by huge and pervasive intelligence agencies – CIA, FBI, MI-6, FSB (KGB), Mossad , BND, SDECE, SISMI and the like – whose cumulative effect is to over-determine or *sur-determine* observed reality.

I therefore contend that the more reliable conceptual model for understanding terrorism is one that situates the secret intelligence agency, or factions thereof, in the center of the process, recruiting prospective terrorists from the immiserated masses and forming them into clandestine organizations which are henceforth subject to guidance from outside, behind, and above. High-profile international terrorism is not spontaneous: it is artificial and synthetic. It requires expert terrorist controllers. Because of this, the starting point for realistic appraisal of 9/11 is not primarily the sociology of the Middle East, but rather the historical record of NATO and CIA state-sponsored terrorism in western Europe and elsewhere in the post-World War II period. For it is here, and surely not in some distant cave of the Hindu Kush, that we can find the methods and personnel which produced 9/11. If the term *grotesque* originally meant something that came out of a cave, we can justifiably dismiss the official explanation of 9/11 – Bin Laden with his laptop in an Afghan cave – as the grotesque theory of terrorism.

Synthetic terrorism is a strategy used by oligarchs for the purpose of waging war on the people – particularly on the middle class, in Machiavelli's sense of *popolo*. Terrorism must therefore be opposed. My own understanding of these events is informed by having experienced first hand, as analyst, journalist, and author, the Italian and German terrorism of the 1970s and 1980s.

In June 1978, while working as a correspondent in Rome, I was contacted by Giuseppe Zamberletti of the Italian Christian Democratic Party. The kidnap-murder of former Italian Prime Minister Aldo Moro had reached its tragic climax in May 1978, when Moro's body was found in the trunk of a car in Via Caetani in downtown Rome, three blocks from my office at that time. Zamberletti had been one of the very few Italian political leaders who had suggested a NATO role in the attack on Moro. Two days after Moro was kidnapped and his bodyguards murdered, Zamberletti attracted the attention of the British press, which wrote that "Signor Zamberletti, an intelligent Christian Democrat who has worked as deputy Interior Minister in charge of the Italian secret services, made a number of interesting comments about NATO. It seems that Zamberletti said that de Gaulle left NATO because of the dozens of assassination attempts against him, and that France, after that, and by implication as a result of that, had succeeded in keeping terrorism under control." (*The Times*, London, March 17, 1978) In another interview, Zamberletti said that an effective defense against terrorism would have to be vigilant in all directions – "360 degrees," as he put it. (*Panorama*, July 4, 1978) Here was de Gaulle's celebrated formula of defense *"tous azimuths,"* against nominal allies as well as adversaries, West as well as East, US and UK as well as USSR. With this, Zamberletti became the target of the Anglo-American party in Italy.

Zamberletti asked me to prepare a study of how the mass media had treated the Moro case, which had been the dominant news story for two months. I gathered a group of friends and co-workers from the *Executive Intelligence Review,* the EIR news agency I was working for at the time, and told them of the proposal. Out of a desire to defeat the nightmare of terrorism and provide justice for Moro, most of them – Italians and a couple of Americans – volunteered to spend their month-long summer vacation assembling the study that Zamberletti had requested. No money was ever involved. The more we looked, the more we found, and soon our study – entitled *Chi ha ucciso Aldo Moro?* (*Who Killed Aldo Moro?*) had grown far larger than the brief overview Zamberletti seemed to have in mind. The writing was done during the summer of 1978 in what was then the EIR European headquarters in the Schiersteinerstrasse in Wiesbaden, Germany, not far from Frankfurt airport.

The resulting product was released at a press conference in Rome in September 1978. It was extensively if unfavorably reviewed in the news magazine *Panorama*. The main finding was that Moro had been killed by NATO intelligence, using the Red Brigades as tool and camouflage at the same time. The cause of the assassination was Moro's determination to give Italy a stable government by bringing the Italian Communist Party into the cabinet and the parliamentary majority. This plan was opposed – as a violation of the Yalta spheres of influence, which made Italy a vassal of the US – by the Henry Kissinger wing of the US foreign policy establishment, as well as by certain factions of the Italian ruling elite grouped around the reactionary P-2 lodge, which was still secret at that time. Accordingly, my study named Kissinger, NATO, and British intelligence as prime suspects, and not the Warsaw Pact embassies named by the Italian media. Later, Moro's widow revealed that her husband had been directly threatened by a leading US figure over the issue of expanding the majority to include the PCI. This figure had told Moro that any attempt to bring the PCI into the government would bring terrible consequences for him personally. Some commentators identified this US figure as Kissinger, and here they were on firm ground. With this, the thesis of the study, *Chi ha ucciso Aldo Moro*, was vindicated. I therefore have a track record as someone who opposes terrorism; I have shown in practice that I understand how terrorism works. This is something which sets this book apart from the babblings of the tribe of "terror experts" who populate cable television and purvey disinformation.

Another thesis of the 1978 study was that those who glorify and lionize terrorism, providing the terrorists with ideological cover, should be investigated as its accomplices. One pro-terror ideologue whom I singled out in this regard was Antonio Negri, Professor of Doctrine of the State at the University of Padua, near Venice. Later, in April 1979, Judge Calogero of Padua issued arrest warrants for Toni Negri, Franco Piperno, and other leaders of the allegedly defunct Potere Operaio group. They were charged with being not just the ideologues and sympathizers, but part of the leadership of the Red Brigades. It was said that Calogero had been influenced by my Moro dossier. Today Negri is still operational from his jail cell, helping to inspire a regroupment of violent anarchist "criminal energy" groups like the Black Bloc, which represent the culture medium from which future terrorists are being recruited by intelligence agencies in Europe. After the publication of *Imperial Hubris*, this thesis should be applied to the CIA, home of what appears to be the most influential chapter of the Bin Laden fan club – about which more later.

I have also learned much from three European experts. One is Brigadier General Paul Albert Scherer of Germany, one of the truly great counter-intelligence specialists of recent decades. Scherer, a Social Democrat, was the chief of the Militärischer Abschirmdienst (MAD), the West German military counterintelligence service, in the early 1970s. Between 1985 and 1994 I had the opportunity of spending many hours with General Scherer, primarily discussing Soviet questions, but also branching out into historical matters and other themes.

This book is, after all, an exercise in counterintelligence. I do not know what he will think of my present conclusions, but I have derived permanent benefit from his insights, and I thank him.

Another who deserves my thanks is the late G. L. Bondarevsky, the distinguished Soviet orientalist and member of the Russian Academy of Sciences. A Russian Jew born in Odessa, Bondarevsky became the dean of Soviet, and later, Russian experts on the five republics of central Asia and beyond into the Middle East; he was the author of the definitive scholarly study on the pre-World War I Berlin-to-Baghdad railway project. At a conference in Germany in the spring of 1991, when the world was still reeling from the shock of the First Gulf War, I briefed Bondarevsky on some preliminary research into George H. W. Bush and his clan. I stammered out an important conclusion in my substandard Russian: "Ego otets zaplatil Gitleru!" – his father, meaning Prescott Bush, paid Hitler, was what I wanted to express. "Vy you don't tell vorld real story of bastard Bush?" replied Bondarevsky in his unique English. It was thanks to Bondarevsky's interest and engagement that I was able to overcome the bureaucratic inertia of EIR, still my employer at that time, and obtain the time necessary to write the 1992 *George Bush: The Unauthorized Biography* together with Anton Chaitkin. Bondarevsky, who at the age of 83 was also one of the world's leading experts on the petroleum industry, was found dead in his apartment on August 8, 2003, the victim of a mysterious murder, most likely arranged by the Anglo-American oil cartel or their agents. His friends are determined to keep his memory alive, and to secure justice for him some day.

The third recipient of my thanks is the late Professor Taras Vasilievich Muranivsky of the Moscow State University of the Humanities. Professor Muranivsky was the President of the International Ecological Academy of Moscow and later of the Schiller Institute of Russia at the time I was President of the Schiller Institute of the United States, and he made it possible for me to visit the Russian capital in October 1993, just after Yeltsin's tanks had bombarded the Russian White House. He nominated me as a consultant to the IEA, one of the first intellectual associations to be formed in Russia after the loosening of the police state. Thanks to Muranivsky, I worked in Moscow under the curfew for two weeks, and had the opportunity to stand before the White House, looking up at the fire-blackened structure. I saw the daily tragedy of the Soviet middle class in the streets. Russia, it was plain to see, was being destroyed by the Anglo-American finance oligarchs. Who would be next? Muranivsky died on July 17, 2000. During one visit to the United States, Muranivsky had said in a briefing: "The US would like to treat Russia like a banana republic. But it's a nuclear banana." The reality of this thermonuclear danger is present in these pages.

The present study embodies a number of criteria which I believe derive directly from the 9/11 events. 9/11 was an example of state-sponsored, false-flag, synthetic terrorism, hereinafter called simply synthetic terrorism. My thesis is that the 9/11 events were organized and directed by a rogue network of high government and military officials of the United States, with a certain participation by the intelligence agencies of Britain and Israel, and with a more general backup from the intelligence agencies of the other Echelon states (Australia, New Zealand, Canada). This US network represents the current form of the Dulles Brothers-Lemnitzer-Lansdale network of the early 1960s, of the Bay of Pigs-Kennedy assassination-Gulf of Tonkin networks, and of the invisible government/secret government/parallel government/shadow government that was widely understood to have been the prime mover of the Iran-Contra affair.

The 9/11 rogue network subsumed some of the "asteroids" of the 1990s, that is to say, the privatized intelligence enterprises operating under Reagan's Executive Order 12333. The September criminals were financiers, top-level bureaucrats, flag-rank military officers, top intelligence officials, and technical specialists; the prime focus of their operations was in all probability a series of private-sector locations, where confidentiality could be best assured by excluding elements loyal to the Constitution. It is therefore probably misleading to think of people like Cheney as the hands-on field commanders of the terrorist forces of 9/11, although Cheney appears to have been complicit in other ways. Bush was expendable enough to undergo an assassination attempt that morning; he owes his continued tenure in office to his speedy capitulation to the demands of the September criminals. As time has gone on, Bush has undoubtedly learned something more about the invisible government he allowed to take over his administration. By 2004, Bush had to be considered as witting as it was possible for a person of his faculties to be about the basic facts of terrorism.

Because of the wretched performance of the Kean-Hamilton 9/11 commission, many well-established facts and timelines pertaining to 9/11 have been blurred and defaced. The 9/11 commission has corrupted and confused public awareness of the basic facts of 9/11 far more than it has enhanced it. It is a rule of thumb for researchers that some of the most revealing information on a cataclysmic event like 9/11 generally becomes available in media reports in the immediate aftermath of the event. This is before the editors and producers have fully assimilated the party line of the oligarchy on what has happened, so they may well publicize facts which are incompatible with the official, mythical version of events. As time goes by, such heuristic revelations become rarer, although they may yet inflict fatal blows on the official story, particularly if the official story is beginning to break up. The 9/11 commission represents the triumph of oligarchical scholasticism, the embalming of what had been a living tragedy into a smoothed-over textbook account from which virtually all of the truth has been drained. This book therefore often gives priority to materials generated soon after 9/11, before the mind-control line of the regime became totally hegemonic.

The reader will understand this book better after a short note on the criteria of selection which have informed it. There already exist encyclopedias and encyclopedic timelines on 9/11 by such writers as Nico Haupt and Paul Thompson, to both of whom I am indebted for much empirical material. My aim has not been to compete with them in exhaustive completeness, but rather to offer a definite hypothesis about what happened on 9/11. This book has therefore been constructed along the following conceptual lines:

Mass gullibility about the events of 9/11 is based on unmediated sense certainty re-enforced by merciless and repetitious media bombardment. Receptivity to the 9/11 myth is correlated with a Hollywood-style, sense-impressionist naïve epistemology (methodology of knowledge), complicated by the schizophrenic and autistic elements present in Anglo-American culture. Belief in the 9/11 myth is agreeable to a way of thinking in the tradition of John Locke's empiricism, which is here formally rejected and repudiated. I do not offer information so much as a method, and the method used here is that of Plato, Machiavelli, and Leibniz. I join Plato in refusing the Illusions of the Cave in favor of dialectical reason. I assert that understanding 9/11 requires a conceptual framework; my approach is therefore conceptual and empirical, but not empiricist. ("Empirical" means basing theories on observation, while an "empiricist" believes that knowledge is nothing but the sum of experiences.) The framework here is that of patsies, moles, and expert professionals discussed below.

1. This book stresses those aspects of 9/11 which indicate state sponsorship by a rogue network or invisible government operating inside the US government and military. Other aspects are given less consideration or omitted entirely.

2. This book stresses those aspects of the official version which are physically impossible. Many dubious aspects and contradictions of the official story are not treated if they can be construed as a matter of opinion, rather than being susceptible to rigorous physical proof. The same goes for physical evidence, such as pictorial evidence, where individual interpretations of what is seen may diverge. At the same time, I urge researchers interested in these aspects of the problem to continue their efforts so that the catalogue of physical impossibilities can be expanded as it doubtless deserves to be.

3. I have sought to be guided by Machiavellian political realism, in the positive sense, rather than by the irrational appeals of propaganda.

I express my gratitude to my old friend Raynald Rouleau of Quebec City for his matchless computer expertise. Finally, this book would have been impossible without the patience and good will of my publisher, John Leonard.

Thesis: A Rogue US Network – the 1986 Iran-Contra / Invisible / Parallel / Secret or Shadow government (Sen. Inouye).
- **Top officials** of White House, executive departments, military, intelligence agencies.
- **Loyal to a private network** with a **privatized command center** (Executive Order 12333).
- **Transverses** agencies and focal points.

Webster Griffin Tarpley
Washington DC
September 11, 2004

I
THE MYTH OF THE
TWENTY-FIRST CENTURY

> In some ways she was far more acute than Winston, and far less
> susceptible to Party propaganda. Once when he happened in
> some connection to mention the war against Eurasia, she startled
> him by saying casually that in her opinion the war was not
> happening. The rocket bombs which fell daily on London were
> probably fired by the Government of Oceania itself, "just to
> keep the people frightened." – Orwell, *1984*, 127.

With the publication of the Report of the Commission to Investigate Terrorist Attacks upon the United States (also known as the Kean-Hamilton Commission after its chairman and vice-chairman), the pattern of cover-up and incompetence on the part of the officially constituted investigative agencies of the United States Government is complete. Since September 11, 2001, no part of the United States Government has offered a convincing, coherent, or complete explanation of the events of that day, and of other events related to them. Indeed, no US government agency has ever so much as proposed to prove the truth of the official account, not even in the way the Warren Commission attempted to demonstrate the veracity of its version of the Kennedy assassination.

The Kean-Hamilton Commission called no hostile witnesses, no skeptics, no devil's advocates. It ignored a growing number of book-length studies which have appeared in English, French, German, and other languages around the world. It never invited to its plenum FBI whistleblowers like Colleen Rowley (who shared *Time Magazine's* Person of the Year honors at the end of 2002), nor did it call on FBI agent Kenneth Williams, the author of the famous Phoenix memo, to testify in its plenary meetings. The Commission was, by contrast, happy to invite the obsessive anti-Iraq ideologue Laurie Mylroie, a fanatic so notorious that she is dismissed with contempt as "totally discredited" even by Richard Clarke in his book, *Against All Enemies*. (Clarke 232) As we will show at various points in this study, the Kean-Hamilton Commission represents a cynical and meticulously orchestrated exercise in cover-up and obfuscation. The net overall result of the Kean-Hamilton Commission has been to obscure even those few relevant facts which had become well established in the mainstream media prior to its inception.

Before the Kean-Hamilton Commission, the chronology of events regarding the interplay among the Federal Aeronautics Administration (FAA), the North American Aerospace Defense Command (NORAD), and other government agencies had been fairly well established by the 9/11 truth movement. The deliberately doctored chronologies offered by the Kean-Hamilton staff have turned that clear picture into chaos. Before the Kean-Hamilton operation went to work, there was an important debate about whether phone calls received at the White House on the morning of September 11 had indicated that unauthorized persons were in possession of top-secret US government code words. The Kean-Hamilton Commission has now assured us that this crucial incident in effect never happened. Before Kean-Hamilton, Congressional Committees and the National Institute of Standards and Technology had been forced to grapple in public with the blatant anomalies of three modern steel skyscrapers collapsing on the same day as the result of fire – something that has never happened even once on any day in world history.

For the Kean-Hamilton Commission, this problem simply does not exist – it has disappeared from the official narrative. No account has been taken of critical or skeptical commentaries, even when these have been the centerpieces of books which have reached the top of the best-seller charts in important countries like France, Germany, Italy, and elsewhere, or have been telecast in prime time in these same places. The demands of the bereaved families of 9/11 have been ignored – even though it was because of the persistent lobbying of these families that the Kean-Hamilton Commission ever came into being in the first place. A cruel hoax has been practiced on these families. Those who thought that an attempt to cooperate in good faith with the Kean-Hamilton Commission could guide it toward the truth have received a bitter disappointment. The Kean-Hamilton Commission in short has shown no decent respect for the opinions of mankind, and has submitted no important facts to a candid world.

The Kean-Hamilton Commission has turned out to be nothing more than a colossal exercise in begging the question. Everything that was controversial, everything that was dubious in the eyes of billions around the world has been simply assumed to be true and posited as the starting point for the entire inquiry. As a fallacy this has been around since the medieval schoolmen, who called it *petitio principii*. In the hands of the Kean-Hamilton Commission, begging the question is meant to work as an arrogant, bureaucratic act of superior power. Believe this, said the Inquisition, or be damned. Believe this, says the Kean-Hamilton Commission, or be vilified as a paranoid obsessed with conspiracies. Thus, when the 9/11 commission was created, it formed nine investigative teams. The first of these was entitled: "Al Qaeda and the Organization of the 9/11 Attack." That is a clear case of rush to judgment and jumping to conclusions, since such a finding should be the end result of an inquiry, and not its starting point.

For the Kean-Hamilton Commission is not a contribution to scholarly debate. It is just as much a part of the US government's assault on the world as an F-16 bombing Fallujah. For the Kean-Hamilton Commission is an act of ideological terrorism worthy of Senator Joe McCarthy. Behind it stands the taboo proclaimed by the figurehead of the regime:

We must speak the truth about terror. Let us never tolerate outrageous conspiracy theories concerning the attacks of September the 11th, malicious lies that attempt to shift the blame away from the terrorists themselves, away from the guilty. (G. W. Bush before the UN General Assembly, November 10, 2001)

It is a point of view at variance with the best moments in American history, as we intend to show. But no amount of bureaucratic arrogance has been able to paper over the manifold absurdities, the contradictions, the impossibilities, the outrageous flaws that infest the official version of the 9/11 events. The Kean-Hamilton Commission simply has no answer for questions about how the alleged hijackers were identified, how they were able to operate, why WTC Building 7 collapsed, why air defense was non-existent, what hit the Pentagon, what happened over Shanksville, what happened to the insider trading, and many more. For any serious, intelligent person – and there are many – the Kean-Hamilton pastiche can only be rejected.

The failure of the Kean-Hamilton Commission leaves the world with the imbecilic myth: the four airliners were hijacked by nineteen Arabs, from Saudi Arabia, Egypt, and Kuwait. Their squad leaders were Atta, Shehhi, Hanjour, and Jarrah. Their "mastermind" was Khalid Sheikh Mohammed. Their rear echelon was Ramzi Binalshibh. Their guru was Osama bin Laden, the terrorist pope who lives in a cave. From his distant grotto in the mountains of Afghanistan, Osama bin Laden, the diabolical genius of the twenty-first century, directed the worldwide network that attacked the United States.

THE SEPTEMBER CRIMINALS
ARE STILL AT LARGE

At a deeper level, closer to the heart of the matter, Kean-Hamilton has failed to indict the real September criminals. It leaves untouched the network of moles in the US government without whose efforts, both in preparation and in cover-up, the events of 9/11 could never have happened. It has not identified the clandestine command center which directed the operation. It has taken not one step towards locating the technocrats of death who actually had the physical and technical capability to make these events happen, in contrast to the supermarket-caliber terrorists who are supposed to have caused them.

All of these networks remain in place, and remain anxious to avoid detection. The September criminals with their project, the clash of civilizations in the form of a new Thirty Years War, remain at large, their desperation magnified, but their power undiminished. Think of this when you hear the strident clatter of the Bush regime as it warns the public that a new wave of terror attacks is inevitable, quite possibly using weapons of mass destruction of the atomic, bacteriological and chemical varieties. The government has failed us, and the Kean-Hamilton Commission has failed us, before, during and after 9/11. The September criminals remain in place, with every intention of striking again, then to take cover behind the shield of martial law.

We are opposed to terrorism. We seek to prevent a new wave of terrorism. We want to identify the September criminals and bring them to justice, because no one has laid a glove on them so far. We have no illusions about the psychotic Arab patsies whose antics are being used to cover up what was in reality a coup d'état *made in the USA*, a coup d'état not against Bush but in favor of a specific policy, that of the clash of civilizations. We condemn terrorism because terrorism is the means used by oligarchs to wage secret war against the people. But the terrorism we fight is the real terrorism of the real world, not the idiotic distortions dished up by the regime and the media.

The official 9/11 account has by now taken on all the characteristics of a myth. In the minds of many, credulousness in regard to the myth has taken on the overtones of religious sanctity. It has taken root deeply in the dark places of the American mind. The myth is a sensitive subject, hedged round with powerful reaction formations and fearful taboos. Challenge these and the subject will often respond with irrational anger and indignation. Nevertheless, the fact remains: the official version has never been proved. It is an unproven assertion, and in the end a myth.

Attempts to base an entire world order on unproven assertions and lies did not fare well in the twentieth century: the war guilt clause of the Versailles Treaty of 1919, which assigned exclusive responsibility for the war to Germany and her allies, while completely exonerating the British allies, was intended to extort some 55 billion gold dollars in reparations. But it turned out to be the key to Hitler's successful demagogy, and generally one of the main causes for fascism, Nazism, and World War II. Let us not build our political house on unproven assertions. Indeed, we should recall that it was the Nazis themselves who avidly embraced myth as the basis for politics: the official chief ideologist of the Nazi movement was Alfred Rosenberg, and his famous work was *The Myth of the Twentieth Century*. The story of Osama in the distant cave is already the myth of the twenty-first century.

Because of the events of 9/11, the regime proclaims, the world as we knew it has disappeared. We are confronted with a new world of preventive and pre-emptive war, of first use of nuclear weapons, of unilateral aggression, of barbarian racism and hatred, of the glorification of violence and killing, of force and the threat of force. Yet before we go willingly into this monstrous new world, it is our right to demand that the events of 9/11 – precisely because they are said to have caused all this – be more thoroughly examined. Before we accept the neocon death warrant for civilization, culture, and every human value, we demand the right of an appeal to the court of reason.

That project will be undertaken in this book. We will draw on the extensive research completed by the 9/11 truth movement during the time since that catastrophic day. Specific indebtedness and especially meritorious works will be acknowledged in the text, or in the footnotes. Participants in the 9/11 truth movement have almost always been private citizens, more or less isolated, more or less bereft of means, but nevertheless determined to seek the truth. The researchers, writers, scientists, historians, websites, and activists of the 9/11 truth movement have upheld the values of universal intellect – *la république des lettres* – as these were spurned by the mass media, the US government, and most academics. They have produced what can now be seen as a coherent body of work which is readily accessible to anyone who wants to learn. This field is no more free from aberrant theories, petty squabbles, and crank positions than any other, and not everything can be taken for pure gold, but the difference between this honest research and the corrupt, controlled corporate media and official pronouncements is as day and night. The 9/11 truth movement is a work in progress which has already accomplished much, and which now awaits wider discussion and the further refinement which that greater exposure will undoubtedly bring.

We urge you to grapple with the issues presented in this book. This is important because of the imminent threat of new terrorist attacks, organized in large part by the original September criminals. It is important also because this is a time of aggravated world economic, political, and strategic crisis, wars, depression, and breakdowns, as we will have occasion briefly to show as part of our explanation of why the 9/11 attacks happened. We must also be aware of the underlying long waves of American history. As we will outline towards the end of this book, the 2004 election completes a fateful cycle of that history – the pattern of party re-alignment which has recurred every 36 or so years since the ratification of the federal Constitution, taking place in 1828, 1860, 1896, 1932, and 1968. We are due for a profound shakeup in the party structure and the basic pattern of political life in this country.

The reason for sending this book into the world is this: if the 9/11 myth can be dismantled, discredited, and denounced before the masses, there is hope that the party re-alignment may unfold in a progressive direction, perhaps with the collapse of the Republican Party, perhaps with the split of the Democratic Party into factions representing roughly the views of Senator Lieberman and those of Senator Kennedy. Under these conditions, the wars in Iraq and Afghanistan can be terminated, and new aggressions warded off. The neocons can be brought to justice. International monetary reform, world reconstruction and economic development, vast projects of infrastructure can be addressed. But if the 9/11 myth is allowed to stand intact as the basis for US national life, for the current regime, and the Republican and Democratic Parties, then there is every reason to fear that the likely party re-alignment will represent the transition to fascism in some form whose outlines we can already see.

The dominant oligarchies of the United States and several other countries committed a serious error when they decided to accept the crude conspiracy theory peddled by the Bush regime concerning 9/11. This was a matter where a careful and judicious ruling class would have exercised more restraint, and kept more options open. The wholesale endorsement of the official 9/11 myth by the controlled corporate news media, by the two major political parties, and by large parts of academia has created a situation in which the 9/11 myth is now the indispensable basis of large sectors of American life. Many institutions have in effect wedded their entire credibility to the myth. This was very unwise. We cannot be entirely certain that the truth about 9/11 will ever become generally accepted by the masses, but if such revelations should ever occur, they will now destroy far more than the 9/11 myth.

The dismantling of the myth in favor of an account at least closer to reality will have the most profound institutional implications. The Republican Party, because it has presided over the institutionalization and exploitation of the myth, would tend toward extinction. The contradictions inside the Democratic Party would explode. Many careers would go by the boards. Because the entire society is so heavily invested in the myth, the entire social order would be called into question. Even the prevalent property relations, at least in regard to media, defense industries, oil and some other sectors, would inevitably be called into question. The current status of the 9/11 myth as the substratum of so many hegemonic institutions helps to explain the absolute hysteria of the ruling elite whenever substantive critiques of the myth arise, as they must ever tend to do.

Everything depends on intellectual activists like you. The 9/11 myth is the last line of defense of a bankrupt regime. Was the Iraq war based on lies? Do the atrocities of Abu Ghraib violate the laws of war and the Geneva Convention? Is the middle class being crushed? The regime, with its back to the wall, has only one answer, "9/11." The mantra of 9/11 is the carte blanche for black propaganda, war crimes, a police state, and thievery until the end of time, if we listen to those now in power.

And there is an irony: if the regime itself has been able to cite the need for wartime solidarity in regard to Afghanistan, the Democratic Party has had only the litany of 9/11 to fall back on. The Democratic Party has portrayed itself as the true believers in the 9/11 myth, eyes fixed on the quest to find bin Laden, while the Republicans were going astray in Mesopotamia. Senator Kerry, until he can be convinced to think otherwise, is more married to the 9/11 myth than Bush is. The Democrats are Johnny One-note, while Bush has the means to modulate. Result: 9/11 is the lever used by all factions of the oligarchy to keep the masses in submission. This lever we will break before their faces.

WHAT DO YOU KNOW AND
HOW DO YOU KNOW IT?

Many readers are by now spluttering with indignation. We can hear them expostulating: "The official version of 9/11 a myth and a lie?!" – followed by a string of obscenities worthy of Dick Cheney. But think for a minute: if you think you know all about 9/11, how do you know what you think you know?

The first identification of Osama bin Laden and al Qaeda as the perpetrators came during the day on September 11, as various commentators and announcers for cable, broadcast, and public television began floating the charge that bin Laden and al Qaeda were behind the attacks. Apparently CNN was the first to mention bin Laden, and the other myth-mongers immediately followed its lead. In retrospect, we know that many of these leaks came from two important functionaries in the Washington bureaucracy. These were George Tenet, the Director of the Central Intelligence Agency, who should have been fired that same day, but who was allowed to resign in disgrace in June 2004, on the eve of the publication of a Senate Intelligence Committee report which pilloried him and his agency for gross incompetence. This was the same Tenet who later assured Bush that the case for weapons of mass destruction in Iraq as a pretext for a US invasion was a "slam dunk."

The other prime myth-monger was Richard A. Clarke, the former terror czar of the Clinton administration who had been kept on by Bush. Clarke had a long history, of which many of his gulled victims at those hearings were unaware. He had been dropped from the State Department by James Baker III because he was accused of concealing Israeli exports of US military technology to the People's Republic of China which were banned under US law, and which the Israelis had agreed in advance not to carry out. In some quarters, Richard Clarke's name was mentioned at the time of the hunt for Mega, the Israeli mole thought to be operating in the White House. Clarke is a close friend of Israeli defense officials, among them David Ivry of the Israeli Defense Ministry.

As Clarke recounts in his recently published memoir: "At the outset of the first Gulf War, Ivry and I conspired to get our governments to agree to deploy a US Army Patriot unit in Israel. No foreign troops had ever been stationed before in Israel. We also worked together to sell Patriots to Israel, and to tie in the Kiriat [the Israeli Pentagon] with American satellites that detected Iraqi Scud missile launches towards Israel. After the war, the CIA circulated unfounded rumors that Israel had sold some of the Patriots to China. Many in the State Department who thought I was 'too close to Israel' sought to blame me." (Clarke 46) Clarke was a protégé of Arnold L. Raphael (killed in the same plane crash with Gen. Zia of Pakistan), and worked closely with Morton Abramowitz.

On the morning of Sept. 11, as the White House was being evacuated for fear that it could be hit after the strikes against the World Trade Center and the Pentagon, the first top official to say "This is Al Qaeda!" had been Richard Clarke. (*New York Times*, December 30, 2001). When Clarke arrived at the White House a little after 9 AM on 9/11, he found Cheney and Condoleezza Rice alone in Cheney's office. "What do you think?" asked the horrified Cheney. Clarke's immediate reply: "It's an al Qaeda attack and they like simultaneous attacks. This may not be over." (Clarke 2) This is the moment of conception of the 9/11 myth. At this moment Clarke, as a New Yorker would say, didn't know from nothing. Had he ever heard of strategic deception? Had he ever heard of diversionary tactics? Had he ever heard of feints?

Clarke tells us in his memoir that he attempted to collect his thoughts about the events going on around him as he walked from the White House Secure Videoconferencing Center just off the Situation Room across the White House to the Presidential Emergency Operations Center, which was Cheney's underground bunker:

> In the quiet of the walk, I caught my breath for the first time that day: This was the "Big al Qaeda Attack" we had warned was coming and it was bigger than almost anything we had imagined, short of a nuclear weapon. (Clarke 17)

This is already one of the most fateful snap judgments in world history. Had Clarke utterly forgotten the lessons of Oklahoma City, when leakers had inspired the report that the explosion was the work of Muslims? Clarke had no proof then, and has come forward with none since.

Rushing to overtake Clarke as the leading hipshot in snap strategic diagnosis was CIA Director Tenet. While Bush was cowering in his spider hole at Offutt Air Force Base in Nebraska, he conducted a National Security Council meeting by means of teleconference screens. "Who do you think did this to us?" Bush asked Tenet. Tenet was emphatic: "Sir, I believe it's al Qaeda. We're doing the assessment, but it looks like, it feels like, it smells like Al Qaeda." (Bamford 2004 91) In other words, Tenet also had no proof, no evidence, no case – just his crude Lockean sense certainty, real or feigned.

Later, after World Trade Center 7 had gone through its inexplicable and embarrassing collapse at about 5:20 PM, Clarke addressed a high-level interagency meeting from the Situation Room. Present by video link were Armitage of State, General Myers of the Joint Chiefs of Staff (JCS), and other important officials. Clarke stated: "Okay, we all know this was al Qaeda. FBI and CIA will develop the case and see if I'm right. We want the truth but, in the meantime, let's go with the assumption it's al Qaeda. What's next?" (Clarke 23) Before he went to bed in the White House, Bush jotted a note to himself: "The Pearl Harbor of the 21st century took place today. We think it's Osama bin Laden." (Bamford 2004 92)

Given the fecklessness of Bush, Cheney, and Rice, Richard Clarke was running the US government on 9/11, and it was he who made the myth of the exclusive responsibility of al Qaeda/bin Laden into the official policy of the US. Clarke can thus claim pride of place as the originator of the 9/11 myth. And Clarke was more than a mythograph. Clarke also shared in the responsibility for the bungling and stupid attack on an aspirin factory in Khartoum, Sudan, after the bombing of US embassies in east Africa in the summer of 1998. If there were an Oscar for deception, Clarke's performance at the Kean-Hamilton Commission hearings in April 2004 would have won it. It was that virtuoso performance which launched Clarke on his current career as a television commentator predicting imminent WMD terrorist attacks on this country and advocating the speedy imposition of martial law. We will hear more about this gentleman later.

All we need to note right now is that anyone would be foolish to buy a used car from Clarke or Tenet.

Another early official fingering of Osama bin Laden as the guilty party came from Secretary of State Colin Powell on September 13. At this point Powell was competing for attention with the fulminations and *Schrecklichkeit,* the awfulness of neocons like Wolfowitz, who was ranting that the US would "end states harboring terrorism," and would do so unilaterally, without reference to the collective security of the United Nations. Already voices of caution were being raised about another ill-prepared rush to judgment. Professor Paul Rogers, of Bradford University's peace department, warned against assuming Middle East extremists were behind the tragedy. "We've been here before. With Oklahoma, everybody assumed it was Middle East [terrorists], then it turned out to be home-grown Timothy McVeigh," he said. "Again with the pipe bomb in Atlanta, it turned out to be domestic." (*Guardian,* September 11, 2001)

In any event, this was the same Colin Powell who perjured himself before the United Nations Security Council in February 2003 on the question of Iraq's alleged weapons of mass destruction. This was the same Colin Powell who alleged mobile biological weapons labs, chemical weapons dispensers, and tubes being used for centrifuges in the process of uranium enrichment. This was the same Colin Powell who committed the most spectacular perjury in the history of the United Nations Security Council.

On September 14 the FBI, which had known nothing about anything before the attacks, published its infamous list of nineteen hijackers. As we will soon see, the mortality rate among those supposed kamikazes was less than 100%, with five, maybe seven of the suspects named turning up alive and well in the days after this list was published. More importantly, this was a list prepared by the same FBI which had been responsible for the Waco, TX massacre of men, women, and children in 1992, the agency that illegally withheld documents in the capital murder trial of Timothy McVeigh – an abuse which ought to have caused his conviction to be thrown out, but which only caused it to be delayed. This is the agency whose vaunted Crime Lab turned out to be a sewer of incompetence and corruption. This is the same FBI which clumsily attempted to entrap and frame the innocent Richard Jewel during the 1996 Atlanta Olympic games, while the real culprit went free. This is the same FBI which persecuted the Chinese-American scientist Wen Ho Lee without any grounds, accusing him of having transferred secrets to the People's Republic of China. This is the same FBI which permitted the Soviet mole Robert Hanssen to operate inside it for fifteen years. This is the agency which ostracized John O'Neill, and which ignored the Phoenix memorandum and Colleen Rowley's warnings from Minneapolis. This is the same FBI which could not capture the Unabomber over decades, until his own brother turned him in. This is the same agency which, over the previous months, in the words of Governor Kean of the 9/11 commission, "failed and failed and failed and failed and failed."

Are we then to believe that on September 14 this troubled and incompetent agency enjoyed a brief interlude of success, as represented by the list of the 19? And if they did succeed that day, they must have soon lapsed back into incompetence again, as seen in their utter failure to prevent the October 2001 anthrax attacks, or ever to identify the perpetrator, perhaps because the anthrax in question was weapons-grade material which had come from a US military lab, probably Fort Detrick, Maryland. This was the same FBI whose main activity after 9/11 seemed to consist in confiscating relevant evidence and tampering with witnesses, telling them they had not seen what they knew they had. Anyone familiar with the record will have a very hard time taking seriously such allegations coming from the discredited, dysfunctional FBI.

BUSH AS INVETERATE LIAR

The definitive identification of Osama bin Laden and al Qaeda as the authors of the atrocity came only on September 20, in Bush's address to a joint session of Congress. Bush stated:

> The evidence we have gathered all points to a collection of loosely affiliated terrorist organizations known as al Qaeda. They are the murderers indicted for bombing American embassies in Tanzania and Kenya, and responsible for the bombing of the USS *Cole*. [...] This group and its leader – a person named Osama bin Laden – are linked to many other organizations in different countries, including the Egyptian Islamic Jihad and the Islamic Movement of Uzbekistan. There are thousands of these terrorists in more than 60 countries. They are recruited from their own nations and neighborhoods and brought to camps in places like Afghanistan, where they are trained in the tactics of terror. They are sent back to their homes or sent to hide in countries around the world to plot evil and destruction. The leadership of al Qaeda has great influence in Afghanistan and supports the Taliban regime in controlling most of that country. In Afghanistan, we see al Qaeda's vision for the world. [...] And tonight, the United States of America makes the following demands on the Taliban: deliver to the United States authorities all the leaders of al Qaeda who hide in your land. [...] These demands are not open to negotiation or discussion. The Taliban must act, and act immediately. They will hand over the terrorists, or they will share their fate. [...] Our war on terror begins with al Qaeda, but it does not end there. It will not end until every terrorist group of global reach has been found, stopped, and defeated. (Bush 10-11)

Here we can see how inextricably the naming of bin Laden and al Qaeda is bound up with the unilateral preventive-war doctrine, the attack on Afghanistan, and the aggression against Iraq. But let us put these remarks into context. Some months later, delivering his January 2003 State of the Union address from the same podium in the well of the House of Representatives, this same Bush intoned:

> The British government has learned that Saddam Hussein recently sought significant quantities of uranium from Africa. (January 28, 2003)

These infamous sixteen words added up to one Big Lie in Dr. Goebbels' sense, as has been amply demonstrated. In the same speech this same Bush claimed:

> We've also discovered through intelligence that Iraq has a growing fleet of manned and unmanned aerial vehicles that could be used to disperse chemical and biological weapons across broad areas. We're concerned that Iraq is exploring ways of using these UAVs for missions targeting the United States. (January 28, 2003)

No such vehicles ever existed. This same Bush also alleged:

> From three Iraqi defectors we know that Iraq, in the late 1990s, had several mobile biological weapons labs. These are designed to produce germ warfare agents and can be moved from place to place to evade inspectors. Saddam Hussein has not disclosed these facilities. He has given no evidence that he has destroyed them. (January 28, 2003)

Mobile labs of the type described by Bush have never been found in Iraq. Experts have speculated that these wildly exaggerated reports were based on vans used for public health purposes, or perhaps ice cream trucks. On another occasion the very same Bush asserted:

> The evidence indicates that Iraq is reconstituting its nuclear weapons program. Saddam Hussein has had numerous meetings with Iraqi nuclear scientists, a group he calls his "nuclear mujahedeen," his nuclear holy warriors. (October 7, 2002)

But the renewed nuclear program turned out to be a chimera, most likely invented by the neocon darling, convicted bank embezzler, and betrayer of American state secrets, Ahmed Chalabi, to justify his $400,000 monthly stipend provided by the American taxpayer. This was the same Bush who had conjured up the specter of an Iraqi nuclear attack on the United States:

> Facing clear evidence of peril, we cannot wait for the final proof, the smoking gun that could come in the form of a mushroom cloud. (Cincinnati, Ohio, October 2, 2002)

The Internet teems with websites dedicated primarily to keeping up with Bush's legendary, picaresque mendacity. Bush has lied about the cost of his prescription drug boondoggle, about nonexistent economic reports he claimed had buttressed his economic prognostications, about all spheres of policy. He has lied about funding first responders, grants for port security, payments to children's hospitals, and veterans' benefits. The tenant of the White House has a troubled relation to the very concept of truth.

This is the man who has acquired an unparalleled reputation at home and abroad as a liar – except in those quarters, like the Office of Canadian Prime Minister Chrétien, where he was dismissed as a moron. This is an administration in which blatant lying has become part of the daily routine – in part because of neocon guru Leo Strauss's theory that truth is dangerous for the masses, and rulers therefore have to be esoteric, that is, lie through their teeth. But whether Bush is a cretin or a liar, his statements offer no sufficient basis for falling in with the neocons in their march towards endless war against the entire world.

Knowing what we knew as of late 2004, no person of good judgment could ever accept statements from the current regime at face value. Nevertheless, otherwise intelligent people who would not dream of believing Bush about Iraq or other issues are content to swallow his biggest whopper of them all: his 9/11 story. This doublethink must end. The Bush regime is a castle of lies and fabrications, and the keystone of all of them is the 9/11 myth.

It is now proverbial in Washington to remark that there is no proof linking Saddam Hussein to 9/11, and this is certainly true. But, by the very same token, there is also no proof in the public domain anywhere that adds up to a case against Osama bin Laden and al Qaeda. We should point out that we hold no brief for the misfit sheikh and his sociopathic followers. Bin Laden was a creation of the CIA, and his al Qaeda followers, to the extent that they exist at all, are doubtless individuals characterized by a surfeit of criminal intent. But we must not join the anonymous CIA agent author of the recent book *Imperial Hubris* in portraying the inept and unstable bin Laden as a genius. Taken by themselves, bin Laden and his band represent supermarket-caliber terrorists, capable of bombing a shopping center, or of destroying a bus. Any capabilities above and beyond this can only be explained through assistance provided by intelligence agencies, primarily but not limited to the American ones.

Presumably, there is no doubt that bin Laden and his benighted gaggle would have desired to inflict destruction on the scale of 9/11. What is at issue is their physical and technical capability of doing so on their own in the universe as we otherwise know it to be constituted. From this point of view, bin Laden and company emerge perhaps as actors in the plot, but playing the parts of patsies, dupes, fall-guys, or useful idiots. The main point remains that Tenet, Clarke, Powell, the FBI, and Bush have produced no convincing evidence to establish the 19 Muslim men, al Qaeda, and bin Laden as the authors of the crimes.

Another Bush administration mythograph has been Donald Rumsfeld, the Secretary of Defense. But Rumsfeld as well has a troubled relation to truth. In a press conference, he was asked if he planned to lie in order to protect state secrets. Rumsfeld boasted that he was clever enough to keep secrets in other ways, but that his underlings might have to preserve secrecy any way they could:

Rumsfeld: Of course, this conjures up Winston Churchill's famous phrase when he said – don't quote me on this, okay? I don't want to be quoted on this, so don't quote me. He said sometimes the truth is so precious that it must be accompanied by a bodyguard of lies.... That is a piece of history, and I bring it up just for the sake of background. I don't recall that I've ever lied to the press, I don't intend to, and it seems to me that there will not be reason for it. There are dozens of ways to avoid having to put yourself in a position where you're lying. And I don't do it.

Reporter: That goes for everybody in the Department of Defense?

Rumsfeld: You've got to be kidding. (Laughter.)

(September 25, 2001)

Theodore Olson, together with his wife Barbara Olson, had been the host of a salon which served in 1998-1999 as a meeting place for one of the principal cliques supporting the Clinton impeachment. This group included the late *Wall Street Journal* editor Robert Bartley, Supreme Court Justice Clarence Thomas, Federal Appellate Judge Robert Silberman, failed Supreme Court candidate Robert Bork, and other militant reactionaries. Olson had on one occasion lectured the US Supreme Court that "it is easy to imagine an infinite number of situations...where government officials might quite legitimately have reasons to give false information out." (Yahoo News, March 22, 2001) Mrs. Olson was later counted among the victims of 9/11; we will return to her story.

In neocon philosophy, lying has been raised to a fine art. Let us take the case of William Kristol, a leading Washington Straussian, and founder of the Project for a New American Century, a congeries of warmongers. Kristol told Nina J. Easton, the author of a profile of some top neocon leaders of the 1990s, *Gang of Five,* that "One of the main teachings [of Strauss] is that all politics are limited and none of them is really based on the truth. So there's a certain philosophic disposition where you have some distance from these political fights....You don't take yourself or your causes as seriously as you would if you thought this was 100% 'truth.' Political movements are always full of partisans fighting for their opinion. But that's very different from 'the truth.'" With the help of money from Rupert Murdoch, Kristol has cultivated the art of the Goebbels Big Lie since 1995 in his weekly magazine, the *Weekly Standard,* the neocon house organ.

But discredited as Tenet, Clarke, Powell, the FBI, Rumsfeld, Kristol, and Bush may appear, perhaps other proof has been offered since? No.

In the days right after the attacks, Colin Powell promised the world a white paper or white book to set forth the contentions of the United States government about what had happened, with supporting evidence. Powell did this on NBC's *Meet the Press,* where the following exchange occurred on September 23, 2001:

Question: Are you absolutely convinced that Osama bin Laden was responsible for this attack?

Secretary Powell: I am absolutely convinced that the al Qaeda network, which he heads, was responsible for this attack. [...]

Question: Will you release publicly a white paper, which links him and his organization to this attack, to put people at ease?

Secretary Powell: We are hard at work bringing all the information together, intelligence information, law enforcement information. And I think, in the near future, we will be able to put out a paper, a document, that will describe quite clearly the evidence we have linking him to the attack. And also, remember, he has been linked to previous attacks against US interests and he was already indicted for earlier attacks against the United States. (www.state.gov/secretary/rm/2001/5012.htm)

The following day, September 24, saw a front-page article in the *New York Times* which bragged that Powell's evidence "reaches from the southern tip of Manhattan to the foothills of the Hindu Kush mountains of Afghanistan." However, there was clearly something wrong with this; since Powell somewhat obliquely retracted his promise in an appearance with Bush at the White House rose garden, also on September 24. And on that same afternoon, Bush's spokesman Ari Fleischer, a past master of mendacity, said that Powell had been the victim of a misunderstanding. No white paper would be forthcoming, he suggested. According to Fleischer, much of the information on bin Laden was classified, and making it public would compromise US intelligence methods and sources.

Even the press trollops in the White House briefing room rebelled at this attempted sleight of hand. A reporter challenged Ari, asking if there was in fact "any plan to present public evidence so that the average citizen, not just Americans, but people all over the world can understand the case against Bin Laden." Fleischer disappeared in a cloud of verbiage: "In a democracy it's always important to provide the maximum amount of information possible. But I think the American people also understand that there are going to be times when that information cannot immediately be forthcoming." As of this writing, it still has not been forthcoming.

Bush himself rejected any white paper. He said that any such publication may "make the war more difficult to win." (AP, September 24, 2001) Amidst much embarrassment, the Bush regime quickly fell back on the following ploy: they would assemble a watertight case against bin Laden, but this was so sensitive that it could only be shown to governments. We must always bear in mind that these assertions were not presented in the manner of a scholarly debate, but as part of brutal pressure on sovereign states to yield to Bush's Manichean *Diktat*.

Even though Bush did not have enough information on the 9/11 events to put out a credible white paper, he nevertheless ordered the FBI to curtail their investigation of the case. The FBI order to stop probing described the investigation done so far as "the most exhaustive in its history." A government official said in an understatement that "The investigative staff has to be made to understand that we're not trying to solve a crime now."

BANKRUPT LEFTISTS

Not just the impotence, but the intellectual and moral bankruptcy of many US leftists was pitilessly displayed by the events of 9/11. Many who would never dream of believing Bush or the FBI on matters far less important were willing to swallow the entire official story this time around. Noam Chomsky went so far as to issue a lengthy interview in the wake of 9/11; he even had it published as a small book. This passage is at the heart of the matter:

> Q: NATO is keeping quiet until they find out whether the attack was internal or external. How do you interpret this?

> Chomsky: I do not think that is the reason for NATO's hesitation. There is no serious doubt that the attack was "external." [...]

> Q: Could you say something about connivance and the role of America secret service?

> Chomsky: I don't quite understand the question. This attack was surely an enormous shock and surprise to the intelligence services of the West, including those of the United States. (Chomsky 17)

This leaves our poor Chomsky far to the right of the 9/11 euroskeptics – and that means foreign ministers, defense ministers, and generals – in the NATO ministerial council! Michael Parenti's book on the terrorism trap falls into it, at least as far as the 9/11 official story is concerned. Amy Goodman of the *Democracy Now!* radio program banned all criticism of the official 9/11 story, while proclaiming her own superlative courage in tackling issues like East Timor. When she finally let the dignified academic David Ray Griffin come on her show, she insisted on balancing him with the bilious character assassin Chip Berlet, who knows less than nothing about 9/11. Perhaps his qualifications are elsewhere; according to leftgatekeepers.com, Goodman and Berlet are both financed by the Ford Foundation.

The left wing of the Democratic Party, grouped around *The Nation* magazine, was rudderless. Some time after 9/11 this magazine produced an anthology of its most important post-9/11 articles. A key contributor to this collection was Jonathan Schell, who wrote in his introduction: "It was clear from the start that Islamic fundamentalists were responsible, almost certainly in the service of the Al Qaeda terrorist organization, but the magnitude of the force involved remained hazy in the extreme." (Vanden Heuvel xv) Other articles in the collection, some by very distinguished and well-meaning authors, may have more or less merit, but they do not rise above this inadequate level.

The US left might object all it liked to the consequences which Bush derived from his fabricated 9/11 premise, but unless those leftists were willing to attack the premise, it was clear that their efforts would not be effective. Even in the pages of *The Nation*, it was the neocon bully Christopher Hitchens, billed until only yesterday as the "last Marxist," who seemed to carry the day, thanks to the refusal of all the others to challenge the myth he shamelessly used to club them into submission.

Some governments found ways to leak their estimate of Bush's alleged proof. One was the government of Pakistan, which had been placed under a US war ultimatum to cooperate in an attack on Afghanistan. Here the distinguished retired military leader General Mirza Aslam Beg told an interviewer some months after the fact that the "evidence" provided to Pakistan's Musharraf government "would not hold in a court of law, because of the inherent weaknesses." (EIR, December 10, 2001) In a newspaper interview, Gen. Beg insisted that the attacks had been the work of highly-trained experts "who used high technology for destruction." He argued that even ordinary trained pilots could not have carried out the missions observed. (*Nawa-Waqt*, September 13, 2001)[1]

Egyptian strategic analyst Tal'at Muslim argued in *al-Akhbar* of Cairo that the resources available to Arab and Islamic terror organizations were "well below" what was plainly necessary to carry out operations on the scale of 9/11. (September 13, 2001) In the Palestinian paper *al-Quds*, Hatim Abu Sha'ban found that the US authorities were searching for the perpetrators in entirely the wrong places. "They accused...the least likely to be perpetrators in light of the operation's nature, which requires great planning capabilities, knowledge of information, and mobility on the part of the criminals who committed this terrorist operation." (September 18, 2001)

The Saudi government complained that its citizens were being accused of crimes, but that the US had provided no hard evidence. Saudi Interior Minister Prince Nayef said that he viewed Osama bin Laden more "as a tool" than as mastermind of the September 11 attacks. "He's at the top of the pyramid from the media point of view, but from my personal views and conviction, I don't think he's at the top of the pyramid," commented Prince Nayef. US officials were claiming that 15 of the 19 hijackers were Saudis. But Nayef noted that "until now, we have no evidence that assures us they are related to September 11. We have not received anything in this regard from the United States." (*New York Times*, December 10, 2001)

Some indication of the problems encountered by the US bureaucracy in trying to pin 9/11 on bin Laden were reflected in a *Wall Street Journal* article entitled "Faint Trail: It's Surprisingly Tough To Pin Terror Attacks on the 'Prime Suspect.'" Here the paucity of evidence was the dominant note. Such evidence as did exist was largely circumstantial, the *Journal* noted, such as ties of suspected

---

[1] Citations from newspapers of the Arab and Islamic world are from Cameron S. Brown, "The Shot Heard Round the World: Middle East Reactions to September 11," in *Middle East Review of International Affairs*, vol. 5, no. 4, December 2001.

hijacker Mohammed Atta to Egyptian Islamic Jihad, which allegedly was part of bin Laden's al Qaeda; the presence of one hijacker in Malaysia in January 2000, meeting with someone linked to the bombing of the USS *Cole*, which was in turn allegedly linked to bin Laden; communications intercepts showing Al Qaeda operatives had some advanced knowledge of the strikes; or that two of the suspected hijackers were perhaps linked to a suspected bin Laden operative in Boston. The *Journal* conceded that the issue of proof was a key component of US ability to enlist support of Islamic countries such as Pakistan, Saudi Arabia, Egypt, Jordan, and perhaps Syria. "The issue of proof is no small matter," one Administration official was cited as observing. But the US case was plainly a lame one, with an unidentified intelligence official concluding weakly that "no information has come up that suggests that bin Laden wasn't involved." None of this could even begin to explain how these rag-tag forces could mount such a spectacular action. Here was surely no justification for abandoning the entire edifice of international law, which had been formed in large part as a result of wars in which tens of millions of people had perished.

BLAIR'S 9/11 DOSSIER: THE CLIFF'S NOTES VERSION

With the US regime struggling, into the breach rushed Tony Blair, a glib and slippery apologist for war. On October 2, Blair's office in Number 10 Downing Street released the first of his celebrated dossiers. It was entitled "Responsibility for the Terrorist Atrocities in the United States." Unfortunately, Blair's dossier was obliged to begin on an uncertain note: "This document does not purport to provide a prosecutable case against Osama bin Laden in a court of law." Why not, given what is at stake? Answer: "Intelligence often cannot be used evidentially, due both to the strict rules of admissibility and to the need to protect the safety of sources. But on the basis of all the information available HMG [Her Majesty's Government] is confident of its conclusions as expressed in this document." Of course, this means that since the proof may be insufficient, we are expected to believe Blair & Co. on the basis of their general integrity and credibility. This is a controversial point, to which we will soon return.

Blair's main finding:

> The clear conclusions reached by the government are: Osama bin Laden and al-Qaeda, the terrorist network which he heads, planned and carried out the atrocities on 11 September 2001; Osama bin Laden and al-Qaeda retain the will and the resources to carry out further atrocities; The United Kingdom, and United Kingdom nationals are potential targets; and Osama bin Laden and al-Qaeda were able to commit these atrocities because of their close alliance with the Taliban regime, which allowed them to operate with impunity in pursuing their terrorist activity." (Blair at www.counterpunch.org/dossier1.html, 1)

Blair's dossier then went on for 16 of its 19 pages reciting the nefarious deeds of which bin Laden had been accused: bin Laden has worked with the Taliban, attacked the USS *Cole*, and bombed the US embassies in East Africa. He had doubtless issued bloodthirsty calls for murder against the US and its citizens. As for his purported claims of responsibility, they could simply be the ravings of a megalomaniac. But none of this adds up to 9/11 or anything approaching it. If working in favor of the Taliban were a crime, it would have been necessary to indict Henry Kissinger, who lobbied Congress in favor of Unocal's pipeline project there. And throughout the argument, Blair relied on unnamed intelligence sources for most of his material.

When Blair finally got to 9/11, he proceeded through a chain of unproven assertions, as signaled by a shift into the vagueness of the passive voice: "Nineteen men **have been identified** as the hijackers from the passenger lists of the four planes hijacked on September 11. At least three of them **have already been positively identified** as associates of al-Qaeda." (Blair 21) But all this means is that the FBI is accusing them, which is wholly inadequate.

> From intelligence sources, the following facts have been established subsequent to 11 September; for intelligence reasons, the names of associates, though known, are not given. In the run-up to 11 September, bin Laden was mounting a concerted propaganda campaign amongst like-minded groups of people – including videos and documentation – justifying attacks on Jewish and American targets; and claiming that those who died in the course of them were carrying out God's work. We have learned, subsequent to 11 September, that Bin Laden himself asserted shortly before 11 September that he was preparing a major attack on America. In August and early September close associates of Bin Laden were warned to return to Afghanistan from other parts of the world by 10 September. Immediately prior to 11 September some known associates of Bin Laden were naming the date for action as on or around 11 September. Since 11 September **we have learned** that one of Bin Laden's closest and most senior associates was responsible for the detailed planning of the attacks. **There is evidence of a very specific nature relating to Bin Laden and his associates that is too sensitive to release**. (Blair 22-23, emphasis added)

All we have here is an exercise in check kiting. The CIA had forwarded a bouncing check to MI-6, and MI-6 had sent it back to Washington by simply citing the claims of the CIA as fact, and covering the whole in a mantle of the Official Secrets Act. It is perfectly plausible that bin Laden and his associates were planning a terror attack on the US which seemed large to them. The issue, once again, is their physical and technical ability to bring about destruction in the places and on the scale observed. Blair's document brought the central issue to a head when he asserted:

The modus operandi of 11 September was entirely consistent with previous attacks....The attacks of 11 September are entirely consistent with the scale and sophistication which went in to the attacks on the East African Embassies and the USS *Cole*. (Blair 23)

The problem is that the 9/11 attacks were incomparably larger and more serious than anything attempted by al Qaeda previously – they were in fact several orders of magnitude larger. This is apart from the question, which we will address later, of the degree to which al Qaeda has continued to receive technical assistance from certain rogue elements of US intelligence and others. So Tony Blair's dossier turned out to be a string of unsubstantiated assertions, and thus a miserable excuse for proof.

In addition, later events taught us more about Tony Blair's methods in compiling dossiers.

NUMBER 10 DOWNING STREET – KITCHEN OF LIES

New light on the putative value of intelligence dossiers issued by Tony Blair's office in Number 10 Downing Street was not long in coming. In September 2002, Blair published amid great fanfare his dossier purporting to demonstrate that Saddam Hussein's Iraq currently possessed weapons of mass destruction. This was entitled "Iraq: Its Infrastructure of Concealment, Deception, and Intimidation," and it was clearly crafted to provide a pretext for waging unprovoked and aggressive war against Iraq. This dossier was exposed as a fraud in two distinct waves of demystification. The first exposure took place in February 2003, when it emerged that entire sections of this report, which had been billed as the most up-to-date evaluation that could be offered by the very formidable capabilities of MI-6 and the rest of the British intelligence machine, had simply been lifted, plagiarized without attribution, from older documents in the public domain.

The Iraq dossier had been concocted by Blair and his media guru Alistair Campbell, a figure who combined the worst of image-mongers like Michael Deaver and Karl Rove, using materials provided by British intelligence. Parts of Blair's dossier had been stolen from articles written in 1997 by Sean Boyne of *Jane's Intelligence Review*, who was horrified by the nefarious use to which his work had been put. "I don't like to think that anything I wrote has been used as an argument for war. I am concerned because I am against the war," complained Boyne.

Another source from which Blair had lifted material verbatim was a thesis entitled "Iraq's Security and Intelligence Network," published by a graduate student, Ibrahim al-Marashi, a California resident, in September 2002, but based on documents going back to 1990, before the Gulf War. Al-Marashi was equally indignant: "this is wholesale deception. How can the British public trust the government if it is up to this sort of tricks? People will treat any other informa-tion they publish with a lot of skepticism from now on." And not just from now on: it is our contention here that this disbelief in regard to Tony Blair's work product should also be applied retrospectively.

The British Parliament was appalled by Blair's mendacity, which was so crude that the coded titles of the Microsoft Word documents that made up the dossier remained visible on the Number 10 Downing Street website. Many pointed to Alistair Hamilton as the dervish of spin behind the entire sordid operation. Former Labour Party Defense Minister and current Member of Parliament Peter Kilfoyle observed that Blair's deception merely "adds to the general impression that what we have been treated to is a farrago of half-truths. I am shocked that on such thin evidence we should be trying to convince the British people that this war is worth fighting." Labour MP Glenda Jackson added, "It is another example of how the Government is attempting to mislead the country and Parliament. And of course to mislead is a Parliamentary euphemism for lying." (London *Daily Mirror*, February 8, 2003)

Blair's nonchalance in cribbing together dossiers on subjects of vast import-ance also attracted the barbs of British wits. AheadOfNews.com spoofed Blair's plagiarized Iraq dossier by writing that "a spokesman for Prime Minister Tony Blair acknowledged recently that the report, 'Iraq: Its Infrastructure of Conceal-ment, Deception, and Intimidation,' had been cobbled together from a variety of sources, including old term papers, *Reader's Digest,* and several tabloids. John Miller, Undersecretary for Cutting-and-Pasting, explained that 'plagiarized' sections of the report included spelling errors, such as 'weapons of mass distraction,' and 'Untied States' found in the originals. 'Our deceptions might have succeeded,' he said, 'except for our bloody incompetent proofreaders.'" (February 12, 2003) Blair's Iraq dossier was an international laughingstock, but that had not prevented Colin Powell from praising it in his infamous speech to the United Nations Security Council.

Yet Blair's dossier was in the end no laughing matter: it contributed to the deaths of perhaps 15,000 people in Iraq within a year. It also brought tragedy to one of the British intelligence officials who had collaborated in its creation.

In June, 2003, when the Iraq war had already begun to go badly for the aggressors, BBC News broadcast a story by correspondent Barnaby Mason reporting that Blair and Campbell had personally supervised the concoction of the Iraq WMD dossier, sending proposed drafts back to the Joint Intelligence Committee "six to eight times" to be "sexed up" through the addition of more lurid and sensational details. One of these details was thought to be Blair's fantastic claim that Iraq had WMD which could be launched within 45 minutes. Blair delivered this warning in such a way as to suggest that Iraq would be capable of striking the UK within 45 minutes, despite the fact that Iraq possessed no delivery systems with any such capacities.

The response of the Blair regime to this report was to promote a witch-hunt to ferret out the source inside the government who had leaked such embarrassing material to Barnaby Mason. Officials of the British Defense Ministry allowed journalists to read them lists of persons suspected of being the leaker, and were willing to confirm the identity of their prime suspect as soon as the journalists mentioned his name. In this way, the Defense Ministry in effect betrayed one of its own employees, Dr. David Kelly. A few days later Kelly was found dead in a forest near his home, with his wrists slashed. His death was quickly ruled a suicide by Blair. After Kelly's death, a UN diplomat recalled that he had asked Kelly back in February 2003 what would happen if Tony Blair went through with his plan to join Bush in attacking Iraq. "I will probably be found dead in the woods," was Kelly's prophetic reply.

Blair's fabrications have been covered up with the help of two devious Lords, Lord Hutton and Lord Butler, both of whom have absolved the Prime Minister and his cohorts of deliberately falsifying intelligence. But the London press has dismissed these two reports as "Whitewash" and "Whitewash II" respectively. Each of them is a politically motivated cover-up designed to save the interests of the British oligarchy, which has heavily invested in Blair, the 9/11 myth, and the Iraq war. The probative value of these whitewashes is nil. Lord Hutton was also tasked with the inquiry and verdict on Kelly's strange "suicide."

In the light of all these facts, anyone interested in truth as distinct from propaganda can hardly accept at face value dossiers issued by the man whom his countrymen have now dubbed "Tony Bliar." Such skepticism must apply not only to Blair's Iraq dossier, but also to his earlier bin Laden dossier, which was an important building block in the bin Laden myth.

TORRICELLI: AN IMMEDIATE BOARD OF INQUIRY

In contrast to the relentless stonewalling of the Bush administration on any serious investigation of 9/11, Democratic New Jersey Senator Robert Torricelli soon came forward as the most consistent spokesman for a real probe, accompanied by accountability for the nonfeasance or malfeasance of federal officials. Torricelli represented New Jersey, the state where the largest number of victims of 9/11 had lived, and he appeared to take seriously the need to find out what happened. Torricelli's fate therefore becomes a case study of the workings of the US regime in the wake of 9/11. On September 26, Torricelli made an address to the Senate in which he began by talking about how much New Jersey had suffered:

> There is not a small town or a city in northern New Jersey that has not been touched or changed. At the time the final body has been found and the search has concluded, 2,000 to 3,000 people in New Jersey may have lost their lives. It is estimated there are 1,500 orphans in my State. It struck everywhere.

He then turned to the US intelligence community, which had manifestly failed its citizens in the most grievous way. He talked about the disproportion between the means allocated and the results obtained:

> It is reported in the media that the United States, in what would otherwise be a classified figure, may spend $30 billion per year on intelligence services, including the CIA and the NSA. The *Washington Post* reports the FBI counter-terrorism spending grew to $423 million this year, a figure which in the last 8 years has grown by 300 percent. It is not enough to ask for more. It is necessary to assess what went wrong. Did leadership fail? Were the plans inadequate? Did we have the wrong people, or were they on the wrong mission?

This was a challenge to the CIA, FBI, and the other spy agencies. Torricelli then began to enumerate several concrete examples of incompetence by these same agencies:

> Earlier this week, the *Washington Post* reported that over the past 2 years the Central Intelligence Agency had provided to the FBI the names of 100 suspected associates of Osama bin Laden who were either in or on their way to the United States. Yet the *Washington Post* concludes that the FBI "was ill equipped and unprepared" to deal with this information.

> Some of the allegations reported in the media are stunning and deeply troubling, not simply about what happened but revealing about our inability to deal with the current crisis. Previous terrorist investigations, it is alleged, produced boxes of evidentiary material written in Arabic that remained unanalyzed for lack of translators. During the 1993 World Trade Center bombing trial, agents discovered that photos and drawings outlining the plot had been in their possession for 3 years, but they had not been analyzed.

> Since 1996, the FBI had evidence that international terrorists were learning to fly passenger jets at US flight schools, but that does not seem to have obviously raised sufficient concern, and there was no apparent action.

> In August, the FBI received notice from French intelligence that one man who had paid cash to use flight simulators in Minnesota was a "radical Islamic extremist" with ties to Afghani terrorist training camps. Regrettably, this intelligence information was apparently not seen in the greater context of an actual threat that has now been realized. [...]

Torricelli then raised his key demand, which was for the immediate convocation of a Board of Inquiry on 9/11, modeled on the boards of inquiry which had been convened after the explosion of the USS *Maine*, the Pearl Harbor attack, and the loss of the space shuttle *Challenger*:

On behalf of the people of my State, if I need to return to this Chamber every day of every week of every month, this Senate is going to vote for some board of inquiry. I joined my colleagues after the Challenger accident, recognizing that the loss of life, the failure of technology and leadership, indicated something was wrong in NASA. The board of inquiry reformed NASA and the technology and gave it new leadership, and it served the Nation well.

After Pearl Harbor, we recognized something was wrong militarily. We had a board of inquiry. We found those responsible, we held them accountable, and we instituted the changes.

Torricelli stressed the necessary moment of accountability for the high government officials who had been found wanting:

Indeed, that formula has served this Nation for years in numerous crises. Now I call for it again. First, review the circumstances surrounding this tragedy, the people responsible, the resources that were available, where there was a failure of action, and make recommendations and assign responsibility. Second, develop recommendations or changes of law or resources or personnel so it does not happen again. I cannot imagine we will do less. I call upon us to do more. I will not be satisfied with new assignments of powers or appropriating more money. I want to know what went wrong, and why, and who.

On October 4, Torricelli took the floor again, to repeat his demand for an immediate Board of Inquiry, and to motivate it further:

A number of my colleagues are joining with me in the coming days in introducing legislation to create a board of inquiry regarding the terrorist attacks of September 11. It is my intention to offer it as an amendment to legislation that is currently working its way through the Senate dealing with this tragedy. [...]

I cannot predict any of these answers, but what is important is neither can anyone else in this Congress or the administration because without some analysis, as we have done throughout our country's history, we will never know. Indeed, if we fail to have a board of inquiry in the midst of this crisis about these circumstances, I believe history will instruct us it will be the first time in the history of the Republic that the Government did not hold itself accountable and subject to analysis when our American people have faced a crisis of this magnitude.

The people deserve an answer. The Government should hold itself accountable, and only a board of inquiry, independent of the Congress and the Executive, has the credibility to do it.

Torricelli's proposals had an undeniable power. If a board of inquiry had been possible in desperate days at the beginning of World War II, with a real shooting war being fought against real and formidable enemies, why was it not possible now? Pro-Bush spokesmen were forced into such contortions as arguing that the current situation was infinitely more dangerous than any moment of World War II, or of the Cold War. For those who remembered the Cuban missile crisis, when one hundred million Americans might have died in the first hour of a nuclear exchange, these notions were patently absurd.

Alarmed by the threat of a rapid and credible investigation being raised by the agitation of Torricelli and a small group of like-minded senators, Bush took the highly unusual step of asking House and Senate leaders to limit the inquiry to the House and Senate intelligence committees, whose proceedings are generally secret. Senate Democratic leaders wanted a broader investigation, involving some committees that would be free to air their findings. But even the Democrats had already narrowed the focus to intelligence failures preceding the terrorist attacks. In ruling out any serious probes, Bush attempted to wrap himself in the banner of military necessity in the prosecution of his alleged war on terror; a senior administration official said, "The president thinks it's important for Congress to review events in a way that does not unduly burden the defense and intelligence communities as they are still charged with fighting a war." Bush made this request of Senate Majority Leader Thomas A. Daschle (D-SD) during a breakfast meeting with congressional leaders. Daschle told reporters that Cheney had "expressed the concern that a review of what happened on September 11 would take resources and personnel away from the effort in the war on terrorism."

Daschle said he agreed with the demand by Bush and Cheney to "to limit the scope and the overall review of what happened." In other words, the supposed opposition was agreeing that there was no need to prove the US government's official version of events. What were they hiding? ("Bush Seeks To Restrict Hill 9/11 Probes, Intelligence Panels' Secrecy Is Favored," *Washington Post*, January 30, 2002) The milquetoast Daschle was a poor substitute for a real opposition leader. His capitulation on the board of inquiry issue set the tone for a series of Democratic Party surrenders that lasted for the duration of 2002, and which included abdicating to Bush the constitutional monopoly of the Congress on the power to declare war.

And what happened to Torricelli? He was owed much by his party. As head of the Democratic Senatorial Campaign Committee, he was often given credit for the 2000 election victories that brought Senate Democrats from 45 seats to 50. Soon after that, he became the target of corruption charges regarding his campaign finances and gifts he had allegedly accepted. For years, he had been profiled as a severe critic of the intelligence agencies. In January 2002, Torricelli supporters hailed US Attorney Mary Jo White's decision not to pursue prosecution of Torricelli for accepting illegal gifts as a vindication. But even on that occasion, the *New York Times* kept up the pressure for Torricelli to be skewered, arguing in an editorial that "the allegations against Mr. Torricelli are serious and cry out for prompt investigation and resolution in a manner worthy of public respect. If the [Senate Ethics] committee will not provide it, it might as well disband."

Torricelli's seat was up in 2002, and he was headed for almost certain re-election when the Senate Ethics Committee found he had damaged the reputation of that august body by accepting expensive personal gifts from a campaign contributor. At this point, Torricelli dropped to even with his opponent. Then, a federal judge ordered federal prosecutors to release to the press a letter which some thought suggested that Torricelli might have been guilty of more than taking gifts. A furious press campaign against the senator ensued. At this point, in September, Torricelli's position in the polls collapsed, and he dropped out of contention. The Democratic Party replaced him with former Senator Frank Lautenberg, who won the seat. Most significantly, federal prosecutors have never to this day brought any charges against Torricelli based on the contents of the supposedly incriminating letter, or any other charges. Their interference in Torricelli's re-election campaign thus appears to have been a political dirty trick at the outer limits of legality, designed to drive him out of political life. A reason for this operation is evident: they were defending the establishment's *omertà*, its code of silence, on 9/11.

The initial congressional effort at dealing with the events of 9/11 was the pitiful cover-up offered by the Subcommittee on Terrorism and Homeland Security of the House Intelligence Committee. Most of the subcommittee's work remained cloaked under a veil of secrecy, but a short executive summary containing analysis and a few anodyne recommendations was made available to the public. This simulacrum of a real probe was directed by Republican Rep. Saxby Chambliss of Georgia, an opportunistic scoundrel who, at the same time he was superintending this superficial report, was conducting one of the most shameful Senate campaigns in US history. Chambliss was seeking to unseat Georgia Democrat Max Cleland, a future member of the Kean-Hamilton Commission. Cleland was a war veteran who had left both his legs and one arm on the battlefield – a triple amputee. Chambliss, like Cheney and so many other hypocritical Bush backers, had other priorities during the Vietnam era. But this did not prevent Chambliss from running as a warmonger, while vilifying Cleland, the war hero, as unpatriotic because he refused to support Bush's Iraq adventure. And it worked: Chambliss was elected to the Senate a few months after the report was published. This may have represented the oligarchy's reward to Chambliss for his yeoman service in piloting the first Congressional cover-up of 9/11.

Chambliss billed his handiwork as "a very critical report," but it was nothing of the kind. Starting from a wholly uncritical acceptance of the 9/11 myth as its premise, the report merely attempted to identify shortcomings in US intelligence and to offer helpful hints about how they might be remedied. Although the subcommittee chronicled the well-known failures of FBI, CIA, NSA and others, no disciplinary action against any sitting federal bureaucrat was recommended. According to Rep. Jane Harman, Democrat of California and the ranking member, the report was "designed to give good people better tools, more resources, access to good watch lists, digital technologies, enhanced platforms, better language training, and career support." The subcommittee was of the opinion that the 9/11 attacks could not have been prevented, even if all the intelligence in the possession of the entire US government had been synthesized and brought to bear – an absurd thesis. However, by virtue of so much ineptitude, the tradition of begging the question had been further solidified. (CNSNEWS.com, July 17, 2002)

The healthy skepticism displayed by world public opinion in response to the fantastic and unsubstantiated stories peddled by the dubious US regime rankled with Paul Wolfowitz, the chief neocon and number two in the Rumsfeld Pentagon. When a new bin Laden tape appeared in which bin Laden was understood by some as claiming responsibility for the attacks, Wolfowitz expressed the wish that this new tape would put an end to "conspiracy theories." According to Wolfowitz, the new find "confirms everything we've known about him already. There's nothing new or surprising in it. It's just further confirmation and hopefully, maybe, we'll stop hearing anything more about these insane conspiracy theories that somehow the US has made this up or that somebody else did it." (Sam Donaldson, ABC, December 9, 2001)

The US Congress mounted its inquiry, which was conducted by the Senate Select Committee on Intelligence and the House Permanent Select Committee on Intelligence, acting as the Joint Inquiry into Intelligence Community Activities Before and After (but not during) the Terrorist Attacks of September 11, 2001. The history of this committee, known as the JICI, was a troubled one. Three months into the probe, the original staff director suddenly resigned. This was L. Britt Snider, the former inspector general of the CIA. He was known for being a creature of Tenet, and was considered too eager to spare his former colleagues any embarrassment. But on the other hand, Snider had been favored by Democratic presidential hopeful Bob Graham of Florida, and was opposed by Republican senators. Snider was replaced temporarily by Rick Cinquegrana, another CIA officer, and then permanently by Eleanor Hill.

"Members are trying to say, 'We've got to get to the bottom of what happened' while also saying, 'We don't want to make it into a witch hunt,'" said L. Paul Bremer, who led a previous probe of intelligence agencies after the bombing of US embassies in East Africa. Bremer later became notorious as Bush's proconsul in Mesopotamia. Those impulses, Bremer said, "will be an inherent tension irrespective of who is the staff director." When the JICI's report was published in December 2002, the most notable thing about it was that 28 pages were absolutely blank – redacted at the insistence of the administration. Remarks by Graham and others fueled speculation that the 28 blank pages contained information that somehow implicated Saudi Arabia, and the press made much of this. But the general approach of the JICI was that there had been an intelligence failure, and that there ought to be measures to avoid more intelligence failures – nothing more.

SKEPTICAL GOVERNMENTS

The other factor that ought to give any thoughtful citizen cause to reflect is the significant number of dissenting opinions registered in the months after 9/11. We have assembled some of these here for inspection. Naturally, few if any of these critical strictures on 9/11 were ever presented in the US news media. That was unconscionable, since many of those who manifested serious doubts on the main issues of 9/11 were eminently respectable, experienced persons with decades of background in government, politics, academia, and military affairs. There were prime ministers and ministers, generals, professors, and well-established experts. Even in the midst of the shock and trauma experienced by world public opinion in the wake of 9/11, they were able to formulate coherent objections to the official version, objections which in many cases have been ignored and not answered down to the present day.

The European NATO partners were confronted with the need to evaluate the US version of 9/11 in a very direct way: immediately after 9/11, the Bush regime demanded the activation of Article Five of the North Atlantic Pact, calling upon member states to assist the United States in warding off an attack from abroad. The US, however, had never offered any proof that the 9/11 attacks had indeed come from outside of its own borders. Under the shock of the 9/11 events, and fearing the retribution of a crazed regime that was announcing its determination to "end states," the European allies approved the resolution unanimously, even though no proof had been provided. One who objected to this procedure was Helmut Schmidt, the former Chancellor and Defense Minister of Germany for the Social Democratic Party. Several months after the vote, Schmidt reiterated that the European acquiescence had been a mistake. "For that article to be put into action, proof had to be delivered that the Sept. 11 terror attacks came from abroad. That proof has still not been provided," said Schmidt. (N-TV, December 10, 2001; EIR, December 13, 2001)

Another skeptic was former Italian President, Prime Minister, and Interior Minister Francesco Cossiga, who was in charge of Italy's internal security during the 1978 kidnap-murder of former Prime Minister Aldo Moro. Cossiga indicated his suspicion that the attacks presupposed some form of complicity within the US security system. He observed that the mastermind of the attack must have been a "sophisticated mind, provided with ample means not only to recruit fanatic kamikazes, but also highly specialized personnel. I add one thing: it could not be accomplished without infiltrations in the radar and flight security personnel." As for bin Laden, Cossiga added that "it is not thinkable that he did everything by himself." (*La Stampa*, September 14, 2001; EIR September 15, 2001)

General Heinz Karst was one of the founders of the reconstituted German military forces, or *Bundeswehr*, in the mid-1950s. Like other experienced military men, Karst found the 9/11 story purveyed by the Bush administration suspiciously incomplete. In an interview, he noted that "British secret service coordinator, Pauline Neville-Jones considers – as most experts do – a bin Laden co-authorship likely. But as far as the logistical operation is concerned, she is almost sure that the attacks were planned out in America, over the last six months." Karst put these comments in historical context: "When, in 1995, the Federal building in Oklahoma was blown up and 168 human beings were killed, people first thought of Islamic terrorists. But they were Timothy McVeigh and Terry Nichols, two elite soldiers of the Green Berets. The Americans have a long tradition of assassination attacks and of terrorism. Their most famous President, Abraham Lincoln, was shot dead in the theater. Martin Luther King was shot dead. John F. Kennedy was shot dead. His assassin was shot dead. Bob Kennedy was shot dead. Ronald Reagan survived an assassination attempt. There are rumors that also American ex-military have their hands in many cases." (*Deutschlandmagazin*, December 17, 2001; EIR)

Also in Germany, former Technology Minister and deputy Defense Minister Andreas von Bülow developed a broad critique of the official 9/11 story, to which we will have occasion to refer several times. In early January 2002 von Bülow told the Berlin *Tagesspiegel* that "planning the attacks was a masterwork, in technical and organizational terms. To hijack four big airliners within a few minutes and fly them into targets within a single hour and to do so on complicated flight routes! That is unthinkable, without backing from the secret apparatus of state and industry." He called attention to the fact that covering up the real authorship of a terrorist crime with false tracks for investigators to follow has "been an accompanying feature of covert operations ever since they have been launched by influential agencies." Von Bülow's conclusion was that the full truth about September 11 had yet to be told. (Berlin *Tagesspiegel*, January 13, 2002; EIR)

Another critical view of the 9/11 story came from Dr. Johannes B. Koeppl, a former official in the German Defense Ministry and an advisor to the former NATO General Secretary, Manfred Woerner. Koeppl told Mike Ruppert: "The interests behind the Bush administration, such as the CFR, the Trilateral Commission – founded by Brzezinski for David Rockefeller – and the Bilderberger group, have prepared for and are now moving to implement open world dictatorship within the next five years. They are not fighting against terrorists. They are fighting against citizens." (*From the Wilderness*, November 6, 2001)

A well-informed European source interviewed by EIR News Service on September 24, 2001 was of the opinion that 9/11 had been organized by a highly sophisticated operation *inside* the US. He added that "the Russians are aware of this, and that what is behind the operation is a vast geostrategic arrangement" that touches upon the most sensitive Russian interests. The lack of proof of a foreign role, he thought, "makes all this talk of invoking Article 5 so problematic, because Article 5 is not valid, if the attack emanates from *inside* a NATO country. But the United States is hugely reluctant, to discuss the internal American factors in this. Yet, the fact is, everything that happened on 9/11, was organized, executed, and raised inside the United States. All this obsession on Osama bin Laden is pure nonsense. In fact, this was all well-organized, the people who did it were geniuses, I wish they were on our side." He elaborated that, "as far as the Russians are concerned, there are two elements involved in all this: There is the United States as such, and there is the situation in Central Asia. All this talk of Islamic terrorism, is a cover for the fact that there are vast geostrategic rearrangements afoot, in all this." Asked about how 9/11 came about, this source replied: "This was not primarily Islamic at all. I'm sure there were Islamic elements, but what is behind this, is a deeply embedded conspiratorial and organized operation, that took two-plus years to put together. These were people, who were able to make sophisticated moves on the markets, right before it happened. It was very carefully initiated and carried out, using American dissident groups, of which there are a lot, some quite violent. Probably the militia elements would have been tapped, although you have to keep in mind, they are a cover for something else. In any case, what I can say to you with certainty, this was not done by a handful of Islamic fanatics."

General Mirza Aslam Beg of Pakistan voiced the doubts of his own government, even as Pakistan was being employed as a staging area for the US invasion of Afghanistan. Gen. Beg commented that "Many of us in this region believe that Osama or his al-Qaeda were not responsible for 11 September attacks in New York and Washington, yet the coalition led by United States is busy on 'Afghan bashing,' chasing objectives, which go much beyond Osama bin Laden. The information which is now coming up, goes to prove that involvement by the 'rogue elements' of the US military and intelligence organization is getting more obvious. Osama bin Laden and al-Qaeda definitely do not have the know-how and the capability to launch such operations involving such high precision coordination, based on information and expertise." (EIR, December 10, 2001)

Leading British academics also found the US official version unpalatable. Fred Halliday, London School of Economics Professor of International Relations and a well-known expert on the Middle East, told the BBC on September 11 that he would look for a domestic origin within the US of the September 11 events, along the lines of the 1995 Oklahoma City bombing. He had underlined that it would be a mistake to depend on the bin Laden/Islamist track, since, in the Middle East, bin Laden has often been derided as an American agent. (*London Observer*, November 25, 2001)

The Arab world in general was not buying Washington's account, especially in the absence of concrete evidence. The *Frankfurter Allgemeine Zeitung*, the leading conservative daily in Germany, lamented towards the end of November that the Arab public preferred its own "conspiracy theories" to the assurances offered by the Bush administration. The Arabs, complained the *FAZ*, tend to believe that "American intelligence circles planned and executed the Sept. 11 attacks in order to launch a long-prepared general assault against the Arab and Muslim world." As an example, the *FAZ* cited the November 3 lead editorial by Dr. Mustafa Mahmud in the semi-official Egyptian newspaper *Al-Ahram*: "History has not ended. Slowly the truth is emerging. American groups planned and executed the attacks of Sept. 11. The anthrax cases in the United States are a further indication for this. We don't know what else will come up in the coming days.... History has not ended yet. There are murderers around, who have not been punished, criminals who have not paid the price for their deeds." (*FAZ,* November 23, 2001; EIR)

MUSLIM VOICES CONDEMN 9/11, DENY OFFICIAL STORY

In a talk show broadcast on the Egyptian government's official nation-wide first television channel featuring leading intellectual Professor Mohammed Selim on November 24, all the participants agreed that organizing the 9/11 attacks was simply beyond the ability of Osama bin Laden and company. "No one in Egypt believes that Osama bin Laden did it," the professor noted.

The London-based *Al-Sharq Al-Awsat* is generally viewed as the semi-official organ of the Saudi government and the Saudi royal family, and has the largest circulation in the kingdom. This paper carried a commentary by the former Minister of Culture, Farouk Al-Berbir, which attempted to refute the US official account. According to Berbir, "the war on terrorism is an umbrella for the clash of civilizations. Saudi officials suspect that American terrorists were behind the September 11 attacks." Berbir elaborated that "probably, the statements made by some Saudi officials, who say that they suspect that terrorists from inside the United States itself have been involved in this sophisticated operation, is enough to prove the meaninglessness of accusing bin Laden,...who was financed and armed by the CIA to fight the war against the Soviets."

According to Berbir, the "war against Islamic terrorism" is simply a new cloak for the old familiar American "arrogance of power" and for the powerful Zionist faction in the US administration. In Berbir's view, the "US has failed to prove or present a single tangible proof for" its official 9/11 story. (*Al-Sharq Al-Awsat,* November 30, 2001) The Saudi press also accused the Israeli intelligence service, the Mossad , of complicity in the attacks. Columnist Abd al-Jabbar Adwan wrapped up this paper's view when he pointed to the numerous Armageddon and Apocalypse cults now operating on the American scene, writing: "Perhaps everyone will be surprised to find that, once again, the operation was 'Made in the USA,' as American society is filled with religious groups who consider themselves to be enemies of the state, its mechanisms and its liberal society." (*Al-Sharq Al-Awsat,* September 13, 2001)

Iran's *Siyasat-e Ruz* carried a front-page editorial entitled "A Blow From Within," in which it argued that since the attacks must have been carried out according to "a complicated methodical, technical and intelligence plan, [this] must have been done by a group or organization that has precise intelligence, access to America's vital and sensitive center, access to high quality weapons and explosives and infiltrators in those organs." In this paper's view, the prime suspects were "dissident elements in the American community, especially the

American military, who played the main role in the explosions at the Oklahoma federal center." (September 13, 2001)

Ferdinando Imposimato, one of the most prominent investigating judges in Italy during the years of the Red Brigades, the Moro assassination, and the attempt to assassinate Pope John Paul II, also found it impossible to accept the Bush administration account. Imposimato was also a former senator and television personality. Speaking to students at Rome University on November 8, 2001 concerning the question of the clash of civilizations, Imposimato made clear that his own view of 9/11 centered on "the participation of internal US forces" in the attacks.

Policy elites in western Europe tended towards skepticism, thus prefiguring the clash of many of them with the Bush administration over Iraq and other issues. An influential and well-informed British observer noted that he had "been convinced, that behind the official story, there has been another story that is not being told. But instead of telling the truth, the policymakers are starting new adventures, as a preemptive move, to take our minds off what is really going on, to avoid reality. The dilemma that they face, though, is that they are only creating more and greater problems. It is the famous story of the Chinese box: you solve one crisis in one box, and then another crisis pops up....Instead of honestly facing the implications of that, Washington has hoped to preempt reality, by creating more problems elsewhere, primarily in this Afghanistan-South Asia region." (*EIR*, January 9, 2002)

THE LIES OF THE US PRESS

In the immediate aftermath of 9/11, the US media were gripped by chauvinist hysteria and war psychosis. Two courageous editors, Ron Gutting of the *Texas City Sun* and Dan Guthrie of the Grants Pass, Oregon, *Daily Courier*, were fired for *lèse majesté* (or was it *Wehrkraftzersetzung*?) when they dared to criticize Bush, including for his cowardice on 9/11. [*Lèse majesté:* disrespect to the crown, or treason; *Wehrkraftzersetzung:* capital offense of undermining the war effort, in the Third Reich] Edward Herman, professor of Political Science at the University of Pennsylvania, pointed out that "*Pravda* and *Izvestia* in the former Soviet Union would have been hard-pressed to surpass the American media in their subservience to the official agenda....They have abandoned the notion of objectivity or even the idea of providing a public space where problems are discussed and debated.... It's a scandal that reveals the existence of a system of propaganda, not of serious media so essential in a democratic society." (Meyssan 2002 87)

Of course, the 9/11 myth could not have been generated and propagated by official leaks, statements, documents and reports alone. These had to be dished up to a gullible public by the corporate press, followed by the electronic media. Richard Bernstein and other *New York Times* staffers produced an elaboration of the official version entitled *Out of the Blue: The Story of September 11, 2001,*

From Jihad to Ground Zero. Surely this embrace of 9/11 orthodoxy by the newspaper of record ought to give us some confidence that the basic facts have been checked? But of course the fact that one reads something in the *New York Times* guarantees nothing these days. The problem is not limited to the excesses of Jason Blair, who was terminated. Far more disturbing were the activities of neocon regime stenographer Judith Miller, a crony of the crank author Laurie Mylroie. Miller was responsible for uncritically purveying the lies of the Wolfowitz clique about Iraq's phantomatic weapons of mass destruction. Partly because of Miller's excess of neocon zeal and absolute lack of critical screening, the *New York Times* was forced to apologize to its readers for its defective coverage. But unlike the hapless Blair, the disingenuous Miller, whose falsifications have contributed to a world tragedy, continued to scribble until she was jailed in the Valerie Plame espionage intrigue. If the *New York Times* had to apologize for serving as a megaphone for Bush's lies of 2002 and 2003, how long will it be before they are forced to apologize for trumpeting Bush's even bigger lies of 2001? How long will it be before the *New York Times* has to apologize for its pitiful propaganda piece, *Out of the Blue*?

THE MEACHER CRITIQUE

A decisive turn in the transatlantic 9/11 debate came in the late summer of 2003, when the dimensions of the Anglo-American fiasco in Iraq were becoming evident. Michael Meacher had been a close associate of Tony Blair and one of the most prominent leaders of New Labour. He was a member of Parliament, and held the post of Environment Minister from May 1997 to June 2003. Other members of the Blair cabinet, such as the former Overseas Development Minister, Claire Short, had quit over the Iraq adventure. Meacher was more courageous and more radical: he called into question the heart of the myth which the Bush administration wanted to foist off on the world. Meacher wrote:

> First, it is clear the US authorities did little or nothing to pre-empt the events of 9/11. It is known that at least 11 countries provided advance warning to the US of the 9/11 attacks. Two senior Mossad experts were sent to Washington in August 2001 to alert the CIA and FBI to a cell of 200 terrorists said to be preparing a big operation (*Daily Telegraph*, September 16, 2001). The list they provided included the names of four of the 9/11 hijackers, none of whom was arrested.

> It had been known as early as 1996 that there were plans to hit Washington targets with aeroplanes. Then in 1999 a US national intelligence council report noted that "al-Qaida suicide bombers could crash-land an aircraft packed with high explosives into the Pentagon, the headquarters of the CIA, or the White House."

> Fifteen of the 9/11 hijackers obtained their visas in Saudi Arabia. Michael Springmann, the former head of the American visa bureau in Jeddah, has stated that since 1987 the CIA had been illicitly issuing

visas to unqualified applicants from the Middle East and bringing them to the US for training in terrorism for the Afghan war in collaboration with Bin Laden (BBC, November 6, 2001). It seems this operation continued after the Afghan war for other purposes. It is also reported that five of the hijackers received training at secure US military installations in the 1990s (*Newsweek*, September 15, 2001).

Instructive leads prior to 9/11 were not followed up. French Moroccan flight student Zacarias Moussaoui (now thought to be the 20th hijacker) was arrested in August 2001 after an instructor reported he showed a suspicious interest in learning how to steer large airliners. When US agents learned from French intelligence he had radical Islamist ties, they sought a warrant to search his computer, which contained clues to the September 11 mission (*Times*, November 3, 2001). But they were turned down by the FBI. One agent wrote, a month before 9/11, that Moussaoui might be planning to crash into the Twin Towers (*Newsweek*, May 20, 2002).

All of this makes it all the more astonishing – on the war on terrorism perspective – that there was such slow reaction on September 11 itself. The first hijacking was suspected at no later than 8.20 AM, and the last hijacked aircraft crashed in Pennsylvania at 10.06 AM. Not a single fighter plane was scrambled to investigate from US Andrews Air Force base, just 10 miles from Washington DC, until after the third plane had hit the Pentagon at 9.38 AM. Why not? There were standard FAA intercept procedures for hijacked aircraft before 9/11. Between September 2000 and June 2001 the US military launched fighter aircraft on 67 occasions to chase suspicious aircraft (AP, August 13, 2002). It is a US legal requirement that once an aircraft has moved significantly off its flight plan, fighter planes are sent up to investigate.

Was this inaction simply the result of key people disregarding, or being ignorant of, the evidence? Or could US air security operations have been deliberately stood down on September 11? If so, why, and on whose authority? The former US federal crimes prosecutor, John Loftus, has said: "The information provided by European intelligence services prior to 9/11 was so extensive that it is no longer possible for either the CIA or FBI to assert a defence of incompetence."

Nor is the US response after 9/11 any better. No serious attempt has ever been made to catch Bin Laden. In late September and early October 2001, leaders of Pakistan's two Islamist parties negotiated Bin Laden's extradition to Pakistan to stand trial for 9/11. However, a US official said, significantly, that "casting our objectives too narrowly" risked "a premature collapse of the international effort if by some lucky chance Mr. Bin Laden was captured." The US chairman of the joint chiefs of staff, General Myers, went so far as to say that "the goal has never been to get Bin Laden" (AP, April 5, 2002). The whistleblowing FBI agent Robert Wright told ABC News (December 19, 2002) that FBI headquarters wanted no arrests. And in November 2001 the US airforce complained it had had al-Qaeda and Taliban leaders in its sights as many as 10 times over the previous six weeks, but had been unable to attack because they did not receive permission quickly enough (*Time Magazine*, May 13, 2002). None of this assembled evidence, all of which comes from sources already in the public domain, is compatible with the idea of a real, determined war on terrorism. (Michael Meacher, "This war on terrorism is bogus." *The Guardian*, September 6, 2003)

This is by all odds the most powerful critique of the 9/11 myth to come from an elected official in Britain. One senses the spirit of Tony Benn, the indomitable leader of the Labour left, who gave Meacher moral support. As for Claire Short, when asked in an interview if there was any common ground between Meacher's critique of Blair and her own, she nervously replied that Meacher had taken himself completely "out of the mainstream."

PAUL HELLYER REJECTS THE US ORTHODOXY

Another high-ranking skeptic on the official US account was Paul Hellyer, who had been Defense Minister and Deputy Prime Minister of Canada in three Liberal Party governments of Pierre Elliott Trudeau. Because of this, he brought the expertise of a top-ranking NATO insider to the question under consideration. Some years later, in 2004, Hellyer told an interviewer: "Terrorism is a terrible thing, but this was a police problem and an intelligence problem. What was wrong with your intelligence? Why didn't you know this was going to happen? You spend billions and billions with spooks all over the world and surely you should have known what was going on. And, so I began to be concerned about that. And then questions were raised by others. Why did the President just sit in the schoolroom when he heard the news? Why did he not acknowledge that he already knew what was going on? As a former Minister of National Defense, when the news came out I had to wonder. Why did airplanes fly around for an hour and a half without interceptors being scrambled from Andrews [Air Force Base]? Isn't Andrews right next to the capital?... With a quick action alert they should have been there in five minutes or ten minutes. If not, as the Minister of National Defense, which in the United States is the Secretary of Defense, I would want to say 'why not?'" (911Visibility.org, May 27, 2004)

POVERTY OF PHILOSOPHY

If ever the world needed voices of reason and wisdom, it was in the traumatized days after 9/11. There were still persons in the world who aspired to the title of philosophers; were they able to provide humanity with any guidance? The picture was bleak. Jürgen Habermas, the most prominent representative of what remains of the Frankfurt School, was interviewed in New York in December 2001 by Giovanna Borradori. Habermas managed a certain veneer of skepticism; he noted that "if the September 11 terror attack is supposed to constitute a caesura in world history, as many think, then it must be able to stand comparison to other events of world historical impact." (Borradori 26) He realizes that Carl Schmitt, the philosophical and juridical handmaiden of the Third Reich, was somehow an issue, and he criticized Schmitt as a "fascist." (Borradori 42) He was against Samuel Huntington; he regarded Bush's alleged war on terrorism as "a serious mistake." (Borradori 34) But when we get to the heart of the matter, Habermas remained imprisoned within the Clarke-Tenet-Powell-Blair-Bush official version, although he was clearly uncomfortable in that prison house of the human spirit. "The monstrous act itself was new," Habermas observed. "And I do not just mean the action of the suicide hijackers who transformed the fully fueled airplanes together with the hostages into living weapons, or even the unbearable number of victims and the dramatic extent of the devastation....one factor above all seems to me to be relevant: one never really knows who one's enemy is. Osama bin Laden, the person, more than likely serves the function of a stand-in....The terrorism we associate for the time being with the name 'al Qaeda' makes the identification of the opponent and any realistic assessment of the danger impossible." (Borradori 28-29)

We see that Habermas, however obliquely, was content to accept the official version. Is terrorism political? "Not in the subjective sense in which Mohammed Atta, the Egyptian citizen who came from Hamburg and piloted the first of the two catastrophic airplanes, would offer you a political answer." (Borradori 33) I myself was in Berlin on 9/11, and saw how the lurid tabloid press there, led by the *Bild Zeitung*, attempted to awaken a new sense of guilt in the German population because Atta, the "terror beast," had lived in Hamburg. Postwar German philosophy had been in many ways a campaign of resistance against the *Bild Zeitung* and its world outlook; now Habermas capitulated.

Another leading European philosopher interviewed by Borradori was Jacques Derrida, the deconstructionist. Derrida, as always, was obscured by the clouds of his own verbiage. He had the merit of proposing at least one realistic step for the post-9/11 configuration: "What would give me the most hope in the wake of all these upheavals is a potential difference between the new figure of Europe and the United States. I say this without any Eurocentrism." (Borradori 116) Derrida also sensed that Carl Schmitt was somehow involved. He was well aware that "it was not impossible to foresee an attack on American soil by these 'terrorists.'" (Borradori 91) He knew that the guerrillas who fought in Afghanistan were trained by the US. (Borradori 95) Derrida commented that the values he thought were important – politics, democracy, international law, human rights – "none of this seems to have any place whatsoever in the discourse of 'Bin Laden.'" (Borradori 113) When it came to these values, "I don't hear any such promises coming from 'Bin Laden,' at least not one for *this world*." (Borradori 114)

Again, the unease of the inmate shut inside the prison house of the official version was palpable, but it looked like no jail break would be attempted. Derrida said he used the term "Bin Laden" as a synecdoche, or shorthand, but use it nevertheless he did, and not, for example, "invisible government" or "rogue network." From these two examples we might be tempted to conclude that, on the great questions of human progress, European philosophy represented a spent force – but this may be premature. These philosophers were prisoners of their milieu, one that was oblivious to the elephant of conspiratorial action in its midst.

Probably the leading US philosopher at the moment of 9/11 was the neo-pragmatist Richard Rorty. In the aftermath of 9/11, Rorty moved into a position of critical support for Bush. A year later, Rorty was perhaps less enthusiastic about Bush, but still focused on the "defense of civilization against terrorism" and "the chances of further attacks." According to Rorty, "The catastrophes that rich monomaniacs like bin Laden are now able to cause are more like earthquakes than like attempts by nations at territorial aggrandizement or attempts by criminals to get rich. We are as baffled about how to forestall the next act of terrorism as about how to forestall the next hurricane." (*The Nation*, October 21, 2002) Al Qaeda is thus a force of nature, which will be buffeting us for many years. This paralytic vacuum is much inferior even to Habermas and Derrida.

For even the beginnings of a sensible summary, we must go to Trudy Govier out in Calgary, Alberta, in Canada. Govier lists four alternative theories on 9/11: there is the Zion theory, which blames the Mossad ; the theory of internal collusion, which asserts that the CIA and the FBI let it happen (sometimes abbreviated as LIHOP, let it happen on purpose); the chickens coming home to roost theory (or "blowback"), which explains the attacks as a product of destructive US foreign policies; and the Gandhian internationalist theory, which accepts the official version of 9/11 – the Standard Theory, with which we are already amply familiar – but rejects the aggressive US response. Govier's argument against the internal collusion theory has no rigorous basis in fact or logic, but reduces everything to a matter of personal opinion (in Plato's sense of opinion as inferior knowledge). "Were the attacks a setup?" asks Govier. "I doubt it. The idea that US intelligence operatives would collude in such devastating attacks against their own country, including such potent symbols as the World Trade Center and the Pentagon, strikes me as wildly unlikely." (Govier 127-128)

She therefore capitulates to the Standard Theory, with a nod to John Stuart Mill on the importance of dissent. Govier does not mention the more radical approach which is endorsed here, namely that 9/11 was the product of a network of moles inside the US government and intelligence agencies, backed up by covert action teams of expert professionals, seeking to provoke a war of civilizations as a means of shoring up Anglo-American world domination. The acronym for this approach is MIHOP – made it happen on purpose.

Finally, it is worthwhile to note that the entire question of 9/11 remains taboo in American politics. This may provide the key to the demise to Howard Dean's presidential campaign in the early months of 2004. Whatever else Dean may have been or not been, he was demonstrably the only Democratic candidate who was willing to make 9/11 and Bush's conduct in relation to it into a campaign issue. He did so on December 2, 2003 in a radio interview with Diane Rehm on NPR. Dean suggested that Bush's obsession with withholding documents on 9/11 might be attributable to his having known what was about to happen. "The most interesting theory I've heard so far – which is nothing more than a theory, it can't be proved – is that he was warned ahead of time by the Saudis," Dean remarked.

This was a direct challenge to the heart of Bush's rationale for re-election – his allegedly sterling performance in the so-called war on terror. It also tended to undermine the bipartisan group which had been attempting to pin the 9/11 attacks on Saudi Arabia. Dean was walking on a minefield. He went on to say: "Now, who knows what the real situation is? But the trouble is, by suppressing that kind of information, you lead to those kinds of theories, whether they have any truth to them or not." In the absence of total disclosure, Dean added, such theories will inevitably "get repeated." He concluded that Bush "is taking a great risk by suppressing the key information that should go in the Kean Commission." Dean's acknowledgement that the 9/11 cover-up had become a major issue was received with howls of "conspiracy theorist" from some of the corporate media who mentioned it. This incident was soon followed by a concerted campaign of denigration and ridicule against the former Vermont governor from such organs as the *Washington Post*. Dean, like Torricelli, had violated the oligarchical consensus which demanded silence, *omertá*, on the real issues of 9/11.

THE FAILURE OF THE KEAN-HAMILTON 9/11 COMMISSION

The utter failure of the "Commission to Investigate Terrorist Attacks Upon the United States," popularly known as the 9/11 commission, also as the Kean-Hamilton Commission, requires special attention. The Kean-Hamilton Commission came into the world as an orphan. The Bush regime and the Washington oligarchy in general had never desired its creation. They had successfully fabricated and propagated the 9/11 myth, and they saw no need whatever for any further rummaging through the events of that catastrophic day.

The creation of the 9/11 commission was due largely to the agitational and lobbying efforts of the 9/11 Families Steering Committee, a body largely composed of New Jersey housewives, the widows of men who had died in the twin towers of the World Trade Center. The most active among these widows were the quartet known as the Jersey Girls – Kristen Breitweiser, Patty Casazza, Mindy Kleinberg, and Lorie van Auken. Another group had as its spokesman Stephen Push. After months of trips to Washington to lobby Congress, Kristen Breitweiser was designated by the 9/11 victims' families to testify in the first public hearing of the Joint Intelligence Committee (JICI) Inquiry at the US Capitol. The four widows soon became embittered as they saw that members of

Congress and their staffs were determined to avoid the questions that seemed most important to them. They were indignant that the Ashcroft Justice Department had prescribed that "minders" had to be present whenever the JICI interviewed officials from the intelligence agencies, a rather overt form of witness intimidation which was later continued in regard to the Kean-Hamilton Commission.

They also began to notice that the FBI continued to lie systematically, and in the process they became aware of some of the anomalies in the government story. Two of the accused hijackers, Khalid al-Mihdhar and Nawaf al-Hazmi, had been known to US intelligence agencies well before 9/11, and important facts about them had been languishing unused in federal files for 15 months. As the JICI discovered, these two persons had extensive dealings and even lived with a longtime FBI counter-terrorism informant based in California. The case was very suspicious.

Since the JICI was mandated to cease its operations upon delivering its report at the end of 2003, the four widows and others began pressing for the board of inquiry which Torricelli had demanded, but which Bush had successfully blocked during the months immediately after 9/11. The new proposal was also stubbornly opposed by Bush, who wanted no investigation at all.

In May 2002, Democratic Senate Minority Leader Daschle endorsed the idea of an independent investigating commission. There was a diehard group of partisan Republicans in the House who sought to block the probe as long as they could. They were led by Tom Delay, who ranted that "a public commission investigating American intelligence in a time of war is ill-conceived and irresponsible." (*New York Times*, May 21, 2002) This was of course what Bush and Cheney also thought.

The House finally agreed to the bill for a commission on July 25, 2002. Rep. Tim Roemer was the bill's sponsor, and it was not a coincidence that he was later named to the commission, since he was out of the House and needed a job. After the commission was finally voted up by the Senate in late November 2002, Bush sought to name Henry Kissinger as the commission chairman. With that everyone in Washington knew the fix was in: the establishment intended the new commission to carry forward the cover-up, not discover the truth about what had happened. Kissinger's old adversary Daniel Schorr was one who said so bluntly, adding that the Bush administration was "desperately anxious" to avoid being pilloried for the obvious intelligence failures of that day. (NPR, November 30, 2002)

The bankruptcy of the 9/11 commission is expressed first of all in the conflicts of interests inherent in the pedigrees of the well-heeled insiders who composed it.

The blueblood former New Jersey Governor **Thomas Kean**, currently president of Drew University, was on the board of the Robert Wood Johnson Foundation and the National Council of Prince Philip's and Prince Bernhard's World Wildlife Fund. He has also been on the board of Amerada Hess

Corporation, which has been engaged in a joint venture with Delta Oil of Saudi Arabia. Delta Oil is owned by the bin Mahfouz and al Amoudi families of Saudi Arabia, who have been charged at various times with helping to fund al Qaeda – as for example in the $1 trillion lawsuit brought by 9/11 victims' heirs against Saudi Arabian interests. Kean has been insistently linked to Khalid bin Mahfouz, who was erroneously named by Woolsey of the CIA as a relative of Osama bin Laden by marriage. He is on the board of the National Endowment for Democracy (NED). This is the so-called Project Democracy, a bipartisan organ of quasi-autonomous US government subversion of the rest of the world. The NED is in effect the privatized version of the Cold War CIA under Reagan's Executive Order 12333. This was the mother, so to speak, of the Bush 41– Poindexter–Oliver North double-dealing that history has come to know as the Iran-Contra affair. In a 1987 essay entitled "Project Democracy's Program: The Fascist Corporate State," I had occasion to observe:

> Even in an epoch full of big lies like the late 20ᵗʰ century, it is ironic that the financiers of the Trilateral Commission should have chosen the name "Project Democracy" to denote their organized effort to install a fascist, totalitarian regime in the United States and a fascist New Order around the world. …Project Democracy is fascist, designed to culminate in the imposition of fascist institutions on the United States, institutions that combine the distilled essence of the Nazi Behemoth and the Bolshevik Leviathan. Project Democracy is high treason, a conspiracy for the overthrow of the Constitution. An organization whose stock in trade is destabilization and putsch in so many countries around the world can hardly be expected to halt its operations as it returns to the US border. For Project Democracy, it can happen here, it will happen here." (Tarpley 1987 40)

Lee Hamilton may be the all-time champion as regards the sheer number of commissions he has served on. While working on the 9/11 commission, he moonlighted as president and director of the Woodrow Wilson International Center for Scholars, a thinly veiled intelligence operation. Hamilton served as congressman from Indiana for 34 years, specializing in the House International Relations Committee, which he chaired. He was also on the House Permanent Select Committee on Intelligence, and the Select Committee to Investigate Covert Arms Transactions with Iran – better known as the Iran-Contra committee, which catapulted Oliver North to notoriety.

At that time, Hamilton had commented that indictment or impeachment of Reagan or Bush would not have been "good for the country." Instead, Hamilton supported the indictment of Reagan NSC director John Poindexter, North, and General Richard Secord, while assiduously protecting both Reagan and Vice President George Bush, the latter of whom had directed every phase of Iran-Contra drug-running and gun-running (Tarpley 1992). All in all, Hamilton is 0 for 4 in finding serious malfeasance by top oligarchs in any of the investigating committees or commissions he has worked on.

John Lehman was Secretary of the Navy from 1981 to 1987, during the Reagan-Bush administrations, working with Caspar Weinberger and Frank Carlucci. His current role was that of Wall Street corporate raider in his capacity as chairman of J. F. Lehman & Company, a private equity investment firm specialized in leveraged buyouts. Lehman counts as a Kissinger clone; he got his start as special counsel and member of the senior staff in Kissinger's Nixon-era National Security Council. He was one of the more accomplished practitioners of psychological warfare among the commissioners, as reflected in his expert baiting of the FDNY representatives during the commission's last hearings in New York City. Thanks in part to this arrogant performance, the last commission session in New York almost turned into a riot against the 9/11 commission, and the commissioners were no doubt glad to get out of town that day. Lehman was a signer of the letter from the Project for a New American Century to G. W. Bush on September 20, 2001 calling for a "war on terrorism" against Iraq.

Jamie S. Gorelick, a partner of Wilmer, Cutler, & Pickering, was also the vice-chair of Fannie Mae, a purveyor of mortgage-backed securities which was reportedly in deep financial trouble as a result of the Greenspan housing bubble. She had been deputy Attorney General during the Clinton years. Gorelick, who served on the CIA's National Security Advisory Panel as well as on the President's Review of Intelligence, counted as a personal creature of CIA Director George Tenet, to whom she displayed fawning deference whenever he appeared for testimony before the 9/11 commission. Her lines of questioning typically aimed to deflect guilt and opprobrium away from Langley, and towards such favored scapegoat agencies as the FAA.

James R. "Big Jim" Thompson was a Republican wheelhorse from Illinois, where he had held on as governor from 1977-1991, an all-time record for that state. He was a member of the law firm of Winston & Straw, which finds its niche in defending corporations accused of wrongdoing – among them Philip Morris, the target of numerous class-action lawsuits by tobacco victims. Thompson's caliber may be most easily gauged from examining his role in overseeing a "corporate kleptocracy" as a member of the audit committee of Hollinger Corporation, the British intelligence front which was mercilessly looted over many years by Lord Conrad Black and his rapacious consort, Barbara Amiel, a self-styled "fascist bitch." According to a report prepared for Hollinger by former SEC chairman Richard C. Breeden, between 1997 and 2003 Black and his management cohorts steered 95.2% of Hollinger's income into their personal accounts, robbing shareholders of about $400 million of company funds. Black and Amiel reportedly viewed Hollinger as a personal "piggybank." This neocon power couple, who had played a key role in the Clinton impeachment via their control of the *London Daily Telegraph*, used the Hollinger corporate jet as their personal property, shuttling between Chicago, Toronto, and vacation spots like Palm Springs. One 33-hour junket to Bora Bora alone cost Hollinger shareholders $533,000. Black billed the company $90,000 to refurbish his Rolls Royce, and another $8 million for memorabilia that once belonged to Franklin D.

Roosevelt, about whom Black wrote a book. A birthday party organized by Black for Amiel at New York's La Grenouille cost Hollinger $42,870. Black shoveled $5.4 million to neocon windbag Richard Perle, whom he described as a "trimmer and sharper" in private company emails.

In the midst of this bacchanal sat Big Jim Thompson of the audit committee, flanked by former State Department operative Richard Burt. Thompson came in for harsh criticism in the Breeden report for having done nothing to prevent Black's picaresque looting of Hollinger, which was supposed to be preserved as an asset of the British intelligence community. If Big Jim Thompson could not see the kleptomania raging around him then, how could he be expected to come up with any meaningful facts about 9/11? (*Washington Post*, September 1, 2004)

Former Senator **Slade Gorton** worked with the law firm of Preston, Gates & Ellis LLP. He had represented Washington state in the Senate for 18 years, 1982-2000. He himself attributed his appointment to his close personal friendship with GOP Senate leader Trent Lott, who was soon forced to quit his leadership post because of his effusive praise for Dixiecrat segregationist Strom Thurmond of South Carolina. Gorton can be considered the representative of the smoke-filled room of Republican senators who exert decisive influence in the GOP.

Former Indiana Democratic Congressman **Tim Roemer** was a partner at Johnston and Associates, and a scholar at George Mason University in Virginia. He served on the House Permanent Select Committee on Intelligence. He was part of the JICI cover-up, and was one of the authors of the House bill which set up the 9/11 commission.

Fred Fielding was a senior partner with the Wiley, Rein, & Fielding law firm. He had been Reagan's lawyer between 1981 and 1986. He had been associate counsel to Nixon between 1970 and 1974. His role as Nixon's lawyer was such that, after a multi-year probe, investigative journalism students at the University of Illinois declared that Fielding had been the fabled Deep Throat who fed leads to Woodward and Bernstein about Watergate back in 1972-74. At that time Fielding had worked in John Dean's office.

Former Senator **Max Cleland** of Georgia was the one possible wild card among the commissioners. He had been defeated in his re-election bid in 2002 by an underhanded Republican campaign of character assassination waged by the shameless Saxby Chambliss. Cleland had attempted to preserve union bargaining rights and job security for the employees of the new Department of Homeland Security, but had been wildly defamed by the GOP attack machine, including the juxtaposition of his picture with that of bin Laden. Cleland, we recall, had left two legs and one arm on the battlefield in Vietnam. In the current scoundrel time in Washington, he quickly became persona non grata.

Democratic Commissioner **Richard Ben-Veniste** was a former federal prosecutor from New York City who gained prominence during the Watergate scandal against the Nixon White House in 1973-74, when he was chief lawyer for the Sam Ervin Senate Watergate Committee. Since then he has been a fixture on the Democratic side of various investigations. Currently a member of the law firm Mayer, Brown, Rowe & Maw, Ben-Veniste was previously with Weil, Gotshal & Manges, one of the largest bankruptcy firms in the world, which was reportedly in the process of making some $200 million out of the bankruptcy proceedings of Enron, the company looted by Bush's top backer of 2000, Ken "Kenny Boy" Lay. In the past, Ben-Veniste had represented the Iran-Contra drug smuggler and pilot, Barry Seal.

Commission staff director **Philip Zelikow** was the director of the Miller Center of Public Affairs and White Burkett Miller professor of History at the University of Virginia. He had previously served as the executive director of the National Commission on Federal Election Reform, chaired by Carter and Ford. Zelikow was one of the editors of *The Kennedy Tapes*, a collection marked by flawed editorial criteria and thus of dubious value to scholars. Zelikow was co-author with Condoleezza Rice of *Germany Unified and Europe Transformed*. As a partner with Rice in a book venture, Zelikow thus had a further crippling conflict of interest. He was also the director of the Aspen Strategy Group, a program of the utopian Aspen Institute. He is a Bushman, and was a part of the 2000-2001 Bush-Cheney transition team. Rice, for example, had been accused of covering up for a payment of some $100,000 sent to lead patsy Mohamed Atta by General Mahmoud Ahmad of the Pakistani Interservices Intelligence in September 2001, almost certainly at the behest of the CIA.

Zelikow was appointed by the Bush administration to the President's Foreign Intelligence Advisory Board (PFIAB) on October 5, 2001; the PFIAB chair at that time was the lugubrious General Brent Scowcroft, formerly of Kissinger Associates. At several points in the investigation, Zelikow was forced to recuse himself, since he had been a part of the actions being probed. In another case, he was interviewed by other representatives of the 9/11 commission in relation to his role in pre-9/11 intelligence. At this rate Zelikow could have simplified the investigation by interviewing himself.

The resident lawyer of the 9/11 commission was **David Marcus** of the arch-establishment law firm of Wilmer, Cutler and Pickering. One of the clients of this law firm was Saudi Prince Mohammed al Faisal, who was named as one of the three most important financiers of 9/11 in the $116 trillion families' lawsuit. (Michel Chossudovsky, "Who's Who on the 9/11 'Independent' Commission," globalresearch.ca; Joyce Lynn, "The 9/11 Cover-Up Commission," www.communitycurrency.org/joycelynn.html)

Four out of the ten commissioners – Kean, Hamilton, Lehman, and Gorelick – were members of the elitist Council on Foreign Relations in New York City. As if to document its lack of seriousness, the 9/11 commission was indifferent to a glaring case of perjury that occurred on the part of witnesses testifying under oath. In one session, former FBI Acting Director Thomas Pickard testified that Attorney General John Ashcroft had told him before 9/11 not to provide any more briefings on the terrorist threat, since he was not interested in hearing them.

Ashcroft later directly denied that this was true. One of the two, most likely Ashcroft, was lying on a matter of considerable materiality. But the 9/11 commission never acted.

The 9/11 families had expected that at least one of their number would be named as a member of the new commission which they had bludgeoned a very unwilling Washington establishment into setting up. When the appointments came out, the commission was composed of hacks, wheelhorses, and professional insiders from the two political parties. The most the families and their allies could manage was to get Mindy Kleinberg on the agenda for a hard-hitting presentation to one of the early public plenary sessions of the commission. The commissioners listened politely, thanked Ms. Kleinberg extensively, and proceeded completely to ignore the letter and the spirit of her remarks. (*New York Observer*, September 14, 2003)

The 9/11 commission was never a fighting investigation, like the Church Committee and the Pike Committee back during the Ford administration. The Pike Committee, we must recall, once issued a richly deserved contempt of Congress citation against Henry Kissinger. The only time it looked like the Kean-Hamilton Commission might actually be going somewhere came towards the end of 2003, when Commissioner Max Cleland became indignant about the high-handed arrogance with which the Bush White House was insisting on conducting its cover-up. The Commission, although it was armed with subpoena power, had chosen to negotiate with Bush about access to important White House documents, notably the presidential daily briefings about which certain details had come out through the earlier probes. Bush was offering to let two members of the commission see a pre-censored selection of the sensitive documents in question, in a guarded room, without the possibility of taking notes.

Cleland, for whom the defeat at the hands of Saxby Chambliss in the 2002 election still rankled, became indignant with the sort of righteous anger which is so seldom seen in today's Washington. Calling the Bush proposal "disgusting," and warning against dirty deals, Cleland forthrightly demanded that all the commissioners be able to see all the documents they wanted and take all the notes they thought necessary. (*New York Times*, October 26, 2003) If Bush chose to oppose this, then the commission would have to use its subpoena powers, and let the matter play out through the courts – incidentally inflicting maximum public relations damage on the always-surreptitious Bush. Just as it appeared that Cleland and perhaps one or two other commissioners were about to clash with Governor Kean and Congressman Hamilton, it was announced that Cleland would be departing the commission to accept a post on the board of directors of the Export-Import Bank. According to the statute that set up the commission, these two jobs could not be held at the same time. The old warrior's courage had failed him. Who knows what threats had been issued to secure this outcome?

Cleland's departure meant a vacancy on the commission now had to be filled. This time a group of family activists officially nominated Kristen Breitweiser for the seat being vacated by Cleland. But, in an act of cynical contempt for the families and their sacrifices, Senator Daschle, in whose power it was to nominate a successor, chose instead to name former Nebraska Senator Bob Kerrey, currently the head of the New School University in New York City. Kerrey was an austerity Democrat and deficit hawk from the right wing of his party who had developed into a very vehement warmonger and xenophobe in the days after 9/11. Subjects like Osama bin Laden and al Qaeda could evoke from him adamant demands for US military retaliation that bordered on psychotic episodes.

Kerrey was not only a troubled man; he was reportedly a war criminal of the Vietnam era. As recounted by *Newsweek* correspondent Gregory L. Vistica in his article "One Awful Night in Thanh Phong" (*New York Times Magazine*, April 25, 2001), one night in 1969 "Kerrey's Raiders" had attacked the Vietnamese hamlet of Thanh Phong, slaughtering at least 13 civilians, including women, old men, and children. This account, relying heavily on the testimony of Gerhard Klann, one of Kerrey's fellow Navy Seals, recounts how Kerrey helped Klann dispatch an elderly Vietnamese man, holding him down while Klann cut his throat with a bayonet. Disturbingly, Kerrey reportedly claims nowadays that he does not remember his role in the slaying of the old man. If true, this obviously suggested that his mental equipment was not up to the task of serving on such an important commission. (See also Justin Raimondo, "Is Bob Kerrey a War Criminal? Yes." www.antiwar.com, April 27, 200)

The 9/11 commission was stonewalled by the FAA, JCS, CIA, NORAD, and Homeland Security. FAA and NORAD were so reticent that subpoenas were finally issued to get them to disgorge documents. At first, witnesses before the 9/11 commission were not even sworn in under oath. This changed under pressure from the bereaved families. The administration intimidated witnesses, with minders – overseers from the agency they worked for – present during the testimony at all times to make sure they did not get too talkative. The final report of the 9/11 commission was "vetted," meaning censored or screened, by the Bush White House.

The apex of interest in the 9/11 commission was the Clarke testimony of April 2004, which resulted in the declassification and publication of Clarke's famous Presidential Daily Briefing of August 6, 2001 entitled "Bin Laden Determined to Strike in US." This was a document which Rice had claimed contained merely historical data. However, the net effect was to strengthen the myth, not to broaden the horizons of the public. This, of course, was Clarke's intent. Condoleezza Rice first refused to appear, until public pressure became unbearable. But when she did show up the results were disappointing.

When the 9/11 commission report was released on July 22, 2004, it received the approval of a bipartisan oligarchical consensus. The ruling elite approved of the cover-up, and also approved of the recommendations for structural reform, notably the idea of having a single intelligence czar of cabinet rank to preside over CIA, DIA, NSA, and the rest. In reality, the nation would be better served by keeping the present fragmented system, since it provided a pluralism of opinion, and could not so easily be dragooned in a given direction. What if the intelligence czar were a neocon of the ilk of Feith, Luti, or Schulsky? Under the current system, there was always the chance that one intelligence agency might help the country by investigating the crimes of another intelligence agency. But that seemed to be precisely what the Kean-Hamilton consensus did not want.

There were a few dissident voices in the controlled corporate media. William Raspberry condemned the 9/11 commission report as "a childlike explanation" which "managed to avoid any semblance of individual responsibility," analogous to a child's saying "The lamp broke." Raspberry quoted CIA alumnus Ray McGovern of Veteran Intelligence Professionals for Sanity commenting that "the whole name of the game is to exculpate anyone in the establishment...why is it that after all this evidence and months and months of testimony, the commission found itself unable even to say if the attacks could have been prevented?" McGovern's overall estimate of the 9/11 commission itself: "This commission is not representative of America or of the families of those who died in 9/11. It is an archetypically establishment body, consisting of people who, with the exception of a token white woman, look exactly like me. They are all lawyers or politicians or both – and all acceptable to Vice President Cheney, who didn't want a commission in the first place. The result is facile, mischievous, and disingenuous." (*Washington Post*, July 26, 2004)

As a result of the official failure to provide a competent investigation of the 9/11 events, there has been absolutely no accountability or responsibility for what occurred. The JICI and the Kean-Hamilton Commission agreed in essence that, although certainly there was an intelligence failure, it was systemic, meaning that no individuals were responsible. In bureaucratic usage, the proposition that everyone is responsible means that in practical terms no one is responsible. The only official of any note whose career seems to have been harmed by 9/11 was the security director of the FAA, and even he was allowed to resign.

In the US Navy, a captain who runs his ship aground is relieved of command, no matter whose fault it turns out to be. In many countries, if the national team does poorly in the World Cup soccer championships, the sports minister must resign. In other countries, if a train wreck occurs, the transportation minister is automatically required to step down. This is the principle of ministerial responsi-bility, the overall political responsibility of the head of an executive department.

After 9/11, the Bush administration did not observe this principle. Instead, figures like Ashcroft argued in effect that the greater the disasters that occurred on their watch, and the more numerous their failures, the more emergency powers they deserved. Their maxim was "the more I fail, the more dictatorial powers I deserve to have." Ashcroft seemed to think that he was entitled to bungle his way into a dictatorship. Such an arrangement provides a positive stimulus for bureaucrats to be less than zealous in preventing the visitation of disasters upon the citizens. The principle of ministerial responsibility provides the most rudimentary and the most essential reality principle for government officials: the sure knowledge that if catastrophes take place on their watch, they will be sacked. In an oligarchical system like ours, this is absolutely necessary to create a minimum common interest between security officials and the citizens. The alien neocon notion of martial law abolishes this reality principle by threatening to freeze the failed officials in power as a reward for their own bungling incompetence – or for their treasonous complicity.

The following comments on the Gunpowder Plot of nearly four hundred years ago bear an eerie resemblance to the 9/11 operation: "The determined manner in which this object was ever kept in view, the unscrupulous means constantly employed for its attainment, the vehemence with which matters were asserted to have been proved, any proof of which was never seriously attempted – in a word, the elaborate system of falsification by which alone the story of the conspiracy was made to suit the purpose it so efficiently served, can inspire us with no confidence that the foundation upon which such a superstructure was erected, was itself what it was said to be. On the other hand, when we examine into the details supplied to us as to the progress of the affair, we find that much of what the conspirators are said to have done is well-nigh incredible, while it is utterly impossible that if they really acted in the manner described, the public authorities should not have had full knowledge of their proceedings." (Gerard 16-17) These comments on the Gunpowder Plot of 1605 are equally applicable to the 9/11 attacks of four centuries later. The Anglo-American financier faction, whose birth was marked by terrorism under James I, has resorted to even more spectacular terrorism in the epoch of its historic decline.

And so we say to all persons of good will: you would never believe the utterances of Bush & Co. about any issue of importance without independently verifying the facts. Why do you persist in believing Bush on the most central question of our time, 9/11? Are the implications too enormous? That enormity will itself be dwarfed by the consequences of allowing such corruption to triumph unchallenged, as has already occurred in Afghanistan and Iraq, and soon will elsewhere, even in the US.

On September 14, 2001, the US Congress, contemptuously flaunting the lessons of the infamous and fraudulent Golf of Tonkin resolution of August 1964, which had been paid for with the lives of 50,000 Americans and a million Vietnamese, gave Bush *carte blanche* to wage war, authorizing him to employ "all necessary and appropriate force against those nations, organizations, or persons he determines planned, authorized, committed, or aided the terrorist attacks that occurred on September 11, 2001, or harbored such organizations or persons, in order to prevent any future acts of international terrorism against the United States by such nations, organizations, or persons." The only dissenting voices were Democrats Rep. Barbara Lee, of California, and Sen. Robert Byrd, West Virginia, who defended the honor of the American people with their superb courage in the face of hysteria. It is Bush's determination of those who "planned, authorized, committed, or aided" the 9/11 events which we must now examine.

II
THE THEORY AND PRACTICE
OF SYNTHETIC TERRORISM

And yet the entire Republic is shaken and disconcerted by these
seditious provocations, and precisely by the action of those who
should have been the first to prevent them.... – Sallust

The original title for this chapter was "the theory and practice of state-
sponsored, false-flag, synthetic terrorism, but we shall let "synthetic terrorism"
sum up this entire concept. In any political system which relies to even a small
extent for its continued existence on the consent of the governed, some form of
popular legitimation is necessary. But what happens when the wars, policies and
institutional changes desired by the ruling elite are inimical to the vast majority
of citizens and cannot gain their understanding or support? When the oligarchical
nature of the system endows it with such inertia that it cannot move in the
direction the most powerful oligarchical factions desire? Under these conditions,
especially if the political and economic systems are in crisis, state-sponsored
terrorism may emerge. Here we are not describing the way in which statesmen,
generals and intelligence officers ought to act; we are describing the way in
which they have acted and continue to act.

What we offer here can be thought of as a theory of synthetic terrorism. This
terrorism is synthetic because it brings together the efforts of a number of
disparate components: patsies, moles, professionals, media, and controllers. It is
also synthetic in the sense that it is artificial: it does not grow up spontaneously
out of despair and oppression, but is rather the product of an effort of organization and direction in which factions of government play an indispensable role.

We are not offering erudite scholarship isolated from public affairs, but an
active intervention against the ongoing attempt to build an entire international
system on a monstrous falsehood.

We must stress the idea, unfamiliar and suppressed as it is, that the vast
majority of international terrorism conducted on a spectacular scale is indeed
state-sponsored terrorism. This does not mean that such terrorism is sponsored by
the entire government, down to the last GS-4 clerical worker doing data entry for
the Social Security Administration. It does mean that a faction or network of the
government uses its access to the levers of power to promote the terrorist action
in various ways. In Europe in the 1960s and 1970s, and in the Arab and Islamic
world today, there have been deluded and naïve individuals and institutions who
have somehow associated large-scale international terrorism with revolutionary
or progressive change, or with the establishment of international justice. Nothing
could be further from the truth. If the Italian left of the 1970s and the German left

of the same period sympathized with the Red Brigades or the Baader-Meinhof group/Red Army faction, they only showed their own gullibility, since both of these terrorist operations were created by and controlled by NATO intelligence. Similarly, the Arab who feels sympathy for al Qaeda needs to be forcefully reminded that al Qaeda was created by the CIA and continues to be steered by the CIA, through various intermediaries and cut-outs, or discreet go-betweens. Terrorism, which was advertised as a desperate aid to oppressed peoples, has most often had the opposite effect: the attack on the Munich Olympics in 1972, the first spectacular blowing up of airliners, the *Achille Lauro* – these were actions which set the Palestinian cause back 20 years, and continue to do so indefinitely.

Terrorism in the modern era is the means by which oligarchies wage secret wars against the people which it would be politically impossible to wage openly. Oligarchy, in turn, always has one and the same political program, which has not changed since the time of Thucydides, Plato and the writer that classical historians call The Old Oligarch: the purpose and program of oligarchy is to perpetuate oligarchy. The specific political and economic form of the oligarchy is much less important. The *nomenklatura* of the old Union of Soviet Socialist Republics was supposedly based on state property of the means of production, the primacy of the Communist Party, and Marxist ideology, but they proved more than willing to throw all that out the window when they saw that their oligarchical status and special privilege could not be preserved under communist auspices. Having realized this, the Soviet oligarchs were eager to transform themselves into stock-jobbers, speculators, profiteers, and young wolves (as Zhirinovsky put it) under the auspices of wild laissez-faire capitalism. What was important to them was to preserve their status as an oligarchy. This is an important lesson, since it shows that we must be deeply suspicious of the ruling elite of the United States, which is of course also an oligarchy, but an oligarchy which operates behind the mask of democratic institutions and formal democracy. The experience of the USSR suggests that the US oligarchy will be more than willing to trade in its democratic costumes for a bureaucratic-authoritarian or even totalitarian garb if the democratic forms prove to be impossible to maintain, most likely because of financial and economic difficulties.

The naïve view of terrorism is that it grows up directly out of oppression, economic misery, and political despair. Oppressed and exploited people, or those who have been colonized by a foreign power, supposedly come together spontaneously in ones and twos, create an organization, and after a certain time of preparation go over to armed struggle against their oppressors or occupiers. But this is the rarest of exceptions.

This naïve view is blind to the most important institutional actors in the world of terrorism – secret intelligence agencies like CIA, FBI, NSA, KGB, Stasi, MI-6, and the rest. Secret intelligence agencies are institutions in which the very essence of oligarchy is at work: as the enjoyment of oligarchical privileges comes inevitably at the expense of the people, covert methods of control become indispensable. Secret intelligence agencies in their modern forms go back to the Republic of Venice, which was famous for its intelligence directorate, the Council of Ten, and its pervasive network of spies, informers, and provocateurs – and the Republic of Venice was the longest-lasting oligarchical system in world history. Despite their cultural differences, all of these secret intelligence agencies are fundamentally alike. Terrorism generally starts within these secret agencies, or nowadays more likely in their privatized tentacles – such as the intelligence community in the United States has had since President Reagan's Executive Order 12333.

Secret intelligence agencies are fatalist or realist in that they regard all large-scale sociological and political changes as inevitable. As soon as they identify a budding phenomenon which they have not yet penetrated, their only thought is how to infiltrate their agents and assets into it, so they can steer or influence it as it ripens. Whenever the leaders of intelligence agencies see a train leaving the station, their only thought is to climb on board, quite irrespective of the destination, as Gen. Paul Albert Scherer, the former head of West Germany's Military Counter-Intelligence (*Militärischer Abschirmdienst*) and one of the greatest experts in this field, assured me some years back. This applies to terrorist groups most emphatically. Here the attention of the secret intelligence agencies is so strongly focused that their task is most often that of founding, and much more seldom that of infiltrating and taking over some group which already exists.

The world of secret intelligence agencies is a realm of falsehood, camouflage, deception, violence, unspeakable cruelty, treachery, and betrayal. It is the most desolate and grim sector of human endeavor, where no human values can subsist. It knows neither hope nor mercy nor redemption. It is the one area of human life where Hobbes's maxim holds true – it is the war of all against all. But not as chaos – rather as an ultimately controlled phenomenon upholds the state power the intelligence agencies serve. During the Cold War, the conflict of CIA, MI-6, SDECE, KGB, BND, Stasi and the rest was called the wilderness of mirrors, a desert populated by agents, double agents, triple agents, multiple agents, their case officers, their counterintelligence opponents, and the omnipresent specialists in *mokrie dela* – wetwork, as the KGB described assassinations.

We start from the strong presumption that terrorism is intrinsically an activity which is controlled by a faction of government, probably acting under the influence of financier factions which are generally the ultimate source of authority in the globalized universe after 1991. Terrorism cannot be described as a spontaneous sociological phenomenon, as the old saying goes – it must rather be seen as a phenomenon developed by sociologists, along with psychologists, profilers, psychiatrists, case officers, handlers, and cut-outs. For every terrorist and terrorist group in the field, an extensive bureaucratic support system is necessary. Spontaneous combustion is the last thing that should be expected.

This is an important point, to which we will return. The naïve or spontaneous theory of terrorism sees the terror group as sprouting up directly out of the compost of misery, poverty, and desperation. Our point here is that this explanation neglects the crucial, indispensable role of the secret intelligence agency, which is usually present at the creation of the terror group, or very soon thereafter. The well-known Indian author Arundhati Roy told the American Sociological Association in San Francisco on August 16, 2004 that "terrorism is the privatization of war" and that "terrorists are the free marketers of war." These are striking formulations, but this does not prevent them from leading in the wrong direction. Synthetic terrorism remains very much under state control; it is only that the puppetmaster's strings are well concealed from those who do not know what to look for, or who do not want to know. Thus, a CIA front corporation is not really part of the free-market private sector – it is an emanation of Langley just as surely as the local station chief and his staff.

It should also be clear that state-sponsored terrorism cannot call itself by its own real name. It must necessarily masquerade as an authentic voice of the oppressed – be they Arabs, Muslims, workers, national minorities, or whatever. The terror groups cannot be labeled CIA or KGB – they must call themselves Red Brigades, Red Army faction, ETA, or al Qaeda. The false flag and false ideology allows the terror group to pretend to be something it is not, and to convince billions of naïve viewers of CNN or al Jazeera that the false dumb-show is reality.

In the nineteenth century, the great headquarters of international terrorism was London. The defense of the Empire required operations which the public decorum of the Victorian era could not openly avow. The main vehicle for British terrorist operations in Europe was Giuseppe Mazzini and his phalanx of organizations starting from Young Italy: Young Germany, Young France, Young Poland, Young Turkey, Young America. Mazzini was a paid agent of the British Admiralty, and received his funding through Admiralty official James Stansfeld. Mazzini's terrorism was directed against what the British called "the arbitrary powers:" Prussia, Russia, and Austria.

Each of these had a large population of oppressed nationalities, and Mazzini created a terrorist group for each one of them, often promising the same territory to two or more of his national sections. The important thing was that rulers and officials be assassinated, and bombs thrown. The net effect of all this can be gauged by the complaint of an Austrian about Mazzini's operations in Italy: Mazzini aimed at making Italy turbulent, he lamented, which was bad for Austria, but without making Italy strong, which might be bad for the British. Mazzini operated out of London during his entire career, which simply means that he was officially sanctioned, as were anarchists like Bakunin and a whole tribe of nihilists. Mazzini worked well for the British in Europe, including the Ottoman Empire, and in the Americas. For other parts of the world, the Admiralty had specialized operations.

State-sponsored terrorism can have a number of goals. One of these is to eliminate a politician or business leader. Back around 1500, Niccolò Machiavelli included a long chapter on conspiracies in his masterwork, *The Discourses*. For Machiavelli, a conspiracy meant an operation designed to assassinate the ruler of a state, and to take his place by seizing power. Modern terrorism is more subtle: by eliminating a leading politician, it seeks to change the policy direction of the government that politician was leading. The paradox here is that a faction or network penetrating the state sometimes undertakes the elimination of the head of state or head of government, and often a very eminent and beloved one.

A good example is the French Fifth Republic under President Charles de Gaulle. De Gaulle would not accept the demand of the US and UK to dictate policy to France as a member of the Atlantic Alliance. De Gaulle took France out of the NATO supranational command, ejected the NATO headquarters from its home near Paris, condemned the Vietnam war, refused the British entry into the European Economic Community, challenged the US to pay its foreign obligations in gold rather than paper dollars, called for a free Quebec, and otherwise demonstrated creative independence from the Anglo-Americans. The result was a series of approximately 30 assassination attempts, carried out by French right-wing extremists. but with the Anglo-American secret services lurking in the background. None of the attempts to assassinate de Gaulle succeeded.

Another example was Enrico Mattei, head of the Italian state oil company ENI. Mattei challenged the hegemony of the US-UK Seven Sisters oil cartel. He offered Arab oil producers a 50-50 split of the profits, far more than the Anglo-Americans were offering, and he was willing to help the Arabs with their own economic development. Mattei was growing powerful enough to challenge the subordination of Italy to the US-UK domination of NATO, when his private jet crashed near Milan in October 1962, an event which can be attributed to sabotage on the part of the CIA and its alliances, among them some of the French Algerian *colons* who were also the enemies of de Gaulle. After Mattei's death, ENI began to abide by the rules of the Anglo-American oil cartel.

The classic example of political assassination was the murder of President Kennedy. Kennedy had been alerted by the Bay of Pigs debacle to the treachery and incompetence of CIA director Allen Dulles, whom he fired. He refused to listen to the adventurist advice of former Secretary of State Dean Acheson. He overrode his main military advisers, Lyman Lemnitzer and Curtis LeMay, who wanted to make the Cuban missile crisis the occasion for general thermonuclear war with the USSR. Kennedy clashed with Roger Blough of US Steel, who was acting as a representative of Wall Street. Kennedy challenged the power of the Federal Reserve to be the sole controller of the US money supply. Kennedy seemed determined to return to the New Deal policies of Franklin D. Roosevelt, and also to the strong presidency Roosevelt had embodied, but which the US oligarchy was determined never to permit again. (There had in any case been an attempt to assassinate FDR in Florida before he was even inaugurated.) Kennedy was probably planning to fire FBI boss J. Edgar Hoover, who regarded himself as an unaccountable state within the state. Documents indicate that Kennedy was scaling down the US presence in Vietnam, rather than escalating it as his incompetent hawkish advisers wanted, and that he may have been preparing to liquidate the Vietnam matter entirely after his re-election in November 1964. Kennedy was assassinated in Dallas in November, 1963.

Somewhere in the mid-1960s a watershed in the annals of terrorism is passed. Up to this point, key person assassinations are carried out by disgruntled officers or colonial refugees, and may be tagged to itinerant misfits like Oswald, or are simply anonymous. After this point, assassinations start to be attributed to revolutionary or subversive groups. During the 1980s and 1990s, those groups gradually drop their Marxist-Leninist camouflage and in many cases assume a right-wing anarchist or Islamist coloration.

In Germany, Detlev Karsten Rohwedder was the chief of the Trusteeship Agency (*Treuhandanstalt*), which in 1991 was the largest corporation in the world. In the communist German Democratic Republic, all industry was the property of the state, and when the GDR collapsed in 1989, this property was transferred to the Trusteeship Agency. Rohwedder, as the head of this entity, preferred to keep the vast state property of the GDR as a state sector during the transition, trying to maintain existing levels of employment and production so as to facilitate the absorption of the East German regions into unified Germany. Anglo-American financiers, however, wanted all the GDR state property to be put on the auction block at once, so that it could be sold off at bargain basement prices from which Wall Street and the City of London had everything to gain. When Rohwedder proved reluctant to accept this policy, he was assassinated around Easter 1991, just after the first Gulf War, by elements claiming to be the Baader-Meinhof group, also known as the Red Army Faction. Rohwedder's successor immediately began selling off GDR state property the way the Anglo-Americans wanted.

Aldo Moro was the head of the Italian Christian Democratic Party. During the 1970s he was the leading advocate of a policy of bringing the Italian Communist Party (PCI) into the government. This would have given the Italian government a solid majority for the first time in many decades, putting an end to the constant parade of government crises and weak, unstable coalitions cobbled together with the help of splinter parties. As Moro's widow later reported, he was warned by a key US figure (identified by some as former US Secretary of State Henry Kissinger) to cease his efforts to bring the PCI into the government. In March, 1978 this warning was followed by a terrorist attack on Moro's motorcade, in which several of his security detail were killed. Moro himself was abducted, and responsibility was claimed by the Red Brigades. After two months of captivity, Moro was killed by his captors and his body found in the trunk of a car in downtown Rome. After his death, the PCI was not allowed to enter the government.

As the examples have suggested, the leading terrorist state of the post-1945 era in Europe was unquestionably the United States, often acting together with the British MI-5 and MI-6 in the framework of NATO intelligence. US state-sponsored terrorism generally aimed at maintaining what can be called the division of the world into spheres of influence as established at the Big Three (US, UK, USSR) conference at Yalta in the Crimea in early 1945. Since the US could not simply arrest and execute its opponents the way Stalin could, terrorism was a favored tool of the US in attempting to maintain domination and discipline within the western bloc. Terrorism was thus used against political challenges, like that of Moro, against economic challenges, like those of Mattei and Rohwedder, or against figures who represented multiple challenges, like President de Gaulle. In the cases of President Kennedy and his brother Robert Kennedy, terrorism was employed to prevent reforms of the system which decisive groups did not desire, and which they despaired of blocking through normal political means. The anti-slavery reforms of the Gracchi brothers were the only way to preserve the Roman Republic, but the latifundists and slaveholders felt mortally threatened by them, so the Gracchi were both assassinated.

Terrorism can also be employed to create a radical change in a political situation or political process. A good example from the postwar period is the terrorist bombing attack on a bank located in Piazza Fontana in Milan, Italy, on December 12, 1969, killing 16 and seriously injuring 88 more – a shocking toll in those days, and a source of horror for public opinion in general. This bombing took place at the height of the biggest strike wave that Italy had seen since the end of World War II, the so-called Hot Autumn, in which the automobile workers and metal workers had proven to be especially aggressive and militant. The bombings achieved the remarkable feat of stopping this broadly based and energetic strike wave dead in its tracks. All strikes were called off as the police ran wild, hauling suspected leftist sympathizers in for questioning and intimidating their families. This successful method of social control was called the "strategy of tension;" the name was well-chosen, since tension is a key factor in psychological conditioning. It included emergency laws against suspected terrorists and other favorite measures of Ashcroft today.

The Piazza Fontana bombs were blamed by the police and the press on a pathetic group of anarchists, the Bakunin Club. Among the members of the Bakunin Club, which had been thoroughly penetrated by the Italian intelligence service, the SID, were the railroad worker Giuseppe Pinelli and the male dancer Pietro Valpreda. Pinelli was pushed to his death from a fourth-story window in police headquarters, while Valpreda was vilified as a subhuman beast by the mass media. When the absurd attempt to pin the atrocity on the anarchists collapsed of its own weight, the next prime suspects became Freda and Ventura, two self-styled "Nazi-Maoists." More than twenty years after the fact, information came into the public domain that the bombs of Piazza Fontana had been placed by a secret network called GLADIO operating under the control of NATO intelligence, which evidently feared that the success of the strike wave might lead to the entry of the PCI into the government, which in turn might have led to the erosion of the NATO alliance as against the Soviet-controlled Warsaw Pact.

All during the 1970s and into the 1980s, US, NATO and Italian ruling circles were obsessed with keeping the PCI out of the government, and with breaking the back of workers militancy. Terrorist incidents included a bomb which went off during a trade union demonstration against fascism at Piazza della Loggia in Brescia in May 1974 (8 dead, 100 injured), a bomb on the Italicus express train in August 1974 (12 dead, 48 injured), and many more. The most spectacular event in this series was the bomb at the Bologna railway station on August 2, 1980, which killed 85 and injured some 200. This was the biggest terrorist attack in Europe before the Madrid train bombings of March 11, 2004, and shows a similar modus operandi.

Terrorism thus has been known to provide a means of social control. Parts of the US oligarchy are today almost euphoric about the seemingly endless panorama of possibilities for exploiting terrorism they believe they see before them. But it is not wise to try to build an entire state and social order on terrorism.

Another major goal of terrorism has been to provoke war. In this variant, state-sponsored false-flag terrorist groups carry out an attack against the power that wants to go to war, which uses the attacks as a moral pretext to rally its own population for conflict, whipping up sentiment by waving the bloody shirt of the victims, the insult to the national honor, and the monstrous evil of the sub-human perpetrators.

The logic here is that of the provocation which can be observed along the fringes of any demonstration which the government does not want to take place. The demonstration proceeds peacefully and responsibly, with marchers walking in orderly fashion within the cordons of parade marshals who are there to prevent trouble. Families with children, elderly people, and youth are all petitioning effectively for the redress of their grievances. The political effect is potentially quite positive. All of a sudden, a group of radical demonstrators, calling themselves anarchists but in reality police agent provocateurs, breaks away from the main body of the demonstration and begins smashing the windows of stores along the route. The anarchists have Molotov cocktails in hand, and they hurl them at the first units of riot police who arrive, injuring some of them seriously. The police, by now thoroughly provoked indeed, begin to fire tear gas grenades in all directions, and wade in to the peaceful crowd with their truncheons, mercilessly beating everyone who falls into their hands. Demonstrators are herded into blind allies, beaten, arrested, and carted off. It will be a long time before some of them come to another demonstration. Television coverage focuses on the violent minority, trying to make it look like the anarchist police agents are typical of the demonstration as a whole. Pundits pontificate; George Will is particularly indignant. This is the model for provocations of all types. It represents a spectacle for the gullible, a theatrical if bloody manipulation of staged pseudo-reality, and it points toward the reality of 9/11.

War commonly begins with provocations of this sort. The colossal blood-letting of World War I began in Sarajevo, the capital of Bosnia with the assassination of Archduke Franz Ferdinand and his wife by a Serbian nationalist fanatic named Gavrilo Prinkip, an activist of the group called the Black Hand, a Mazzini-style Serbian underground national liberation group. But the Black Hand was controlled by Serbian military intelligence. Colonel Apis of Serbian military intelligence was in turn an asset of the Okhrana, the Russian intelligence, through the Russian military attaché in Belgrade, and he and Prinkip may also have been under the influence of the British-backed Grand Orient freemasons, which had been working towards a general European war since about 1906 or 1907.

Another case was the explosion of the battleship USS *Maine* in the harbor of Spanish-controlled Havana, Cuba in 1898. The jingoistic Hearst and Pulitzer newspapers, the archetypes of modern yellow journalism, blamed the Spanish government and called for war against Spain, which soon ensued. The Hearst papers argued that the US warship had been sunk by the detonation of a Spanish mine, and drew imaginative cartoons to show how this might have happened.

This war is a fateful turning-point in world history, since it marks the launching of US imperialism on the world stage. But an inquiry conducted decades later by retired Admiral Hyman Rickover, the father of the US nuclear Navy, led to the conclusion that the explosion had taken place inside the *Maine*, probably as the result of sparks amidst the coal dust of an empty coal bunker, a fairly well-known danger in those days. But it may also be that the internal explosion was not an accident, but rather the result of a deliberately placed bomb.

World War II also began with a provocation, at least as far as Germany is concerned. When Hitler wanted to invade Poland in September 1939, he knew the majority of the German population did not want war. He accordingly hatched a plot which centered on the Gleiwitz radio station, a German broadcasting station located near the border with Poland. In late August 1939, Hitler obtained a group of German convicts, and had them dressed in Polish army uniforms. These wretched men were then taken to the Gleiwitz radio station and machine-gunned to death. Their bodies were arranged around the radio station in such a way as to suggest that they had been shot while storming the building. Nazi agents inside the radio station then broke into the ongoing program to read a raving anti-German declaration in Polish, proclaiming that Polish forces had taken over Gleiwitz and the radio there. This crude farce, when amplified and repeated hundreds of times by Dr. Goebbels' propaganda machinery, secured at least minimal acceptance by the German population of the inevitability of war, which broke out with Hitler's attack on Poland, September 1, 1939.

The classic case of strategic terrorism of this type is doubtless the Gunpowder Plot of November 5, 1605, a day that is still marked each year in the English calendar as Guy Fawkes' Day. In 1605 James I Stuart, a Protestant who united in his person the crowns of Scotland and England for the first time, was considering a policy of accommodation with the Spanish Empire, the leading Catholic power. James was also considering some measures of toleration for Catholics in England, where the majority of the landed gentry in the north of the country was still loyal to Rome. An influential group in London, backed by Venetian intelligence from abroad, wanted to push James I into a confrontation with the Spanish Empire, from which they hoped among other things to extract great personal profit. They also thought it was politically vital to keep persecuting the Roman Catholics. Chief among the war party was the royal chancellor, roughly equivalent to prime minister, who was Lord Robert Cecil, the Earl of Salisbury. Cecil set out to sway James I to adopt his policy, by means of terrorism.

Acting behind the scenes, Cecil cultivated some prominent Catholics, one of them Lord Thomas Percy from the famous Catholic Percy family, and used them as cut-outs to direct the operations of a group of naïve Catholic fanatics and adventurers, among them a certain gullible gentleman named Guy Fawkes. Thomas Percy was supposedly a Catholic fanatic, but in reality was a bigamist. This group of Catholic fanatics hatched the idea first of tunneling into the basement of the Houses of Parliament from a nearby house, and then simply of renting the basement of the Houses of Parliament, in order to pack that basement with explosives for the purpose of blowing up King, Lords, and Commons when James I came to open the Parliament early that November. But instead Guy Fawkes was caught going into the basement the night before the great crime was scheduled to occur. Fawkes and the rest of the plotters were tortured and hanged, and several Catholic clergy were also scapegoated. James I put aside his plans for toleration of Catholics, and England set out on a century of wars against the Spanish and Portuguese Empires, from which in turn the British Empire was born. Guy Fawkes Day became the yearly festival of "no popery" and hatred of Spain.

Concerning the Gunpowder Plot, the Jesuit Gerard concludes that "for purposes of State, the government of the day [meaning Cecil] either found means to instigate the conspirators to undertake their enterprise, or, at least, being, from an early stage of the undertaking, fully aware of what was going on, sedulously nursed the insane scheme till the time came to make capital out of it. That the conspirators, or the greater number of them, really meant to strike a great blow is not to be denied, though it may be less easy to assure ourselves of its precise character; and their guilt will not be palliated should it appear that, in projecting an atrocious crime, they were unwittingly playing the game of plotters more astute than themselves." (Gerard 17) Here we have an excellent definition of state-sponsored terrorism. Gerard's method of proof is this: "It will be enough to show that, whatever its origin, the conspiracy was, and must have been, known to those in power, who, playing with their infatuated dupes, allowed them to go on with their mad scheme, till the moment came to strike with full effect." (Gerard 55) This can also be applied to 9/11.

It should be added that James I does not seem to have been aware of the operation in advance. The plot was not directed against him; it rather intended to push him in a specific policy direction. After the event, James I does appear to have realized what Cecil's role had been, at least to some extent. Father Gerard speaks of Thomas Percy, Cecil's agent in the Gunpowder Plot, as a "tame duck employed to catch the wild ones." (Gerard 152) But the fact that he was Cecil's agent did not prevent Percy from being killed as part of the cover-up after November 5. At the risk of mixing metaphors, we can cite the opinion of a contemporary observer that Cecil, once he had secured the game birds he was seeking, hanged the spaniel who had actually caught them for him, "that its master's art might not appear." (Gerard 153)

Towards the end of the 1600s, some leaders of the Whig ministry decided that France, not Spain, was now the leading Catholic power. In 1678 they brought forth the charlatan Titus Oates to allege that he had proofs of a "popish plot" backed by France to restore Catholicism in England, including by manipulating the royal succession. Oates may be usefully compared to the many "anti-terrorism experts" who appear on television news broadcasts to report on what the terrorists are doing, since it is clear that most of what these commentators say they have simply invented. When Oates began to recite his charges there was mass hysteria in England, and several Jesuits were hanged. The diarist John Evelyn had never seen "the nation in more apprehension and consternation." So great was the fear that "…before the end of 1678 not only did a majority of the English people believe that there was such a plot, but anyone who ventured to deny it ran the risk of impeachment as an accessory. 'Twas worse than plotting to suspect the Plot.'" (Hay 122) The popish plot had enormous mass appeal: "the extravagant frenzy of the London mob took most people by surprise…London witnessed an exhibition of emotional fanaticism which has seldom been equaled in the history of a civilized nation. Mobs have often been as wicked, but not often so stupid. 'The imposture known as the Oates Plot,' wrote Lingard, 'supported by the arts and declamations of a numerous party, goaded the passions of men to a state of madness, and seemed to extinguish the native good sense and humanity of the English character.'" (Hay122-3) The great sponsor of Titus Oates was Anthony Ashley Cooper, Lord Shaftesbury, the founder of the Whig Party and a member of the oligarchical cabinet called the CABAL after the initials of its members: Clifford, Arlington, Buckingham, Ashley, and Lauderdale. The philosopher John Locke was Ashley's secretary. In the late summer of 1679 the hysteria began to subside, and it became apparent that Titus Oates was a fraud and an imposter. At this point King Charles II put Ashley on trial for treason. Ashley escaped conviction but had to flee to Holland, where he died.

We now turn to a structural analysis of modern false-flag terrorism of the type that is commonly sponsored by factions or networks embedded in the secret intelligence agencies of modern states, drawing on the work of Andreas von Bülow, Gerhard Wisnewski, Gianfranco Sanguinetti, and on my own research on the Moro assassination, the Red Brigades, and Italian terrorism in general.

PATSIES

> "I'm just a patsy."
> – Lee Harvey Oswald, November 1963

Speaking of Guy Fawkes and his confrères, Father Gerard comments that "many intelligent men took for granted that in some way or other the actual conspirators were but the dupes and instruments of more crafty men than themselves, and in their mad enterprise played the game of ministers of State." (Gerard 43) In this sense, Guy Fawkes may represent an archetype of the category of person known in modern intelligence parlance as the *patsy* (from the Italian *pazzi*, meaning fools and madmen; which in turn may be from the Pazzi family, who bungled a mad conspiracy to overthrow the Medicis by murder.)

If the real authorship of state-sponsored terrorism is to be successfully concealed, then a collection of scapegoats is the first ingredient required. These may be defined as the patsies, or alternatively as fall-guys, scapegoats, useful idiots, stooges or dupes. It is necessary that they be of low mental ability and great gullibility, since their mission is to be part of false-flag groups which pretend to be working for a cause, while in reality they are under the control of a private network inside the US government; so much the better if the cause is an impractical one, such as the restoration of the caliphate, or Islamic empire. It is vital for the terrorist controllers that the patsies not realize that this or that comrade in arms is actually a double agent, a provocateur working for the parallel CIA or some other complicit agency, of which more will be said later. The best candidates for the patsy role are psychotics, psychopaths, or sociopaths. They may be fanatics bursting with criminal energy and criminal intent, or they may be pathetic ideologues and naifs. Frequently they are also misfits, bunglers, and generally maladroit in what they undertake.

According to research sponsored in 1999 by the Library of Congress, in a 1972 study "psychologist B.J. Berkowitz describes six psychological types who would be most likely to threaten or try to use WMD: paranoids, paranoid schizophrenics, borderline mental defectives, schizophrenic types, passive-aggressive personality types, and sociopath personalities. He considered sociopaths the most likely actually to use WMD. Nuclear terrorism expert Jessica Stern disagrees. She believes that 'Schizophrenics and sociopaths, for example, may want to commit acts of mass destruction, but they are less likely than others to succeed.' She points out that large-scale dissemination of chemical, biological, or radiological agents requires a group effort, but that 'Schizophrenics, in particular, often have difficulty functioning in groups....'" (Hudson)

Because the patsies are usually such low-grade subjects, they require comprehensive support of many kinds. They may need help in renting an apartment or in finding a cover job. They always seem to be getting in trouble with the police, and then it is necessary to see that they get out on bail as quickly as possible. If they are lonely, they may need specially trained sex operatives to comfort them or even to marry them (the KGB and the Stasi called their sex troops "The Swallows"). Above all they require constant financial assistance to be able to travel around the world, as they so frequently seem to be able to do without any visible means of support. The most important thing about patsies is that they are almost always physically, mentally and technically unable to carry out the crimes of which they are accused. This is a matter of insufficient ability and capability, and not of the lack of criminal intent, which is often abundant.

Patsies can then be used in many combinations. They can be merged together in false flag terror operations. These organizations will assume a distinct ideological or religious coloration and will advertise it, and that will become the key to the process of creating or reinforcing the enemy image desired by the terrorist controllers after the terrorist action has been successfully carried out. That coloration or affiliation will constitute the false flag, and it will be assiduously prepared. Here some of the members may be witting; these are the double agents and police informers. Other components are not witting, at least about the most important things. What patsies can accomplish by themselves is often supplemented by the actions of informers, double agents, and doubles, who do things for them when they can not show up. Sometimes patsies are sent to make contact with other groups, a process known as sheep-dipping. If a terrorist controller wants to implicate the Podunk Democratic Party in terrorism, then he sends a patsy to sign up with them and attend their meetings before the terrorist act is carried out. That gives the police a good reason to raid the Podunk Democratic Party headquarters.

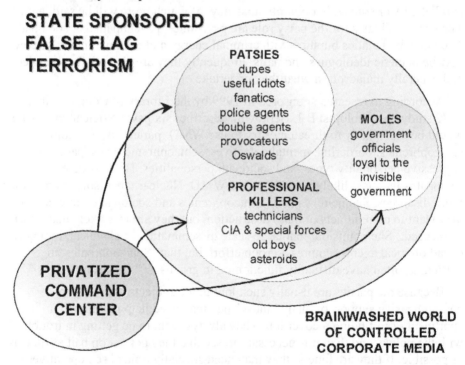

Thus, in 1992 and 1993, the New York City FBI informant and agent provocateur Emad Salem repeatedly tried to implicate the Sudanese UN Mission in his own "Islamic terror cell" World Trade Center bomb plot conspiracy. Here we see how a false flag terror cell sheep-dips its dupes into contact with a target, which then becomes the object of police investigation, and possibly later of military attack.

In January 2002, the Supreme Court of Germany had to call off all proceedings in the ongoing constitutional trial concerning the Schroeder government's attempt to ban the extreme right-wing or reputedly neo-Nazi National Democratic Party of Germany because it turned out that the government's chief witness, a member of the national NPD party executive, had worked as an informant for the German Constitutional Protection Agency (*Verfassungsschutz*, comparable to the FBI), for many years. The Court ruled that the trial could not go forward until this issue was clarified.

Osama bin Laden, the rich misfit, has often been described in terms which seem to suit him for this category. A CIA agent named Beardman has asserted that Osama bin Laden, during the entire time that he was organizing his mujahideen fighters to do battle with the Soviets in Afghanistan, never realized that the operation was being financed and directed by the CIA. The CIA's Beardman confirmed, in this regard, that Osama bin Laden was not aware of the role he was playing on behalf of Washington. In the words of bin Laden (quoted by Beardman): "neither I, nor my brothers saw evidence of American help." Bin Laden thus may also qualify as a clueless dupe.

The patsies ultimately have three vital functions. The first is that they have to be noticed. They must attract lots and lots of attention. They may issue raving statements on videotape, or doubles can be used to issue these statements for them if they are not up to it. They need to get into fights with passersby, as Mohammed Atta is said to have done concerning a parking space at the airport in Boston early in the morning on September 11. Even if they are presumed dead they must remain prominent, as in the case of the hijacker's passport, which is alleged by the FBI to have survived the fiery collapse of the World Trade Center towers to be found undamaged and unsinged on a nearby street. Even when presumed dead they must be eloquent about themselves and their activities, as the accused 9/11 hijackers when they left behind a copy of the Koran, airline schedules, terrorist literature and videotapes, and Atta's crudely forged last will and testament in a car and in luggage.

Despite the need to be noticed as much as possible, the patsies have to stay out of jail. If they are all in jail, the planned terror action cannot take place. This is not because the patsies are needed to carry it out, but rather because they must be on hand in order to be blamed for it, whether they are on the scene or far away. If the patsies are in jail, they cannot be scapegoated. Therefore a lawyer and bail money must be provided, or a complicit judge told to release the defendant. Immigration authorities and Customs must be told to look the other way. To keep the patsies out of jail so they can serve their vital purpose is the job of the moles, as will soon be shown.

Finally, if all else goes well, it is the destiny of the patsies to take the blame for the terror action once it has happened. At this point the moles in the government apparatus, who had earlier been the patsies' greatest friends and protectors, become their most implacable enemies. The patsies must be hunted down and, preferably, liquidated on the spot, as the British Special Air Services anti-terrorist force always prefers to do, with a maximum of firepower. Their faces and stories will be demonized as the latest manifestation of absolute evil. The nationality, philosophy, or religion which the media portray them as representing will become the target of raving vilification, arrest, economic sanctions, cruise missile retaliation, and armed invasion, as the case may be.

A pathetic case in point is Richard Reid, the shoe bomber of December 2001. Shortly after Reid was arrested for attempting to blow up the transatlantic airliner he was traveling in with the help of explosives planted in the soles of his shoes, sources in the Washington DC mosque said that they had acquired the following profile of Reid from Dr. Abdul Haqq Baker of Brixton Mosque in London. According to Baker and others from Brixton, Richard Reid could only be described as mentally deficient. "He was not someone who would be medically classified as mentally retarded," the source reported, "but he was definitely slow." He could not have hatched any kind of terror attack on his own, and could not have even put the shoe bombs on his own feet without help, the source had been told by officials of the Brixton Mosque.

Yet, according to news accounts, Reid spent time in Iran three or four years before his terror attempt, and traveled to Tel Aviv from Heathrow Airport near London in the summer of 2001. He was thoroughly frisked before being allowed on to the El Al flight, and was forced to sit next to a sky marshal at the back of the plane. Israeli officials claimed to know nothing about what Reid was doing in Israel. From Israel, Reid went to Egypt, and then to Turkey, before returning to London Heathrow. Reid had been sleeping on the floor at the Brixton Mosque, had no visible means of support, etc. Reid's father, who had converted to Islam, and encouraged his son to do the same, told the American press that his son must have been brainwashed by radical Islamists to undertake the suicide attack. (*New York Times* and *Washington Post*, December 29, 2001)

Another case may well be that of José Padilla, the man who was arrested at Chicago's O'Hare airport, and who has been designated as an enemy combatant by Attorney General Ashcroft and held incommunicado without charges or a lawyer for months. Although he may only be a walk-on in Ashcroft's larger spectacle, what kind of an Islamic fighter was Padilla supposed to be? According to Maureen Dowd, this "plotter was a Chicago street punk named José Padilla, a hothead with a long criminal record who was thrown in jail in Florida for shooting at a motorist in a road-rage incident. The mind games of fear begin with Abu Zubaydah, the US captive, one of Osama bin Laden's top lieutenants, who fingered Padilla." (*New York Times*, June 12, 2002)

The most famous patsy is of course Lee Harvey Oswald, the archetype of the embittered, lonely misfit and drifter. But he was a misfit with a difference, one who was able to move from the Marine Corps to émigré status in the USSR, then back to Texas and New Orleans as an activist for the Fair Play for Cuba Committee. Oswald was someone who seemed to go out of his way to be abrasive and to attract attention. He handed out leaflets for the Fair Play for Cuba Committee and got involved in altercations with anti-Castro Cubans. He appeared in a radio debate, and was interviewed on television. He took a surprise trip to Mexico City to visit the Soviet Embassy there. He did everything possible to get noticed. Indeed, he got noticed so much that at various times there may have been two or even three Oswald doubles running around, something that would have required the resources of a major intelligence organization like the CIA or the FBI. But Oswald was also unable to manage the petty details of his own everyday life without the assistance of others, notably of the European aristocrat Georges de Morenschildt, a patrician who had George H. W. Bush's name and phone number in his address book.

Oswald was most likely an FBI informant, working for Special Agent Guy Bannister in New Orleans. But this did not protect him from being fingered as the assassin, nor did it save him from being silenced by Jack Ruby before he could ever testify in his own defense. The problem with Oswald, as with so many patsies, is that he was neither physically nor technically capable of carrying out the crime which has been ascribed to him: using his antiquated Italian 1917 Mannlicher-Carcano rifle with its crude little telescopic sight, it is clear that Oswald could never have fired with sufficient speed and accuracy the four or five shots (at minimum) that were actually heard on Dealey Plaza that day, and which are necessary to account for the number of wounds suffered by President Kennedy and Governor Connally, plus other shots that missed their target.

This question of *physical impossibility* is often the most obvious weak point of the official explanations of terrorist actions. In the Kennedy assassination, it was expressly to address the problem of the physical impossibility of Oswald's acting as a lone assassin that Arlen Spector, a staff member of the Warren Commission, invented his magic bullet theory. Spector asserted that the same slug had caused seven wounds: an entry wound in Kennedy's back, an exit wound at the base of his throat, then an entry wound in Connally's back, an exit wound in Connally's chest, an entry wound in Connally's wrist, and exit wound from the other side of Connally's wrist, and finally an entry wound in Connally's leg.

At the end of all this, the bullet was supposedly found in virtually pristine condition lying in a stretcher at Parkland Hospital after Kennedy had died. Even after these incredible contortions, requiring that the same bullet change course in mid-air at least twice, the problem of physical impossibility had not been solved, since there were still four or five shots on the audio tape which had recorded the sounds of the assassination through the open microphone of a Dallas police officer's radio. It was this insuperable problem which led the House Assassinations Committee of 1978 to rule that Kennedy's death was the result of a probable conspiracy, and not simply of the actions of a deranged lone assassin.

As Sanguinetti sums up, "the outrages that are accomplished directly by the intelligence agencies and secret services of the State are not usually claimed by anybody, but are each time imputed or attributed to some convenient 'culprit,' like Pinelli or Valpreda. Experience has proved that this is the weakest point of such terrorism, and that which determines the extreme fragility of it in the political usage that certain forces want to make of it. It is starting from the results of the same experience that the strategists of secret services of the State seek, from this point on, to lend a greater credibility, or at least a lesser inverisimilitude to their own work ...by claiming them directly through such-and-such initials of a ghostly group...." (Sanguinetti 2)

THE PATSY MILIEU

> You give yourself for an agent provocateur. The proper business
> of an agent provocateur is to provoke.
> – Joseph Conrad, *The Secret Agent* (1907).

The patsies inhabit a scene of their own, a place on the outskirts of society where terrorists, naïve or romantic dupes, provocateurs, sting operatives, double agents, *Doppelgänger* and informers congregate. There was something of this nature among southern European fascist extremists in Madrid, Athens, and Rome during the 1960s and 1970s; the denizens of this milieu played their parts in the "black terrorism" of those years. There was a parallel milieu of anarchists, Maoists, left communists, Trotskyists, and anarchosyndicalists in many cities of Europe during that same time frame. In the 1980s and 1990s, a patsy milieu developed among right-wing militia activists and paramilitaries in the Great Plains and upper Midwest of America. During the 1970s, 1980s, and 1990s, a patsy milieu has grown up not just in the Middle East, Afghanistan, Pakistan, and Indonesia, but also in western Europe and the United States. In fact, the classic patsy milieu of the 1990s was in London.

The patsy milieu has been skillfully evoked by Joseph Conrad in his fascinating novel, *The Secret Agent* (1907). Here we have the agent provocateur Verloc meeting with his confrères of the International Red Committee; Verloc is in the pay of the Russian Embassy, among others, and attempts to organize a bombing of the prime meridian at Greenwich Observatory. The Russian Embassy wants the attentat in order to motivate the international Milan conference to crack down on nihilists, revolutionaries, and bomb-throwers all over Europe. A movie which accurately depicts the world of patsies, moles, and expert professionals is *The Package*, written by John Bishop, starring Gene Hackman and Tommy Lee Jones. During the Gorbachev era, a group of US and Soviet generals opposed to disarmament decide to sabotage an upcoming treaty by assassinating Gorbachev during a visit to Chicago. Tommy Lee Jones is the expert professional who operates in complete anonymity – he is smuggled into the US under a fake identity. There is also a pathetic patsy, recruited by one of the mole generals from a military prison and sent to Chicago to attract attention as a neo-Nazi.

The following schematic diagram shows how synthetic terror functions as a pillar of the oligarchical state.

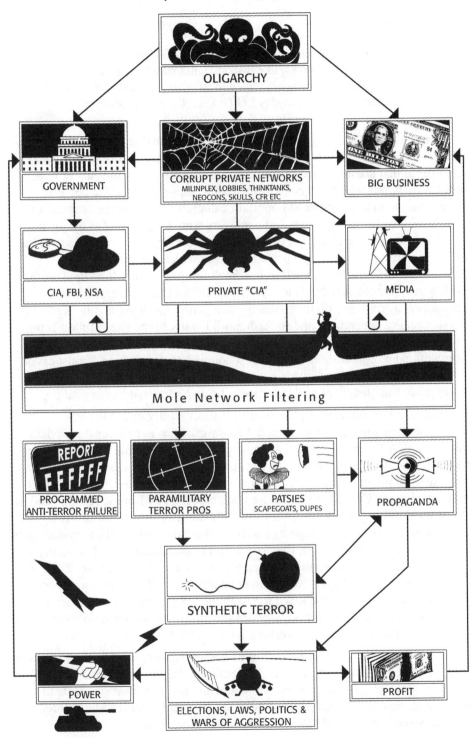

MOLES

> ...jokes were actually made that the key FBIHQ personnel had
> to be spies or moles, like Robert Hanssen, who were actually
> working for Osama bin Laden to have so undercut Minneapolis'
> effort. – Colleen Rowley to FBI Director Robert Mueller

As has already been suggested, the patsies are incapable of operating on their own for any length of time, and certainly do not have the ability to carry out the vast crimes that are attributed to them. The assistance which the patsies require in order to carry out their roles come from another sub-system of the terrorist enterprise, the moles. The most important category of moles is constituted by high-level government officials and managers who are not loyal to the agencies they work for, and certainly not to the Constitution they are sworn to serve, but rather operate as members of a private network which has infiltrated the government and ensconced itself in it, sometimes over a very long time. In fact, the US government as it exists today is the result of many generations of penetration by moles, with the moles of each generation assisting the careers of the succeeding generation, and so forth, until loyalty to the Constitution is the exception rather than the rule. One definition of a mole is "A spy who operates from within an organization, especially a double agent operating against his or her own government from within its intelligence establishment." Thus the intelligence establishment itself may function as a subversive organization.

Foreign moles have been able to operate successfully inside the US government for long periods. Aldrich Ames worked as a mole for the Soviets inside the CIA for many years. The same goes for Soviet mole Robert Hanssen of the FBI, who was discovered in the spring of 2000. In 1997 the press carried a news item about an Israeli mole code-named Mega , who was allegedly ensconced in the Clinton White House and controlled by Danny Yatom, head of the Mossad. (*Washington Post*, May 7, 1997) But here we are not primarily concerned with outright foreign moles, but rather with moles whose loyalty goes to networks based on religion, finance, or other associations based primarily in the US, although here foreign influence certainly cannot be ruled out. Even so, the fact that high-level spies were able to operate for so long suggests a certain nonchalance about the presence of moles in the US government bureaucracy. Certainly a mole working for a US-based subversive network would have a much easier time operating than one working for the USSR.

So far, the classic mole suspect of 9/11 according to most published accounts is Dave Frasca, the head of the radical Islamic fundamentalist bureau of the FBI, the point at which the Phoenix memorandum and the Minnesota requests to search Zacarias Moussaoui's laptop evidently converged, only to be ignored, sabotaged, and sanctioned. As *Time* magazine commented:

...in its most searching passage, Rowley's letter lays out the case that the FBI made fateful miscalculations by failing to see a possible connection between the Minneapolis investigation of flight student Moussaoui and the hunch of Phoenix agent Kenneth Williams – posited in a report to HQ two months earlier – that al-Qaeda operatives were attending US flight schools. Law-enforcement and congressional sources told Time that both reports landed on the desk of Dave Frasca, the head of the FBI's radical-fundamentalist unit. The Phoenix memo was buried; the Moussaoui warrant request was denied. (*Time*, May 27, 2002)

Other accounts differ as to the identity of the main blocker of the Phoenix memorandum and the Minneapolis proposals. According to former CIA agent Ray McGovern, the official who sat on this material was Spike Owen, who nevertheless "received a $20,000 cash award from the administration for his duties in safeguarding the American people." (*Washington Post*, July 26, 2004) Was this a mole?

The Phoenix memorandum, written by Kenneth Williams, an agent in Phoenix, was sent to FBI headquarters as an electronic computer message on July 10. It was reviewed by mid-level supervisors who headed the bureau's Bin Laden and Islamic extremist counter-terrorism units. The Phoenix memorandum urged FBI headquarters to investigate Middle Eastern men enrolled in American flight schools, and cited bin Laden by name, and suggested that the men might be training for terror operations against the United States. (*New York Times*, May 15, 2002)

Frasca is not mentioned once in the final report of the Kean-Hamilton Commission, and whistleblower Colleen Rowley, despite having been featured on the cover of *Time* as person of the year, never testified in public, and gets only one fleeting mention of her interview with the 9/11 commission in footnote 94, page 557, towards the back of the book.

Rowley's memo to FBI Director Mueller has been published, and is worth examining at length. The Supervisory Special Agent to whom she repeatedly refers is once again presumably David Frasca. Rowley reports:

The Minneapolis agents who responded to the call about Moussaoui's flight training identified him as a terrorist threat from a very early point. The decision to take him into custody on August 15, 2001, on the INS "overstay" charge was a deliberate one to counter that threat and was based on the agents' reasonable suspicions. While it can be said that Moussaoui's overstay status was fortuitous, because it allowed for him to be taken into immediate custody and prevented him from receiving any more flight training, it was certainly not something the INS coincidentally undertook of their own volition. I base this on the conversation I had when the agents called me at home late on the evening Moussaoui was taken into custody to confer and ask for legal advice about their next course of action. The INS agent was assigned to the FBI's Joint Terrorism Task Force and was therefore working in tandem with FBI agents. To say then, as has been iterated numerous times, that probable cause did not exist until after the disastrous event occurred, is really to acknowledge that the missing piece of probable cause was only the FBI's (FBIHQ's) failure to appreciate that such an event could occur.

Even without knowledge of the Phoenix communication (and any number of other additional intelligence communications that FBIHQ personnel were privy to in their central coordination roles), the Minneapolis agents appreciated the risk. So I think it's very hard for the FBI to offer the "20-20 hindsight" justification for its failure to act! Also intertwined with my reluctance in this case to accept the "20-20 hindsight" rationale is first-hand knowledge that I have of statements made on September 11th, after the first attacks on the World Trade Center had already occurred, made telephonically by the FBI Supervisory Special Agent (SSA) who was the one most involved in the Moussaoui matter and who, up to that point, seemed to have been consistently, almost deliberately thwarting the Minneapolis FBI agents' efforts.... Even after the attacks had begun, the SSA in question was still attempting to block the search of Moussaoui's computer, characterizing the World Trade Center attacks as a mere coincidence with Minneapolis' prior suspicions about Moussaoui.

The fact is that key FBIHQ personnel whose job it was to assist and coordinate with field division agents on terrorism investigations and the obtaining and use of FISA searches (and who theoretically were privy to many more sources of intelligence information than field division agents), continued to, almost inexplicably, throw up roadblocks and undermine Minneapolis' by-now desperate efforts to obtain a FISA search warrant, long after the French intelligence service provided its information and probable cause became clear. [The special court that grants requests for FISA warrants had denied only one out of 12,000 requests in its entire history.] HQ personnel brought up almost ridiculous questions in their apparent efforts to undermine the probable cause. In all of their conversations and correspondence, HQ personnel never disclosed to the Minneapolis agents that the Phoenix Division had, only approximately three weeks earlier, warned of Al Qaeda operatives in flight schools seeking flight training for terrorist purposes! Nor did FBIHQ personnel do much to disseminate the information about Moussaoui to other appropriate intelligence/law enforcement authorities. When, in a desperate 11th hour measure to bypass the FBIHQ roadblock, the Minneapolis Division undertook to directly notify the CIA's Counter Terrorist Center (CTC), FBIHQ personnel actually chastised the Minneapolis agents for making the direct notification without their approval!

Eventually on August 28, 2001, after a series of e-mails between Minneapolis and FBIHQ, which suggest that the FBIHQ SSA deliberately further undercut the FISA effort by not adding the further intelligence information which he had promised to add that supported Moussaoui's foreign power connection and making several changes in the wording of the information that had been provided by the Minneapolis Agent, the Minneapolis agents were notified that the NSLU Unit Chief did not think there was sufficient evidence of Moussaoui's connection to a foreign power. Minneapolis personnel are, to this date, unaware of the specifics of the verbal presentations by the FBIHQ SSA to NSLU or whether anyone in NSLU ever was afforded the opportunity to actually read for him/herself all of the information on Moussaoui that had been gathered by the Minneapolis Division and the French intelligence service. Obviously verbal presentations are far more susceptible to mischaracterization and error. The e-mail communications between Minneapolis and FBIHQ, however, speak for themselves and there are far better witnesses than me who can provide their first hand knowledge of these events characterized in one Minneapolis agent's e-mail as FBIHQ is "setting this up for failure."

My only comment is that the process of allowing the FBI supervisors to make changes in affidavits is itself fundamentally wrong, just as, in the follow-up to FBI Laboratory Whistleblower Frederic Whitehurst's allegations, this process was revealed to be wrong in the context of writing up laboratory results. With the Whitehurst allegations, this process of allowing supervisors to re-write portions of laboratory reports, was found to provide opportunities for over-zealous supervisors to skew the results in favor of the prosecution. In the Moussaoui case, it was the opposite – the process allowed the Head-quarters Supervisor to downplay the significance of the information thus far collected in order to get out of the work of having to see the FISA application through or possibly to avoid taking what he may have perceived as an unnecessary career risk. I understand that the failures of the FBIHQ personnel involved in the Moussaoui matter are also being officially excused because they were too busy with other investigations, the *Cole* bombing and other important terrorism matters, but the Supervisor's taking of the time to read each word of the information submitted by Minneapolis and then substitute his own choice of wording belies to some extent the notion that he was too busy.

To sum up her frustration, Rowley wrote: "I know I shouldn't be flippant about this, but jokes were actually made that the key FBIHQ personnel had to be spies or moles, like Robert Hansen [sic], who were actually working for Osama bin Laden to have so undercut Minneapolis' effort." These lines speak for themselves. Evidently Frasca was not alone, since he was able to stay on the job with impunity even after 9/11, and even received a promotion. Rowley stresses the lack of any accountability whatsoever in the FBI's internal process, which seems to be made to order for facilitating the unhampered operations of moles.

> Although the last thing the FBI or the country needs now is a witch hunt, I do find it odd that (to my knowledge) no inquiry whatsoever was launched of the relevant FBIHQ personnel's actions a long time ago. Despite FBI leaders' full knowledge of all the items mentioned herein (and probably more that I'm unaware of), the SSA, his unit chief, and other involved HQ personnel were allowed to stay in their positions and, what's worse, occupy critical positions in the FBI's SIOC Command Center post September 11th. (The SSA in question actually received a promotion some months afterward!) It's true we all make mistakes and I'm not suggesting that HQ personnel in question ought to be burned at the stake, but, we all need to be held accountable for serious mistakes. (*Time*, May 27, 2002)

An internal FBI memo, which became public in May 2002, revealed that FBI agents had destroyed evidence gathered in an investigation involving Osama bin Laden's network after its e-mail wiretap system mistakenly captured information to which the agency was not entitled. This was supposedly because the FBI software being used, called Carnivore, not only picked up the e-mails of its target, "but also picked up e-mails on non-covered targets," said the memo, which was written in March 2000 to agency headquarters in Washington. According to the memo, "The FBI technical person was apparently so upset that he destroyed all the e-mail take, including the take on" the suspect. These events allegedly took place during an investigation in Denver in which the FBI's bin Laden unit was using the bureau's Carnivore system to conduct electronic surveillance of a suspect under a Foreign Intelligence Surveillance Act warrant. The memo was addressed to M.E. "Spike" Bowman, the FBI's associate general counsel for national security. Another mole?

The Justice Department's Office of Intelligence and Policy Review claimed to be furious after learning the evidence captured by the e-mail wiretap system was destroyed because of the glitch, the memo states. "To state that she was unhappy at ITOS (International Terrorism Operations Center) and the UBL (bin Laden) unit is an understatement," the memo stated, quoting a Justice official. This incident came to light in the course of a court battle over whether the Carnivore system was being used illegally by the FBI to scoop up emails that were not covered by a warrant. The main reform undertaken by the FBI in this matter would appear to have been to change the name of Carnivore to DCS-1000. (D. Ian Hopper, "Memo: FBI Destroyed Evidence in Bin Laden Case After Glitch With E-mail Surveillance System," Associated Press, *Boston Globe*, May 28, 2002)

Then there is the case of Kevin Delaney, an official of the Federal Aviation Administration. During the day of 9/11, supervisors had asked air traffic controllers and other officials to talk about their experiences, and had taped these statements. It later came to light that this evidence had been subsequently destroyed by an FAA official named Kevin Delaney. Press reports in the spring of 2004 confirmed that Delaney had burned the tapes. Was he a mole? The 9/11 commission was not interested in this highly significant and highly indicative matter, and did not bother to include Delaney's name in its final report. How many other Kevin Delaneys still infest the federal bureaucracy may never be known with precision. But, according to press accounts, federal agency records with possible bearing on 9/11 were "routinely destroyed" between September 11, 2001 and the launching of the 9/11 commission in the spring of 2003. (*New York Times*, May 6, 2004)

Another FBI whistleblower was Robert Wright, whose case was taken up by David Schippers, the lawyer who prosecuted the impeachment of Bill Clinton before the House of Representatives, and later by Larry Klayman of Judicial Watch. According to Klayman, Wright had been sounding an alarm within the FBI for years before 9/11 about terrorists within the United States. Rather than act on Wright's warnings, the FBI deflected and obstructed his efforts to curtail dangerous movements by agents of Hamas and Hezbollah. Wright's work within the FBI was geared towards thwarting money-laundering activities by these agents, and after going public he claimed that his efforts were stymied because of an official desire to coddle pro-Palestinian groups to protect the reputation of Yasser Arafat. But Wright's expertise does not reach up that high; all he knew was what he saw, and the explanations he cites are hearsay or speculation.

The important thing is the phenomenon. In the course of Wright's probing, a Saudi businessman named Yasin Kadi had become implicated in the terrorism funding. Wright was careful to note that, one month after the 9/11 attacks, Kadi was named by the Federal government as a financial supporter of Osama bin Laden. Wright's frustration about the FBI's inaction regarding his warnings led him to write a 500-page manuscript detailing the Bureau's anti-terrorism failings entitled "Fatal Betrayals of the Intelligence Mission." At a press conference in May, 2002, Wright summed up: "My efforts have always been geared towards neutralizing the terrorist threats that focused on taking the lives of American citizens, in addition to harming the national and economic security of America. However, as a direct result of the incompetence, and at times intentional obstruction of justice by FBI management to prevent me from bringing terrorists to justice, Americans have unknowingly been exposed to potential terrorist attacks for years." He went on to state, "Knowing what I know, I can confidently say that until the investigative responsibilities for terrorism are removed from the FBI, I will not feel safe." (William Rivers Pitt, *Truthout*, May 31, 2002)

For analytical purposes, we must stress once again that these activities of reputed FBI moles all have to do with the key mole mission of preventing the patsies from being rounded up and put out of action. The patsies, we recall, are not the actual authors of the crime, but their presence as the scapegoats is indispensable to the entire operation. And if the patsies are to operate, their support network, including funding, must operate undisturbed. Ironically, shutting down the patsies tends to shut down the operation. Even though the patsies are not part of the operation itself, they are needed for its propaganda exploitation. The question of the actual authors of the crime will be dealt with shortly.

But is there any hope that things may have gotten better after 9/11? Let us look for a moment at the FBI's own in-house investigation of what went wrong. According to the *Washington Post*, the leader of this internal inquiry turns out to have been the official whose most important achievement in his previous career had been the stubborn obstruction of the inquiry into the Waco massacre by former Senator and current US Ambassador to the UN John Danforth. The FBI official in question was Thomas A. Kelley, the head of the team looking into what the FBI knew and didn't know prior to Sept. 11 for the JICI. Kelley had previously been the deputy general counsel of the FBI. In that capacity he obstructed Danforth's investigation into the FBI's role at the Branch Davidian compound in Waco in the spring of 1993. A December 2000 internal FBI memo reported that Kelley "continued to thwart and obstruct" the Waco investigation to the point that Danforth was forced to send a team to search FBI headquarters for the documents he needed. The memo said that Kelley should have been investigated by the Office of Professional Responsibility for "unprofessional conduct, poor judgment, conflict of interest, hostile work environment and retaliation/reprisal" in connection with his role in the Waco investigation.

Sen. Charles Grassley (R-IA), in a letter to the leaders of JICI, expressed concern about Kelley's presence in the investigation, and noted that Kelley retired from the FBI before a probe by the Office of Professional Responsibility (OPR) could get off the ground. JICI officials said they were waiting for confidential memos and other documents relating to the allegations against Kelley before deciding how to proceed. Danforth himself, in an interview last year, faulted the FBI's "spirit of resistance" to outside scrutiny. He said getting the information he needed for his investigation "was like pulling teeth." (*Washington Post*, June 22, 2002)

In the recent history of terrorism, we have been able to observe situations in which the moles inside the state apparatus and the terrorists in the field have become almost impossible to distinguish. In other words, the moles have gone out into the field in the guise of double agents and infiltrators. One such case involves the shadowy Greek terrorist group, November 19. This group advertises itself as a reaction to the US-backed fascist colonels' coup in Greece in 1967. More recently, November 19 has inveighed in its communiqués against US imperialism, the capitalist class, the European Community, and Germany, which it has defined as the "Fourth Reich," a slogan which smacks of the Thatcher-Ridley regime in Britain in 1989-90. It was the November 19 group which in December 1975 claimed responsibility for the assassination of Richard Welch, the CIA station chief in Athens. This crime was especially useful to the CIA, to its incoming chief, George H. W. Bush, and to the Ford administration in general, who had been on the defensive in intelligence matters for many months because of the aggressive investigations of the Church Committee in the Senate and the Pike Committee in the House, which had unearthed much evidence of illegal and questionable activity by the US spy agencies. The Pike Committee had even issued a contempt of Congress citation against none other than Henry Kissinger, the strongman of the Ford regime. Columnists friendly to the CIA impudently blamed the death of Welch directly on the Church and Pike committees, although neither of them had ever mentioned Welch or Athens. (Tarpley 1992 300-301)

Over the years the November 19 organization, while carrying out some 40 armed attacks and assassinations, demonstrated a remarkable ability to escape capture, evading the most carefully prepared traps and ambushes. Gradually the awareness spread that November 19 somehow had access to information from the secret councils of the Greek anti-terror authorities. After four November 19 operatives escaped a police ambush in March 1992, the case broke open to some extent. The boss of the Greek anti-terror unit EKAM, Mihalis Mavroleas, was ousted from his job. It soon became evident that the investigators and the terrorists were in fact the same persons! The Greek Minister for Public Order and the national Chief of Police were obliged to come forward with the extremely embarrassing revelation that November 19 possessed a network of spies within the police. The EKAM, which had been founded in 1990 as the anti-terror *corps d'élite*, had allegedly been completely penetrated! About half of the anti-terror personnel were fired.

But the Athens authorities were clearly doing their best at damage control. As damaging as their revelations were, they were not as damning as the obvious truth, which was that November 19 was in fact a wholly owned subsidiary of the Greek police and intelligence services, perhaps with ties to the CIA and to NATO intelligence. This impression is confirmed by persistent reports of the existence in Greece of a paramilitary formation founded some decades back and supposedly dedicated to the task of organizing guerrilla warfare against Soviet occupying forces in case Greece were conquered in the course of some future war. This unit would thus fit the logic of the stay-behind organization, which has been amply documented in the case of Italy in the case of Gladio, which we describe below. (Wisnewski 1994 395-400)

Something quite similar has been established in regard to the Italian Red Brigades. In 1982 an important official of the Italian Justice Ministry in Rome, Giovanni Senzani, was arrested on the charge of being the head of the Red Brigades in the Naples area. Senzani had been the object of a campaign in the Rome press about the need to discover the identity of *la talpa*, the mole in the state bureaucracy. Senzani was in close relations to SISMI, the Italian military intelligence service, an agency which had been implicated in the Milan bomb of 1969 and other terrorist atrocities. This would indicate that at least part of the Red Brigades structure was directed from inside the government.

The Red Brigades had been created in the late 1960s at the Sociology Department of the University of Trento in northern Italy. The original members had displayed sociopathic symptoms, and they had gradually been eliminated by arrests and shootouts with the police. The Italian investigating judge Ferdinando Imposimato asserted in 1982 that the Red Brigades had been infiltrated by the Israeli Mossad no later than 1978. Based on testimony from two jailed former members of the Red Brigades, Imposimato reported that the Mossad had provided the Italian terrorists with weapons, money, and information. As the original members suffered attrition, they were replaced by new recruits. One of these was Mario Moretti, reputedly the leader of the Red Brigades during the Moro kidnapping. More senior members complained from their jail cells that Moretti failed to pass on warnings of coming police raids, and sabotaged attempted jail breaks. Moretti advocated a policy of constantly escalating violence, and was widely considered an *agent provocateur* of the CIA.

In these cases, it is not the terrorist organization which has infiltrated the state apparatus, but the state apparatus which finds it convenient to practice a virtual interchangeability with top members of the terrorist organization. Sanguinetti notes that in certain safe houses or lairs of the Red Brigades there was found "an abundance of ultra-confidential material issuing from police headquarters, central police stations and even from ministries. In view of such eloquent facts, spectacular information [i.e. new broadcasts] always claimed to explain them by emphasizing the ultra-efficient organization of the terrible Red Brigades, and by adding, in order to enhance this wonderful godsend for advertising, the fact that these clandestine militants, so hunted-down but so tentacular, have infiltrated everywhere, even ministries and central police stations." This, as we will see, is like some 9/11 researchers who conclude that, since the attacks took place on a day when so many special exercises were taking place, al Qaeda must have infiltrated the Pentagon in order to know exactly when to strike. Naturally Sanguinetti cannot entertain such nonsense. His conclusion: "It is not the Red Brigades who have infiltrated the central police stations and ministries, but agents of the State, issuing from the central police stations and ministries, who have infiltrated the Red Brigades by design, and not only their top leadership, to be sure." (Sanguinetti 21)

SIBEL EDMONDS: INSIDE THE FBI MOLEHILL

A similar and highly significant case has come to the surface in connection with 9/11. This involves Sibel Edmonds, who worked as a translator for the FBI's Washington field office. Edmonds' story may give some the impression that the FBI has been penetrated by some subversive Middle East organization, but a careful reading suggests the penetration was in the opposite direction. Edmonds became known to the public as a whistle blower protesting very strange activities in her FBI work place. As a result, she was accused of having breached FBI security, and was fired. The heart of Edmonds's allegation is that the FBI office where she worked was staffed by members of the very same Middle Eastern organization whose wiretapped conversations the office was working to translate. The FBI, of course, denied everything, but Edmonds recounts that when she told Dennis Saccher, a special agent in the Washington field office who was conducting the surveillance, about her co-worker's actions, Saccher had replied, "It looks like espionage to me." However, he refused to comment for the press. Edmonds was fired in March 2002 after she reported her concerns. Government officials said the FBI fired her because her "disruptiveness" hurt her on-the-job "performance." Edmonds said she believes she was fired in retaliation for reporting on her co-worker.

Edmonds began working at the FBI in late September 2001. She later reported that she had become particularly alarmed when she discovered that a recently hired FBI translator was going around saying that she belonged to precisely the same Middle Eastern organization whose taped conversations she had been translating for FBI counterintelligence agents. FBI officials did everything they could to prevent the name of the target group from being revealed to the public, allegedly for national security reasons. This case became public when a *Washington Post* reporter discovered Edmonds's name in her whistle-blowing letters to federal and congressional officials and approached her for an interview. Edmonds said that on several occasions, her fellow translator had tried to recruit her to join the targeted foreign group. "This person told us she worked for our target organization," Edmonds said in an interview. "These are the people we are targeting, monitoring." Of course, what all this means is that the target organization was also controlled by the FBI, or was itself part of the FBI – not that the FBI had been infiltrated.

The other translator was an unidentified 33-year-old US citizen whose native country is home to the target group. This is also the country were Edmonds was born, and is probably Turkey or Iran. Both Edmonds and the other translator are US citizens. The other woman, who is still working under contract for the FBI's Washington field office, refused to comment. Edmonds also reported that the woman and her husband, a US military officer, suggested that Edmonds become a member of their group during a hastily arranged visit to Edmonds' Northern Virginia home on a Sunday morning in December 2001. "He said, 'Are you a member of the particular organization?" Edmonds recalled the woman's husband saying. The military officer went on to add: "It's a very good place to be a member. There are a lot of advantages of being with this organization and doing things together and one of the greatest things about it is you can have an early, unexpected retirement. And you will be totally set if you go to that specific country." Edmonds also reported that the military officer assured her that she would easily be admitted to the group, especially if she said she worked for the FBI. Later, Edmonds said, the same woman approached her with a list dividing up individuals whose phone lines were being secretly tapped: under the plan, the woman would translate conversations of her fellow members of the target organization, and Edmonds would handle other phone calls. Edmonds said she refused and that the woman told her that her lack of cooperation could put her family in danger.

Edmonds also brought her concerns to her supervisor and other FBI officials in the Washington field office. When no action was taken, she also reported to the FBI's Office of Professional Responsibility, then to the Justice Department's inspector general. "Investigations are being compromised," Edmonds wrote to the Office of the Inspector General (OIG) in March 2002. "Incorrect or misleading translations are being sent to agents in the field. Translations are being blocked and circumvented." Edmonds had also written to Dale Watson, the bureau's counter-terrorism chief. Her case has been referred to the OIG. (*Washington Post*, June 19, 2002) But in the meantime, the Ashcroft Justice Department has taken the extraordinary step of declaring the Edmonds case a state secret, meaning that literally everything is classified. Sibel Edmonds was interviewed by the 9/11 commission, and makes it into the commission report just once, in footnote 25, page 490, in the course of a discussion about how important it is to have good translators. But the substance of her case goes completely unreported. This is not surprising, since the entire case has been classified by Ashcroft as a state secret.

After the 9/11 commission had issued its report, Edmonds sent an open letter to Kean and Hamilton pointing out that much of the evidence she had delivered to the commission had simply been ignored. She also escalated her critique by naming the names of FBI supervisors, some of whom qualify for our purposes here as potential moles. Edmonds' letter provides another rare glimpse at how moles operate inside intelligence agencies to sabotage law enforcement and make sure patsies are not rounded up nor effective warnings given until it is too late.

Melek Can Dickerson, a Turkish translator, was hired by the FBI after September 11, and was placed in charge of translating the most sensitive information related to terrorists and criminals under the Bureau's investigation. Melek Can Dickerson was granted Top Secret Clearance, which can be granted only after conducting a thorough background investigation. Melek Can Dickerson used to work for semi-legit organizations that were the FBI's targets of investigation. Melek Can Dickerson had on going relationships with two individuals who were the FBI's targets of investigation. For months Melek Can Dickerson blocked all-important information related to these semi-legit organizations and the individuals she and her husband associated with. She stamped hundreds, if not thousands, of documents related to these targets as 'Not Pertinent.' Melek Can Dickerson attempted to prevent others from translating these documents important to the FBI's investigations and our fight against terrorism. Melek Can Dickerson, with the assistance of her direct supervisor, Mike Feghali, took hundreds of pages of top-secret sensitive intelligence documents outside the FBI to unknown recipients. Melek Can Dickerson, with the assistance of her direct supervisor, forged signatures on top-secret documents related to certain 9/11 detainees. After all these incidents were confirmed and reported to FBI management, Melek Can

Dickerson was allowed to remain in her position, to continue the translation of sensitive intelligence received by the FBI, and to maintain her Top Secret Clearance. Apparently bureaucratic mid-level FBI management and administrators decided that it would not look good for the Bureau if this security breach and espionage case was investigated and made public, especially after going through Robert Hanssen's case (FBI spy scandal). This case (Melek Can Dickerson) was confirmed by the Senate Judiciary Committee....

Here we have a serious allegation of serious federal crimes, far worse than Sandy Berger stuffing some old documents into his pants at the National Archives. It also raises the question: is Mike Feghali a conscious, witting mole, or merely an incompetent? Given the chaos inside the FBI, it is sometimes hard to tell. Edmonds also shows that there is no effective discipline or accountability inside the FBI molehill:

Today, more than two years since the Dickerson incident was reported to the FBI, and more than two years since this information was confirmed by the United States Congress and reported by the press, these administrators in charge of FBI personnel security and language departments in the FBI remain in their positions and in charge of translation quality and translation departments' security. Melek Can Dickerson and several FBI targets of investigation hastily left the United States in 2002, and the case still remains uninvestigated criminally. Not only does the supervisor facilitating these criminal conducts remain in a supervisory position, he has been promoted to supervising Arabic language units of the FBI's Counter-terrorism and Counterintelligence investigations.

Edmonds also revealed a specific pre-9/11 warning on patsy activities which was simply ignored by the FBI, and then ignored again by the 9/11 commission:

Over three years ago, more than four months prior to the September 11 terrorist attacks, in April 2001, a long-term FBI informant/asset who had been providing the bureau with information since 1990, provided two FBI agents and a translator with specific information regarding a terrorist attack being planned by Osama bin Laden. This asset/informant was previously a high-level intelligence officer in Iran in charge of intelligence from Afghanistan. Through his contacts in Afghanistan he received information that: 1) Osama bin Laden was planning a major terrorist attack in the United States targeting 4-5 major cities, 2) the attack was going to involve airplanes, 3) some of the individuals in charge of carrying out this attack were already in place in the United States, 4) the attack was going to be carried out soon, in a few months. The agents who received this information reported it to their superior, Special Agent in Charge of Counter-terrorism, Thomas Frields, at the FBI Washington Field Office, by filing 302 forms, and the translator translated and documented this information. No action was taken by the Special Agent in Charge, and after 9/11 the agents and the translators were told to 'keep quiet' regarding this issue. The translator who was present during the session with the FBI informant, Mr. Behrooz Sarshar, reported this incident to Director Mueller in writing, and later to the Department of Justice Inspector General. The press reported this incident, and in fact the report in the *Chicago Tribune* on July 21, 2004 stated that FBI officials had confirmed that this information was received in April 2001, and further, the *Chicago Tribune* quoted an aide to Director Mueller that he (Mueller) was surprised that the Commission never raised this particular issue with him during the hearing.

Was Frields a mole? This is the kind of question the 9/11 commission should have asked, but which it always ducked. Edmonds goes on to mock the clichés about connecting the dots and sharing intelligence which are the stock in trade of the controlled corporate media. She points out that the Phoenix memo, the Minneapolis alarms, and the Sarshar material all converged in the J. Edgar Hoover Building in Washington DC. The FBI had all that it needed to know that a large operation was afoot, which it could have disrupted by rolling up parts of the patsy network. But the FBI did nothing, and the 9/11 commission dropped the ball here as well, as Edmonds stresses:

All this information went to the same place: FBI Headquarters in Washington, DC, and the FBI Washington Field Office, in Washington DC. Yet, your report claims that not having a central place where all intelligence could be gathered as one of the main factors in our intelligence failure. Why did your report choose to exclude the information regarding the Iranian asset and Behrooz Sarshar from its timeline of missed opportunities? Why was this significant incident not mentioned; despite the public confirmation by the FBI, witnesses provided to your investigators, and briefings you received directly? Why did you surprise even Director Mueller by refraining from asking him questions regarding this significant incident and lapse during your hearing (Please remember that you ran out of questions during your hearings with Director Mueller and AG John Ashcroft, so please do not cite a 'time limit' excuse)?

Mike Feghali appears in Edmonds' account as a consummate bureaucratic bungler and dissembler. But the question stubbornly arises: was he a mole as well? And what about the bureaucrats who promoted him? Here Feghali is sabotaging translations requested by field agents:

In October 2001, approximately one month after the September 11 attack, an agent from a (city name omitted) field office, re-sent a certain document to the FBI Washington Field Office, so that it could be re-translated. This Special Agent, in light of the 9/11 terrorist attacks, rightfully believed that, considering his target of investigation (the suspect under surveillance), and the issues involved, the original translation might have missed certain information that could prove to be valuable in the investigation of terrorist activities. After this document was received by the FBI Washington Field Office and re-translated verbatim, the field agent's hunch appeared to be correct. The new translation revealed certain information regarding blueprints, pictures, and building material for skyscrapers being sent overseas. It also revealed certain illegal activities in obtaining visas from certain embassies in the Middle East, through network contacts and bribery. However, after the re-translation was completed and the new significant information was revealed, the unit supervisor in charge of certain Middle Eastern languages, Mike Feghali, decided NOT to send the re-translated information to the Special Agent who had requested it. Instead, this supervisor decided to send this agent a note stating that the translation was reviewed and that the original translation was accurate. This supervisor stated that sending the accurate translation would hurt the original translator and would cause problems for the FBI language department. The FBI agent requesting the re-translation never received the accurate translation of that document. (Sibel Edmonds, Letter to Thomas Kean, August 1, 2004)

Before we leave the moles, we must make one further important method-ological point. Before the terrorist action occurs, the moles appear as embedded in a government bureaucracy which is resisting the new course which they wish to impose. After the fact, providing that the terrorist action has gone off successfully, the entire government seems to be made up exclusively of moles. Now the moles no longer appear isolated. In fact, the entire government is speaking the language which before the terror attack seemed to be the factional distinction of the moles, to the extent that they said anything.

The government bureaucracy can be thought of as a gigantic freight train. With the successful terrorist act, a switch is turned, and the entire train goes rumbling in a new direction. The transformation achieved by a successful act of spectacular terrorism goes beyond what can be achieved by mere directives emanating from the office of the president or some cabinet secretary. Public opinion is shocked and stunned; the Congress is stampeded; the entire bureaucracy senses that the terrorist controllers have proven that it is they who are the strongest. After all, in Byzantine and neocon theory, law is an act of the will of the stronger over the weaker. The neocons regard a successful act of force as a valid act of legislation in that sense. The bureaucracy therefore inclines to the side of the plotters.

Once the new policy has been institutionalized, every bureaucrat will attempt to defend it as a matter of self-preservation. Bureaucratic inertia will now adapt itself to the new party line. This is why, in retrospect, it looks as if the entire government is composed of nothing but moles. But this impression is misleading.

It is not feasible for every high government official to be a witting party to the terrorist action. Some, of course, can be given a specific task on a need to know basis, and they may or may not be able to intuit the larger design in which they are a cog. Others need to know everything. But the fully witting participants will number in the hundreds, not the thousands. This is Machiavelli's most vehement advice in the chapter on conspiracies in *The Discourses*: keep the number of witting participants low, limiting it if possible to oneself and at most one other person. In today's society that would be too few.

Of course, after the fact, more officials figure out what is going on, and thus join the ranks of the witting. But it ought to be axiomatic that the entire command structure cannot be in on the secret; what if somebody objects to the planned operation, and has the courage to do something about it? This might become very embarrassing for the plotters. Those who persist in seeing the whole state apparatus or US command structure as being behind 9/11 face the problem of what to do about the Phoenix memorandum and the Minneapolis actions, followed by the Rowley whistleblower memo. Here were government officials who were subjectively opposed to the 9/11 operation, even if they were only able to express this opposition in regard to the patsy network with which they were dealing.

EXPERT PROFESSIONALS

Much low-level terrorism consists of crude local attacks on buses, super-markets, hotels, and the like. Such actions are sometimes within the capability of low-level activists, but when we go beyond such actions, special technical preparation and training become necessary. When we get to the level of spectacular international terrorism of the type represented by 9/11, it is clear that only skilled professionals have the physical ability to produce the effects observed. The third sub-system which must be examined to account for modern synthetic terrorism is therefore that of the expert professionals.

They are the well-trained, well-equipped operatives who really do have the technical, physical, and mental ability to bring about the terrorist acts which the public sees. They are the members of the team which was indeed able, using the best state-of-the-art sniper rifles and related equipment, to fire the requisite number of shots in Dealey Plaza, and to fire them with sufficient accuracy within the objective time limits imposed by the situation. They are the ice-cold technocrats of death who were able to direct the aircraft into the World Trade Center and the Pentagon. The expert professionals are the persons who can accomplish the amazing feats which the media attribute to the pathetic patsies.

The expert professionals and the patsies differ in many fundamental ways. The expert professionals do not have to be ideologues, they are not raving fana-tics in the way that the patsies tend to be. They are proud of their professional competence. Not infrequently, they are mercenary in their motivation. They do not try to get noticed. They are not abrasive, and they do not go out of their way to pick quarrels with passersby. They do not give interviews, and would never hand out leaflets. Their goal is the lowest possible profile, even complete anonymity. They would always like to escape attention, and to melt away into the shadows. They come from out of town, and disappear as soon as their work is done. Their main occupational hazard is not that of arrest by the police, but the risk of being liquidated by their own employers as a basic security measure.

Because of these factors, we know much less about the expert professionals than we do about the patsies, about whom so much gossipy detail is circulated, or about the moles, who cannot always escape detection after the fact. The attempt to identify the expert professionals is the same as the attempt to name the snipers of Dallas on November 22, 1963: we have no certitude, but only speculation. Were they disgruntled members of the French OAS? Were they central European fascists left over from World War II? We do not know.

There are, however, some instances in which something more about the expert professionals may be learned. At the end of the Cold War it turned out that the prime suspects in many of the terrorist attacks in Italy and other countries were in fact members of a CIA-sponsored stay-behind network, the Italian branch of which was called Gladio. The existence of Gladio was revealed to the Italian Parliament, which had never been informed, in a report issued by then-Prime Minister Giulio Andreotti on February 26, 1991. Apparently a secret clause of the North Atlantic Alliance required member states who might be subject to Soviet invasion and occupation to make some provision in advance for promoting armed resistance and guerrilla warfare against the feared Soviet occupiers of the future – that was, at least, the cover story.

In 1951 the Italian military intelligence, perhaps punningly abbreviated as SIFAR, signed an agreement with the CIA on the creation of the infrastructure of a totally secret, clandestine stay-behind operation. This underground group was called Gladio, the Italian word for the Roman sword. Gladio was tasked with espionage, sabotage, guerrilla warfare, and propaganda in the event of a Soviet occupation. Its headquarters were located on the island of Sardinia, which the Italian general staff thought it could control even if mainland Italy had fallen to the Red Army.

In 1959, Gladio became an integral part of the Clandestine Planning Committee (CPC) at SHAPE, the Supreme Headquarters Allied Powers Europe. Later, in 1964, it was included in the Europe-wide apparatus managed by the Allied Clandestine Committee (ACC) of NATO, along with US, UK, France, Belgium, the Netherlands, Luxemburg, and West Germany. When SIFAR became SID and later SISMI, Gladio continued to operate as its secret arm. Gladio was set up according to a cell structure, meaning that each team was compartmentalized and separated from all the other teams – a good idea in case of Soviet invasion, but also the best way for a single cell to become the vehicle for spectacular terrorism if it happened to be composed of persons with a certain outlook. In peacetime, Gladio's activity was devoted largely to training and recruitment of new members. Some of the training was placed in the hands of the Training Division of MI-6, the British Secret Intelligence Service, an institution that was directing terrorist operations on a grand scale when the CIA did not yet exist. Other training courses were set up at the CIA's so-called farm in Virginia. Operative links with the CIA were always present. Gladio had 40 cells: 6 for espionage, 10 for sabotage, 6 for propaganda, 6 for getting key people out of the Soviet-occupied zone, and 12 for guerrilla warfare. The sabotage and guerrilla warfare cells amounted to secret units of highly trained special forces commandos. This structure was somewhat revamped in 1974-76. There were 622 official members of Gladio, 83% of whom had been born before 1945, 16% between 1945 and 1960, and the rest after 1960. These were of course cadres, or officers, around whom a much larger number of operatives would be assembled. We must also assume that this official report represents a modified limited hangout, designed to reveal a few facts, hide many more, and accustom public opinion to the existence of the secret structure by minimizing its importance. Other estimates of Gladio's numerical strength range up to 15,000, a more realistic figure.

In addition to the cells, Gladio also possessed large amounts of weapons and explosives. There were 138 secret arms deposits, most often buried in cemeteries, containing stocks of portable weapons, explosives, hand grenades, precision sniper rifles, radios, and other equipment. These were sealed in plastic containers to prevent rust and deterioration. According to Andreotti's report, these arms caches were buried during the 1960s. When they were all finally dug up again between 1973 and 1990, it turned out that two caches with 6 containers of arms and explosives in the province of Udine near the Yugoslav border had been pilfered. These would have been more than enough to provide the raw materials for the strategy of tension between 1967 and 1985, approximately. These weapons have never been recovered. Andreotti announced the dismantling of Gladio in 1990. According to the report, Belgium, France, Luxemburg, and Switzerland terminated their own secret stay-behind programs in 1990; Austria was said to have done so in 1970. As for Greece and Germany, it is not clear that the stay-behind networks were ever terminated.

The hypothesis is unavoidable that Gladio had drawn its recruits from the fascists of Mussolini's Italian Social Republic of 1943-1945 in northern Italy, behind German lines. Since Gladio's mission was allegedly to prevent the country from becoming a permanent Soviet satellite, its commanders in SIFAR-SID-SISMI, CIA and MI-6 may have decided to act pre-emptively: to use the secret Gladio capabilities plus its arms deposits to prevent the Italian Communists and their trade union allies from ever participating in the government, which they would have seen or pretended to see as a step towards Soviet domination. The circumstantial case is very strong that the Gladio teams provided the well-trained, well-equipped professionals who placed the bombs in Milan in 1969, in Brescia and the Italicus express in 1974, and at the Bologna railway station in 1980. In this, the Gladio people may have been assisted by such notorious SID-SISMI assets as Stefano delle Chiaie, a terrorist who made his base in Madrid until the death of Franco and the fall of Spain's fascist regime in 1976.

The case implicating Gladio as a state-sponsored terrorist underground grows stronger if we also consider the role of the P-2 or Propaganda Due freemasonic lodge. The existence of this secret power center became public knowledge in the early 1980s. Among the P-2 members were many of the most prominent political, financial, economic, media, and military leaders of Italy, including Andreotti and the current prime minister, Silvio Berlusconi. There were no communists and no labor leaders present. The P-2 was most likely a descendant of a pro-Mazzini Masonic lodge sometimes identified as Propaganda Uno, which would have been functioning during the second half of the nineteenth century and into the twentieth. P-2 was notable for its overwhelming links to the US. In the view of some, P-2 grandmaster Licio Gelli, a former fascist, and his assistant Umberto Ortolani, may have represented a command center for terror operations in Italy, including those carried out by the trained professionals of the Gladio network. Or, more likely, they may have represented a conduit for instructions from higher up to be passed along to the various personalities of the local establishment.

Gladio in any case represents an extremely instructive example for students of 9/11. Here we have one of the five advanced industrial countries, a founding member of the European Community, and a member of NATO, in which state-sponsored terrorism would appear to have been practiced for about 15 years on a very large scale, all as a matter of *raison d'état*, specifically because of the Soviet threat. The human toll over this time numbers certainly in the hundreds, about one order of magnitude less than 9/11, but in a country about one fourth the size of the US. There seems to have been very little compunction about turning lethal terrorism against one's own population. As for those who believe that a self-inflicted wound on the scale of 9/11 is morally and humanly impossible to be organized by US intelligence networks, they will gain no support from this example.

OPERATION NORTHWOODS

In July 1961, Democratic Senator William Fulbright of Arkansas, noting the activities of General Edwin Walker, called for an investigation of the Institute for American Strategy, the Richardson Foundation, the National War College, and the Joint Chiefs of Staff – all for subversive activity. Fulbright compared the mentality of some US military men to that of the OAS (Secret Army Organization) in Algeria, which plotted against General de Gaulle and was implicated in various assassination plots against him. All in all, there were about thirty attempts to kill the French President. (Démaret, *Target de Gaulle*)

Fulbright's warnings were more accurate than he knew at the time. The crucial exhibit in this regard is Operation Northwoods, a plan to provoke a war with Cuba, which was supported by the entire Joint Chiefs of Staff and their

Chairman, General Lyman Lemnitzer. This document, titled "Justification for US Military Intervention in Cuba" was provided by the JCS to Secretary of Defense Robert McNamara on March 13, 1962, as the key component of Northwoods. Written in response to a request from the Chief of the Cuba Project, General Edward Lansdale, the Top Secret memorandum describes US plans to covertly engineer various pretexts that would "justify" a US invasion of Cuba. The documents of Operation Northwoods were first published in Australia by John Elliston in his *PsyWar on Cuba: The Declassified History of US Anti-Castro Propaganda* (1999). They became prominent around the time of 9/11 thanks to the study *Body of Secrets* by James Bamford, a former ABC newsman.

Lemnitzer had worked with Allen Dulles during World War II, and was part of Dulles' Operation Sunrise, the separate surrender of German forces in Italy by SS General Karl Wolf. Lemnitzer had helped to assemble the first stay-behind networks of the Gladio type, which were often staffed by former Nazis and fascists. Lemnitzer, along with Curtis LeMay of the Air Force, favored using the Cuban missile crisis of October 1962 to provoke general nuclear war with the USSR. Robert Dallek's new biography of Kennedy documents the reckless and irresponsible advice Lemnitzer gave Kennedy on a number of military problems; it usually came down to recommending nuclear weapons under all circumstances as the only way to guarantee victory.

In 1962 Lemnitzer was denied his ambition of being re-appointed to a second term as JCS chairman, but he was given the post of NATO Supreme Commander, where he presided over the creation of the first Gladio arms and explosives caches on the Italian front. Lemnitzer did not retire from active duty until 1969. President Gerald Ford asked Lemnitzer to join the agitation of the Committee on the Present Danger, a retread of a CIA front group from the early 1950s. The CPD was the private-sector arm of CIA Director George Bush's Team B, an exercise in anti-Soviet alarmism that foreshadowed the Feith-Luti-Shulsky Office of Special Plans in the Pentagon. Ford also promoted General William H. Craig, who had been a part of the Northwood cabal, to be the head of the Army Security Agency, an arm of the super-secret National Security Agency, the center of electronic surveillance. Lemnitzer died in November 1988.

Senator Albert Gore senior, the father of the later vice president, thought that Lemnitzer was a part of the subversive machinations associated with General Edwin Walker, who distributed inflammatory anti-Kennedy propaganda to his troops in Germany. When Walker returned to the US, he organized a racist riot against the hiring of a black professor at the University of Mississippi, and was prosecuted by Attorney General Robert Kennedy for sedition, insurrection, and rebellion. Walker was thought to have joined with French OAS military in plotting to kill de Gaulle; these same circles are also suspect in the Kennedy assassination. A little later, in 1963 and 1964, George H. W. Bush ran for the Senate in Texas on a platform that included the overthrow of Castro and the use of tactical nuclear weapons against North Vietnam. (Meyssan 2002 139-146)

General Edward Lansdale was one of the most prominent practitioners of special forces, special operations, and related utopian military methods during the Cold War. He was one of the leading architects of the catastrophic US involvement in Vietnam. Lansdale was the founder of the US Special Warfare School at Fort Bragg, North Carolina. Lansdale worked closely together with Allen Dulles, the Wall Street lawyer who became the head of the CIA during the Eisenhower administration, and who cooked up the plan for the Bay of Pigs and foisted it off on the newly inaugurated President Kennedy. When the Bay of Pigs failed, and Kennedy wisely decided to cut his losses by not throwing more military assets into what was already a hopeless debacle, the Allen Dulles clique and many counterinsurgency-oriented military officers blamed not their own incompetent planning, but Kennedy. In February, 1962, Robert Kennedy told Lansdale that his covert Operation Mongoose, a plot to kill Castro, should be frozen, and the emphasis shifted to gathering intelligence.

The Dulles-Lemnitzer-Lansdale networks should not be thought of as an extinct feature of the past, but rather as a living presence in the Pentagon, CIA, NSA, and other agencies. Given the track record of this network, they must necessarily come under scrutiny in the context of 9/11.

The Northwoods documents start from the premise that the US should be seeking war with Cuba over the short term for the purpose of regime change: "[T]he Joint Chiefs of Staff recommend that a national policy of early military intervention in Cuba be adopted by the United States. They also recommend that such intervention be undertaken as soon as possible and preferably before the release of National Guard and Reserve forces presently on active duty." Part of the effort would be to demonize Castro and his communist government. The Northwoods planners thought that "world opinion, and the United Nations forum, should be favorably affected by developing the international image of the Cuban government as rash and irresponsible, and as an alarming and unpredictable threat to the peace of the Western Hemisphere." How could Castro be demonized? Northwoods: "Exploding a few plastic bombs in carefully chosen spots, the arrest of Cuban agents and the release of prepared documents substantiating Cuban involvement also would be helpful in projecting the idea of an irresponsible government." In addition, "hijacking attempts against civil air and surface craft could appear to continue as harassing measures condoned by the Government of Cuba."

Northwoods planners did not hesitate to prescribe attacks on US ships, planes, or installations: "We could blow up a US ship in Guantanamo Bay and blame Cuba," they wrote; "casualty lists in US newspapers would cause a helpful wave of national indignation." Northwoods had not forgotten the *Maine* incident of 1898. Nor did they hesitate to propose a murderous campaign of terror against US civilians: "We could develop a Communist Cuban terror campaign in the Miami area, in other Florida cities and even in Washington," proposed the JCS planners. "The terror campaign could be pointed at Cuban refugees seeking haven in the United States." So much for any notions that rogue Pentagon and

CIA elements have any profound metaphysical inhibitions about killing their own troops or US citizens in general; this is an important lesson to bring to the analysis of 9/11.

In the search for a pretext, the JCS planners also considered a massacre of foreign citizens: "We could sink a boatload of Cubans en route to Florida (real or simulated). . . . We could foster attempts on lives of Cuban refugees in the United States even to the extent of wounding in instances to be widely publicized."

The most complicated project proposed by the Northwoods brainstormers:

~~TOP SECRET SPECIAL HANDLING NOFORN~~

ANNEX TO APPENDIX TO ENCLOSURE A   UNCLASSIFIED

PRETEXTS TO JUSTIFY US MILITARY INTERVENTION IN CUBA

8. It is possible to create an incident which will demonstrate convincingly that a Cuban aircraft has attacked and shot down a chartered civil airliner enroute from the United States to Jamaica, Guatemala, Panama or Venezuela. The destination would be chosen only to cause the flight plan route to cross Cuba. The passengers could be a group of college students off on a holiday or any grouping of persons with a common interest to support chartering a non-scheduled flight.

a. An aircraft at Eglin AFB would be painted and numbered as an exact duplicate for a civil registered aircraft belonging to a CIA proprietary organization in the Miami area. At a designated time the duplicate would be substituted for the actual civil aircraft and would be loaded with the selected passengers, all boarded under carefully prepared aliases. The actual registered aircraft would be converted to a drone.

b. Take off times of the drone aircraft and the actual aircraft will be scheduled to allow a rendezvous south of Florida. From the rendezvous point the passenger-carrying aircraft will descend to minimum altitude and go directly into an auxiliary field at Eglin AFB where arrangements will have been made to evacuate the passengers and return the aircraft to its original status. The drone aircraft meanwhile will continue to fly the filed flight plan. When over Cuba the drone will being transmitting on the international distress frequency a "MAY DAY" message stating he is under attack by Cuban MIG aircraft. The transmission will be interrupted by destruction of the aircraft which will be triggered by radio signal. This will allow ICAO radio

[International Civil Aviation Organization]

stations in the Western Hemisphere to tell the US what
has happened to the aircraft instead of the US trying to
"sell" the incident.

As will be seen, this was a precise template for the remote control and plane-
switching theory that is able to explain so many discrepant facts about 9/11 –
down to the final detail of feigned cluelessness.

When Colonel John Glenn was about to attempt his orbital flight, Lemnitzer
and the Northwoods cabal were ready. They did not explicitly prepare to
sabotage Glenn's rocket, but they were ready to exploit any mishap to attain the
goal which, as always, was the invasion of Cuba. Lemnitzer proposed that an
astronaut disaster could be turned into a pretext for war "by manufacturing
various pieces of evidence which would prove electronic interference on the part
of the Cubans." Thus the NOFORN classification, meaning the project was to be
kept secret from all foreign nationals, even those with security clearances.

The inventiveness of the Northwoods cabal seems endless; quite likely, the
single sample that came here to light was drawn from a much larger stock of
patterns for subterfuge. The plotters were eager to stage "a series of well
coordinated incidents to take place in and around" the US Navy base at
Guantanamo Bay, Cuba. This would entail a group of anti-Castro Cubans decked
out in Cuban army uniforms who would "start riots near the main gate of the
base. Others would pretend to be saboteurs inside the base. Ammunition would
be blown up, fires started, aircraft sabotaged, mortars fired at the base with
damage to installations."

Another path to war might be through embroiling the Cubans in conflict with
other Caribbean nations through covert operations and US provocations:
"Advantage can be taken of the sensitivity of the Dominican [Republic] Air
Force to intrusions within their national air space. 'Cuban' B-26 or C-46 type
aircraft could make cane burning raids at night. Soviet Bloc incendiaries could be
found. This could be coupled with 'Cuban' messages to the Communist
underground in the Dominican Republic and 'Cuban' shipments of arms which
would be found, or intercepted, on the beach. Use of MiG type aircraft by US
pilots could provide additional provocation."

Finally, there was a plan to "make it appear that Communist Cuban MiGs
have destroyed a USAF aircraft over international waters in an unprovoked
attack." It was a particularly believable operation given the decade of
shootdowns that had just taken place. Lemnitzer was emphatic that the Joint
Chiefs of Staff, and not the CIA, ought to be in charge of these covert operations:
"It is recommended," he concluded, "that this responsibility for both overt and
covert military operations be assigned to the Joint Chiefs of Staff."
(http://www.gwu.edu/~nsarchiv/news/20010430/) This is an interesting parallel
with trends in the current administration.

Northwoods was never carried out in regard to Cuba. However, this does not
mean that these concepts were never implemented. In the Gulf of Tonkin incident

of August 1964, two US destroyers were operating along the coast of North Vietnam very near South Vietnamese ships which were raiding and bombarding the north. The Pentagon then announced that the two destroyers, the Maddox and the Turner Joy, had been attacked by North Vietnamese torpedo boats. President Johnson then ordered US air strikes on nearby North Vietnamese ports and naval bases, and also used this incident to extort the infamous Gulf of Tonkin resolution from the Congress, which gave him unlimited power to wage war.

Later, it turned out that there probably had not been any North Vietnamese torpedo boats, but more likely only ghost images on the radar screens of the destroyers – here again, we have a parallel, to the "war games" and "fake radar blips" experienced by FAA flight controllers on 9/11. After the Gulf of Tonkin incident, Johnson was clearly embarked on the path of escalating the Vietnam war, with disastrous consequences for all concerned. The mind which produced Northwoods and the Gulf of Tonkin affair is a mind which would have no difficulty in producing 9/11. And there is no sign that those networks have ever been eradicated.

THE MOSSAD'S FALSE FLAG AL QAEDA CELL

Rashid Abu Shbak, the head of Palestinian Preventive Security in the Gaza Strip said on Friday, December 6, 2002 that his forces had identified a number of Palestinian collaborators who had been ordered by Israeli security agencies to "work in the GazaStrip under the name of Al-Qaeda." Al-Jazeera TV reported that the Palestinian authorities had arrested a group of Palestinian "collaborators with Israeli occupation" in Gaza, who were trying to set up an operation there in the name of bin Laden's Al Qaeda. The Palestinian Authority spokesman said the members of the group had confessed that they were recruited and organized by the Israeli intelligence, Mossad. Sharon had personally claimed on December 4, 2002 that he had proof of Al Qaeda operations in Gaza, and used the allegations to justify brutal Israeli Defense Forces attacks in the Gaza Strip the next day– which was the start of the Islamic holiday, Eid, celebrating the end of Ramadan. Ten civilians were killed in the IDF assaults.

Reuters published an extensive featured story on the affair by Diala Saadeh on December 7, 2002, under the headline "Palestinians: Israel Faked Gaza Al Qaeda Presence." The article quoted President Arafat, who told reporters at his West Bank Ramallah headquarters, "It is a big, big, big lie to cover [Sharon's] attacks and his crimes against our people everywhere." Information Minister Yasser Abed Rabbo explained: "There are certain elements who were instructed by the Mossad to form a cell under the name of Al Qaeda in the Gaza Strip in order to justify the assault and the military campaigns of the Israeli occupation army against Gaza." (*Ha'aretz*, Reuters and Al Jazeera, December 7, 2002) Sharon is of course a past master of false-flag tactics like these, having been implicated in the direction of the Abu Nidal organization and also in the setting up of Hamas.

On Sunday, December 8, 2002, Nabil Shaath, the Palestinian Authority Planning and International Cooperation Minister, held a press conference with Col. Rashid Abu Shbak, head of the PA's Preventive Security Apparatus in the Gaza Strip, to release documents and provide further information about the Israeli intelligence creation of a self-styled Al Qaeda cell. Shaath called on the diplomats to "convey to their countries that they assume the responsibility of exerting pressure on the Israeli government to stop the Israeli aggression," and announced that the PA had handed ambassadors and consuls of the Arab and foreign countries documents revealing the involvement of the Israeli Intelligence in recruiting citizens from Gaza Strip in a fake organization carrying the name of al Qaeda.

The goal of the operation was to create a new pretext for aggression against the inhabitants of the GazaStrip. Shbak said that the PA had uncovered eight incidents of fake Al Qaeda recruiting over the previous nine months. Three Palestinians were arrested, while another 11 Palestinians were released, "because they came and informed us of this Israeli plot." The PA Security Service had traced mobile phone calls and e-mails, purportedly from Germany and Lebanon, back to Israel; these were messages asking Palestinians to join Al Qaeda. One e-mail even bore the forged signature of Osama bin Laden. "We investigated the origin of those calls, which used roaming, and messages, and found out they all came from Israel," Shbak said. The recruits were paired with collaborators in Gaza, and received money and weapons, "although most of these weapons did not work." The money was provided by collaborators, or transferred from bank accounts in Israel and Jerusalem. (Palestine Ministry of Public Information, IslamOnline, December 9, 2002)

TERRORIST MURDER AS BRITISH STATE POLICY

In April 2003, Great Britain was rocked by one of the greatest secret intelligence scandals in the entire postwar period. Metropolitan Police Commissioner Sir John Stevens, the most senior police official in Great Britain, delivered the third installment of his report documenting that a special branch of British army intelligence had coordinated the murders of some thirty Roman Catholics in Northern Ireland in the years 1989-1990. Stevens had begun his investigation already back in 1989, but the report was not published until 2003, after two postponements during 2002.

The Stevens investigation centered on the British Army intelligence's Force Research Unit (FRU), for working in collusion with Protestant loyalist paramilitary groups to kill Catholics. An aggravating factor was that the head of the FRU at the time when these murders were being committed, in 1989-90, was an army officer named Gordon Kerr. Until February 2003, Kerr was the British military attaché in Beijing, one of the highest military posts for a British military officer. Sir John Stevens confirmed that in that same month of February 2003 he was preparing papers for the Director of Public Prosecutions (DPP) relating to a prosecution of Kerr. At that point Kerr, by then an army brigadier general, was moved to Kuwait, and was serving in Iraq when the Stevens report came out. (BBC, April 17, 2003)

The Stevens report represented, in its author's words, "the largest investigation undertaken in the United Kingdom," with 9,256 statements recorded, 10,391 documents logged (over 1 million pages), and 16,194 evidentiary exhibits seized. By April 2003, the Stevens probe had generated 144 arrests and 94 convictions. (Stevens 17) Stevens' findings centered on collusion in the Finucane and other murders. "Collusion is evidenced in many ways. This ranges from the willful failure to keep records, the absence of accountability, the withholding of intelligence and evidence, through to the extreme of agents being involved in murder." (Stevens 18)

It was evident to all that Kerr and his FRU could never have committed such atrocities on their own, but would have required "orders from the highest level," that is, from Prime Minister Margaret Thatcher's office. Whether the Stevens investigation would implicate Thatcher remained to be seen. The British press was focused on the fact that Kerr's chief FRU operative for coordinating the Ulster Defence Association (UDA) in the commission of at least 30 murders was a certain Brian Nelson. Nelson, under Kerr's direction, had intrigued to become the UDA's intelligence chief. In January 1990, the Stevens team identified Nelson as a key suspect, and planned to arrest him and others in a dawn raid. The officers went to their secure investigation headquarters, hours before the planned arrests, to find a fire raging in their offices, with fire alarms, telephones, and heat-sensitive intruder alarms not working, and with many of their files destroyed. This was an obvious case of arson.

To top off the story, Brian Nelson died the week before Stevens III was issued, supposedly of a brain hemorrhage. The Stevens investigation had been launched in 1989, following the murder of top Catholic lawyer Pat Finucane. Finucane's family had always insisted that the security forces were involved in his murder, and dismissed the Stevens report as inadequate. Finucane's widow, Geraldine, demanded a full judicial inquiry as the only way to deal with the issue. Alex Maskey, the Lord Mayor of Belfast, commented on the Stevens report: "This is not about rogue elements with the British system. It is about a state policy sanctioned at the highest level."

The Stevens inquiry did not develop in a vacuum. It had been stimulated by the work of film-maker and author Sean McPhilemy, whose book, *The Committee: Political Assassination in Northern Ireland*, had appeared in 1998. McPhilemy systematically documented the murderous collusion among the British government, the British military, the Royal Ulster Constabulary, Loyalist paramilitary death squads, and respected Protestant citizens in planning and perpetrating the murders of Republican paramilitaries and Catholics.

The roles of the RUC, its Special Branch, the Force Research Unit, and British Army agent Brian Nelson in the murder of human rights attorney Pat

Finucane and others were revealed in McPhilemy's book. McPhilemy also provided evidence implicating British domestic intelligence (MI-5) and Secret Air Services (SAS) commandos in these operations. In spite of these revelations, opinion-makers persist in pointing to Northern Ireland as a prime example of spontaneous, religiously-inspired violence requiring a colonial police power to maintain order.

CONTROLLED CORPORATE MEDIA

It almost goes without saying that the effective political exploitation of a large-scale terrorist operation like 9/11 depends to an extraordinary degree on the complicity of the controlled corporate media. So far we have discussed moles primarily as a private network inside the visible government, but the media are honeycombed with moles as well: these are persons whose task it is to support the terror project in its totality. On 9/11, it was the media moles who first began churning out the mythical party line about bin Laden and al Qaeda. They are in this sense the main propagators of the myth, with Bush and others bringing up the rear. We have already suggested that a majority of the leaks implicating bin Laden and al Qaeda on the basis of no evidence whatsoever probably came from Richard Clarke and George Tenet.

It is no secret that the CIA has long recruited media managers and media personalities to be its agents of influence. The corporate bosses of the media conglomerates, in their capacity as powerful oligarchs, may also be more or less witting parties to the unfolding operation, and may therefore instruct their own media personalities on the line to espouse. In any case, they subscribe to the policy directions the myth leads to.

A COMMAND CENTER

This panoply of elements – patsies, moles, professionals, and media – clearly presupposes an additional element: a center of command and coordination to guide all these operational components towards the desired outcome. A number of accounts of 9/11 have gone so far as to suggest that President Bush himself was the coordinator, but it must be countered in all seriousness that this is impossible, and not only for the reason of mental and technical inability which must always be applied in questions of terror.

As a matter of propaganda it is permissible and probably necessary to direct mass anger against Bush as the person generally responsible for 9/11; since he does qualify for this opprobrium in various ways, although not in the simple, linear way that some people might think. However, when we are attempting to analyze in detail how 9/11 came about, it is equally clear that in any serious conspiracy, a figure of the caliber of Bush 43 would normally be one of the last to know. He is after all merely a figurehead, a front man for the CIA-Brown

Brothers Harriman-Skull & Bones-neocon-Bush family faction, which is itself an oligarchical congeries, not a disciplined, centralized apparatus.

It is hardly likely that the command center of 9/11 could have been in the upper reaches of government, and far more likely that it was outside of government altogether. Since Reagan's first term, the US intelligence community has been largely privatized under the aegis of Executive Order 12333. This means that the really crucial capabilities for an operation like 9/11 are no longer to be sought in the George Bush intelligence center in Langley, Virginia which houses the headquarters of the CIA, but rather in a myriad of private military firms, technology companies, think tanks, law firms, public relations firms, and front companies of all types. It is here, rather than a secret government office, that the planning and command center for 9/11 would normally be sought. However, given the considerable audacity of the operation, it cannot be excluded that some specific subdivisions of government agencies may have been involved. Possible candidates here might include a focal point operation within the Defense Department, or a special, secret military unit.

For those who find it incredible that terrorism against the Pentagon should be directed from inside the Pentagon, we recall that French President François Mitterrand, Italian Prime Minister Bettino Craxi, and Italian financier Michele Sindona each at one time or another caused a near-miss terror attack against himself, presumably as a means of garnering public sympathy. The basic principle is as mundane as insurance fraud.

CONDUCTED BY A NETWORK

It is important to stress that large-scale synthetic terrorism of the 9/11 type is generally conducted, not so much by identifiable institutions acting as a totality, but rather by a network or faction of like-minded plotters which cuts across the institutions transversally. It is not the visible, elected government which plots terrorism, but rather the parallel, invisible, or secret government, and that secret government is hidden inside the public and elected one.

The essence of this phenomenon is a private network which has ensconced its operatives in decisive, influential positions, from which entire bureaucracies can be controlled, manipulated, or paralyzed. To take an extreme case, it might be argued that the FBI belongs completely to a network of moles. But even though the power of the moles in the FBI is admittedly very great indeed, the Phoenix memo and the Colleen Rowley memo are enough to show that even the FBI is not composed exclusively of moles. That the FBI generally acts like a mole organization pure and simple is due to the preponderant power of certain well-placed moles who can make the institution do what their faction wants on key issues.

The secret, private network at the higher levels of the US government which was behind 9/11 has been around for some time. We see its footprints in such events as the U-2 crisis, the Bay of Pigs, the JFK assassination, the Martin Luther King and Robert Kennedy assassinations, parts of Watergate, Iran-Contra, the bombing of Kosovo (and of the Chinese embassy in Belgrade), the *Kursk* incident, and other operations, not counting precursors going back to the 19th century. This list could be extended. It is an aggressive, imperialistic, murderous network, restlessly seeking to preserve itself through conflict and confrontation.

In waging political conflict, it is often necessary and indispensable to personalize matters by encouraging citizens to direct their anger at an odious leader of the opposing faction; this often allows a more efficient mobilization than calling for the defeat of an abstraction or of a collectivity. In this sense, it is good politics and close to the truth to blame Bush for 9/11, but not in the simple way that many might think. It is a naïve argument to say that if there was US government collusion in 9/11, which there certainly was, then this proves that the titular head of the US government and tenant of the White House, G. W. Bush, must have been the leader of the plot. This reflects a media-conditioned overestimation of the powers of the presidency.

After the death of Franklin D. Roosevelt, the US oligarchy made a collective pledge that never but never would they ever allow an elected leader actually to exercise the constitutional powers of the presidency. This was codified in the term limit contained in the XXII Amendment of 1947-1951, which has weakened the office of the presidency in comparison to earlier times.

Then began the parade of puppet presidents: Harry S Truman was always susceptible to blackmail for his role in the crooked Pendergast machine of Missouri; Truman meekly took his orders from a committee that included Clark Clifford, Dean Acheson, Averill Harriman, and Robert Lovett, and the oligarchy has held him up as exemplary ever since.

Eisenhower was the easy-going chairman of the board who did not force Montgomery and Patton to coordinate during World War II; much of the real power was exercised by the Dulles brothers. The oligarchy considered Kennedy a playboy and sex maniac; he turned out to be a man of much positive principle. Kennedy showed his willingness to put the Federal reserve on a leash, forced Wall Street in the person of US Steel to back down, and refused to let his advisers (EXCOMM) use the Cuban missile crisis to launch world war against the USSR, and the response of the oligarchy came the following year.

Lyndon B. Johnson's pathologies crippled him, despite his apparent power, and made him accept the Vietnam adventure Kennedy had refused. Doris Kearns Goodwin has studied this matter well enough in her book on LBJ. Richard Nixon had been through a kind of nervous breakdown during the 1960s through his loss of the 1962 California gubernatorial election and the death of his mother; he was willing to take orders from Kissinger, who took them from the Rockefeller brothers, etc. Ford, according to LBJ, was so mentally impaired that he was not capable of walking and chewing gum at the same time. Carter had gone through a nervous breakdown of his own after being ousted as Governor of Georgia.

Reagan had learned to mask his mean and vindictive tendencies behind a mask of avuncular joviality; he acted the role of the good uncle, one of the archetypes of the American ideology, but he delegated most decisions, after Haig was forced out, to Bush and Baker. In the meantime, Reagan dozed and drooled; by 1987 his mental impairment was obvious enough to cause a scandal.

Bush 41 was a very sick man by the second half of his presidency; his thyroid problem was the symptom of psychosomatic disorders which live on in the various syndromes exhibited by his son, such as the penchant for snap decisions. (Tarpley 1992) Bush 41 had made his career thanks to Kissinger, and he let Kissinger's partners Scowcroft and Eagleburger share power with Baker. On big issues, like the Kuwait crisis, Bush took orders from Thatcher. Dukakis, the Democratic competitor in 1988, was also a seriously disturbed personality, as I pointed out at the time.

Clinton was profiled, like JFK, as a sex maniac and Anglophile, but he turned out to be more intelligent than the oligarchs had reckoned with. He was accordingly allowed to serve two terms, but real power was seized after January 1998 by the principals' committee acting under cover of impeachment. The mental wreck that is Bush 43 is described in detail in another section of this book. In addition, the many crimes of the Bushes make them a convenient target for blackmail.

All in all, the oligarchy favors candidates who are intellectually and morally incapable of governing according to the full powers of the office, and who are therefore willing to have their options pre-determined by servants of finance oligarchy from the Washington establishment. In any case, much of the original power of the presidency has been transferred to the unelected and unaccountable Federal Reserve Board.

During the Reagan years, a high administration official told me that the permanent bureaucratic class considered Reagan a perfect president. His job, said this official, was to be a head of state, which meant that his task came down to ministering to the emotional and symbolic needs of the country during moments of great sorrow and stress – given that there were now more disasters than victories. The assistant secretaries and the deputy assistant secretaries actually ran the government through the interagency groups and special interagency groups – and these were the figures who controlled the principals in the later principals' committee. The presidency was symbolic, while the permanent bureaucracy (plus the White House palace guard) made up a kind of collective prime minister who actually made decisions and ran the government – and even that within the parameters defined by the controlled corporate media.

Given all this, the notion that the US president possesses real power, or makes real decisions, is slightly fantastic. According to Bush 43's own testimony, he saw himself as a symbolic figure needing to project strength, rather than as a crisis manager, during the crucial minutes at the Booker School, during the reading of "My Pet Goat." The government was being run by Richard Clarke of the permanent bureaucracy, who also made the call on al Qaeda.

David Ray Griffin's *The New Pearl Harbor* has represented a significant progress in 9/11 research, but this book has the defect of listing as suspects only identifiable institutions, such as the intelligence agencies, the Pentagon, and the White House. In reality, the likely suspect is a network of moles that cuts across all of these, but which most likely keeps its center of gravity and command center somewhere in the privatized public sector.

P2OG AS OFFICIAL AGENTS PROVOCATEURS

Newspaper readers may have not believed their eyes when they read the following story:

WASHINGTON, Sept. 26, 2002 (UPI) – The United States should create an elite group of counter-terror operatives to make the war on terrorism pre-emptive and proactive, duping al Qaida into undertaking operations it is not prepared for and thereby exposing its personnel, a Pentagon report advocating more than $7 billion in new spending will recommend. The counter-terror operations group alone would require 100 people and at least $100 million a year. Rather than simply trying to find and foil terrorists' plans – the approach that characterizes the current strategy – the "Proactive Pre-emptive Operations Group" – known as P2OG – would devise ways to stimulate terrorists into responding or moving operations, possibly by stealing their money or tricking them with fake communications, according to the report.

The group would be comprised of specialists in information operations, psychological operations, computer network attack, covert activities, signal intelligence, human intelligence, special operations forces and deception operations. The Defense Department already maintains a secretive counter-terror operations group known as Delta Force that is called in when a crisis happens; P2OG would focus its efforts on preventing those crises from even occurring in the first place.

The starting point for this operation appears to be Rumsfeld, who said in May 2002: "Prevention and preemption are ... the only defense against terrorism. Our task is to find and destroy the enemy before they strike us." This is plainly a proposal for the creation of de facto terror cells under the authority of the Pentagon. If the goal is to provoke terror, there is nothing to prevent P2OG from infiltrating agents into existing terror groups, or creating its own terror groups, with the mission of causing those groups to engage in specific terrorist attacks. There is no form of supervision or oversight which could ever guarantee that abuses of this type would not take place; they would be inherent in the design of the project itself. Indeed, just the fact that the project outline exists strongly suggests that P2OG also exists, and has presumably been at work.

III
THE ROOTS OF 9/11:
THE GLOBALIZED CRISIS OF THE 1990S

I'm not going to start the Third World War for you.
– General Sir Michael Jackson to Wesley Clark, June 1999

Contrary to popular belief, the 9/11 events were anything but a bolt out of the blue. They grew out of the severe and increasing global instability of the world and of the United States during the 1990s. These years were marked by repeated trips to the brink of systemic breakdown crisis of the world financial and monetary systems, against a backdrop of recrudescence of the great-power tensions among the US, Russia, and China which had supposedly been relegated to the past at the end of the Cold War. The US political system was exhibiting many of the crisis symptoms of Weimar Germany (1919-1933). The common denominator of the tempests of the 1990s was financial globalization as expressed in the form of the Washington Consensus, which proved itself to be an absolutely unworkable way of organizing the economic life of the world.

Within this crisis, there were aggressive, militaristic and lawless networks at work within the United States. The events of 9/11 should re-direct our attention to these lawless networks inside the US government which have periodically asserted themselves, with devastating consequences. One of these was the Dulles Brothers-Lemnitzer-Lansdale network as it had emerged from the Iran-Contra years; this was the world of the asteroids, or privatized intelligence community operations.

This is the network which we can associate with the U-2 crisis, with the Bay of Pigs, the Kennedy assassination, the Gulf of Tonkin incident, the Martin Luther King assassination, the Robert Kennedy assassination, Watergate, Iran-Contra, and a score of lesser events. Another aggressive and adventurous network was the neocon network, always calling for new wars to be fought by other people's children.

As Sanguinetti points out, modern states tend to resort to terrorism and violence during their birth, when they are in severe crisis, and in the process of their extinction. In the 9/11 instance, the roots of terrorism are to be sought only marginally in events taking place in the Middle East, and certainly not in any distant cave in Afghanistan. Monocausal explanations embraced by corporate elites, such as the Hubbert "peak oil" thesis, are also unsatisfactory, since we are dealing not with geological events *per se*, but rather with the breakdown crisis of a political economy.

OLIGARCHICAL MALTHUSIANISM
THEN AND NOW

From 9/11 to "peak oil" is a dangerous leap, and from "peak oil" to population reduction is more dangerous still. Because oligarchs have always held humanity in general in contempt, they have from time immemorial exhibited the outlook which has, during the last 200 years, been called Malthusian. Back among the early Greeks, one school of thought explained the Trojan War as necessary to remove the weight of the masses of mankind which were oppressing the breast of Mother Earth. Together with the axiomatic notion of overpopulation has gone a profound hostility to science and technology, especially because of their egalitarian effects. During the time of Thucydides in Athens, the writer called the Old Oligarch complained that the high-tech Athenian navy was helping the plebs to achieve upward mobility, while the equally high-tech long walls between Athens and Piraeus kept the armies of oligarchical Sparta at bay. During the agony of the Roman Empire, the decrees of the Emperor Diocletian in effect banned technological progress by making it illegal to alter the equipment and property of any guild. During the decline of the Venetian Empire, the decadent Giammaria Ortes (1713-1798) elaborated the notion that the earth had an absolute and unalterable maximum carrying capacity, which he set at 3 billion persons.

Ortes was the original from which the English Reverend Thomas Malthus copied. Malthus' well-known contention that population increases geometrically while food supply increases arithmetically stands in contradiction with thousands of years of successful human development. Malthus' real interest, it should be remembered, was to convince capitalists that they had to pay to maintain a numerous state church made up of people like himself, whose consumption would make sure that no crises of overproduction occurred. This was Malthus' notorious slogan, "The church with a capacious maw is best." Malthus was in turn the key to the bankruptcy of Darwin, who based himself on the greedy prelate. There is no doubt about evolution, but Darwin is a completely separate kettle of fish, especially his wayward thesis about the "blind watchmaker," meaning that the universe is a totally random process. The present writer agrees rather with Leibniz's view of a least-action universe which has a definite in-built tendency towards greater order, greater energy organization, and greater development.

The fatal flaw of Keynesian economics is that they are based on Malthusian premises: there is a surplus which has to be consumed, and Keynes is unable to distinguish between productive and parasitical ways of doing this. In more recent times, the Malthusian outlook has been promoted with great success by the sinister Club of Rome, founded by Alexander King and Aurelio Peccei. The Club of Rome sponsored that infamous hoax, Meadows and Forrester's 1968 *The Limits to Growth*. This fraudulent study took a snapshot of the then-known reserves of the main industrial commodities, and then simply extrapolated when these would be gone, based on the current rate of consumption. Almost forty years later, not one of these dire predictions has come to pass, and known reserves of many raw materials are greater than they were in 1968.

In 1971-1973, the long period of world economic expansion associated with Franklin D. Roosevelt's Bretton Woods system and postwar economic reconstruction came to an end in a series of monetary crises that destroyed the most successful monetary arrangement the world had ever seen. Since 1971-73, long-term economic growth in the main industrial countries has been cut in half, from about 5% per year to about 2.5% per year. This, plus the later push for de-industrialization, is the main reason why living standards in the US have declined by about 50% over the same period, and the costs of essential services like health care and education have gone into the ionosphere. After 1971-73, we are no longer dealing with a normal economy, but with an increasingly sick one.

THE FAKE OIL SHOCKS OF THE 1970s

Building on the lies of the Club of Rome and the *The Limits to Growth*, Wall Street, the City of London, and the Federal Reserve, backed by the Seven Sisters Anglo-American oil cartel, decided to jack up the price of oil to save the dollar while making western Europe and Japan foot the bill. This cynical maneuver was associated with Henry Kissinger's Middle East Yom Kippur War of October 1973. After the hostilities began, the Organization of Petroleum Exporting Countries (OPEC) announced an Arab oil boycott. In late December 1973, the OPEC speeches had become the pretext for a 400% increase in the price of oil carried out by banks and speculators in the commodity trading pits of New York and Chicago. OPEC was blamed, but OPEC was never the real cartel. OPEC was largely a Potemkin cartel. The real cartel were the Seven Sisters. Without the connivance of the Seven Sisters and their Royal Dutch Shell/British Petroleum leadership, none of OPEC's antics could have been made to stick. In reality, there had been no reduction in oil deliveries to the US. In December 1973, oil-bearing supertankers of the leading oil companies were put into a holding pattern on the high seas because storage facilities were already full to bursting with crude. But that did not stop greedy speculators from bidding up the price.

The plan for the entire exercise had been provided by Lord Victor Rothschild, the sometime head of a think tank attached to Royal Dutch Shell, the dominant force within the Seven Sisters oil cartel. The operation had been discussed at a meeting of the self-styled Bilderberger Group of finance oligarchs held at Saltsjöbaden, Sweden on May 11-13, 1973. The effect of the oil price hike was to create a massive artificial demand for US dollars, thus effectively saving the greenback from a short-term collapse which would have ended its role as a reserve currency, and would have also ended the ability of US-UK finance to loot the world using this mechanism. In particular, if the posted price of oil were no longer expressed in dollars, then New York and London would no longer exercise *de facto* control over the oil reserves of the world. The 1973 oil crisis, followed by petrodollar recycling from the OPEC countries to David Rockefeller's Chase Manhattan Bank, kept the dollar in demand and thus prevented it from being dumped. Of course, the world paid the price for all this wizardry in the form of the deepest recession since World War II.

In 1978-79, Carter and Brzezinski, acting in the service of Brzezinski's lunatic thesis that Islamic fundamentalism was the greatest bulwark against Soviet communism, toppled the regime of the Shah of Iran. In line with this project, the US also made sure that the Shah was replaced by Khomeini, who embodied the negation *in toto* of modern civilization. Having done so well on the fake 1973-74 oil crisis, the New York and London finance oligarchs decided to repeat the operation, this time using the specter of Khomeini's self-styled Islamic revolution. This time prices went up by another 200%. When 1979 was over, it emerged that world oil production had not fallen, but the prices stayed up anyway. The 1979 doubling had more dramatic economic effects than the 1973 quadrupling, since the world economy was much weaker by 1979.

CHENEY WANTS $100-A-BARREL OIL

When we see a book like Paul Roberts' *The End of Oil* being hyped by Lou Dobbs on CNN, accompanied by a barrage of articles in the controlled corporate media on this same line, we can see that an Anglo-American consensus in favor of $100 per barrel oil is developing. The rationale is not hard to find, and has little to do with geological facts: the US dollar is once again in terminal crisis, and oil at $100 per barrel would create a new wave of artificial demand, making the dollar a little more attractive for oil producers and others, and perhaps staving off for a few more years the end of its reserve currency and posted price status. It is reported that the center of the agitation for $100 a barrel oil is, not surprisingly, the Vice Presidential office of Dick Cheney, managed by the ruthless neocon operative Lewis I. "Scooter" Libby.

As far as the substantive argument about oil reserves is concerned, it is clear that oil should be used less and less as a fuel, and employed rather for petro-chemicals. It is also clear that the internal combustion engine is now a technology that is over 100 years old, and due to be replaced. However, it is also clear that a growing world population and, hopefully, increased levels of world economic development will require greater energy sources. Every fixed array of human technology in world history has always defined certain components of the biosphere as usable resources, with the inevitable corollary that these resources would one day be exhausted. Thus the great imperative of human evolution cannot be retrenchment and austerity, but rather innovation, invention, discovery, and progress. If existing energy sources are insufficient, then science will have to find new ones, without ideological preclusions. Solar energy gathered outside the ionosphere in earth orbit might be one future solution. The one thing we must not do is to leap from a rising oil price to coerced population reduction, since that represents the core program of the Malthusian Anglo-American oligarchy, and has been in place as a policy goal since Kissinger's infamous NSSM 200 [2] and the Global 2000/Global Futures campaigns of the Muskie State Department under the disastrous Carter administration.

The pervasive oil and raw material grabs of today's world suggest nothing more than world economic breakdown and imminent world war. In 1941, Japan's main war aim was to secure the oil of the Dutch East Indies. Hitler's *Panzer* divisions in Operation Barbarossa were pointed towards Baku, which was Stalin's oil aorta. Stalin's own attack plan aimed at Ploesti in Romania, Germany's sole source of oil. Each of these plans sought to deny oil to an adversary and procure it for their authors as a means of winning a war. Much the same dynamic is afoot today, partially under the cover of "peak oil."

US OLIGARCHICAL CONSENSUS FOR TERRORISM

During the 1990s, the US oligarchy came to a consensus regarding the need for synthetic terrorism to preserve its system of rule under conditions of increasing economic and financial breakdown. This consensus was elaborated through commissions associated with names like Hart and Rudman, Gillmore, Rumsfeld, and the New York Council on Foreign Relations. Terrorism, the oligarchy concluded, was needed to maintain the cohesion of the hierarchical system, and the legitimacy of irrational domination. This was in line with the Carl Schmitt "enemy image" thesis, as elaborated more recently by Samuel Huntington.

Terrorism was also needed as an instrument of maintaining Anglo-American world domination, especially to wage oblique warfare to isolate, weaken, and contain powers like Russia, China, Japan, and some others who were too strong to be openly attacked on the Iraqi model. This type of terrorism was a continuation of the NATO geopolitical terrorism, whose goal was to maintain the Yalta division of the world against the self-asserting and self-liberating tendencies of countries like Germany, Italy, and others. Terrorism would serve as well to prevent threatened defections from the dollar zone, and shore up the battered greenback as the world's residual reserve currency. Terrorism would also help to consolidate US-UK control over oil, strategic metals, and other critical raw materials, in part by weakening and destabilizing economic nationalist or pro-development third world regimes.

9/11 must rather be viewed as a symptom of a perhaps insoluble crisis inside the US political and economic system. Whether or not the crisis of the 1990s

---

[2] US National Security Council, "Implications of Worldwide Population Growth for US Security and Overseas Interests," National Security Study Memorandum 200, December 10, 1974. This document posited a "special US political and strategic interest" in population reduction or limitation in many developing sector nations because of potential competition with the US for access to natural resources and raw materials. This amounted to a strategy of thinly veiled genocide, and facilitated US support for the murderous Pol Pot regime in Cambodia.

represents the first phase of the terminal crisis of the United States as presently constituted remains to be seen; by contrast, there can be little doubt that the post-1945 hegemony of the US dollar as the world's reserve currency is now ending, and that is more than enough to generate the cataclysmic events observed. Complacent and superficial commentators like David Brooks have attempted to portray the 1990s as a time of idyllic tranquility, when the polyanna US failed to pay attention to the gathering storm of terrorism "out there." In reality, the 1990s were a period of aggravated financial and economic breakdown and of severe if masked tensions among the US, China, the USSR, and other states.

The United States devastated Iraq at the beginning of the decade, destroying the civilian infrastructure with the cowardly and duplicitous "bomb now, die later" policy. The US said at the time that coalition aircraft had flown 120,000 sorties over Iraq. If each sortie had killed just one Iraqi, that would already have been 120,000 dead; the reality was probably three or four times greater. The unspeakable suffering in Iraq was made much worse by the US-backed and UN-enforced economic sanctions of 1990-2003, which, in violation of all relevant international law, banned the import of food and medicine completely, until certain limited purchases were allowed under the UN oil-for-food program in the later 1990s. The estimates of the number of Iraqi victims of these murderous sanctions vary widely, but it seems likely that the number of fatalities involved is between 500,000 and 1,000,000, with infants, children, and elderly people – all non-combatants – accounting for the majority. Some estimates take the death toll above 2 million Iraqis.

When once asked about this sacrifice, Madeleine Albright replied that in her opinion it was "worth it" to contain Iraq. During the 1990s, the present writer warned repeatedly that the economic sanctions were sowing a harvest of hate among Iraqis with which the US would one day have to reckon. The harvesting of that accumulated hate began in 2003, with a vengeance. All this was compounded by the unilateral imposition by the US and UK of no-fly zones in northern and southern Iraq, which involved the almost daily bombing of Iraqi targets during the entire decade of the 1990s. The Gulf crisis of 1990-91 disrupted the regional economy and led to the collapse of Somalia, where the lame duck Bush intervened just after Thanksgiving 1992. This was billed as a humanitarian mission, but US political meddling led to resistance by certain groups, and an orgy of gratuitous killing of black-skinned Arabs resulted.

THE 1990s: DECADE OF US FINANCIAL CRISIS

During these years the US was lurching from one financial crisis to the next. For a full account of this process, see my *Surviving the Cataclysm* (1999). The entire energy of the system was expended on impossible efforts to shore up the speculative edifices of stocks, bonds, and derivatives, which were always on the brink of panic collapse. The specter of some bankruptcy or panic setting off a systemic crisis, the implosion of the entire world dollar-based system, was a constant threat during the 1990s. US financial policy makers have been caught for decades in an impossible predicament. If they lower interest rates to keep the domestic system solvent, hot money will flee abroad, tending to collapse the overvalued dollar. If they raise interest rates to make the dollar more attractive, domestic bankruptcies begin to multiply. Fed governor Paul Volcker's worst nightmare had been an accelerating dollar collapse which could not be stopped.

The stock market crash of 1987 was in reality sandwiched in between two dollar crises which had the potential of sinking the battered and bloated greenback. That same stock market crash of 1987 brought on a collapse of the commercial real estate market in many cities, causing the bankruptcy of real estate firms like Olympia and York in 1992. As the real estate market collapsed, it undermined the main US money center banks. In 1990 the Bank of New England went bankrupt. Just as bankrupt from a technical point of view, but too big to fail because of the economic and political repercussions, were the twin giants of US banking, Chase Manhattan and Citibank. In July 1990, bank analyst Dan Brumbaugh stated on the ABC network program *Nightline* that not only Citicorp, but also Chase Manhattan, Chemical Bank, Manufacturers Hanover and Bankers Trust were all already insolvent. During September 1990, there was an electronic near-panic run on Citibank, while Chase Manhattan, and other New York money center banks were also under increasing pressure. Around Thanksgiving 1990, Citibank was quietly seized by federal regulators who then proceeded to run it for more than a year; the controlled media were silent to prevent panic runs, although they did not wholly succeed. In August 1991, Rep. John Dingell (D-Michigan) observed that Citibank was "technically insolvent" and "struggling to survive." Lloyd's of London also defaulted around this time. In the background, Russia had lost two thirds of her productive activity as the result of IMF shock therapy.

By the middle of the decade, former Secretary of the Treasury Brady reported that there was $1 trillion per day in currency speculation alone. Much of this was related to a new, parasitical, and highly unstable form of financial vehicle – derivatives. Felix Rohatyn of Lazard Freres admitted in the spring of 1994 that he was nervous about the derivatives crisis "because the genie is out of the bottle and could touch off a financial nuclear chain reaction, spreading around the world with the speed of light." By the end of the year Orange County, California had gone bankrupt because of derivatives dealings, reporting a two-billion dollar loss. But that was peanuts.

In January 1995 Mexico went bankrupt, bringing the world banking and financial system to about 48 hours from a total world-wide meltdown; at stake here was implicitly the huge mass of debt owed by the developing countries, which had reached $1.6 trillion. The tequila crisis required a $50 billion bailout which was thrown together *in extremis* by the Clinton administration. Camdessus of the IMF noted with much alarm on February 2, 1995 that "Mexico was in imminent danger of having to resort to exchange controls. Had that happened, it would have triggered a true world catastrophe." A few weeks later Barings Bank of London, one of the world's oldest financial institutions, went belly up, and contrived to blame the default on a rogue trader.

AUGUST-SEPTEMBER 1998: RUSSIA AND LTCM TAKE WORLD TO BRINK

In 1997 the Asian contagion crisis began in earnest; it was in reality another crisis of the world dollar-based system. This led on August 17, 1998 to the default and state bankruptcy of Russia, with a series of banking panics wiping out the savings of the middle class. Russian economic reform, better known as IMF shock therapy, had been the great international financier project of the first half of the 1990s, and it ended in dust and ashes. Anti-oligarchical Russian economist Tatyana Koryagina observed around this time that "the world economy has reached the point where – if economic liberalism is a dead-end street, it has hit the concrete wall at the end of the street. This liberalism will explode the entire economy and then there will be global chaos, which will be economic fascism. A 'New World Order' is economic fascism, when a huge number of people are thrown into desperate poverty, and only the speculators make any profit. We are on the verge of a particular sort of anti-financier revolution – a revolution against financial speculators." (Tarpley 1999 chapter 1)

When Russia blew up, real panic spread around the world. The newspaper that expresses the views of the Swiss financial community noted with consternation: "With the ruble collapse and the de facto state bankruptcy of Russia, the crisis which has been boiling for a year is now threatening to turn into a global *GAU*" – *Größten aller Unfälle*, or worst possible catasrophe, wrote this paper. "Like dominoes, one currency after another, one financial market after another, are falling all over the globe. The specter of a worldwide recession is spreading." (*Neue Zürcher Zeitung*, August 29, 1998)

The Russian state bankruptcy in turn provoked the failure of Long Term Capital Management (LTCM), a giant Connecticut hedge fund with close ties to the US Federal Reserve. With LTCM, the world banking system was once more on the brink of systemic meltdown. Only a crony capitalist bailout of LTCM's creditors by Greenspan prevented the immediate collapse of the US money center banks, the US securities markets, and the reeling US dollar. LTCM had posed the immediate danger of a chain-reaction bankruptcy of the entire world banking system, leading to financial and monetary chaos. The New York Fed, in the person of its president William McDonough, undertook an emergency bailout as lender of last resort for the syndicate of big banks that were scrambling to save themselves by taking over LTCM, which was bankrupt with a reported $1 trillion in derivatives outstanding.

Long Term Capital Management was leveraged at 500:1, but what of that? J.P. Morgan was leveraged at over 600:1, with $6.2 trillion in derivatives against just $11 billion in equity capital. The story was broken by David Faber of CNBC on the afternoon of Wednesday, September 23, 1998. Within a few days, Union Bank of Switzerland announced a $685 million loss, and Dresdner Bank said it was $144 million to the downside. LTCM's total loss was about $4 billion. If the US banks had gone under, the FDIC would have had to pay depositors, and the taxpayers would soon have had to bail out the FDIC. Between August 29 and October 19, currency in circulation grew at an annual rate of 16.4%, and the M3 money supply grew at 17% annually. Greenspan was using system repurchase agreements, coupon passes, and open market operations to churn out liquidity. The dollar softened and the gold price spiked upward: there were reports that central banks were replenishing their gold stocks in the face of the hurricane. Between late September and early October, the dollar managed to fall ¥ 10 (or, in forex jargon, "ten big figures") in just 10 days. In August and September 1998, the world finance oligarchy had been forced to look into the glowing bowels of Hell. The half-million bankers and fund managers who are the chief beneficiaries of the globaloney system had felt the icy breath of panic on their necks. But their near-death experience had not impelled them to consider any serious reforms.

By the end of 1998, the debt superpower of Brazil was on the brink of default, once more threatening to bring down the banks of Wall Street. George Soros demanded that the banks be protected by a "wall of money," and Greenspan complied. Using the pretext of providing liquidity to cushion the shocks of the transition from 1999 to 2000, when multiple computer breakdowns were feared, Greenspan began to print fresh US dollars at an unprecedented rate. Much of this new cash rushed into the NASDAQ stock market, where it stoked the merging dot.com bubble. But by the early months of 2000, it was clear that the dot.com companies still had no profits, and their high burn rate of cash on hand spelled the end of the bubble. In a spectacular decline that did not stabilize until the middle of 2002, the NASDAQ lost a breathtaking 75% of its value.

Many hedge funds, banks, and insurance companies were on the verge of imploding, but Greenspan kept pumping new dollars to stave off chain-reaction bankruptcies. Interest rates reached new historical lows, and oil producers began to consider dumping the dollar in favor of the more stable euro, which was now available as an alternative. A housing bubble and a bond market bubble now emerged in the US. Greenspan's response was to tout the "wealth effect," meaning that the housing bubble was raising the fictitious value of private homes, allowing home owners to take out second mortgages and use the cash to speculate in the stock market. The bond bubble began to falter in the spring of 2004. In the meantime the entire system had been back to the brink in late 2001 and early 2002 with the declaration of a formal debt moratorium – a payment halt – by Argentina. Derivative financial instruments were always close to detonating a systemic crisis; there is some evidence that a derivatives disaster of the first magnitude had overtaken Citibank around the middle of 2001, but was papered over by Federal Reserve loans under the cover of 9/11. Citibank was forced to sell Travelers Insurance for $4 billion, apparently to raise cash to plug a considerable hole.

Towards the end of the decade, Eisuke Sakakibara of the Japanese Finance Ministry a well-known official who had earned the nickname of "Mr. Yen" in the world press, had summed up the problems of the US-UK system as follows: "… I think the financial system we have today is inherently unstable. We need to set up a new system to stabilize financial markets. Otherwise, the repetition of crisis after crisis . . . is going to result in a major meltdown of the world financial system." – (Japanese Finance Ministry, January 22, 1999)

TO THE BRINK OF SYSTEMIC BREAKDOWN:
Financial Crises and Panics 1987 – 2003

1	October 1987	American stock market and futures market crash
2	December 1987 – January 1988	Greenspan dollar crisis
3	January – February 1990	Bankruptcy of Drexel-Burnham-Lambert, RJR-Nabisco default threat, Campeau stores bankruptcy, junk bond collapse
4	1990-1991	Failure of Bank of New England, threatened insolvency of Citibank, Chase, and other US banks
5	September 1992	European Rate Mechanism crisis
6	August 1993	Second speculative assault on European Rate Mechanism, leading to permanent loosening of fixed parities
7	February 1994 – February 1995	World bond market crisis, Orange County-Mexico-Barings
8	August – September 1995	Japanese banking crisis: $1 trillion in bad loans
9	November 1995	Daiwa Bank threatened by insolvency in wake of $1.1 billion bond trading losses
10	June 1996	Sumitomo copper futures trading crisis; 31% decline in world copper price
11	July – November 1997	Southeast Asia currency and stock market crisis, featuring Thailand, Philippines, Malaysia, Hong Kong, Singapore, Indonesia, South Korea, with world stock market panic
12	November 1997	Japanese banking crisis

13	December 1997	South Korean insolvency crisis
14	November 1997 – April 1998	Indonesian crisis
15	May 1998 and July – August 1998	Russian monetary, stock market, and interbank crisis starting in May 1998. Failure of IMF bailout attempt, July-August 1998. Russian default, August 1998
16	September 23, 1998	Long Term Capital Management insolvency with bailout by New York Federal Reserve. Threat of world banking panic and interbank settlements freeze
17	December 1998 – January 1999	Brazilian crisis and Soros "wall of money"
18	March 2000 – August 2002	Collapse of NASDAQ bubble, down 75%
19	Summer 2002	J. P. Morgan Chase derivatives monster implodes
20	2002 ff.	Argentine crisis with debt default
21	May 2003	US dollar in bear market; world dumping of dollar looms

END OF DOLLAR HEGEMONY?

Perhaps most serious for the Anglo-American system of world domination was the impact of these events on the fate of the US dollar. By virtue of the Bretton Woods agreement of 1944, the dollar had replaced the British pound as the world's reserve currency. The Bretton Woods system disintegrated in 1971-73, and we are now living among its rubble, but the primacy of the dollar has remained unchallenged. This means that most world trade was and still is conducted in dollars, including Eurodollars based in London. The prices for the main raw materials, and especially oil, are quoted in US dollars. If Europe wants Russian or Saudi oil, it must pay in dollars, thus creating demand for a currency which otherwise might find few buyers, since the US produces so little to sell.

This allows the US-UK banking community to skim 5-10% off all world trade by providing import-export financing; this used to be called invisible earnings. More important still, if the dollar is the only way you can buy oil, then whoever controls the dollars – meaning the US – will in effect control the oil, whether it is nationalized or not, no matter who formally owns it. The role of the dollar in the posted priced for Gulf crude is thus the central symbol of the world dominance of the dollar. And the dollar is the nerve and fist of US world domination.

As an anonymous expert quoted by William Clark correctly pointed out in early 2003: "The Federal Reserve's greatest nightmare is that OPEC will switch its international transactions from a dollar standard to a euro standard. Iraq actually made this switch in November 2000 (when the euro was worth around 80 cents), and has actually made off like a bandit considering the dollar's steady depreciation against the euro. (http://globalresearch.ca/articles/CLA302A.html) The dollar declined 17% against the euro in 2002.

IRAQ

For Iraq, the decision to quit the dollar for the euro was an explicitly political one. Iraqi Finance Minister Hekmat Ibrahim al-Azzawi announced the move by saying: "The dollar is the currency of an enemy state, and must be abandoned for other currencies, including the euro." The Iraqi central bank announced in October 2000 that it had begun to buy European currencies. (AFP via energy24.com, October 12, 2000) Saddam Hussein stopped accepting dollars for oil in November 2000, and at the same time shifted ten billion dollars on deposit in the UN oil-for-food fund into the euro. Sure enough, the 2003 US occupation regime put Iraqi oil exports back on a dollar, rather than a euro, standard. The US invasion also helped to intimidate any nation which might have been considering switching to the euro. Since late 2001, the dollar was steadily declining and the euro was steadily gaining, with periodic plateaus, so those who chose the euro were rewarded to the tune of 20% or more. The second country in Bush's axis of evil, North Korea, switched to the euro on December 2, 2002. Here the economic impact was limited, but the political symbolism was still quite strong.

IRAN

The third Bush bugaboo and number two OPEC producer Iran was also considering a move out of the dollar, and the arrival of US military forces next door was doubtless designed to dissuade the Iranians from such thoughts. The Iranian approach was less flamboyant and confrontational, but the threat to the dollar was there none the less. Iranian sources were quoted in September 2002 as remarking that "Iran's proposal to receive payments for crude oil sales to Europe in euros instead of US dollars is based primarily on economics." Still, an anti-US political animus could not be denied, since dumping the dollar would be an "opportunity to hit back at the US government, which recently labelled it part of an 'axis of evil.'" As this proposal was considered, Iran was moving currency assets out of the dollar anyway. Russia and China announced during 2003 that they were doing the same thing.

VENEZUELA

And what of Venezuela, the number four producer of oil? Here the CIA, with the help of Iran-Contra veteran Otto Reich, attempted to overthrow President Chavez with a botched coup in April 2002. Many saw this as a move to secure oil supplies in case the attack on Iraq got messy. But a year before the coup, Venezuela's ambassador to Washington, Francisco Mieres-Lopez, apparently floated the idea of switching the posted price for Venezuelan crude to the euro. Under Chavez, Venezuela also embarked on a policy of direct barter deals for oil, which had been concluded with about a dozen Latin American countries. In these cases the dollar was cut out of the oil transaction cycle, and the ability of the Wall Street banks to skim off these transactions was eliminated. Venezuela had for example a deal with Cuba under which Cuban doctors and health workers served in the Venezuelan countryside, while Castro got his crude oil needs covered in return, thus meeting a need that had been acute since the collapse of the USSR cut off oil deliveries to Cuba from Soviet fields.

INDONESIA

Pertamina, the Indonesian oil giant, showed every sign of jumping on the bandwagon. According to a Jakarta paper, in April 2003, "Pertamina…dropped a bombshell….. It's considering dropping the US dollar for the euro in its oil and gas trades." The paper pointed to the "major implications for the world's biggest economy." ("Indonesia May Dump Dollar, Rest of Asia Too?" *Jakarta Post*, April 22, 2003) In the same issue, two economists, Nur Azis and Jason Meade, from the Center for Indonesian Reform, Jakarta, urged that Indonesia cast off its dollar dependence. They argued that the dollar would "remain weak over the next decade at least, for a number of reasons."

MALAYSIA

The former Malaysian Prime Minister, Mahathir Mohamed, was perhaps the most outspoken against the dollar. He repeatedly called on oppressed Arabs to turn away from suicide bombing, and fight the US-UK combine with the far more potent weapon of dumping the dollar in favor of the euro. Mahathir was blunt about the need to replace the world dollar standard. In early 2003, Mahathir told a group of reporters that the international community needed to be encouraged to use other currencies or even gold as the benchmark in international trade. This was because the domination of the US dollar in global transactions was distorting the world's economy. Mahathir suggested that the euro, yen, or even gold should be used for transactions. "We should be given the choice to use whatever currency that we want," he said at a meeting with 31 foreign editors and senior journalists. He pointed to the greater danger of manipulation when international business is all conducted in one nation's currency. "For the purpose of trade, we shouldn't say that oil should be quoted only in US dollars. Today, the oil price has gone up, but the value of the US dollar has gone down, something that the people do not point out," he added. "The oil price today was not actually US $36 if this was compared with the value of the dollar a year or three years ago."

Mahathir said he had read an article which pointed out that the United States was actually living on borrowed money and that it always faced a huge deficit. Despite that, he said, the US economy continued growing at a tremendous rate for the past 10 years while Japan, which had made a lot of money and had very healthy reserves, was facing economic problems. "This is a contradiction. Why is this happening? It is simply because we are giving value to the US dollar which it doesn't really have. There is nothing to back the US dollar other than people's belief in it." (*The Star*, February 28, 2003) Later in 2003, Mahathir, noting the fall of the dollar against the euro, told the Nikkei Forum in Tokyo: "The US dollar is not a stable currency at all. We have to think of some other ways of determining exchange rates. We need to rethink whether we can depend on the US dollar or not. Initially yes, we have to depend on the US dollar, but we should move away from the US dollar." (*The Edge Daily*, June 6, 2003)

SAUDI ARABIA: THE PARTING OF THE WAYS WITH THE US, AUGUST 2001

Most significant of all were the signs that even Saudi Arabia, long considered a client state or even a ward of the United States, was considering breaking away from the US system. Here the falling dollar, Bush's slavish support of Sharon, and preparations for new US attacks on Arab states were doubtless playing a role. According to the *Wall Street Journal*, Saudi Crown Prince Abdullah sent a letter to Bush at the end of August 2001 – before the events of September 11 – and warned him, in reference to the US-Saudi relationship, that "a time comes when peoples and nations part." The letter went on to say that "it is time for the United States and Saudi Arabia to look at their separate interests. Those governments that don't feel the pulse of the people and respond to it will suffer the fate of the Shah of Iran."

Prince Abdullah read from this letter at a meeting of 150 prominent Saudis in October 2001, in an effort to convince them that the Saudi government is defending Arab and Muslim interests. During a phone call with Bush around the same time, Abdullah again called for the US to restrain Israel. Diplomats said that there was considerable debate within the Saudi royal family over the US war in Afghanistan and the cost of the US-Saudi relationship. One Western diplomat said that the failure to resolve the Middle East conflict was going to make it harder for Saudi Arabia to continue its relationship with the US in the same manner. (*Wall Street Journal*, Oct. 29, 2001) Saudi Arabia was a pillar of the US empire; without it, the empire would collapse. For the imperialists, action was imperative to prevent this critical defection.

The dubious Michael Moore along with a gaggle of fellow travelers and self-styled 9/11 skeptics parroted the Mossad line that Saudi Arabia was responsible for 9/11. It is more likely that the stolen passports and unproven allegations about Saudi hijackers were cooked up as a means of blackmailing the Saudis, who were evidently ready to distance themselves from Washington. (Indeed, the financier faction at least may have more than a defensive gambit in mind, judging by probes in the media about opening up the Saudi national oil company to plunder by foreign capital, under the guise of "liberalization" and "privatization.")

THE EUROPEAN UNION

Europe for its part was eager to eliminate the dollar. Jacques Santer, former president of the European Commission, called on Gulf Arab oil exporters to price their crude in the euro rather than the US dollar as a means to stabilize the oil market. "It could be the instrument to consolidate oil markets" and would be less affected by US foreign policy, he told a Gulf-Euro conference in Dubai. ("Santer calls for oil to be priced in euros," *The Irish Times* October 8, 2000) The biggest issue here was whether Russia would phase out the dollar in favor of the euro, as the Germans and others were proposing. In addition, dumping the dollar was popular politics. Newspaper columnists and antiwar activists in countries from Morocco to Indonesia shared the sentiments expressed in a Nigerian street protest witnessed by a *Wall Street Journal* reporter during the run-up to the Iraq war: "Euro yes! Dollar no!" (http://journeyman.1hwy.com/J-Big_OneIIIb.html)

US elites had long been painfully aware of the colossal vulnerability represented by the world's dollar overhang – the masses of dollars held outside of the United States. Republican Senator Pete Dominici of New Mexico commented on May 18, 1995: "What would happen if the Saudi Arabians said they didn't want to be paid [for oil] in dollars anymore, but wanted instead, to be paid, say in yen. There would be inflation that would make the 15 to 20 percent inflation in the early '80s look good." (C-SPAN II, May 18, 1995)

The impact of a world move to dump the dollar can be deciphered from the following commentary from an insider newsletter: "The US dollar is 'over-owned.' 77.7% of world central bank reserves are in US dollars. That's disproportionate to the US share of world trade. There'll now be some diversification, especially to the euro. Just as central banks sold gold, they'll now sell US dollars. A study revealed at a central bank confab at Jackson Hole by Professors Obstfeld and Rogoff suggests the US dollar could drop 24%-40% if foreigners move quickly to exchange dollars. Foreigners own a record 38% of the US Treasury market (44% excluding Federal Reserve holdings), 20% of US corporate bonds, and 8% of US stocks. A change of sentiment, now suddenly in the air, could start a dollar brushfire." (*The International Harry Schultz Letter,* January 19, 2001)

If oil producers in general were to make the leap from the dollar to the euro, many central banks would have to shift reserves into the European currency. The value of the dollar might crash between 20 and 40%, as Clark's article points out. The impact of this inside the US could even be hyperinflation of 1000% or more per year. As the expert cited by Clark summed up: "One of the dirty little secrets of today's international order is that the rest of the globe could topple the United States from its hegemonic status whenever they so choose, with a concerted abandonment of the dollar standard. This is America's pre-eminent, inescapable Achilles Heel for now and the foreseeable future. That such a course hasn't been pursued to date bears more relation to the fact that other westernized, highly developed nations haven't any interest to undergo the great disruptions which would follow – but it could assuredly take place in the event that the consensus view coalesces of the United States as any sort of 'rogue' nation. In other words, if the dangers of American global hegemony are ever perceived as a greater liability than the dangers of toppling the international order. The Bush administration and the neo-conservative movement have set out on a multiple-front course to ensure that this cannot take place, in brief by a graduated assertion of military hegemony atop the existent economic hegemony. The paradox I've illustrated with this one narrow scenario is that the quixotic course itself may very well bring about the feared outcome that it means to pre-empt. We shall see!" (http://globalresearch.ca/articles/CLA302A.html)

The US economy was very sick indeed. Electrical infrastructure was at the breaking point, with major blackouts every summer. The air transportation system was bankrupt. Commuter and freight railroads were subject to constant breakdowns. The budget deficit was rising towards $500 billion – or $750 billion, and the merchandise trade deficit was rising towards $500 billion; for the first time in memory, the US even became a net importer of foods. The public debt was headed towards $6.5 trillion, with over $4 trillion in foreign debt. The military forces were comprised of ten hollow infantry divisions – hardly an adequate force to conquer the world, except in a neocon fantasy.

THE CATASTROPHE OF GLOBALIZATION

After the fall of the East German communist regime in 1989, and the extinction of the USSR in December 1991, the United States presided over the inauguration of a new era, that of the globalized world economy. I have discussed the main features of globalization in *Surviving the Cataclysm* (1999), my study of the world financial crisis. For our present purposes, it is enough to focus on the consequences of globalization. Globalization has completed the destruction of the United States as a political economy, and has substantially wrecked the entire world economy, as was evident to clear-minded observers no later than 1992, when globalization began the demolition of the Russian economy. Together with globalization came the ascendancy of parasitical financier elites oriented exclusively towards short-term speculative gain in such areas as derivatives speculation, and perfectly incompetent in regard to the economic requirements of civilized progress. It was not September 11, 2001 which destroyed the world as we had known it; it was the marauding and immiserating march of economic globalization.

The great lesson of the twentieth century was that financial disintegration and economic depression set the stage for world war. The same dynamic was at work during the 1990s. For most people in the United States, western Europe and Japan, this underlying dynamic was masked by a currency arrangement centering on the dollar which tended to shield these parts of the world from the full fury of globalization, while inflicting intensified looting and impoverishment on the underdeveloped countries. But even so, the economic decline in the supposedly rich countries was breathtaking.

As the United States became financially more unstable and economically less viable, ruling elites began to exhibit greater readiness for military adventures abroad. This aggressivity was common to the Republican and Democratic wings of the oligarchy, but was somewhat alleviated by Bill Clinton's personal distaste for foreign military adventures and keen awareness of the risks they posed for himself politically. But after the Monica Lewinsky crisis emerged at the beginning of 1998, executive authority was increasingly usurped by a group of high officials calling themselves the principals' committee, who carried out the bombing of Iraq (Operation Desert Fox) at the end of 1998, and who then turned to the bombing of Serbia in the spring of 1999. Not to be outdone, the neoconservative faction of the oligarchy attempted at the same time to stir up conflict with China, whose high rates of economic growth posed in their eyes the threat of the emergence of a new and competing superpower. Conflict with Russia, always latent, threatened at various junctures to erupt into more visible hostility.

The prevalent conception of Russia on the part of US foreign policy elites is that of a strategic adversary. Russia has retained significant parts of the strategic missile forces built during the Soviet era, and has supplemented them with new developments such as the Topol missile. Traditional strength in basic science may put Russia ahead of the US in certain key areas of military technology although engineering problems still hold them back. The Russian middle class has been bankrupted twice, once in the 1300% hyperinflation of 1992-93, and a second time in the banking panic associated with the Russian state default in August and September 1998. This fact alone is very ominous. The last time the middle class of a great power was subjected to two waves of bankruptcy was in Weimar Germany, when the middle class lost all its savings and investments through the combination of the hyperinflation of 1923, followed by the deflationary depression of 1929.

Under Yeltsin, Russia was the playground of a group of rapacious financiers who arrogantly called themselves the oligarchs – these were figures like Berezovsky, Potanin, Smolensky, Friedman, and Khodorkhovsky. Khodorkhovsky seized control over most of the Siberian oil reserves, and appeared ready to sell them off to the Anglo-American oil cartel. The beginning of the end for the oligarchs came with the resignation of Yeltsin and the elevation of Putin to the Russian presidency on December 31, 1999. The KGB officer Putin tended to repress the oligarchs in conformity with the usual Russian statist model of political economy. Putin's arrival was punctuated by bombings of apartment houses in Moscow which were attributed to Muslim Chechen terrorists. This terror wave helped to consolidate Putin's power through the usual stampeding effect, but this may not be the whole story. The entire Chechen insurrection has been sponsored by the US and the British within the framework of what Brzezinski calls the "grand chessboard," and its leaders are reputed to be assets of the CIA. Perhaps the CIA and MI-6 had provided the terror wave upon which Putin rode to power. The precedent of the Soviet Afghan war is all too suggestive: a conflict incited by the US which brought down the Soviet Union.

US AS WEIMAR GERMANY

One of the favorite theses of the neocons is that the United States today can be directly compared to the Weimar Republic, that is to say, to Germany between 1919 and 1933. Here the neocons are correct, although it must be added that one of the main factors contributing to the similarity is the role of the neocons themselves. Weimar was financially unstable, as seen in the hyperinflation of 1923 and the deflationary depression of 1929. It was also politically unstable, with right-wing coup attempts (like the Kapp-Luttwitz putsch of 1920 on the part of army officers and top bureaucrats, the Hitler-Ludendorff Munich beer hall putsch of November 1923) alternating with attempts at communist insurrection (the Bavarian Soviet republic and the German Communist Party's coup attempts). This kind of instability finds a precise analogue in the globalized United States starting at the end of the 1990s. We have had at least one coup or coup attempt per year, starting in 1998.

ONE COUP PER YEAR: USA, 1998-2005		
1998	Impeachment coup against Clinton	successful
1999	Conviction coup against Clinton	failed due to mass support for Clinton
1999	Principals' committee coup; bombing of Serbia	successful
2000	Bush stolen election coup	successful
2001	9/11 terror coup	successful
2002	War powers coup by Bush	successful
2003	Iraq war coup by Bush	successful
2004	Threatened 2nd wave terror coup; 2nd stolen election coup	?
2005	Threat of war with Iran, Sudan, Syria, Russia	?

During 1994, a remarkable pattern of events emerged. One of Clinton's helicopters crashed, killing the pilot; Clinton was not on board. A Clinton ally, the black politician John Wilson, head of the Washington DC City Council, was found hanged in his home. Vincent Foster, Clinton's old friend, was found dead along the George Washington Parkway, not far from CIA headquarters. This was pronounced a suicide. Neofascist opponents of Clinton raved that there was a Murder Incorporated operating out of the White House which had killed Foster, but this was absurd.

On September 11, 1994, Frank Eugene Corder crashed his Cessna 150 L into the White House lawn two floors below Clinton's bedroom, killing himself in the process. Clinton was not there. These events marked an attempt by the permanent Washington oligarchy – the Establishment – to break the will of Clinton, a person for whom many of them felt a wholly irrational but intense hatred. So the White House lawn was hit by a plane on September 11, 1994.

In the late summer of 1995, the Gingrich Republicans attempted to permanently weaken the constitutional powers of the presidency by unilaterally dictating the federal budget. This was an attempted coup by the GOP congressional leadership. They announced their willingness to deny spending authority to the Treasury in such a way as to provoke the default of the United States – an unprecedented event which would have meant national bankruptcy and chaos. Clinton held firm as the government shut down, and the population turned against Gingrich, permanently weakening him. The Republicans were forced to back down, and the budget was enacted according to the relevant constitutional norms.

During 1998, the impeachment of Bill Clinton was prepared and carried out by a coalition of oligarchical reactionaries. The pre-history of this coup goes back to the beginning of the Clinton presidency, when stories about sexual excesses in the White House were circulated by disgruntled pro-Bush elements in the Secret Service. After 12 years of feeding at the public trough, the Bush faction and its allies experienced loss of power as a kind of traumatic cold turkey, and their response was an aggressive rage against Clinton, which fed on the relatively minor positive achievements of the new president.

The impeachment coup was promoted by the reactionary millionaire Richard Mellon Scaife, and by the Hollinger press empire of Conrad Black, with its flagship London *Daily Telegraph* and its star reporter Ambrose Evans-Pritchard, a man known to be in contact with British intelligence. Another contributing group was the Barbara and Ted Olson salon in northern Virginia, which was attended by such reactionary gurus as Clarence Thomas, failed Supreme Court candidate Robert Bork, Lawrence Silberman of the DC circuit court of appeals, Robert Bartley of the *Wall Street Journal*, and others. The spearhead of impeachment in the House was Tom "the Hammer" Delay, a former pest exterminator. (See Tarpley in Hidell)

The scandal escalated in January 1998 as a result of Linda Tripp's illegal taping of her conversations with the pathetic Monica Lewinsky. Tripp had been encouraged by Lucienne Goldberg, a hardened Republican operative. Tripp was a GS-16 federal bureaucrat with a background in Army Intelligence. During the Iran-Contra era, Tripp had served as personal secretary to General Richard Secord of the Army Delta Force; she had also been involved in one of the front companies on Oliver North's flow chart. When Tripp revealed the Clinton-Lewinsky story to GOP zealot special prosecutor Ken Starr, Starr redirected his probe from Whitewater to Monica, and the US presidency was paralyzed for two years.

The impeachment propaganda of the Republicans resonated deeply within the military, where the relatively new presence of female officers and enlisted personnel had led to a series of sexual abuse and sexual harassment scandals. Most famous of these was the 1991 Tailhook affair, involving an orgy in which naval aviators and female officers participated, some under duress. Resentment grew over cases like that of Rear Admiral Ralph L. Tindal, who was ousted in December 1995 for sex harassment and adultery. Serving and retired military whose careers had been damaged or terminated by charges of sexual misconduct became enraged against Clinton, for whom they thought a double standard was being applied. Although such rage by itself might never add up to an attempted coup, it could help set the stage for one. Widespread hatred for President Kennedy in the CIA, its Cuban paramilitaries, and the US military after his failure to escalate the Bay of Pigs crisis and the Cuban missile crisis certainly helped to weaken the defenses of the presidency, and may have contributed something to the ease of recruitment of key officers to the plot and above all to the cover-up.

In December 1998, with Clinton facing immediate impeachment by the House of Representatives, the principals' committee effectuated a minor coup within the White House bureaucracy. The visible expression of this was the bombing of Iraq just before Christmas under the code name of Operation Desert Fox. At the beginning of 1999, the attempted ouster of Clinton from the presidency was a coup that failed. Clinton's survival was the result of his continued strong public support, expressed in part as unusual off-year gains for Democratic congressional candidates.

Pro-impeachment oligarchs registered foaming rage and resentment not just against Clinton, but against the US population as a whole, which they claimed had not paid enough attention to the moral rectitude of the impeachers. Paul Weyrich of the Mellon-Scaife-funded Free Congress Foundation talked of withdrawing from political affairs altogether, without making clear what the alternative field of endeavor might be. This incident tended to heighten the bureaucratic-authoritarian and totalitarian tendencies inside the reactionary wing of the US oligarchy. Since it was evident that the population was not convinced by arguments which seemed self-evident to the oligarchy, one may say that these events educated them in the need for a fascist transformation of some sort.

Nevertheless, a successful coup d'état did take place in 1999. It involved the seizure of power by an organism known as the principals' committee, which was composed at that time of Vice President Gore and his dubious national security adviser Leon Fuerth, Defense Secretary William Cohen, Secretary of State Madeleine Albright, National Security Council director Samuel Berger, and Gen. Hugh Shelton, the chairman of the Joint Chiefs of Staff. George Tenet of the CIA was sometimes present, and the bureaucratic *eminence grise* of the committee was terror czar Richard Clarke, the star of the Kean-Hamilton Commission in 2004.

The pretext for ascendancy of the principals' committee was the fighting in the former Yugoslavia, which had begun in June 1990, when Yugoslavia started to break up. After massacres of Muslims by Serbs at Srebrenica in July 1995, the US and NATO undertook a bombing campaign against the Bosnian Serb positions around besieged Sarajevo. These air strikes lasted from August 28 to September 13, 1995, with about 3400 missions flown, and finally put an end to the Yugoslav civil war, which had claimed the lives of 250,000 dead, and had seen numerous war crimes by Bosnian Serb leaders Karadjic and Mladic and others.

Ex-Yugoslavia was finally pacified when all parties signed the Dayton accords on November 21, 1995 at Wright-Patterson Air Force Base. US and other NATO peacekeepers entered Bosnia in December. Then, in 1997, Albania, which neighbors Serbia and the province of Kosovo, which has an ethnic Albanian and Muslim majority, collapsed as a result of an orgy of financial speculation and Ponzi schemes. Weapons which had been the property of the Albanian government were pilfered, and found their way into Kosovo, where they were used to arm the emerging Kosovo Liberation Army (KLA), a US-backed organization which relied on drug running for much of its financing.

Clashes between the KLA and the Serbian military and police started in February-March 1998, and were soon seized upon by Madeleine Albright as a means of making an example of Serbia and of intimidating the world community in general, and in particular Russia, the traditional Orthodox backer of the Serbs. Fighting in Kosovo intensified during the summer of 1998. Responding to the threat of NATO air strikes, the Yugoslav leader Milosevic pulled most Serb units out of Kosovo.

But in the spring of 1999 the fighting flared up again. Now a crisis summit was convened at Rambouillet, near Paris. Here the KLA half-accepted the solution demanded by Albright, while the Serbs rejected it outright, since it included a clause giving US and NATO forces the right to go anywhere and everywhere in Serbia, while seizing buildings and commandeering supplies. The Serbian national identity was based on a fierce commitment to independence, which had been expressed as guerrilla warfare against the Nazis, and then in successfully facing down Stalin at the height of his power.

In response to the predictable Serb refusal, Albright became hysterical, feeling her entire secretaryship was in danger of collapse. She then sent Richard Holbrooke to Belgrade to give Milosevic an ultimatum: capitulate or face NATO bombing. Milosevic, realizing that giving up Kosovo and letting NATO forces into his country would mean his own political doom, rejected the US ultimatum.

At this point Russian Prime Minister Yevgeni Primakov was en route to Washington, seeking to help mediate a negotiated solution for the crisis. There is good reason to believe that serious talks between the US and Primakov would have allowed a peaceful solution, since it was a Russian mediation that finally did bring a cessation of the bombing. But with Primakov over the Atlantic, Vice President Al Gore, acting on behalf of the principals' committee, insisted on giving the order to start the bombing. Seeing an affront, Primakov turned back to Moscow.

Now began 78 days of merciless bombing of Serbia, directed by General Wesley Clark, the NATO commander. Serbian civilian dead were estimated at 10,000 or more – at least three times the death toll of 9/11, all imposed as part of a proxy war designed to humiliate Russia and break the will of small countries who might want to resist the Anglo-American universal bullies.

APRIL 9, 1999: YELTSIN WARNS OF WORLD WAR

The bombing of Kosovo was a giant step towards the international anarchy that manifested itself during the Iraq war of 2003. Russia and China were opposed to the bombing, but their peace plan was vetoed by the US, Britain, and France. However, NATO bombed without the benefit of a UN security council resolution. US-Russian relations reached a post-1991 low, with militant demonstrations at the US embassy in Moscow every day. The bombing of Kosovo duplicated the cowardly "bomb now, die later" method pioneered in the first Iraq war of 1991, with civilian power stations, water systems, and sewage treatment plants all being targeted. The bridges over the Danube were destroyed, an act of despicable vandalism which paralyzed Europe's most important waterway.

As the bombing went on week after week without any Serb capitulation, NATO leaders were seized by the hysterical fear that if NATO's first war were to end in a draw, the now wholly artificial alliance would begin to collapse. The US needed NATO as a tool for out-of-area deployments, meaning attacks on developing countries. Tony Blair began proposing an invasion of Serbia with land forces, an option which Clinton had explicitly ruled out. Joining Blair in this insane proposal was General Wesley Clark. On April 9, 1999 Russian President Yeltsin predicted that an invasion of Serbia by land forces would lead to "European war for sure, and possibly a world war." Russian General Seleznyov reminded NATO that Russian nuclear missiles were still pointed towards the western powers. This was the first serious mention of world war by a major international figure during the 1990s. Not caring about Yeltsin's warnings, Blair attempted to use his visit to Washington for the NATO 50th anniversary on April 23 to convince Clinton to start the ground invasion, but he was rebuffed.

NATO tried to justify its bombing by citing the large numbers of Albanian refugees leaving Kosovo. There were also wild reports of Serb massacres of ethnic Albanians in Kosovo. Many of these exaggerations were conduited from US State Department spokesman Jamie Rubin to his wife, the meretricious CNN correspondent Christiane Amanpour. The US claimed that 100,000 Albanians had been massacred and placed in mass graves; postwar investigation showed that there were perhaps 3,000 – a tragedy, but consistent with a guerrilla war of the type started by the KLA. The motivation for the bombing was therefore a big lie, manufactured by the US government and its media minions. (www.antiwar.com/justin/j082100.html)

How far was the aggressive clique within NATO prepared to go? According to Louis Sell, Milosevic was bludgeoned into capitulation by a threat by Finnish NATO spokesman Ahtisaari, who told the Serbs that "if he refused the deal, NATO was prepared to attack a much broader range of targets – including the remaining bridges across the Danube, the power and heating systems, and the telephone network." (Sell 311) This was a program of genocidal bombing with devastating delayed-action demographic impact – the "bomb now, die later" method employed in Iraq.

"I'M NOT GOING TO START WORLD WAR III FOR YOU"

Russia, now in the person of Chernomyrdin rather than the ousted Primakov, was finally able to induce Milosevic to capitulate in early June. The Russian army, anxious to demonstrate solidarity with the Serbs, and resentful of NATO attempts to deny Russia an occupation zone in Kosovo, on June 12 carried off a *coup de main.* They quickly shifted a couple of companies of armored vehicles to the airport in Pristina, the capital of Kosovo and not far from the border of Serbia proper. At this point General Wesley Clark (later Michael Moore's favorite presidential candidate in 2004) became frantic, and ordered the NATO ground commander, British General Sir Michael Jackson, to deny the Russians the use of the airport. There were reports that Russia was about to send a sky train of paratroopers to back up its demand. General Jackson flatly refused to carry out Clark's order, making the now-famous reply:

I'm not going to start the Third World War for you.

General Jackson later told the BBC: "We were [looking at] a possibility....of confrontation with the Russian contingent which seemed to me probably not the right way to start off a relationship with Russians who were going to become part of my command." Clark planned to order British tanks and armored cars to block the runways to prevent any Russian transport planes from landing. Clark said he believed it was "an appropriate course of action." But the plan was again vetoed by Britain. Here was a second serious warning about world war. (BBC, March 9, 2000)

It is evident in retrospect that the Kosovo operation was a proxy war between the United States and Russia, in which NATO's mauling of the Serb civilian population was supposed to illustrate to Russia the formidable military potential of the US-led alliance. The Pristina crisis cooled down, but US-Russian relations were dangerously strained. Milosevic had been indicted for war crimes in May 1999. As NATO troops streamed into defeated Serbia, they were accompanied by suitcases full of US dollars to be used by the National Endowment for Democracy to organize the overthrow of Milosevic, which duly followed in the spring of 2000, when the dictator was toppled by a textbook CIA "people power" revolution. In mid-2001, a couple of months before 9/11, Milosevic was illegally kidnapped from Serbia and taken to stand trial at a kangaroo court in The Hague.

MAY 7, 1999: US BOMBS CHINESE EMBASSY

The Kosovo adventure ruined US relations with China as well. On May 7, a US stealth bomber destroyed the Chinese embassy in Belgrade, killing a number of Chinese. This incident may have disrupted a potential agreement that might have ended the bombing a month earlier. The Chinese leadership orchestrated a vehement anti-US campaign, with mass demonstrations everywhere. Albright's deputy James Pickering flew to Beijing on June 16 to deliver the official US apology and claim the attack was an accident, but this was brusquely rejected by the Chinese government. Matters were complicated by the arrest of US scientist Wen Ho Lee, who had been charged in March with spying for China. On May 25, 1999, the Cox Committee of the US House of Representatives delivered an exaggerated and provocative report about Chinese espionage in the US. US-Chinese relations were now dangerously strained.

This was followed by what some journalists saw as a possible brush with actual thermonuclear war between the US and Russia. The occasion was the mysterious sinking of the newest and most powerful Russian nuclear submarine, the *Kursk*, in the Barents Sea during maneuvers on August 12, 2000. Russian officials reported that there had been a NATO submarine in the area when the *Kursk* was lost. NATO denied any involvement. The *Kursk* had been launched in 1994. During the Cold War and well into the 1990s, the Barents Sea had been the scene of dangerous underwater cat-and-mouse games between the US and Russia, with hunter-killer subs trailing ballistic missile subs on each side.

US and Russian subs had last collided in the Arctic Ocean on March 20, 1993, when the USS *Grayling* crashed into a Russian Delta III class ballistic missile sub carrying 16 SS-N 18 submarine-launched ballistic missiles (SLBMs) about 105 miles north of the Soviet fleet base at Murmansk, during what was alleged by the US to be a routine patrol. At that time the Russian Defense Ministry had stated that the "high command of the Russian military fleet expresses its extreme concern over the latest incident of dangerous maneuvering by foreign submarines in military training zones."

THE *KURSK*: "WORLD WAR III COULD HAVE BEGUN SATURDAY"

While American and European media have jumped the gun in attributing the *Kursk* sinking to onboard explosions, probably caused by a battery fire or torpedo detonation, the preponderance of evidence in fact suggests that the *Kursk* collided with another vessel – a US or British submarine, or drone vehicle – or, in the extreme case, was possibly hit by a torpedo. A commission of Russian Navy officers officially endorsed the finding that the *Kursk* had been destroyed by a collision with a foreign sub. The *Kursk*, with a crew of 118 sailors and officers, was found at the bottom of the sea. The crew members were instantly killed in what Russian officials asserted was a collision with the second vessel. On August 21, the Russian news agency Interfax reported that Russian rescue workers had found a fragment of a submarine, "most likely British," near the *Kursk*. This followed earlier reports that emergency buoys, also identified as British, were seen floating near the collision site.

On August 22, 2000, Pravda.ru ran a story on the *Kursk* disaster under the headline: "World War III Could Have Begun on Saturday." According to this piece, "On Saturday, August 12, an incident occurred in the Barents Sea, where the Russian Federation's Northern Fleet was conducting exercises, which nearly led to the outbreak of full-scale combat–a third world war.... For several days the world hung by a thread, and one false political move could have led to an exchange of nuclear strikes." Citing hydroacoustical evidence of three explosions, "indicating the possibility that the *Kursk* had suffered a torpedo attack." Pravda.ru described the incident as a possible *casus belli,* but concluded, "Happily, the incident in the Barents Sea was successfully resolved by political means. Agreement to 'end the affair in peace' was reached during a telephone conversation between Vladimir Putin and Bill Clinton. The Presidents' conversation lasted 25 minutes, and nothing of its content was reported in the mass media." (*New Federalist*, August 28, 2000)

On August 22, John Helmer, a Moscow-based journalist who wrote for the *Journal of Commerce* and the *Moscow Times,* commented in the Singapore-based *Straits Times* that "the Russian sub drama looked like war at the start." Dismissing the hysterical Western media criticism of President Putin, who remained at the "vacation Kremlin" at Sochi, Helmer wrote, "If you were the ruler of Russia, and you were told late one night that one of your most powerful and secret submarine weapons had been hit by a mysterious explosion, and sent to the bottom without word from the crew, would it be prudent for you to suspect an attack? An attack by a nuclear superpower and old rival? And if it is your sworn duty to defend your country from attack, would it be reasonable for you to determine whether there was a cause for war, or an accident?" Also noteworthy was Putin's growing convergence with the former Prime Minister Yevgeni Primakov, an advocate of a Eurasian perspective for Russia, who on August 23 delivered a strongly worded statement warning the West and the Russian oligarchs not to try to exploit the near-war crisis. (*EIR*, September 1, 2000)

The US claimed that an anti-submarine rocket fired from the *Kursk* had gotten jammed in a firing tube, causing the deadly explosion. But Russian authorities insisted that a foreign sub of the same general type as the *Kursk* had been present. As the US media were concerned, the *Kursk* crisis calmed down after a surprise visit to Moscow by CIA Director Tenet, but tensions between the two powers remained extreme. This is the background to Vladimir Putin's telephone call to Bush on the morning of September 11, 2001.

THE NEOCONS ANTAGONIZE CHINA

The great neocon project of the late 1990s was that of a US confrontation with China. Huntington's *Clash of Civilizations* crisis cookbook had identified two challengers to Anglo-American world domination: the Muslims, because of their population growth, and China, because of its economic growth. Neocon thinking oscillates between these two as the more immediate threat. After the Taiwan Straits confrontation of 1996, the bombing of the Chinese Embassy in Belgrade in May 1999, the Wen Ho Lee case, the Cox report on alleged Chinese espionage, and the Chinagate accusations of Beijing funding for Clinton, US-Chinese relations were at a low ebb.

As former US Ambassador to Beijing James Lilley pointed out, ":...there has been a dramatic change that is pervasive and, at times, ugly. After the Belgrade bombing accident in May of 1999, we saw the full face of anger, hostility, and even hate on the faces of the Chinese attacking our embassy." Lilley went on in a threatening tone: "If China continues to expand its military parameters, it will encounter our power. China can avoid this confrontation by buying into economic globalization, and lowering nationalistic tensions. To do otherwise is to risk tearing down the whole structure." (*Newsweek*, April 16, 2001)

The good will expressed towards the US by the Chinese students in Tien An Men Square in 1989 had completely dissipated, and was replaced by loathing – well before 9/11 and Iraq. Something similar had happened in Russia and elsewhere – also before 9/11.

Bush's first months in office were dominated by an incident involving the mid-air collision between a US EP-3E Aries II spy plane and a Chinese F-8 fighter jet just off the coast of China near the main base of the Chinese South Sea Fleet in Zhangjiang. Here US planes on electronic surveillance missions had long been regularly buzzed and harassed by Chinese interceptors. During one such encounter the Chinese fighter collided with the larger and slower US plane; the Chinese jet crashed and the pilot was lost, while the US plane had to make an emergency landing at a Chinese airport on Hainan Island. The plane and its crew of 19 were detained for a couple of weeks before being returned to the US.

The Chinese demanded a formal apology, which the pugnacious Bush administration was reluctant to make. The Chinese press ran pictures of the downed US spy plane with headlines reading "Proof of Bullying," and contemptuous attacks on "Little Bush." Chinese Internet chatrooms buzzed with talk of imminent war; "Are you ready? This is war," said one posting. The neocon *Weekly Standard* headlined its story about the Hainan incident "A National Humiliation," and authors William Kristol and Robert Kagan, both prominent chickenhawk warmongers, accused the newly installed Bush 43 of "weakness" in handling the affair. The neocons were disturbed by Colin Powell's reliance on diplomacy to get back the plane and crew for the US, and especially by the attitude of the US business community, which was more interested in profitable deals than in seconding the neocons' distorted view of national honor. (*Newsweek* April 16, 2001)

The whole experience was an object lesson to the neocon clique and the military provocateurs. For eight years they had writhed in bitterness because of Clinton's sane reluctance to resort to military force. Now, after the tremendous effort required to put Bush into the White House, the result was not much more satisfactory. We can safely assume that neocons and provocateurs drew the obvious lessons: that they must begin thinking along more grandiose lines, and planning for an outside event several orders of magnitude greater than any attempted thus far.

Tensions increased elsewhere as well. During the 1990s, Moscow and Beijing were repeatedly and pointedly reminded of the presence of an aggressive faction inside the US government and military which was intent on provoking periodic incidents to exacerbate tensions among the major powers. From Kosovo to Belgrade, from the Barents Sea to the South China Sea, from Iraq to Somalia, this aggressive faction had provoked clashes, manufactured pretexts for intervention, and fought a proxy war near the heart of Europe. The 1990s were anything but idyllic; they were a period of escalating economic and strategic crisis. The sympathetic interest in US life seen in 1989-1991 in Russia and China had by mid-2001 been replaced by overwhelming hostility.

At the same time, the aggressive and adventurous network inside the US government was deeply dissatisfied with their own failure to achieve decisive results. Every passing year brought population increases throughout the Muslim world, and 10-15% economic growth rates to China, while the US real economy (apart from Wall Street's paper swindles) continued to stagnate. Like the British contemplating German economic growth in 1905-1907, the US war faction concluded that a long period of world peace could only result in the further relative decline of the US. To create the political preconditions for what they wanted to do, the US war party therefore began to feel an overwhelming need to become the party of synthetic terror.

The groundwork for the aggressive and terror-based consensus at the end of the 1990s had been laid starting in March 1992, when Paul D. Wolfowitz, then the Pentagon's Under Secretary for Policy submitted his long-term Defense Planning Guidance to then Secretary of Defense Dick Cheney. As the press wrote at that time, the Pentagon policy paper asserted "that America's political and military mission in the post-cold-war era will be to insure that no rival superpower is allowed to emerge in Western Europe, Asia or the territory of the former Soviet Union." The role of the UN would dwindle to insignificance, the paper indicated, and US unilateral action would dominate the world. Wolfowitz's plan also stressed "using military force, if necessary, to prevent the proliferation of nuclear weapons and other weapons of mass destruction in such countries as North Korea, Iraq, some of the successor republics to the Soviet Union and in Europe."

Direct nuclear blackmail of Russia was also prominent; the Wolfowitz document underlined that American strategic nuclear weapons would continue to target vital aspects of the former Soviet military establishment. The rationale for this targeting policy was that the United States "must continue to hold at risk those assets and capabilities that current – and future – Russian leaders or other nuclear adversaries value most" because Russia would remain "the only power in the world with the capability of destroying the United States." The essence of US policy was seen in intimidation, "convincing potential competitors that they need not aspire to a greater role," thus guaranteeing that no rival superpower would be allowed to emerge. (*New York Times,* March 8, 1992)

Richard Perle later elaborated an aggressive strategy for Israeli politician Beniamin Netanyahu known as the "Clean Break" policy, which was based on rejecting a negotiated peace with Arabs and Palestinians in favor of endless war. Brzezinski's 1997 *Grand Chessboard* touted the benefits of US meddling in central Asia for geopolitical reasons; this study was similar in spirit to the Karl Haushofer's 1934 *Weltpolitik von heute*, the manual of Nazi geopolitics. But how to manipulate the American people into accepting the burdens and human losses associated with such meddling? Brzezinski, a petty Polish aristocrat, replied: "The attitude of the American public toward the external projection of American power has been much more ambivalent. The public supported America's engagement in World War II largely because of the shock effect of the Japanese attack on Pearl Harbor." (Brzezinski 24-25)

An even more explicit call for US world domination came from the Project for a New American Century, a neocon movement that provided most of the top officials for the Bush 43 administration. After discussing their imperialist plans, the PNAC authors, led by chickenhawk William Kristol, focused on the way of duping the American people into supporting the raft of new foreign adventures: "…the process of transformation is likely to be a long one, absent some catastrophic and catalyzing event – like a new Pearl Harbor." (PNAC, September 2000) It is in this restless mood, desirous of a new global conflict to pre-empt the emergence of challengers to a new Anglo-American world order, viewing the democratic system as unresponsive to their elitist warmongering, and eager for the assistance that a spectacular external attack would bring, that the roots of 9/11 are to be sought.

IV

AL QAEDA:
THE CIA'S ARAB LEGION

"I thought these guys [Atta & Co] were double agents." – former
executive, Huffman Aviation, Venice FL (Hopsicker 150)

Al Qaeda and its best-known leader bin Laden would not exist without the
help of the United States, which created them for use against the USSR in
Afghanistan, and which continues to support them until this day. At various
times, the US Special Forces have been bin Laden's valets; the State Department
has acted as his defense counsel and his travel bureau, and the CIA has furnished
his public relations advisors and his preferred health plan; the British government
has acted as his Human Resources department to recruit new personnel.

Osama bin Laden is a rich recluse who speaks to the world by means of video
and audio tapes whose validity cannot be determined. Bin Laden may be dead, or
he may be one of the CIA's several hundred ghost prisoners, who are being held
in secret prisons around the world in violation of the Geneva Convention. There
is no evidence to support the authenticity of any of bin Laden's tapes. The
statements and even the physical appearance of the figure representing bin Laden
are contradictory. For example, in the weeks after 9/11, a Pakistani newspaper
published an interview with "Osama bin Laden" in which we find the following
denial of any role in 9/11:

> I have already said that I am not involved in the 11 September attacks in
> the United States. As a Muslim, I try my best to avoid telling a lie. I had
> no knowledge of these attacks, nor do I consider the killing of innocent
> women, children and other humans as an appreciable act. Islam strictly
> forbids causing harm to innocent women, children and other people.
> Such a practice is forbidden even in the course of a battle. It is the
> United States, which is perpetrating every maltreatment on women,
> children and common people of other faiths, particularly the followers
> of Islam. All that is going on in Palestine for the last 11 months is
> sufficient to call the wrath of God upon the United States and Israel.
> There is also a warning for those Muslim countries, which witnessed all
> these as a silent spectator. What had earlier been done to the innocent
> people of Iraq, Chechnya and Bosnia? Only one conclusion could be
> derived from the indifference of the United States and the West to these
> acts of terror and the patronage of the tyrants by these powers: that
> America is an anti-Islamic power and it is patronizing the anti-Islamic
> forces. Its friendship with the Muslim countries is just a show, rather
> deceit. By enticing or intimidating these countries, the United States is

forcing them to play a role of its choice. Put a glance all around and you will see that the slaves of the United States are either rulers or enemies of Muslims.

The countries which do not agree to become the US slaves are China, Iran, Libya, Cuba, Syria [Afghanistan, Pakistan, Bangladesh, Iraq, Sudan, Indonesia, Malaysia] and Russia. Whoever committed the act of 11 September are not the friends of the American people. I have already said that we are against the American system, not against its people, whereas in these attacks, the common American people have been killed. According to my information, the death toll is much higher than what the US Government has stated. But the Bush Administration does not want the panic to spread. The United States should try to trace the perpetrators of these attacks within itself; the people who are a part of the US system, but are dissenting against it. Or those who are working for some other system; persons who want to make the present century as a century of conflict between Islam and Christianity so that their own civilization, nation, country, or ideology could survive. They can be anyone, from Russia to Israel and from India to Serbia. In the US itself, there are dozens of well-organized and well-equipped groups, which are capable of causing a large-scale destruction. Then you cannot forget the American-Jews, who are annoyed with President Bush ever since the elections in Florida and want to avenge him.

Then there are intelligence agencies in the US, which require billions of dollars worth of funds from the Congress and the government every year. This [funding issue] was not a big problem till the existence of the former Soviet Union but after that the budget of these agencies has been in danger. They needed an enemy. So, they first started propaganda against Osama and Taliban and then this incident happened. You see, the Bush Administration approved a budget of 40 billion dollars. Where will this huge amount go? It will be provided to the same agencies, which need huge funds and want to exert their importance. Now they will spend the money for their expansion and for increasing their importance. I will give you an example. Drug smugglers from all over the world are in contact with the US secret agencies. These agencies do not want to eradicate narcotics cultivation and trafficking because their importance will be diminished. The people in the US Drug Enforcement Department are encouraging drug trade so that they could show performance and get millions of dollars worth of budget. General Noriega was made a drug baron by the CIA and, in need, he was made a scapegoat. In the same way, whether it is President Bush or any other US President, they cannot bring Israel to justice for its human rights abuses or to hold it accountable for such crimes. What is this? Is it not that there exists a government within the government in the United

States? That secret government must be asked as to who carried out the attacks. (*Ummat,* Karachi, September 28, 2001)

This may be the voice of one of several bin Ladens, or it may be the Pakistani voice of one bin Laden. Several weeks after this interview a tape surfaced in which a rather different bin Laden seemed to acknowledge, at least obliquely, that he was involved in 9/11. This bin Laden comments that

> The brothers, who conducted the operation, all they knew was that they have a martyrdom operation and we asked each of them to go to America but they didn't know anything about the operation, not even one letter. But they were trained and we did not reveal the operation to them until they are there and just before they boarded the planes.(Meyssan 2002 196)

Osama the Gaunt as portrayed in mass media, Dec. 1998

Osama the Stout as portrayed in mass media, Nov. 2001

Which, if either, is the real Bin Laden? There is no way of knowing, so every assertion made about the mysterious, mercurial, and erratic Saudi millionaire is an exercise in speculation. (Paul, Hoffman, iii)

AL QAEDA, BIN LADEN: THE ACCUSED

Osama bin Laden appears as a rich misfit, certainly a sociopath, and doubtless obsessed with his own fanatical ideological vision of what the world should be. His main goal would appear to be the restoration of the caliphate, the combined emperor and pope of the Islamic world, an institution which was until about 1924 embodied in the figure of the Ottoman Turkish Sultan. Of course, this utopian Pan-Arab program means that bin Laden is automatically the enemy of any existing state in the Arab or Islamic world, and thus allows him to conduct what amount to Anglo-American destabilization operations against these states under a cloak of radical Islamic historical legitimacy which certain rulers are clearly hard put to answer.

But bin Laden is not the greatest political genius of today's world, as the "anonymous author" of *Imperial Hubris* attempts to convince us. Bin Laden is a dilettante who could not survive very long without powerful protectors and a comprehensive support network, including kidney dialysis. Rather than a political genius, we evidently see in bin Laden a clueless dupe, a patsy who cannot comprehend the forces around him which make his day-to-day activity and above all his universal notoriety possible. As previously noted, if we are to believe one of bin Laden's handlers by the name of Beardman, during the Afghan years bin Laden was not aware of the role he was playing on behalf of Washington. In the words of bin Laden (quoted by Beardman): "neither I, nor my brothers saw evidence of American help." (Meyssan 2002 7) In an interview with Frontline, Prince Bandar, the Saudi Ambassador to the United States, said that when he first met bin Laden, in the nineteen-eighties, "I thought he couldn't lead eight ducks across the street."

Osama bin Laden was one of dozens of children in the bin Laden harem, which was presided over by the patriarch of the bin Laden's Saudi construction company fortune. Osama's mother was not the number one wife or *valide sultan* in this seraglio; on the contrary, she was one of the least favored and least important of the numerous spouses. This peculiarity made Osama what we would call in the language of European feudal aristocracy a cadet or younger son, and cadet sons are by definition expendable. The bin Laden family was one of the wealthiest in Saudi Arabia, and functioned as compradors of the British and the US, including the dirty operations of MI-6 and CIA; Osama was for example a relative by marriage of the Iran-Contra businessman Adnan Khashoggi. Since he was a cadet son and not one of the Saudi royals, he was doubly expendable.

Osama was allegedly asked in 1979 by Prince Turki of Saudi intelligence to mobilize money and volunteers for operations against the Soviet forces in Afghanistan. Prince Turki wanted a Pan-Arab force to go and fight the Red Army and the Kabul regime. Part of Osama's role was simply to be a bagman for Saudi government funds being sent to the Afghan fighters. In these efforts, bin Laden worked closely with the Pakistani Interservice Intelligence, and thus also with the CIA and MI-6.

The CIA had teams in Afghanistan in early 1979, well before the Soviet invasion which Brzezinski provoked. According to former CIA Director Robert Gates, the big expansion of the US covert operation in Afghanistan began in 1984. During this year, "the size of the CIA's covert program to help the Mujahideen increased several times over," reaching a level of about $500 million in US and Saudi payments funneled through the Zia regime in Pakistan. As Gates recalled, "it was during this period [1985] that we began to learn of a significant increase in the number of Arab nationals from other countries who had traveled to Afghanistan to fight in the Holy War against the Soviets. They came from Syria, Iraq, Algeria, and elsewhere, and most fought with the Islamic fundamentalist Muj groups, particularly that headed by Abdul Rasul Sayyaf. We examined ways to increase their participation, perhaps in the form of some sort of 'international brigade,' but nothing came of it. Years later, these fundamentalist fighters trained by the mujahideen in Afghanistan would begin to show up around the world, from the Middle East to New York City, still fighting their Holy War – only now including the United States among their enemies. Our mission was to push the Soviets out of Afghanistan. We expected a post-Soviet Afghanistan to be ugly, but never considered that it would become a haven for terrorists operating worldwide." (Gates 349) But the international brigade Gates talked about was in fact created – as the group now known as al Qaeda.

The story is then that bin Laden was shocked and alienated by the arrival of US forces in Saudi Arabia for operation Desert Shield, after Saddam Hussein's takeover of Kuwait. The FBI and CIA have accused bin Laden in the World Trade Center bombing in 1993 that killed six people, two bombings in Saudi Arabia in 1995 and 1996 in which 24 American servicemen died, and the bombings of two American embassies in East Africa in 1998 that killed 224 people, as well as the attack on the USS *Cole* in 2000 which killed 19 sailors. (*New York Times*, September 9, 2001)

FBI Director Robert Mueller confessed to the Commonwealth Club of San Francisco on April 19, 2002 that after six months in Afghanistan the US forces had found absolutely no documentary evidence there relating to 9/11. This was a huge scandal, just as big as the later failure to discover the phantomatic weapons of mass destruction in Iraq. Mueller admitted: "The hijackers also left no paper trail. In our investigation, we have not uncovered a single piece of paper – either here in the US or in the treasure trove of information that has turned up in Afghanistan and elsewhere – that mentioned any aspect of the September 11th plot. The hijackers had no computers, no laptops, no storage media of any kind. They used hundreds of different pay phones and cell phones, often with prepaid calling cards that are extremely difficult to trace. And they made sure that all the money sent to them to fund their attacks was wired in small amounts to avoid detection."

Clearly the US would now rather not see bin Laden, if he still exists, be taken alive, for fear of what his testimony might be. On November 21, 2001, Rumsfeld was quite explicit on this point, saying on the CBS *60 Minutes II* program he would prefer that Osama bin Laden be killed rather than taken alive. "You bet your life," he said.

It became known shortly after 9/11 that Osama bin Laden's half-brother Salem was an investor in Arbusto Petroleum in the late 1970s, and thus can be counted as a former business partner of George W. Bush. Two weeks after 9/11, the London tabloid *Daily Mail* carried the banner headline: "Bin Laden's Amazing Business Link with President Bush." George W. Bush and Salem bin Laden were both present at the creation of Arbusto Energy, an oil company in Texas. Salem bin Laden had very close business ties to a friend of George W. Bush, a certain James Bath. According to researchers, it is likely that the $50,000 that Bath invested in Arbusto in 1978 actually came from Salem bin Laden. Salem bin Laden died in a plane crash in Texas in 1983. This *Daily Mail* story was singled out on BBC's *European Press Roundup* the following morning, but these facts have never been given adequate coverage by the US media. The Bath angle was, however, stressed by Michael Moore in his *Fahrenheit 911*. (*Daily Mail*, September 24, 2001)

The bin Ladens were benefactors of Harvard University, where fellowships were offered bearing their name. This attracted the attention of the media, but the willingness of Harvard students to accept the bin Laden money appeared undiminished after 9/11. Andy Tiedemann, a spokesperson in the Harvard University development office, said no Harvard students had called to object to the bin Laden fellowships. The bin Laden family's endowed fellowships totaled $2 million, for use at Harvard's law and design schools. (*Harvard Crimson*, October 5, 2001)

ALBRIGHT SABOTAGES EXTRADITION OF BIN LADEN BY SUDAN

During the mid-1990s, bin Laden established himself in Sudan. By 1996, he had become an embarrassment to the rulers of that country, General Bashir and Hassan Turabi. Sudan had shown in 1994 that it wanted nothing to do with terrorism when it turned the legendary terrorist Carlos the Jackal over to French authorities, who put him away for good. Early in 1996, the Sudanese government offered to deliver bin Laden to the Saudis, who declined on the grounds that any prosecution of the fanatical sheikh in his home country might cause a split in the ruling elite, to say nothing of public disorder. In March 1996, Sudan offered to deliver bin Laden to the US government. Instead of gratefully accepting the extradition of the man who was already one of the world's top terrorists, Secretary of State Madeleine Albright chose this moment to provoke a new wave of tensions with Sudan, even contriving – no doubt as a clever diversion – to shut down the US Embassy in Khartoum because of alleged terrorist threats. The Sudanese offer remained on the table until May 19, 1996, when bin Laden departed Sudan for Afghanistan, but Albright invented pretext after pretext to say no. Here we have a crucial experiment that proves the duplicity and hypocrisy of the US regime: they could have had bin Laden's head on a platter, and they turned it down. Bin Laden, after all, had a great career ahead of him – he was destined to become the great false-flag counter-gang leader of Islamic opposition to the US empire.

CIA Director George Tenet told the Senate Select Committee on Intelligence on October 17, 2002 that the CIA officially knew nothing about a Sudanese offer to give bin Laden to the US: "Mr. Chairman, CIA has no knowledge of such an offer," said Tenet. The 9/11 commission announced in one of their staff reports that they found no evidence that Sudan had offered to deliver bin Laden directly to the US, but they did establish that Sudan was willing to extradite him to Saudi Arabia. (9/11 commission staff report, March 24, 2004) The 9/11 commission final report, ever true to form, simply ignores the public record and with it the key issue of why the Albright State Department refused to accept bin Laden's extradition or rendition. (9/11 commission 61-62)

The Sudanese offer was documented by Barton Gellman in the *Washington Post* soon after 9/11. According to Gellman, in 1999, Sudanese President Omar Hassan Bashir referred elliptically to his government's 1996 willingness to send bin Laden to Saudi Arabia. What remained to be added was the role of the US government and a secret channel from Khartoum to Washington. Gellman wrote:

> The government of Sudan, employing a back channel direct from its president to the Central Intelligence Agency, offered in the early spring of 1996 to arrest Osama bin Laden and place him in Saudi custody, according to officials and former officials in all three countries.

> Clinton administration struggled to find a way to accept the offer in secret contacts that stretched from a meeting at a Rosslyn hotel on March 3, 1996, to a fax that closed the door on the effort 10 weeks later. Unable to persuade the Saudis to accept bin Laden, and lacking a case to indict him in US courts at the time, the Clinton administration finally gave up on the capture. (*Washington Post*, Wednesday, October 3, 2001)

The Sudanese envoy to the US in this attempted rendition was Sudan's 2001 UN ambassador, major general Elfatih Erwa, Sudan's minister of state for defense in 1996, who flew from Khartoum to Washington for secret negotiations with the CIA.

Anthony Lake, then US national security adviser, says Washington was skeptical of Sudan's offer – meaning that there was an offer. Lake told the *Village Voice* that Sudan brought up the story after 9/11 because it feared US bombing attacks during the war on terrorism. The Sudanese offer of bin Laden was also obliquely confirmed by Susan Rice, a former assistant secretary of state for African affairs who was then senior director for Africa on the NSC. Rice's variation is the claim that Sudan made the offer knowing the US couldn't accept it. "They calculated that we didn't have the means to successfully prosecute bin Laden. That's why I question the sincerity of the offer." Rather than indulge in such hairsplitting, why not test Sudanese sincerity by accepting bin Laden's extradition? One US intelligence source in the region seemed to be close to an answer when he called the lost opportunity a disgrace. "We kidnap minor drug czars and bring them back in burlap bags. Somebody didn't want this to happen." (*Village Voice*, October 31, 2001) Indeed: a most valuable patsy had to be protected.

The US refusal to take bin Laden from the Sudan remains an important point, embarrassing enough to engage Richard Clarke, the true high priest of the bin Laden myth. Clarke writes in his memoir:

> Turabi and Bin Laden parted as friends, and pledged to continue the struggle and to use Khartoum as a safe haven. In recent years Sudanese intelligence officials and Americans friendly to the Sudan regime have invented a fable about Bin Laden's final days in Khartoum. In the fable

the Sudanese government offers to arrest Bin Laden and hand him over in chains to FBI agents, but Washington rejects the offer because the Clinton administration does not see Bin Laden as important or does and cannot find anywhere to put him on trial. The only slivers of truth in this fable are that a) the Sudanese government was denying its support for terrorism in the wake of the UN sanctions, and b) the CSG [Counter-terrorism Security Group] had initiated informal inquiries with several nations about incarcerating Bin Laden, or putting him on trial. There were no takers. Nonetheless, had we been able to put our hands on him we would gladly have done so. US Attorney Mary Jo White in Manhattan could, as the saying goes, "indict a ham sandwich." She certainly could have obtained an indictment for Bin Laden in 1996 had we needed it. In the spring of 1998, she did so. The facts about the supposed Sudanese offer to give us Bin Laden are that Turabi was not about to turn over his partner in terror to us and no real attempt to do so ever occurred. (Clarke 142)

This cover story falls to the ground without any refutation because of its own internal contradictions. Clarke is simply lying, and his statements about terrorism need to be read with full awareness of the mendacity of which he is capable. In addition, if the US waited until 1998 to indict bin Laden, this confirms the story told in *La verité interdite* that the US had failed to issue an Interpol warrant for bin Laden after the Khobar Towers attack of 1996. (Brisard and Dasquié 136)

It is enough to repeat that the reason bin Laden was not taken into US custody was to preserve a patsy of incalculable value. We should recall once again that Clarke was reportedly ushered out of the James Baker State Department for covering up Israeli violations of the US arms export laws involving the illegal Israeli sale of Patriot missile systems to China. In August 1998, Clarke was reportedly one of the key figures who planted false information about Sudan's involvement in the East Africa US Embassy bombings, which led to US cruise missile attacks on a Sudanese pharmaceutical company in Khartoum which turned out to be producing nothing but aspirin. In this incident, Clarke is said to have retailed disinformation from British-Israeli covert operations stringer Yossef Bodansky that provided a pretext for the targeting of Sudan. The Sudan extradition story was confirmed in "Targeted: Bin Laden," broadcast by the History Channel on September 15, 2004, with interviews by Anonymous, Steve Coll, Saudi Prince Turki, Robert Baer, and others. In reality, Sudan cooperated before and after 9/11 in legitimate international anti-terrorism efforts. One such case came in late spring 2002, when Sudan arrested Abu Huzifa, a suspected Al Qaeda-linked terrorist, at the request of the United States. Abu Huzifa detailed his infiltration of Saudi Arabia, to profile vulnerability of US troops to terrorist attack, and described how he had fired a SAM missile at a US warplane near the Prince Sultan Air Base, one of the headquarters of the US Afghan military operations. According to former Clinton-era ambassador to Sudan Tim Carney,

Sudan had been totally cooperative with the United States in the war on terror. (*Washington Post*, June 14, 2002)

FBI TOLD BY BUSH TO BACK OFF BIN LADENS

FBI agents have testified that Bush 43 ordered the bureau to relax their surveillance of the bin Laden family members living in the United States. According to BBC *Newsnight* of November 6, 2001, the FBI "was told to back off bin Laden family." The program said it had been told by a highly placed source in a US intelligence agency there had always been "constraints" on investigating Saudis, but under President George Bush these had become much worse. After the 2000 elections, the intelligence agencies were told to "back off" from investigating the bin Laden family and the Saudi royals. BBC2's *Newsnight* also said that it had secret documents from the FBI investigation into the terrorist attacks which showed that despite claims that Osama bin Laden was the black sheep of the family, at least two other US-based members were suspected of having links with a possible terrorist organization. The BBC report was based on a secret FBI document numbered 199I WF213589 and emanating out of the FBI's Washington field office. One of the organizations that the FBI was supposedly ordered to ignore was the "Saudi-funded World Association of Muslim Youth (WAMY), a suspected terrorist organization." WAMY's accounts were frozen by Pakistan after 9/11, and India "claimed that this group was linked to an organization involved in bombing in Kashmir."(*Times of India*, November 8, 2001) Whatever the specifics, this is the familiar pattern of police agencies finding reasons for not rolling up the financial infrastructure required to keep their indispensable patsies in the field, at least until the big hit has been accomplished.

Just after 9/11, FBI agents swooped down on the Boston suburb where around twenty wealthy relatives of bin Laden lived, and questioned them at a condominium complex in Charlestown. Agents even visited nightclubs to collect credit cards of younger members of the family. Bin Laden's younger brother Mohammed, who was said to have moved back to Saudi Arabia with his wife and children several years before, owned a ten-bedroom mansion in nearby Wayland. Another younger brother, Abdullah, was a 1994 graduate of Harvard Law School. But despite the official US story demonizing their maverick half-brother, the plutocratic bin Ladens had nothing to fear. Soon reports began circulating widely that the Bush regime organized special flights out of the US for members of the bin Laden family and some other wealthy Saudis. Craig Unger and others have told the story of these special flights which whisked the bin Ladens and other Saudis out of the US during a time when civil aviation was still suspended. The 9/11 commission denies that these took place between Tuesday and Sunday, that is to say during the days when all US commercial aviation was grounded. The *Tampa Tribune* carried a story about a Lear Jet which took off from Tampa on September 13 and flew to Lexington, Kentucky with Saudi plutocrats on board. The plane started from a private hangar at Raytheon Airport Services in

Tampa. It is possible that this Lear Jet was rented from Wally Hilliard, the man who financed Rudi Dekkers' Huffman Aviation in nearby Venice, Florida, where Atta and Shehhi took flight lessons. (Hopsicker, Mad Cow Morning News 11)

In Afghanistan and Iraq, the US forces constantly imitated the Israeli practice of simply seizing family members of accused terrorists and holding them as hostages. If these illegal methods are good enough for the little people, and if bin Laden was the heart and soul of world terrorism, why were the opulent bin Ladens not simply declared enemy combatants and hustled off to Guantanamo for a round of sleep deprivation and other torture, until the family disgorged the fugitive sheikh? US methods, although they are certainly brutal and illegal, are not consistent.

Quite apart from these flights, the US State Department has long functioned as al Qaeda's virtual in-house travel agency. The former head of the American visa bureau in Jeddah from 1987 to 1989, Michael Springmann, told BBC *Newsnight* in the fall of 2001: "In Saudi Arabia I was repeatedly ordered by high-level State Department officials to issue visas to unqualified applicants – people who had no ties either to Saudi Arabia or to their own country. I complained there. I complained here in Washington ... and I was ignored." He added: "What I was doing was giving visas to terrorists, recruited by the CIA and Osama bin Laden to come back to the United States for training to be used in the war in Afghanistan against the then Soviets."

BUSH 41 WORKS FOR BIN LADENS VIA CARLYLE GROUP

The business cooperation of the Bush and bin Laden families did not stop with Arbusto. A few weeks after 9/11, readers of the *Wall Street Journal* were more than mildly surprised to learn that the 41st president of the United States, George H. W. Bush, the father of the current tenant of the White House, was in effect a paid part-time employee of the Saudi Bin Laden Group, the bin Laden family business in Saudi Arabia, through the intermediary of the Carlyle Group, an international investment and consulting firm, in which the bin Ladens invested. There had been at least two documented meetings of Bush 41 with the bin Laden business clan, and in reality there had doubtless been more on social occasions and the like. Other top Republicans were also associated with the Carlyle group, such as former Secretary of State James A. Baker, Bush 43's lawyer during the 2000 stolen election, and Iran-Contra heavy Frank Carlucci, a former Secretary of Defense. Also working with Carlyle were Reagan Treasury official Richard Darman, and Bush 41's White House chief of staff, John Sununu, and John Major, prime minister between Thatcher and Blair, from 1990 to 1997. The *Journal* story repeated the cover story that Osama bin Laden had supposedly been "disowned" by his family, which was running a multi-billion dollar business in Saudi Arabia and was a major investor in the senior Bush's firm. Other reports have questioned, though, whether members of his Saudi family have truly cut off Osama bin Laden. It was also reported that the FBI had subpoenaed the bin Laden family business's bank records. (*Wall Street Journal*, September 27, 2001; Judicial Watch, September 28, 2001)

Almost everything about Osama bin Laden remains uncertain, down to the question of whether he is dead or alive, free or in captivity, and whether he is one person or a group of doubles, *Doppelgänger*. But there is no doubt that CIA, MI-6, and their satellites have showed a remarkable loyalty to bin Laden, building him up and lionizing him at every opportunity. These agencies do this because they need to establish the credibility of their patsy. Because of his notorious track record as a CIA asset, bin Laden needs all the public relations assistance the agency can give him. In the days after 9/11, a large demonstration was held against terrorism by the middle classes of Teheran, Iran, and one of the most prominent signs read "Bin Laden = CIA agent."

One of bin Laden's flacks is none other than Bernard Lewis of the Institute for Advanced Study in Princeton, New Jersey, the author of the operational US-UK-Israel long-term strategic plan for the dismemberment and Balkanization of the Arab and Islamic states of the Middle east and of the "arc of crisis" which we see in action in Iraq and elsewhere today. Lewis bent over backward to establish the Islamic legitimacy and bona fides of bin Laden in an interview given about two months after 9/11.

BERNARD LEWIS: BIN LADEN'S FLACK

Lewis argued that bin Laden's brand of Islamic terrorism was completely consistent with classical Islam, which is committed to the subjugation of the infidels to Islamic law. Lewis documented bin Laden's place in the great tradition of the Muslim world by citing the passage in bin Laden's recent videotape in which he spoke of "humiliation and disgrace ... for more than 80 years," a reference to the dismemberment of the Ottoman Empire by Britain and France after 1918. Lewis located bin Laden in the tradition of jihad, "bequeathed to Muslims by the Prophet." In principle, Lewis went on, the world was divided into two houses: the House of Islam, in which a Muslim government ruled and Muslim law prevailed, and the House of War, meaning the rest of the world, which was still inhabited and, more important, ruled by infidels. Between the two, there was to be a perpetual state of war until the entire world either embraced Islam or submitted to the rule of the Muslim state. Among all the different "infidels" ruling the House of War, according to Lewis, Christianity was singled out as "their primary rival in the struggle for world domination." In a masterpiece of *Geschichtskletscherei* (fake historical parallels), Lewis cited slogans painted on the walls of the Dome of the Rock from the 7th Century assailing Christianity. Next, Lewis asserted that the evolution of modern Islamic terrorism, specifically al Qaeda terrorism, had a long history within Islam, dating to the Assassins of the 11th to 13th Centuries. He also identified Saudi Arabia and Egypt as the two regimes singled out by the Islamic jihadists for their corruption by modernism. He concluded ominously: "For Osama bin Laden, 2001 marks the resumption of the war for the religious dominance of the world that began in the 7th Century.... If Bin Laden can persuade the world of Islam to accept his views and his leadership, then a long and bigger struggle lies ahead, and not only for America. Sooner or later, al-Qaeda and related groups will clash with the other neighbors of Islam – Russia, China, India – who may prove less squeamish than the Americans in using their power against Muslims and their sanctities. If Bin Laden is correct in his calculations and succeeds in his war, then a dark future awaits the world, especially the part of it that embraces Islam." (*New Yorker*, November 19, 2001) Lewis' gloating provides a candid glimpse of the intent behind western fostering of Islamism, as we shall see in Chapter XV.

THE LANGLEY BIN LADEN FAN CLUB

The most comprehensive document of Bin Ladenolatry so far produced comes from the bowels of the CIA, the workplace of Anonymous, the author of *Imperial Hubris*. This book can only be interpreted as a semi-official compendium of CIA doctrine on today's world. Anonymous is sure that bin Laden will strike the US again, most likely with a weapon of mass destruction, but he still offers the erratic millionaire praise without stint:

> Viewed from any angle, Osama bin Laden is a great man, one who smashed the expected unfolding of universal post-Cold War peace. The New York and Washington attacks, Andrew Bacevich and Sebastian Mallaby wrote in the *Wilson Quarterly*, "revealed that the pilgrimage to perfection was far from over," though "not for a moment did they cause American political leaders to question the project's feasibility." Post-11 September, Dr. Bruce Hoffman also offered an acute judgment of Bin Laden's impact. "Whatever else," Hoffman wrote, "Bin Laden is one of the few persons who can argue that they changed the course of history."...All told, Bin Laden in certainly the most popular anti-American leader in the world today. His name is legend from Houston to Zanzibar to Jakarta, and his face and sayings are emblazoned on T-shirts, CDs, audio and videotapes, posters, photographs, cigarette lighters, and stationery across the earth. "Afghanistan's children," Daniel Bergener wrote in the *New York Times Magazine* in July 2003, "suck on Bin Laden candies, sugary balls in wrappers showing the leader's face, his pointed finger and the tip of a rocket." So too with his name: "one of the most common names for newborn males is Osama," James Kitfield reported in the *National Journal* in November 2002. "Even among those who publicly denounce his terrorist methods, the namings indicate the nearly mythical status the Islamic world has bestowed on Osama bin Laden." (Anonymous 104-105)

Our anonymous CIA agent waxes positively indignant about those in Saudi Arabia and around the world who impugn Bin Laden's world-historical genius.

He is especially upset about certain Saudis who have worked closely with bin Laden in the past, and who find it impossible to believe that he is now functioning as the evil demiurge of the twenty-first century. Anonymous detects a "theme of Bin Laden's limited mental and leadership abilities" which has been spread by "a number of Saudi officials and writers. Their intent seems simple enough: to prove that Bin Laden is intellectually incapable of managing al Qaeda and designing its operations." (Anonymous 107) As an example of this line, Anonymous quotes an account given by Saudi Prince Mahmoud bin Abdel Aziz to the US press. The Prince recalled

> that night a decade ago when Osama bin Laden attended an evening salon to describe his exploits fighting in Afghanistan....[The prince] remembers young Osama floundering when guests questioned him about the interpretation of religious texts. "Finally, I had to signal with my hands for them to stop it," said the prince. "He really is quite a simple man." (Anonymous 108)

Here we have a rich misfit and fanatic who cannot hold his own in theological debates, which should supposedly be his strongest suit. In Anonymous' view, "the most common form of the Saudis' defamation of Bin Laden is done by having his friends in the kingdom describe him as a gentle, amiable, and relatively unintelligent man." (Anonymous 108) But the yelping detractors of bin Laden do not stop here. According to Anonymous: "A final side to the effort in the Muslim and Western worlds to denigrate Bin Laden's brains and talents lies in the studied attempt to depict Bin Laden as a simpleton who is directed by that evil terrorist genius Ayman al-Zawahiri, former chief of Egyptian Islamic Jihad and now bin Laden's deputy in al Qaeda. 'My knowledge of bin Laden makes me unable to conceive what is happening now,' said Dr. Abdullah al Muayyad, a former director general of the Saudi finance ministry who worked with bin Laden during the Afghan jihad.'" (Anonymous 107) Like a good CIA agent, Anonymous tries to make his readers think that the Saudis are passing the buck to the nefarious Egyptians, but this is hogwash. Zawahiri, once again, was a key part of the Sadat assassination, and afterwards was protected by London. The world needs to remember Sadat's widow, Jehan Sadat, recalling in a television interview after 9/11 that Zawahiri, a murderer of her husband, had lived in London for years after that crime, while extradition to Egypt was always refused by the UK. The guess here would be that Zawahiri is a double agent working for MI-6, while bin Laden is indeed a fanatical, deluded patsy and dupe; at any rate, if this is bin Laden's mentality, it would make him the ideal type for the role he is presently carrying out.

Anonymous devotes a lyrically fulsome passage to evoking bin Laden's status as a beloved figure among the Muslims; the Muslim love for Osama, he argues, is

> love not so much for Osama bin Laden the person – although there is much of that – but love for his defense of the faith, the life he lives, the

heroic example he sets, and the similarity of that example to other heroes in the pantheon of Islamic history. (Anonymous 124)

Anonymous concludes this paean to his hero bin Laden by favorably comparing the psychotic sheikh to Abraham Lincoln. This is all coming, we recall, from a high-level CIA officer, one of the founding members of the "Manson family," as the original CIA bin Laden station called itself. If Arabs and Muslims can be convinced that bin Laden is really their leader, and not a creature of the CIA, then they will never accomplish the modernizing reforms which the progressive nationalists promised. They will spend their time fighting among themselves in the name of re-creating the caliphate. They will be unable to make alliances against the Anglo-Americans with Europe, with the Orthodox, the Hindus, the Buddhists, the Confucians, the atheists, or anybody else; they will self-isolate themselves in endless backwardness. Bin Laden's mass line is, after, all, that it is the duty of every Muslim to kill infidels wherever they are found. If applied literally, this would even cut off all scientific and commercial exchanges in a kind of murderous self-embargo. All these factors will make the Muslim *ummah* ever so much easier to divide and defeat. No wonder the CIA is so proud of having made bin Laden a folk hero of the Muslim world, with the help of the 9/11 attacks which the unstable dreamer could never have carried out by himself: literally billions of dollars of publicity for the Saudi misfit have paid off in one of the greatest psychological warfare operations of all time. Any cause that chooses bin Laden or some similar figure as its leader, we may be certain, is damning itself to a lonely and ignominious defeat at the hands of the laughing CIA *kuffar* (infidels).

Even more notable are the support services which the CIA and it minions continue to provide bin Laden. Here the evidence is fragmentary but persistent and finally overwhelming. According to CBS News, "the night before the September 11 terrorist attack, Osama bin Laden was in Pakistan. He was getting medical treatment with the support of the very military that days later pledged its backing for the US war on terror in Afghanistan....Bin Laden was spirited into a military hospital in Rawalpindi for kidney dialysis treatment." (Barry Peterson, "Hospital Worker: I Saw Osama," CBS News, January 29, 2002) Before we criticize Pakistan, though, we should realize that the ISI in this case was probably acting on US instructions, as it generally does.

LE FIGARO: BIN LADEN TREATED AT AMERICAN HOSPITAL, JULY 2001

On October 31, 2001, *Le Figaro*, the leading French conservative newspaper, published a front page story about medical treatment received by bin Laden in Dubai in the summer before 9/11. This remarkable revelation came in an article by Alexandra Richard entitled "*La CIA a rencontré Ben Laden à Dubaï en juillet,*" (The CIA met Bin Laden in Dubai in July). At around the same time, similar facts were reported by Agence France Presse and Radio France International, the French external broadcasting service. The AFP dispatch read in part:

Bin Laden Underwent Treatment in July at Dubai American Hospital

Osama bin Laden underwent treatment in July at the American Hospital in Dubai where he met a US Central Intelligence Agency (CIA) official, French daily *Le Figaro* and Radio France International reported. Quoting "a witness, a professional partner of the administrative management of the hospital," they said the man suspected by the United States of being behind the September 11 terrorist attacks had arrived in Dubai on July 4 by air from Quetta, Pakistan. He was immediately taken to the hospital for kidney treatment. He left the establishment on July 14, *Le Figaro* said.

During his stay, the daily said, the local CIA representative was seen going into bin Laden's room and "a few days later, the CIA man boasted to some friends of having visited the Saudi-born millionaire."

Quoting "an authoritative source," *Le Figaro* and the radio station said the CIA representative had been recalled to Washington on July 15. Bin Laden has been sought by the United States for terrorism since the bombing of the US embassies in Kenya and Tanzania in 1998. But his CIA links go back before that to the fight against Soviet forces in Afghanistan.

Le Figaro said bin Laden was accompanied in Dubai by his personal physician and close collaborator, who could be the Egyptian Ayman al-Zawahiri, as well as bodyguards and an Algerian nurse. He was admitted to the urology department of Doctor Terry Callaway, who specializes in kidney stones and male infertility. Telephoned several times, the doctor declined to answer questions. Several sources had reported that bin Laden had a serious kidney infection. He had a mobile dialysis machine sent to his Kandahar hideout in Afghanistan in the first half of 2000, according to "authoritative sources" quoted by *Le Figaro* and RFI. (AFP, Wednesday October 31, 2001, 2:04 PM)

The CIA was quick to deny these embarrassing facts reported by real investigative journalists, who apparently still exist in France. A spokeswoman at CIA Langley, VA headquarters described the *Le Figaro* article as "complete and utter nonsense. It's nonsense, it's absurd, it's ridiculous, it's not true." The CIA said it intended to protest to *Le Figaro*. The American Hospital in Dubai denied that bin Laden had been a patient. (*The Scotsman*, November 1, 2001) But the French author and RFI editor-in-chief Richard LaBevière countered that Osama bin Laden had been working for the CIA since 1979, a fact which was generally accepted in Europe. (October 31, 2001) Radio France International stuck to its guns and followed up on its story with further details about bin Laden's CIA handler and case officer, Larry Mitchell: "The local representative of the CIA who visited Osama bin Laden last July 12 at the American Hospital in Dubai is called Larry Mitchell. If his visiting card specifies that he is a "consular agent," everyone in Dubai knows, especially in the small expatriate community, that he is working under cover. To say it openly, Larry Mitchell belongs to the 'big house', otherwise known as the CIA. He himself does not hide it." RFI went on: "An expert in the Arab world and especially in the Arabian peninsula, Larry Mitchell is a colorful personality who livens up the somewhat drab evenings of the expatriates of Dubai. One of his friends likes to say that his natural exuberance often gets into classified matters. That is perhaps one of the reasons why he was called back to the United States last July 15. About twenty days after the September 11 attacks, in a statement dated October 5, the CIA dismissed as baseless rumors the story that the agency had had contacts with bin Laden and his group in the past, especially at the time of the war against the USSR in Afghanistan. It happens that this communiqué of the CIA is in complete contradiction with the earlier official statements of several representatives of the US administration itself." (http://www.rfi.fr/1 novembre 2001)

It is thus clear that the CIA was providing vital support services to bin Laden long after he had allegedly turned into the world's leading anti-American monster. The reality is that bin Laden and al Qaeda have never stopped serving the CIA strategic agenda, whatever that happened to be. As Thierry Meyssan writes, "In reality, the CIA continued to have recourse to Osama bin Laden's services against Russian influence as it had done against the Soviets. You don't change a winning team. The 'Arab Legion' of Al Qaeda was used, in 1999, to support the Kosovar rebels against the dictatorship in Belgrade. It was also operational in Chechnya, at least until November 2001, as was attested to by the *New York Times*. (Michael Wines, December 9, 2001) The alleged hostility of bin Laden against the United States permitted Washington to deny responsibility for these dirty operations." (Meyssan 2002 106-7)

In a discussion of the impact of the anonymous *Imperial Hubris* CIA tract during the summer of 2004, the *Washington Post* provided a succinct summary of al Qaeda's strategic services to the CIA: "Al Qaeda's camps were staffed by veteran fighters who trained insurgents who fought and trained others to fight, not only against the Northern Alliance in Afghanistan, but also against national armies in Indian Kashmir, Chechnya, Uzbekistan, Eritrea, Yemen, Saudi Arabia, Algeria, Tajikistan, Egypt, Bosnia, western China, Indonesia, Malaysia, Macedonia, Kosovo, and the Philippines." (Review of Anonymous, *Imperial Hubris*, *Washington Post*, July 11, 2004) Notice that all these states were or are targets of US destabilization. And even this list is far from complete; it leaves out Libya, for example.

The Iranian press also noted the strange affinities of al Qaeda for figures who were clearly still on the US payroll. While panning the 9/11 commission report, the *Teheran Times* observed that none other than KSM, "Khalid Sheikh Mohammed, the reported mastermind of the 9/11 attacks, was a longtime associate of Abdul Rasul Sayyaf, a leader of the Afghan Northern Alliance and current ally of the US-backed Afghans president, Hamid Karzai." (*Teheran Times*, July 27, 2004)

AL QAEDA AND NATO'S BALKAN DRUG RUNNING

Another thing that is known about al Qaeda is that bin Laden's supposed followers are drug pushers in grand style – once again a foible they share with MI-6 and CIA. During a fall 2001 strategic briefing, Gwen McClure of Interpol's Criminal Subdivision officially informed a group of parliamentarians from NATO countries that Interpol had evidence that the bin Laden group "is linked to Albanian gangs who have taken over the growing web of crime across Europe. The investigations of Interpol have also shown that bin Laden deployed one of his top military commanders for an elite KLA unit during the NATO Kosovo war." The Interpol official also stated that a special meeting took place in Albania in the presence of bin Laden, according to Albanian police. Several Algerian terrorists were present at the meeting. "It was during this meeting," the official stressed, "that many structures and networks were established for propaganda and fund raising activities and for providing the Algerian armed groups with logistical support." During and immediately after the Kosovo war, when the KLA took over the Kosovo, heroin and weapons traffic exploded unchecked. The so-called "Albanian mafia" ended up controlling 80% of the heroin distribution in Western Europe, using the NATO Kosovo protectorate as its base. The criminal and the terrorist networks became indistinguishable, with a multiplying destructive effect. "These crime syndicates have formed alliances of convenience and are willing to cooperate or make business arrangements with other organized crime groups," the Interpol official told the parliamentarians. She also said Interpol had evidence of the involvement in the criminal and terrorist activities of the Chechnya terrorists. According to Balkan sources and other records, the man in charge for the Balkan terrorism-organized crime connection was bin Laden's chief adviser – or controller – the head of the Egyptian Jihad, Ayman al Zawahiri. Zawahiri's brother Mohamed was reported to be in Macedonia just after 9/11, leading a gang of ideological mercenaries to launch another major KLA assault against the country. Ayman al Zawahiri was in Albania to play a leading role in the KLA/NATO offensive against Serbia in 1999. (*Independent*, October 24, 2001) According to some experts, the al Qaeda/KLA united front had taken over the 1980s "Bulgarian connection" or Balkan Route, a gigantic arms-for-drugs traffic with the involvement of numerous NATO, Warsaw Pact, and other intelligence services and various ethnic mafias. The Bulgarian connection had come under intense scrutiny after the assassination attempt against Pope John Paul II on May 13 1981. (*The Independent*, October 24, 2001)

ZAWAHIRI AND NATO'S DARLING, THE KLA

The brother of bin Laden's second in command, Ayman al Zawahiri, was reported after 9/11 to be taking part in terrorist actions in Northern Macedonia, where NATO's puppet Albanian KLA had started a new terror campaign. The Zawahiri connection surfaced on October 25, 2001, when the "new" KLA in Macedonia, the Albanian National Army (ANA), claimed responsibility for the bombing of the police station and municipal building of Tearce in northern Macedonia. Tearce was one of the Macedonian towns – previously assaulted, occupied and "cleansed" of its Macedonian inhabitants – which became the scene of a symbolic policing by a mixed police patrol of ethnic Albanians and Macedonians.

BRITISH TERROR SCHOOLS FOR PATSIES

A window into the London state-sponsored synthetic terror milieu came in December 2001, when British authorities were forced to arrest and question Mark Yates, a self-styled security expert who ran a firearms training camp in Alabama. Yates was suspected of helping Islamic terrorist patsies from Britain who were to hone their marksmanship skills on American soil before going off to fight for Islamic causes around the globe. Yates, a British bodyguard and firearms trainer who had operations in both the United Kingdom and the United States, allegedly offered "live fire" weapons training in America for aspiring holy warriors. British police thought that Yates was involved on the US end of the "Ultimate Jihad Challenge" training program offered on the London market by the Sakina Security Services company, owned by Suleiman Bilal Zain-ul-abidin. Yates, who was also the operations and training director at the Ground Zero firearms training camp outside Marion, Alabama, denied everything.

"Ultimate Jihad Challenge" included instruction in the "art of bone breaking," and learning to "improvise explosive devices." British Muslims would be given the opportunity to squeeze off up to 3,000 rounds at a shooting range in the United States before heading off to fight for Islamic causes around the world. "All serious firearms training must be done overseas" because of British gun laws, advertising for the course noted. British prosecutors said their investigators had searched Zain-ul-abidin's apartment and seized documents believed to be related to suspected terrorist mastermind Osama bin Laden and his al Qaeda network, anti-Semitic material and what appeared to be disabled firearms, including a rifle and two handguns. The *Sunday Telegraph* reported on another military training course, this time at a secret camp near the village of Yetgoch in southern Wales. Young Muslims and others learned how to use Uzi machine guns at the camp, which was run by Trans Global Security International.

The reports of the Welsh training camp rekindled a debate in Britain over how the UK had become a hotbed for military recruitment by radical Islamic elements. Sheik Omar Bakri Mohammed, a firebrand Islamic leader in London, founder of the fundamentalist al-Muhajiroun organization, and bin Laden's sometime spokesman, said in 2000 that between 1,800 and 2,000 British Muslims were going abroad each year for military training. "We find young men in university classes or mosques, invite them for a meal and discuss ... ongoing attacks being suffered by Muslims in Chechnya, Palestine or Kashmir," Bakri Mohammed said. "We ... make them understand their duty to support the jihad (holy war) struggle verbally, financially and, if they can, physically in order to liberate their homeland." Bakri's al-Muhajiroun group, like al Qaeda, advocated wiping out the world's 50-plus existing Muslim-majority states and replacing them with a single "khilafah" (caliphate), or Islamic state. (*Sunday Telegraph*, MSNBC, December 27, 2001)

Records of a satellite phone used by Osama bin Laden from 1996 to 1998 revealed that "Britain was at the heart of the terrorist's planning for his worldwide campaign of murder and destruction," according to the London *Sunday Times*. Bin Laden and his most senior aides made more calls to Britain than to any other country; they made more than 260 calls from Afghanistan to 27 numbers in Britain. According to documents from the trial of the East African US embassy bombings, the telephone was bought in 1996 with the help of Dr Saad al Fagih, 45, the head of the London-based Movement for Islamic Reform in Arabia. Al Fagih had been regularly used by the BBC as an expert on bin Laden. His credit card was also used to buy more than 3,000 minutes of pre-paid airtime. The records showed calls to ten other countries, the next most frequent after the UK being Yemen, home of the bin Laden family. There were no calls to Iraq. (*London Sunday Times*, March 24, 2002)

AL QAEDA AND LONDONISTAN

The role of London as the leading center of Islamic radicalism has been an open secret for years, but has never been reported by the US controlled corporate media. In the nineteenth century, when Mazzini and Marx operated out of London, the slogan was that "England supports all revolutions but her own." In the post-colonial world, the British have found it to their advantage to encourage violent movements which could be used for destabilizations and assassinations in the former colonies, which their ex-masters did not want to see become strong and effective modern states. Between 1995 and 1999, protests were lodged by many countries concerning the willingness of the British government to permit terror groups to operate from British territory. Among the protestors were: Israel, Algeria, Turkey, Libya, Yemen, India, Egypt, France, Peru, Germany, Nigeria, and Russia. This is a list which, if widely known, might force certain US radio commentators to change their world picture about who is soft on terrorism.

A number of groups which were cited as terrorist organizations by the US State Department had their headquarters in London. Among them were the Islamic Group of Egypt, led by bin Laden's current right-hand man, Zawahiri, who was a known participant in the plot to assassinate Egyptian President Sadat;

this was also the group which had murdered foreign tourists at Luxor in an attempt to wreck the Egyptian tourist industry. Also present in London were Al Jihad of Egypt, Hamas of Palestine, the Armed Islamic Group (GIA) of Algeria (responsible for large-scale massacres in that country), the Kurdish Workers' Party (PKK), which attacked targets in Turkey, and the Liberation Tigers of Tamil Eelam (Tamil Tigers) of Sri Lanka, who assassinated Indian Prime Minister Rajiv Ghandi. Sheikh Bakri, a bin Laden spokesman, was openly active in London into mid-1998 and later; he gave a press conference after the bombings of the US East African embassies. The killings of figures like Sadat and Rajiv Ghandi should indicate the scale of the destabilization in developing countries of which some of these groups are capable.

Non-Anglo-Saxon press organs have from time to time pointed up the role of London in worldwide subversion. "The track of … the GIA leader in Paris leads to Great Britain. The British capital has served as logistical and financial base for the terrorists," wrote *Le Figaro* on Nov. 3, 1995, in the wake of a murderous terror attack carried out in France. A report by the French National Assembly in October 2001 alleged that London played the key role as clearinghouse for money laundering of criminal and terrorist organizations. On March 3, 1996: Hamas bombed a market in Jerusalem, leaving 12 Israelis dead. A British newspaper reported soon after: "Israeli security sources say the fanatics…are funded and controlled through secret cells operating here.…Military chiefs in Jerusalem detailed how Islamic groups raised £7 million in donations from British organizations." (*Daily Express*, London, March 5, 1996)

In the midst of a campaign of destabilization against Egypt in the mid-1990s, the semi-official organ of the Egyptian government pointed out that "Britain has become the number one base in the world for international terrorism." (*Al Ahram*, Cairo, September 7, 1996) Egyptian President Hosni Mubarak noted that "…some states, like Britain, give political asylum to terrorists, and these states will pay the price for that." (*Al-Hayat*, September 18, 1996) British newspapers were also alarmed by the level of Islamic extremist activity they saw around them. By the late 1990s, there were so many Islamic extremists in London that the city had acquired the nickname of "Londonistan."

The leading right-wing paper in the UK wrote: "Britain is now an international center for Islamic militancy on a huge scale…and the capital is home to a bewildering variety of radical Islamic movements, many of which make no secret of their commitment to violence and terrorism to achieve their goals." (London *Daily Telegraph*, November 20, 1999) President Putin of Russia saw a direct link between the London Islamic scene and terrorism in his own country. He said in an interview with a German news magazine: "In London, there is a recruitment station for people wanting to join combat in Chechnya. Today–not officially, but effectively in the open–they are talking there about recruiting volunteers to go to Afghanistan." (*Focus*, September 2001)

Brixton Mosque was one of the notorious centers for terrorist recruitment in the heart of London. This was the home base of Zacarias Moussaoui, the French citizen put on trial in Alexandria, Va. It was also the home of Richard Reid, the shoe bomber of December 2001. Imam Qureshi of Brixton and others were allowed by the British authorities to preach anti-US sermons to the some 4,000 Muslim inmates in British prisons, and thus to recruit new patsies for the world-wide terror machine. According to bin Laden's spokesman Bakri, 2,000 fighters were trained yearly during the late 1990s, including many in the US because of the lax firearms legislation. The rival of Brixton Mosque was the equally redoubtable Finsbury Mosque, home of the Saudi demagogue al Masri, who was finally taken into custody in the spring of 2004. There is every reason to believe that London is one of the main recruiting grounds for patsies, dupes, fanatics, double agents, and other roustabouts of the terrorist scene.

AL QAEDA AND MI-5 AGAINST LIBYA

Muammar Qaddafi of Libya, who had been bombed by the US in the mid-1980s, not coincidentally became a target of al Qaeda. In March 1994, bin Laden supporters killed two German agents in Libya. In November 1996, there was an MI-5 assassination attempt against the Libyan dictator with the help of the local bin Laden organization, in which several people were killed. Here is a prime example of al Qaeda being employed by UK intelligence for purposes of state-sponsored terrorism with the goal of eliminating a political leader who was not appreciated by London. (Hollingsworth and Fielding) The conclusion is clear: al Qaeda is a subsidiary of Anglo-American intelligence.

According to the French authors Brisard and Dasquié, bin Laden's controllers had been using him to cause trouble for Qaddafi since the early 1980s, when bin Laden had demanded permission to set up a base of operations in Libya, but was rebuffed by Qaddafi. "Enraged by Libya's refusal, bin Laden organized attacks inside Libya, including assassination attempts against Qaddafi," Dasquié told IPS press service. The French authors cited the Islamic Fighting Group, head-quartered in London, as the Libyan opposition group most closely allied with bin Laden. Author Dasquié told IPS, "Qaddafi even demanded that Western police institutions, such as Interpol, pursue the IFG and bin Laden, but never obtained co-operation. Until this very day [late 2001], members of IFG openly live in London." In 1998, former MI-5 officer David Shayler told reporters that the British secret services had financed the assassination attempt against Qaddafi. (Inter Press service, November 15, 2001)

A rare moment of truth about the infrastructure of international terrorism was provided in October 2001 by Qaddafi, who was aware of al Qaeda's track record of attempting to eliminate him in the service of the US and UK. In an appearance on the popular Al-Jazeera program "The Opposite Direction," Qaddafi condemned the 9/11 attacks, and referred to bin Laden's Arab Afghans as "stray dogs" and terrorists. But then Qaddafi began to talk about the support network for al Qaeda:

> I am actually puzzled. I mean, if America were serious about eliminating terrorism, the first capital it should rock with cruise missiles is *London*.

> Interviewer: London!?

> Qaddafi: London. It is the center of terrorism. It gives safehousing to the terrorists. I mean, as long as America does not bomb London, I think the US is not serious, and is using a double standard. I mean, on the contrary, London is far more dangerous than Kabul. How could it rock Kabul with missiles and leave London untouched? (Al-Jazeera, Qatar-Tripoli, October 25, 2001)

The interviewer, a former BBC employee, quickly changed the subject before the mercurial dictator could say more. At this time, al Jazeera was closely monitored by all the international wire services, since it had the best reporting from inside Afghanistan. But none of them reported these illuminating remarks from Qaddafi.

NEOCONS PLAN FOR AL QAEDA'S GLOBAL FUTURE

Voices from the Washington neocon oligarchy leave no doubt that the US establishment's reliance on al Qaeda as its tool for ordering world affairs is intended to be a long-term one. The neocon retired army colonel Robert Killebrew considers al Qaeda as the "once and future threat," since he believes that "the al Qaeda we will face in 2010 will be an even more dangerous threat to Americas than the al Qaeda our troops are fighting today." According to Killebrew, "we can expect that within a decade al Qaeda will open one, or possibly several, political fronts in predominantly Islamic states, transforming itself from a deadly but diffuse terrorist movement into implacably hostile governmental factions throughout the Middle East that will pose critical geostrategic challenges to America and our allies....the political transformation of al Qaeda into a radical pan Islamic movement would divide the world between the progressive West and a number of deeply reactionary, nuclear-armed states, and raise the possibility of far more serious conflict." (*Washington Post*, August 8, 2004)

Here we see the oligarchy's intent of employing the benighted ideology of al Qaeda to organize the Arab and Islamic worlds for their own destruction. As we will see, neocolonial and neo-imperial powers have always feared secular Arab nationalism of the Nasser type, and have been eager to foment fundamentalist alternatives in the hope of perpetuating backwardness and isolation. The big danger for the US has always been that Arab oil producers would reach their own economic development accords with western Europe, Japan, and the larger third world nations, such as Brazil. Al Qaeda fanaticism makes precisely these types of understandings impossible, preventing the forms of cooperation which would do the most to rival the US. The US is the biggest backer of al Qaeda, in just the same way that the Bank of England, Royal Dutch Shell, the City of London, and Wall Street were the biggest boosters of Hitler: if you know that you may face an adversary, the reasoning goes, then try to make sure that adversary will have a raving, incompetent, fanatical leader who will be structurally incapable of making successful alliances with your other foes.

BUSH FAMILY NAZI LINKS

Perhaps this is what Bush 43, whose family tradition includes grandfather Prescott Bush's implication in the Thyssen Nazi financial infrastructure, meant when he said in late 2001 that the United States has "the best intelligence we can possibly have," and what Porter J. Goss, the Florida Republican who chaired the House Permanent Select Committee on Intelligence in 2001, meant when he denied that any intelligence failure had taken place around 9/11. (R.W. Apple, *New York Times*, December 14, 2001; *George Bush: The Unauthorized Biography*, Tarpley and Chaitkin)

PRELIMINARIES:
TERRORISM IN THE 1990s

> Guys, now you saw this bomb went off and you both known we could avoid that. – Emad Salem to the FBI, 1993

Synthetic terrorism is an enterprise that terrorist controllers often choose to escalate gradually, partly to enhance their own technical preparedness, and partly as a means of progressively degrading public intelligence while institutionalizing fantastic lies about what is going on. The Italian terrorism of 1967-1985, for example, which was directed by NATO intelligence, MI-6, the CIA, and SISMI, shows an unmistakable pattern of escalation, inasmuch as each terrorist attack became the stepping stone of the successive one, with an overall tendency towards larger and more complicated operations with higher and higher numbers of victims, reaching a culmination at Bologna in 1980.

If we look at terrorism in the US during the 1990s, we see a similar pattern. One has the impression of looking at a crescendo of terror attacks, in which each new attack introduces new elements which will be important in the attacks to come. It is worth pointing out that, during the 1990s, few if any wealthy oligarchs became victims of terrorism; the dead were almost always the little people, the masses, and so it was to remain on 9/11. In addition, each new distortion accepted by the public increased the overall gullibility of the political system.

THE WORLD TRADE CENTER 1993: THE FBI SET IT UP AND LET IT HAPPEN

The bomb detonated in the underground parking garage at the World Trade Center on February 26, 1993 killed six people, resulted in injuries to a thousand more, and threw lower Manhattan into chaos. At the center of the terror cell was a bombmaker who had been in the Egyptian army. He was also a paid informer and provocateur for the FBI. Other participants in the terror operation had entered the country with the connivance of the CIA, despite the fact that normally they would not have been allowed in. The FBI was aware of every phase of the plot, but refused to exploit numerous opportunities to stop it. The first WTC bomb of 1993 went off with the full complicity of the FBI, which tried repeatedly to pass off the blame to the Sudanese mission to the United Nations. The Kean-Hamilton Commission has nothing to say about this.

A detailed narrative of these events has appeared under the title *The Cell*. It is a cover-up, written by participants in the operation. This book ignores the central and most dramatic event of the entire affair, which was the publication of the tapes secretly made by FBI provocateur Emad Salem of his own conversations with his FBI controllers – tapes which he wisely surmised he might need later as an insurance policy. Salem appears to have been passed from British intelligence to the FBI.

Even without the Salem tapes, *The Cell* presents a story of criminal incompetence within the FBI. The story starts with the November 1990 assassination in New York City of Rabbi Meir Kahane, an Israeli terrorist leader who had founded the Jewish Defense League several decades earlier. The accused assassin of Kahane was El Sayyid Nosair, an Egyptian fanatic. But Nosair was not just a drifting fanatic: when the police searched his apartment, "there were training manuals from the Army Special Warfare School at Fort Bragg. There were copies of teletypes that had been routed to the Secretary of the Army and the Joint Chiefs of Staff. How had Nosair come up with those? Clearly, he had a source in a sensitive position in the US military." (*Cell* 45) Much more likely, his terrorist controller occupied a sensitive position in the US military, as any fool can see.

Nosair's Arabic-language files were said to contain the detailed plan of a series of future terrorist acts, including the 1993 WTC bombing. But the FBI was not interested in having these documents translated; it simply put them into storage and ignored them until it was too late. This vital evidence, according to our authors, "entered a black hole."

Sheikh Abdel Rahman, known to Kean-Hamilton Commission devotees as the Blind Sheikh, was a known terrorist, a friend of the CIA's favorite Afghan warlord Gulbuddin Hekmatyar and of Osama bin Laden. He had been placed under house arrest in Egypt. Nevertheless, he was allowed to enter the US, coming from Sudan. In the light of the subsequent demonization of the blind Sheikh as one of the key terrorist plotters of the 1990s, we are entitled to ask why he was allowed to come to the US in the first place. The preferred answer: "Abdel Rahman's visa was signed by a CIA officer stationed at the Sudanese consulate, and one theory advanced by FBI agents is that the Agency sponsored his immigration. The CIA, in that scenario, may have wanted to nurture its ties to the Egyptian fundamentalists in order to avoid a replay of Iran in 1979, when the overthrow of the Shah left US intelligence out in the cold. Another theory was that the officer had 'gone bad.'" (*Cell* 54)

More likely, the CIA or the moles within it simply wanted to use the Sheikh for terror operations against Egypt and/or the US. As for the Shah, he was deliberately overthrown by the US in the framework of Brzezinski's Islamic fundamentalism strategy, with the CIA as an active participant. (See Dreyfus)

The key wrecker in this episode seems to be one Carson Dunbar, an FBI manager working in the FBI National Security Division who oversaw the activities of the FBI's Joint Terrorism Task Force (JTTF) in New York City. Salem's two controllers were Louie Napoli and John Anticev, who reported to Dunbar. Even though Salem was supposedly providing good information, Dunbar "was reluctant to trust too much" in him. (*Cell* 70-71) Salem for his part did not want to wear a wire when talking to his terrorist confrères, since that would mean he would have to testify in court, which would put an end to his career as an infiltrator. Dunbar increasingly insisted that Salem wear a wire, and Salem kept refusing. This then led to the alleged "firing" of Salem as an FBI informant by Napoli, acting under pressure from Dunbar. The cover story" "...many people in the Bureau, especially street agents, blamed Dunbar for dropping Salem." (*Cell* 75) A more sophisticated interpretation would be that Dunbar was deliberately wrecking the surveillance of the terror cell. Was Dunbar a mole?

When alleged terror planner Ramzi Yousef comes on the scene, the INS inspector at the airport suggests that he be locked up. But by some strange coincidence "there was not enough room in the INS lockup, so he was released with the promise that he would turn up at a hearing later." (*Cell* 77)

When the terrorists in the cell decide that they need training, they turn to Garrett Wilson, a former Army Ranger who worked as a military police officer at a naval base near Philadelphia. Wilson was an agent of NCIS, meaning naval intelligence. The idea was now supposedly that while Wilson provided the training – allegedly for Jihad in Bosnia, which matched US government policy at the time – the FBI could monitor the comings and goings of the terrorists, and track each one of them to his home and job. Dunbar once again attempted sabotage: "Dunbar was concerned that the Bureau was training potential terrorists, holy warriors who may not be breaking the law now, but who might one day turn the skills they were acquiring against the US...Dunbar...was uncomfortable with the entire mission." (*Cell* 88) Because of these scruples, Dunbar was able to contrive an outcome in which the terrorists got their training, while the FBI was deprived of the promised harvest of valuable information.

On a certain weekend in January 1993, about a month before the WTC bombing, the terrorists had all gathered on a farm near Harrisburg, Pennsylvania. The FBI had the place staked out and surrounded. All that was needed was the patience to wait until the terrorists got into their cars and drove off for home, and the FBI would know precisely where each of them lived and slept, making it possible to roll up the entire cell on demand. But at this critical moment, Dunbar decided that this was nothing but a waste of manpower. He called all the FBI agents back to New York, preventing them from tailing their suspects home. He also wanted to dump the entire investigation on the FBI's Newark office, washing his hands of it.

> The JTTF was just a whisper away from the World Trade Center plot. But once more Dunbar lost patience with the operation....At that point, JTTF's jihad investigation was effectively dead in the water, killed by an investigative stroke of the pen. (*Cell* 91)

The way was now clear for the attack on the WTC a few weeks later. The FBI had thoroughly bungled the case:

> There were very few strangers to law enforcement among the men who blew up the World Trade Center. Mohammed Salameh and Mahmoud Abouhalima had been collared by Eddie Norris's detectives after the Rabbi Kahane murder, but then let go under pressure from the NYPD brass. JTTF's people had surveilled a number of the other bombers at the shooting range in Calverton, even before the Kahane case. Emad Salem had become a trusted member of the group's larger circle, with close links to Abdel Rahman Nosair, Abouhalima and el Gabrowny. He'd been in the thick of the original 'twelve Jewish locations' plot and a hair's breadth away from the actual World Trade Center bombers.

Tommy Corrigan's colleagues had tailed several more of their associates to the training camp in Harrisburg just a few months ago. In fact, the last of the surveillances had run up until just a few weeks before the bombing, when one group seemed to be asking the other if they knew how to get detonators....the two cases were both shut down based on a series of FBI management concerns that were more administrative than exigent. (*Cell* 98)

Thus far the cover-up, which appears damning enough in its own way. But *The Cell* constitutes only a limited hangout, conceding incompetence in the hopes of obscuring real treason. The procedure is not a new one, having been outlined some four hundred years ago by Paolo Sarpi of Venetian intelligence, who perfected the technique of speaking well of someone while pretending to speak ill. The technique amounts to criticizing a valued asset because he beats his wife, while remaining silent on the fact that he is also a serial killer.

We get far closer to reality with the following article by Ralph Blumenthal from the *New York Times* which appeared on October 28, 1993:

Tapes Depict Proposal to Thwart Bomb Used in Trade Center Blast

Law enforcement officials were told that terrorists were building a bomb that was eventually used to blow up the World Trade Center, and they planned to thwart the plotters by secretly substituting harmless powder for the explosives, an informer said after the blast.

The informer was to have helped the plotters build the bomb and supply the fake powder, but the plan was called off by an FBI supervisor who had other ideas about how the informer, Emad Salem, should be used, the informer said.

The account, which is given in the transcript of hundreds of hours of tape recordings that Mr. Salem secretly made of his talk with law-enforcement agents, portrays the authorities as being in a far better position than previously known to foil the February 26th bombings of New York's tallest towers.

Supervisor 'Messed It Up'

After the bombing, [Salem] resumed his undercover work. In an undated transcript of a conversation from that period, Mr. Salem recounts a talk he had had earlier with an agent about an unnamed FBI supervisor who, he said, "came and messed it up."

"He requested to meet me in the hotel," Mr. Salem says of the supervisor.

"He requested to make me testify, and if he didn't push for that, we'll be going building the bomb with a phony powder, and grabbing the people who was involved in it. But since you, we didn't do that."

The transcript quotes Mr. Salem as saying that he wanted to complain to FBI headquarters in Washington about the Bureau's failure to stop the bombing, but was dissuaded by an agent identified as John Anticev.

Mr. Salem said Mr. Anticev had told him, "He said, I don't think that the New York people would like the things out of the New York Office to go to Washington DC."

Another agent, identified as Nancy Floyd, does not dispute Mr. Salem's account, but rather appears to agree with it, saying of the 'New York people': "well, of course not, because they don't want to get their butts chewed."

Salem was later given $1.5 million by the FBI to keep his mouth shut. This extraordinary article, and the transcripts upon which it is based, leave no doubt that a faction within the FBI was determined to have the first WTC bombing take place, and sabotaged any and all serious law enforcement efforts which non-witting FBI personnel and New York police undertook in good faith to try to avoid this disaster. FBI managers wanted a real bomb, and at the same time wrecked the surveillance operation that had been watching the terrorist cell. So far as is known, none of the FBI moles involved has ever been called to account. The Kean-Hamilton Commission has nothing whatever to say about this "intelligence failure." In any sane society, the active participation of the FBI in the first WTC bomb plot conspiracy would have been the occasion for the breakup of this dysfunctional agency, or at the very least a thorough purge of the officials involved. The silence of the 9/11 commission on this matter is yet another indicator of its moral and conceptual bankruptcy.

OKLAHOMA CITY

The attack on the Federal Building in Oklahoma City killed 168 people, and marked a definite escalation in the pattern of synthetic terrorism. Here many of the components of the 9/11 attacks were experimented with and tested, partly to gauge the degree to which the public would believe that the techniques being used were what the FBI claimed that they were. Local media coverage concurred that there had been more than one explosion at the Federal Building, and at first the national media attempted to suggest that a Middle East terror organization had been involved. Soon Timothy McVeigh and Terry Nichols were arrested, and McVeigh in particular was subjected to a thorough demonization by the controlled corporate media. The casualties and building damage were attributed according to the official account to a single truck bomb containing some 4,800 pounds of ammonium nitrate transported in a Ryder van, and parked in front of the building. All reference to multiple explosions soon disappeared.

Retired Brigadier General Benton Partin of the US Air Force, an expert in explosives, including nuclear detonations, came forward with a convincing analysis showing that the official explanation was physically impossible, given what is known about the propagation of a shock wave through the atmosphere. Air, Partin stressed, is a very inefficient coupling mechanism when it comes to directing such a shock wave against heavily reinforced concrete beams and columns. Blast damage potential, according to his analysis, decreases more rapidly than an inverse function of the cube of the distance, so there was no way that a fertilizer bomb could have accounted for the extensive damage observed. Partin concluded:

"The Murrah Federal Building was not destroyed by one sole truck bomb. The major factor in its destruction appears to have been detonation of explosives carefully placed at four critical junctures on supporting columns within the building. The only possible reinforced concrete structural failure solely attributable to the truck bomb was the stripping out of the ceilings of the first and second floors in the 'pit' area behind columns B4 and B5. Even this may have been caused by a demolition charge at column B3. It is truly unfortunate that a separate and independent bomb damage assessment was not made during the cleanup – before the building was demolished on May 23 and hundreds of truck loads of debris were hauled away, smashed down, and covered with dirt behind a security fence… All ambiguity with respect to the use of supplementing demolition charges and the type of truck used could be quickly resolved if the FBI were required to release the surveillance camera coverage of this terribly tragic event." (www.whatreallyhappened.com/RANCHO/POLITICS/OK/PARTIN/ok2.htm)

Soon after the explosion, Controlled Demolition Inc. was called in to destroy those parts of the building which had remained standing, and to speedily dispose of all the rubble of the building. This, of course, prefigures the blatant tampering with a crime scene which became the hallmark of Mayor Giuliani's approach to the World Trade Center, again using CDI.

We need have no illusions about Gen. Partin, who belonged to a dubious organization called the Rushmore Foundation, which occupied itself with working with and studying the right-wing militias that proliferated during the 1990s. Partin made special reference to the problems posed by tampering with the crime scene in a July 30, 1995 letter to GOP Senate Majority Leader Trent Lott. Here Partin wrote that "no government law enforcement agency should be permitted to demolish, smash, and bury evidence of a counter-terrorism sting operation, sabotage, or terrorist attack without a thorough examination by an independent, technically competent agency. If an aircraft crashed because of a bomb, or a counter-terrorism sting or an FAA controller error, the FAA would not be permitted to gather and bury the evidence. The National Transportation Safety Board would have been called in to conduct an investigation and where possibly every piece of debris would have been collected and arrayed to determine cause of failure."

But nobody in power was willing to protect the crime scene or force the FBI to disgorge the evidence it had sequestered. The suggestible public had been given a spectacular example of the supposed fragility of steel-reinforced concrete buildings in the delusional world of synthetic terrorism, and the precedent of bringing in Controlled Demolition to destroy the evidence had also been established for all to see. These advances on the part of the terrorist controllers would become components in the future synthetic terrorism of 9/11.

Before leaving Oklahoma City, we should recall that the prevalent form of counter-gangs which were fielded during the 1990s by the intelligence agencies of the US and Britain was precisely these right-wing militias. They were a widespread phenomenon during that decade but now, from the point of view of the controlled corporate media, they have simply disappeared. But such a large recruiting ground for trained manpower does not disappear from one decade to the next. Some of the case officers who directed the duped rank and file of the right-wing militias have doubtless found their way into the clandestine ops/special forces element which made its contribution to 9/11.

TWA 800

On July 17, 1996, TWA Flight 800, a Boeing 747, crashed off the coast of Long Island, killing all 230 persons on board. Pierre Salinger, the former White House press secretary to President Kennedy and a former ABC newsman, soon came forward with the charge that the plane had been destroyed by a US Navy missile which had gone astray. At a press conference in Paris, Salinger offered a 69-page document and a set of radar images to bolster his case. The FBI, Pentagon and federal air safety investigators simply rejected this theory, which spread over the Internet following the July 17, 1996 crash. National Transportation Safety Board Chairman James Hall called Salinger's allegations "irresponsible." Salinger and Mike Sommer, an investigative reporter and former Salinger colleague at ABC News, claimed the 'missile' was fired during a "super-secret" US Navy exercise off Long Island and was meant to target a Tomahawk missile, but hit Flight 800 instead when it "lost its lock on its original target." They alleged that the missile was either a kinetic energy missile or a continuous rod missile; the continuous rod missile would "slice through" the plane. Salinger alleged that witnesses monitoring secret Navy anti-terrorism exercises heard a male voice say, "Oh, my God, I just hit that plane." Salinger also asserted that two Russian satellites active above the scene of the disaster had recorded images showing a missile hitting the TWA aircraft. Salinger's personal stature makes it necessary to take his charges seriously, but this case has remained clouded by mystery. (CNN, March 13, 1997)

US SPECIAL FORCES SERGEANT ALI MOHAMED: BIN LADEN'S PERSONAL ASSISTANT

The other detail about the 1993 WTC bombing which we need to know is that the bombers were in fact trained by the picaresque Sergeant Ali Mohamed of the United States Army Special Forces. At different stages of his colorful career,

Mohamed worked, or seemed to work, for the Egyptian Army, the Egyptian Islamic Jihad, the CIA, the FBI, the US Army Special Forces, the al Kifah Refugee Services Office, the Afghan mujahideen and Osama bin Laden.

Ali Mohamed was born in Egypt in 1952. He attended the Military Academy in Cairo and gained promotion in the Egyptian Special Forces and military intelligence, rising to the rank of major. In 1981 he came to train with the US green berets at Fort Bragg, North Carolina. While still in Egypt, he had become associated with the blind Sheikh, Omar Abdel Rahman, who was allegedly part of Egyptian Islamic Jihad. It was four officers from Ali Mohamed's unit who carried out the October 1981 assassination of Egyptian President Anwar Sadat. Ali Mohamed was attending courses in Fort Bragg at the time, and he was never implicated in the plot. But, supposedly because he was considered a sympathizer with the assassins, Ali Mohamed was obliged to resign his commission.

In 1984, Ali Mohamed began working as a security adviser for Egypt Air. He tried to go to work for the CIA, but after a short time on the job he was dumped for having unreported contacts with Hezbollah, and his name was placed on the State Department watch list. Despite this, he was nevertheless allowed to enter the US in 1986. Ali Mohamed married an American woman who worked in Silicon Valley, and became an American citizen, despite his well-established terrorist links.

In 1986, Ali Mohamed enlisted in the US Army Special Forces, although still on the watch list. He was recruited by Lt. Col. Steve Neely to give lectures on Islamic culture and politics to the anti-bin Laden units being trained at Fort Bragg.

In 1987, Ali Mohamed told Lt. Col. Neely that he wanted to use a 30-day leave to go to Afghanistan, where guerrilla warfare was raging against the Soviet Red Army occupiers. This might have created a grave incident with the Soviets, and Lt. Col. Neely sent a report about Mohamed's plan to his superiors, who failed to intervene. When Mohamed came back from Afghanistan, he told Lt. Col. Neely that he had taken part in combat and had wiped out more than one Russian patrol. Neely composed a report on Mohamed's findings about the Soviet *spetsnaz* special forces. Ali Mohamed left the army when his enlistment expired, but he remained in the reserves; he was in the Fort Bragg 5th Special Forces Group (Airborne) throughout this period. A retired special ops source has stated that particularly this unit involves a virtual lifetime and informal membership; "they never drop off the radar screen."

From 1989 to 1992-93, Ali Mohamed gave paramilitary training in the New York City area to the "Islamic terror" clique convicted for the 1993 bombing of the World Trade Center. It was he who trained Nosair, and he might also have been the source of the secret documents found in Nosair's apartment. (*The Cell* 140 ff) The training took place at an Islamist center in Brooklyn. According to the London *Independent*, a CIA internal review conducted in 1998 would reveal that the Agency was "partly culpable" for the WTC bomb of 1993.

Another of Sgt. Ali Mohamed's supervisors at Fort Bragg was Col. Norville de Atkine of the Fort Bragg Special Forces School, who later turned up as the co-author with anti-Muslim agitator Daniel Pipes – appointed by Bush to the board of the US Institute of Peace – in a 1995 piece entitled "Middle Eastern Studies: What Went Wrong" in Pipes' *Middle East Quarterly.*

Ali Mohamed now attempted once more to go to work for the CIA. Starting in 1990, he attempted to enter the FBI as a translator. During his interview process he told the FBI about a passport-forging operation run by Hamas, and became an FBI informant. Twice during the early 1990s, Ali Mohamed brought the person the corporate media today call Bin Laden's right-hand man, Ayman al-Zawahiri, to the US for fund-raising tours in California. The second tour came in 1995, exactly the time Zawahiri and his brother were beginning the mujahideen deployment into the Balkans under protection of corrupted networks within NATO. This channel became a key component of the NATO-run KLA guerrillas in Kosovo. Also in 1995, Ali Mohamed had applied for a security job in the high security area of a Department of Defense subcontractor near his home in Santa Clara, CA. He was interviewed three times by the Defense Security Service (DSS). Ali Mohamed's friend in Santa Clara, Abu El-Dahab, ran a phone patch communications link for the alleged "bin Laden Network" around the world.

In 1991, Ali Mohamed worked as a personal assistant to Osama bin Laden, helping with security and other matters when bin Laden moved his operation from Pakistan to Khartoum, Sudan. Ali Mohamed performed other services for bin Laden. "In 1992, I conducted military and basic explosives training for al Qaeda in Afghanistan," Ali Mohamed told US authorities in 1999. "I also conducted intelligence training for al Qaeda. I taught my trainees how to create cell structures that could be used for operations." (*The Cell* 145) Supposedly the FBI, in the person of agent John Zindt, got its first news of al Qaeda from an interview with Ali Mohamed in May 1993. Toward the end of the 1990s, the FBI would arrest Ali Mohamed as the prelude to putting him on the permanent payroll as an informer.

In 1993, Ali Mohamed who was traveling in the company of an al Qaeda terrorist, was arrested by the Royal Canadian Mounted Police (RCMP); the FBI intervened, with Ali Mohamed's FBI case officer asking the RCMP to release Mohamed. According to the *Toronto Globe and Mail*, Ali Mohamed was "working with US counter-terrorist agents, playing a double or triple game, when he was questioned in 1993."

Patrick J. Fitzgerald, who prosecuted Ali Mohamed twice as US Attorney for Northern Illinois, told the 9/11 commission that Ali Mohamed was a top al Qaeda agent who "trained most of al Qaeda's top leadership" including "the persons who would later carry out the 1993 World Trade center bombing."

Ali Mohamed was put on trial in 2000 for his role in the 1998 bombings of US Embassies in Kenya and Tanzania, which the Washington establishment had rushed to blame on Osama bin Laden and al Qaeda, in part because of their sophisticated coordination. Ali Mohamed was allowed to cop a plea bargain. As part of the deal, Mohamed revealed that he had trained the 1993 WTC bombers. According to a State Department summary of Ali Mohamed's testimony, he was ordered by the FBI in 1994 to fly from Kenya to New York, and he complied. He was debriefed by an FBI agent in the context of the upcoming trial of the blind Sheikh Abdel Rahman on charges stemming from the 1993 WTC attack. Mohamed stated: "I flew back to the United States, spoke to the FBI, but I didn't disclose everything that I knew."

After Ali Mohamed had been released by the RCMP on orders from the FBI, he flew to Nairobi, Kenya, where he photographed the US Embassy. According to Mohamed's 2000 confession, "Bin Laden looked at the picture of the American Embassy and pointed to where a truck could go as a suicide bomber."[3] Another cluster of attacks ascribed to bin Laden was the bombings of US East African embassies in Nairobi, Kenya, and Dar es Salaam, Tanzania.

In the 9/11 commission's report we read: "As early as December, 1993, a team of al Qaeda operatives had begun casing targets in Nairobi for future attacks. It was led by Ali Mohamed, a former Egyptian army officer who had moved to the United States in the mid-1980s, enlisted in the US Army, and became an instructor at Fort Bragg. He had provided guidance and training to extremists at the Farouq Mosque in Brooklyn, including some who were subsequently convicted in the February 1993 attack on the World trade Center." (68)

Since September 11th, many publicly available leads pointing to bin Laden in fact draw on the corrupted investigation and trial results from the 1993 WTC and 1998 African embassy bombings, a timeframe in which Ali Mohamed was in repeated contact with the FBI and Department of Defense, and was permitted to operate in the modus operandi of an officially sanctioned rogue intelligence operative. Ali Mohamed must be considered one of the most successful double agents of the party of international terror ensconced in the US government.

EGYPTAIR 990: THE DEBUT OF GLOBAL HAWK?

October 31, 1999 was Halloween, and this day was marked by the mysterious crash of Egyptair Flight 990, a Boeing 767 bound from New York's JFK to Cairo. At a little before 2 AM, the plane abruptly descended from its normal altitude of 33,000 feet and, after some desperate maneuvers, crashed into the sea. The US government, in the person of the National Transportation Safety Board (NTSB), alleged that the plane had been deliberately crashed by Co-pilot Gameel al-Batouti. The US case was built on the cockpit voice recorder, which, the NTSB claimed, had registered Batouti's Islamic prayer, "I rely on God," just

---

[3] Peter Dale Scott, 9/11 commission Misses FBI's Embarrassing al Qaeda Dealings," www.dissidentvoice.org, June 27, 2004.

before the plane started its dive, and again at several points on the way down. Batouti was thus accused of being the first Islamist suicide pilot of the current phase. The Egyptian government rejected this explanation, and demanded a more objective investigation.

Of this incident, the 9/11 commission writes: "In late 1999, a great deal of discussion took place in the media about the crash off the coast of Massachusetts of Egyptair Flight 990, a Boeing 767. The most plausible explanation that emerged was that one of the pilots had gone berserk, seized the controls, and flown the aircraft into the sea. After the 1999-2000 millennium alerts, when the nation had relaxed, Clarke held a meeting of his Counter-terrorism Security Group devoted largely to the possibility of a possible [sic] airline hijacking by al Qaeda." (345) Clarke, as we see, was always anxious to build up the reputation of al Qaeda in the US government. The 9/11 commission also does not mention that this flight carried a group of Egyptian military officers who had just been trained in the United States to fly Apache helicopters, despite strenuous objections on the part of the government of Israel. (von Bülow 207 ff; 264 n. 204)

This case became widely known because of an article by William Langewiesche in the *Atlantic Monthly* which was published shortly after 9/11 ("The Crash of Egyptair 990," November 2001). According to Langewiesche, the supposed "suicide bomber" was a 60-year old *bon vivant* three months away from his retirement. He was married and had five children, one of whom was a girl who suffered from lupus but who had been receiving successful treatment in Los Angeles. Batouti had a comfortable home in Cairo and a vacation home by the Mediterranean. He was carrying with him an automobile tire he had bought in New Jersey the day before, and had a number of Viagra samples to distribute to his friends as gifts. Any attempt to depict this man as a suicide pilot is destined to shipwreck on the shoals of absurdity.

According to Langewiesche's tendentious account, at 1:48 the flight's pilot, Captain Habashi, went to the bathroom, leaving Batouti alone at the controls. At 1:48:30 an unintelligible sound was recorded on the CVR, which he claims was "control it" or "hydraulic." The word was probably in English, with three syllables, and the accent was on the second syllable. What this might mean remains a mystery. Then Batouti repeated four times as the aircraft descended: "I rely on God."

Absolutely no cockpit voice recorders from 9/11 have ever been made available in full to the general public or to researchers; the FBI and the government obviously have a great deal to hide. If the CVRs from 9/11 could speak, they might sound something like this dialogue from the ill-fated Egyptair flight:

Habashi: What's happening? What's happening?

Batouti: I rely on God. I rely on God.

Habashi: What's happening, Gameel? What's happening?

Habashi: What is this? What is this? Did you shut the engines?

Habashi: Get away in the engines! …shut the engines!

Batouti: It's shut.

Habashi: Pull! Pull with me! Pull with me! Pull with me!

[Silence]

Perhaps Egyptair 990 was no longer under the control of its pilots, but was now being remotely controlled by the US Force's Global Hawk system, the same technology used to guide the Predator drone used in Afghanistan about which Richard Clarke had so much to say at the 9/11 commission in April 2004. Perhaps Egyptair 990 was the Boeing 767 chosen for the dress rehearsal for 9/11. In the light of subsequent events, this hypothesis is far more credible than the absurd explanation espoused by the NTSB and its minion, Langewiesche.

It was later found from the flight data recorder that the elevators on the tail were split, with one in position to lower the nose of the plane, and the other positioned to raise it. "The ailerons on both wings had assumed a strange upswept position, normally never seen on an airplane." (46) These anomalies did not interest the NTSB, which had espoused the "suicide pilot" thesis.

The Egyptian representatives at the NTSB proceedings pointed out that when Batouti idled the engines, it was to keep from gaining speed as the plane had begun its dive. When he cut the engines, Batouti was carrying out the prescribed restart procedure, because he erroneously believed – based on the low oil pressure warning light that was flashing in the cockpit – that the engines had flamed out. Habashi was apparently under the same impression. When Habashi called on him to pull, Batouti did so, as the FDR showed. Despite so much uncertainty, the US government arrogantly pushed forward with its own improbable version of the event – Vice President Al Gore reportedly angered Egyptian President Hosni Mubarak during his state visit to Washington by making a crack about "the suicide flight." The reality may have been the debut of Global Hawk as a system for synthetic terrorism.

Tarek Selim, the chief pilot of Egypt Air, told a British reporter that the plane was going so fast that it must somehow have lost its tail assembly. Selim called the FBI's theory that one of the pilots had deliberately crashed the plane in a suicide action as "ridiculous" and "nonsense." Selim's view was that the Egyptian aircraft "had been brought down by either a bomb or a missile that hit the plane's tail." (Al-Ahram Weekly, *The Guardian,* November 26, 1999)

As for Langewiesche, the primitive level of his propaganda style can be seen in the passage in which he attempts to win his readers' gullible devotion for the NTSB. According to its apologist Langewiesche, the NTSB is shielded from the political currents of Washington; it "represents the most progressive American thinking on the role and character of good government...." (44) Langewiesche goes on: "In part because the NTSB seems so lean, and in part because by its very definition it advocates for the 'right' causes, it receives almost universally positive press coverage. The NTSB is technocratic. It is clean. It is Government Lite." (44) Egypt Air, by contrast, is portrayed as a sinister enterprise, operating out of Stalinist-style office buildings, which refuses to be privatized. Our reporter's lack of impartiality could hardly be more evident.

Of course, the specialty of the NTSB in the 1990s was to run interference for the asset-strippers and corporate wreckers who had taken over the freight railways of this country with every intention of running them into the ground while extracting the maximum of loot from the deteriorating fixed capital. They did this by ruling that train wrecks were human error, and not the fault of the railroads. One such case was the February 17, 1996 crash of a freight train with a local commuter train on the Chesapeake and Ohio tracks near Silver Spring, Maryland. Eleven persons were killed and 24 were injured when an Amtrak train collided with a Maryland Rail Commuter (MARC) train. The cause of the crash was clearly the railroad's lack of upkeep on the signal system, but the NTSB ruled that the cause was human error – on the part of the engineer who was dead. The NTSB is mandated by law to provide a timely accident investigation for all fatal transportation mishaps in the US or involving US carriers abroad; so far the NTSB has failed to report on the four plane crashes believed to have occurred on 9/11. Perhaps it is not so well insulated from dirty Washington politics as it would like to make people think.

Langewiesche established his credentials for dishonesty so well in this article that he was immediately assigned to cover the WTC crime scene, where he managed to write 200 pages without saying anything about the illegal removal of evidence in a criminal case that was going on all around him, as we will soon see.

AMERICAN 587

Two months after 9/11, American Airlines Flight 587 – an Airbus 300-600 – left John F. Kennedy International Airport en route to the Dominican Republic. Less than three minutes after takeoff, the aircraft crashed in a blazing inferno in the heart of a Queens neighborhood. All 265 people aboard perished. According to the NTSB, the tail fin and rudder of the plane sheared off as it accelerated. This was the second deadliest crash in US history, but it also "was the first example where we had an in-flight failure of a major structural component of an aircraft that in fact was made of composite materials," said National Transportation Safety Board Chairwoman Marion Blakey.

In the case of American Airlines Flight 587, federal officials seemed interested in avoiding the question of terrorism, so they released detailed information about the cockpit voice recorder within less than 36 hours. (*Philadelphia Daily News*, November 15, 2001) While this crash also remains very suspicious, and exhibits some technical parallels to Egyptair 990, it appears impossible to come to a definite conclusion at this time as to what causes were involved.

V
COULD THE ALLEGED HIJACKERS FLY THE PLANES?

Bertram: Well, how are they gonna bring it down?
Byers: Same way a dead man can drive a car.
– *The Lone Gunmen*

We must now begin to discuss the specific patsies of 9/11. Much detail about them will have to be ignored; much of it is disinformation which deserves to be ignored anyway. This entire area is dominated by hearsay evidence purveyed by the fiction-mongers of the FBI. Many of the identities offered are frauds, composites, or legends. What will interest us in the stories of the patsies are those singularities which show them for what they are, and which point beyond the superficial world of the patsies towards the underlying reality shaped by intelligence agencies and moles.

At least five of the persons accused by the FBI in the 9/11 atrocity apparently turned out to be alive; the FBI has never provided any proof that those accused were actually involved. Indeed, FBI Director Muller has admitted that his case against the notorious nineteen would never stand up in a real court of law. It would therefore be perfectly proper to reject the entire list of nineteen out of hand as just another effluvium of the FBI molehill – and, in effect, we do. At the same time, we find that at least some of the nineteen are double agents and tainted by criminal intent. But we also wish to examine the list of nineteen to discover the inherent complicities and contradictions in the government's case. In this way, the list of the nineteen can be used to cast light upon the operations of moles and terrorist controllers.

The FBI and the 9/11 commission have uniformly alleged that the leader of the mythic 19 hijackers who commandeered the aircraft was Mohammed Atta, a well-to-do Egyptian who they say was a very intolerant, puritanical, and doctrinaire Muslim. Reality looks much different, and rules out any notion that Atta could have accepted the mission of a suicide pilot because of profound religious convictions. He was in fact not a practicing Muslim, but rather a devotee of alcohol, cocaine, call girls, and pork chops. These biographical details are vital because they demolish any notion of Atta as a fanatic kamikaze. He was a sybaritic playboy or worse, addicted to the pleasures of the flesh, and no ascetic to immolate himself for a cause of faith. He emerges rather as a much more complicated figure, surely a sociopath, and in all probability a patsy who was being told one thing by his patrons and controllers while he was steered to act in ways which set him up in the role he played, and in all probability for liquidation.

In order to be accused of playing the role of suicide pilots, the 9/11 patsies needed to have a smattering of flight training. What actual expertise they were able to acquire in this process is something that we will examine, but it is already clear that the flight lessons were mostly for show. Ironically, they were conducted in south Florida, in a neighborhood which is redolent of the CIA covert operations of yesteryear, from the Bay of Pigs to Watergate to Iran-Contra. The school for patsies was located in the back yard of CIA Miami station, and just down the road from the US Central Command.

These matters have been illuminated by the reporting of former network newsman Daniel Hopsicker of the *Mad Cow Morning News*, who has shown much more real interest in the behavior and personality of Atta and his associates than the FBI ever has. Hopsicker has documented that Atta in particular was a piece of human refuse, a mixture of bungling ineptitude with psychopathic rage. Atta's mental impairment is such that it is very hard to attribute to him the remarkable feats of aviation skill which are ascribed to him by the mythmakers of the FBI and the 9/11 commission. Yet Hopsicker insists that Atta was indeed capable of flying his plane into the WTC north tower by the seat of his pants. Hopsicker also appears focused on the Saudi Arabian track, which leads away from the essential role played by the network of moles operating within the US government.

FLIGHT SCHOOLS FOR PATSIES

Atta, along with Shehhi, trained at the Huffman Aviation flight school in Venice, Florida, a small town on the Gulf coast between Tampa and Naples, inhabited mostly by retirees. Ramzi Binalshibh, who the official version claims was originally slated to be the twentieth hijacker, was on his way to Venice when he was stopped because of visa problems. Venice had two flight schools, both owned and operated by newly emigrated Netherlands nationals: Huffman Aviation was run by Rudi Dekkers, while Florida Flight Training Center, was run by Arne Kruithof, also from the Netherlands. The third accused suicide pilot, Siad al Jarrah, trained at Kruithof's center. Kruithof claimed privately that he had been trained at a US military installation in southeast Missouri. Atta and al Shehhi supposedly paid Dekkers more than $38,000, hardly the bargain rates that supposedly drew the two to Huffman in the first place.

Two Dutch nationals running flight schools at the same small airport which were attended by three out of the four alleged hijackers is a remarkable pattern. Both Dutchmen arrived in Venice in 1998. According to intelligence sources quoted by Hopsicker, "two Dutch boys buying adjacent flight schools which shortly thereafter get overrun by terrorists is one Dutch boy too many." Three alleged terrorists at two flight schools located at one small airport, when there are some 200 flight schools in Florida, is also a curious circumstance. (Hopsicker, *Mad Cow Morning News* 2, 7, 8)

On March 6, 2002 the US Immigration and Naturalization Service sent Dekkers letters telling him that Atta and Shehhi – now allegedly deceased – had met the necessary requirements and were now eligible to apply for extensions of their visas to stay in the US. How had the INS made this blunder in two of the best-known cases having to do with 9/11? "The error seemed particularly difficult to explain, sniffed the *New York Times*, because Mr. Atta and Mr. Shehhi were among the most infamous of the 19 hijackers." Media coverage focused on the "troubled" INS, but this incident is totally consistent with the hypothesis that the names of Atta and Shehhi had been flagged in government computers with national security overrides, which had served to make them virtually immune from watch lists, criminal checks, and the like. A lazy mole had evidently neglected to remove the override when the usefulness of these two patsies had come to an end, and so the posthumous visa approval forms were sent out. A similar case is the CIA cable announcing the presence of accused hijacker Al Hazmi in the US in March 2000, which was marked "Action Required: None." (JICI, September 20, 2002)

Atta's name had been on the CIA-FBI-INS watch list for many years, since an older person with the same name bombed an Israeli bus in the occupied territories of the West Bank on October 12, 1986. (Hopsicker 144-145) This indicates that the name was flagged with a national security override to allow him to enter the country. Atta was stopped by police for a traffic violation in Broward County, Florida on the night of April 26, 2001; he was even arrested for not having a drivers license. But he was soon released on bail – presumably the national security override again.

The FBI arrived at Venice airport no later than 2:30 AM in the morning of September 12, which indicates that they had known something about Atta's and Shehhi's being there. According to some accounts, the FBI arrived within a few hours, by the middle of the afternoon. An aviation businessman and employee of Huffman told Hopsicker, "They [the FBI] were outside my house four hours after the attack." This suggested that the FBI had known where Atta and Shehhi were all along. Hopsicker adds: "Like many eyewitnesses we spoke with, this longtime aviation executive spoke of being intimidated and harassed by FBI agents. They didn't strong-arm him to make him think harder and cough up some useful leads, but to ensure he kept his mouth shut. We've heard about this from other people, haven't we? It's becoming a refrain." This source had the following to say about Atta and his friends: "I thought these guys [Atta & Co.] were double agents." (Hopsicker 150) But Dekkers, who might easily have been arrested as a material witness, instead became a media personality, appearing on the Larry King interview program on CNN.

THE FALSE-FLAG AIR FORCE

According to some press accounts, as many as 27 al Qaeda operatives took flying lessons in the US in the months before 9/11. Before 2001, Dekkers had launched an aggressive marketing campaign in Europe to get foreigners to come to his flight school for training. One of his selling points was that it cost less to learn to be a pilot in the US than in Europe. Soon 80% of the students enrolled at Huffman Aviation were from abroad, and many were Arabs. About 400 foreign nationals were graduating every year from Huffman.

According to some reports, some Arab flight trainees who had been taking lessons at Huffman disappeared around the time of 9/11 – either a few days in advance or more or less simultaneously with the terror attacks. This is a hint of the hidden hands pulling the strings: intelligence agencies love to have a few spare patsies around who can be thrown into action at a moment's notice if some other patsy is arrested, killed, or incapacitated. After John Hinckley Jr.'s attempt to kill President Reagan in 1981, more than a dozen deranged loners with obsessions similar to Hinckley's were reported from police blotters in various parts of the US, according to intelligence reports at that time. The organizers of that hit, like the organizers of 9/11, took no unnecessary chances; they had redundant backup echelons of patsies ready to go in case they were needed.

Working with Dekkers and providing most of the funds was Wally J. Hilliard, who also had an interest in a nearby Lear Jet rental service. Hilliard had a special interest in Rum Cay in the Bahamas, a suspicious island patrolled by a single policeman. This island was said to be the scene of operations linked to Saudi moneybags Adnan Khashoggi, who figured prominently in Bush 41's and Oliver North's Iran-Contra gun-running operations during the 1908s. A Lear Jet belonging to Hilliard was seized by the DEA in July 2000 when it was found to be carrying 15 kilos of heroin on a flight back from Venezuela – a sizable amount. Hilliard and his company alleged that they were unaware of the narcotics, which they said had been brought on board by a passenger without their knowledge. Hilliard appeared also to have operated a more or less regular commuter air link with Havana, Cuba, something that is theoretically illegal because of the US embargo on all trade and other contacts with Castro's island – suggesting an operation sanctioned by the shadow world. (*Mad Cow Morning News* 32)

General aviation and commuter air services between Florida and the nearby islands are inextricably linked with drug-running, which was highlighted during the Iran-Contra hearings of the late 1980s, and which of course has never ceased. These operations are associated in the popular mind with Oliver North, but it should be recalled that the covert operations czar of the Reagan administration was of course Vice President George Bush, who directed every phase of Iran-Contra with the help of figures like Felix Rodriguez. (Tarpley 1992) This pattern was later confirmed by former DEA agent Celerino Castillo, who personally confronted Bush about drug running, but got no response. The DEA estimates that two thirds of the illegal drugs coming into the US pass through the Bahamas.

Journalists have speculated that Dekkers and Kruithof were cut-outs for a US intelligence operation at the Venice airport. Huffman Aviation was also the location of offices of Britannia Aviation, a small and undercapitalized company which surprisingly beat out better-known and better-connected firms to win a contract to provide maintenance services at Lynchburg Regional Airport in Virginia. At a hearing, one of Britannia Aviation's executives, Paul Marten, said that one of his main customers was Caribe Air, a reputed CIA proprietary which reportedly took part in Iran-Contra drug smuggling. Aircraft belonging to Caribe Air were seized by prosecutors at the airport in Mena, Arkansas, during that phase. Caribe Air had moved its headquarters to the island of Dominica. A source said that Britannia Aviation was a firm favored by the US Drug Enforcement Administration, from which it had received "a green light."

In the summer of 2002, Kruithof narrowly escaped death when the Twin Beech E 18 aircraft in which he was flying to Cancun, Mexico, crashed. At the same time, deportation procedures and fraud charges were in progress against Dekkers, who was involved in a helicopter crash in January 2003. Efforts were clearly being made to intimidate these two key witnesses, or to silence them. The Kean-Hamilton Commission had no time for Dekkers and Kruithof. (*Mad Cow Morning News*)

The accused hijackers' choice of Venice, Florida also allows us to locate them better in the recent history of covert operations. If we take the Bay of Pigs (1961), the Kennedy assassination (1963), Watergate (1972-74), Iran-Contra (exposed in 1986), and 9/11, we find that there is a single common denominator: Florida, the Miami Cubans, and Cuba generally. For the Bay of Pigs, Watergate, and Iran-Contra, the links are obvious: there is a continuity of people who populate these scandals, people like Felix Rodriguez who took part in the Bay of Pigs and then served as Bush 41's operative in Iran-Contra, or Frank Sturgis and his crew who link Howard Hunt's role in the Bay of Pigs with Watergate.

In the case of the Kennedy assassination the links are not quite so evident, but evident enough: Oswald was an activist of the Fair Play for Cuba Committee, the Bay of Pigs survivors hated Kennedy, and there is a persistent connection between Operation Mongoose, the US government plan to assassinate Castro, and the killing of JFK. George Bush 41 allegedly chartered the ships used by the CIA in the Bay of Pigs invasion, was part of the Kennedy assassination cover-up, was a leading Watergate figure, and directed most of what is known as Iran-Contra. Underlying many of these connections is the sinister presence of CIA Miami Station, which was created in the early 1960s as the CIA's large-scale domestic facility. This is the infamous JM/WAVE which is described in the unauthorized biography of George Bush. (Tarpley 1992) Not far away is the Hobe Sound/Jupiter Island complex, the wintering place for some of the most prominent oligarchical masters of human destiny.

Venice Airport was built by the government during World War II for pilot training. Not far away in Tampa is the headquarters of US Central Command, which wages the wars in Afghanistan and Iraq. Central Command is located at MacDill Air Force Base. There are indications of an NSA presence in Venice, as well. The legendary Mena, Arkansas airport was one of the airports used for gun running and drug running, but so was Homestead Air Force Base in Florida. In fact, there was hardly an airport in Florida and in the southern US generally that was not involved, and there is every reason to think that Venice was as well.

According to Hopsicker, "many of the flight trainers who had trained the Arab terrorist pilots had also flown missions out of the Venice-Sarasota airport for such Christian missionary services as televangelist Pat Robertson's Operation Blessing." One of the pilots who did the training at Huffman was Mike Mikarts, also a pilot for the fundamentalist "Agape Flights" of Sarasota which runs air missionary activity with obvious destabilization overtones in Haiti and the Dominican Republic.

After Venice, Atta and Shehhi rented planes from Kemper Aviation at North Palm Beach Airport near Miami in August 2001. Owner Joe Kemper spent 20 years in Peru and Bolivia as a "missionary pilot" for the evangelical-run SAMAIR (South American Mission Air) which worked to bring fundamentalism to Andes mountains Indio tribes. SAMAIR is a part of an international evangelical/Pentecostal air wing, often drawing on former military pilots, who are not accidentally often found in areas in the middle of civil wars, drug gangs, and mercenary intelligence operations in Third World countries. Additionally, Joe Kemper's chief pilot trainer between 1989 and 1999 was Jean-François Buslik, who was later arrested on murder charges filed in Belgium. Buslik was implicated in the 1982-85 Brabant killings, a wave of serial killings and de facto strategy of tension which claimed the lives of over 30 victims at supermarkets in the Brussels suburbs. These were no ordinary flight schools. (*Mad Cow Morning News* 41; EIR, October 26, 2001)

MOHAMED ATTA, PORK CHOP FUNDAMENTALIST

Atta's father was a well-to-do Egyptian lawyer. Atta was a mediocre student of architectural engineering at Cairo University, and his family wanted him to obtain an advanced degree. Atta's life changed when he was selected to participate in an elite exchange program originally set up between the US and Germany which had been expanded to include engineers from other countries as well. Atta was befriended in Cairo in 1992 by an obscure German couple who had taken him under their wing. Between 1995 and 1997, Atta was a member of the Congress-Bundestag Program, a joint project of the US State Department and the German Ministry of Economic Cooperation and Development. This program was administered by the Carl Duisberg Gesellschaft. located in Köln. (*Frankfurter Allgemeine Zeitung*, "Atta Was Tutor For Scholarship Holders," October 18, 2001; *Chicago Tribune*, March 7, 2003) Later, as a student in Hamburg, Atta had worked along with Shehhi and Binalshibh for Hay Computing Service GmbH in Hamburg. There has been speculation that this company was a front for intelligence agencies.

Atta arrived in Venice in late April or early May 2000. Hopsicker shows that during his time in Venice, Atta did not behave like a puritanical Wahhabite

Islamic fundamentalist of the bin Laden school. He rather appeared as a sybaritic hedonist and promiscuous playboy. He loved to attend topless bars, where he would order lap dances at the Pink Pony, or else stuff twenty dollar bills into the g-strings of the dancers at the Olympic Garden nightclub. He was also a regular at Harry's Bar in Naples. Atta's favorite nightspots were the Cheetah in Venice, and Margarita Maggie's in Sarasota. FBI investigators showing pictures of Atta after 9/11 found that he had been drinking Stolichnaya vodka for three hours recently; with him was accused suicide pilot Marwan al Shehhi, who preferred rum. Atta was also a frequent cocaine user. He would habitually snort rows of cocaine with a dollar bill. His source of cocaine was apparently located at or near Kruit-hof's Florida Flight Training Center at Venice airport. When Atta went back to Hamburg, he was under surveillance by the CIA. (*Mad Cow Morning News* 27)

Atta also cohabited with a 22-year old call girl who may also have been a sex operative for one of the intelligence agencies. Amanda Keller worked for a "lingerie model escort service" in Sarasota called Fantasies & Lace. Her personal appearance was described as "slutty;" she dressed "like a hooker," according to published reports. Her hair was dyed hot pink during the time she was with Atta. This was Amanda Keller, who was inexplicably ignored by the tabloids and intimidated by the FBI. Her constant refrain was: "I can't really discuss anything. I'm afraid I'll get in trouble." Not only Keller, many witnesses in and around Venice have been harassed and intimidated by the FBI. (Hopsicker 63-68)

On one occasion Atta took Amanda and two other friends on a three-day orgy and bender of nightclubs, drinking, and cocaine in Key West. A waitress recalled seeing Atta wearing lots of jewelry, perhaps including a large crucifix – "a big gaudy gold cross" and a "big watch." The waitress said that the conversation she overheard involving Atta and some others involved references to $200,000 and the need to answer to the "Family." Atta was also an eager eater of pork chops, another explicit violation of Islamic law. Atta's musical tastes inclined to the Beastie Boys. (*Mad Cow Morning News* 20, 30)

Atta and Amanda Keller lived together for two months. Keller says that her breakup with Atta began when he embarrassed her at the night club Margarita Maggie's in Sarasota. She recalled bitterly that "Mohammed, like a dumbass, was standing on top of a speaker dancing. The man could not dance to save his life. He was real stiff, just kind of shaking, doing the 'Roxbury head bob' thing. He just embarrassed me instantly with the people there, and I just pretended I didn't know him." Keller's attraction to Atta probably had something to do with money. Although he seemed to live in modest circumstances, Atta always had plenty of cash. He thought nothing of leaving a twenty dollar bill to cover a bar tab of $4.

According to Amanda Keller, Atta was also a cat-torturer. After she had thrown him out of the apartment they shared, Atta got back in and disemboweled her pet cat, leaving the remains on her kitchen table. He also dismembered five out of six kittens. As Keller remembered, "There were baby cat parts all over the place."

Atta was in Venice at least three times during the six weeks immediately before 9/11. He was seen in friendly conversation with Dekkers. Atta in particular had mastered the fine art of getting himself noticed and remembered when he wanted to. One witness spoke of Atta as a menacing presence: "He just stood back and glared at you with his dark eyes. It gave me a frightening feeling you wouldn't want to be caught in the parking lot at night with him." Another specialty was a nasty shout of "You do not speak to me unless I speak to you first" for anyone who approached him. Atta exchanged emails with employees at companies like Virtual Prototypes, a Canadian firm which works on sensitive projects for the Pentagon. He sent another email complaining that the American University in Cairo had dismissed a female student who had insisted on coming to class in her *niqab*, or face veil.

TERRORISTS FROM US MILITARY BASES

The other peculiarity about the alleged hijackers of 9/11 is that so many of them were directly linked to US military bases. According to press accounts, Atta attended the International Officers School at Maxwell Air Force Base in Montgomery, Alabama. Abdulaziz Alomari had attended the Aerospace Medical School at Brooks Air Force Base in Texas. Saeed Alghamdi had been to the Defense Language Institute at Monterrey, California. (*Washington Post*, September 15 and 17, 2001) According to *Newsweek* three of the FBI's group of 19 terror suspects had received training at Pensacola Naval Air Station in Florida, and listed their address as locations on that base. Most foreign students at these facilities are there because they are sponsored by governments within the US orbit. But some may be sponsored by the US directly – especially if agent recruitment is the object.

The *Newsweek* coverage, entitled "Alleged Hijackers May Have Trained at US Bases: The Pentagon has turned over military records on five men to the FBI," by George Wehrfritz, Catharine Skipp and John Barry, is especially instructive, and reads in part:

> Sept. 15 – US military sources have given the FBI information that suggests five of the alleged hijackers of the planes that were used in Tuesday's terror attacks received training at secure US military installations in the 1990s. Three of the alleged hijackers listed their address on drivers licenses and car registrations as the Naval Air Station in Pensacola, Fla.–known as the "Cradle of US Navy Aviation," according to a high-ranking US Navy source.

> Another of the alleged hijackers may have been trained in strategy and tactics at the Air War College in Montgomery, Ala., said another high-ranking Pentagon official. The fifth man may have received language instruction at Lackland Air Force Base in San Antonio, Tex. Both were former Saudi Air Force pilots who had come to the United States, according to the Pentagon source. But there are slight discrepancies

between the military training records and the official FBI list of suspected hijackers – either in the spellings of their names or with their birth dates. One military source said it is possible that the hijackers may have stolen the identities of the foreign nationals who studied at the US installations.

The five men were on a list of 19 people identified as hijackers by the FBI on Friday. The three foreign nationals training in Pensacola appear to be Saeed Alghamdi and Ahmad Alnami, who were among the four men who allegedly commandeered United Airlines Flight 93. That flight crashed into rural Pennsylvania. The third man who may have trained in Pensacola, Ahmed Alghamdi, allegedly helped highjack United Airlines Flight 175, which hit the south tower of the World Trade Center. Military records show that the three used as their address 10 Radford Boulevard, a base roadway on which residences for foreign-military flight trainees are located. In March 1997, Saeed Alghamdi listed the address to register a 1998 Oldsmobile; five months later he used it again to register a second vehicle, a late model Buick. Drivers licenses thought to have been issued to the other two suspects in 1996 and 1998 list the barracks as their residences. (*Newsweek*, September 15, 2001)

US government spokesmen issued less than ironclad denials, alleging that because of confusion among Arabic names, the accused hijackers had "probably" not been part of activities on the military bases cited. They were being confused with other Arabs with the same names, the military spokespersons suggested. The controlled corporate media soon stopped paying attention to this story. The *Newsweek* story quoted a former Navy pilot's comment that, during his years on the base, "we always, always, always trained other countries' pilots. When I was there two decades ago, it was Iranians. The shah was in power. Whoever the country *du jour* is, that's whose pilots we train." Evidently the country du jour was now "al Qaeda."

The intelligence community record in regard to two accused 9/11 suicide operatives was less than sterling. According to Michael Isikoff, these two were for a time the roommates of a seasoned informer. The two hijackers, Khalid Al-Mihdhar and Nawaf Al-Hazmi, had been known to the CIA since January 2000, when the two Saudi nationals showed up at a Qaeda summit in Kuala Lumpur, Malaysia. One had been a part of the attack on the USS *Cole*. As Isikoff reports:

Upon leaving Malaysia, Almihdhar and Alhazmi went to San Diego, where they took flight-school lessons. In September 2000, the two moved into the home of a Muslim man who had befriended them at the local Islamic Center. The landlord regularly prayed with them and even helped one open a bank account. He was also, sources tell *Newsweek*, a 'tested' undercover 'asset' who had been working closely with the FBI office in San Diego on terrorism cases related to Hamas. (*Newsweek*, September 15, 2001)

The FBI, of course, came up with the cover story that their paid informer had failed to inform the Bureau of the true identity of his two mysterious house-guests. The informant's name was Abdusattar Shaikh. The FBI later refused to let the JICI Congressional investigators talk to him, claiming that he could not add anything of interest. The JICI did not exercise its power of subpoena in order to hear this important witness. Nor did the 9/11 commission.

But the FBI also had to admit that the San Diego case agent involved knew that visitors were renting rooms in the informant's house. On one occasion, a source reported, the case agent called up the informant and was told he couldn't talk because 'Khalid'–a reference to Al-Mihdhar–was in the room. This makes it look like the case officer knew precisely who Khalid was. Isikoff cited I. C. Smith, a former top FBI counterintelligence official, as commenting that the case agent should have been more carefully supervising the people with whom his informant was fraternizing – among other things, to recruit the houseguests as possible informants. "They should have been asking, 'Who are these guys? What are they doing here?' This strikes me as a lack of investigative curiosity." He is on firm ground there; other counterintelligence people were "stunned" by the FBI's lassitude.

About six weeks after moving into the house, Al-Mihdhar left town, explaining to the landlord he was going back to Saudi Arabia to see his daughter. Al-Hazmi moved out at the end of 2000. It was not until August 23, 2001, that the CIA sent out an urgent cable to US border and law-enforcement agencies identifying the two men as possible terrorists. By then it was too late. The FBI did not realize the San Diego connection until a few days after 9/11, when the informant heard the names of the Pentagon hijackers and called his case agent. "I know those guys," the informant purportedly said, referring to Al-Mihdhar and Al-Hazmi. "They were my roommates."

FBI Director Mueller has repeatedly insisted there was nothing the bureau could have done differently to penetrate the 9/11 plot. That claim is patently absurd. In addition to the FBI, the alleged future hijackers were also under the scrutiny of the Israeli Mossad. The Mossad maintained a stakeout in Hollywood, Florida, and operated a safe house of their own close to the apartment where Atta and Shehhi lived. (*Die Zeit*, October 1, 2002)

COULD ATTA, SHEHHI, HANJOUR AND JARRAH PILOT LARGE AIRLINERS?

In addition to whether they were US agents or not, the big question regarding Atta, Shehhi, Hanjour, and Jarrah, just as it was in regard to Lee Harvey Oswald and Timothy McVeigh, is still: were they physically and mentally capable of carrying out the criminal actions ascribed to them? Patsies can always talk the talk – but can they walk the walk, meaning, is it within their power, above and beyond all criminal intent, to create the effects observed? If not, we have a case of physical impossibility – as we had in the cases of Oswald and McVeigh – and we must look further for the true culprits. Here follows an account from the mainstream press:

Atta, the alleged hijacker of Flight 11, and Shehhi, alleged hijacker of Flight 175, both of which crashed into the World Trade Center, attended hundreds of hours of lessons at Huffman Aviation. They also took supplementary lessons at Jones Aviation Flying Service Inc., which operates from the Sarasota Bradenton International Airport. According to the *Washington Post*, neither experience was successful. A flight instructor at Jones who asked not be identified said Atta and Al Shehhi arrived in September or October [2000] and asked to be given flight training. Atta, the instructor said, was particularly difficult. "He would not look at your face," the instructor said. "When you talked to him, he could not look you in the eye. His attention span was very short." The instructor said neither man was able to pass a Stage I rating test to track and intercept. After offering some harsh words, the instructor said, the two moved on .... "We didn't kick them out, but they didn't live up to our standards." (*Washington Post*, September 19, 2001) Could these substandard pilots execute the difficult feat of hitting the towers at high speed, flying by the seat of their pants?

HANI HANJOUR, MISFIT

So far we have heard little of Hani Hanjour, who is accused by the FBI of piloting American Airlines Flight 77 into the Pentagon. According to press reports, Hanjour had visited Bowie's Maryland Freeway Airport just north of Washington DC three times since mid-August 2001 as he attempted to get permission to use one of the airport's planes. But Hani Hanjour was simply too clumsy, too inept. The question is crucial, because the plane that hit the Pentagon performed a stunning maneuver of which many a seasoned pilot would have been proud. Instead, Hani Hanjour turns out to have been a pathetic misfit. The following account is from *The Prince George's Journal* (Maryland), September 18, 2001:

> Marcel Bernard, the chief flight instructor at the airport, said the man named Hani Hanjour went into the air in a Cessna 172 with instructors from the airport three times beginning the second week of August and had hoped to rent a plane from the airport. ...Hanjour had his pilot's license, said Bernard, but needed what is called a 'check-out' done by the airport to gauge a pilot's skills before he or she is able to rent a plane at Freeway Airport, which runs parallel to Route 50.

> Instructors at the school told Bernard that after three times in the air, they still felt he was unable to fly solo and that Hanjour seemed disappointed ... Published reports said Hanjour obtained his pilot's license in April of 1999, but it expired six months later because he did not complete a required medical exam. He also was trained for a few

months at a private school in Scottsdale, Ariz., in 1996, but did not finish the course because instructors felt he was not capable.

Hanjour had 600 hours listed in his log book, Bernard said, and instructors were surprised he was not able to fly better with the amount of experience. Pete Goulatta, a special agent and spokesman for the FBI, said it is an on-going criminal investigation and he could not comment.

Hani Hanjour is supposed to have executed a breathtaking 270-degree turn while descending from an altitude of 7,000 feet to below treetop level to hit the Pentagon, probably the most difficult maneuver performed by any of the kamikaze planes on 9/11. But he was not considered capable of flying solo in a Cessna! And what of Jarrah, the accused suicide pilot of United Airlines Flight 93, the plane that was destroyed near Shanksville, Pennsylvania? He was not much better as a pilot. Arne Kruithof later explained that, when Jarrah arrived to start taking lessons, "We had to do more to get him ready than others. His flight skills seemed to be a little bit out there." Jarrah did succeed in getting a pilot's license, but he was never able to qualify as a commercial pilot, despite 200 hours of flight time logged. According to Kruithof, "he was a guy who needed some more."

Jarrah's roommate was Thorsten Biermann of Germany. Although Biermann got along fairly well with Jarrah, he soon refused to fly anywhere with Jarrah at the controls. This was because of Jarrah's foolhardy refusal to refuel before a flight in bad weather. When they landed, the tank was almost empty. Biermann: "I decided I did not want to fly with him any more. Everyone I knew who flew with him felt the same way." (Longman 91-92)

AL QAEDA STALWARTS: DUMB AND DUMBER

Alleged Flight 77 hijackers Nawaf al-Hazmi, Khalid Al-Midhar and Hani Hanjour all spent time in San Diego, where they sought flight training. According to published accounts, "Two of the men, Alhazmi and Al-Midhar, also briefly attended a local flight school, but they were dropped because of their limited English and incompetence at the controls…. [In the spring of 2001], two of the men visited Montgomery Field, a community airport ... and sought flying lessons. They spoke to instructors at Sorbi's Flying Club, which allowed them to take only two lessons before advising them to quit. 'Their English was horrible, and their mechanical skills were even worse,' said an instructor, who asked not to be named. 'It was like they had hardly even ever driven a car ...They seemed like nice guys,' the instructor said, 'but in the plane, they were dumb and dumber.'" (*Washington Post*, September 24, 2001)

Rick Garza, Sorbi's chief flight instructor, told Al-Mihdhar and Al-Hamzi after two flights: "This is not going to work." Garza later said that the two "had no idea what they were doing." (*Washington Post*, September 30, 2001) They were always prattling about flying big jets, but when Garza asked one of them to draw a picture of a plane, **"He drew the wings on backwards."** (*Chicago Tribune*, September 30, 2001) "It was clear they weren't going to make it as pilots." (*London Observer*, October 7, 2001) These two would-be pilots, although they were allegedly the most experienced and hardened terrorists in the entire group of 19, were subject to panic attacks in the cockpit, at which time they would begin praying out loud. The official version does not assert that they acted as pilots, but the basis of this part of the official story is wrapped in mystery, like the rest of it.

In addition to the supposed four suicide pilots, the story told by the 9/11 commission also includes some 15 "muscle hijackers." These were the members of the suicide teams whose task it would be to break into the cockpits, overpower the pilot, copilot and other flight personnel using box cutters and knives, keep the passengers under control, and guard the door to the cockpit once it had been seized. According to the 9/11 commission, "the so-called muscle hijackers actually were not physically imposing, as the majority of them were between 5' 5" and 5' 7" in height and slender in build." (Staff Statement No. 16, 8) These, then, were the ferocious fighters that were expected to quell the resistance of airline pilots, most of them from military aviation, and many of them war veterans, to say nothing of flight attendants, stewardesses, and the general public.

What was the caliber and actual effectiveness of these figures? US propaganda has a vested interested in building them up as capable, even formidable individuals who had the ability to carry out the spectacular terrorism of 9/11. But sometimes the pathos of the patsies comes through. In Staff Report 16, "Outline of the 9/11 Plot," we read that Khalid Sheikh Mohammed (KSM, touted by the Bush regime as the "mastermind of the entire plot) "and Binalshibh have both stated that, in early 2000, Shehhi, Atta, and Binalshibh met with KSM in Karachi for training that included learning about life in the United States and how to read airline schedules." If they were still unable to read airline schedules on their own in the spring of 2000, these strange figures had a long way to go before 9/11. Be that as it may, the eyewitness accounts collected just after 9/11 seem to converge on the diagnosis that they were bunglers. According to one wag, they were the sort of people who could probably not obtain a drivers license in any state except New Jersey.

Accounts inspired by the official story generally try to portray the feats of Atta, Shehhi, and Hanjour as relatively easy. But when it comes to United 93 over Shanksville, the tone suddenly changes. Now the official version has to explain why the passengers, assuming they had already succeeded in taking back the cockpit from Jarrah & Co., were not able to land the plane. One of the passengers on United 93 was an experienced pilot of light planes who had also trained on a Falcon corporate jet simulator. Could this passenger have landed United 93? In his book on United 93, Jere Longman of the *New York Times* quotes Hank Krakowski, a 737 captain who was responsible for United's flight operations on 9/11. According to Krakowski, "If the guy was a professional pilot flying all the time, it would have been possible. If he was an occasional pilot, it would have been a pretty big challenge. You can get a boat into a dock, but it's a lot harder getting a cruise ship into a dock. The problem is the mass of the machine, the energy, the feel. It doesn't have the response of a smaller plane. It has much more kinetic energy. It takes training to get a feel for that." (Longman 188) These are of course the same problems that would have been faced by the hijackers, not in landing, but in hitting their targets. The prognosis for success in their case, without some form of outside help, could hardly have been much better.

WHY WERE THEY NOT ARRESTED?

During the summer of 2001, US intelligence agencies received numerous warnings from their foreign counterparts about the danger of coming terror attacks. MI-6 says that it alerted the US in 1999 to al Qaeda plans to use commercial aircraft as "flying bombs." In early August 2001, this warning was reiterated, this time specifying multiple airliner hijackings. Around the same time, the Cayman Islands told the US that al Qaeda was "organizing a major terrorist act against the US via an airline or airliner." In late July, Egypt informed the US that 20 al Qaeda agents were in the US, and that four had received flight training. In June, Germany warned the US that Middle Eastern terrorists were planning to use commercial airliners as weapons to attack "American and Israeli symbols which stand out." On September 7, Italy sent word of an attack on the US and UK using airplanes as weapons; the source was Father Jean Marie Benjamin, a leading expert on the Muslim world. In the late summer, Jordan sent the contents of an intercepted message, according to which a major attack, code named the Big Wedding, was imminent. It was to take place inside the US and employ aircraft, says this report. In August, Russia alerted the US to an attack by about 25 terrorists, including suicide pilots, who would attack "important buildings like the Pentagon."

In July, Taliban Foreign Minister Wakil Ahmed Muttawakil discovered that bin Laden is planning a "huge attack" inside the US. He sent an emissary to convey this information to the US consul general, and also to a US intelligence officer. In late July 2001, the Argentine Jewish community obtained news of a coming big attack against the US, Argentina, or France. This was passed on to the US. On July 16, MI-6 reported to Tony Blair that al Qaeda is "in the final stages" of a serious terrorist attack against the west. This was based on a reading of information from GCHQ, the British NSA, and also from the CIA and the NSA, which the British share according to a long-standing agreement with the US. In June, three Pakistani men in the Cayman Islands were overheard discussing a hijacking attack on New York. US intelligence was alerted. At the end of August, Egyptian President Mubarak personally warned US officials that bin Laden was about to attack an American target inside the US. France sent a generic warning in late August that something big was up. India added its own warning in mid-July. Israel, in early August, said that 50 to 200 al Qaeda terrorists are inside the US and intended "a major assault" aimed at "a large scale target." On August 23, Israel sent a list of 23 terrorists which contained the names of four later fingered by the FBI, including Atta. Also in August, Morocco warned of large-scale operations in New York in the autumn, possibly targeting the World Trade Center. Again in August, a Gulf prince told CIA veteran Robert Baer that a "spectacular terrorist operation" would take place shortly. Baer told a senior CIA official and the CIA's Counter-Terrorism Center. (cooperativeresearch.org)

Naturally, every government that could do so wanted to look good after 9/11, and putting out a report that they had tipped off the US in advance did wonders for the *amour-propre* of MI-6, Mossad, SDECE, SISMI, FSB, and the other agencies involved. So we have to take these reports *cum grano salis*. US officials deny that some of these reports were ever delivered, even the one that came from Mubarak personally, and that might even be true in some cases. But if even a quarter of these after-the-fact claims are true, that is a damning revelation for CIA, FBI, NSA, and the rest of the bloated, $40 billion per year intelligence community. And of course the 9/11 commission had no interest in foreign intelligence warnings; their report has no mention whatever of the intelligence superpowers MI-6 and Mossad, two of the most formidable and dangerous organizations on the planet, which any serious report would carefully scrutinize.

The reader should not be confused by the fact that many of these reports refer to al Qaeda and/or bin Laden. This organization exists after a fashion, but it exists in the specific form of a false flag operation: the sign above the door and the badges of the members, so to speak, say al Qaeda, and the ranting motivation-al speaker more often than not bin Laden. It is therefore perfectly possible for a witting mole, sitting in the CIA or FBI offices, to be edified by reading incoming reports about what his own patsies have been observed preparing. And we must remember that one of the specialties of patsies is getting noticed.

In the spring of 2002, the Bush regime went through an orgy of breast-beating about how impossible it would have been to stave off the 9/11 attacks. "I don't think that anybody could have predicted that these people would take an airplane and slam it into the World Trade Center, take another one and slam it into the Pentagon, that they would try to use an airplane as a missile," said the scowling Miss Rice. (May 16, 2002) Bush chimed in that "based on everything I've seen, I do not believe that anyone could have prevented the horror of September the 11th." (June 7, 2002) This is self-serving rhetoric.

However, in the summer of 2001, the Italian government received and acted on a similar series of warnings. At the time of the July 2001 world economic summit of the G-8 countries, the Italians cordoned off large areas of downtown Genoa which were declared off limits to unauthorized persons. Fighter jets patrolled overhead, while brigades of riot police dominated the streets. One can be sure that all leaves were cancelled for Italian police and troops in the area, and that no maneuvers were scheduled during those days to compete for manpower and attention with the anti-terror deployment. The entire air space above Italy's busiest port city was closed. Bush for his part stayed overnight on a US warship offshore. Some approximation of these measures might have materially altered the outcome on September 11.

WHAT DID THE HIJACKERS THINK THEY WERE DOING?

Patsies are led by deception, and deception is the art of making a person do something for one reason when the real reason is something quite different. If we are willing to make the rather large assumption that the 19 hijackers indeed boarded the four lost planes, of which there is no proof, they must have thought they were doing something. That is, they must have had some subjective intent of some kind. Did they believe that they were on a suicide mission? We are in the realm of pure speculation here, but there is no real proof of this either. Quite to the contrary: it is hard to imagine Atta, the assiduous drinker of vodka and frequenter of strip clubs, as a suicide operative, and the same goes for his confrères. Perhaps they thought this was going to be a traditional hijacking of some kind, from which they could hope to escape alive.

In any case, they took care to leave an abundant trail of evidence designed specifically to be found. This applies to the contents of the rented car found at the airport in Maine, and of the luggage supposedly left behind by Atta when his flight took off. Here the inventory includes an alleged last will and testament by Atta, which betrays the amateurish attempt of some half-baked area specialist to sound Islamic, as Robert Fisk and others have shown. We will not attempt to explain the miraculous survival of the hijacker's passport alleged to have been discovered near the World Trade Center after the fact. In order to fulfill their function, patsies must be directed to leave a trail of clues and evidence which will tie them and the larger target group they supposedly represent to the heinous actions they will be accused of. But in the 9/11 case, none of this material rises to the level of being convincing, on the contrary. We are left with the enigma: what did the hijackers, assuming that there were any, think they were doing on 9/11?

WERE THE ACCUSED HIJACKERS PHYSICALLY CAPABLE OF PILOTING THE PLANES?

The best opinions on the official story of hijackers piloting the airliners into buildings might come from experienced commercial airline pilots. There are few available opinions on this matter, as is understandable. The hegemony of the 9/11 myth has been very great among the population in general, and airline pilots as a group have special problems. Most of them are retired military officers, and they often move in circles where people with military backgrounds are common. If they are employed, they have to worry about their jobs. If they are retired, they may see no reason to get involved in a controversy that promises no gain, but only needless trouble for them personally. Nevertheless, there is enough evidence to substantiate the doubt that the four inept persons named in the official version would have been able to operate the aircraft in the way the observed phenomena indicate.

Flying a large modern commercial airliner is not especially demanding as long as the plane is taking advantage of its built-in guidance systems and computerized automatic pilot, which depend in turn on radio beacons, navigation aids, Global Positioning Satellites, and the like. As long as the plane sticks to its pre-arranged flight path, the pilot acts more like a superintendent than a driver. But the enterprise attributed to the hijackers changes all this. The hijackers are supposed to have abruptly wrenched the airliners out of the influence of all navigation aids, beacons, and positioning systems, and flown them by the seat of their pants to hit three demanding targets under conditions of conflict and stress inside the planes, and with the constant fear that fighter aircraft would soon pull up alongside, demanding to be followed. The issue is the transition from instrument flight techniques to visual flight rules and techniques in a context where all the usual instrument aids would have been inoperative.

Apart from the operation of the controls, there is also the question of how the hijackers could have navigated. On a fine clear day like September 11, 2001, it might be possible to follow certain natural features from one point to another, using landmarks for additional guidance. For the planes coming from Boston, one obvious expedient would have been to fly west, find the Hudson River, and then turn left towards New York City. But this is not what is shown on the maps offered by newspapers at the time. Instead of orienting towards natural features and landmarks, the planes fly strange detours, ignoring rivers and related navigation reference points. Real hijackers would have been concerned with reaching their targets as fast as possible, before they were overtaken by air defenses. But the 9/11 aircraft think nothing of deviating 50 miles in the wrong direction. All of this makes the official story implausible.

The 9/11 commission provided its own maps of the flight routes flown by the hijacked planes. Here there are pervasive anomalies that should have attracted the commission's curiosity, but did not. The hijackers did not choose the most direct routes to their targets, but flew long and dangerous detours. Real hijackers would have known that the greatest danger to their project was interception of their hijacked planes by US military aircraft. They could not have tolerated even the most minimal deviations from the direct path towards their goal. Another obvious course for American 11 would have been southwest across Rhode Island and Connecticut to the shore of Long Island Sound and thence down the East River to hit the North Tower. This would also have simplified navigation because of the constant orientation provided by the Connecticut coast, the Sound, and the north shore of Long Island. Instead, when it left its prescribed course, American 11 turned northwest, and came close to clipping the southwest corner of Vermont. It went well north of Albany before carrying out a 270-degree turn to then head approximately south, more or less following the Hudson River to New York City.

For United 175, the same course over Rhode Island, Connecticut, along Long Island Sound, and down the East River would have been the most direct and the most practical for amateur pilots of light planes. But according to the 9/11 commission's own map, this plane supposedly flew across southern New York state, across northern New Jersey, and entered Pennsylvania before finally turning back onto a northeasterly course towards the WTC south tower.

American 77 is even more difficult to discuss because of numerous anomalies. According to the 9/11 commission's own map, this plane is alleged to have flown all the way out to the meeting point of southern Ohio, Kentucky, and West Virginia before allegedly turning back towards Washington DC. The 9/11 commission map suppresses a five-minute jug-handle detour by this flight over the West Virginia panhandle along the way, which had attracted much curiosity and suspicion when it appeared in *USA Today* and other papers.

Finally, United 93, which took off last, went all the way across Pennsylvania, entered northern Ohio, and was west of Cleveland when it finally turned back towards the east.

Real hijackers could never have indulged in these interminable detours. Time was of the essence for the success of their crimes, and they would have had to choose far more direct routes in the case of each and every one of the 9/11 aircraft. This pattern raises the level of suspicion about the coherence of the official version, and suggests that reality was not what the 9/11 commission and its predecessors claimed it was.

MUBARAK'S CRITIQUE

In a CNN interview on September 15, 2001, Egyptian President Hosni Mubarak commented about the 9/11 events. His testimony is of interest because he spent his military career as a fighter pilot in the Egyptian Air Force. Mubarak was also one of the world leaders who had tried to warn the US government about what was coming in the summer of 2001. Mubarak said first of all that he found the US government's official version, which was then taking shape, technically implausible. Mubarak: "Not any intelligence capability in the world could say they are going to use commercial planes with passengers on board to crash the towers, to crash the Pentagon, those who did that should have flown in the area for a long time, for example. The Pentagon is not very high, a pilot could come straight to the Pentagon like this to hit, he should have flown a lot in this area to know the obstacles which could meet him when he is flying very low with a big commercial plane to hit the Pentagon in a special place. Somebody has studied this very well, someone has flown in this area very much."

Sensing a challenge to the orthodoxy of the official version, the CNN reporter countered: "Are you suggesting it was an inside operation? I may ask, who do you think was behind this?" Mubarak: "Frankly speaking, I don't want to jump to conclusions…something like this done in the United States is not an easy thing for pilots who had been training in Florida, so many pilots go and train just to fly and have a license, that means you are capable to do such terrorist action? I am speaking as a former pilot, I know that very well, I flew very heavy planes, I flew fighters, I know that very well, this is not an easy thing, so I think we should not jump to conclusions for now." (Meyssan 2002 26) One senses that Mubarak is restraining his skepticism for diplomatic reasons; he does not believe the official story, and he has good reasons for not doing so. (www.ahram.org.eg/weekly/2001/557/intrvw.htm)

NIKKI LAUDA: ACTUAL FLIGHT EXPERIENCE ON BOEINGS WAS REQUIRED

On the day after 9/11, two experienced German airline pilots, both veterans of many hours at the controls of Boeing 757s and 767s, agreed in the course of a September 12 prime time television broadcast that neither a real professional flight simulator, nor less flight simulation software on a PC even less, could ever suffice to impart the skills demonstrated by the supposed 9/11 suicide pilots. They were asked by host Guenter Jauch whether the hijackers could have flown the planes.

Captain Joerg Kujak's evaluation: "No. It's not that simple," whatever many laymen might think. "That wouldn't work. An amateur is not capable of steering a large commercial airliner anywhere with accuracy, neither with the automatic pilot, nor, with his hands on the controls. He would need training for that, and that does not necessarily have to last three years, the way normal pilot training in a flight school goes, but it has to go on for a certain amount of time. He needs basic training in the specific type of plane or on a jet in general, and through that he has to learn how to fly manually. With a PC you don't get the same feeling, for example for the trim tabs, for the steering yoke, for the change of situations. If you put your foot on the gas, then a jet rears up, because it has its engines under the wings, and that would be too much for an amateur, that can't be done without training."

Nikki Lauda, a legendary Formula One race driver, was a pilot and the founder of his own airline. He was asked by Jauch: "Is it easy to learn, we've seen that a video was found in a car near the Boston airport, and people think that the car belonged to a kidnapper, who had used it to bone up in advance on what the inside of a cockpit looks like. Is it so simple, for example, to learn that with the help of a computer simulator?"

Lauda judged that "these gentlemen were properly trained to fly a plane like that." In particular, he stressed that "you have to know exactly what the turning radius of a plane like that is, if I am trying to hit the World Trade Center. That means, these had to be fully trained 767 or 757 pilots, because otherwise they would have missed. It certainly could not be the case that some half-trained pilot tries it somehow, because then he will not hit it. That's not so easy, coming out of a curve....If he's coming out of a curve, then he has to know precisely the turning radius that derives from the speed of the plane in order to be able to calculate it, so that he will hit right there."

Jauch asked which was harder to hit, the World Trade Center or the Pentagon. Lauda: "Well, what impressed me is the organization of this whole operation, since without good weather it would have not been possible at all, because then you can't see anything. These were visual flights, using VFR [visual flight rules] as we call them. And so the World Trade Center is relatively easy to find, because it is stands out so tall.... The Pentagon is another matter again, because it is a building that is relatively flat. That means, they had to be trained well enough that they had flown around in the air in the New York area, I would speculate, so they could see the scene from above of where the building is located and how you could best reach it." To hit a flat building like the Pentagon is "an even more difficult case" than the World Trade Center. Lauda: "That means, to fly downwards out of a curve, and still hit the building in its core, I would have to be the best trained of all. I would speculate that a normal airline pilot would have a hard time with that, because you are simply not prepared for things like that. That means, they must have had some super-training to have been able to handle an airliner so precisely."

Could this have been done with the best, most expensive professional flight simulator, asked Jauch. For Lauda, the flight simulator was only a prerequisite. "I don't think a simulator by itself would be enough to know all the New York landscapes, and to know exactly what angle to use to fly in there. I believe that these people had actually flown these airliners; they could have been pilots from some airline or the other, just to get this feeling for the plane – in real flight, not on a simulator – so they could then carry out this act of terror." (Wisnewski 38-40) Of course, not even the FBI has ever ascribed such thorough training to the accused suicide pilots; practice on a 757 or 767 was not available at Huffman Aviation.

THE GRANDPRE SEMINAR

In the days after 9/11, a private group of US military and civilian pilots held a seminar to evaluate this crucial feature of the official story – could the hijackers have flown the planes with the requisite accuracy? After 72 hours of deliberation and discussion, they issued a press release summarizing their findings: "The so-called terrorist attack was in fact a superbly executed military operation carried out against the USA, requiring the utmost professional military skill in command, communications and control. It was flawless in timing, in the choice of selected aircraft to be used as guided missiles and in the coordinated delivery of those missiles to their pre-selected targets." The seminar report expressed grave doubt as to whether the alleged hijackers, supposedly trained on Cessna light aircraft, could have located a target dead-on 200 miles or more from their takeoff point. The participants also called into question the ability of the hijackers to operate within the intricacies of the instrument flight rules (IFR) during the interval between their takeover of the planes and the moment of impact. One of the organizers of the seminar, retired Colonel Donn de Grand-pre, said that it would be impossible for novices to have taken control of the four aircraft and orchestrated such a complicated operation, which obviously had as a prerequisite military precision of the highest order. The seminar concluded that it was likely that the hijackers were not the ones in control of the aircraft. One participant in the seminar was a US Air Force officer who flew over 100 sorties during the Vietnam war. This experienced combat pilot concluded that "Those birds either had a crack fighter pilot in the left seat, or they were being maneuvered by remote control."

Another spokesman for the group was identified as Captain Kent Hill (USAF retired), who was reportedly a friend of Chic Burlingame, the pilot of the plane that crashed into the Pentagon. Hill recalled that the US had already carried out multiple flights of an unmanned aircraft, similar in size to a Boeing 737, between Edwards Air Force base in California across the Pacific to South Australia. Hill said this plane had flown on a pre-programmed flight path under the supervision of a pilot in an outside station.

Other expert witnesses at the inquiry were of the opinion that airliners could be controlled by electromagnetic pulse or radio frequency instrumentation from command and control platforms based either in the air or at ground level. Captain Hill maintained that the four airliners must have been choreographed by an Airborne Warning and Control System (AWACS). This system can engage several aircraft simultaneously by knocking out their on-board flight controls.

According to press accounts, the pilot seminar also pointed to the inherent problems of the official account. In this, they drew on their own experience and the likely reactions of pilots like themselves. "All members of the inquiry team agreed that even if guns were held to their heads, none of them would fly a plane into a building. Their reaction would be to ditch the plane into a river or a field, thereby safeguarding the lives of those on the ground. A further question raised by the inquiry was why none of the pilots concerned had alerted ground control. It stated that all pilots are trained to punch a four-digit code into the flight control's transponder to warn ground control crews of a hijacking – but this did not happen." The veteran pilots were also surprised by what had not happened. They noted that the pilots and crews of the hijacked aircraft had not taken any evasive action to resist the supposed hijackers. They had not attempted any sudden changes in flight path or nose-dive procedures – which led them to believe that they had no control over their aircraft.

A reporter from the *Portugal News*, the largest English-language publication in that country, sought an independent evaluation of these findings from Captain Colin McHattie of Algarve, Portugal. McHattie, a pilot with 20 years' experience, was then currently working for Cathay Pacific. He agreed with the independent commission's findings. He added that, while it is possible to fly a plane from the ground, the installation of the necessary equipment is a time-consuming process, and needs extensive planning. The pilots' seminar sent a copy of their findings to the White House, but there was no response. (*Portugal News*, August 3, 2002)

HYPOTHESIS: GLOBAL HAWK

The insuperable problems posed by the notion that the four misfits and patsies of the official version actually flew the planes can, however, be satisfactorily explained with the help of a hypothesis involving the application of a technology which is known to exist. This is Global Hawk, a guidance system developed by the Defense Advanced Research Projects Agency (DARPA) for the Pentagon. Global Hawk is a robot plane, the modern form of remote control, which has been a familiar concept for decades – at the very least since the 1950s, when Nike missiles and Skysweeper radar-controlled antiaircraft guns used remote-controlled drones for testing. Global Hawk is a somewhat more advanced and sophisticated version of the guidance system of the Predator drone, which has been used to attack supposed targets (and a wedding party) in Afghanistan. Predators were available during the later years of the Clinton administration.

Global Hawk became widely known as a result of its first transpacific flight, which took place in April 2001. The new weapons system was touted by the media in glowing terms:

> The Global Hawk, a jet-powered aircraft with a wingspan equivalent to a Boeing 737, flew from Edwards Air Force Base in California and landed late on Monday at the Royal Australian Air Force base at Edinburgh, in South Australia. The 8600 mile (13840 km) flight, at an altitude of almost 12.5 miles (20 km), took 22 hours and set a world record for the furthest a robotic aircraft has flown between two points. The Global Hawk flies along a pre-programmed flight path, but a pilot monitors the aircraft during its flight via a sensor suite which provides infra-red and visual images.

According to Rod Smith, who managed the Australian end of the Global Hawk project, "The aircraft essentially flies itself, right from take-off, right through to landing, and even taxiing off the runway." The robot plane version of Global Hawk reportedly could fly non-stop for 36 hours. "Emerging systems such as the Global Hawk offer Australia great potential for surveillance, reconnaissance and ultimately the delivery of combat power," crowed Brendan Nelson, parliamentary secretary to the Australian defense minister. (ITN Entertainment April 24, 2001)

The existence of this technology in a fully operational form raises the possibility that it might have been installed in commercial airliners, and further that it may have been such airliners under the control of a Global Hawk equivalent which crashed into the WTC and the Pentagon. This entire matter is covered with secrecy, but it is clear that it is technically quite feasible that commercial jets were equipped with remote control systems capable of piloting them to landings (or to crashes) under the pretext of an anti-terrorism measure. The rationale would have been that, if terrorists took over the plane, authorities on the ground would be able to frustrate the terrorists by seizing control of the hijacked airliners and flying them to safety. However, for such a system to be effective, it would have to include the ability of ground controllers to deny the personnel occupying the cockpit – the terrorists and the pilots under their control – any ability to steer the plane. Activating it would simultaneously de-activate the cockpit controls, making them useless. Otherwise, the hijackers might find ways to override the commands to the servomechanisms, flight surfaces and avionics being issued through Global Hawk from the ground. Total control of the plane, in other words, would have to be on the ground.

The advantages of such a system against classical hijack scenarios are clear. If the hijackers tell the pilot, "Fly to Cuba," and threaten to kill him if he does not do so, the plane can be landed in Miami no matter what the hijackers do or do not do, all thanks to Global Hawk. But what happens if the Global Hawk ground control center falls into the hands of a group of moles bent on insurrection and subversion, and determined to use aircraft as missiles in support of their attempt to re-order world affairs along the lines of the clash of civilizations doctrine? Here we can see that Global Hawk has an enormous potential for abuse. There is every reason to believe that the events of 9/11 were rendered possible, not by superhuman piloting skills on the part of the patsies, but by competent professionals using Global Hawk and operating out of a ground control center or an airborne command center such as AWACS.

There would be nothing new about any of this. Modern aircraft are equipped with a "Flight Control System" or FCS, which is integrated with sophisticated avionics capable of automatically landing the aircraft in zero visibility conditions. Even the takeoff and landing of large jets in largely automated, and the role of the pilots is more and more that of standing by for the unlikely eventuality that the guidance systems fail. To produce events of the type seen on 9/11, it would only be necessary for the computer access codes of an aircraft equipped with Global Hawk to fall into the hands of moles and professional experts with treasonous designs.

As aeronautical engineer Joe Vialls has pointed out, the main prerequisite for the use of Global Hawk in the manner suggested would be the installation of a back door on a plane's computer system so as to allow an interface with the Global Hawk command post located elsewhere. Vialls says that DARPA has indeed provided these back doors on certain aircraft. These aircraft came to be equipped with "a primary control channel for use in taking over the flight control system and flying the aircraft back to an airfield of choice, and secondly a covert audio channel for monitoring flight deck conversations. Once the primary channel were activated, all aircraft functions came under direct ground control, permanently removing the hijackers and pilots from the control loop." Vialls states that he is a former member of the Society of Licenced Aeronautical Engineers and Technologists, London, but this could not be corroborated.

The Global Hawk hypothesis also helps explain one of the singularities of 9/11, which is that none of the transponders in the hijacked planes ever broadcast the coded message telling ground controllers that the planes had been hijacked. The transponder is a combined radio transmitter and radio receiver which sends out signals announcing each flight's airline name and flight number, and thus indicating the plane's position. This is a supplement to radar, and becomes more important than radar for flight controllers in busy aviation corridors. Vialls' hypothesis is that Global Hawk operated by taking over the transponder channel and monopolizing it for the purpose of controlling the plane. So no airliners signaled that they had been hijacked, because the transponder channel which could have sent this code had been usurped for remote control. Vialls regards the lack of such coded hijack warning signals as "the first hard proof that the target aircraft had been hijacked electronically from the ground, rather than by motley crews of Arabs toting penknives."

According to Vialls, the remote control "listening device on the flight deck utilizes the cockpit microphones that normally feed the Cockpit Voice Recorder (CVR), one of two black boxes armored to withstand heavy impact and thereby later give investigators significant clues to why the aircraft crashed." But once the remote control protocol has been activated, the "CVRs are bypassed and voice transmissions are no longer recorded on the 30-minute endless loop recording tape." In this case, after 30 minutes the CVR, which is designed to record the last minutes before a crash, will end up totally blank. This would explain the fact that the CVRs from the Pentagon and Pittsburgh aircraft were both claimed by the FBI to have been blank. For Vialls, this would be an additional indication that remote control had been employed.

It is not known if other US commercial aircraft have been equipped with back doors and interfaces permitting remote control by means of a technology cognate with Global Hawk. Vialls tells the story of a European carrier, possibly Lufthansa, which removed the flight control computers which had come with its Boeings as original equipment, and replaced them with computers impervious to Global Hawk, but this has yet to be confirmed. He also speculates that up to 600 US aircraft may still be vulnerable to Global Hawk. (www.pratyeka.org/wtc/wot/home_run.htm)

After 9/11, a special aviation radio was found in a safe in the Millennium Hilton Hotel near the World Trade Center. The radio was a transceiver of the type used by pilots to communicate air-to-air and air-to-ground. The FBI detained Abdallah Higazy, the son of an Egyptian diplomat, who was staying in the room in which the safe with the transceiver was located. Higazy was released on January 17, 2002 when it was established that the transceiver belonged to another hotel guest who was a private pilot. Since this pilot was neither Egyptian nor Arab, he was automatically exempted from suspicion – another example of the racist incompetence of the FBI. This transceiver might have been a radio beacon or a positioning or homing device of some kind. During the 1999 bombing of Serbia, the government there accused NATO agents of placing radio beacons at key points in Belgrade to aid in the bombing campaign. (Associated Press, January 17, 2002)

THE 9/11 SCENARIO ON FOX ENTERTAINMENT

As so frequently happens in the world of US intelligence, the concept for this operation was popularized before the fact in a scenario film. This drama was entitled "The Lone Gunmen," and was broadcast by the Fox Entertainment Network on March 4, 2001. The writers were John Shiban, Vince Gilligan, and Frank Spotnitz, the director Rob Bowman. The filming was done in New York City and Vancouver, Canada between March 20 and April 7, 2000. Among the stars were Tom Braidwood, Dean Haglund, Bruce Harwood, and Zuleikha Robinson. This was the pilot for a series of thirteen episodes, after which Fox discontinued the series.

In this film, the good guys board Atlantic National Flight 265 for its 6:50 PM takeoff from gate 34 at Boston's Logan Airport – just like Atta and Shehhi in the official story. The good guys are fighting a governmental power named Overlord which they believe is going to try to destroy Atlantic National 265. The good guys think they are dealing with a bomb, so they bring along some mini hydro-carbon sniffers to locate the explosives. But Overlord is not using bombs this time: the airplane is seized by a mysterious remote control system against which the pilot is helpless; the controls do not respond. The plane seems headed to-wards New York City, and soon the twin towers of the World Trade Center loom ahead. Realizing what is happening, the good guys use their laptop to attempt to hack into the Overlord computer. At first it seems like it will take seven to ten days to defeat Overlord's defenses, but the good guys access the remote control system just in time with the help of the new Octium IV computer chip. They take back control of the airplane, which misses the World Trade Center towers by a hair. (http://www.tvtome.com/servlets/EpisodeGuideSummary/showid-38/.)

DOPPELGÄNGER, PHANTOMS, AND APPARITIONS

In 1995, Ziad Jarrah rented an apartment in Brooklyn, and reportedly worked as a photographer. The signed and dated lease is convincing proof of the presence of this Ziad Jarrah in New York. But there was another Ziad Jarrah, who was 20 years old and living with his family in Beirut, Lebanon. This Jarrah left home in 1996, when he went to study in Germany, where he found an ethnic Turkish fiancée to whom he was engaged to be married; their engagement was cut short by 9/11. One Ziad Jarrah was questioned on January 30, 2001 at Dubai Airport at the request of the CIA on suspicion of involvement in terror activities. The other Ziad Jarrah, a student at Kruithof's Florida Flight Training Center in Venice, was visiting his family and sick father in Beirut. Jarrah was among the more convivial of the accused terrorists, and would go for beers with Kruithof. It would appear that the fake (Brooklyn) Jarrah obtained a pilot's license in Hamburg before the real (Beirut) Jarrah got his in Florida. Jarrah clearly had a double – or *Doppelgänger*, from the German – who resembled him to some extent. Doubles are an infallible sign of an intelligence agency operation. (www.cooperativeresearch.org/essay.jsp?article=essayjarrah)

During the month of August 2001, the San Diego trio of Al-Hamzi, Al Midhar and Hanjour went traveling. One or two of them were at various times reported as sighted in Falls Church, Virginia getting illegal drivers licenses. They were in Las Vegas, and then in Baltimore, followed by ten days in New Jersey. Sightings were then reported in southern Maryland. However, their neighbors at the Parkwood Apartments in San Diego said that Al Hazmi, Al Midhar, and Hanjour had all stayed put in San Diego until about September 1, or perhaps as late as September 8. The use of doubles is standard intelligence practice in synthetic terrorism. If there is something the terrorist controllers need a patsy to do, but which the patsy is unwilling or incapable of accomplishing, then a double will step in to see that the necessary action is indeed carried out. At times in 1963 there were two or perhaps even three Lee Harvey Oswalds.

"KSM"

In the spring of 2002, it was announced that a certain Khalid Sheikh Mohammed had been the "mastermind" of 9/11. When this same KSM was allegedly captured by the US, this event was hailed by Porter Goss as an event equal in world-historical importance to the liberation of Paris from the Nazis in 1944. From the very beginning, the overblown KSM story has been a magnet for world skepticism. When the US media showed a video tape of what was supposed to be the capture of KSM, Geraldo Rivera reported that "foreign journalists looking at it laughed and said this is baloney." (Fox News, Hannity and Colmes, March 10, 2002) Gerhard Wisnewski has shown that the account of KSM presented by Nick Fielding and Yosri Fouda in their study *Masterminds of Terror* – billed as the last word on KSM – lacks all probative elements. (Wisnewski 203 ff) The US government has never produced KSM for a trial, so everything that is alleged about him is pure hearsay, and thus to be discounted. One of the glaring incongruities of the 9/11 commission report is the degree to which unsubstantiated allegations about al Qaeda operations are regarded as proven simply because they allegedly came from KSM, who ranks as one of the star witnesses of the final report. He was later pressed into service as the alleged murderer of *Wall Street Journal* reporter Daniel Pearl in Pakistan.

THE LIVING DEAD

There is also the possibility that Nawaf Al Hazmi and Salem Al Hazmi are still alive. According to press accounts, accused hijackers Salem Al Hazmi was reported alive and well and working at a petrochemical plant in Yanbu, Saudi

Arabia after 9/11. (*Guardian*, September 21, 2001) Of the others on the FBI's list, a Waleed al-Shehri turned out to be alive in Casablanca, Morocco, working as a pilot with Saudi Arabian Airlines. An Abdulaziz al-Omari was also reported alive, and complaining that he had lost his passport in Denver. A Saeed al-Ghamdi was also alive and working as a pilot in Saudi Arabia. Khalid al-Midhar was also reported alive. (Marrs 17-18) Saudi Arabian Foreign Minister Saud al-Faisal noted that "it was proved that five of the names included in the FBI list had nothing to do with what happened" after his meeting with Bush on September 20, 2001. The FBI, contemptuous as always of both the truth and world public opinion, has stubbornly refused to revise the list of accused hijackers.

BEHIND THE AIR DEFENSE DEBACLE: 9/11 MANEUVERS

On 9/11, US air defense collapsed. Before and after 9/11, US air defense functioned more or less normally. What happened on 9/11 to create this paralysis, and why was that date such an anomaly in comparison to the previous and subsequent operation of the Federal Aeronautics Administration/North American Aerospace Defense Command tandem? The heart of the cover-up of these events performed by the 9/11 commission can be found in the section sub-headed "Clarifying the Record," on page 31. The 9/11 commission here concedes that "the defense of US airspace on 9/11 was not conducted in accord with pre-existing training and protocols." (31) Why then were the well-established procedures suddenly abandoned, for that one day? On this crucial point the 9/11 commission's impressionist-empiricist account is silent.

What the 9/11 commission should have done, but did not do, was to prepare an honest timeline and then compare that timeline to the notification times as they would have been had the standard procedures been followed, rather than mysteriously thrown out the window. They would have found that American 11 (North Tower) stopped transmitting its IFF beacon and veered sharply off course at 8:20 AM. It was thus at 8:20 that FAA should have notified NORAD, and NORAD should have scrambled interceptors. Instead, the FAA waited until 8:38, and NORAD pilots at Otis AFB on Cape Cod were not informed of the emergency until 8:40, were not ordered to take off until 8:46, and did not actually get into the air until 8:52. By this time American 11 had already hit the World Trade Center, at 8:46. The pilots flew slowly and did not arrive over New York in time to protect the WTC South Tower, which was hit at 9:03. At this time the Otis jets were still 71 miles away.

Similarly, the hijacking of United 175 was evident at 8:42, when the aircraft went off course and its transponder was turned off. This time NORAD was told within a minute, by 8:43, but was unable to scramble any additional planes from bases in New Jersey, despite the fact that multiple hijackings were now evident.

The 9/11 commission also found that on that day US air defense "was improvised by civilians who had never handled a hijacked aircraft that attempted to disappear, and by a military unprepared for the transformation of commercial aircraft into weapons of mass destruction." (31) This is dishonest in the extreme. The long-established defenses against traditional, classical, or normal hijacking would also have been effective against the suicide hijacking that the 9/11 commission claimed was involved this time. One suspects that Philip Zelikow, the controversial Executive Director of the 9/11 commission, is attempting to provide cover for his former business partner Condoleezza Rice, who had made that absurd remark on precisely this subject ("I don't think anybody could have predicted that these people would take an airplane and slam it into the World Trade Center, take another one and slam it into the Pentagon, that they would try to use an airplane as a missile, a hijacked airplane as a missile." [May 16, 2002]) As Miss Rice knew or should have known, these scenarios had been prominent since the mid-1990s, since the Atlanta Olympics, since the threatened attack on the Eiffel Tower in Paris, since the 2001 Genoa summit, and were routinely one of the main themes of military exercises on various levels. Zelikow and Rice were both rewarded with promotions, with Zelikow serving as Counselor to Rice in her new post as Secretary of State.

Why was it necessary to improvise US air defense? Before and after 9/11, the air defense system was noted primarily for its stability and regularity in responding to any emergency. An emergency was defined objectively as a plane that went off course, a plane that did not respond to radio communication, a plane whose transponder went off, or a plane that refused to obey the instructions of an air traffic controller. If any one of these conditions were fulfilled, an emergency had to be declared, and fighters had to be scrambled for intercept. Intercept did not mean shooting down any aircraft; intercept simply meant that fighters would join the aircraft in trouble, carry out visual observation, and signal the pilot to follow them to a landing place. Only if these attempts failed, would shooting down an aircraft become an option. And shooting down would have to be approved by the President.

The great virtue of its system was its automatic functioning, which was recognized by all concerned. The criteria were all objective. If there were any doubt that an incident had to be treated as an emergency, it was automatically upgraded to an emergency. Nothing fell between the chairs as long as the guidelines were observed. Before and after 9/11, the FAA/NORAD link worked like a well-oiled machine. Sixty-seven cases of successful intercept were carried out by the FAA-NORAD combination between January 1 and September 10, 2001.

STANDARD PROCEDURES: PAYNE STEWART, 1999

On October 26, 1999, a Lear Jet carrying the famous golfer Payne Stewart veered off course and traveled for 1500 miles across the United States before crashing into a field near Mina, South Dakota. Stewart had intended to fly to

Love Field in Dallas for a business meeting. Stewart took off from Orlando, Florida at 9:19 in the morning. His plane apparently lost oxygen pressure, leading to the deaths of the passengers. The plane proceeded on automatic pilot. The air traffic controllers stopped getting responses to their radio contacts with Stewart's plane. Following established procedures, FAA air traffic controllers called NORAD to inform them that something had gone wrong with a plane in the air. As soon as it was clear that Stewart's plane was in distress, the US Air Force scrambled two F-15s from Eglin Air Force Base, Florida, which intercepted the plane and followed it to Missouri. According to published accounts, fighter jets intercepted Stewart's jet in either 15 or 21 minutes after his plane first lost contact. An F-16 fighter aircraft came up behind it and did a visual inspection. The pilot said the windows of Stewart's plane were frosted over.

Two F-15s from Tyndall Air Force Base in Florida had also been sent to track the Lear Jet, but they turned away when the Eglin planes got there first. After the Lear Jet reached the Midwest, the two Eglin F-16s returned to base and four F-16s and a midair refueling tanker from the Tulsa National Guard followed it. Finally, four F-16s from Fargo, North Dakota moved in; they also helped to clear air space. According to the Air Force, additional F-16s were also scrambled from the Oklahoma Air National Guard unit in Tulsa, but were not used because the Fargo planes arrived first. Two additional F-16s on "strip alert" at Fargo, South Dakota, were armed, but never took off. This is a fair sample of the capabilities NORAD could normally deploy if it wanted to.

The Pentagon said it never came close to shooting down Stewart's plane in order to prevent a crash into a heavily populated area. Pentagon spokesman Ken Bacon said, "Once it was determined it was apparently going to crash in a lightly populated area, we didn't have to deal with other options, so we didn't." The FAA routed air traffic around the Lear Jet and prevented other planes from flying underneath it, in case it should suddenly lose altitude. (CNN, ABC, October 26, 1999) Andrews Air Force Base is 12 miles from the White House, and on 9/11 was the home of a fighter squadron of F-16s as well as one of F/A-18 Hornets.

A change in the standard operating procedures was introduced on June 1, 2001; this inserted the Secretary of Defense into the bureaucratic chain. This marked a radical departure from procedures which had been in successful operation for some 35 years. Now, the approval of the Secretary of Defense was required for the scrambling of aircraft. The authority to order the shooting down of an aircraft remained with the president. There may have been something more afoot here than simply adding another layer of bureaucracy. The authors of this change may have been seeking to introduce that element of disorder and uncertainty which might be necessary in order to allow the success of the upcoming operation. Who was responsible for this needless change, which amounted to a kind of passive stand-down order? The 9/11 commission, as usual, is silent.

THE 9/11 COMMISSION'S FUDGED TIMELINES

The 9/11 commission was also guilty of doctoring the timelines of the key events of the day. These timelines had been established and empirically validated by a number of researchers, including Mike Ruppert, Paul Thompson, and others. The timelines had been assembled by an exhaustive collation of media reports, and, apart from a detailed analysis which need not detain us here, they provided conclusive demonstration that NORAD had ample time to scramble fighter jets to intercept American 77 (Pentagon) and United 93 (Shanksville). If the system had performed according to its own strict protocols, there would also have been a fighting chance to intercept American 11 (North Tower) and United 175 (South Tower).

But the 9/11 commission, in a sweeping and breathtaking revision of everything that was known about the chronology of the day, writes: "As it turned out, the NEADS air defenders had nine minutes' notice on the first hijacked plane, no advance notice on the second, no advance notice on the third, and no advance notice on the fourth." (31) NEADS is NORAD's Northeast Air Defense Operations Center. For the 9/11 commission, it would appear that the longer the crisis went on, the less the lead time available for NORAD. During the time between 8:55 and 9:41 the whole world knew (or thought it knew) that American 77 was headed east towards Washington; when even the Washington news stations were warning that the capital was a likely target, NORAD was incapable of providing two planes over Washington DC to provide a minimal screen against the threatened decapitation of the federal government.

The 9/11 commission hypocritically pretended that it was setting the record straight: "More than the actual events, inaccurate government accounts of those events made it appear that the military was notified in time to respond to two of the hijackings, raising questions about the adequacy of the response. Those accounts had the effect of deflecting questions about the military's capacity to obtain timely and accurate information from its own sources. In addition, they overstated the FAA's ability to provide the military with timely and useful information that morning." (34)

Underlying this obfuscation is a strategic decision by the 9/11 commission to scapegoat the FAA, while attempting to lead investigators away from NORAD track, which in reality is likely the more important one. The 9/11 commission cites the testimony of NORAD officers that NEADS had learned from the FAA of the hijacking of United 93 at 9:16. The 9/11 commission report claimed that there had been no such notification, since United 93 had not yet been hijacked at that time. In the last sessions of the 9/11 commission, we had the absurd spectacle of NORAD officers thanking the commissioners for helping them to straighten out their own erroneous and fragmentary in-house chronologies. Perhaps NORAD had decided early in the game to spread the chaff of disinformation as a means of foiling the radar of any future inquiries. If so, it appeared to have worked.

One of the more obvious absurdities recounted by NORAD personnel during the 9/11 commission hearings was their fairy tale to the effect that NORAD radar was only able to look outwards from US coasts, and that their radar capability for tracking events in US airspace was zero. NORAD, they claimed, could look out, but could not look in. In the May 2003 hearings, we have this exchange:

> Mr. Ben-Veniste: And so on the day of September 11th, as you can see these dots – I know it may be difficult to see – NORAD was positioned in a perimeter around the United States, but nothing in the central region, nothing on the border with Canada?

> Gen. McKinley: That's correct, sir.

This is a crude subterfuge. Would the NORAD generals have us believe, for example, that a Russian submarine-launched cruise missile, once it had penetrated the US coastline in New Jersey, would have nothing more to fear from NORAD and could proceed on its leisurely way to Detroit or St. Louis, without any risk of further interference? Or, would they have us believe that a Russian Bear bomber, having once gotten into Minnesota, could fly on unmolested to destroy Chicago, because NORAD could no longer detect it? These nonsensical arguments refute themselves. NORAD was known to possess phased array warning system radars (PAWS) of various types which provided a comprehensive overview of US airspace and beyond.

CHENEY'S TERRORISM TASK FORCE

In May of 2001, one week before the execution of Timothy McVeigh, Bush issued an Executive Order making Cheney the leader of a new terrorism task force. Cheney's job was the development of "a coordinated national effort so that we may do the very best possible job of protecting our people from catastrophic harm," Bush said. The threat of chemical biological or nuclear attack on the US "while not immediate – is very real. "Should our efforts to reduce the threat to our country from weapons of mass destruction be less than fully successful, prudence dictates that the United States be fully prepared to deal effectively with the consequences of such a weapon being used here on our soil."

The executive order gave Cheney authority over the anti-terror operations of 46 government agencies. Cheney said that his new task force would "figure out how we best respond to that kind of disaster of major proportions that in effect would be manmade or man-caused." Cheney said the threats under his purview would include "a hand-carried nuclear weapon, or biological or chemical agent." "The threat to the continental United States and our infrastructure is changing and evolving and we need to look at this whole area oftentimes referred to as homeland defense," said Cheney. Cheney also announced in an interview with CNN television that Bush was creating an office within the Federal Emergency Management Agency to coordinate the government's response to any biological, chemical or nuclear attack. Cheney added that his task force would cooperate with FEMA Director Joe Allbaugh. Cheney's task force was supposed to report to the Congress and the National Security Council by October 1, 2001, according to press reports. (AP, CNN, MSNBC, Bloomberg May 8, 2001)

Many observers have concluded that Cheney's supposed terrorism task force was nothing but a boondoggle, and that this group never did anything; references to a "do-nothing" anti-terror task force abound. But perhaps Cheney's task force was a good deal more sinister. Since Cheney is a candidate for witting participation in the rogue network in a way that Bush himself can hardly be, we must wonder about how Cheney may have deliberately abused his authority over the anti-terrorism capabilities of those 46 agencies. Did his sweeping authority extend to military maneuvers as well? If the proof of the pudding is in the eating, then we must conclude that Cheney must bear a good deal of the responsibility for the total disarray of the US anti-terror posture on the morning of 9/11. Indeed, Cheney's task force appears to be the universal common denominator for that pattern of chaos and confusion.

COVERT USES OF MILITARY EXERCISES

In addition to being a day of terrorism, 9/11 was also a day of military and civilian maneuvers. These may turn out to have been more closely connected than many people might think. Let us recall a recent coup d'état of US history, that of March 30, 1981. On that day John Hinckley Jr. attempted to assassinate President Reagan. Scott Hinckley, the elder brother of the would-be assassin, was a personal friend of Neil Bush, the son of the Vice President who would have assumed the presidency if Reagan had died that day. George H. W. Bush presided over a cabinet meeting that same day which declared it to be the official policy of the US government that Hinckley was a lone assassin who had acted by himself, without any accomplices. But the question of the close relations between the Bush and Hinckley families has never been cleared up. (Tarpley 1992)

The aspect of the attempted assassination of Reagan which concerns us here is the fact that the shooting had occurred on the eve of two important maneuvers, one military and one civilian. As I described these events in my 1992 *Unauthorized Biography* of Bush the elder:

.... Back at the White House, the principal cabinet officers had assembled in the situation room and had been running a crisis management committee during the afternoon. Haig says he was at first adamant that a conspiracy, if discovered, should be ruthlessly exposed: "It was essential that we get the facts and publish them quickly. Rumor must not be allowed to breed on this tragedy. Remembering the aftermath of the Kennedy assassination, I said to Woody Goldberg, 'No matter what the truth is about this shooting, the American people must know it.'" But the truth has never been established. Defense Secretary Caspar Weinberger's memoir of that afternoon reminds us of two highly relevant facts. The first is that a "NORAD [North American Air Defense

Command] exercise with a simulated incoming missile attack had been planned for the next day." Weinberger agreed with General David Jones, the chairman of the Joint Chiefs of Staff, that this exercise should be cancelled. Weinberger also recalls that the group in the Situation Room was informed by James Baker that "there had been a FEMA [Federal Emergency Management Administration] exercise scheduled for the next day on presidential succession, with the general title 'Nine Lives.' By an immediate consensus, it was agreed that exercise should also be cancelled." (Tarpley 1992, Chapter XVII – The Attempted Coup d'Etat of March 30, 1981)

The FEMA exercise was much more than an uncanny coincidence – that a presidential succession exercise was planned for the day after a real presidential succession was supposed to take place. It is very unlikely that Hinckley acted alone, and it is likely that whoever prodded him to act when he did could well have been aware of the upcoming presidential succession exercise. This suggests that we need to think about the ways in which military maneuvers which seem to be coincidental and routine events can prepare and promote other types of actions, including important terrorist attacks.

Military exercises come in two varieties – there are the field exercises or live-fly exercises, war games in which real tanks or real planes move around in the fields or the sky. There are also staff exercises, which mainly involve officers assigned to the headquarters, who move markers in a sandbox, map grid, or computer screen.

The classic use of war games has been to prepare a sneak attack. The aggressor army announces that it is holding its summer maneuvers near the border of the target state. The deployment takes place under the cover of press releases announcing that these are merely maneuvers. When the troops are in position, they receive an order for a real attack. If field exercises can be used for fooling the adversary, then staff exercises are more useful for deceiving ones own side. In December 1975, in the wake of the US defeat in Vietnam, when the Pentagon was smarting from the reverse and looking for ways to redress the balance, there were certain circles in NATO who considered using the staff exercise HILEX 75 to set up a confrontation with the Warsaw Pact in Europe. Staff officers of countries who were not party to that plan were told not to be alarmed by the war preparations they saw; after all, those were only part of a staff exercise. Fortunately, due to the efforts of a network of alert citizens in a number of NATO countries, word got out about the really explosive potential of HILEX 75, and the confrontation option was abandoned. But these are at least two models of how maneuvers can be used for deception that we should keep in mind; there are more.

Staff exercises or command exercises are perfect for a rogue network which is forced to conduct its operations using the same communications and computer systems used by other officers who are not necessarily party to the illegal operation, coup or provocation as it may be. A putschist officer may be working at a console next to another officer who is not in on the coup, and who might indeed oppose it if he knew about it. The putschist's behavior is suspicious: what the hell is he doing? The loyal officer looks over and asks the putschist about it. The putschist cites a staff maneuver for which he is preparing. The loyal officer concludes that the putschist's activities are part of an officially sanctioned drill, and his suspicions are allayed. The putschist may even explain that participation in the staff exercise requires a special security clearance which the loyal officer does not have. The conversation ends, and the putschist can go on with his treasonous work.

Most civilians would assume that a military exercise or drill, be it a field or live fly exercise, or a staff drill, would tend to enhance the readiness of the military units taking part. This was the view expressed by 9/11 widow Mindy Kleinberg to the 9/11 commission in March 2003, when she remarked that: "… on September 11, NEADS (the North East Air Defense System of NORAD) was several days into a semiannual exercise known as 'Vigilant Guardian.' This meant that our North East Air Defense System was fully staffed. In short, key officers were manning the operation battle center, 'fighter jets were cocked, loaded, and carrying extra gas on board.'" (Testimony to 9/11 commission, March 31, 2003) But in reality the maneuvers may have introduced confusion and scattered available resources. The drills included false radar blips, military aircraft pretending to be hijacked, and the transfer of many NORAD fighters to northern Canada and Alaska.

AMALGAM VIRGO: COVER STORY FOR 9/11

The military exercise called Amalgam Virgo bore a close relationship to the events of 9/11. Amalgam Virgo was a military drill that had to do with hijacked airliners, sometimes from inside the United States, and sometimes used as weapons. A cruise missile was included at least once. The best working hypothesis is that Amalgam Virgo was the cover story under which the 9/11 attacks advanced through the bureaucracy. Preparations for carrying out 9/11 were conducted under the cover of being preparations for Amalgam Virgo. Most of those who took part in Amalgam Virgo could hardly have been aware of this duplicity.

One of the military officers who had been responsible for organizing Amalgam Virgo '01 was Colonel Alan Scott. Scott testified on May 23, 2003 at the 9/11 commission hearings:

> …MR. ALAN SCOTT: Yes, sir. Specifically Operation Amalgam Virgo, which I was involved in before I retired, was a scenario using a Third World united – not united – uninhabited aerial vehicle launched off a rogue freighter in the Gulf of Mexico.

> MR. BEN-VENISTE: That was Operation Amalgam Virgo. In fact, this exercise – in this exercise we used actual drones – NQM-107 drones,

which are about the size of a cruise missile, to exercise our fighters and our radars in a Gulf of Mexico scenario....

MR. BEN-VENISTE: You are referring to Amalgam 01, are you not?

MR. SCOTT: Yes, sir, Amalgam 01.

MR. BEN-VENISTE: I am referring to Amalgam 02, which was in the planning stages prior to September 11th, 2001, sir. Is that correct?

MR. SCOTT: That was after I retired, and I was not involved in 02.

MR. BEN-VENISTE: Will you accept that the exercise involved a simultaneous hijacking scenario?

MR. SCOTT: I was not involved in 02.

GEN. MCKINLEY: Sir, I do have some information on 02, if you would allow me to read it for the record.

MR. BEN-VENISTE: Please.

GEN. MCKINLEY: [Reads from briefing book.] Amalgam Virgo in general, 02, was an exercise created to focus on peacetime and contingency NORAD missions. One of the peacetime scenarios that is and has been a NORAD mission for years is support to other government departments. Within this mission falls hijackings. Creativity of the designer aside, prior motivations were based on political objectives – i.e., asylum or release of captured prisoners or political figures. Threats of killing hostages or crashing were left to the script writers to invoke creativity and broaden the required response of the players.

What this means is that the scenario papers prepared for the officers participating in the drill by collaborating writers included crashing planes into targets; these papers were evidently an integral part of the drill. McKinley is explicitly acknowledging that the drills did indeed include the concept of hijacked aircraft being used as weapons. Ben-Veniste, feigning not to understand this, thought McKinley's answer was "fatuous," and added ironically "It wasn't in the minds of script writers when the Algerians had actually hijacked the plane, when they were attempting to fly into the Eiffel Tower....Don't you agree we could have been better prepared?"

But Amalgam Virgo was not fatuous, it was sinister. Here was an exercise which included many of the elements which were put into practice on 9/11. Amalgam Virgo thus provided the witting putschists with a perfect cover for conduiting the actual live fly components of 9/11 through a largely non-witting military bureaucracy. Under the cover of this confusion, the most palpably subversive actions could be made to appear in the harmless and even beneficial guise of a drill. In addition, a red herring was built in for the purpose of confusing investigators arriving after the fact: the hijacked planes involved were generally imagined as coming from abroad. But even that covering detail was dubious.

These exercises came up again in the April 2004 hearings of the 9/11 commission. In her much-touted appearance, NSC director Condoleezza Rice repeated her well-known and discredited contention that the White House had not contemplated hijacked airliners being used as weapons. Bush himself had chimed in, asserting that "Nobody in our government, at least, and I don't think the prior government, could envision flying airplanes into buildings on such a massive scale." As the hearings showed, during the two years before the 9/11 attacks, NORAD conducted exercises using hijacked airliners as weapons to crash into targets and cause mass casualties. Another scenario involved crashing an airliner into the Pentagon, but this was not conducted after the Defense Department objected that it was too unrealistic. But it was done as a staff exercise – one might say, as a rehearsal. Perhaps it was too realistic, too revealing. One drill, planned for July 2001 but not conducted until later, involved planes from airports in Utah and Washington which were hijacked for the purposes of the drill. These aircraft were then escorted by US and Canadian interceptors to airfields in British Columbia and Alaska.

A NORAD statement issued in April 2004 confirmed that "Numerous types of civilian and military aircraft were used as mock hijacked aircraft. These exercises test and track detention and identification; scramble and interception; hijack procedures; internal and external agency coordination and operational security and communications security procedures." According to NORAD, these were regional drills, not regularly scheduled continent-wide drills. (*USA Today*, April 18, 2004) Not surprisingly, there is absolutely no mention of Amalgam Virgo in the report of the 9/11 commission.

Mike Ruppert has contributed much on the causes of the "complete paralysis of fighter response on 9/11…" Ruppert wrote in June 2004 that he had "obtained an on-the-record statement from someone in NORAD, which confirmed that on the day of 9/11 the Joint Chiefs (Myers) and NORAD were conducting a joint, **live-fly**, hijack Field Training Exercise (FTX) which involved at least one (and almost certainly many more) aircraft under US control that was posing as a hijacked airliner." Ruppert also concluded that "There never was a stand down order issued. That would have been way too incriminating and risky a piece of evidence." (*From the Wilderness*, June 6, 2004)

The exercises that were conducted on 9/11 were these:

1. Vigilant Guardian

From what is known about Vigilant Guardian, it is clear that it closely mimicked the actual events of 9/11. Vigilant Guardian was thus the source of much confusion among the non-witting NORAD personnel. As we will see, NORAD personnel were bewildered as to whether the reports they were getting represented fictitious events within the exercise, or whether they were dealing with a real emergency. (*Aviation Week and Space Technology*, June 3, 2002) This was a joint US-Canada exercise, and was designed to test the coordination of the two defense establishments. According to GlobalSecurity.org: "The

VIGILANT GUARDIAN (VG) is a VIGILANT OVERVIEW Command Post Exercise (CPX) conducted in conjunction with USCINCSTRAT-sponsored GLOBAL GUARDIAN and USCINCSPACE-sponsored APOLLO GUARDIAN exercises. The exercise involves all HQ NORAD levels of command and is designed to exercise most aspects of the NORAD mission. One VG is scheduled each year and the length will vary depending on the exercise scenario and objectives." (www.globalsecurity.org/military/ops/vigilant-guardian.htm) According to another source, "The planning for Vigilant Guardian Exercise-2001 probably began in 2000; and it was responding to a growing uneasiness of the US government and intelligence reports, world-wide – including NORAD – about plans for terrorist seizure of commercial air planes to be used as missiles against American targets." (www.911teachin.net/L5A.html)

The 9/11 commission had this to say about Vigilant Guardian: "On 9/11, NORAD was scheduled to conduct a military exercise, Vigilant Guardian, which postulated a bomber attack from the former Soviet Union." This is a very narrow definition of the drill in question, and is probably intended to mislead. The 9/11 commission continues: "We investigated whether military preparedness for the large-scale exercise compromised the military's response to the real-world terrorist attack on 9/11. According to General Eberhart, 'it took about 30 seconds to make the adjustment to the real-world situation.' (Ralph Eberhart testimony, June 17, 2004). We found that the response was, if anything, expedited by the increased number of staff at the sectors and at NORAD because of the scheduled exercise. See Robert Marr interview (Jan. 23, 2004)" (911 commission 458 n. 116) Eberhart's braggadocio was transparent, and the commission's verdict was a lie. Here is one example of the profound confusion engendered by the simultaneous occurrence of drill and real emergency:

> **FAA**: Hi. Boston Center TMU [Traffic Management Unit], we have a problem here. We have a hijacked aircraft headed towards New York, and we need you guys to, we need someone to scramble some F-16s or something up there, help us out.
>
> **NEADS**: [Staff Sergeant Jeremy Powell, Air National Guard] Is this real-world or exercise?
>
> **FAA**: No, this is not an exercise, not a test. (9/11 commission report 20)

Here is the same scene of confusion as described from the standpoint of another participant:

> On Sept. 11, as Americans watched horror rain upon New York and Washington, command teams at a little-known military outpost in Rome, N.Y., worked feverishly to restore safe skies and rouse a slumbering homeland defense.
>
> At the Northeast Air Defense Sector, radar operators who constantly scan the continent's boundaries suddenly faced a threat from within and a race they could not win.

Four months after the terrorist attacks, there are still untold stories. This is one.

6 A.M.: WAR GAMES

Lt. Col. Dawne Deskins figured it would be a long day.

Sept. 11 was Day II of "Vigilant Guardian," an exercise that would pose an imaginary crisis to North American Air Defense outposts nationwide. The simulation would run all week, and Deskins, starting her 12-hour shift in the Operations Center as the NORAD unit's airborne control and warning officer, might find herself on the spot.

Day I of the simulation had moved slowly. She hoped the exercise gathered steam. It made a long day go faster.

8:40 A.M.: REAL WORLD

In the Ops Center, three rows of radar scopes face a high wall of wide-screen monitors. Supervisors pace behind technicians who peer at the instruments. Here it is always quiet, always dark, except for the green radar glow.

At 8:40, Deskins noticed senior technician Jeremy Powell waving his hand. Boston Center was on the line, he said. It had a hijacked airplane.

"It must be part of the exercise," Deskins thought.

At first, everybody did. Then Deskins saw the glowing direct phone line to the Federal Aviation Administration.

On the phone she heard the voice of a military liaison for the FAA's Boston Center.

"I have a hijacked ," he told her.

Three minutes later, the drill was still a factor of confusion for Lt. Deskins in the form of a simulated hijacked plane heading for JFK Airport in New York City:

Deskins ran to a nearby office and phoned 1st Air Force Chief Public Affairs Officer Major Don Arias in Florida. She said NEADS had a hijacked plane no, not the simulation likely heading for JFK.

"The entire floor sensed something wrong," Chief of Operations Control Lt. Col. Ian Sanderson said. "The way this unfolded, everybody had a gut sense this wasn't right." ("Amid Crisis Simulation, 'We Were Suddenly No-Kidding Under Attack,'" Newhouse News Service, January 25, 2002)

It is not clear from this account whether the "simulation" in question was an artificial radar blip inserted on the NEADS screens, or an actual aircraft (piloted or remote controlled) going towards the New York airport.

2. Vigilant Warrior

This drill was identified by Richard Clarke in his recently published memoir. Here is what he writes:

"I turned to the Pentagon screen. 'JCS, JCS. I assume NORAD has scrambled fighters and AWACS. How many? Where?'

'Not a pretty picture, Dick.' Dick Meyers, himself a fighter pilot, knew that the days when we had scores of fighters on strip alert had ended with the Cold War. 'We are in the middle of Vigilant Warrior, a NORAD exercise, but...Otis has launched two birds toward New York. Langley is trying to get two up now. The AWACS are at Tinker and not on alert' Otis was an Air National Guard base on Cape Cod. Langley Air Force Base was outside Norfolk, Virginia. Tinker AFB, home to all of America's flying radar stations, was in Oklahoma."

'Okay, how long to CAP over DC?' Combat Air Patrol, CAP, was something we were used to placing over Iraq, not over our nation's capital.

'Fast as we can. Fifteen minutes?' Myers asked, looking at the generals and colonels around him. It was now 9:28." (Clarke 5)

3. Northern Vigilance

Operation Northern Vigilance involved deploying fighter interceptors to air bases in northern Canada and Alaska. Northern Vigilance was supposedly mounted by NORAD to counter a Russian maneuver going on at the same time. It could have been planned in advance, provided the timing of the Russian drill had also been known in advance. It was announced publicly in a NORAD press release of September 9, 2001 under the headline "NORAD Maintains Northern Vigilance." Here we read:

CHEYENNE MOUNTAIN AFS, Colo. – The North American Aerospace Defense Command shall deploy fighter aircraft as necessary to Forward Operating Locations (FOLS) in Alaska and Northern Canada to monitor a Russian air force exercise in the Russian arctic and North Pacific ocean. "NORAD is the eyes and ears of North America and it is our mission to ensure that our air sovereignty is maintained," said Lieutenant-General Ken Pennie, Deputy Commander-in-Chief of NORAD. "Although it is highly unlikely that Russian aircraft would purposely violate Canadian or American airspace, our mission of vigilance must be sustained." NORAD-allocated forces will remain in place until the end of the Russian exercise. NORAD conducted operation Northern Denial from December 1 to 14, 2000 in response to a similar, but smaller scale, Russian deployment of long-range bombers at northern Russian air bases. NORAD-allocated forces were deployed to three FOLS, two in Alaska and one in Canada. More than 350 American and Canadian military men and women were involved in the deployment.

The net effect of Northern Vigilance was drastically to reduce the number of fighter interceptors available at airports in the lower 48 states of the continental US. It is not known exactly how many planes moved north.

4. Northern Guardian

This drill is the least documented. It may have involved a complement to Northern Vigilance; one group of planes might have played the attackers, while another group played the defenders. A reference to this drill was found in the *Toronto Star*, December 9, 2001. At the very minimum, the drill was apparently centered on northern Canada and Alaska, which would also have siphoned off planes from the lower 48 states.

5. National Reconnaissance Office Drill

This drill simulated an airplane crashing into the headquarters of the National Reconnaissance Office (NRO) in Chantilly, Virginia, near Dulles Airport. It meant that the employees of the NRO were evacuated from their buildings just as the 9/11 attacks were actually taking place. The AP ran a story about this drill under the headline "Top US Intelligence Agency was to simulate plane crash into government building on September 11, 2001." The story stated that "a US intelligence agency was planning an exercise last Sept. 11 in which an errant aircraft would crash into one of its buildings." (AP, August 21, 2002)

The NRO was a super-secret agency responsible for spy satellites and other eavesdropping from space. It was created in 1960, and its existence was not officially acknowledged for some 32 years. The NRO draws its personnel from the military and the Central Intelligence Agency and has a budget equal to the combined budgets of both the CIA and the National Security Agency. On 11 September 2001, the NRO director was Keith R. Hall, who had headed the agency since 1996. In his capacity as DNRO, Hall was responsible for the acquisition and operation of all United States space-based reconnaissance and intelligence systems. At the same time Hall also served as Assistant Secretary of the Air Force for Space. As Nico Haupt has pointed out, Booz Allen Hamilton is a prominent subcontractor for the NRO. The obvious effect of evacuating the NRO was at least temporarily to blind institutional US intelligence to events which could have been monitored from space. NRO could have provided a real-time view of the air space over North America; as a result of the evacuation, this may not have been available. The advantages for the perpetrators are obvious.

6. Tripod II

Tripod II was a biological warfare exercise conducted jointly by the US Department of Justice and the City of New York; it was scheduled for September 12, 2001, and formally speaking never took place. Its obvious relevance was to provide a cover for various pre-9/11 activities in New York City.

It would seem that the code name "Tripod II" was revealed for the first time in testimony by former New York Mayor Rudy Giuliani at the 9/11 commission;

however, the basic facts about this exercise had been described by Giuliani in his self-serving memoir, *Leadership*, published in 2002. Here the former Mayor wrote:

> For months, we had in place an exercise in which we'd drill on our response to a biochemical attack, specifically practicing for the distribution of medication. The planned date: Wednesday, September 12. We had stored much of the materials for that drill at Pier 92. Pier 92 offered 125,000 square feet of open space and easy transportation to and from Ground Zero by way of boat and the West Side Highway. Moreover, because it was already in use by the military, the points of access were relatively easy to guard." (Giuliani 355)

After Giuliani's unusable command center in WTC 7 had been destroyed by the inexplicable collapse of that large building, he transferred his command post to Pier 92. The ease of the transition is suspicious in and of itself: had Giuliani known in advance that he would need this fallback option?

7.   Finally, a number of jets from the Washington DC area were on an informal training flight over North Carolina on 9/11, a circumstance that took them away from the national capital airspace. (*Aviation Week*, 9/9/2002)

Vigilant Guardian in particular compels our attention because it appears to have been transformed from a staff or command post exercise to a live fly exercise. Specifically, VG had all the earmarks of an anti-terrorism live fly exercise. According to research by Mike Ruppert presented at the Toronto 9/11 Inquiry, Vigilant Guardian included the use of military aircraft to simulate hijacked commercial airliners.

In his book, Richard Clarke recalls being told by an official on the morning of 9/11, "we have reports of eleven aircraft off course or out of communication, maybe hijacked." Clarke said he repeated this number, "Eleven." (Clarke 4) This figure of eleven has come to be seen as the canonical maximum of the aircraft reported hijacked for whatever reason at the height of the emergency. Because of the post-Cold War defense build-down initiated by Cheney when he was Secretary of Defense under Bush 41, the air defenses of the US had been drastically denuded.

Ruppert estimates that, on 9/11, there were just 8 fighter jets at the ready in the northeast US. Since these jets generally fly in pairs, this meant that there were four pairs of aircraft ready to be scrambled to intercept four aircraft. Therefore, there were at least 11 possible targets as compared to a total of four defensive asset packages available to cover them.

According to Ruppert, leaks of classified information suggest that the number of airliners reported or feared hijacked had at one point risen to 21. Some of the extra hijacks were represented by false blips made to appear on FAA and NORAD radar screens as part of the exercises that have been discussed. Other hijacks would have been accounted for by the actual military aircraft which were playing the roles of hijacked aircraft in the drills. Blips and dummy hijacks combined to create an insuperable confusion. This would have made the predicament of any loyal air defense commanders even more difficult. Keeping this in perspective, however, the collapse of the towers on 9/11 was not caused by the airplanes, as we shall see: the crashes were a diversion from the destruction by explosives of not just two buildings, but ultimately the entire New York World Trade Center.

Who in the Pentagon coordinates military maneuvers, be they of the command post or live fly variety? There must be some focal point where alternative dates are weighed, and conflicts foreseen, and minimum defense capabilities calculated. Whatever office in the bowels of the Pentagon does this, it is an urgent candidate for being swept for the presence of moles. However, even these insights do not by any means explain the failure to deploy fighter interceptors on 9/11.

Any military commander would have realized that all available assets had to be scrambled, at the latest by the point at which the second WTC tower was hit. In particular, any military commander would have been alert to the imminent threat of the decapitation of the national command structure centered in Washington. All the commanders running the show had been schooled in the Cold War, when a Soviet submarine-launched ballistic missile detonating over Washington was regarded as the most plausible overture for the third world war. The eight lanes of superhighway leading from Washington DC to Dulles Airport are monuments to the all-encompassing concern of the US federal bureaucracy for its center in Washington. The autonomic reaction of the military establishment would normally have been to place at least one pair of jets over Washington, whatever else was done or not done. The fact that even this was not done until well after the Pentagon had been hit indicates a remarkable density of moles at high levels of the US command structures.

AL QAEDA MOLES OR US GOVERNMENT MOLES?

The 9/11 terrorist attacks and the maneuvers enumerated above all took place on the same day. Some of the exercises were public knowledge, but some were not. If the actions of the hijackers (assuming there were hijackers) and the US military maneuvers were coordinated, what does this suggest? Did al Qaeda have a spy inside the US government, or was the US government directing or influencing the actions of al Qaeda? One who believes that al Qaeda had penetrated the US government in order to learn the day of the many simultaneous maneuvers is Barbara Honegger, the former Reagan Administration official and author of *October Surprise,* an account of Bush 41's secret negotiations with Iran during the 1980 election campaign. Ms. Honegger is currently with the US Naval Postgraduate School, and frequently posts to 9/11 truth activist chat lists. She rightly calls attention to the salient fact that the terror attacks and the US government exercises took place on the same day. She argues for the growing reasons to believe that the date for the attack was not 'chosen' by the hijackers at all, but that one of them learned that a counter-terror war-game/exercise simulating a scenario like the one that actually took place on 9/11 was planned for that morning, and then 'piggybacked' the 'real thing' on top of it.

But for Ms. Honegger, all of this does not point to the obvious reality that al Qaeda, notorious as the CIA's Arab Legion, was marching to the tune of a rogue network of rebel moles inside the US state apparatus. In order to avoid this evident conclusion, she reaches for a *deus ex machina* in the person of the myth-drenched Khalid Sheikh Mohammed. Not only does she mobilize KSM: she presents him as a wily *triple agent* who has successfully bamboozled the chief personalities of the US regime. After describing the question of the coordination of the terrorist attacks with the day of drills, Ms. Honegger writes that

> For all of this to 'work', the bad guys had to have at least one person among them who had fooled US intelligence into believing that he was 'one of us.' That person, almost certainly, is Khalid Sheikh Mohammed – the only person about whom all information is still classified, even his name, even though reams have already been written about him in the open press. And for good reason. Vice President Cheney, President Bush, CIA Director George Tenet, CIA officer and chief of NRO's strategic gaming division for their 9/11 'plane-into-building' exercise, John Fulton, and all the others who were so stupid as to risk thousands of innocent American lives on the bet that their star 'informant', Khalid Sheikh Mohammed, had really been 'turned' to the US 'side' – don't want him to talk about what he knows. And he knows a lot. On Sept. 10, 2002, Knight Ridder quoted a top UN counter-terror expert that Mohammed is probably the *only* person who has *all* the pieces to the 9/11 puzzle."

At this point 9/11 the day of the drills becomes 9/11 the day of the dupes. In reality the fancied superman KSM, to the extent that he exists at all, does so as a patsy and operative of US intelligence – perhaps a "superdupe." The orchestration of the terror attacks and the 9/11 drills was the handiwork of the rogue network inside the US government, and not a product of an Afghan cave or the teeming slums of Karachi.

In support of her thesis, Ms. Honegger also over-interprets the term "match" as used in the supposed communication between Atta and the phantomatic Khalid Sheikh Mohammed on September 10, 2001, but not translated until after the attacks. The text of this message was: "The Match is about to begin. Tomorrow [i.e., 9/11] is zero hour." (AP February 8, 2003) Ms. Honegger notes that Cheney was so incensed when this became public that he ordered an FBI investigation of members of the JICI to find out who might have leaked it. According to Ms. Honegger, "match' is "what you would expect if the speaker were referring to his discovery of the date that the US Government had selected to conduct its counter-terror simulation/exercise on the scenario of plane(s) crashing into government buildings – one that was about to turn very real when the terrorists 'piggybacked' their long-planned plot onto it." But this interpretation is strained. If the speaker was speaking English, "match" would simply mean "game." If the speaker was speaking Arabic, then we need to be aware of the multiple problems faced even by competent Arabic translators. So the philological and linguistic problems involved with this term "match" finally appear insuperable; it tells us nothing reliable. It is another example of disinformation pointing to an "Arab hackers with Arab hijackers" scenario, i.e., the myth of the infiltration of the intelligence services by their own patsies. (Barbara Honegger, "The US Government, Not the Hijackers, 'Chose' the Date of the 9/11 Attacks.")

MODES OF STANDING DOWN

The obvious lack of any air defense on 9/11, combined with the flagrant disregard for well-established and long-institutionalized procedures involving the FAA air traffic controllers and NORAD, led soon after 9/11 to the notion that an order or guideline must have been issued that was responsible for the paralysis of the usual intercept routine. A written "stand down" order *per se* has never been found, but this does not mean that it did not exist, possibly in some non-written form. Orders can be conveyed in verbal form, or better yet the expectations of a superior can be conveyed by indirection. But the surest way to make sure that nothing gets done is to make sure that moles, more or less witting partners in the covert operation, occupy the key nodal points in the bureaucracy on the day of the big event. And since we ascribe responsibility for 9/11 to precisely such a network of moles, this is the conclusion that is offered here.

If the FAA guidelines had been observed, an exchange like this one between the FAA Command Center and the FAA headquarters from 9:49 AM would have been simply unthinkable:

> FAA Headquarters: They're pulling Jeff away to go talk about United 93.
>
> Command Center: Uh, do we want to think, uh, about scrambling aircraft?
>
> FAA Headquarters: Oh, God, I don't know.
>
> Command Center: Uh, that's a decision somebody's gonna have to make probably in the next ten minutes.
>
> FAA: Uh, ya know everybody just left the room. (9/11 commission 29)

Was one or both of these speakers a mole? As they knew well, since the plane was off course, not responding to the radio, not following orders, and had its transponder turned off, there was absolutely no doubt that fighters had to be scrambled automatically and immediately, and not in ten minutes. In fact, any one of these conditions would have been enough to scramble fighters.

Another example of extremely suspicious behavior on 9/11 – this time from the private sector rather than the government – became known after June 4, 2004, when the FBI finally allowed a group of victims' families gathered at Princeton, New Jersey to hear a tapes of the responses of managers and officials of American Airlines to the obvious fact that American 11 and United 175 had been hijacked.

The FBI had tried as usual to intimidate the families with nondisclosure agreements and a ban on note-taking. However, some of the content of this tape seeped out, and was reported by Gail Sheehy of the *New York Observer*. One crucial passage recorded at the headquarters of American Airlines in Fort Worth, Texas, beginning about 8:21 AM on September 11, showed that American Airlines managers had done everything possible to prevent the news of a hijacking from leaking out. Here is a segment, according to the best recollection of family members of the deceased:

> Don't spread this around. Keep it close.
>
> Keep it quiet.
>
> Let's keep this among ourselves. What else can we find out from our own sources about what's going on?

These were the words of two managers at American Airlines Systems Operations Control. According to the recollection of another family member, their words were: "Do not pass this along. Let's keep it right here. Keep it among the five of us." When a United Airlines dispatcher was told by his superiors to transmit the order that all planes had to land, he was also told, "Don't tell the pilots why we want them to land."

We cannot know if the unnamed speakers were moles within the American Airlines bureaucracy, but this is certainly what moles would have done on such an occasion. Family members noted that if the news of the hijack of American 11 had been transmitted with the necessary rapidity, United 93 might never have taken off from Newark Airport. When Gerald Arpey, the president of American Airlines, testified before the 9/11 commission, he never mentioned the existence of the tapes played in Princeton on June 4. Clearly Arpey had not been served with a *duces tecum* subpoena, instructing him to present the 9/11 commission with all relevant records and exhibits. ("9/11 Tapes Reveal Ground Personnel Muffled Attacks," *New York Observer*, June 17, 2004) As for the FBI, they were indignant that their non-disclosure had been violated, not that airline officials blocked timely notification about a hijack. This was another example of the FBI's abuse of the Moussaoui case to withhold vital information from the public.

As for the FAA, it issued an official gag order for all of its employees in the immediate aftermath of 9/11, and for a long time what little was known had been divulged in violation of that gag order. Even some twelve FAA directives and warnings sent out during the summer of 2001 were reportedly classified. The mystery enveloping the actions of the FAA on 9/11 was made deeper by the notorious Kevin Delaney, the FAA official who deliberately destroyed audio tapes of the reports and recollections of New York air traffic controllers about what they had done and seen on the morning of 9/11. (*New York Times*, June 6, 2004) If those tapes still existed, they might shed some more light on the air defense stand-down of 9/11.

RESIDUAL ANOMALIES

Using documentation from press reports, Woody Box and Nico Haupt have concluded that two distinct aircraft took off from Boston on the morning of September under the designation of American Flight 11. "Where did Flight 11 start?" writes Box. "There are two answers: Gate 26 and Gate 32. And both answers resist any attempt to refute them." American 11's departure was regularly scheduled for 7:45 AM from Terminal B, Gate 32 of Boston's Logan Airport. This was American 11's departure gate on 9/11, as shown in a transcript of radio communications between American 11 and the Logan tower published in the *New York Times*: "7:45:48 – Ground Control 1: American eleven heavy Boston ground gate thirty two you're going to wait for a Saab to go by then push back" (*New York Times*, October 16, 2001) But many press reports indicate that passengers on American 11 embarked at Gate 26 (*Washington Post*, September 15, 2001, and other newspapers) Gate 26 is located in another wing of Terminal B, and is about 1000 feet away from Gate 32. Gate 26 is the majority view.

One paper, the *Boston Globe*, mentioned both gates on successive days. In an extra of the *Boston Globe* published on September 11, we find: "One airport employee, who asked not to be identified, said the American flight left on time from Gate 32 in Terminal B, and that nothing unusual was apparent." One day later, in the *Boston Globe* article entitled "Crashes in NYC had grim origins at Logan", we read: "The American flight left from Gate 26 in Terminal B, and the United flight from Gate 19 in Terminal C. One airport employee said nothing unusual was apparent when the American flight left." Was this the same employee as the day before? The Gate 26 flight pushed back later than its scheduled departure time of 7:45 AM.

Was one of these two flights a dummy flight, a decoy being used in one of the live fly hijacking exercises described above? Did its unannounced presence contribute even more to the confusion that reigned in US airspace on the morning of 9/11? Or was there some other, more devious purpose?

There are also reports of another mystery flight landing in Cleveland. And then there is a cryptic remark by Richard Clarke in his White House narrative of the morning of 9/11. Clarke reports hearing: "We have a report of a large jet crashed in Kentucky, near the Ohio line." (Clarke 13) At any rate, in the next chapter we shall see that the discourse concerning the airliners easily tends to obscure the core issue of the collapse of the World Trade Center, since crashing airplanes nor fire cannot and never have demolished steel buildings.

VI
THE COLLAPSE OF
WORLD TRADE CENTER 1, 2, AND 7

We now reach the center of the tragedy, the hecatomb of innocent airline passengers and office workers in the unprecedented and inexplicable collapse of the two World Trade Center towers. Here is where vast numbers of ordinary persons were immolated by the terrorist controllers for the sake of their insane geopolitical plans. Coming from a family which lived in New York for six decades after about 1910, having lived in New York City (Flushing, Queens) from the age of 4 to the age of 16, having attended New York City public schools from the first grade through the twelfth (PS 23, PS 20, JHS 185, Flushing High School), having worked in the city for a year as an adult living in Brooklyn, and having had an uncle who was a New York City policeman, the author is as much of a New Yorker as anyone. 9/11 has marked a decisive new step downward in the city's decline, and the bitter recognition of this tragic situation can only spur on the exposure of the actual process involved in 9/11.

THE KEY: SECONDARY EXPLOSIONS

According to the official version, which the 9/11 commission hardly comments on, the twin towers fell because of the impact of the planes and of the effects of the subsequent fires. The problem is that this is physically impossible, as we will show. The fall of the towers thus depends on some other cause: controlled demolition of some kind is the only possible hypothesis. The key to seeing beyond the official version is to chronicle the presence of secondary explosions, since these are the tell-tale signs of controlled demolition. When we examine the literature, we find a multitude of references to such secondary explosions.

Louie Cacchioli, aged 51, was a firefighter attached to Engine Company 47, based uptown in Harlem. "We were the first ones in the second tower after the plane struck," Cacchioli recounted later. "I was taking firefighters up in the elevator to the twenty-fourth floor to get in a position to evacuate workers. On the last trip up a bomb went off. We think there were bombs set in the building." Cacchioli was trapped in an elevator but was able to escape with the help of some fireman's tools. (*People Weekly*, September 24, 2001)

Auxiliary Fireman Lt. Paul Isaac Jr. also spoke of bombs in an interview with Internet reporter Randy Lavello. Isaac had served with Engine Company 10 in lower Manhattan during the late 1990s, so he knew the area around the WTC. Isaac said that many New York firemen were very concerned about the ongoing cover-up of why the World Trade Center collapsed. "Many other firemen know there were bombs in the buildings," he revealed, "but they are afraid for their jobs to admit it because the higher-ups forbid discussion of this fact. There were definitely bombs in those buildings." Among those suppressing real discussion about what had happened, Isaac cited the neocon heavy James Woolsey, CIA Director under Clinton and now the New York Fire Department's anti-terrorism consultant. (Marrs 34)

Teresa Veliz was a manager for a software development firm. She was on the 47th floor of the North Tower when American 11 struck. Veliz was able to reach the ground level at about the same time that the South Tower collapsed. Flung to the ground in total darkness, Veliz and a colleague followed another person who happened to have a flashlight. As she narrated later: "The flashlight led us into Borders bookstore, up an escalator, and out to Church Street. The explosions were going off everywhere. I was convinced that there were bombs planted all over the place and someone was sitting at a control panel pushing detonator buttons. I was afraid to go down Church Street towards Broadway, but I had to do it. I ended up on Vesey Street. There was another explosion. And another. I didn't know which way to run." (Murphy; Marrs 34)

Ross Milanytch viewed the scene from the 22nd floor of a nearby building. He reported seeing "small explosions on each floor. And after it all cleared, all that was left of the buildings, you could just see the steel girders in like a triangular sail shape. The structure was just completely gone." (*America at War*; Marrs 34)

Steve Evans, a reporter for the BBC, happened to be in the South Tower that morning. "I was at the base of the second tower, the second tower that was hit," he reported. "There was an explosion – I didn't think it was an explosion – but the base of the building shook. I felt it shake ... then we were outside, the second explosion happened and then there was a series of explosions....We can only wonder at the kind of damage – the kind of human damage – which was caused by those explosions, those series of explosions." (Christopher Bollyn, *American Free Press*; Aug. 9, 2002)

Fox 5 News, a New York television channel, was able to catch on videotape a large white cloud billowing out near the base of the South Tower. The newsman commented: "There is an explosion at the base of the building....white smoke from the bottom ...something has happened at the base of the building... then, another explosion. Another building in the World Trade Center complex...." (Marrs 35)

Tom Elliott was at work at his desk in the offices of Aon Corp. on the 103rd floor of the South Tower just before 9 AM. When the North Tower was hit, he decided to leave the building and began walking down the stairs with a small group of people. At the 70th floor, Elliott was encouraged by a woman to disregard the announcement on the public address system that there was no need to evacuate. When Elliott had reached the 67th floor, United 175 struck the South Tower, above where he was. Elliott later told a reporter what he was able to observe after that: "Although its spectacularly televised impact was above Elliott, at first he and those around him thought an explosion had come from below. An incredible sound – he calls it an 'exploding sound' – shook the building and a tornado of hot air and smoke and ceiling tiles and bits of drywall came flying up the stairwell. "In front of me, the wall split from the bottom up," Elliott recounted. Elliott was able to get out of the South Tower by 9:40. (*Christian Science Monitor*, September 17, 2001)

At 11:56 AM, NBC News broadcast a segment in which reporter Pat Dawson summarized a conversation he had just had with Albert Terry of the FDNY. Terry had told the reporter that he had about 200 firefighters in the WTC buildings at around 9 AM. Then, Terry said, he had heard a kind of secondary explosion. Dawson:

> Just moments ago I spoke to the Chief of Safety for the New York City Fire Department, who was obviously one of the first people here after the two planes were crashed into the side, we assume, of the World Trade Center towers, which used to be behind me over there. Chief Albert Terry told me that he was here just literally five or ten minutes after the events that took place this morning, that is the first crash. The Chief of Safety of the Fire Department of New York City told me that shortly after 9:00 he had roughly ten alarms, roughly 200 men, trying to effect rescues of some of those civilians who were in there, and that basically he received word of a secondary device, that is another bomb, going off. He tried to get his men out as quickly as he could, but he said that there was another explosion which took place. And then an hour after the first hit here, the first crash, that took place, he said there was another explosion that took place in one of the towers here. So obviously, according to his theory, he thinks that there were actually devices that were planted in the building. One of the secondary devices, he thinks, that [detonated] after the initial impact he thinks may have been on the plane that crashed into one of the towers. The second device, he thinks, he speculates, was probably planted in the building. So that's what we have been told by Albert Terry, who is the Chief of Safety for the New York City Fire Department. He told me that just moments ago. (Wisnewski 135-136)

Proponents of the official version have attempted to explain some of these explosions as having been caused by gas escaping from leaks in gas mains, but this cannot account for the phenomena described by Terry. Nor can such other explanations as exploding transformers, etc.

Ann Thompson of NBC reported that she had reached the corner of Broadway and Fulton on her way to the World Trade Center that morning when she heard an explosion and a wall of debris came toward her. She took refuge in a building. When she came out again about 10:30, she heard a second explosion. Firemen warned her about a further explosion. (Wisnewski 136; Trinkhaus, 4 ff.)

The eyewitness Michael Benfante told a German TV camera team: "As I was leaving, I heard it. I looked back, and the top of the North Tower was exploding.

And even then I did not believe that the whole tower could fall. I thought, only the top exploded and is now going to fall on me. I turned around again and ran away. I felt the rumble of the explosions, the thunder of the collapsing building." (German ARD network, *"Tag des Terrors – Anschlag aus heiterem Himmel,"* August 30, 2002, Wisnewski 136)

A reporter tried to film a standup with the WTC in the background, but was interrupted by the sound of an explosion: "We can't get any closer to the World Trade Center. Here you can see the firemen who are on the scene, the police and FBI officers, and you see the two towers – A huge explosion! Debris is coming down on all of us!" *("Verbrechen gegen die Menschheit,"* West German Television, Cologne, July 24, 2002; Wisnewski 136)

Yet another eyewitness reported: "We heard a huge explosion, and everything got black. Glass was falling down, people were getting hurt when the glass hit them. It was a big explosion, everything got dark, this here is not snow, it's all from the building, a horrible nightmare... I was on Sixth Avenue and I had just tried to call somebody when I heard an explosion and saw how the people were throwing themselves on the ground, screaming and crying, I looked up and saw all that smoke, as the tower came down, and all that smoke in one tower." (Segment by Oliver Voegtlin and Matthias Fernandes, NTV, September 11, 2001)

Another European documentary showed a man with glasses recovering in a hospital bed who recalled: "All of a sudden it went bang, bang, bang, like shots, and then three unbelievable explosions." *("Terror gegen Amerika,"* RTL, September 13, 2001)

An eyewitness who worked in an office near the WTC described his experiences to a reporter for the *American Free Press*. He was standing in a crowd on Church Street, about two and a half blocks from the South Tower. Just before the South Tower collapsed, he saw "a number of brief light sources being emitted from inside the building between floors 10 and 15." He saw about six of these flashes and at the same time heard a "a crackling sound" just before the tower collapsed." (Christopher Bollyn, *American Free Press*, December 2, 2001; Wisnewski 137)

Kim White, 32, who worked on the 80th floor of the South Tower, was another eyewitness who reported hearing an explosion. "All of a sudden the building shook, then it started to sway. We didn't know what was going on," she told *People* magazine. "We got all our people on the floor into the stairwell . . . at that time we all thought it was a fire . . .We got down as far as the 74th floor . . . then there was another explosion." (Christopher Bollyn, *American Free Press*, December 2, 2001)

A black office worker wearing a business suit that was covered with dust and ashes told the Danish television network DR-TV1: "On the eighth floor we were thrown back by a huge explosion." (Wisnewski 138)

The German network SAT 1 broadcast a report featuring survivors who also were talking about explosions. One of these eyewitnesses, by the name of Tom Canavan, was cut off in mid-sentence by two FBI agents who barged in, grabbed him as he was speaking, and hustled him away; this scene was captured on tape. (Wisnewski 138)

NBC TAPES SHOW CONTROLLED DEMOLITION EXPLOSIONS

In his best-selling study and also in his prime-time special broadcast on German television in August 2003, Gerhard Wisnewski employed out-takes from NBC News cameras near the World Trade Center to provide actual examples of what are almost certainly controlled demolition charges being detonated. On the NBC tape, we see the two towers burning and emitting clouds of black smoke. Then, at about frame 131 of the tape, there emerges a cloud of white-grey smoke along about two thirds of the 79th floor of the South Tower. Two thirds of the southeast façade correspond to the dimensions of the central core column complex, which would be where controlled demolition charges would have to be placed. This line of white-grey smoke billows up, contrasting sharply with the black smoke from the fire. At about frame 203, another line of white-grey smoke emerges several floors below the first, and billows up in its turn. This represents decisive photographic evidence of controlled demolition charges being triggered in the World Trade Center. (Wisnewski 216)

Andreas von Bülow, the former Social Democratic Technology Minister of Germany under Chancellor Helmut Schmidt, noted in his study of 9/11 that news tapes show smoke being forced out of the hermetically sealed windows of both towers in the minute or so just before they fell. (Von Bülow 146-147) This is very likely also evidence of controlled demolition charges or other artificial processes going on inside the buildings.

FIREMEN WERE CONFIDENT OF EXTINGUISHING THE FIRE

The Giuliani administration in New York City, and its successor, the Bloomberg administration, refused for a long time to allow the public to hear tapes of the radio conversations among the FDNY firemen on the scene at the WTC. In the summer of 2002, press accounts surfaced which indicated that firemen had been able to climb to the Sky Lobby on the 78th floor and been able to survey the extent of the fire from there. The fuselage of United 175 had struck the 80th floor, and one of its wings had clipped the 78th floor itself. The FDNY officers describe a situation with only two pockets of fire, and they express confidence that they will be able to fight the fire successfully with two hose lines. Two officials who are mentioned by name on the tape are Battalion Chief Orio J. Palmer and Fire Marshal Ronald P. Bucca, both of whom died when the South

Tower collapsed. "Once they got there," the NY *Times* says, "they had a coherent plan for putting out the fires they could see and helping victims who survived." According to the *New York Times* summary, the two officers "showed no panic, no sense that events were racing beyond their control.... At that point, the building would be standing for just a few more minutes, as the fire was weakening the structure on the floors above him. Even so, Chief Palmer could see only two pockets of fire and called for a pair of engine companies to fight them...."

The limited transcripts made available on the Internet were as follows:

> Battalion Seven...Ladder Fifteen, we've got two isolated pockets of fire. We should be able to knock it down with two lines. Radio that, 78th floor numerous Code Ones.

The audio tape has never been released to the public. The Justice Department claims that it is evidence in the trial of Zacarias Moussaoui in Alexandria, Virginia. (*New York Times*, August 4, 2002) Christopher Bollyn, already cited, commented: "The fact that veteran firefighters had 'a coherent plan' for putting out the 'two pockets of fire' indicates they judged the blazes to be manageable. These reports from the scene of the crash provide crucial evidence debunking the government's claim that a raging steel-melting inferno led to the tower's collapse." (Marrs 38-39)

Earlier in the morning, Pete Ganci, the Chief of the Department, and thus the highest-ranking uniformed firefighter in the city, had told Giuliani: "We can save everybody below the fire. Our guys are in the building, about halfway up the first tower." (Giuliani 8) Ganci was killed in action later in the day.

THE CASE OF WTC 6

CNN broadcast the image of smoke rising up from street level near the base of Building 6, the Customs House. This video footage had originated at 9:04, about one minute after United 175 struck the South Tower. Remember that WTC 6 was on the north side of the North Tower, so any explosions there cannot be regarded as having been generated by the impact to the South Tower. A powerful explosion inside WTC 6 had hurled a cloud of gas and debris 170 meters high. A CNN archivist commented, "We can't figure it out." (Marrs 36) This incident was soon eclipsed by the collapse of the South Tower, and has tended to be forgotten. The various official reports have had precious little to say about WTC 6. Overhead views of the ruins later showed a large crater in the steel structure of WTC 6; it was clear that this crater could not have been caused by fire. (Von Bülow 163-164)

THE AGONY OF THE FDNY

FDNY lost 343 firefighters that day, more than their casualties in the previous hundred years. It is worth asking why this came about. In the case of fires in high-rise skyscrapers, outside ladders cannot be used above a certain level. Therefore, the firemen are trained to use staircases to climb up to the fire and fight it within the building. They could do this with a fair degree of confidence because no modern, steel-framed, fireproof building has ever collapsed as a result of fire. Yet on 9/11, three of them – WTC 1, WTC 2, and WTC 7 – all collapsed. Veteran firefighters knew what they were doing. Their losses are not attributable to any mistake on their part, but to the fact that the twin towers and WTC 7 were brought down by some form of controlled demolition.

The 1 Meridian Plaza fire in Philadelphia had burned lustily for many hours in 1991, but came nowhere near collapsing. The 1 Meridian fire burned for 19 hours, leaping from floor to floor and burning out as combustible materials were used up. There was no significant damage to structural members. On May 4-5, 1988, the 62-story First Interstate Bank Building in Los Angeles – a structure that was more or less comparable to the twin towers – burned for more than three hours, with bright, intense flames licking up the sides of the building. In a post-blaze assessment, Iklim Ltd., a company that specializes in building inspections and structural analyses after fires, concluded: "In spite of the total burnout of four and a half floors, there was no damage to the main structural members and only minor damage to one secondary beam and a small number of floor pans."

These comparisons were noted with some discomfort by the *New York Times*, which commented that "High-rise buildings are designed to be able to survive a fire, even if the fire has to burn itself out. The strategy is to ensure that the steel support structures are strong enough or protected well enough from fire that they do not give way in the time it takes for everything inside an office building, like furniture, to burn. In major high-rise fires elsewhere in the country, such as the 1 Meridian Plaza fire in Philadelphia in 1991 and the First Interstate Bank fire in Los Angeles in 1988, this approach has worked. But the fires at 7 World Trade Center raged mainly on lower floors and never burned out, and in the chaos of Sept. 11, the Fire Department eventually decided to stop fighting the blazes." One can sense the acute embarrassment of the mythographs; this is all just absurd. "What the hell would burn so fiercely for seven hours that the Fire Department would be afraid to fight it?" said one member of the investigation team quoted in this same article. (*New York Times*, March 2, 2002)

THE ROMERO ANALYSIS

An important early contribution to the discrediting of the official version regarding the WTC came in an interview with a New Mexico expert in mining technology which appeared a few days after 9/11. This highly realistic analysis appeared in the *Albuquerque Journal* of September 14, 2001 under the headline "Explosives Planted in Towers, New Mexico Tech Expert Says," the byline belonged to Olivier Uyttebrouck.

Televised images of the attacks on the World Trade Center suggest that explosive devices caused the collapse of both towers, a New Mexico

Tech explosion expert said Tuesday. The collapse of the buildings appears "too methodical" to be a chance result of airplanes colliding with the structures, said Van Romero, vice president for research at New Mexico Institute of Mining and Technology.

"My opinion is, based on the videotapes, that after the airplanes hit the World Trade Center there were some explosive devices inside the buildings that caused the towers to collapse," Romero said. Romero is a former director of the Energetic Materials Research and Testing Center at Tech, which studies explosive materials and the effects of explosions on buildings, aircraft and other structures.

Romero said he based his opinion on video aired on national television broadcasts. Romero said the collapse of the structures resembled those of controlled implosions used to demolish old structures. "It would be difficult for something from the planeto trigger an event like that," Romero said in a phone interview from Washington, D.C.

Romero said he and another Tech administrator were on a Washington-area subway when an airplane struck the Pentagon. He said he and Denny Peterson, vice president for administration and finance, were en route to an office building near the Pentagon to discuss defense-funded research programs at Tech.

If explosions did cause the towers to collapse, the detonations could have been caused by a small amount of explosive, he said. "It could have been a relatively small amount of explosives placed in strategic points," Romero said. The explosives likely would have been put in more than two points in each of the towers, he said.

The detonation of bombs within the towers is consistent with a common terrorist strategy, Romero said. "One of the things terrorist events are noted for is a diversionary attack and secondary device," Romero said. Attackers detonate an initial, diversionary explosion that attracts emergency personnel to the scene, then detonate a second explosion, he said. Romero said that if his scenario is correct, the diversionary attack would have been the collision of the planes into the towers. (http://www.abqjournal.com/aqvan09-11-01.htm – removed from archive; see http://emperors-clothes.com/news/albu.htm)

Here was an honest appraisal from a qualified expert. Romero successfully identified some of the main anomalies presented by the spectacle of collapse, and proceeded from there to the only tenable hypothesis: controlled demolition. He was also acutely perceptive in seeing that the aircraft impacts could not in themselves have been the cause of the fall of the twin towers; they rather had to be regarded as a diversion. However, the America of late September 2001 was marked by a climate of neo-McCarthyite hysteria wholly antithetical to public truth; Van Romero later retracted his highly insightful remarks, and is rumored to have since found preferment from the federal government.

But numerous foreign experts arrived independently at similar conclusions. Steffen Kretz, the news anchor of the Danish television channel DR-1, reported that "the World Trade Center Tower collapsed after two more explosions." In a commentary of this same network, it was stated that the World Trade Center collapsed after an *additional* explosion. (Wisnewski 138) On 9/11, Denmark's DR-1 broadcast an interview with Jens Claus Hansen, a high-ranking officer of the Danish Military Academy. His view was: "Additional bombs must have been placed inside the WTC towers – otherwise they would not have collapsed as they actually did." Another guest was the former NATO General Keld Hillingsøe, who commented: "Additional bombs must have been installed in the buildings." (Wisnewski 138) The Danish newspaper *Berlingske Tidende*, the leading conservative paper in the country, published an interview with the explosives expert Bent Lund, who pointed out that fire alone could not have caused the collapse of the twin towers. He estimated that about a ton of explosives must have exploded inside the buildings in order to bring them down in this way. (*Berlingske Tidende*, September 12, 2001; Wisnewski 138)

THE VIEW OF A SWISS ENGINEER

Another leading authority who raised the issue of sabotage from within the towers was Hugo Bachmann, professor emeritus of building dynamics and earthquake engineering at the world-famous Swiss Eidgenössische Technische Hochschule in Zürich – where Einstein had taught. As Bachmann told the *Neue Zürcher Zeitung Online* on September 13, 2001, at first glance there seemed to be two possibilities in the fall of the towers. The first was the fire and its effect on the steel supports. But Bachmann had an alternative: "In the second scenario, an additional terrorist action would have caused the collapse of the buildings. In this way, according to Bachmann, buildings like the World Trade Center can be destroyed without great logistical exertion." The article went on to say that "Bachmann could imagine that the perpetrators had installed explosives on key supports in a lower floor before the attack."

If the perpetrators had rented office space, then these "explosive tenants" could have calmly placed explosive charges on the vulnerable parts of the building "without having anyone notice." Bachmann thought that it was less likely that explosives in the parts of the building below ground could have caused the collapse. Here the logistical problems would be harder to solve in order to put the charges in the right places, and the foundations were probably of more stable construction than the steel towers. Bachmann commented that "the question of whether in fact one of these two scenarios is applicable cannot be answered at this time." But he felt it was a central issue that the second scenario should get more attention, whether or not it applied to the WTC. Bachmann observed that anyone who had enough knowledge of static structures and explosives technology could in principle destroy any building, since every structure has its Achilles heel. An attack aimed at that weak point would be relatively easy to carry out, but would require careful and time-consuming planning. Not all buildings were equally vulnerable, but the twin towers of the World Trade Center were in Bachmann's opinion probably among the more sensitive targets. (Wisnewski 141-143)

OPPORTUNITIES FOR TAMPERING

There are numerous pieces of anecdotal evidence suggesting strange and unusual activities in the World Trade Towers in the days and weeks before their destruction. One New York businessman told me in an interview three years after the fact that he had visited a client in one of the towers numerous times during the months preceding the attack, and had always found that certain elevators were out of service. Another report came from Scott Forbes, an employee of Fiduciary Trust, a firm which was located on floors 90 and 94-97 of the South Tower. Eighty-seven employees of Fiduciary Trust were killed on 9/11. In an email account, Forbes reported that over the weekend of September 8-9, 2001, floors 50 and above of the South Tower experienced a "power down," meaning that all electrical current was cut off for about 36 hours. The reason officially cited was that the electrical cables in the building were being upgraded. Forbes was an information technology officer in charge of Fiduciary Trust's computer network; his attention was engaged by the power down because it fell to him to shut down all the company's computers and related systems before the power went out. After the power down, he had to turn the computers back on again, and restore service on the network. Because there was no electric power above the fiftieth floor, there were also no security cameras and no security locks. However, there were many outside engineering personnel coming in and out of the tower at all hours during the weekend. Forbes lived in Jersey City and could see the WTC towers from his home; when he saw the conflagration on the morning of 9/11, he immediately related it to the events of the previous weekend. (www.serendipity.li/wot/forbes01.htm)

SEISMIC EVIDENCE

The seismic effects of the collapse of the towers were observed and measured by Columbia University's Lamont-Doherty Earth Observatory just up the Hudson River in Palisades, New York. Here seismographs recorded two spikes reflecting two shock waves in the earth on the morning of 9/11. The crucial fact is that these two spikes came just *before* the collapse of the towers began. Specifically, Columbia scientists at the facility registered a tremor of 2.1 on the Richter scale at 9:59:04 EDT, just before the beginning of the collapse of the South Tower, and a 2.3 shock just as the North Tower began to come down at 10:28:31 EDT. Both tremors were recorded before the vast majority of the mass of the buildings hit the ground. Although they were not of earthquake proportions, these were considerable shocks, about twenty times more potent than any previously measured shock wave generated by a falling building. The

1993 WTC truck bomb had produced no seismic effects at all – it had failed to register. At 5:20 local time on the afternoon of 9/11, there was also a 0.6 tremor from the collapse of WTC 7, also at the beginning, rather than the end, of this building's collapse. Dr. Arthur Lerner-Lam, the director of the Columbia Center for Hazards and Risk Research, commented that "during the collapse, most of the energy of the falling debris was absorbed by the towers and neighboring structures, converting them into rubble and dust or causing other damage – but not causing significant ground shaking." But Lerner-Lam declined to draw any conclusions from the glaring anomaly represented by his data, which the 9/11 commission has also avoided. (Marrs 39 ff.)

After most of the pile was removed, experts found that there were pools of what appeared to have been molten metal which had congealed on foundations of the buildings many levels underground. Some steel appeared to have partially melted, other steel had undergone alternations to its crystalline structure, and still other steel was full of holes, like a Swiss cheese. Puddles of molten steel were reported up to a week after the collapse. This may be consistent with the use of thermite, a demolition agent that works by melting steel where it is applied.

GIULIANI OBLITERATES THE WTC CRIME SCENE

Mayor Giuliani, by pedigree, was a creature of the highly repressive bureaucratic-authoritarian apparatus which had consolidated itself in the Justice Department during the Reagan years. He now performed yeoman service in defense of the 9/11 myth, a myth which had its most obvious vulnerability in its most spectacular point: the unprecedented and physically inexplicable collapse of the twin towers. Giuliani used the pretext that his term was ending on December 31, 2001 to organize the massive and hasty obliteration of the WTC as a crime scene. Parallel to this, Giuliani engineered a confrontation with the New York firemen, both to divert public attention from his tampering with the evidence, and also to neutralize the potential of the firemen, the one group which might have denounced the presence of controlled demolition charges in WTC 1, 2, and 7, of which, as we have seen, they were well aware.

During the crisis, Giuliani had been eager to exploit for his own political image the immense admiration and gratitude which had been expressed around the nation and the world for the epic feats of the New York firefighters. The firemen were now the most revered symbols in the country: typical was the cover of *Newsweek*'s post-9/11 issue, which showed some firemen raising a flag over the ruins, with an evident allusion to the flag raising on Iwo Jima. Giuliani made a practice of appearing in public wearing a baseball cap emblazoned with the letters "FDNY." The police he relegated to his windbreaker, which bore the legend "NYPD." Giuliani proved to be treacherous in practice to both, and he did this by playing the firefighters against the police, and vice versa – all in the service of the 9/11 cover-up. The firemen, once revered, would soon be "inexcusable," according to Giuliani.

CONTROLLED DEMOLITION AGAIN

Giuliani brought in Controlled Demolition, the same highly suspect firm which had finished the demolition of the Murragh Federal Building in Oklahoma City in 1995, and which had disposed of the evidence there in the process.

This contract was let surreptitiously just eleven days after 9/11, and empowered Controlled Demolition to recycle the steel of the World Trade Center. Giuliani has not a word to say about this in his memoirs. The city accepted rock-bottom prices for the steel; the priority was to make it disappear fast. Trucks hauling the steel away were equipped with $1,000 Global Positioning System locators to ensure that none of them went astray, and that no suspect steel ended up in the back yard of a maverick 9/11 researcher, although the steel was ostensibly being handled as scrap of little value. All investigators, in fact, were banned from Ground Zero. Now Controlled Demolition would eradicate any chance of using the abundant physical evidence present in "the pile," as the mass of twisted rubble of the WTC quickly came to be called. It was a scene out of Kafka – it was impossible to find out which officials were superintending the destruction of the evidence, to save a myth that was being used to set in motion a world war.

Giuliani, along with ghostwriter Ken Kurson, has produced a relentlessly self-laudatory and self-promoting autobiography entitled *Leadership*. This work constitutes a monument of hypocrisy. During one of his visits to the WTC site, the Mayor noticed that many visitors were taking pictures of the site. Because there was so much to hide, he found this troubling: "I noticed a disturbing phenomenon – hundreds of people carrying disposable cameras and handheld video cameras. I understood the impulse – this was a historic event, and experiencing it up close had a tremendous impact. At the same time, this was a crime scene, and a dangerous one. I did not want anyone to get hurt, or to damage evidence as they scouted out the best angle for their snapshots. If we didn't do something about it immediately, it would soon be out of control, a voyeur's paradise, and we risked the site developing a distasteful freak show aspect." (Giuliani 49) An independent photographic documentation of the crime scene, one the FBI would not be able to confiscate? Horrors! Giuliani promulgated his infamous order that all photos were illegal in the area around the WTC complex. Those who risked a snapshot also risked going to jail.

When it was a question of preventing public scrutiny, Giuliani considered the WTC pile a crime scene where there was evidence that had to be preserved. But when it was a question of sending the crucial evidence to the other end of the world, Giuliani's motto became "scoop and dump" – with the help of Controlled Demolition. As Thomas Van Essen, Giuliani's fawning appointee as Fire Commissioner, described the scene: "…a full-blown recovery operation was under way, and the site had become an enormous construction zone. Trucks and plows rolled around everywhere. Giant cranes lofted massive steel beams over the heads of the men below." (Van Essen 263) The steel was sent to the Fresh

Kills salvage yard in New Jersey that cut it up for recycling to blast furnaces, many of them overseas.

According to Van Essen, by the end of October Giuliani was filled with humanitarian concern about the danger of accidents to those working on the pile. One of the main groups present there were firefighters who were seeking the bodies or other remains of their hundreds of fallen comrades. According to the literary provocateur Langewiesche, "there were some among the construction workers and the police who grew unreasonably impatient with the firemen, and became overeager to repeat the obvious – in polite terms, that these so-called heroes were just ordinary men. On the other hand, the firemen seemed to become steadily more self-absorbed and isolated from the larger cleanup efforts underway. " (Langewiesche 158) "Firemen were said to prefer watches from the Tourneau store, policemen to opt for kitchen appliances, and construction workers (who were at a disadvantage here) to enjoy picking through whatever leftovers they came upon – for instance, wine under the ruins of the Marriott hotel, and cases of contraband cigarettes that spilled from the US Customs vault in the Building Six debris." (Langewiesche 159) Langewiesche reported with great gusto the discovery of evidence that the firemen had been looting even before the towers came down. "Fifty feet below the level of the street they began to uncover the hulk of a fire truck that had been driven deep by the collapse." According to Langewiesche, the field superintendent who only wanted to get on with the job at hand felt "delight, then, after the hulk of the fire truck appeared, that rather than containing bodies (which would have required decorum), its crew cab was filled with dozens of new pairs of jeans from The Gap, a Trade Center store. When a grappler pulled off the roof, the jeans were strewn about for all to see. It was exactly the sort of evidence the field superintendent had been waiting for. While a group of initially bewildered firemen looked on, the construction workers went wild." (Langewiesche 161)

The firemen, we must remember, were those who knew most about the controlled demolition of the World Trade Center, and they were also the group most likely to tell what they knew. In this sense, the firemen posed perhaps the greatest immediate threat to the 9/11 myth upon which the oligarchy had staked so much. The obvious campaign of psychological warfare against the firemen, therefore, was of world-historical importance. Given the stakes, it would be impossible to exclude that the dungaree incident which Langewiesche found so delightful had been cynically staged as a means of keeping the angry and rebellious firemen off-balance, distracted and confused. The jeans could easily have been planted at a quiet moment during the graveyard shift. Langewiesche's reporting came out during the fall in the *Atlantic Monthly*, and rankled deeply among the angry firemen and the bereaved families.

On October 31, Halloween, Giuliani decreed without any meaningful consultation that there would be an upper limit of 25 firefighters on each shift at the WTC pile, along with 25 New York City policemen and 25 Port Authority patrolmen. Soon "the rescue workers were up in arms. Stories went around that we had simply given up on finding bodies; that the mayor wanted to speed the cleanup so it would be finished before he left office; that we had recovered gold from the trade center and didn't care about anything else....Union officials started telling the workers we were haphazardly trucking everything to Fresh Kills – a 'scoop and dump' operation." (Van Essen 265)

Langewiesche defends the Mayor's justification of cutting the firemen's representation on the pile: "when Giuliani gave 'safety' as the reason for reducing their presence on the pile, he was completely sincere." (Langewiesche 161) In his view, the big problem on the pile was "firemen running wild." (Langewiesche 162) In mid-October, an audience of firemen, policeman, widows, and orphans loudly booed several members of the Giuliani administration, but also Senator Hillary Clinton and a local Democratic politician. (Van Essen 258) On Friday, November 2, Giuliani was able to harvest the results of his provocations. In the morning, more than 1,000 firemen came together at the WTC. Their chants included: "Bring the brothers home! Bring the brothers home!", "Do the right thing!", "Rudy must go!", and "Tom must go!", a reference to Fire Commissioner Thomas Van Essen, a Giuliani appointee. Their signs read, "Mayor Giuliani, let us bring our brothers home." Speakers denounced Giuliani's hasty carting off of wreckage and remains to Fresh Kills as a "scoop and dump" operation. One well-respected former captain appealed to the crowd: "My son Tommy of Squad 1 is not home yet! Don't abandon him!" This was met with a cry of "Bring Tommy home!" from the assembled throng. This scene soon degenerated into an altercation between the firefighters and the police guarding the site, and then into a full-scale riot. Twelve firefighters were taken to jail, while five policemen were injured. Giuliani had gladly sacrificed the 9/11 myth of national solidarity to the needs of his campaign of psychological warfare and provocations against the firemen. It was All Souls Day, the day of the dead, November 2, 2001.

At a press conference that same day, Giuliani hypocritically condemned the actions of the firemen as inexcusable. The police wanted to make more arrests, and were scanning videotapes of the riot to identify firefighters. The city was appalled by what had happened; many newspapers were anti-Giuliani this time. One firefighters' union leader, Peter Gorman, called Giuliani a "fascist," and referred to Police Commissioner Kerik and the Fire Commissioner as Giuliani's "goons."

On Monday, November 11, Giuliani and his officials were again confronted by 200 angry firefighters and bereaved families at a meeting. Giuliani was accused again and again of running a "scoop and dump" operation. One widow protested: "Last week my husband was memorialized as a hero, and this week he's thought of as landfill?" When Van Essen stammered that the department had been overwhelmed, a widow replied, "Stop saying you are overwhelmed! I am overwhelmed! I have three children and my husband is dead!" Dr. Hirsch of the "biological stain" theory discussed below tried to defend Giuliani by arguing that nothing resembling an intact body was being found any longer, but he was shouted down by firemen who knew from their experience on the pile that this was not so. Van Essen was forced to concede that, based on photographic evidence he personally examined, remains were indeed still being found that had to be "considered intact bodies." (Van Essen 270-271)

Giuliani's rush to eradicate the crime scene without regard to the preservation of human remains thus served two important goals. He was able to destroy much pertinent evidence, and he succeeded in throwing the firefighters on the defensive and playing them off against the police, the construction workers, and other groups. He was able to split the firefighters themselves. The firefighters were tied into knots emotionally, and were left with no time or energy to pursue the issue of justice for their heroic fallen comrades, which could only have been served by directly raising the issue of the indications of controlled demolition in numerous points of the World Trade Center complex. Nor was the cynical oligarchical strategy limited to Giuliani: at the 9/11 commission's last set of hearings in New York City, the FDNY, NYPD, and other line departments of the city were mercilessly baited by the likes of former Navy Secretary John Lehman, who told them that their operational coordination was inferior to that of a Boy Scout troop. So far the firefighters have not been able to mount a challenge to the 9/11 myth, which necessarily portrays them as incompetent, in spite of their heroism and huge losses. Only by demolishing the myth, only by unearthing the story of controlled demolition, can the immense historical merits of the firefighters be duly recognized.

Giuliani's memoir is mainly for self-aggrandizement, but it also attempts to shore up the official version at certain key vulnerable points, since the Giuliani legend and the 9/11 myth are now inextricably intertwined. The following remarks are attributed to Dr. Charles S. Hirsch, the Medical Examiner of New York City in the late afternoon of 9/11: "Most of the bodies will be vaporized. We're going to end up with biological stains, where the tissue has become shapeless, amorphous masses of matter." According to Giuliani, Hirsch estimated that the temperature inside the building had reached 2,000 degrees (presumably Fahrenheit). Such a temperature from fuels like kerosene and furnishings is impossible in the physical universe as we otherwise know it to be constituted. (Giuliani 22)

CONGRESSIONAL HEARINGS: "BORDERLINE CRIMINAL"

The scandalous eradication of the WTC crime scene was one of the main themes of hearings held by the House Science Committee on March 2, 2002. Congressman Anthony D. Weiner, a New York Democrat, led off by contrasting the businesslike handling of the crash scene of Flight 186 on November 12, 2001 with the chaos and disdain for the integrity of evidence that had prevailed on the WTC pile under Giuliani's management: "Within literally moments of that plane crash, the National Transportation Safety Board was on the ground sequestering evidence, interviewing witnesses, subpoenaing information, if necessary, and since then, they have offered periodic reports. One month and a day earlier, when the World Trade Center collapsed, nothing could have been further from the truth. According to reports that we have heard since, there has been no comprehensive investigation. One expert in fire engineering concluded that there was virtually a nonexistent investigation. We haven't examined any aspects of the collapse that might have impacted rescue worker procedures even in this last month. Second, reports have emerged that crucial evidence has been mishandled. Over 80 percent of the steel from the World Trade Center site has already been sold for recycling, much of it, if not all of it, before investigators and scientists could analyze the information."

Weiner pointed out that at the Flight 186 Rockaway crash scene on November 11, he had been able to "watch the National Transportation Safety Board point to pieces of evidence, [and] say to local law enforcement, don't touch this or it is going to be a felony if you do." (House March 104) That had been the procedure before 9/11, and it had become procedure once again after 9/11; only in regard to the 9/11 events did these methods, mandated by federal law, go out the window. It was a massive breakdown of the rule of law, and all in the service of the cover-up.

Weiner pointed out that there was also plenty of blame to go around for the federal government as well. This centered on inter-agency turf wars, always a favorite means used by moles to disguise the scope and motivation of what they are really doing: "...we have allowed this investigation to become woefully bogged down in fighting and lack of cooperation among agencies. Researchers from FEMA did not get timely access to the designs of the building. News accounts have said there has been friction between engineers in FEMA because of concerns about where the information would wind up. Even the National Science Foundation, which has awarded grants to several scientists to study the collapse, didn't coordinate these efforts with FEMA or the American Society of Civil Engineers."

The reality was even worse. FEMA's Building Performance Assessment Team (BPAT) investigation was carried out not by full-time government officials, but rather by a group of volunteer investigators, with a budget of just $600,000. (Ken Starr's budget for hounding Clinton: more than $40 million.) FEMA volunteers had no subpoena power, and could not stay the hand of steel recyclers or confiscate evidence if they required it. They were denied the blueprints of the buildings. They generally could not enter ground zero, apart from an early walking tour. They never saw a piece of steel wreckage until October. Out of millions of fragments, the FEMA BPAT was able to save only 156 from the recyclers.

Weiner also deplored the parsimonious budget that had been granted to the investigation: "...finally, we have seen and noted painfully that the financial commitment to this investigation simply is not there. It is not uncommon to spend tens of millions of dollars investigating why a plane crashed. But we have yet to spend even a million dollars on this investigation, and the Bush

Administration has refused to commit to release the full funding necessary."
(House March 48)

In a later hearing, Weiner elaborated that "thousands of tons of steel were
carted away and recycled before any expert could examine what could have been
telltale clues. Support trusses, fireproofing fragments, and even burned-out
electrical switches that might have given scientists and engineers insight were
lost forever even before an investigation was underway. (House May 20-21)

Weiner was also well aware that the Giuliani administration, just like the
Bush regime in Washington, was behaving with implacable hostility towards any
and all investigations. "We just heard testimony that the city was the opposite of
cooperative. That they had refused to provide basic information," said Congressman Weiner at the March hearings. He told the government witnesses from
FEMA and other agencies: "The idea that there was some level of cooperation, I
have to tell you, the anecdotal record is replete with stories of people having
cameras confiscated from them, being stopped at checkpoints. You are officials
of the United States Government. The idea that this should have to be a subject of
a long negotiation over what information would be at your disposal, to me is
most troubling." (House March 133) Indeed, FEMA's Building Performance
Assessment Team (BPAT) was not even allowed on the scene until October.

Weiner's concerns were shared by Virginia Republican J. Randy Forbes, who
complained that he was "disappointed to learn that investigators were unable to
examine recovered pieces of steel from the Twin Towers before they were
recycled. I am also troubled that investigators had difficulty in obtaining
blueprints, design drawings, and maintenance records because of liability
concerns from the buildings' owners. (House March 55) It even turned out that,
despite repeated urgent requests, the investigators were being denied the out-
takes of the video tapes shot by the various television networks operating around
the WTC on 9/11. This is a reminder that moles are sometimes just as necessary
in the private sector as they are in government.

Glenn P. Corbett, Professor at the John Jay College of Criminal Justice,
reminded the committee that "handling the collapse study as an assessment has
allowed valuable evidence – the steel building components – to be destroyed.
The steel holds the primary key to understanding the chronology of events and
causal factors resulting in the collapse. The collapse of the World Trade Center
towers were the largest structural collapses in world history. A disaster of such
epic proportions demands that we fully resource a comprehensive, detailed investigation. Instead, we are staffing the BPAT with part-time engineers and scientists on a shoestring budget." (House March 78) Corbett called for a World Trade
Center Disaster Commission, but the Bush administration was not interested.

Abolhassan Astaneh-Asl, a Berkeley professor of civil engineering, related his
own shock in discovering that the structural steel was simply being shipped out:
"I believe I was the first one to find out that the steel was being recycled. *New
York Times* reporter Jim Glanz told me two weeks after the quake – after the

collapse. And I tried to contact the city and also the *New York Times* reporters tried to make sure we could have access to the steel to do the research. It was not happening. And I went myself – directly contacted the recycling plant and made the arrangement." (House March 128) Even so, most of the steel was soon gone.

Congressman Crowley of New York correctly suggested that the flagrant illegalities and abuses of the crime scene would permanently undercut whatever explanation the government was seeking to purvey: "I do believe that conspiracy theorists are going to have a field day with this. They are going to make the Warren Commission look like a walk in the park. And that is unfortunate not only for the Members of Congress who are trying to work on this issue, but for all the families out there that are listening very carefully to what we are talking about today, what these experts are saying. And I just think there is so much that has been lost in these last six months that we can never go back and retrieve. And that is not only unfortunate, it is borderline criminal." (House March 129)

Congressman Christopher Shays of Connecticut, a liberal Republican like Giuliani, ran interference for the Mayor. He rejected the idea that the WTC was a crime scene where there was still something to be discovered, something to be proven; Shays said he had "a particular bias that the actions against us weren't criminal acts, they were acts of war, acts of terror. And I kind of bristle when I think of our treating this as a criminal act in which we have to prove, beyond a shadow of a doubt, that someone did it and they were at the scene or whatever you need to deal with in a crime." (House May 115) This chauvinistic rhetoric was a cover for the urgent need of annihilating the evidence. For this school of thought, there was no need for evidence because there was nothing to prove and nothing to learn; they thought they knew what happened *a priori* thanks to CNN and Bush. The supposed government of laws was in eclipse.

Small wonder, all in all, that the august, 125-year old fireman's trade paper *Fire Engineering* blasted the entire inadequate investigation process in a January 2002 editorial. Editor Bill Manning wrote that "For more than three months, structural steel from the World Trade Center has been and continues to be cut up and sold for scrap. Crucial evidence that could answer many questions about high-rise building design practices and performance under fire conditions is on a slow boat to China, perhaps never to be seen again in America until you buy your next car." Manning charged that "Fire Engineering has good reason to believe that the 'official investigation' blessed by FEMA and run by the American Society of Civil Engineers (ASCE) is a half-baked farce that may already have been commandeered by political forces whose primary interests, to put it mildly, lie far afield of full disclosure." "The destruction and removal of evidence must stop immediately," Manning demanded. Elsewhere in the same issue, a fire official deplored that "we are literally treating the steel removed from the site like garbage, not like crucial fire scene evidence." (*Fire Engineering*, January 2002)

An extremely serious aspect of the botched investigation of the World Trade Center events involved the issue of the four black boxes from the two planes (American 11 and United 175) – a cockpit voice recorder and a flight data reporter from each plane. The official version, as codified by the 9/11 commission, claims that not one of these black boxes was ever found. But a New York City firefighter named Nicholas De Masi claimed that he escorted FBI agents into the WTC ruins and helped them to find and recover three of the four missing black boxes. DeMasi's account is supported by the WTC volunteer Mike Bellone, who said that he had seen at least one black box being taken from the wreckage. The three black boxes were removed from the wreckage with the help of DeMasi's all terrain vehicle, according to this account. Then the three black boxes were taken away by the FBI, and have never been heard of again. The black boxes of the two planes that apparently hit the WTC were the only ones which have never been recovered from jetliners. DeMasi wrote about this experience in his book *Ground Zero: Behind the Scenes*, which was published by Trauma Recovery and Assistance for Children (TRAC Team) in 2003. Here DeMasi recalls: "There were a total of four black boxes. We found three." DeMasi's story has been denied by the FBI and the FDNY. It has been largely ignored by the controlled corporate media, except for an article in the neocon *New York Post* which alleged that TRAC team was heavily in debt. (*Philadelphia News*, October 28, 2004)

THE FEMA BPAT REPORT OF MAY 2002: "A HALF-BAKED FARCE"

The worthy culmination of this "half-baked farce" was the FEMA BPAT report issued in May 2002. A key section is the one entitled "Structural Response to Fire Loading," where the central tenets are developed in all their intimate poverty. According to the FEMA/ASCE experts:

> As fire spread and raised the temperature of structural members, the structure was further stressed and weakened, until it eventually was unable to support its immense weight. Although the specific chain of events that led to the eventual collapse will probably never be identified, the following effects of fire on structures may each have contributed to the collapse in some way. Appendix A presents a more detailed discussion of the structural effects of fire.

> As floor framing and supported slabs above and in a fire arm are heated, they expand. As a structure expands, it can develop additional, potentially large, stresses in some elements. If the resulting stress state exceeds the capacity of some members or their connections, this can initiate a series of failures.

> As the temperature of floor slabs and support framing increases, these elements can lose rigidity and sag into catenary action [i.e., supporting

by suspension, as a chain]. As catenary action progresses, horizontal framing elements and floor slabs become tensile elements, which can cause failure of end connections and allow supported floors to collapse onto the floors below. The presence of large amounts of debris on some floors of WTC 1 would have made them even more susceptible to this behavior. In addition to overloading the floors below, and potentially resulting in a pancake-type collapse of successive floors, local floor collapse would also immediately increase the laterally unsupported length of columns, permitting buckling to begin. As indicated in Appendix B, the propensity of exterior columns to buckle would have been governed by the relatively weak bolted column splices between the vertically stacked prefabricated exterior wall units. This effect would be even more likely to occur in a fire that involves several adjacent floor levels simultaneously, because the columns could effectively lose lateral support over several stories.

As the temperature of column steel increases, the yield strength and modulus of elasticity degrade and the critical buckling strength of the columns will decrease, potentially initiating buckling, even if lateral support is maintained. This effect is most likely to have been significant in the failure of the interior core columns.

Concerning the twin towers, FEMA had only agnostic conclusions to offer: "With the information and time available, the sequence of events leading to the collapse of each tower could not be definitively determined." Concerning WTC 7: "The specifics of the fires in WTC 7 and how they caused the building to collapse remain unknown at this time. Although the total diesel fuel on the premises contained massive potential energy, the best hypothesis has only a low probability of occurrence. Further research, investigation, and analyses are needed to resolve this issue." (911research.wtc7.net) The World Trade Center disaster was the centerpiece of an event which the Bush administration had seized on to start what may well turn out to be a world war, but that main event could not be explained, many months after the fact.

The FEMA report is redolent of conscious distortion and of fraud. The illustrations in the spring 2002 FEMA report do everything possible to make the twin towers look like flimsy, unstable structures. In one cross-section (Figure 2-1 in the report), the core columns are depicted in about one third of their actual dimensions. FEMA gives short shrift or no shrift at all to the cross-bracing core beams and the core columns. One picture (D-13) shows what is purportedly a core column with a construction hard hat on it to convey its dimensions, but this column is about half the size of the real core columns.

FEMA's illustrations offered in support of their theory of truss failure (2-20, 21, 22) show no steel columns in the core of the building at all. These fake diagrams duly impressed the radical empiricists at the *New York Times*, who quickly reported that the interior core of the buildings was a hollow steel shaft, not 47 massive steel box columns.

The heart of the FEMA argument is that the astronomical temperatures allegedly reached by the fires weakened the floor trusses, causing each floor to pancake onto the one below. As the floors fell away, the columns in the façade as well as the core columns remained standing, but they then quickly buckled at the points where they were bolted together, and came crashing down. This theory is not based on observation, but on pure speculation. It is a purely cinematic explanation of what happened – it tries to account for the phenomenon of collapse, but takes no notice of whether such a process could occur in the real world. In fact, the floor truss/pancake theory cannot function in the real world. Even if the floors failed, the strong structure of the 47 central columns, minus a very few which might have been severed by the impact of the airlines (even fewer in the South Tower) would have remained standing. That would have left a 110-floor steel spine intact, and this is not what was observed. Many of the deceptive drawings contained in the FEMA report then became the inspiration for the graphics used in the NOVA documentary program on this subject which was aired on PBS.

Because of the difficulties of the pancake theory, busy academics have whipped up new theories to try to meet obvious objections. Apologists for the official version start with the mythical notion of *killer fires* – fires which, even though they are fed by carpets, paper, and office furniture, are able to melt steel. From here they develop the notion of *progressive total collapse* – the buildings do not fall to one side, but simply collapse in place upon their own foundations. Since no modern steel-framed skyscraper had ever succumbed to fire, the attempted cover-up then required new pseudo-theoretical constructs. One of these was the *column failure*, or wet noodle, theory. This suggested that fires melted the core columns, and that was that. Of course, even the cover-up cannot change the fact that the fires were not hot enough to melt the core columns. Steel is a very effective conductor of heat, meaning that a serious hot spot on one floor is likely to be dissipated up and down the columns that pass through that hot spot. The internal and external columns, that is to say, act as cooling ribs. According to a study by Corus Construction cited at www.911research.wtc7.net, the highest temperature reached by steel in the presence of hydrocarbon fires was logged at about 360 degrees Fahrenheit – far below what is needed to weaken steel. Moreover, to collapse symmetrically, rather than toppling, the weakening would have to be precisely symmetrical, a clear impossibility.

Given the disadvantages of the column failure theory, the *truss failure* theory was advanced. The trusses were relatively lightweight metal structures which attached the metal decks bearing the concrete slabs of each floor to the core columns and the columns in the façade. The trusses offered the added advantage of being invisible from the outside, so that it was possible to assert without fear of being refuted that they had gotten extremely hot.

MIT Professor Thomas Eagar is one who has rushed into the many breaches of the FEMA report in an attempt to shore up its credibility. Not content with *trusses* and *pancakes*, Eagar has propounded the *zipper* theory, which he has judiciously combined with the *domino* effect. Eagar's argument is that if the angle clip on one side of the building had given way, then the unbearable load on the other angle clips would have caused the entire floor to become totally unzipped in just a few seconds. According to Eagar, "If it had only occurred in one little corner, such as a trash can caught on fire, you might have had to repair that corner, but the whole building wouldn't have come crashing down. The problem was, it was such a widely distributed fire, and then you got this domino effect." (www.911research.wtc7.net/talks/wtc/trusseseagar.html) In reality, the buildings had been designed to resist a Boeing 707, not just a trash can fire.

FACT CHECK

The melting point of steel is 1,538 degrees Celsius, equal to 2,800° Fahrenheit, although it will weaken and buckle at somewhat lower temperatures. But the absolute maximum that can be achieved with hydrocarbons, such as the kerosene-like mixture used for jet fuel, is 825° C or 1517° F – unless the mixture is pressurized or pre-heated through the admixture of fuel and air, which in this case it could not be. Diffuse flames burn at a lower temperature, and fires fed by inadequate oxygen are cooler still. The best estimate is that the fires in the towers were burning at a temperature substantially less than 800° C. Tests have shown that fires in steel buildings do not exceed 360° C, but steel does not even begin to weaken at temperatures below 800° C. Yet even if it had, moderate weakening would have had no effect, since the building was designed to carry five times the expected loads. And even then if the steel still had weakened, the buildings would have twisted and toppled to one side, rather than taking the path of greatest resistance straight through the core. The unprecedented collapse of the towers from the effects of fire is thus an absolute physical impossibility.

LOIZEAUX PREDICTS THE COLLAPSE

In the March hearings of the House Science Committee, Robert F. Shea, the Acting Administrator of the Federal Insurance and Mitigation Administration noted that "the World Trade Center was a tragedy. And, frankly, it was an anomaly. No one who viewed it that day, including myself, believed that those towers would fall. Our collective thought process for laymen and engineers and firefighters changed that day forever." (House March 60)

At those same hearings, a leaflet was distributed by the Skyscraper Safety Campaign, an organization which included many members of the victims' families. Here the Congressmen were reminded: "The collapse of the Twin Towers caused the biggest loss of life in a single incident on US soil since the Civil War. Their collapse constituted the first failures of high-rise protected steel structures in history. Not a single structural engineer, including those working for the firm that built the Twin Towers and those working in the Fire Department of New York, seems to have anticipated their collapse, even when those individuals saw the extent of the fires raging in the buildings. The Twin Towers were designed to withstand the impact of the largest passenger jets of their day, a Boeing 707…." (House March 167)

However, it turned out that there was at least one expert who claimed that he had immediately intuited that the towers could collapse. As John Seabrook wrote in the *New Yorker*, "among the dozens of people I have spoken to recently who are experts in the construction of tall buildings (and many of whom witnessed the events of September 11th as they unfolded), only one said that he knew immediately, upon learning, from TV, of the planes hitting the buildings, that the towers were going to fall. This was Mark Loizeaux, the president of Controlled Demolition Incorporated (www.controlled-demolition.com), a Maryland-based family business that specializes in reducing tall buildings to manageable pieces of rubble. 'Within a nanosecond,' he told me. 'I said, "It's coming down." And the second tower will fall first, because it was hit lower down.'" Loizeaux was billed as a "structural undertaker" whose job was to destroy old buildings. Here is Loizeaux' version of how he foresaw the disaster:

> I thought, "Somebody's got to tell the Fire Department to get out of there… I picked up the phone, dialed 411, got the number, and tried it – busy. So I called the Mayor's Office of Emergency Management" – which was in 7 World Trade. "All circuits were busy. I couldn't get through."

But how could Loizeaux know what no other expert claimed to know, and which went against a hundred years accumulated by civil engineers in building skyscrapers? If suspects are those who had the means, the motive and the opportunity, then Loizeaux may well have had the means. According to the demolitions man:

> First of all, you've got the obvious damage to the exterior frame from the airplane – if you count the number of external columns missing from the sides the planes hit, there are about two-thirds of the total. And the buildings are still standing, which is amazing – even with all those columns missing, the gravity loads have found alternate pathways. O.K., but you've got fires – jet-fueled fires, which the building is not designed for, and you've also got lots of paper in there. Now, paper cooks. A paper fire is like a coal-mine fire, it keeps burning as long as oxygen gets to it. And you're high in the building, up in the wind, plenty of oxygen. So you've got a hot fire. And you've got these floor trusses, made of fairly thin metal, and fire protection has been knocked off most of them by the impact. And you have all this open space – clear span from perimeter to core – with no columns or partition walls, so the airplane is going to skid right through that space to the core, which doesn't have any reinforced concrete in it, just sheetrock covering steel,

and the fire is going to spread everywhere immediately, and no fire-protection systems are working – the sprinkler heads shorn off by the airplanes, the water pipes in the core are likely cut. So what's going to happen? Floor A is going to fall onto floor B, which falls onto floor C; the unsupported columns will buckle; and the weight of everything above the crash site falls onto what remains below – bringing loads of two thousand pounds per square foot, plus the force of impact, onto floors designed to bear one hundred pounds per square foot. It has to fall." (*The New Yorker,* November 19, 2001)

Naturally, the pancake theory was original neither to Loizeaux nor to FEMA. The pancake theory had been advanced by "Osama bin Laden" in the remarks attributed to him, allegedly made in mid-November 2001, and widely publicized by the US government in December 2001. Here bin Laden is alleged to have commented: "We calculated in advance the number of casualties from the enemy, who would be killed based on the position of the tower. We calculated that the floors that would be hit would be three or four floors. I was the most optimistic of them all. (Inaudible) Due to my experience in this field, I was thinking that the fire from the gas in the plane would melt the iron structure of the building and collapse the area where the plane hit and all the floors above it only. This is all that we had hoped for." But there are indications that the stocky figure shown on the tape may not be the reputedly ascetic bin Laden at all, but a double or ham actor; see photos on page 138. (Meyssan 2002 192)

REDUCTIO AD ABSURDUM: WTC 7

In the May House Science Committee W. Gene Corley, the American Society of Civil Engineers representative on the BPAT, conceded that "Building 7, which was across the street from the main towers, also collapsed and provided us with the first example that we recognized of a building collapsing as a result of fire." (House May 30) WTC 7 presents the image of a classical controlled demolition. Whereas the twin towers are seen to explode, WTC 7 implodes – it falls in upon itself with none of the spectacular mushroom plumes of smoke and powder which had marked the demise of the larger twin towers. The foundations collapse before the façade, the middle of the building collapses before the outer walls, and streamers of smoke are emitted from the façade; see photographs on page 246. WTC 7 did imitate the twin towers by collapsing almost exclusively upon its own foundations. WTC 7 contained electrical generators and a supply for diesel fuel to operate these, and apologists of the official version like Gerald Posner have seized on this circumstance to make the collapse of this building plausible. But there has been no sign of raging diesel fuel fires, as can be seen from the photos of the fall of WTC 7, so the apologists are grasping at straws.

The owner of the WTC complex was Larry Silverstein, a friend of Israeli prime ministers, who recounted the fall of WTC 7 in the September 2002 PBS documentary, *America Rebuilds,* complete with this astounding revelation: "I remember getting a call from the...fire department commander, telling me that they were not sure they were going to be able to contain the fire, and I said, 'we've had such terrible loss of life, maybe the smartest thing is to pull it. And they made the decision to pull and we watched the building collapse." "To pull" would appear to be the jargon term in controlled demolition circles for the deliberate detonation of charges leading to the destruction of a building. And if WTC 7 was pulled, why not WTC 1 and 2? (Marrs 43) Silverstein was already awarded an insurance profit of a half billion dollars on WTC 7 and stands to net another billion in insurance gains from the Twin Towers – although he had leased them only six weeks before.

ANOMALIES OF THE WTC COLLAPSE

The twin towers did not simply collapse as a result of gravity; they were violently pulverized in mid-air in an explosive process which hurled debris hundreds of meters in all directions – they were vaporized by an explosive force. Anomalies abound. The North Tower was hit first, was hit hardest in its core columns, and had more jet fuel burn inside its structure than the South Tower – but the North Tower exploded later. The South Tower was hit later, with a more glancing blow which had less impact on its core columns, and which also caused more jet fuel to be consumed outside of the building in a spectacular plume; the South Tower's fires were less severe – but the South Tower fell first. WTC 7 was never hit by a plane, and had minor fires only on two floors (there are no photos of WTC 7 enveloped in flames and smoke) – but WTC 7 fell anyway. WTC 6 witnessed an explosion and fire which has never been explained or even addressed.

Finally, we have the embarrassing fact that steel frame skyscrapers are virtually indestructible by fire. The official version of events argues that, at least as far as the towers are concerned, it was the combined effect of crash impact plus fire which caused the collapses. But even the South Tower collapsed well after most of the jet fuel had burned away, and a fire based on paper, rugs, and furniture melts steel even less than one based on jet fuel. By all indications, the South Tower began the collapse sequence precisely at the moment when, well after the impact had been absorbed, the fires too were subsiding. The hole made in the North Tower by American 11 had cooled so much that, just before the collapse of the North Tower, survivors were observed looking out through the gash in the side of the building. (Marrs 41)

The upper floors of both towers, after showing symptoms of high pressure which forced smoke out through the widows, exploded into spectacular mushroom clouds. Debris and other ejecta were thrown at speeds of 200 feet per second to distances of up to 500 feet in all directions. The clouds then descended, always emanating from the towers as these fell. The mushroom clouds had expanded to two or three times the diameter of the towers after five seconds, and had expanded to five times the diameter of the towers after 15 seconds. Blast waves broke windows in buildings over 400 feet away. In the thick mushroom clouds, solid objects were hurled out ahead of the dust, another telltale sign of explosive demolition.

One might have expected the buildings to tip over at an angle starting at the points where they had been hit like a tree which leaves a stump as it falls towards the side where it has been most chopped, but they did not topple and there were no stumps; apart from some initial asymmetry in the top of the South Tower, the two towers both collapsed down on themselves in a perfectly symmetrical way – a suspicious sign and one of the prime goals and hallmarks of controlled demolition.

The fall of the twin towers took place at breathtaking speed. The tops of the buildings reached the ground as rubble no more than 16 seconds after the collapse process had begun. A weight in a vacuum would have taken 9.2 seconds to cover the same distance. This meant that air resistance and little else had slowed the fall of the upper stories. This indicates that the lower floors must have been demolished and pulverized before the upper stories fell on them. The building, in other words, had been pulverized, and in many areas vaporized, in mid-air. No gravity collapse could have created this phenomenon.

The non-metallic elements of the twin towers, especially the cement slabs which formed the horizontal surface of each floor, were pulverized into a fine dust, with particles of less than 100 microns in diameter. This was the dust which pervaded lower Manhattan as the explosive clouds spread from hundreds of yards in all directions. This dust took a long time to settle, but the Giuliani administration tried to convince office workers in the area that there was no danger. All the steel in the building superstructures was simply shredded. The exceptionally strong central core columns were neatly diced into 10 or 20 floor segments, something which the mythographs have never explained – except accidentally, in the marketing literature of Controlled Demolition Inc., which boasts of their ability to dice debris to lengths to fit their clients' dump trucks.

Jim Hoffman, the source heavily relied on here, is a leading expert on the collapse of the World Trade Center, co-author of *Waking Up from Our Nightmare* and author of the website wtc7.net. Hoffman calculates that the energy necessary to create the mushroom clouds, expand them to the extraordinary dimensions actually observed, pulverize virtually all the concrete in the towers, and to chop the steel into segments, is on an order of magnitude greater than the gravitational energy represented by the buildings.

Hoffman points out that the Twin Towers were demolished "in a decidedly different manner from conventional demolitions to make it [appear] consistent with the story that the towers collapsed as a result of the jet impacts and fires.... Explosions started at the impact zone and proceeded down the intact portion of the tower and up the overhanging portion, instead of starting at ground level.... Much more powerful explosives were used than in a conventional demolition... The Twin Towers exploded rather than imploded." In a classic demolition from ground level, like the implosion of WTC 7, gravity brings the mass of the building down; but in the twin towers, much of it was pulverized and ejected outwards as dust. Hoffman further notes a number of features of the Twin Towers' collapse which suggest that they may have been "demolished through some entirely different process, perhaps involving some form of directed energy weapon," in addition to explosives. For a possible explanation of what kind of energy source could have been at work, we must turn our attention to the realm of new physical principles, and thus to the class of directed-energy weapons which are probably most familiar to the general public in connection with President Reagan's so-called Star Wars speech of March 23, 1983.

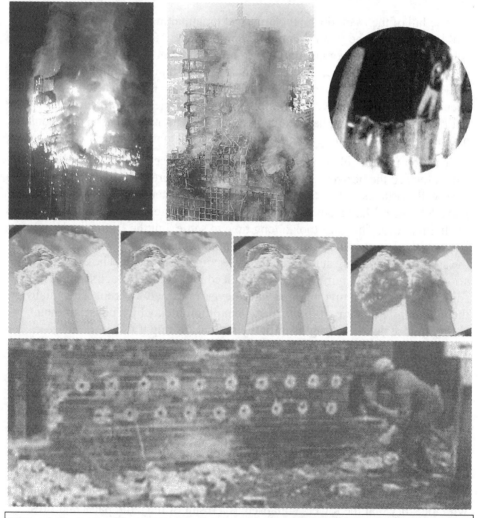

Upper left, center: Hotel Windsor Madrid burned fiercely for 24 hours; after the blaze, the structural skeleton remained intact. Right: women sitting and standing as they peer out from gash where plane hit North Tower – at room temperature. Middle: Demolition charges sequenced top down at speed of falling to simulate a spontaneous collapse. Bottom: typical placement of a row of explosive charges.

High energy microwave interferometry using coaxial beams for constructive and destructive interference might be a possibility. However, engineer Ken Jenkins has pointed out that this would require so much energy that, if it had to be delivered as conventional electric current, it would necessitate a cable about half a meter in diameter – and there is no evidence of this. So the problem remains intractable, and will require more time and research.

Toppling Tower and Exploding Tower: Please see captions on page 248.

THE TWIN TOWERS WERE ROBUST STRUCTURES

The structure of the twin towers was represented first of all by an internal core of 47 steel box columns which measured 36 by 90 centimeters; the steel was thickest near the base, where it attained a thickness of 10 centimeters (about four inches), and tapered gradually down to 6 centimeters on the upper floors. There were 236 exterior columns in the buildings' façades; these were 10 centimeters thick at the base, but only 6 millimeters thick in the highest floors. Each floor was a steel plate into which concrete had been poured. In the center of the building was a reinforced core featuring four steel columns encased in concrete.

The structure is abundantly cross-braced, so that stress in one sector could be efficiently shifted to other parts of the structure. All steel columns rested directly on the bedrock under Manhattan. These structures were designed to withstand 140 mph winds, and had resisted them successfully for more than thirty years. They were designed by Lee Robertson, the structural engineer who built the towers to absorb the impact of a Boeing 707, an aircraft roughly comparable in size and fuel capacity to the aircraft that appear to have struck the towers on 9/11.

47th floor, going down. The sudden, apparently unprovoked collapse of WTC 7 is for many 9/11 skeptics the smoking gun *non plus ultra* of 9/11. This tower was never hit by any plane. There are no photographs of large fires, but there *are* photos showing only two small ones that the fire department is not bothering to fight – and without a single broken window from the ground to the 47th floor. The FEMA report was obliged to discuss WTC 7, but could draw no conclusions about it.

For the 9/11 commission report, the collapse is no part of the Al Qaeda myth, so it simply did not happen. The corporate media studiously ignore it. Public opinion is effectively manipulated by focusing attention on the drama of the Twin Towers, obfuscating the issues around that incident, and hushing up the unexplainable of Bldg. 7. See text *REDUCTIO AD ABSURDUM: WTC 7* on **page 241 ff.** and video clips of the smoothly gliding collapse at wtc7.net or www.hugequestions.com. Compare also www.controlled-demolition.com.

The Pride of Controlled Demolition Inc.

Photo Captions: Page 245, Toppling Tower. The official conspiracy "theory" (or hoax) has nothing going for it except gravity and gravitas. If gravity and not explosives brought down the towers, then the tipping top of the South tower had to keep falling by inertia and plunge into the street, not turn back onto its foundations. The section was reportedly leaning over 23° – half-way to a 45° angle – when it disappeared in a cloud of dust and debris. It appears a detonation timing error had been corrected by further charges which pulverized the wayward top section.

Page 245, Exploding Tower. Demolishing the Twin Towers required explosives to first shatter the 47 massive core columns. The arrow points to a "squib" or smoke plume from a row of such charges within the building. Compare the smoke puff at the top of page 247. After the steel girders were severed, more explosives blew away the cement of the floors and walls in massive plumes, shooting 70 meters outward and upwards at high speed, as can be viewed at www.reopen911.org.

Page 247. Controlled Demolition Inc. Coffee-Table Book dustjacket. Compare CDI chief Loizeaux' confabulation about how the towers self-destructed (p. 241) to this bragging in the CDI book: "Weeks and even months of preparation are required for a successful implosion... Demonstrating expert choreography, the building bends and folds in on itself... Demolition of these three 18-story buildings was so carefully controlled that all of the debris was contained within the footprint of these structures." (Liss 44, 45, 51) Ch. 1: Demolition and Political Change. Ch. 2: Demolition as Offense...

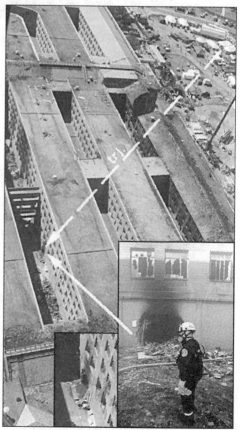

This page (p. 248). A bunker-busting Boeing? "Whatever it was that hit the Pentagon" penetrated at least six exterior walls – it was decidedly not a hollow aluminum tube like a 757. What fits the evidence seems to be a small drone aircraft which launched a bunker-busting missile as it crashed into the Pentagon. Inset shows exit hole of the missile inside the third ring. See p. 258.

Next page (p. 249). Where's the plane? No debris on the lawn, no pieces of wings, tail or fuselage. The lawn is unscratched, although the aircraft hit the building so low that a 757's low-slung engines would have been underground. Also, the outer hole is narrower than the 757's wingspan. See p. 251.

VII
What Hit The Pentagon?

The speed, the maneuverability, the way he turned, we all
thought in the radar room, all of us experienced air traffic
controllers, that that was a military plane. – Danielle O'Brien

The official version and the 9/11 commission report claim that it was
American 77, a hijacked Boeing 757, which struck the side of the Pentagon. Here
the official version is again at its most vulnerable: the impact hole in the side of
the building is far too narrow and deep for a Boeing 757, and there is almost no
recognizable aircraft debris. Beyond these insuperable problems with the physical evidence, the reports of eyewitnesses, while contradictory, show that many
thought they had seen a flying object much smaller than a Boeing 757. Some
spoke of a missile, and at least one of the smell of high explosives in the air.

Perhaps because of these grave difficulties, it was the Pentagon chapter of the
official 9/11 story which came under attack soonest. The timely exposure of the
absurdities of the official story was largely due to the clarity and the courage of
Thierry Meyssan of the Réseau Voltaire in Paris, who used his website to
demystify what had happened. Meyssan's success in making telling points on the
Internet and on French national television even motivated *Le Monde*, the leading
French center-left newspaper, to attempt a grotesque and degrading defense of
the US official account in February and March 2002. *Quelle honte! (For shame!)*

Three days before Meyssan's pioneering book *L'effroyable imposture* (*The Big Lie*) was published, the FBI gave CNN a meager five frames from a surveillance video camera which purported to show how the Pentagon was hit – although these images proved nothing of value to shore up the official version. The pictures were reported in the *Washington Post* of March 7, 2002, and televised on March 8, 2002, certainly not by coincidence.

The defenders of the official story can point to a number of eyewitnesses who claim to have seen something like a Boeing 757 on its way to impact the Pentagon wall. But one problem is that many of these witnesses are military officers, Pentagon contractors, or federal government employees. This gives them all a very evident conflict of interest as witnesses, and renders their testimony *a priori* suspect. The other problem is that the Pentagon was hit much later in the morning than the World Trade Center. The Pentagon was in fact struck at 9:43 AM, that is to say about one hour and 29 minutes after American 11 had gone off course and entered the hijacked category at 8:15 AM.

The irony is that it had been an open secret for almost a full hour that American 77 was a potential threat to the capital; American 77 had gone off course at 8:46. The local cable television news outlet, Newschannel 8, had been telling its viewers of an imminent threat for many minutes before the actual impact at the Pentagon. We should also recall that Andrews Air Force Base, with its two combat-ready fighter wings, was only 11 miles from the Pentagon – just a few minutes' flying time away. Nevertheless, the Air Force proved incapable of getting their assets airborne in time to prevent what could easily have been a decapitation attack on the national capital. It was a record of indescribable ineptitude, which was itself only a cover for active complicity by some key officers in the attack and its geostrategic goals.

Since eyewitnesses who work for the military must be eliminated from consideration, and since so much of the traffic on the roads around the Pentagon owe their daily bread to the US federal government, eyewitness accounts must be relegated to a subordinate position. It is always good forensic practice to accord primacy to the irrefutable physical evidence, as against the testimony of witnesses. Some have asserted that there were two aircraft: a large jet as a diversion, and a smaller one, probably with a missile, and have alleged that one purpose could have been to test a bunker-buster missile against a newly reinforced construction.

The southwest face of the Pentagon was undergoing renovation, and it was therefore more sparsely populated than any other part of the building. The section that was impacted was scheduled to house the command center of the US Navy. The Navy top brass was not present that day. In fact, it is notable that no top-level civilian officials or military officers were killed in the attack. Many of the dead were construction workers and low-level Defense Department employees. The oligarchy, in short, did not pay a serious price for the strike against the Pentagon.

The flying object, whatever it was, could have most easily hit the Pentagon from above, in a vertical dive-bombing run. But the flying object went out of its way to hit the empty quarter of the building. As CBS News reported on September 12, 2001, "Radar shows that Flight 77 did a downward spiral, turning almost a complete circle and dropping the last 7,000 feet in two and a half minutes." (Hoffman 6) In addition to multiplying the difficulties, this maneuver also meant that the attacking craft was in the air and exposed to fighter interceptors for an additional two minutes, and that in the most sensitive and presumably well-guarded air space in the world. It is hard to see why real hijackers, intent only on striking the heart of imperialism or of the infidels, would not have hit the eastern part of the building, where they might have been able to number Rumsfeld and other top officials and officers among their victims.

THE PHYSICAL EVIDENCE

The flying object which hit the Pentagon cannot have been American 77. American 77 was a Boeing 757-200, a type of aircraft which is 155 feet long and which has wingspan of 125 feet. When the landing gear are retracted in flight, the plane measures 18 feet from the bottom of its engine to the top of its fuselage. The height of the plane from the bottom of the engines to the top of the tail is 45 feet. The fuselage is 13 feet in diameter.

The original impact punched a hole estimated by Marrs as between 15 and 20 feet wide, and by Meyssan as between 15 and 18 feet wide – barely wide enough for the fuselage of a 757. Above the impact hole is an intact wall which is not more than 25 feet above the ground, some 20 feet too low to accommodate the tail. The flying object that collided with the Pentagon could not have been a Boeing 757-200.

Each of the five faces of the Pentagon is 280 meters long. A major physical problem of the official version is that, even after the collapse of the building façade on either side of the original small impact hole, the collapsed section of wall measures only 19 meters, in contrast to the plane's 38 meter wing span. Even after the fire had collapsed the section of wall, the hole was only half as wide as it needed to be. This problem was made worse by the fact that, according to the Pentagon and press accounts, the alleged plane came in almost perfectly level, but at an oblique angle of about 45 degrees with the southwest façade of the building. This angle of attack would have increase the stretch of wall impacted by the plane and its wings to some 177 feet.

Given that the position of the impact hole was so close to the ground, attention naturally turned to the Pentagon lawn between the building and a multi-lane highway that passes nearby. Strikingly, the Penta-lawn (as it came to be called) was totally pristine and untouched. It looked like the most perfect putting green at an opulent country club. One or two lamp posts had been knocked down, but others were intact. Of the few vehicles parked near the lawn, one or two had burst into flames, but the others were intact. There are simply none of the inevitable physical hallmarks of a crashed jetliner.

OBSTACLES IN THE FLIGHT PATH

In order to fulfill the specifications of the official version, it must be assumed that American 77 flew across the Penta-lawn at well below treetop level – the plane must be thought of as skimming along just inches above the ground. The flight path is known with some precision because a number of lamp posts were knocked down. But there were other, more serious obstacles: American 77 had to fly across a construction site which was surrounded by a chain link fence. There was a generator located about where the right engine of the plane would have passed. There were also large spools of cable or wire. The fence, the generator, and the spools present serious difficulties for the official version. The jet engines of a Boeing 757 are about 10 feet in diameter, and the engine assemblies extend 5 feet below the fuselage.

NO COMMERCIAL AIRLINER DEBRIS

Another great anomaly of the Pentagon crash scene is the total absence, with only one very suspicious exception, of identifiable aircraft debris outside the building. The Pentagon was unable to show any jet engines, any landing gear, any tail section, any wing fragments, any sections of fuselage, any seats, any bodies, any luggage. The small metal fragments which were shown to the press were about enough to fill a small washbasin. Where was the plane?

After the fact, a search line of about 20 men in uniform appeared on the Penta-lawn in front of the impact zone. Men wearing white shirts and ties also appeared on the lawn and carefully gathered up various fragments of debris that had been scattered there. If this had indeed been the scene of an airplane crash, the National Transportation Safety Board should have gone into action, securing important pieces of evidence and holding all other agencies at bay under the threat of felony prosecution. But at the Pentagon there was no sign of the NTSB. After a while a group of military men in uniform carried away what appeared to be a large container wrapped in a tarpaulin with something large but not excessively heavy inside. One photograph was published claiming to show the turbofan of a 757; but in a recent OnlineJournal article, Karl Schwarz and his research team have identified it as a part from the much smaller A3 Skywarrior.

Since the Pentagon is located in Arlington County, Virginia, it was the Arlington County Fire Department which had the primary responsibility for fighting the Pentagon fire. The Arlington County Fire Chief was Ed Plaugher. The Arlington County firefighters were not allowed to approach the immediate impact site; they fought the fire at a distance, from the outside lawn and inside the Pentagon. They were kept away from the place where the airliner was supposed to be by a special Urban Search and Rescue Team from FEMA.

Even so, Ed Plaugher's testimony is valuable. Plaugher was allowed to speak at a Pentagon press conference held on September 12, and run by Victoria Clarke, the Assistant Secretary of Defense for Public Affairs, and thus the chief Pentagon spokeswoman. Chief Plaugher was unable to answer some very basic, common-sense questions about what is alleged by the government to have occurred at the Pentagon. Here is an excerpt:

Reporter: Is there anything left of the aircraft at all?

Plaugher: First of all, the question about the aircraft, there are some small pieces of aircraft visible from the interior during this fire-fighting operation I'm talking about, but not large sections. In other words, there's no fuselage sections and that sort of thing. [...]

Reporter: Chief, there are small pieces of the plane virtually all over, out over the highway, tiny pieces. Would you say the plane exploded, virtually exploded on impact due to the fuel or...?

Plaugher: You know, I'd rather not comment on that. We have a lot of eyewitnesses that can give you better information about what actually happened with the aircraft as it approached. So we don't know. I don't know. [...]

Reporter: Where is the jet fuel? Just...?

Plaugher: We have what we believe is a puddle right there that the...what we believe is to be the nose of the aircraft. (*The Big Lie* 23)

The unique piece of apparent aircraft wreckage associated with the Pentagon crash was found on the Penta-lawn. This fragment matched the color scheme of American Airlines, and seemed to bear a part of the letter "n." A consensus of analysts assembled by Jim Hoffman tends to view this fragment as belonging to the starboard forward portion of the fuselage of a Boeing 757. There is no sign of fire damage, no soot, no black coating as would be typical of a jet fuel fire. The fact that this lone piece of evidence turned up in such utter isolation increases the natural suspicion that it was simply planted as part of an effort to shore up the credibility of the Pentagon's claim that a commercial airliner had hit the building.

COVERUP

The overall impression of a rather maladroit coverup is increased by the behavior of the FBI at and around the crime scene. First, all available video tape from surveillance cameras which might have captured the flying object was confiscated with the speed of lightning. This included video tape from the gas station that was directly under the flight path of the object, and from another gas station a hundred yards or so to the west. It also included video tape from a camera maintained by the Sheraton Washington Hotel. It included every business in the area. The FBI has never released these tapes, and they were not made public by the 9/11 commission. All that has been released has been five frames from a surveillance camera, heavily edited to remove the frame or frames which might have shown the actual flying object itself; or perhaps the number of frames is small because they owe more to original art than photography. The contents of the flight data recorder and the cockpit voice recorder have never been released, under the claim that they were rendered inoperable by the fire. Initially, the FBI claimed that it was assembling the pieces of wreckage or at least inventorying them, but no more was ever heard about any such effort. For our own inventory of facts, though, the list price of a new Boeing 757 is on the order of $80 million. Whatever else it may be, the cloak-and-dagger industry is also a lucrative racket.

EYEWITNESSES

We now cite several eyewitness reports, frankly focusing on those which contradict the official version. FAA air traffic controllers assigned to Dulles Airport, near Washington in northern Virginia, picked up a flying object coming towards Washington DC at high speed. "The first Dulles controller noticed the fast-moving plane at 9:25 AM. Moments later, controllers sounded an alert that an aircraft appeared to be heading directly toward the White House." (*Washington Post*, November 3, 2001)

Danielle O'Brien, an air traffic controller at Dulles Airport, said in an interview with ABC News that she and her colleagues had observed the radar blip approaching the Pentagon as it carried out this remarkable maneuver. Here is what she later said they all concluded at that time: "The speed, the maneuverability, the way he turned, we all thought in the radar room, all of us experienced air traffic controllers, that that was a military plane." (ABC News, October 24, 2001) This reflects the CBS report we have already examined, according to which "Flight 77 did a downward spiral, turning almost a complete circle and dropping the last 7,000 feet in two and a half minutes." (Hoffman 6)

Army Captain Lincoln Liebner claimed that he had distinctly seen an American Airlines airliner coming towards the Pentagon at high speed and at a low altitude. (Marrs 29) But army captains are not likely to undercut the official version; they are under military discipline, and therefore not their own men.

Steve Patterson told a reporter: "The airplane seemed to be able to hold between eight and twelve persons." (*Washington Post*, September 11, 2001)

Tom Seibert: "We heard something that made the sound of a missile, then we heard a powerful boom." (*Washington Post*, September 11, 2001)

Mike Walter told CNN: "A plane, a plane from American Airlines. I thought, 'That's not right, it's really low.' And I saw it. I mean, it was like a cruise missile with wings." (Marrs 29)

April Gallop, a Pentagon employee, was working at her job on the morning of 9/11. She was getting ready to take her son to his day care when the impact occurred. "I thought it was a bomb," she recounted later. "I was buried in rubble and my first thought was for my son. I crawled around until I found his stroller. It was all crumpled up into a ball and I was very afraid. But then I heard his voice and I managed to locate him. We crawled out through a hole in the side of the building. Outside they were treating survivors on the grassy lawn. But all the ambulances had left, so a man who was near the scene stepped up, put us in his private car, and drove us to the hospital. The images are burned into my brain."

While in the hospital, Gallop received a series of visits from men in suits, presumably FBI agents. "They never identified themselves or even said which agency they worked for. But I know they were not newsmen because I learned that the Pentagon told news reporters not to cover survivors' stories or they would not get any more stories out of there. The men who visited all said they couldn't tell me what to say, they only wanted to make suggestions. But then they told me what to do, which was to take the [victim compensation fund] money and shut up. They also kept insisting that a plane hit the building. They repeated this over and over. But I was there and I never saw a plane or even debris from a plane. I figure the plane story is there to brainwash people." (Marrs 26)

Christine Peterson: "My mind could not comprehend what happened. Where did the plane go? ... But there was no plane visible, only huge billows of smoke and torrents of fire." (911research.wtc7.net)

DeChiaro: "My brain could not resolve the fact that it was a plane because it only seemed like a small hole in the building. No tail. No wings. No nothing." (911research.wtc7.net)

Moran: "I saw the flash and subsequent fireball rise approximately 200 feet above the Pentagon. There was a large explosion noise and the low frequency sound echo that comes with this type of sound. Associated with that was the increase in air pressure, momentarily, like a small gust of wind. For those formerly in the military, it sounded like a 2000-lb bomb going off 1/2 mile in front of you." (911research.wtc7.net)

Perkal: "Even before stepping outside I could smell the cordite. Then I knew explosives had been set off somewhere." (911research.wtc7.net)

Joel Sucherman thought that he had seen an American Airlines plane, "But whoever was flying the plane made no attempt to change direction. It was coming in at a high rate of speed, but not at a steep angle – almost like a heat-seeking missile was locked on its target and staying dead on course." ("Journalist Witnesses Pentagon Crash," eWeek, September 13, 2001)

Dick Cheney later recalled how he had first learned of the attack on the Pentagon: "The first reports on the Pentagon attack suggested a helicopter and then a private jet." (*Los Angeles Times*, September 17, 2001)

Later, in an interview with *Parade Magazine*, Defense Secretary Rumsfeld himself also referred to the object which hit the Pentagon as a "missile." (Marrs 29) Was this a Freudian slip by the loquacious defense chief?

The lead pilot of the interceptor group sent from Langley AFB said later: "I reverted to the Russian threat....I'm thinking cruise missile threat from the sea. You look down and you see the Pentagon burning and I thought the bastards snuck one by us....[Y]ou couldn't see any airplanes, and no one told us anything." (9/11 commission 45) This pilot is in effect reporting that the damage he observed at the Pentagon was compatible with a cruise missile explosion. His explicit citing of a cruise missile should not be neglected.

What then is the origin of the claim that the Pentagon was hit by a Boeing 757, and specifically by American 77? During the first 9/11 official press conference by the Defense Department, Navy spokesman Rear Admiral Craig Quigley was unable to offer any specifics about what he was at that time calling an "allegedly hijacked commercial aircraft." (Defense Link DOD, 11 September 2001) During the course of the afternoon, the new party line that American 77 had hit the Pentagon was spread by anonymous military leakers. According to the *Los Angeles Times* of 9/11, officials "speaking under the condition of anonymity" had briefed journalists that the flying object which had crashed into the Pentagon was American 77.

THE FIVE BELATED FRAMES OF MARCH 2002

The only available photographic evidence for the events at the Pentagon emerged on March 6, 2002, when five US news organizations were able to obtain a limited number of frames from a security camera in a Pentagon parking lot somewhat to the west of the point of impact. (*Washington Post*, March 7, 2002)

One frame showed a bright, orange-colored fireball, but there was no sign of an American Airlines jet. The *Washington Post* thought it saw a small, blurry white object. Whatever is shown in this frame has a tail that is at most half as tall as the Pentagon façade, but the tail of a real Boeing 757 would be almost as tall as the Pentagon itself, and possibly taller, depending on how close to the ground it was flying. American Airlines, furthermore, has always preferred to keep the fuselages of its planes gleaming silver, not white. The frames also show a thin trail of white smoke left behind by the flying machine. This should not be confused with the condensation trails which are left behind by planes flying in the extremely cold air of the higher altitudes. Apart from a slight darkening, jets flying near the ground leave very little trail of any kind behind them. As Gerhard Wisnewski points out, "Such a smoke trail does not speak at all for the presence of a jet, but for a rocket." (Wisnewski 154)

Thierry Meyssan's *Pentagate* contained an authoritative assessment of the explosion at the Pentagon, taking into account what was seen on the selected and censored frames of video tape released by the FBI after many months. This study was contributed by Colonel Pierre-Henri Bunel. Bunel, a French artilleryman and graduate of the world-famous École Militaire of St. Cyr, the French equivalent of West Point and Sandhurst, was a battlefield damage assessment officer who served in the first Gulf War of 1991. One of Bunel's fundamental points is a discussion of the different types of explosions. His focus is the speed of the shock wave which each type of explosion produces:

> Explosive materials are divided into two groups, according to their progressiveness [i.e., the speed of propagation of their shock wave]. Explosives produce a shock wave whose speed of propagation is superior to a value of about six thousand feet per second. One says that they "detonate." Explosive materials whose shock wave speed is lower than that do not detonate. They deflagrate. This is the case, for example, of gunpowder or hydrocarbons.

> Jet fuel, which is similar to kerosene, does not possess the high explosive power of cordite or other materials used for making bombs and conventional missile warheads. The most jet fuel can manage is deflagration; it is not powerful enough to generate a detonation. The frames of the Pentagon being hit show a fireball which is a white-hot, brilliant fireball attaining some 130 feet in height, thus indicating a powerful detonation, most likely caused by high explosives of some type. Compare this to the jet fuel explosion involving the South Tower of the World Trade Center, where a cloud of jet fuel went from yellow to orange to black as the fuel was consumed. The evidence again suggests that a large commercial airliner was not involved, but rather some form of missile.

> This argument is supported by the white vapor or exhaust trail of the flying object as shown on the Pentagon's own video frames. This is not the exhaust of fan jets running on kerosene fuel, since this exhaust trail would be darker if it were visible at all so close to the ground. (Pentagate 67 ff.)

So much for the exhaust trail and fireball observed at the outer façade of the Pentagon. Another issue posed by the Pentagon events is the ability of the flying object to penetrate several rings of the large building's structure. Bunel reminds us here of the bunker-busting bombs used during the Gulf War of 1991, and much improved since. Bunel notes that "for certain very hard fortifications, one even finds that there are multi-charged weapons. The first charges fracture the concrete, while the later one or ones penetrate and detonate. In general, anti-concrete charges are hollow charges. The jet of energy and melted materials penetrates the fortification and spreads quantities of hot materials inside which are propelled by a column of energy which pierces the walls like a punch. The great heat produced by the detonation of the hollow charge sets fire to everything that is combustible inside." (Pentagate 71)

Colonel Bunel discusses the flight patterns of cruise missiles, which generally have a launch phase, a cruise phase, and an acceleration phase as they are approaching the target, so that they attain their maximum speed just before impact. He also points out that cruise missiles also carry out an end-course correction in order to impact the target at precisely the point and angle of attack desired. According to Bunel, "that is why it so often happens that the missile ends its cruising flight with a tight turn that allows it to adopt the right alignment. A witness might observe that the missile reduces its engine power before throttling back up." (Pentagate 72) This would account for the spectacular 270 degree turn carried out by the flying object that hit the Pentagon, while descending 7,000 feet in two minutes. It is far more plausible that this extremely demanding maneuver was carried out by the computerized, pre-programmed guidance system of a cruise missile, than that it was due to the dubious flying skills of the notorious bungler, Hani Hanjour.

Bunel also points out that the firemen shown fighting the Pentagon fire in the available photographs are not using foam, as they would for a jet-fuel fire, but a water-based mixture. They are using water hoses, not foam cannons. There is some evidence of foam, but this appears to be limited to one or two vehicles on the Pentagon lawn that burst into flames as the flying object hit; their gasoline fuel tanks were what required the foam, and not the larger fire in the Pentagon building itself.

Bunel examines the pictures published by the Department of Defense as allegedly showing the maximum penetration of the flying object that hit the Pentagon, which managed to punch a hole 7 feet in diameter in the inner wall of the third ring in from the outside façade.

> The appearance of the perforation in the wall certainly resembles the effects of anti-concrete hollow charges that I have been able to observe on a number of battlefields. These weapons are characterized by their "jet"…this jet pierces concrete through many feet of thickness. It could thus pierce five thick walls of the building without any problem. Five walls out of six because the façade was already perforated by the delivery system itself. (Pentagate 84)

Based on these considerations, and with special reference to his analysis of the photo of the inner wall of the third ring, Colonel Bunel offers the following hypothesis:

> This photo, and the effects described in the official version, lead me therefore to think that the detonation that struck the building was that of a high-powered hollow charge used to destroy hardened buildings and carried by an aerial vehicle, a missile. (Pentagate 85-86)

WHY NO AIR DEFENSE OF THE PENTAGON?

In 2001, the Pentagon should have been one of the best-defended points on earth. Nevertheless, it was hit by a flying object carrying a warhead at 9:43 AM, one hour and twenty-nine minutes after American 11 had been hijacked. For the official version, this remains an acute embarrassment and an insoluble mystery. It is widely reported, and even more widely assumed, that the Pentagon was equipped with powerful batteries of surface to air missiles. This is virtually impossible to confirm, since the details of defense dispositions are all strictly classified.

The hypothesis of a cruise missile fired off by a military unit in support of the 9/11 putsch helps solve problems here as well. Military aircraft of all types, including cruise missiles, are equipped with a friend-foe indicator which allows the US side to distinguish its own (and allied) air assets from hostile objects. If it was indeed a US cruise missile which hit the Pentagon, then it is likely that such a cruise missile would have carried a friend-foe indicator signaling that it was a military asset of the US side. This feature may well have helped to neutralize or defeat the Pentagon's air defense system: the incoming object may have been perceived as a friendly one. But there may be further complications.

In testimony to the 9/11 commission, Transportation Secretary Norman Mineta recounted what he had seen in the White House Bunker. Mineta had arrived at the Presidential Emergency Operating Center soon after the South Tower had been hit. Mineta testified:

> During the time that the airplane was coming in to the Pentagon, there was a young man who would come in and say to the Vice President, "The plane is 50 miles out." "The plane is 30 miles out." And when it got down to "the plane is 10 miles out," the young man also said to the Vice President, "Do the orders still stand?" And the Vice President turned and whipped his neck around and said, "Of course the orders still stand! Have you heard anything to the contrary? Well at the time, I didn't know what all that meant…. [That was the] flight that came into the Pentagon." (Marrs 30)

To the question of whether the orders being referred to involved shooting down the incoming flying object, Mineta replied:

> Well, I don't know that specifically. I do know that the [interceptor] airplanes were scrambled from Langley or from Norfolk, the Norfolk area, and so I did not know about the order specifically other than to listening to that other conversation….Subsequently, I found that out.

This exchange poses a number of important issues. It has been interpreted as the repeated confirmation of an order to shoot down wayward aircraft that refused to respond to orders. If these conversations actually happened, and if Cheney had indeed issued the order to "take out" planes that did not respond to orders from air traffic controllers, then we must wonder why the aircraft approaching the Pentagon was not in fact shot down. Since that did not happen, it may be that the unstated terms of Cheney's exchanges with the "young man" were based on something else. Was the premise here in fact the elusive stand-down order which in the opinion of some would have been necessary to cripple US air defense to the extent that occurred on September 11? If this is so, then what was being repeatedly confirmed here was an order not to shoot down the incoming flight. This latter interpretation best fits the words Mineta says he heard.

VIII
SHANKSVILLE

United 93 took off from Newark Airport at 8:42 after a 40-minute delay. It left the ground just as the hijacking of United 175 out of Boston was becoming known to the FAA. The airplane headed west, and its hijacking became known at 9:36. At this point United 93 turned off its transponder and headed back towards the east. Again, the moment the transponder channel ceased to operate is the likely moment when Global Hawk or some other system of remote control assumed control of the aircraft.

Around this time, Bush and Cheney were discussing the need to authorize shoot-downs of civilian airliners by the pilots in the Combat Air Patrols the Air Force was now straining to deploy. Richard Clarke told the teleconference of key agencies: "Three decisions. One, the President has ordered the use of force against aircraft deemed to be hostile. Two, the White House is also requesting fighter escort of Air Force One. Three, and this applies to all agencies, we are initiating COG. Please activate your alternate command center and move staff to them immediately." (Bamford 2004 66) COG was Continuity of Government, the centerpiece of the long-standing machinery for emergency rule from bunker complexes which had been developed over the years, including with the help of figures like Oliver North and Buster Horton. Clarke spoke at around 9:55 AM.

Soon after, the authorization to open fire on hijacked aircraft that refused to obey the instructions of interceptor jets passed down the chain of command. Bamford, with access to interviews with 9/11 insiders, portrays this moment: "Sitting in the glassed-in Battle Cab of NORAD's Northeast Air Defense Operations Center [NEADS] at Rome, New York, Air Force Colonel Robert Marr received the call. Then he sent out word to air traffic controllers to instruct fighter pilots to destroy the United jetliner and any other threatening passenger plane. 'United Airlines Flight 93 will not be allowed to reach Washington DC,' said Marr. Maj. Daniel Nash, the F-15 pilot from Cape Cod, heard the message while patrolling over Manhattan. 'The New York controller did come over the radio and say if we have another hijacked plane we're going to have to shoot it down,' he said. 'From where we were sitting, you could see there were people dying and it had to stop. So if that's what it's going to take, that was our job. We would have done it.'" (Bamford 2004 66)

So what was the US air defense posture over southern Pennsylvania at about 10 a.m. – 74 minutes after the first plane struck the World Trade Center and about a half-hour after air traffic controllers and United started to suspect that Flight 93 had been hijacked? The 9/11 commission claimed that NORAD pilots never got a shoot-down order in time to impact the course of United 93: "The Vice President was mistaken in his belief that shootdown authorization had been passed to the pilots flying at NORAD's direction." (44) According to the commission, the first fighters to operate under a shootdown order were fighters of the 133rd Wing of the District of Columbia Air National Guard, operating from Andrews Air Force Base in Maryland, and responding to a direct appeal from the Secret Service. The first of these fighters, the 9/11 commission says, took off at 10:38, and then established a Combat Air Patrol over the capital by 10:45. At 9:55, the Secret Service ordered all pilots to defend the White House at all costs. Around this time also, Cheney had his ambiguous exchanges with the "young man" who kept asking him whether his orders stood as a plane approached Washington DC. The young man told Cheney that Air Force fighters were close to the hijacked plane.

CBS reported before 10:06 – just as the flight of United 93 was ending – that two F-16s were on the tail of United 93. (AP, September 13, 2001; *Nashua Telegraph*, September 13, 2001) Some time later, an Air Traffic Controller working for the FAA, ignoring the blanket ban imposed on public statements by government officials with inside knowledge of the 9/11 events, said that an F-16 had closely followed United 93, even making 360-degree turns to stay in close range of the airliner. The federal flight controller said the F-16 was "in hot pursuit" of the hijacked United jet. "He must have seen the whole thing," an unnamed aviation official said. (*The Independent*, August 13, 2002; CBS News)

According to a Reuters report dated September 13, 2001 the FBI was at that point refusing to rule out that Flight 93 was shot down by a US fighter jet before it crashed in Pennsylvania. Citing indications that this plane was indeed shot down, this report stated: "Pennsylvania state police officials said on Thursday [September 13] debris from the plane had been found up to 8 miles away [from the crash site] in a residential community where local media have quoted residents as speaking of a second plane in the area and burning debris falling from the sky." Finding debris so far from the crash site indicates that the aircraft was disintegrating well before it hit the ground, as would be the case if it had been shot down. The *Pittsburgh Post-Gazette* reported on September 12 that among debris found miles from the crash site were "clothing, books, papers and what appeared to be human remains."

Shortly after the crash, rumors began circulating in the local community that United 93 had been shot down by a US fighter jet, but had no authoritative confirmation. The news desk at the *Pittsburgh Post-Gazette* was contacted September 22 by the *Idaho Observer*. The editor confirmed the news release and stood by the information contained in it. The editor also said that, although the FBI later changed its story, "The FBI confirmed to us that the debris came from that airliner!" (*The Idaho Observer*, October 2001)

Rumsfeld, the FBI, and NORAD soon united on a common line: United 93 had not been shot down. The Bush administration was transparently eager to avoid the opprobrium of having shot down a commercial airliner carrying American citizens; this would have exposed the regime as impotent to defend the lives of its own citizens, but able to kill some of those citizens to protect top oligarchs in the White House and other Washington buildings. This would have led to an outcry from the victims' families far beyond anything that was in fact observed.

The other complicating factor was that United 93 appeared to have been the scene of a partially successful US citizens' counterattack against the shadowy enemy, on a day which otherwise offered only stories of US incompetence, bungling, and abject defeat. This was the version of events which was developed around a cell-phone call made around 9:45 EDT by United 93 passenger Todd Beamer to Lisa Jefferson of the GTE Airfone Customer Care Center in Oakbrook, Illinois near Chicago. This call lasted slightly more than 15 minutes, according to published accounts. It was towards the end of this conversation that Todd Beamer told Lisa Jefferson that he and a group of other passengers had decided to storm the cockpit and overpower the hijackers. Todd asked Lisa to recite the Lord's Prayer with him, and then he pronounced the famous words: "Let's roll!"(Beamer 216) "Let's roll!" became the symbol of the resistance of the American people against terrorist fanatics and murderers.

Todd Beamer had been on the phone with Lisa Jefferson, and not with his own wife, Lisa Beamer. According to her account, Jefferson had offered to put the call through to Lisa Beamer, but Todd had, strangely enough, declined. It was from Ms. Jefferson that Mrs. Beamer obtained the story which made her husband and herself famous. Ms. Beamer soon appeared on Good Morning America, Primetime, NBC Dateline, CNN's Larry King Live, and other television programs. She was then invited to attend Bush's address to the joint session of Congress, where she sat next to Joyce Rumsfeld, the wife of the Pentagon boss. Early in his speech, Bush intoned:

> In the normal course of events, presidents come to this chamber to report on the state of the union. Tonight, no such report is needed. It has already been delivered by the American people. We have seen it in the courage of passengers who rushed terrorists to save others on the ground. Passengers like an exceptional man named Todd Beamer. And would you please help me to welcome his wife, Lisa Beamer, here tonight?"

> As Ms. Beamer retells it, "The room erupted in applause....The entire Congress of the United States of America rose to its feet in one motion, so almost instinctively, I rose as well. The Congress applauded and applauded, and it was the most humbling experience of my life to know that they were applauding me, in an indirect effort to express their appreciation to Todd and the other heroes aboard Flight 93. I was overwhelmed." (Beamer 247-248)

With that, the reality of United 93 had been eclipsed by the propaganda needs of the Bush machine. The "Let's roll!" story originally had the passengers breaking into the cockpit and struggling for the controls with the hijackers, resulting in the crash. Later, during 2003, the FBI backed away from this story and fell back on a second version which described the hijackers deciding to crash the plane into the ground as passengers were about to force their way into the cockpit. The FBI has never let the general public have a transcript of the cockpit voice recorder, which apparently survived. The FBI has played that CVR tape to a gathering of the United 93 victims' families, but only after swearing them to secrecy. Finally, small portions of the tape were played during the 9/11 commission hearings in the spring of 2004.

The official story has evolved over time. As CNN noted just before the release of the 9/11 commission report in late July 2004: "In the weeks and months after the attacks, there were reports that officials believed passengers had overtaken the plane, forcing it to crash in the field in Pennsylvania. However, last year, officials began backing away from that theory. [The 9/11 commission report] gives no indication that passengers ever broke through the cockpit door, but it makes clear that passengers' actions thwarted the plans of the terrorists." (http://edition.cnn.com /2004/US/07/22/911.flight.93/index.html)

The "Let's roll!" story, despite some doubts about the technical feasibility of the in-flight cell-phone call to Lisa Jefferson, may be real. It certainly does appear that the passengers were about to take back the plane. It also appears that Global Hawk, or whatever system of remote control was supposed to take control of United 93, had malfunctioned on this flight. The pilot and co-pilot had reportedly been killed, but on board United 93 was Donald F. Greene, an experienced pilot of an amphibious, single-engined, four-seater private plane which he used to fly from his home near Greenwich, Connecticut to northern Maine. There was also Andrew Garcia, a former Air Traffic Controller with the California National Guard. (Longman 182) These two, with much assistance from Air Traffic Controllers and other personnel, might well have been able to land the aircraft. But this would have posed immense problems for the entire official 9/11 story.

An aircraft safely landed meant, in all probability, living hijackers who could have been interrogated. What would their cover story have been? What would they have revealed about their own intentions and their own understanding of what they were doing? Would their testimony have exploded the official version? And what if there simply were no hijackers on board? The official version would fall to the ground. It was a risk that the terrorist controllers could not afford to run. And then again, there was the aircraft. Would a forensic examination have revealed the presence of Global Hawk, defective or otherwise, or of some other remote control guidance system? Would the FBI have succeeded in destroying this evidence as well? Despite the prolific capabilities of the FBI in destroying evidence, this might have been beyond their powers. These considerations point, along with abundant physical evidence and a large portion of the eyewitness accounts, towards the conclusion that United 93 was shot down to destroy evidence and silence suspects and witnesses forever.

UA93 was identified as a hijack at 9:16 AM. At 9:24, NORAD ordered three F-16s from Langley Air Force Base in Virginia to scramble. They were airborne at 9:30. Deputy Defense Secretary Paul Wolfowitz confirmed a few days later on TV that "we were already tracking that plane that crashed in Pennsylvania." At 9:35 AM, the three F-16s were ordered to "protect the White House at all costs" when the airliner turned towards the capital. At 10:06 AM it crashed at Shanksville, just minutes' flying time from Washington at full throttle.

Based on the plane's easterly course, the official consensus view was that Flight 93 was headed toward Washington for a strike on the White House or the Capitol. The 9/11 commission has endorsed this notion. But in 2002, the *London Times*, quoting US intelligence sources and noting the plane's low altitude and erratic course, suggested that the real target might have been a nearby nuclear power plant. The Three Mile Island plant, near Harrisburg, was about 10 or 15 minutes' flying time away. An attack on a nuclear reactor might have caused severe disruptions, although it should also be stressed that the protective shell of a US nuclear reactor is designed to protect the vessel by resisting the impact of a crashing airliner. Oliver North told Fox News that he thought Flight 93 was headed towards Fort Detrick, Maryland, near Frederick, where the national emergency military command center is located.

At approximately 9:58 AM, roughly eight minutes before impact, a 911 emergency dispatcher in neighboring Westmoreland County, Pennsylvania, took a call from a distraught passenger, Edward Felt, who said he had locked himself in the bathroom of Flight 93, and reported that the plane had been hijacked. The caller said there had been an explosion aboard the plane and that he could see white smoke. Authorities have never been able to explain this report, and the 911 tape itself was immediately confiscated by the inevitable FBI. In addition, the supervisor who took the call has been gagged by the FBI. The FBI evidently has not made the full recording of this call public, despite their evident desire to discredit this report. Cell-phone calls from the passengers all stopped about 9:58 AM – roughly the same time that the caller to 911 in Westmoreland County reported an explosion. The plane didn't come down until 10:06 – leaving an 8-minute gap of unexplained flying time, and thus a great mystery. (*Philadelphia Daily News*, November 15, 2001)

PHYSICAL EVIDENCE

The former mine where the plane crashed is composed of very soft soil, and searchers said that much of the wreckage was found buried 20-25 feet below the large crater. But despite that, there was also widely scattered debris in the immediate vicinity and also some much farther away. Considerable debris washed up more than two miles away at Indian Lake, and a canceled check and brokerage statement from the plane were found in a deep valley some eight miles away later that week.

The official version insists the plane exploded on impact, yet a one-ton section of the engine was found over a mile away and other light debris was found scattered over eight miles away. This account is confirmed by a number of media accounts. Some of the details may vary – at least one version has a half-ton piece of jet engine being found over a mile away – but most accounts converge on concentrations of debris two, three, and eight miles away.

Needless to say, this indicates that the end of United 93 was caused by an explosion within the aircraft or a missile – almost certainly fired by the US Force pursuant to an order from Bush and Cheney – rather than a crash provoked by an altercation between passengers and hijackers in the cockpit, or as a result of a desperate decision by the hijackers to dive the plane into the ground because they feared that the seizure of the cockpit by passengers was imminent.

The FBI has tried to account for the widely scattered debris by citing the wind. As we read in Jere Longman's rendering of the official version: "Debris was found as far as eight miles from the crash of Flight 93, in a southeast direction, but this airborne material had traveled from the crater in the direction of the prevailing wind." But this only makes sense if the plane had broken up in mid-air, which is exactly the conclusion which the FBI was seeking to disprove.

While the FBI has asserted the plane was largely obliterated by the roughly 500 mph impact, they also conceded that an engine – or at least a 1,000-pound fragment of one – was found "a considerable distance" from the main impact crater. That information further buttresses the shoot-down theory, since a heat-seeking, air-to-air Sidewinder missile from an F-16 would likely have impacted one of the Boeing 757's two large engines.

The mayor of Shanksville, Ernie Stull, changed his story several times after giving interviews to reporters and investigators. (Wisnewski 2003 197-198; *Der Spiegel*, September 8, 2003) But one of his first comments after the demise of United 93 was that he knew of two people who had heard a missile. (*Philadelphia Daily News*, November 15, 2001)

The presence of debris at Indian Lake, between 1.5 and 2 miles away, also supports the theory that there had been a mid-air explosion of some kind before United 93 hit the ground. Debris rained down on the lake; this is impossible if the plane was intact when it hit the ground. "It was mainly mail, bits of in-flight magazine and scraps of seat cloth," according to witness Tom Spinelli. "The authorities say it was blown here by the wind." But there was only a 10-mph breeze. Light debris was also found eight miles away in New Baltimore. The FBI said the impact bounced it there... But the few pieces of surviving fuselage, in the words of local coroner Wallace Miller, were "no bigger than a carry-on bag."

EYEWITNESSES

Laura Temyer, who lives in Hooversville, several miles north of the crash site, was hanging some wash on the line outside when she heard an airplane pass overhead. That struck her as unusual since she had just heard on TV that all flights had been ordered grounded.

She told the *Philadelphia Daily News*: "I heard like a boom and the engine sounded funny. I heard two more booms – and then I did not hear anything." Temyer's explanation for what she heard is this: "I think the plane was shot down." Temyer told a reporter she had twice told her story to the FBI. She also insists that people she knows in state law enforcement agreed with her story, namely that the plane was shot down and that decompression sucked objects from the aircraft, which would account for the wide debris field.

Nevin Lambert, a neighbor, had a different account. According him, the plane seemed to be fully, or largely, intact. "I didn't see no smoke, nothing," said, this elderly farmer, who witnessed the crash from his side yard less than a half-mile away. Lambert added that he also later found a couple of pieces of debris, one, a piece of metal, less than 12 inches across, with some insulation attached. A caller to the Howard Stern Radio Show related the story of how he saw Flight 93 in flames while it was in the air and also saw two other aircraft circling it. (Howard Stern Show, April 21 2004)

OTHER AIRCRAFT

A minimum of six witnesses claimed to have seen a small military-type plane in the vicinity shortly before UA93 crashed. Some spoke of a mysterious white jet which they had observed in the vicinity. The FBI stubbornly denied the presence of any other aircraft. The London *Daily Mirror* wondered later whether "in the moments before the airliner piled into the black, spongy earth at 575 miles per hour did an American fighter pilot have to do the unthinkable and shoot down a US civil airliner?"

Susan McElwain, 51, who lived two miles from the crash site, told a British reporter that she had seen a white aircraft pass directly over her head.

> It came right over me, I reckon just 40 or 50 feet above my mini-van. It was so low I ducked instinctively. It was traveling real fast, but hardly made any sound. Then it disappeared behind some trees. A few seconds later I heard this great explosion and saw this fireball rise up over the trees, so I figured the jet had crashed. The ground really shook. So I dialed 911 and told them what happened. I'd heard nothing about the other attacks and it was only when I got home and saw the TV that I realized it wasn't the white jet, but Flight 93. I didn't think much more about it until the authorities started to say there had been no other

plane. The plane I saw was heading right to the point where Flight 93 crashed and must have been there at the very moment it came down. There's no way I imagined this plane – it was so low it was virtually on top of me. It was white with no markings but it was definitely military, it just had that look. It had two rear engines, a big fin on the back like a spoiler on the back of a car and with two upright fins at the side. I haven't found one like it on the Internet. It definitely wasn't one of those executive jets. The FBI came and talked to me and said there was no plane around. Then they changed their story and tried to say it was a plane taking pictures of the crash 3,000 feet up. But I saw it and it was there before the crash and it was 40 feet above my head. They did not want my story – nobody here did. (London *Daily Mirror*, 2002)

Ms. McElwain, a special education teacher, refused to accept the official version of what she saw, in part because of a conversation she had several hours after the fact with the wife of friend of the family who is in the Air Force. According to McElwain, that friend "said her husband had called her that morning and said 'I can't talk, but we've just shot a plane down.'" "I presumed they meant Flight 93. I have no doubt those brave people on board tried to do something, but I don't believe what happened on the plane brought it down. If they shot it down, or something else happened, everyone, especially the victims' families, have a right to know." (London *Daily Mirror*, 2002)

Lee Purbaugh, aged 32, was the sole person to see the final seconds of Flight 93 as it descended on the former strip-mining land at precisely 10.06 AM – and he also saw the white jet. He was at his job at the Rollock Inc. scrap yard on a ridge overlooking the point of impact, less than half a mile away. "I heard this real loud noise coming over my head," he told a journalist of the London *Daily Mirror*. "I looked up and it was Flight 93, barely 50 feet above me. It was coming down in a 45 degree angle and rocking from side to side. Then the nose suddenly dipped and it just crashed into the ground. There was this big fireball and then a huge cloud of smoke." Lee Purbaugh also saw the mysterious other plane: "Yes, there was another plane. I didn't get a good look but it was white and it circled the area about twice and then it flew off over the horizon."

Tom Spinelli, 28, was working at India Lake Marina, a mile and a half away. "I saw the white plane," he reported. "It was flying around all over the place like it was looking for something. I saw it before and after the crash."

At 9:22 AM a sonic boom, almost certainly caused by supersonic flight, was registered up by a seismic monitoring station in southern Pennsylvania, 60 miles from Shanksville. (London *Daily Mirror*, 2002)

Kathy Blades, who was in her small summer cottage with her son about a quarter mile from the impact site, also reported seeing a white aircraft. Blades and her son ran outside after they heard the crash and saw the jet, which according to them had sleek back wings [sic] and an angled cockpit, race overhead. "My son said, 'I think we're under attack!'" Blades remembered.

A few days after the crash, the FBI tried to provide a plausible explanation for this embarrassing and mysterious white jet which the various witnesses had identified. The FBI now claimed that a private Falcon 20 jet bound for nearby Johnstown was in the vicinity and was asked by authorities to descend and help survey the crash site. But the authorities failed to provide the identify of the owner of the jet, and also could not justify why it was still flying some 40 minutes after the Federal Aviation Administration had ordered all planes to land at the nearest airport. "I think it was shot down," was the opinion of Dennis Mock, who did not see United 93 come down, but who lived closest to the crash site, immediately to the west of the crater. "That's what people around here think," he added. (London *Daily Mirror*, 2002)

Even though United 93 had supposedly been flying at an altitude of less than 10,000 feet, there was no tail section, no jet engines, no large sections of fuselage in view anywhere near the impact crater. This can be compared to the crash scene at Lockerbie, Scotland, in 1988. Here a Boeing 747 was destroyed by a bomb at an altitude of 30,000 feet. One whole side of the forward part of the plane and many other pieces were clearly identifiable as coming from a large commercial airliner. If there were a plane in Shanksville, it appeared to have disappeared into the ground – as in the case of the Valujet which had crashed into the Everglades swamp in 1994. But the Pennsylvania countryside was not the Everglades. Here is the depiction of the last moments of United 93 from former *New York Times* reporter Jere Longman's *Among the Heroes*, probably the most sustained attempt to present the official version of this flight:

> Traveling at 575 miles per hour, the 757 had inverted and hit the spongy earth at a 45-degree angle, tunneling toward a limestone reef at the edge of a reclaimed strip mine. Because the plane crashed upside down, the engines and stowed landing gear thrust upward and forward. The ground became littered with the fractured underbelly of the plane, electronics, shredded wiring. The cockpit and first class shattered like the point of a pencil, and remnants sprayed into a line of hemlock pine trees. The fuselage accordioned on itself more than thirty feet into the porous, backfilled ground. It was as if a marble had been dropped into water. (Longman 215)

Longman is not interested in the shootdown hypothesis, nor does he wonder much about the presence of other aircraft in the area. But Longman must also deal with the amazement of the local emergency workers, who found that they were not dealing with a normal crash site. Here is Longman's reconstruction of what one rescuer saw as he approached the crash site:

> As he approached the scene, adrenaline thoughts raced through [the rescuer's] head. *What are we going to see? Is there going to be a fire in*

the fuselage? Will people be trapped? He jumped out of his truck and noticed small fires in different places, but he could not see the plane.

Where is it?

He was sure a commercial airliner had crashed, but he saw only small broken pieces. A 757 is composed of six hundred twenty-six thousand parts, fastened by six hundred thousand bolts and rivets, connected with sixty miles of wire. That's all that he could see now, fragmented parts and rivets and wires, a catastrophic uncoiling. Other firemen and townspeople at the scene had the same quizzical looks. Metal and plastic and paper were everywhere, in the trees, on the ground, a shirt, a shoe, underwear, a backless seat sitting in its aluminum track, a remnant of seat cushion smoking on the roof of a nearby cabin. The pine trees were peppered with shrapnel. King saw the pushed-up earth and crater that measured thirty feet or more in diameter, and he knew it had been the point of impact. He sent a crew to hose down the smoldering debris, but still he did not realize what had plunged into the disturbed ground. 'Never in my wildest dreams did I think half the plane was down there," King said.

Maybe it wasn't a commercial airliner.

The rumors started. There were two hundred people on the plane, four hundred. There were no passengers, only mail. Bewilderment prevailed. No one knew anything for certain. King sent his men into the woods to search for the fuselage, and they kept coming back and telling him, 'Rick. There's nothing.' (Longman 215-216)

Longman struggles to account for the pulverized state of the aircraft, which is simply not consistent with the crash of an airplane which had not already broken up in mid-air:

In the hours after the crash, Pennsylvania state troopers said that they had seen no piece of the plane larger than a phone book. Later, an eight-by-seven foot section of the fuselage containing several windows would be found. It was about the size of the hood of a car. A piece of one engine, weighing a thousand pounds, landed more than a hundred yards from the crater, apparently jettisoned upward in a tremendous arc. The cockpit data recorder, one of the so-called black boxes, would be excavated fifteen feet into the crater and the cockpit voice recorder at twenty-five feet. Ash and paper, a canceled check, a charred brokerage statement, traveled eight miles from the crash on a prevailing wind. Brush fires would spark up in the woods for more than a week. *Where were the people? Where were the bodies?* (Longman 215-216)

Notice that Longman slyly diverges from the eyewitness accounts in attempting to locate the jet engine wreckage much closer to the impact crater –

100 yards instead of about a mile. But Longman cannot avoid the extraordinary pulverization of the plane: "'You couldn't take a step without stepping on some part of that aircraft,' said Craig of the FBI....two weeks before Christmas, rivets and wires littered the field as if someone had spilled a plane-building kit. Ninety-five percent of the airplane had been recovered, the FBI said, but thousands of splintered pieces lay about in the field." (Longman 262)

There was also the gruesome detail that the human remains collected were not commensurate with the number of passengers. "The collective weight of the forty-four people aboard the plane was seven thousand five hundred pounds, the coroner said. Only six hundred pounds of remains were discovered...." (Longman 260) According to a reporter: "the largest piece of human tissue found was a section of spine eight inches long." (London *Daily Mirror*, 2002)

The FBI was adamant that there was no evidence of explosives of any kind having been used. All of this led to speculation not only that United 93 had been shot down by the US Force, but that the plane had been destroyed – pulverized in mid-air – by a futuristic weapon based on new physical principles. Wallace Miller, the coroner, commented that he believed the plane had not been shot down, "unless there is some new technology we don't know about." (Longman 264) According to Longman, there was a military aircraft, a Lockheed Hercules C-130 transport plane, about 17 miles away. Such a plane could easily have carried a powerful airborne chemical laser, and this type of directed-energy weapon based on new physical principles might have accounted for the physical effects actually observed on the scene.

The FBI was not curious to find out what had actually happened. Coroner Wallace Miller and Dennis Dirkmaat, a forensic anthropologist from Mercyhurst College in Erie PA, had proposed a detailed analysis of the crash site; they wanted to divide the area up into a grid with 60-foot squares. Distribution patterns would have cast light on how the plane struck the ground. The FBI, true to form, refused to allow this investigation. To justify this, they invented a soap opera theory that the investigation was designed to reveal in an invidious fashion who had stormed the cockpit and who had not. According to the FBI: "There was no mystery to solve about the plane. Everyone knew what happened with the plane." (Longman 262) Or thought they did; precisely what is well-known is least understood, as Hegel might have argued.

The FBI, which assumed control of the accident investigation from the National Transportation Safety Board, continues to refuse to make public the complete data from either of the black boxes, the cockpit voice recorder and the flight data recorder. The pretext is, as always, the exigencies of the alleged war on terrorism. It is worth recalling that in the case of American Airlines Flight 587, which crashed in Queens in November 2001, NTSB officials made public detailed information about the cockpit voice recorder within less than 36 hours. (*Philadelphia Daily News*, November 15, 2001; London *Daily Mirror*, 2002)

Before departing, the FBI made sure that the crime scene was rendered totally opaque. The crater was filled in with dirt, to be followed by a layer of topsoil. The scorched trees were cut down and shredded into mulch. The FBI was gone two weeks after the crash. (Longman 258) More evidence had gone into the FBI's black hole in a molehill. Still, relatives of the victims had persistent questions for the FBI. Bob Craig of the FBI's evidence-gathering team tried to convince them of the official account: "Turn the picture of the second plane hitting the World Trade Center on its side, and, for all intents and purposes, the face of the building is the strip mine in Shanksville. Look at the fireball in the picture. That's what happened." (Longman 260) According to Longman, "conspiracy theorists continued to assert that the plane was shot down, but evidence indicated otherwise."

The FBI later announced that the cockpit voice recorder had been recovered. The FBI at first kept the tape secret, but then agreed to let the bereaved families hear it. The tape was played at Princeton, New Jersey on April 18, 2002. Before they could hear the tape, the families had to sign a special waiver agreeing not to sue the government about any issue arising from the tape. They were forbidden to record the tape, or to take notes. Later, note taking was allowed. The FBI claimed that these procedures were necessary to prevent any damage to the prosecution of Zacarias Moussaoui. The families listened through headphones while an FBI transcript was projected on a screen. Some family members later said that the tape raised more questions than it had answered. (Longman 270)

The tragedy of United Airlines Flight 93 ended at 10:06 AM Eastern Daylight Time. This was a full 110 minutes, one hour and fifty minutes, after the hijack of United Flight 11 from Boston. The US air defense system, usually a well-oiled machine, had failed utterly and completely. Had the air defense system compounded its own failure by shooting down United 93 to prevent the interrogation of hijackers, and the inspection of an aircraft that might have been equipped with Global Hawk? Had the air defense system in this last phase performed the same function as Jack Ruby in the Kennedy assassination – the elimination of patsies whose testimony might have been fatal to the myth which the leakers and the media were busily constructing even before the tragedy of United 93 was complete?

Or were they silenced beforehand? The absence of Arab names on the published lists of passengers was one of the first glaring discrepancies in the official story. In 2003, motivated by concern over the run-up to the Iraq War, skeptic Thomas Olmsted filed a Freedom of Information Act request for the results of DNA tests made at the Pentagon crash site. Fourteen months later, he finally received and published them in the online *Sierra Times* under the title "Autopsy: No Arabs on Flight 77."

IX
"ANGEL IS NEXT" –
THE INVISIBLE GOVERNMENT SPEAKS

> From 10:00 a.m. to approximately 8:00 p.m. (on Sept. 11), US
> government officials were not thinking that this was the work of
> Arab terrorists, but rather that it was an expression of a military
> coup being carried out by US-based extremists who were
> capable of provoking a nuclear war.
> – Réseau Voltaire, Paris, September 27, 2001

> Sheikh: They [the Americans] were terrified thinking there was
> a coup.
> – "Bin Laden" tape of December 2001 (Meyssan 2002 197)

The current tenant of the White House most probably was not familiar in advance with a detailed outline of the 9/11 plot. He was assisted in not knowing and not acting by his cognitive impairment, his contempt for detailed, accurate information, and his habitual mental lethargy. Whether or not he suspected that something was coming, whether or not he knew this or that detail, are all matters to be determined with the help of open archives and cross-examination of the subject. The guess here is that Bush knew far less than many of his most severe critics might surmise. Bush's crime was not the crime of knowing everything in advance; it was rather the crime of not knowing what he should have known, and of then compounding that by capitulating, by turning the US government and polity in the direction demanded by the terror plotters. Better than "Bush knew," as we will see, is "Bush surrendered." "Bush knew" makes a good political slogan, but it cannot be a guide to understanding the true scope of what actually happened. Students of 9/11 who build their work around the thesis that "Bush knew" are on treacherous ground.

As I pointed out in my 1992 study of Bush 41, the typical model of a Bush presidency is that of a weak and passive executive who comes into office with few ideas beyond the basic desire to rule and to appoint rich cronies to key posts, and who sits in the White House waiting for his networks to tell him what it is he must do. These impulses, naturally, are mediated through the handlers of the White House palace guard. But here lies the danger: when Bush was running for office, it was widely conceded by his supporters that their candidate was a moron, but a moron who would hire the best advisers available, who would guide him through the crises of his presidency. In this sense, both Bush presidencies were oligarchical presidencies, with the chief magistrate in fact functioning as the front man for a committee.

The events of 9/11 showed the grave danger of such an oligarchical presidency: what happened if the advisors turned out to be traitors, misfits, or absent, as they did on 9/11: the presidency itself was paralyzed and incapable of acting, as occurred during the dark eternity of horror the world experienced as Bush busied himself with reading "My Pet Goat."

If the forces favorable to a policy of open-ended clash-of-civilizations warfare had been in total control of the government, they might have been able to orchestrate the outbreak of war directly, through an incident involving a target country like Iraq – somewhat along the lines of the Gulf of Tonkin incident. This would have been enough to convince the mass media and the population. But the coup faction, the golpistas, felt that they needed to convince the state apparatus as well, to shake the state to its foundations, threaten the life of Bush in a number of ways, and run the risk of being caught in some highly treasonous activities, in order to get what they wanted. This can be shown through an analysis of Bush's conduct on 9/11. As indicated below, many of the citations furnished in this section are drawn from Allan Wood and Paul Thompson, "An Interesting Day."

As part of his "endless summer" approach to the presidency which had seen him on vacation for over 40% of his time in office up to 9/11, Bush was spending the evening of September 10 at the Colony Beach and Tennis Resort on Longboat Key, a narrow coral island in the Gulf of Mexico, off Sarasota, Florida. This resort, a favorite destination for plutocrats, was billed as "America's greatest tennis resort." Here Bush dined on the evening of September 10 with his brother Jeb, the governor of Florida, and a group of Republican politicians and rent seekers (e.g., lobbyists seeking favors from the public purse).

Bush awoke at 6 AM on the morning of September 11, 2001, and went for his habitual jog. But in the night of September 10 to 11, Bush's security detail received a warning that he was in imminent danger. The Sarasota ABC affiliate reported on 9/11: "The warning of imminent danger was delivered in the middle of the night to Secret Service agents guarding the President," said reporter Monica Yadov, "and it came exactly four hours and thirty-eight minutes before Mohammed Atta flew an airliner into the World Trade Center. (Hopsicker 2004 40)

ASSASSINATION ATTEMPT

On the evening of September 10, Zainlabdeen Omer, a Sudanese national who was a local resident, reported an assassination threat against Bush to the Secret Service. Omer said an acquaintance named Ghandi had made violent threats against Bush and was now in town, so Omer was worried about Bush's safety. The next day, 9/11, the Secret Service searched a Sarasota apartment in connection with this report. "Three Sudanese men were questioned for about ten hours. The Secret Service also raided a beauty supply store in Sarasota, whose owner, identified as "Hakim," told the agents that "Ghandi" was a member of the Sudanese People's Liberation Army, a group fighting against the Muslim government in Sudan." (Wood 2003; Hopsicker 2002) The SPLA, led by US agent John Garang, is an asset of the CIA and the Mossad. It is not possible to determine whether this story represents the danger about which the local ABC station said Bush was warned.

It was at Longboat Key that Bush was the target of a possible assassination attempt. As Bush was preparing for his morning run, a van carrying several Middle Eastern men pulled up to the security post at the Colony's entrance. "The men said they were a television news crew with a scheduled 'poolside' interview with the president. They asked for a certain Secret Service agent by name. The message was relayed to a Secret Service agent inside the resort, who hadn't heard of the agent mentioned or of plans for an interview. He told the men to contact the president's public relations office in Washington, DC, and had the van turned away." (Wood 2003; *Longboat Observer*, Sept. 26, 2001; Hopsicker 2004 39-48.)

This technique may have been the same one used to eliminate General Ahmed Shah Massoud two days earlier. Here a television camera crew composed of suicide bombers had gained access to the legendary anti-Soviet fighter and leader of the Afghan Northern Alliance. After setting up their equipment, a bomb inside their camera had detonated, killing Massoud and others. The official version sees this event as a preparation for 9/11, through attempting to cripple the Northern Alliance which the CIA was sure to use against the Taliban regime.

But there is a more cogent view: Massoud was a proud nationalist who would not have taken orders from the CIA and UNOCAL, so it was urgent for the CIA to eliminate him. In the latter case, Bush may have come close to joining Massoud as the victim of the same rogue network of US intelligence which planned 9/11. In any case, the fact that a likely assassination attempt had been foiled would normally have been the basis for canceling the rest of Bush's schedule for the day and for quickly hurrying him back to Washington or some other secure destination. But on 9/11, the most minimal precautions were flaunted. Was it security stripping?

"Bush's appearance at the Emma E. Booker Elementary School in Sarasota, Florida, on September 11, 2001, had been in the planning stages since August, but was only announced publicly on the morning of September 7. (White House, September 7, 2001) Later that same day, [alleged] 9/11 hijackers Mohamed Atta and Marwan al Shehhi traveled to Sarasota and enjoyed drinks and dinner at a Holiday Inn only two miles down the sandy beach from where Bush was scheduled to stay during his Sarasota visit." (*Longboat Observer*, November 21, 2001; *Washington Post*, January 27, 2002; Wood 2003) Was this a coincidence, or did it have something to do with a possible assassination attempt on Bush?

On the surface, Bush's security arrangements at the Colony appeared elaborate. "Surface-to-air missiles were placed on the roof of the resort (*Sarasota Herald-Tribune*, September 10, 2002), and an Airborne Warning and Control System (AWACS) plane circled high overhead." (Wood 2003; Sammon 25)

"At about 8:50 AM (when reports of the first World Trade Center crash were first broadcast), while standing on the Sarasota bay front waiting for the presidential motorcade to pass by, [a passerby] saw two Middle Eastern men in a dilapidated van "screaming out the windows 'Down with Bush' and raising their fists in the air.'" (Wood, 2003) The FBI supposedly questioned the source of this report, but it is not clear if this was the same van that had appeared at the Colony security checkpoint. (*Longboat Observer*, September 26, 2001)

When did Bush learn that American Flight 11 had hit the North Tower? There are several reports that Bush was told of the first crash before he arrived at the Booker school. The initial flashes of American 11's crash into the World Trade Center began around 8:48 AM, two minutes after the crash happened. (*New York Times*, September 15, 2001) Nevertheless, at 9:03 AM, fifteen minutes after a grave emergency was obvious, Bush sat down with a classroom of second-graders and began a 20-minute photo opportunity?

Part of the answer to this may lie in Bush's mental inertia and weak hold on external reality. But it may also be that Bush was being subjected to some form of security stripping by the networks who were carrying out the 9/11 attacks. It should be recalled that the assassination of President Kennedy in Dallas was greatly facilitated by the absence of many of the redundant layers of security that usually envelop a traveling president. The many lapses in Bush's personal security on 9/11 suggest that the Secret Service was anything but immune to the rogue network operating behind the scenes.

An alert security detail would have taken Bush out of the Booker school at the first news that American 11 had hit the North Tower. A local reporter commented: "[Bush] could and arguably should have left Emma E. Booker Elementary School immediately, gotten onto Air Force One and left Sarasota without a moment's delay.... But he didn't." (*Sarasota Herald-Tribune*, September 12, 2001)

Months later, Bush offered his famous garbled and impossible account of how he learned of the first plane impacting the WTC. On December 4, 2001, Bush was asked: "How did you feel when you heard about the terrorist attack?" Bush answered, "I was sitting outside the classroom waiting to go in, and I saw an airplane hit the tower – the TV was obviously on. And I used to fly, myself, and I said, well, there's one terrible pilot. I said, it must have been a horrible accident. But I was whisked off there, I didn't have much time to think about it." (White House, 12/4/01)

Many commentators have noted that the only known film of American 11 hitting the North Tower, the Naudet video, was not broadcast until many hours later. Some have verged into real nonsense, imagining that a secret camera had filmed the first impact and transmitted the pictures to a special television screen set up in the school, all for the edification of Bush. This vastly overestimates the importance of Bush, who was after all just another puppet president. More likely, this garbled account is simply another index of Bush's well-known mental impairment.

The children were opening their books to read a story together when Bush's White House Chief of Staff Andrew Card entered the room and whispered to Bush: "A second plane hit the second tower. America is under attack." (*San Francisco Chronicle*, September 11, 2002) Bush did not respond. He did not ask questions. He wanted no further information. He gave no orders or directives. He tasked no bureaucracies. He did literally nothing. Bush had run for president with the admission that he was a person of limited mental ability, but one who would hire the best advisers available. This moment showed the fatal weakness of that formula, of the oligarchical presidency. Now there was no time for options to be prepared; quick action, crisp orders were required – orders to mobilize all air defenses, to evacuate key sites, to investigate what was happening. Bush had never been qualified for the presidency, and at this moment he proved it: he froze. As Dr. Franks has pointed out, Bush clings obsessively to his routine as a means of preventing the public disintegration of his personality. On 9/11, Bush clung to a routine with a vengeance, even as the world was crumbling around him. And when a head of state and a head of government fumbles, the goal line is wide open behind him.

This was the defining moment of the Bush 43 presidency: the raging infantile id paralyzed by fear and dread. And this was Bush's pattern: When an American EP-3E spy plane had been forced down on the coast of China in the spring of 2001, "neither Bush nor Rice seemed anxious about the situation's deteriorating into a hostage crisis....Bush went to bed around his usual time, before midnight. ... In the White House, it was mostly business as usual. Bush came back from Camp David early on Sunday, not because of the crisis, but because bad weather interfered with his outdoor recreation." (*Newsweek* April 16, 2001)

"MY PET GOAT"

Bush's defense, as summarized by the 9/11 commission was that "the President felt he should project strength and calm until he could better understand what was happening." (9/11 commission report 38) This is exactly the ceremonial conception of the weak presidency, which sees the office as a symbol and object of popular emotional cathexis or focus, rather than as a policy-making post oriented toward action in the real world. It was left to the foreign press to ask the obvious question: whatever Bush's animadversions might have been, why was he not picked up and carried out? A Canadian reporter noted that "for some reason, Secret Service agents (did) not bustle him away." (*Globe and Mail*, September 12, 2001) There had in fact been one attempt. A member of Bush's entourage, variously identified as a Secret Service agent or as a Marine from the communications detail, had said, "We're out of here. Can you get everyone ready?" (*Sarasota Herald-Tribune*, September 10, 2002) But nothing happened. What strange process was at work behind the scenes to leave Bush as a sitting duck in a highly publicized location at a time of gravest danger? Was security stripping going on in the background? This lackadaisical response of Bush's

Secret Service detail contrasts sharply with the aggressive manhandling of Cheney, who was lifted up by main force and carried toward the PEOC, the White House bunker, by Secret Service agents.

As for Bush, he was taking orders from his handlers, as usual. From the back of the room, Press Secretary Ari Fleischer held up a sheet of paper with the words "DON'T SAY ANYTHING YET" written on it in big block letters. (*Washington Times*, October 7, 2002) In the interval, Bush was listening to a pupil read the celebrated story of "My Pet Goat," while the crisis unfolded around him. This is the interval portrayed so graphically in Michael Moore's *Fahrenheit 911*; how long did Bush stay in the classroom after he was told of the second attack. The *Tampa Tribune* thought he had remained there "for eight or nine minutes" – until sometime between 9:13 and 9:16. (*Tampa Tribune*, September 1, 2002) At a certain point a reporter asked Bush, "Mr. President, are you aware of the reports of the plane crash in New York? Is there anything..." Bush, obedient to the instructions of Ari Fleischer to keep his mouth shut on this topic, responded, "I'll talk about it later." But even now the president did not depart. He tarried to shake hands with Ms. Daniels, the second grade teacher. It was evident that Bush felt no urgency to take any action in particular. "He was taking his good old time. ... Bush lingered until the press was gone." According to Bill Sammon, a Bush backer who wrote for the Moonie-controlled Washington Times, Bush here earned the title of "the dawdler in chief." (Sammon 90)

This singularly lethargic conduct by Bush attracted criticism very early on. 9/11 widow and activist Kristen Breitweiser said on the Phil Donahue show: "It was clear that we were under attack. Why didn't the Secret Service whisk [Bush] out of that school? ... (H)e is the commander-in-chief of the United States of America, our country was clearly under attack, it was after the second building was hit. I want to know why he sat there for 25 minutes." (Donahue, August 13, 2002) This critique is all the more justified because of the security warning of the previous night, and the attempted assassination attempt earlier that same morning.

One way to account for Bush's behavior in the classroom that morning, and perhaps the most likely one, is the notion that Bush simply froze in fear and insecurity about what to do. "We've seen Bush's sense of omnipotence threatened before – in the hours following the attacks on the World Trade Center and the Pentagon," wrote Dr. Frank. "All of us were understandably frightened, but Bush's fear at first appeared paralytic: he continued reading to the second grade class he was visiting for a full twenty minutes after he was told that the first tower had been hit. Then he fled for an entire day, serpentining across the country until the coast was clear and he could finally make it back to Washington." (Frank 99)

The 9/11 commission accepted without criticism and even without comment Bush's absurd decision to continue reading the story about the goat while the country was under attack, along with his explanation that this was motivated in his own mind by the desire to project an image of strength – an answer which suggests that he was more concerned about maintaining appearances in his own delusional world than he was about providing concrete measures of national defense in this world.

Bush went to a private room in the school and conferred with his advisors. Then, at 9:30, he read the following statement:

> THE PRESIDENT: Ladies and gentlemen, this is a difficult moment for America. I, unfortunately, will be going back to Washington after my remarks. Secretary Rod Paige and the Lt. Governor will take the podium and discuss education. I do want to thank the folks here at Booker Elementary School for their hospitality.
>
> Today we've had a national tragedy. Two airplanes have crashed into the World Trade Center in an apparent terrorist attack on our country. I have spoken to the Vice President, to the Governor of New York, to the Director of the FBI, and have ordered that the full resources of the federal government go to help the victims and their families, and to conduct a full-scale investigation to hunt down and to find those folks who committed this act.
>
> Terrorism against our nation will not stand. And now if you would join me in a moment of silence. May God bless the victims, their families, and America. Thank you very much.
>
> END 9:31 A.M. EDT

The operative term here is "apparent terrorist attack." Later that day Bush remarked, "The resolve of our great nation is being tested. But make no mistake: We will show the world that we will pass this test." As Meyssan argues, the general tone of Bush's remarks, including especially the term "test," might suggest a military conflict or internal insurrection just as easily as terrorism. (Meyssan 2002 47)

Soon after this, Bush left the Booker School for the nearby Sarasota Airport. But before he left, the Secret Service was to receive news of another threat to Bush: As the local paper reported a few days later: "Sarasota barely skirted its own disaster. As it turns out, terrorists targeted the president and Air Force One on Tuesday, maybe even while they were on the ground in Sarasota and certainly not long after. The Secret Service learned of the threat just minutes after Bush left Booker Elementary." (*Sarasota Herald-Tribune*, September 16, 2001)

Another account confirms that the Secret Service learned of a new threat to Bush and Air Force One "just minutes after Bush left Booker Elementary." Karl Rove, who was traveling with the president, commented: "They also made it clear they wanted to get us up quickly, and they wanted to get us to a high altitude, because there had been a specific threat made to Air Force One.... A declaration that Air Force One was a target, and said in a way that they called it credible." (*New Yorker*, October 1, 2001)

Air Force One took off from Sarasota between 9:55 and 9:57 AM, as many news reports confirm. The takeoff was a hurried one, followed by a steep climb to higher altitudes. Communications Director Dan Bartlett remembered, "It was like a rocket. For a good ten minutes, the plane was going almost straight up." (CBS, September 11, 2002) Air Force One began to roll down the Florida runway just as WTC 2 was about to collapse. "As the President sat down in his chair, [he] motioned to the chair across from his desk for me to sit down," recalled Karl Rove. "Before we could, both of us, sit down and put on our seat belts, they were rolling the plane. And they stood that 747 on its tail and got it about 45,000 feet as quick as I think you can get a big thing like that up in the air." (Bamford 2004 63)

However, despite the pattern of grave threat, Air Force One took off without any military fighter protection. This was about one hour after the impact on the South Tower. There was no lack of nearby air bases which should have been on continuous alert: Homestead Air Station was 185 miles from Sarasota, and Tyndall Air Station was 235 miles away. It should have been possible to improvise a small fighter escort in that interval. This poses the question: was fighter cover being denied to Bush by the rogue network, as part of the pattern of security stripping? This question is made more urgent by the fact that, according to most accounts, Air Force One did not get a fighter escort until well over one hour after it had made its emergency takeoff.

"AIR FORCE ONE IS NEXT"

Once in the airplane, Bush was in continuous contact with Cheney and others. Around this time, officials feared that as many as 11 airliners had been hijacked. (CBS, September 11, 2001) Some reports place Bush out of the loop because of communication difficulty, but "out of the loop" was his father's line from Iran-Contra.

"Shortly after takeoff, Cheney apparently informed Bush of "a credible threat" to Air Force One. (AP, September 13, 2001) US Representative Adam Putnam "had barely settled into his seat on Air Force One ... when he got the news that terrorists apparently had set their sights on the plane." (*Orlando Sentinel*, September 14, 2001) The Secret Service had received an anonymous call: "Air Force One is next." The caller [spoke in the code words] relating to Air Force One procedures. Pilot Col. Mark Tillman was told of the threat and he asked that an armed guard be stationed at the cockpit door. The Associated Press reported that the threat came "within the same hour" as the Pentagon crash – before 10:00 AM, roughly when the plane took off." (Wood 2003; AP, September 13, 2001)

The threat contained in this message, "Air Force One is next," would appear to have been distinct from the earlier warning that came upon leaving Booker School, but this cannot be established with total certainty.

Bush wanted to go to Washington, but he was overruled by the White House palace guard. Card told Bush, "We've got to let the dust settle before we go back." (*St. Petersburg Times*, September 8, 2002) The plane apparently stayed over Sarasota until it was decided where Bush should go. Accounts conflict, but through about 10:35 AM (*Washington Post*, January 27, 2002), Air Force One "appeared to be going nowhere. The journalists on board – all of whom were barred from communicating with their offices – sensed that the plane was flying in big, slow circles." (*London Daily Telegraph*, December 16, 2001) What was being discussed on the secure phone during this time? Was Cheney communicating the demands of the coup faction to Bush? Was Cheney reporting these demands, or was he joining in urging Bush to accept them? At various points in the narrative, Cheney appears to be acting not just as relayer of information, but as a spokesman for the secret government network which was in action on 9/11. It is thus Cheney, far more than Bush, who must be considered a prime suspect in any serious investigation of 9/11.

"ANGEL IS NEXT"

According to Bob Woodward's canonical mainstream account: "At about 10:30 AM Cheney reached Bush again on Air Force One, which was still on its way toward Washington. The White House had received a threat saying, 'Angel is next.' Since Angel was the codeword for Air Force One, it could mean that terrorists had inside information." Allegedly because of this report, Cheney argued that Bush should not return to Washington. "There's still a threat," said Cheney. (Woodward 18) Within minutes, the plane changed course and flew to Louisiana instead. (*Washington Post*, January 27, 2002) Was this now a third threat, after the post-Booker threat and the "Air Force One is next" threat? Did the terrorist controllers now add the code word "Angel" to further document their insider status, and their possible access to nuclear codes? Or are we dealing with two versions of the same threat?

We will return to "Angel is next." This represents the single most important clue as to the sponsorship of 9/11, since it was at this point that the sponsors showed their hand. They were not located in a cave in Afghanistan, but were rather a network located high within the US government and military It was a moment of capital importance, the thread which, if properly pulled, will unravel the entire fabric of 9/11 deceit.

"Around 10:55 AM, there was yet another threat to Air Force One. The pilot, Colonel Mark Tillman, said he was warned that a suspect airliner was approaching from dead ahead. "Coming out of Sarasota there was one call that said there was an airliner off our nose that they did not have contact with.' Tillman took evasive action, pulling his plane even higher above normal traffic. (CBS, September 11, 2002) Reporters on board noticed the increased elevation." (Wood 2003; *Dallas Morning News*, August 28, 2002; *Salon*, September 12, 2001) It has not been possible to establish exactly what the basis of this threat report was. Was the rogue network blackmailing Bush? Was this suspect airliner a military aircraft using participation in Vigilant Guardian/Vigilant Warrior as a cover story for assisting the plot?

Air Force One had some protection against heat-seeking missiles in the form of an infrared jammer code-named "Have Charcoal." There were also other electronic anti-missile countermeasures. The plane is shielded against the electromagnetic pulse effect (EMP) which can be generated by nuclear explosions, and which causes damage even at a considerable distance. (Bamford 2004 84)

At the time of this incident, it is apparent that Air Force One still had no fighter escort. Why were the fighters being withheld, and by whom? It was later reported that, in his 10:32 phone call, Cheney told Bush that another 40 to 90 minutes would be needed to get protective fighters up to escort Air Force One. (Wood 2003; *Washington Post*, 1/27/02.) This would have left Bush without fighter cover until noon. What was the tone of this remark by Cheney? Was it a threat? Was it blackmail? Our only certainty is that at the time of the 10:55 AM evasive action, there was still no fighter escort. By 11:30 there were reportedly six fighters protecting Air Force One. (*Sarasota Magazine*, September 19, 2001) According to another version, when the Air Force sent an AWACS early warning radar aircraft plus two F-16s to escort Air Force One, the presidential party treated them on a need-to-know basis. "We were not told where Air Force One was going. We were just told to follow the President," said Major General Larry Arnold of NORAD (Bamford 2004 87) Was the Bush party suspicious of certain military elements?

BARKSDALE AND NIGHT WATCH

Aboard Air Force One on the way to Barksdale, passengers, including the numerous press corps, were told to turn off their cell phones. The Secret Service then came around and removed the batteries from each phone to prevent the emission of any kind of signal that might reveal the plane's location. These measures turned out to be of dubious value, since the Shreveport television stations had placed at least one camera crew near the main runway. "The strange part about it was, here we were turning off cell phones and taking precautions, and we could see ourselves landing at Barksdale Air Force Base in Louisiana on the TV," recalled Eric Draper, Bush's personal photographer. (Bamford 2004 86)

Air Force One landed at Barksdale Air Force base near Shreveport, Louisiana at about 11:45 a.m. (CBS, September 11, 2002; *Daily Telegraph*, December 16, 2001) "According to intelligence sources, a key reason for deciding to land there was that Barksdale was home to the US Strategic [Air] Command's alternate underground command post, a bunker from which Bush could run a war if necessary. It was also a place where the President could rendezvous with 'Night Watch,' the 'Doomsday Plane.' Once a specially outfitted Boeing 707 known as the National Emergency Airborne Command Post, by 2001 it had become a heavily modified military version of the Boeing 747-200, similar to Air Force One. Renamed the National Airborne Operations Center (NAOC), the aircraft was designed to be used by the President to direct a war in case of nuclear attack. During the Cold War, one of the four Night Watch aircraft was always in the air, twenty-four hours a day. But in the 1990s, the decision was made to keep the alert aircraft on the ground with the ability to take off on fifteen minutes' notice." (Bamford 2004 84)

During the morning, Clarke had instituted Continuity of Government, the measures prescribed for emergency rule in the face of a catastrophic emergency. "Our coordinator for Continuity of Government (we will call him Fred here to protect his identity at the request of the government) joined us. 'How do I activate COG?' I asked him. In the exercises we had done, the person playing the President had always given that order. 'You tell me to do it,' Fred replied." After relaying messages to Bush and Cheney, Clarke added: "'Tell them I am instituting COG.' I turned back to Fred: 'Go.'" (Clarke 8) Clarke, we see again, was running the country, while Bush zig-zagged.

It was at Barksdale that Bush made a second statement for television broadcast; it was taped and put on the air only after he had left the base. Bush said:

> Freedom itself was attacked this morning by a faceless coward, and freedom will be defended. I want to assure the American people that the full resources of the federal government are working to assist local authorities to save lives and to help the victims of these attacks. Make no mistake: The United States will hunt down and punish those responsible for these cowardly acts. I've been in regular contact with the vice president, secretary of defense, the national security team and my Cabinet. We have taken all appropriate security precautions to protect the American people. Our military at home and around the world is on high-alert status and we have taken the necessary security precautions to continue the functions of your government. We have been in touch with the leaders of Congress and with world leaders to assure them that we will do whatever is necessary to protect America and Americans. I ask the American people to join me in saying thanks for all the folks who have been fighting hard to rescue our fellow citizens and to join me in saying a prayer for the victims and their families. The resolve of our great nation is being tested. But make no mistake: We will show the world that we will pass this test. God bless."

The crucial point here is that all reference to terrorism or terrorists had disappeared. Bush was now speaking under the impact of "Angel is next," which had given him the idea that his adversaries were not what the term "terrorists" would normally suggest.

While Bush was reading his 219-word statement, "'he looked nervous,' said *The New York Times* reporters David E. Sanger and Don Van Natta Jr. The *Washington Post* reporters Dan Balz and Bob Woodward agreed. 'When Bush finally appeared on television from the base conference room,' they wrote, 'it was not a reassuring picture. He spoke haltingly, mispronouncing several words as he looked down at his notes." Judy Keen of *USA Today* noted that 'Bush looked grim. His eyes were red-rimmed.' An administration official later admitted, 'It was not our best moment.'" (Bamford 2004 87)

While at Barksdale, Bush "spent the next hour and a half talking on the phone," still disputing with Cheney and others over where he should go next. (*Sarasota Magazine*, November 2001) There was probably much more at issue than Bush's itinerary. Were Bush and Cheney haggling about whether or how to accept the rogue group's demands, such as the war of civilizations? When Bush requested a return to Washington, Karl Rove answered: "Our people are saying it's unstable still." (Associated Press, September 13, 2001) Bush was told he should go to the US Strategic Command center in Offutt, Nebraska, and he agreed to go.

While still at Barksdale, Bush received word of yet another threat. Just after 1:00 PM, Bush reportedly "received an intelligence report from the base commander that a high-speed object was headed for his ranch in Crawford, Texas." It turned out to be a false alarm. (Sammon 117) By 12:16 PM, US airspace was supposedly empty, since all flights were thought to have landed. Was this another psychological warfare ploy by the rogue network in order to keep Bush off balance? (*USA Today*, August 12, 2002) Air Force One left Barksdale for Offutt Air Force Base around 1:30 PM. Perhaps better to mask the nature of Bush's predicament, most of the White House press corps were jettisoned at Barksdale. Bush's party was pared down to a few essential staffers such as Ari Fleischer, Andrew Card, Karl Rove, Dan Bartlett, and Gordon Johndroe (Wood 2003; White House, September 11, 2001), plus a pool of about five reporters. (AP, September 12, 2001) Were these reporters intelligence community assets who could be relied on not to report potentially explosive details? On the flight to Offutt, Bush remained in "continuous contact" with the White House Situation Room and Vice President Cheney.

"By then [as Bush was leaving Barksdale] many in the press were beginning to question why the President hadn't returned to Washington during the grave crisis. The question was put to presidential counselor Karen Hughes, then at FBI headquarters. 'Where's the President?' asked one reporter. 'Is he coming back to DC? asked another. Instead of answering, she simply turned on her heels and walked out of the room. NBC's Tim Russert, host of *Meet the Press* and the Washington bureau chief, also remarked about the nation needing the leadership of its president. Yet, rather than return to Washington, the decision was made to keep moving as quickly as possible in the opposite direction. It was a risky choice. 'If he stayed away,' reported London's *Daily Telegraph*, 'he could be accused of cowardice.'" (Bamford 2004 87)

OFFUTT, NEBRASKA: STRATCOM

Offutt Air Force Base near Omaha Nebraska was the principal headquarters of the US Strategic Command (STRATCOM), the successor organization to Curtis LeMay's Strategic Air Command of Cold War vintage. This base possessed the main military command bunker of the US for nuclear warfighting purposes. Bush arrived here on Air Force One at 2:50 Eastern Daylight Time. He went at once to the bunker, which was several stories underground, and protected by a series of blast doors and the like. The conference room was ABC-proof, that is, secure against atomic, biological and chemical weapons. As Bamford evokes the tableau:

> It was like a scene from *Dr. Strangelove*, or *Seven Days in May*. Never before had all the pieces been in place for the instant launch of World War III. The military alert level was at its highest level in thirty years. The Vice President was in the White House bunker, senior administration officials were at Site R, congressional officials had been flown to Mount Weather, the Secretary of Defense and the Vice Chairman of the Joint Chiefs of Staff were in the Pentagon War Room, and the President of the United States was in the nuclear command bunker at STRATCOM. (Bamford 2004 89)

Was all of this because of terrorism, or was there some more serious threat of subversion to the state, perhaps complicated by the danger of a thermonuclear exchange? All of this behavior suggests at the very least that the White House thought that forces far more formidable than bin Laden and his Afghan troglodytes were involved.

Both movies cited by Bamford involve military madmen attempting either to precipitate general thermonuclear war, or else to stage a coup d'état in the US. A Straussian might see a hidden message here. The US military posture was now Defcon Delta, the highest state of alert short of all-out war. At Malmstrom Air Force Base in Montana, there were 200 Minuteman III ICBM silos, each one ready to launch three warheads. At other bases there were MX ICBM silos, and here each missile carried even more warheads.

Bush convened the NSC as "a teleconference call with Vice President Cheney, National Security Advisor Rice, Defense Secretary Rumsfeld, Deputy Secretary of State Richard Armitage, CIA Director Tenet, Transportation Secretary Norman Mineta, and others. Rice recalled that during the meeting, Tenet told Bush, "Sir, I believe it's al-Qaeda. We're doing the assessment but it looks like, it feels like, it smells like al-Qaeda.'" (Wood 2003; CBS, September 11, 2002) Was Tenet articulating the program of the coup faction, and obliquely demanding that Bush declare that the clash of civilizations in the form of warfighting had commenced?

Omaha's resident plutocrat and world's richest man Warren Buffett was scheduled to appear at Offutt that day, hosting an unpublicized charity benefit inside the base at 8:00 AM. In attendance were business leaders and several executives from the World Trade Center, including Anne Tatlock of Fiduciary Trust Co. International, the source of this story, who likely would have died had it not been for the fortuitous meeting. (*San Francisco Business Times*, February 1, 2002)

Bamford notes that "...it was close to 4:30 on the East Coast, and except for the brief, two-minute taped comments made at Barksdale, no one had seen or heard from the President or even knew where he was. Republicans back in Washington were becoming worried. 'I am stunned that he has not come home,' said one Bush fundraiser. 'It looks like he is running. This looks bad.' William J. Bennett, a former education secretary and a drug czar under former President George Bush, said that it was important for Bush to return to the White House as soon as possible. 'This is not 1812,' he said. 'It cannot look as if the President has been run off, or it will look like we can't defend our most important institutions.'" (Bamford 2004 91)

"Air Force One left Offutt around 4:30 PM and landed at Andrews Air Force Base at 6:34 PM, escorted by two F-15 fighters and one F-16. Bush then took the Marine One helicopter to the White House, arriving shortly before 7:00 PM. Bush gave a nationally televised speech at 8:30 PM, speaking for about five minutes." (Wood 2003)

This speech is too long to be included here, but it is readily available. Indeed, the White House commemorative edition leaves out the earlier two statements, and begins with this one. The change of tone is remarkable. Bush is now possessed of a Manichean certainty about the events of the day. He is back to the line that the perpetrators were terrorists. One important passage came at the beginning, where Bush stated: "Today, our fellow citizens, our way of life, our very freedom came under attack in a series of deliberate and deadly terrorist acts....Thousands of lives were suddenly ended by evil, despicable acts of terror." (Bush 1) Later in this statement, Bush presented the kernel of what would later be termed the Bush doctrine, his declaration of war on the world: "We will make no distinction between the terrorists who committed these acts and those who harbor them." (Bush 2)

What had changed for Bush during the course of the afternoon and early evening? It may have been only at this moment that Bush began to recover from the panic which had gripped him around 9 AM that morning. Clarke noted that "unlike in his three television appearances that day, Bush was confident, determined, forceful." (Clarke 23) As we will argue below, there is persuasive evidence that he had decided to capitulate to the demands of the sponsors of the terrorist attacks by launching the war of civilizations which this network had demanded. This surrender, carried out sometime in the afternoon or evening of September 11, constitutes Bush's great betrayal of the Constitution and his great crime against humanity. Everything Bush has done since, down to the very structure of his personality, has been determined by the moment in which he declined to fight the rogue network, but rather preferred to follow its orders, in violation of his oath of office. Never before had the United States surrendered to an enemy in this way.

After his 8:30 PM television address, Bush met with key officials in the Presidential Emergency Operations Center. According to Clarke, who was there, this was "a place he had never seen." (Clarke 23) This 9:00 PM meeting with Bush's full National Security Council was "followed roughly half an hour later by a meeting with a smaller group of key advisors. Bush and his advisors had already decided bin Laden was behind the attacks. CIA Director Tenet told Bush that al Qaeda and the Taliban in Afghanistan were essentially one and the same." (Wood 2003) When Bush insisted on sleeping in his own bed, he was warned that any threat would require that he go to the bunker. "And sure enough," said Mr. Bush. "We are in bed at about 11:30, and I can hear a guy breathing quite heavily. 'Mr. President, Mr. President! There's an unidentified aircraft heading towards the White House!'" It turned out to be a false alarm – or was it a good night kiss from the rogue network? (*Daily Telegraph*, December 16, 2001) Before going to sleep, Bush wrote in his diary, "The Pearl Harbor of the 21st century took place today.... We think it's Osama bin Laden." (*Washington Post*, January 27, 2002) There is no evidence that Bush, the man who never reads, writes enough to keep a diary. This reference to a diary would seem to be a vehicle to convey that depth of Bush's capitulation to the rogue network behind 9/11, a kind of intimate confession that he truly believed in the new party line he had embraced that afternoon or evening.

There was a brief phase of recrimination against Bush after 9/11, and it was based largely on his evasive retreats to Barksdale and Offutt. *Human Events*, the conservative magazine which had been favored by Reagan, noted that "some in the media were caustic in their description of the flight." The *New York Times* called it a "zigzag course." The *New York Daily News* charged, "A shocked and shaken President Bush – who was hopscotched around the country yesterday in an extraordinary effort to keep him safe...." Journalists were whispering about the president's absence. And even some friends are disturbed by the implications that the president or Washington may not have been safe. One former official with the first Bush administration said he was "deeply disappointed by his zigzagging across the country." "We had control of the skies by 10 o'clock," the source added. "I was hoping to see a Churchillian or Reaganesque sign of defiance. Bush was poorly served by his staff." (*Human Events Online*, 9/17/01)

There are several additional significant incidents which must be taken into account. These vanished early on from narratives of the event; they made the defenders of the official version uncomfortable. The first of these was a fire at the Old Executive Office Building or Eisenhower Building (OEOB), which is where the offices of the National Security Council are located. This is an integral part of the White House compound, and was the work place of such figures as Condoleezza Rice, Stephen Hadley, Elliott Abrams, and others. The ABC television network broadcast live pictures of a fire at the OEOB on 9/11 at 9:42 AM local time. (Meyssan 2002)

Another is the issue of a car bomb at the State Department: "Lisa slipped a note in front of me: 'CNN says car bomb at the State Department. Fire on the Mall near the Capitol." (Clarke 9) According to another account, "at 10:20 a report came in that a huge car bomb had gone off outside the State Department in Washington. It wasn't true, but it changed the picture once more." (*Daily Telegraph*, December 16, 2001) The fire on the Mall near the Capitol is yet another incident. Clarke also recounts receiving a report: "There has been an explosion in the Pentagon parking lot, maybe a car bomb." (Clarke 7)

If we put these events together with the possible early morning attempt to assassinate George Bush, we see that the scope of the 9/11 plot was altogether broader and more inclusive even than the acts of spectacular synthetic terrorism which the world observed that day.

SAFIRE: INSIDE THE BUNKER

An initial exposition of Bush's claim to have acted under threats on 9/11 came in a September 13 *New York Times* column entitled "Inside the Bunker" from William Safire, a hardened old neocon sinner from the Nixon White House. According to Safire, "A threatening message received by the Secret Service was relayed to the agents with the president that 'Air Force One is next.' According to the high official, American code words were used showing a knowledge of procedures that made the threat credible."

Safire identified his source as Karl Rove, Bush's political Svengali. According to Rove, when Bush stubbornly insisted that he was going back to Washington, "the Secret Service informed him that the threat contained language that was evidence that the terrorists had knowledge of his procedures and whereabouts. In light of the specific and credible threat, it was decided to get airborne with a fighter escort." Another Safire source, who was with Cheney in the White House bunker, related that it was Cheney who "suggested Air Force One go to Offutt Air Force Base in Nebraska, headquarters of the Strategic Air Command, with a communications facility where the president could convene the National Security Council."

Safire correctly pointed out that "The most worrisome aspect of these revelations has to do with the credibility of the 'Air Force One is next' message. It is described clearly as a threat, not a friendly warning – but if so, why would the terrorists send the message? More to the point, how did they get the code-word information and transponder know-how that established their *mala fides*? That knowledge of code words and presidential whereabouts and possession of secret procedures indicates that the terrorists may have a mole in the White House – that, or informants in the Secret Service, FBI, FAA or CIA. If so, the first thing our war on terror needs is an Angleton-type counterspy." (*New York*

Times, September 13, 2001) Of course, it may well be that the dubious Angleton networks, given their penchant for fascism, are themselves among the suspects. But that is another story.

The essential details given by Safire were confirmed by an AP wire that same day, also inspired by the opportunistic Rove. Here Ron Fournier wrote:

> Hopscotching across half the country while America was under attack, President Bush vented his frustration with Secret Service officials who told him of an anonymous call saying: "Air Force One is next." According to a senior government official, speaking on condition of anonymity, the caller knew the agency's code words relating to Air Force One procedures and whereabouts. (AP, September 13, 2001)

Foreign press organs, more critical than the controlled corporate media of the US, reported this story straight. The London *Financial Times* wrote that after Bush had taken off from Florida, "within an hour, an anonymous call reached the Secret Service. Using code words known only to the agency's staff, the caller issued a chilling warning: 'Air Force One is next.'" (*Financial Times*, September 14, 2001)

The principal clue leading us to the existence of the rogue network behind 9/11 is the "Angel is next" threat. Since hasty attempts to deny that this ever existed came soon after 9/11, we pause to document the evidence that this call really did take place.

In an interview with Tony Snow on *Fox News Sunday*, National Security Advisor Condoleezza Rice confirmed that the September 11 threat against President Bush's life included a secret code name.

> SNOW: Sept. 11 there was a report that there was a coded message that said, "We're going to strike Air Force One" that was using specific coded language and made the threat credible. Is that true?
>
> RICE: That is true.
>
> SNOW: So we have a mole somewhere?
>
> RICE: It's not clear how this coded name was gotten. We're a very open society and I don't think it's any surprise to anyone that leaks happen. So, I don't know – it's possible the code name leaked a long time ago and was just used.
>
> SNOW: How on earth would that happen?
>
> RICE: I don't know. I don't know. We're obviously looking very hard at the situation. But I will tell you that it was plenty of evidence from our point of view to have special measures taken at that moment to make sure the president was safe.

This exchange was reported by Carl Limbacher of NewsMax.com, who added that "US intelligence officials have not ruled out the possibility that a government mole may have given terrorists the top secret code language they used to deliver the threat 'Air Force One is next' as the World Trade Center and Pentagon were under attack." (NewsMax.com, September 23, 2001) Of course, the real imperative was to consider whether the rogue network behind the attacks extended into the ranks of holders of top secret security clearances.

The threat to Air Force One was repeated by others in the administration. In the September 12 White House briefing, Ari Fleischer told reporters, "We have specific and credible information that the White House and Air Force One were also intended targets of these attacks." The next day Fleischer was asked, "[It was] yesterday reported that some of the people in the Pentagon were a little bit skeptical about your comments yesterday that the White House and Air Force One were attacked – were targets of attack, given that the plane had come from the south. What do you –" Fleischer: "Who are these people?" Reporter: "Well, I don't know. They weren't my sources, so..." Fleischer: "No. There's – I wouldn't have said it if it wasn't true." Reporter: "Can you confirm the substance of that threat that was telephoned in...that Air Force One is next and using code words?" Fleischer: "Yes, I can. That's correct."(September 13)

On *Meet the Press* of September 16, Cheney began to back away from the story, telling Russert: "The president was on Air Force One. We received a threat to Air Force One – came through the Secret Service ..." Russert: "A credible threat to Air Force One. You're convinced of that." Cheney: "I'm convinced of that. Now, you know, it may have been phoned in by a crank, but in the midst of what was going on, there was no way to know that. I think it was a credible threat, enough for the Secret Service to bring it to me." (*Meet the Press*, September 16) Notice that the top-secret code words, the really sensitive point, have now disappeared. Still, the Bushmen were extremely sensitive to any impugning of their man's courage under fire. A journalist who said Bush was "flying around the country like a scared child, seeking refuge in his mother's bed after having a nightmare" and another who said Bush "skedaddled" were fired. (*Washington Post*, September 29, 2001)

In the short term, the Bushmen were eager to use the threat incidents to defend their leader from the charge of cowardice, and also to provide a cover for the reasons that had actually caused him to flee across the country. However, the "Angel is next" story contained an explosive potential for the longer term, since by pointing toward the existence of highly-placed moles within the administration who had access to top secret code words and procedures, it threatened to explode the official myth of 9/11 which was then taking shape.

As Bush gathered momentum with his "war on terrorism" and Afghan invasion, the need to use the "Angel" story for political cover diminished, and the need to protect the coherence of the official myth became paramount. It was at this time that the threat story began to be denied, not by officials speaking on the record, but by mysterious, anonymous leakers. One of these leaks came two weeks after 9/11: "Finally, there is this postscript to the puzzle of how someone presumed to be a terrorist was able to call in a threat against Air Force One using a secret code name for the president's plane. Well, as it turns out, that simply never happened. Sources say White House staffers apparently misunderstood comments made by their security detail." (Jim Stewart, *CBS Evening News*, September 25, 2001) An AP wire of the same day, also based on an anonymous leak, read: "[Administration officials have] been unsuccessful in trying to track down whether there was such a call, though officials still maintain they were told of a telephone threat Sept. 11 and kept Bush away from Washington for hours because of it."(AP, September 25, 2001) But the "Angel" story was persistent. One full year after 9/11, CBS revived the story that terrorists had broken Air Force One's secret codes, even though it was CBS which had aired the leaked denial a year earlier. (CBS, September 11, 2002)

After these leaks, Fleischer also dropped the story. On September 26, a reporter asked about the September 11 warning. Fleischer replied: "I'm not going to comment on any particular threats coming toward the White House. . . it is not an uncommon occurrence for people to threaten the government of the United States, regardless of whether it's President Bush or any of his predecessors. And that's why there are security precautions taken at the White House as a matter of routine." (*Washington Post*, September 27, 2001)

Latent hatred and resentment of Bush made it easy for reporters to trivialize the threat story, and make it appear as a devious invention of the loathsome Karl Rove. In her column in the September 23 *New York Times*, the gossipy Maureen Dowd noted that Karl Rove had "called around town, trying to sell reporters the story – now widely discredited – that Mr. Bush didn't immediately return to Washington on Sept. 11 because the plane that was headed for the Pentagon may have really been targeting the White House, and that Air Force One was in jeopardy, too." Rove was indeed a scoundrel, but there was something much more important at stake.

Especially eager to dispense with the threat story and focus on the soap opera of Bush the skedaddler were the leftists. To illustrate these, we take the case of Joe Conason, who wrote indignantly that "The Bush administration told an outrageous lie that the president was a target of terrorists – and Americans deserve an explanation." Conason, already inclining to defend the most reactionary lie of all, the official version, was especially upset about the reference to "code-word confirmation" – since this was the point that threatened the al Qaeda myth. Conason was even more worried about the demand for an investigation to root out the mole network inside the US government:

> Only when those assertions were shot down by CBS News and the Associated Press did the spinners back down, claiming that it had all been a "misunderstanding" by staffers, with little elaboration. How serious? In addition to undermining public confidence in the White House during a national emergency, this spinning of the president's flight from Washington led *New York Times* columnist William Safire, among others, to demand an internal investigation that would determine

whether an administration "mole" had revealed top-secret information to America's enemies. That paranoid theme was immediately picked up in the foreign media, no doubt worrying allies and potential allies engaged in sensitive discussions with the United States. (*Slate*, October 5, 2001)

Conason's reference to foreign paranoids may have been meant for the Réseau Voltaire, which was already performing yeoman service in dismantling the official version. In the 9/11 commission hearings, it was Ben-Veniste who took care to assert that the story was spurious. As a leading public opponent of the Bush dynasty since the time of Bush 41, I yield to nobody in my determination to put an end to the monstrous prominent role of this family in US public life. However, to think that the moron Bush could have organized 9/11 is absurd. As we have seen, part of the project was evidently to liquidate Bush and pass power to Cheney, whose credentials as a possibly witting plotter are infinitely stronger. By surviving the Colony interview hit, Bush lived to encounter 9/11 as a *fait accompli*, in which he was told at gunpoint to acquiesce, and he promptly did so. To reduce everything to "Bush knew" is a good slogan – far better than the official version – but it does not deal with the rogue network which antedates 9/11, and which remains in place today, posing a constant threat of new terrorist attacks, with or without Bush.

Paul Thompson, whose empirical work on the 9/11 timelines is a valuable resource for all researchers, and Allan Wood, unfortunately buy into the denials of the threat story. After marshalling the available evidence, Thompson and Wood, who pride themselves on their empirical precision, conclude: "Was there a mole in the White House? No. It turned out the entire story was made up." But it is far too simple to let this entire complex of problems and the vast issues it raises be swept under the rug by mere anonymous leaks, no matter how many times they might have been repeated. At stake is the most important clue in the entire 9/11 case. The regime is hiding something crucial here, and they must not be allowed to abscond. "Had terrorists hacked their way into sensitive White House computers?" Thompson asks. But the issue is much larger. If the threat to Bush came encrusted with code words, this means that the terror attacks were organized by high-level moles inside the US government – not that a hacker in an Afghan cave had cracked the Pentagon mainframes.

BUSH AND PUTIN ON 9/11

The potential for a thermonuclear confrontation or even of an all-out thermonuclear exchange growing out of 9/11 has generally been ignored by the US controlled media, but such a potential was clearly present. It was inherently present because of the tense relations among the US, Russia, and China in the wake of the bombing of Serbia and the *Kursk* incident. It was made explicit when a flying object, probably a cruise missile, hit the Pentagon. As the 9/11 commission report notes, one fighter pilot who saw the damage to the Pentagon immediately thought of Russia as the most likely adversary. This innate mental reaction must have been repeated thousands of times in the minds of non-witting military personnel on the day of 9/11. Clarke points out that the US proclamation of Defcon Delta, the level of readiness just below actual war, was inevitably immediately noticed by Russia, and came near causing immediate counter-measures of readiness on the Russian side. This was the first Defcon Delta since Henry Kissinger had ordered a world-wide alert to deter possible Soviet inter-vention in the Yom Kippur War in the Middle East in October 1973. Defcon Delta posed the danger of an escalation of mobilization between the two leading nuclear powers:

> Frank Miller reported that DOD had gone on a global alert, DEFCON 3: "This hasn't happened since the '73 Arab-Israeli War."

> "State, State, go." Armitage acknowledged the call. "Rich, DOD has gone to DEFCON 3 and you know what that means." Armitage knew; he had been an Assistant Secretary of Defense in the first Bush administration.

> "It means I better go tell the Russkies before they shit a brick." Armitage activated the Nuclear Risk Reduction Center, down the hall from the State Department Operations Center. The NRRC was connected directly to the Russian Ministry of Defense just outside of the Kremlin. It was designed to exchange information in crisis to prevent misunderstanding and miscalculation.

> Armitage reappeared. "Damn good thing I did that. Guess who was about to start an exercise of all their strategic nuclear forces?" He had persuaded his Russian counterpart to defer the operation. (Clarke 15-16)

Most US 9/11 commentators have virtually nothing to say about Bush's famous telephone conversation with Russian President Putin; Bamford, Thompson, and others exhibit elaborate disinterest in this matter. And yet, this is another one of the central moments of 9/11. In order to avoid a possible thermonuclear exchange, Putin needed to be reassured that the US Defcon Delta was not a cover for a thermonuclear sneak attack upon his country, something perfectly within the realm of possibility from the Russian view. Putin also needed to be told that thermonuclear launches from the US toward the Middle East or other areas were the work of a rogue network, not of the constituted government. Putin, in short, had to be asked for cooperation and restraint.

During the hours after the 9/11 attacks, Putin became the first world leader to place a call to Bush. Officially, this was done so that Putin could offer his condolences. But in the course of this conversation, Putin told Bush that he had ordered a stand down of Russian strategic forces, meaning that the maneuvers planned for the Arctic Region were cancelled. Putin also sent an official telegram to Washington DC conveying "anger and indignation" against the "series of barbaric terrorist acts directed against innocent people." (See "On Russian President Vladimir Putin's Telegram of Condolence to US President George Bush, 11 September 2001, Russian Ministry of Foreign Affairs website, www.In.mid.ru)[4] Bush later noted his appreciation for Putin's gesture and for Putin's strategic stand down of the Russian strategic rocket troops in deference to the US Defcon Delta. "It was a moment where it clearly said to me that he understands the Cold War is over." (*Washington Post*, October 4, 2004)

In a national television address later that day, Putin vehemently condemned the 9/11 attacks as "an unprecedented act of aggression on the part of international terrorism." These attacks, he claimed, were not a localized American issue but an event that "goes beyond national borders." Terrorism, Putin declared, is the "plague of the twenty-first century" and "Russia knows first hand what terrorism is. So, we understand as well as anyone the feelings of the American people." Putin described 9/11 as "a brazen challenge to the whole of humanity, at least to civilized humanity." Resonating with Bush, Putin set up his own Manichean dichotomy between terrorist barbarism and 'civilized humanity.' Putin assured Bush that "we entirely and fully share and experience your pain. We support you." ("Statement by President Putin of Russia on the Terrorist Acts in the US, Moscow, September 11, 2001," www.In.mid.ru) Putin later declared a national minute of silence in commemoration of the victims of the attacks.

Putin's actions on 9/11 can be seen as a successful attempt at war avoidance *in extremis*. Putin, as a KGB veteran, would have had no doubt that the official US version was hogwash, something a number of prominent Russian military officers expressed in the wake of 9/11. Putin could also see that the rogue network responsible for the bombing of Serbia and the sinking of the Kursk momentarily had the upper hand, and with them negotiation would be fruitless. Putin was determined not to play into the hands of the unhinged US rogue network behind 9/11. At a deeper level, his policy was therefore one of strategic deception or of *maskirovka* – to gain time in the wake of the catastrophe.

Putin must have seen that secret-government madmen ferociously hostile to Russia had now taken over the US regime to an unprecedented degree. He could also see that the neocons, with their obsession with Israel's strategic predicament, might well attack various countries in the Middle East before they got around to attempting to deal with Russia. Such Middle East tar-baby scenarios could only weaken, overextend, discredit, and isolate the United States, thus offering Russia some advantage. Putin was also busily working on the follow-on to the very formidable Topol missile, a weapons system that was probably superior to anything in the US arsenal, which would very likely allow Russia to defeat the US side's primitive off-the-shelf missile defense system. All these considerations suggested that Putin should camouflage himself for the time being as Bush's bosom buddy.

---

[4] For Putin's statements related to 9/11, see John O'Loughlin, Gearóid Ó Tuathail (Gerard Toal), and Vladimir Kolossov, "A 'Risky Westward Turn'? Putin's 9-11 Script and Ordinary Russians."

On September 24, 2001 Putin made a major television address, which grew out of a weekend of strategizing with his top advisors and a forty-minute phone call with President Bush. In this speech Putin accepted the establishment of US bases in the former Soviet republics of central Asia, which the US wanted to set up as staging areas for the imminent invasion of Afghanistan. On the surface this was capitulation, but underneath was still strategic deception. For a time, it appeared that a great US-Russian alliance was in the making, but this was more appearance than substance. Bush joined with Putin at a school in Crawford, Texas on November 15, 2001. The Bush-Putin honeymoon lasted into 2002. By the time Bush began seeking UN carte blanche for his war on Iraq, Russia had been attracted into the French-German continental bloc.

The existence of Russian strategic maneuvers on 9/11 involving bombers had been known to the Pentagon, since it was the explicit premise for the maneuver Northern Vigilance. In this case, it would have been known to the plotters as well. Therefore, the planners of 9/11 were well aware that their incendiary actions would take place against a dangerous backdrop of simultaneous US and Russian aircraft maneuvers.

BAMFORD: THE US INTELLIGENCE VERSION

Bamford compares Bush's actions on 9/11 with the behavior of President Lyndon B. Johnson on the day of the Kennedy assassination. Despite worries that the killing of the president might have been just the beginning of the strategic decapitation of the US under conditions of Cold War confrontation with the USSR, Johnson flew directly back to Washington and gave a short television address just after leaving his airplane. According to the usual procedure, Cheney should have gone to Site R on the Maryland-Pennsylvania border. But he refused to go. Why? "Bush could have easily ordered Vice President Cheney to a secure location outside Washington to preserve the continuity of government and then flown back to Andrews Air Force Base and given a defiant, Johnson-like speech. Then, with the public – and the rest of the world – feeling confident that despite the terrorist actions the US government remained stable and firm, he could have gone back either to the White House or to one of the other highly protected, secure locations. That would have been the courageous thing to do." (Bamford 2004 70)

"Instead, the decision was made to leave Vice President Cheney in the White House while President Bush hopscotched around the country. Though reporters were told of a supposed call to the White House threatening Air Force One – the reason for the President's odyssey – later it was concluded that no such call or threat ever took place. 'They've been unsuccessful in trying to track down whether there was such a call,' one administration official told the Associated Press. CBS News reported the call 'simply never happened,' and the *Washington Post* headlined its article on the subject: 'White House Drops Claim of Threat to Bush.' (Bamford 2004 70) Bamford thus avoids most of the really essential questions about 9/11.

THE ISRAELI INTELLIGENCE VIEW

One of the most detailed accounts of the high-level state secrets possessed by the 9/11 conspirators was provided by the Internet journal Debka, which often reflects the views of the Israeli Mossad . This Israeli analysis stresses the extent of the top-secret information controlled by the plotters, and the extensive network that would be necessary to have gathered such information. According to Debka, the message "Air Force One is next" was received by the US Secret Service at 9 AM. For Debka, Cheney was hustled into the bunker three minutes later. Debka suggests that the code name of Air Force One is changed daily, and that "the terrorists' message threatening Air Force One was transmitted in that day's top-secret White House code words." At the heart of Debka's account is the estimate that

> ...the terrorists had obtained the White House code and a whole set of top-secret signals. This made it possible for a hostile force to pinpoint the exact position of Air Force One, its destination and its classified procedures. In fact, the hijackers were picking up and deciphering the presidential plane's incoming and outgoing transmissions. The discovery shocked everyone in the president's emergency operations center – Cheney, National Security Adviser Condoleezza Rice and Transportation Secretary Norman Mineta. Their first question was: How did the terrorists access top-secret White House codes and procedures? Is there a mole, or more than one enemy spy in the White House, the Secret Service, the FBI, the CIA or the Federal Aviation Administration?

Nor was this all; the reach of the conspirators was even greater: "In the week after the attacks in New York and Washington, more hair-raising facts emerged. The terrorists had also obtained the code groups of the National Security Agency and were able to penetrate the NSA's state-of-the-art electronic surveillance systems. Indeed, they seemed to have at their disposal an electronic capability that was more sophisticated than that of the NSA."

According to Debka's information, the US intelligence community also believed "that terrorists are in possession of all or part of the codes used by the Drug Enforcement Administration, the National Reconnaissance Office, Air Force Intelligence, Army Intelligence, Naval Intelligence, Marine Corps Intelligence and the intelligence offices of the State Department and Department of Energy."

According to Debka, the plotters had even mastered steganography, a technology which "enables users to bypass electronic monitoring by hiding messages randomly in seemingly innocent digital files, such as music files, those of the popular online marketplace eBay, pornographic files or even e-mail headers."

Here were the sure-fire premises for an incontrovertible argument that the 9/11 attacks were the work of a rogue network of dissident moles inside the US government and military. But after having made precisely this case, Debka attempted to lead its audience back to the myth of al Qaeda, this time presented as possessing scientific and technological capabilities superior to those of the US government! As one of the parties guilty of having given al Qaeda the codes, Debka fingered World Space Communication, described as "one of the known bin Laden assets" which the US counter-terrorism agencies, including the NSA, had supposedly been tracking. Debka also alleged that "Bin Laden also has the NSA beat on the employment front," since the wily Saudi had supposedly hired "the best computer experts on the market. One such is Nabil Khan Kani, a Syrian who lived in Barcelona with his Spanish wife, Jenna Florine, in the late 1980s and early 1990s."

Through one *salto mortale* (fatal leap of logic) after another, Debka clawed its way to the astounding conclusion that the only agency which could have secured access to all those code words was – Iraq!! Debka wrote:

> The nagging question of a mole in the highest reaches of the US government and intelligence community – with direct or indirect links with bin Laden – remains. Since no single individual has access to every top-level code at any given time – a single mole would not answer the case; it would have to be a large, widely spread number. US experts do not believe bin Laden was capable of infiltrating double agents into the heart of the US administration on a large scale. They are looking elsewhere, instead, at a country with a very well-oiled intelligence apparatus– Iraq. (Debka, "Digital moles in White House? Terrorists had top-secret presidential codes." *WorldNetDaily.com*, September 22, 2001)

While this conclusion was absurd in the extreme, Debka had provided a valuable estimate of how high up in the US command structure the rogue network reached.[5]

---

[5] This is comparable to the "infiltration of police by the Red Brigades" or the story that the "Saudi-financed" Ptech software firm's penetration of FAA, NORAD and other sensitive databases was the key to the wargames and the attacks of 9/11 – a sleeper story that has been dusted off after the 2004 elections, perhaps signifying a new phase of blackmailing of the Saudis in Bush's second term. An early seed was planted in the report, "Bin Laden's Magic Carpet – Secret U.S. PROMIS Software" by Michael Ruppert (FTW, Oct. 26, 2001): "Bin Laden's reported possession of Promis may also explain the alleged threatening messages that were received by President Bush while aboard Air Force One on September 11th... the likelihood than [sic] bin Laden may have compromised the systems the U.S. government and its allies use to track him is high." And Bin Laden supposedly obtained the software not direct from his sponsors in the CIA, but from his "Russian handlers" [sic] – perhaps during a lull in the Soviet-Afghan war? Other commentators, less solicitous of the CIA or the bin Laden myth, describe Promis as

A CRITICAL FRENCH ACCOUNT

During the weeks after 9/11, the Réseau Voltaire of Paris represented one of the strongest voices calling the official version into question. Réseau Voltaire's most prominent writer was Thierry Meyssan, the well-known civil rights activist. His book on 9/11, *L'effroyable imposture*, was primarily a demonstration that the official thesis of a large commercial airliner striking the Pentagon was absurd and impossible. But Meyssan also focused on the central political-institutional questions posed by 9/11, and especially the "Angel" question. For Meyssan, the plotters' use of top-secret code words suggested that they had access to other codes, including the US nuclear missile launch codes.

At the heart of 9/11 was therefore a blackmail threat to the Bush regime that, if he refused to launch the war of civilizations, the plotters were in a position to do it on their own in a much more sweeping manner, by launching a US nuclear strike against a series of Arab and Islamic capitals. Whatever the Russian and Chinese attitude to such a launch might have been was not specified. Meyssan's thesis was that "from 10:00 AM to approximately 8:00 PM [on Sept. 11], US government officials were not thinking that this was the work of Arab terrorists, but rather that it was an expression of a military coup being carried out by US-based extremists who were capable of provoking a nuclear war." (www.reseauvoltaire.net, September 27, 2001)

On his website, and in his later books *The Big Lie* and *Pentagate*, Meyssan offered a detailed analysis of the events of the day, with special stress on the insurrectionary behavior of the US rogue network. He narrates that

> About 10:05, the Secret Service, in charge of protecting top personalities, reportedly received an encoded telephone call from the assailants. They thus would have had at their disposal transmission and authentication codes for the White House and Air Force One. In other words, the security of the top American leaders is no longer guaranteed and the enemies of America are able to usurp the identity of President Bush, including to order a nuclear launch. According to Brian L. Stafford, director of the Secret Service, it is not a matter of the United

---

a trojan horse, spyware that reports back to its masters on the recipients' doings – perhaps the perfect gift for a patsy like bin Laden. As for Ptech, is it reasonable to imagine that the deep and long entrenched US resident rogue network needed an outsider like CIA cut-out and drug dealer Yasin Kadi in order to surveille their own government? Or rather that the Saudi-sheepdipped Ptech was created by these very networks as a false lead, as part of the hoax? "Ptech" is the incompetence theory, which like "LIHOP" we must reject as a subspecies of the official lie that tells of autonomous terrorists capable of spectacular attacks, and thus worthy of a war of vengeance. Nico Haupt has proposed instead that the real 9/11 (and anthrax) command center may be a CIA front company in Florida.

States' facing terrorist actions, but facing a situation of war. He orders the implementation of the COG (Continuity of Government) plan. This ultra-secret procedure is orchestrated by FEMA...which has already been supervising the rescue operations and working in coordination with the FBI. From this moment, FEMA steps ahead of the FBI and becomes the highest civilian authority of the administration. This agency, which cultivates opacity, is directed by Joe M. Allbaugh, a former campaign treasurer for the Bush family. (www.reseauvoltaire.net)

The keystone of this aspect of Meyssan's analysis is the "Angel" call:

According to sources close to George W. Bush, the Secret Service received during the course of the morning a telephone call from the authors of the attacks, probably to make demands. In order to accredit their call, the assailants revealed presidential transmission and authentication codes. Only a few trusted persons at the apex of the state apparatus could have access to these codes. It therefore follows that at least one of the authors of the September 11 attacks is one of the civilian or military leaders of the United States of America. (www.reseauvoltaire.net)

For Meyssan, the "Angel" call definitely came from the "sponsors of the terror attacks in New York and Washington." He argues that "from 10 AM to 8 PM approximately, American officials did not think that those strikes were the result of Middle Eastern terrorists, but that they manifested an attempted military coup by American extremists capable of provoking nuclear war." The content of the call had been not so much to claim responsibility for the attacks, but to "pose an ultimatum, to force the hand of the President of the United States."

The trump card of the plotters was their possible possession of nuclear launch codes, and to counteract that, "during some 10 hours, President Bush was forced to run away from Washington and to go personally to the US Strategic Command (Offutt, Nebraska) both to take direct control of the armed forces; and especially so that no one could usurp his identity and unleash nuclear war." In Meyssan's view, in the wake of the "Angel" call, "No member of the National Security Council thinks any longer about terrorist attacks, all think about a military putsch which is ongoing. Calm will only be restored at 8:30 PM." (Réseau Voltaire, Information Note 235-236, September 27, 2001)

The call was followed by the descent of Cheney and Rice into the White House bunker. Meyssan sees the defense preparations around the White House as directed against a possible attack by insurrectionary US troops:

Simultaneously, the Secret Service has the Presidential areas evacuated, and deploys special agents and sharpshooters armed with machine guns and rocket-launchers in the surrounding area. It prepares to repel a possible assault by airborne troops. The Secret Service also informs President Bush of the situation; he is on board Air Force One, en route to Washington.

Within this context, Meyssan sees the pattern of threats to Bush and to Air Force One:

> The US Strategic Air Command indicates to the President that it has detected a signal, moving towards Air Force One. Considering the velocity, it is probably a missile. To protect the President, the military demand that Air Force One, despite its profile, continue its flight at tree-top level and follow an evasive course, while the F-15 and F-16 join it and escort it. But the military do not shut off its weather apparatus on board the Presidential plane, such that it continues to emit a signal allowing the international meteorological network to know its position continuously....Over a scrambled phone line, Bush consults the Vice President. He decides to go to Offutt Air Force Base (Nebraska), headquarters of the US Strategic Air Command. If his identity can be usurped by the perpetrators, the only possibility to prevent them from giving orders to the US Army in his place, is for him to be physically where all the weapons of mass destruction are controlled, including nuclear bombs. But Air Force One consumes too much fuel flying at low altitude, and its refueling in flight is impossible for safety reasons. A stop is therefore planned for the military base at Barksdale. (www.reseauvoltaire.net)

Meyssan reported that his research team attempted to determine what network might have been behind the 9/11 attacks. His prime suspect was a group he called the "special forces underground," a terrorist network associated with US-controlled stay-behind networks of the Gladio type which in his opinion maintained close ties to bin Laden among others. (Réseau Voltaire, Information Note 235-236, September 27, 2001)

Meyssan sums up the world-historical significance of 9/11 in these terms: "The attacks were thus not ordered by a fanatic who believed he was delivering divine punishment, but by a group present within the American state apparatus, which succeeded in dictating policy to President Bush. Rather than a coup d'état aimed at overthrowing existing institutions, might it not involve instead the seizure of power by a particular group hidden within those institutions?" (Meyssan 202 48) This means that the September criminals are still at large, still in power, and capable of striking again.

THE RUSSIAN INTELLIGENCE VIEW: NAMAKON

The Russian opposition weekly newspaper *Zaftra*, edited by the maverick Russophile Aleksandr Prokhanov, published on July 16, 2002 excerpts from a German-language EIR news agency report on the background of the attempted internal US coup of 9/11. EIR's thesis was that "the New York and Washington attacks could not have occurred without the witting complicity of high-level rogue elements within the US military intelligence command structures." Together with this material, *Zaftra* included some comments on the 9/11 issue from "Namakon" – the pen-name used by a group of top-level former Soviet intelligence officers. Namakon agreed that the events of September 11 could not have occurred without high-level complicity by a network or faction within the US military. Namakon also emphasized that the decision by President Bush, urged on by Tony Blair and others, on the evening of September 11 to endorse and embrace the bin Laden cover story "meant a de facto capitulation of the US Presidency to the real organizers of the attack, and the adoption of their policy of confrontation with the Islamic world, according to Huntington's formula for a 'Clash of Civilizations.'"

Namakon also called attention to the much-neglected fact that the attempted orchestration of an escalating nuclear alert between the US and Russia was a crucial part of the 9/11 coup plot. Namakon explicitly linked this potential for thermonuclear confrontation with the August 2000 sinking of the Russian nuclear submarine *Kursk*, the full story of which has yet to be told. Namakon wrote that this "hypothesis leads us to ask whether the *Kursk* catastrophe might not also have been an included facet of the operations of the US putsch group, since an attack of such dimensions would necessarily lead to a large-scale reaction by the Russian military and population, creating an atmosphere favorable to provoking nuclear escalation."

The escalation of the *Kursk* incident, which high-ranking Russian military officials repeatedly blamed on the presence of NATO submarines near the site of the sinking in the Barents Sea, came perilously close to succeeding. A serious confrontation was avoided only by a direct hot line consultation between Russian President Putin and then-US President Clinton. This telephone call was followed within 48 hours by a highly unusual visit to Moscow by CIA Director George Tenet. (*Zaftra*, July 16, 2002; EIR, July 22, 2004) In the case of 9/11, the immediate parallel was the telephone conversation between Bush and Putin, which, strangely enough, is never mentioned by an otherwise well-informed author like Bamford.

Many features of the analysis developed here with the help of Israeli, French, and Russian sources in particular have become current among well-informed European circles. On August 23, 2002, at a moment when the neocon drive for war with Iraq appeared stalled, an influential British political figure made the following comments to the late investigative journalist Mark Burdman of EIR:

> I have been noticing, as you have, the growing opposition, in Britain, in the United States, to this Iraq war. Last night, something occurred to me that I think is very relevant. I think the crowd that wants this Iraq war may well do something drastic in the coming days to regain the momentum. Some very big terrorism, perhaps. It is all very well that there are these challenges to the Iraq war. But we should not lose sight of the fact that there are powerful people in Washington, who pulled off this September 11 last year. They have their Plan A, which is now in trouble. But they also have their Plan B, Plan C, Plan D. They may well

have been thinking until very recently that their coup that began on September 11 was going very well. But suddenly, they have to re-think. And I think they are desperate, and capable of a lot. (EIR, August 23, 2002)

In other words, the rogue network was still in place, and it might resort to a new round of terrorism.

SEPTEMBER 11, 2001 – WHAT A REAL PRESIDENT WOULD HAVE SAID

We now leave the terrain of what actually happened, and move to a hypothetical sphere in which we can best try to shed further light on the events of 9/11. At this point a detailed account and timelines of what really happened behind the scenes on 9/11 cannot be attempted. However, we can speculate as to what an honest and courageous president might have done. Such a president might not have immediately understood the full scope of the 9/11 plot, but he would have insisted upon political accountability for appointed officials and on an immediate and thorough investigation. Some guidance might have come from an examination of the Ed Meese press conference of November 1986 which blew the lid off the Iran-Contra scandal, and which was accompanied by the firing of Oliver North and John Poindexter, then the NSC director. The speech on the evening of 9/11 might have sounded something like this:

My fellow citizens:

Today our country and our political system have been targeted by large-scale acts of terrorism. These are monstrous crimes against humanity, and they will not go unpunished. We send our solidarity to the brave firemen, policemen, military people, and office workers who have borne the brunt of this assault. We promise an equitable and equal compensation for the human losses of this day. Insistent and irresponsible voices have been raised in my own White House and in the intelligence agencies, and have inspired media reports attributing these attacks to Arab or Islamic terrorists of the al Qaeda Bin Laden organization. But this is no time for snap decisions or a rush to judgment when we are dealing with the present and future peace of the world. It is true that we have bitter enemies around the world, but the capabilities displayed today appear to go far beyond the technical and physical means available to al Qaeda. We must also recall that, under the reckless and irresponsible policies of my predecessors, the CIA had been one of the main sponsors of Bin Laden and al Qaeda. If we think back to the attack on the federal building in Oklahoma City in 1995, we remember that media voices attempted in the first hours to attribute that tragedy to the Arab world. Although I am convinced that we still do not know the full story of Oklahoma City, it is clear that the Arab world was not involved.

There are too many unanswered questions at this point. How were the terrorists who seem to have been involved allowed to enter the United States and operate freely in this country? Why was there no air defense over a period of one hour and fifteen minutes? I have ordered an immediate inquiry into this question, and in the meantime I have accepted the resignations of Gen. Myers of the Air Force, the deputy chairman of the Joint Chiefs of Staff, and of Gen. Bernhard of NORAD, whose agency failed the people today. There is also evident reason to believe that the CIA, the FBI, the NSA, and the Immigration and Naturalization Service have not performed satisfactorily, based on the fragmentary accounts available so far. I have therefore accepted the resignations of the leaders of those agencies, and of their principal deputies. I have furthermore accepted the resignation of the Secretary of Defense and his deputy, the Attorney General, the Secretary of Transportation, and of my National Security Adviser, since it is evident to me that they could not continue to serve the nation effectively because of the immense tragedy which has occurred on their watch. We rightly demand accountability from teachers, from railroad engineers, and from physicians. We therefore have all the more reason to demand accountability and responsibility from those who have been entrusted with the management of the executive departments, several of which have not served us well today.

Another question involves the collapse of the World Trade Center towers many minutes after they had been impacted by the airplanes. These events, as you know, represent an absolute anomaly in the history of skyscrapers. In particular, there is no explanation whatsoever for the collapse of building seven at five o'clock in the afternoon. Accordingly, and consistent with our urgent measures to save any victims remaining in the rubble, I am ordering the Seventh Mountain Division of Fort Drum, New York, to seize control of the site of the World Trade Center, cordoning it off as a crime scene and taking immediate measures for preserving the evidence we must have to determine what really happened. Not one scrap of metal will be removed before a full forensic survey has been carried out. Contrary to media accounts, we have not been able to identify the flying object which apparently hit the Pentagon, although it seems likely that it was not a Boeing 757, and thus could hardly have been United Flight 77. As for the tragedy over Shanksville, we are investigating whether this aircraft was shot down by our own forces, and why. All crash sites are being secured by military units, acting under my direct orders, whose loyalty to the Constitution is beyond question.

The overriding question is whether the criminals who acted today enjoyed support or collaboration from within our own country and even within our own government. I have created a special unit of federal investigators which will act under my direct orders and which will report to me and to me alone. The first task of that unit will be to determine why there was no air defense, in violation of the standard operating procedures of NORAD and the FAA. Another task will be to examine the entire roster of FBI and CIA double agents presently infiltrating terrorist groups and how they are managed, with a view to identifying possible factors of collusion. Another task will be to determine why our watch list procedures and other forms of vigilance were not effective in screening the criminals out.

As far as the FBI is concerned, I urge the Congress to join me in breaking up this tragically dysfunctional agency. After Ruby Ridge, Waco, the FBI crime lab, Wen Ho Lee, the Atlanta Olympics and Richard Jewel, the withheld documents in the McVeigh case, we now have September 11, 2001. The FBI has never recovered from the corruption and mismanagement instilled during the fifty-year reign of J. Edgar Hoover, a man whom we know today to have been unfit for public office. The FBI has many dedicated public servants, but they are trapped today in a structure of incompetence, corruption, and worse. Accordingly, I am placing the FBI into receivership by executive order with immediate effect; this agency will operate for the time being under the direction of my special assistant for internal security.

In determining the full scope of what happened today, I need the help of all our citizens. If you know something important about what happened today, I want to hear it. Call the White House and talk with one of my staff, who are mobilized to take your calls. If you see anyone, including especially federal agents, attempting to tamper with evidence, or if a federal agent attempts to intimidate you into saying you saw or heard something you did not see, I want to know about that, too.

I am also determined to find out if foreign intelligence agencies or foreign citizens were involved in today's events. I am appointing myself as temporary Director of the CIA, and in that capacity I will undertake a comprehensive review of foreign operations on American soil. No foreign agency will be exempted, and I promise you a full initial progress report.

In addition to the immediate investigations I have mentioned so far, I am also empanelling a board of inquiry to study today's events and offer a second opinion on what may have gone wrong. I am asking Senator Byrd to be the chairman of this body, and Lawrence Walsh, a Republican, the former Iran-Contra prosecutor, to be the vice chairman. I have invited former Secretary of the Treasury O'Neill, former President Carter, General Zinni, former Governor Ryan of Illinois to serve. I am also actively soliciting participation by outsiders and academics who have been critics of our government policies of recent years. I am inviting Susan Sontag, Eric Foner, Noam Chomsky, Chalmers Johnson, Howard Zinn, and Seymour Hersh to become members of the board of inquiry. Let them play the devil's advocates, if they will, so long as we obtain truth and justice. They will all receive the necessary security clearances directly from me personally, if necessary. I will personally supervise the rapid declassification of documents as recommended by the board of inquiry in order to educate the public about the board's findings. We all remember the failure of the Warren Commission; that failure will not be repeated during my presidency.

I recall the words of President Eisenhower in the wake of the Kennedy assassination: the American people, he commented will not be stampeded. I ask you to support your government and its constitutional institutions, and not to give way to the voices of hatred, fear, aggression, and paranoia. I promise that swift justice will be rendered for those who have struck us today, no matter who they turn out to be.

These dastardly attacks will not force this great nation off course; they will not force us to become something we are not. We will remain ourselves. We will go forward in the great American tradition of the Monroe Doctrine, the Good Neighbor Policy, the Bretton Woods system, the Marshall Plan, and the Four Freedoms of the Atlantic Charter, starting with the freedom from fear.

Further attacks cannot be ruled out in the coming days and weeks. Because of the office I hold, and because of the constitutional responsibilities I must meet, I ask for your support – no matter what may happen during the coming days and weeks.

Good night.

SEPTEMBER 25, 2001 – WHAT A REAL PRESIDENT WOULD HAVE SAID

A real president would have glanced at Cicero's orations against Catiline in the Roman Senate to stop the impending coup d'état of the bankrupt aristocrat Lucius Sergius Catilina in 63 BC, who had planned to seize power through a massacre of Roman political leaders. He would have been mindful of General de Gaulle's 1962 speech in which he expressed his determination to defeat the coup attempt of four fascist generals in Algiers.

My fellow citizens:

Tonight I would like to present, as promised, a progress report on the investigations into the events of September 11, investigations which have been the main task of your government over the past weeks. The tidings I bring you this evening are very grave, and they are related to the tempestuous events of the last few days which are known to you in whole or in part.

As many of you may know, during the morning of 9/11 the White House received a telephone call saying, "Angel is next." "Angel" was the top-secret code word designating my official aircraft, Air Force One, so this was a threat to shoot down Air Force One. It was also something more: as I realized immediately, it was quite possible that this telephone call had indeed come from the authors of the 9/11 terror attacks. If that was so, there existed the definite possibility that this group, whoever they were, also had access to other top-secret code words used by our government. This meant that there was imminent danger that the terrorist group might possess the code words and related signals that could be used to target thermonuclear ballistic missiles on targets in foreign countries – or even here at home. A duplicate of the briefcase known as "the football," which follows me everywhere, might be in the hands of the plotters. I decided at once to proceed as quickly as possible to the headquarters of the Strategic Air Command in Nebraska with a small force of bodyguards for the purpose of countermanding, by the immediate physical presence of the commander in chief, any and all illegal attack orders that might be issued by the rogue terrorist network which had so plainly declared war on our country. My intent was to assume direct personal control over the nuclear deterrent forces of this country, wherever they might be located.

During my flight to Nebraska, I received a phone call which presented this threat in the most concrete form. The call came from a man who identified himself as the spokesman for a secret organization of clandestine operatives and special forces – clearly a subversive and insurrectionary group acting as a tool for a coterie of very powerful, wealthy, and ruthless persons. This spokesman told me that his organization had orchestrated the attacks on the World Trade Center and the Pentagon as a means of reversing the inexorable decline of American power in the world – a process which I and my elected predecessors had been wholly negligent in allowing, he asserted. He also demanded that I immediately make a televised public statement identifying al Qaeda, Osama bin Laden, Afghanistan, and Iraq as those responsible for the terror attacks, and announcing our government's plans to invade and occupy these two countries. Iran, Pakistan, and Saudi Arabia, he added, might have to come later. If I failed to accept this ultimatum, the conspirators were determined to use the nuclear launch code words in their possession to destroy Cairo, Baghdad, Teheran, Rabat, Tunis, Karachi, Jakarta, Damascus, Pyongyang, Riyadh, Havana, and possibly other cities. That would start 100 years of war of civilizations, they told me, and once it had started, nothing could stop it. I told this spokesman that he and his group, in addition to being guilty of high treason, were courting suicide. The Russian Federation might interpret the missile firings as the beginning of a US first strike against Russian targets, and might respond by initiating procedures for launch under attack, in an attempt to use their nuclear assets against us before they were destroyed on the ground. The People's Republic of China might respond in the same way. These countries might also conclude that our government had been taken over by madmen, and that their only hope of safety might lie in the use of military means against us. The spokesman for the group of plotters replied that those dangers were real, but that it was up to me to avoid this danger by granting the demands of the terrorist controllers, which came down to US attacks on Afghanistan, and Iraq, with the overthrow of the government of Saudi Arabia likely along the way. The terror group, he boasted, welcomed the bloody global conflict that I seemed to fear, and even regarded the prospect of world war engulfing this planet as preferable to the relative decline of the United States for which he said I and those like me were responsible.

At this moment, our country faced the greatest danger in our entire history. To accept the ultimatum of the plotters and to wage war against their target list of Arab and Islamic states would have cast the United States adrift on an ocean of blackmail, lies, and adventures. Blackmailers always escalate their demands, and the addiction to terrorism of the victorious criminal network might have poisoned our national life for decades, or even for centuries. If I had capitulated, I would have been a puppet of the plotters for as long as I remained in office, indeed for the rest of my life. On the other side, the danger of world war was immediate. I decided that the only honorable course coherent with my oath to preserve, protect, and defend the Constitution was to defy the terrorists. At this point we had reached the SAC headquarters in Nebraska. I terminated my conversation with the spokesman for the plotters.

At this point, I activated several units of the Secret Service and Army intelligence under hand-picked officers whose constitutional loyalty I knew I could trust. I briefed them on what I knew so far, and gave them the task of finding the rogue terror network and rooting it out. These fine patriotic men and women went to work at once, and within 72 hours the main outlines of the plot were evident. Let me sum up what we have learned so far.

A group of al Qaeda operatives, manipulated by a cabal of rogue CIA case officers, had chosen September 11 to hijack several aircraft, force them to land, and use the passengers as hostages to extort the liberation of certain prisoners being held in Egypt and Saudi Arabia. Among these al Qaeda operatives were several double agents, also under the control of rogue elements in our own intelligence community. These were dissolute and evil persons, who had been trained using the infrastructure left over from the Iran-Contra affair.

Air defense that day was completely absent, in part because of four air exercises which were taking place at the same time in various parts of North America. A number of officers in critical positions at NORAD, its regional office in Rome, New York, and in the FAA appear to have been party to the plot. By a kind of collective inertia, they ignored the well-known and long-established , standard operating procedures which govern the cooperation of FAA and NORAD, and were able to misdirect our few remaining fighter interceptors, out over the Atlantic Ocean in one case. More arrests are imminent as a result of ongoing investigations in this area.

What the al Qaeda operatives apparently did not know was that the aircraft they had chosen to hijack had been equipped with a new technology making it possible to seize control of these aircraft and operate them by remote control from a command center on the ground. It was this new technology, and not the dubious skills of the hijackers, which allowed the planes to hit their targets with such precision.

But even direct hits by the two planes could not have been enough to bring down the towers. According to the information we have developed, the collapse of World Trade Center buildings one, two, and seven was the direct result of controlled demolition – the result of explosive charges which had been placed in these buildings over the previous days and weeks by the terror network, who infiltrated the buildings in the guise of cleaning and security personnel. We have not yet been able to solve all the problems posed by the collapse of the twin towers, since energy sources appear to have been at work which go beyond the realm of today's conventional technology. I will have more to report on this later. In the meantime, I regret to report that I have had to order the arrest of the Mayor of New York, who repeatedly attempted to bring about the destruction of evidence at the crime scene.

As for the Pentagon, it was struck by a US Air Force cruise missile fired from an aircraft above West Virginia, and not by one of the hijacked airliners. We have not yet been able to determine what happened to American Flight 77, and we call on citizens to come to our aid in this matter. The launch of the cruise missile was the work of an entire Air Force unit in Ohio, and these traitors have all been taken into custody.

The airplane that crashed in Shanksville was cynically shot down through the actions of a rebel mole placed in a highly sensitive position at NORAD. This mole was aware that the passengers had retaken control of the aircraft from the lightly armed hijackers, and realized that the interrogation of the hijackers on board would have revealed critical dimensions of the real plot in which the hijackers, although certainly acting with criminal intent, were ultimately mere expendable pawns. The NORAD mole also feared that an examination of the aircraft might reveal the presence of the remote control technology, which had for some reason failed to function. Accordingly, the mole cynically directed jet interceptors to destroy this airplane, even though it was far away from any target of interest to the hijackers.

Several FBI officials and agents have been indicted for obstruction of justice; they have been accused of destroying security camera tapes at the Pentagon, and intimidating witnesses at the Pentagon and in Shanksville. Members of the FBI crime lab and the NTSB team have been discovered attempting to sabotage the cockpit voice recorders of the planes in question; the recordings we have heard are consistent with the account of the 9/11 events I have just described.

Sadly, I must address the three mysterious suicides from the highest ranks of our own government which have caused so much speculation over the past several days. The vice president was found dead in his bunker at Site R last Thursday; the coroner has ruled this a suicide, and has established that the cause of death was a potassium cyanide pill. The same finding has been delivered in the case of the former deputy secretary of defense some hours later on that same day. The death of the Vice Chairman of the Joint Chiefs of Staff by a gunshot wound to the head in the Pentagon at around that same time has also been ruled a suicide. I can only confirm that arrest warrants for all three had been issued by a federal grand jury empanelled to investigate the tragic events of September 11.

The mutiny of the Delta Force battalion based near Fort Bragg, North Carolina, has been quelled by loyal troops and planes. The appeal of the rebel commander for a military rebellion against the legal government and for a military coup has been ignored.

As you may also know, a top former anti-terror official and several other high officials of the CIA and FBI have been missing for over two weeks, and are presumed to have fled abroad. I can confirm that arrest warrants have been issued for these persons. A number of journalists have also disappeared, and this may also be related to the recent upheaval. I can assure you that our constitutional procedures are just as vigorous as they have ever been, that habeas corpus remains alive, well, and in full force. We have no secret prisons and no secret prisoners, and I will tolerate none. Our open courts continue to function, and they will continue to do so.

We have uncovered complicity between the rogue network in this country and a number of foreign intelligence agencies. One of these is the British MI-6. After the raid by Scotland Yard on the headquarters of MI-6 in Oxford Circus, and after the resignation of Mr. Blair, I look forward to working with the new Labour Party prime minister to eradicate any remaining insurrectionary elements. We continue to observe the situation in several other countries we believe may have been involved in the 9/11 plot. I regret that General Sharon has refused to cooperate, and I invite the Congress to consider what response may be required.

I would like to thank President Putin of the Russian Federation and the leadership of the People's Republic of China for their wisdom and restraint, especially during the morning of 9/11, when the rebel network engaged in visible preparations for a nuclear launch. I am certain that the great powers, having weathered this storm, will be able to return to the path of confidence-building measures at our summit next week.

More details will be announced as soon as practicable. In conclusion, let me say a few words about the state of the world.

I do not assert that terrorism is a spontaneous outgrowth of poverty and misery. In fact, I assert the opposite: terrorism is usually organized by an outside agency, often by a government or a network operating inside a government. But it is certainly true that poverty and misery provide the indispensable environment in which terrorist groups can recruit, or be created by intelligence agencies. In today's world, there are about 2 billion people who are attempting to get by on less than $1 per day. There are some 600 million homeless – that is equal to about the entire population of Europe. About one and one half billion people do not have clean water to drink. With about one billion people unemployed, the unemployment rate in our world is about 33%, or about one third. When that happened in our own country during the 1930s, we called that a great depression, and we must therefore acknowledge the existence of a world economic depression of unprecedented severity today.

Two thirds of the people in the world – 65% – have never made a phone call. About 40% do not have access to electricity for household use; I would call that a clear need for rural and urban electrification. Every day in this world of ours, some 40,000 human beings perish from malnutrition and from easily treated diseases like diarrhea. Another 40,000 lose their lives each month as the result of warfare, all of which is absolutely futile and which has often been cynically fomented by foreign economic interests; I am thinking here of the crisis in Africa most specifically. In Africa, the standard of living of the average family has declined by 20% over the last twenty years.

Eighty-nine countries are now worse off than they were at the beginning of the 1990s. 175 million people leave their home countries every year in the desperate search for jobs and food – about 3% of humanity. The price of a human slave on the slave markets of southern Europe at this very moment is about 4,000 euros. In the midst of all this, the 258 richest persons in the world own more in the way of assets and other property than the poorest three billion persons. When 258 own more than half the human population of the world, I hope you will agree with me that such a world cannot be stable. Yet, this is the world that lies before us. I plan to use my powers as president to ameliorate this situation with every means at my disposal, and I call upon the Congress and upon all citizens to support these steps for a new world economic order that will be more just, more equitable, more prosperous, and more dynamic.

We have now been tested in the crucible of a brutal crisis. From this experience we must take renewed devotion to our best values. The decade of globalization has been revealed as a colossal failure, for ourselves as well as for others. We must find a better, more humane, more equitable way of organizing the affairs of this planet. To do this, we must work closely with almost 200 sovereign states, and work out the details with them, since every country has an inherent right to economic development, science, technology, and dignity. The old imperialism denied these, and the old imperialism is now on the junk-heap of history. In the days to come, my two lodestars will be peace and economic development, seen as the two sides of the same coin. Our world has turned over several times in the past month, but I am more certain than ever that I can count on the support of the American people in getting the world back on the right track. I ask you once again to remember the victims of the recent tragedy in your prayers. Good night.

CONCLUSIONS

So far we have come to the following conclusions:

1. The government's assertion that the so-called hijackers operated without being detected by official surveillance is **untenable**, and evidence is strong that the alleged hijackers acted in coordination with a faction within the government itself. The hijackers were therefore in all probability expendable double agents or, more bluntly, patsies.

2. The government's assertion that the four supposedly hijacked airliners were taken over and piloted by the four accused hijackers identified by the FBI **is at or beyond the limits of physical and technical reality**.

The planes were in all probability guided to their targets by some form of remote access or remote control.

3. The government's assertion that the failures of air defense were caused by the fog of war is **lame and absurd**. Air defense was in all probability sabotaged by moles operating inside the government.

4. The government's assertion that a Boeing 757-200 hit the Pentagon is **physically impossible**. Some other type of flying object, possibly a cruise missile, must therefore be considered.

5. The government's assertion that the Twin Towers of the World Trade Center collapsed as a result of the impact of aircraft and of the subsequent fire is **physically impossible**. The fall of the towers cannot be explained without the hypothesis of controlled demolition of some form, possibly including unconventional methods employing new physical principles.

6. The government's assertion that World Trade Center 7 collapsed at 5:20 PM EDT on September 11 purely as a result of fire is **physically impossible**. The collapse of WTC 7 is coherent with controlled demolition of the conventional type.

7. The government's assertion that United Flight 93 crashed because of actions by the hijackers or because of a struggle in the cockpit is **physically impossible**, given the pattern in which the wreckage was distributed. All evidence points towards the hypothesis that United 93 was shot down by US military aircraft.

8. The government's refusal to investigate insider trading in American Airlines and United Airlines put options, the wholesale seizure and destruction of evidence, the systematic intimidation of witnesses by the FBI, and a series of other incidents point unmistakably to an attempted **cover-up** on the part of the entire US government and establishment.

BUSH IN HELL

At the bottom of Dante's Inferno, in that third part of the traitors' ninth circle which is called Tolomea, Dante and Vergil encounter a certain Frate Alberigo of Faenza. Tolomea is devoted to that species of traitors who have betrayed their own guests. The peculiarity of Frate Alberigo is that he is apparently alive on earth, even while his soul is being tormented in the depths of Hell. Frate Alberigo explains that in cases of particularly heinous betrayal, the damned soul departs from the body and descends directly into Hell. The body remains alive, but it is operated by a demon during the rest of its natural life span. Something similar happened to Bush when he betrayed his oath of office by turning the US government over to the rogue network on 9/11. The demon has been in control ever since.

X
ANTHRAX

The anthrax incidents of October 2001 must be regarded as an integral part of the entire 9/11 operation. The 9/11 terror attacks were highly effective in terrorizing urban populations, since no one knew when another city might be struck, and with what means. But what of the vast suburbs, and what of rural America? Here kamikaze aircraft, poison gas and dirty bombs were hardly likely. But everyone in the country had a mailbox, and now that mailbox could become the delivery system for a deadly disease. Even the most humble and obscure person living in the most remote location could never be sure that a piece of junk mail in the letterbox had not brushed up against an envelope teeming with lethal anthrax spores. The most harmless daily routine, that of checking the mailbox, suddenly became a tense encounter with the world of biological warfare.

The anthrax attacks also provided a most welcome pretext for the Bush administration and the FBI to scale down and slow down the ongoing probes into 9/11. The anthrax letters provided a reason to re-assign FBI agents to the new danger, before they got anywhere near unearthing the explosive secrets of 9/11. On October 10, FBI assets were shifted away from the 9/11 investigation with the explanation that they were needed for the anthrax emergency.

At the same time the anthrax attacks, if properly regarded, can become the Achilles heel of the entire 9/11 operation, since it is here that the cause-and-effect relationship reaching into the secure weapons labs and military facilities of the US federal government is the most obvious. Anthrax cannot be synthesized by a rag-tag band in a distant cave. Weaponized anthrax can only be obtained at the US Army's biological weapons facility at Fort Detrick, Maryland, and at a very few other centers of the same type controlled by other governments. The existence of weaponized anthrax is ipso facto a strong case for US government collusion in terror attacks on this country.

The anthrax cases also provide a case study in FBI obstruction of justice. After the anthrax letters were used as a pretext for paring down the 9/11 searches, the agents so re-assigned accomplished virtually nothing. For a long time the bureau pretended that any microbiologist could have been the killer. But the pool of potential anthrax suspects was of course much smaller – it numbered in the dozens, or less. In order to define a realistic suspect pool, the FBI would have had to admit that the most likely source of the anthrax attacks was the government labs themselves, and that was something the FBI clearly did not want to do, lest this revelation be projected backwards onto 9/11. After a while Stephen Hatfill, a supposedly disgruntled former bio-war researcher with a sinister résumé and opinions, and thus a probable diversionary scapegoat, was identified as a person of interest. He was vilified by FBI leakers, but never indicted. The FBI made a Potemkin show of an investigation by draining a pond near Frederick, Maryland, but Hatfill was never charged.

We may also note in passing that the US government response to the anthrax cases pointed up the extent of oligarchical stratification in this society. Bush and the White House staff started taking Cipro, an antidote to anthrax, before the attacks even started. Members of Congress and congressional staffers got Cipro as soon as anthrax letters were found on Capitol Hill, and their offices were shut down instantly. In the case of black postal workers, the Postal Service expected them to keep working in tainted facilities, while at the same time there was a marked reluctance to give out free Cipro to these workers. The head of the USPS, a Bush appointee, said that any criticism of how he ran his agency amounted to aid and comfort for terrorists.

We cannot exclude the hypothesis that the anthrax cases were intended to become a much larger epidemic, one that might have claimed thousands of lives rather than just a few. Finally, in the anthrax cases, we have a *prima facie* case for political targeting. The first recipients of anthrax letters were a tabloid newspaper which had been prominent in publicizing the disorderly and at times illegal conduct of Bush 43's two substance-abusing daughters. Other recipients, like Senators Daschle and Leahy, were possible sources of opposition to the Patriot Act and other liberticide measures demanded by Bush and Ashcroft.

Between October 10 and October 11, just one week after the first case of anthrax had been reported, the FBI contacted the University of Iowa in Ames, Iowa. For seventy years this university had maintained a comprehensive repository of samples of every known strain of anthrax pathogen. This university was furthermore the source which provided samples of anthrax pathogen to researchers seeking cures, and also to labs seeking to weaponize the pathogen. Immediately after this phone call by the FBI, the University of Iowa destroyed the Ames anthrax repository. While it is not difficult to imagine the cover stories the FBI might have used to obtain this result, it is also clear that the Ames repository could have been the key to definitively solving the anthrax letters case. Analysis of the anthrax spores in the letters by chemical and DNA techniques identified these spores as belonging to the Ames strain. With the help of the samples collected in the repository, it would have been possible to identify with great precision the specific batch from which the anthrax letters had been filled, along with a paper trail leading to the agency to which the sample had been transferred. As the *New York Times* reported:

> Shortly after the first case of anthrax arose, the FBI said it had no objection to the destruction of a collection of anthrax samples at Iowa State University, but some scientists involved in the investigation now say that collection may have contained genetic clues valuable to the inquiry. Criminal investigators have not visited many of the companies, laboratories, and scientific institutions with the equipment or capability to make the kind of highly potent anthrax sent in a letter to Senator Tom

Daschle, the majority leader. Where investigators have conducted interviews, they often seemed to ask general questions unlikely to elicit new evidence, several laboratory directors said.

Evidence Disappears

Last month, after consulting with the FBI, Iowa State University in Ames destroyed anthrax spores collected over more than seven decades and kept in more than 100 vials. A variant of the so-called Ames strain had been implicated in the death of a Florida man from inhalation anthrax, and the university was nervous about security. Now, a dispute has arisen, with scientists in and out of government saying the rush to destroy the spores may have eliminated crucial evidence about the anthrax in the letters sent to Congress and the news media.

If the archive still existed, it would by no means solve the mystery. But scientists said a precise match between the anthrax that killed four people and a particular strain in the collection might have offered hints as to when the bacteria had been isolated and, perhaps, how widely it had been distributed to researchers. And that, in turn, might have given investigators important clues to the killer's identity.

No matter how scientifically illiterate they might be, the reflex response of any real detective would be to veto the destruction of anything remotely resembling evidence, or even of a key to interpreting evidence. But this time around, the FBI was pleading ignorance. According to Bill Tobin, a former forensic metallurgist who had worked at the infamous and scandal-ridden FBI crime laboratory in Washington DC, "The bureau was caught almost as unaware and unprepared as the public was for these events. It's just not realistic to ask 7,000 agents to overnight become sufficiently knowledgeable about bioterrorist agents [sic] and possible means of theft of those items and how they might be disseminated lethally to an American public."

Dr. Martin Jones, an anthrax expert at Louisiana State University, commented: "If those cultures were still alive they could have helped in clearing up the muddied history" of the spores found in the letters. Ronald M. Atlas, the president-elect of the American Society of Microbiology, the world's largest group of "germ professionals," saw large legal implications in the destruction of evidence. "Potentially," he said, "it loses evidence that would have been useful" in the legal investigation. (*New York Times*, "Experts See FBI Missteps Hampering Anthrax Inquiry," November 11, 2002) The FBI was obviously out to sabotage its own investigation. Here is yet another case of manifest obstruction of justice by the FBI molehill. The 9/11 commission ignores both the anthrax affair overall and the obstruction of justice by the FBI.

Starting about a week after 9/11, anthrax letters began to arrive at the offices of *The Sun*, a supermarket tabloid based in Florida, of Senators Daschle and Leahy, NBC News, and the *New York Post*. On October 5, Bob Stevens, photo editor of *The Sun*, died of anthrax. A number of postal workers in Washington

DC also succumbed. A total of five people died. The anthrax spores found in the letters were the product of very sophisticated milling, and were coated with silica, a process that is unique to US laboratories. Iraqi anthrax, by contrast, is coated with bentonite, a mixture of silica and aluminum.

A great deal of publicity was given to a series of reports by Barbara Hatch Rosenberg, a former government official and microbiologist at the State University of New York who was also working for the Federation of American Scientists. Rosenberg's work was enthusiastically supported by the Stockholm International Peace Institute (SIPRI), and the radical ecologists of Greenpeace. The FBI orchestrated a series of derogatory leaks about Rosenberg, suggesting that a gang/counter-gang operation might be in progress. Rosenberg's basic thesis was that the anthrax attacks were the work of a disgruntled lone assassin who had once worked for the US Army Medical Research Institute for Infectious Diseases (USAMRIID) at Fort Detrick, Maryland, near Frederick, but had subsequently been laid off. Naturally, the lone assassin approach tended to rule out an action by a more extensive network of moles in the federal government, which seems much more probable. Whenever extremely complicated and demanding operations are attributed to a disgruntled loner, we should be on guard against disinformation fabricated by the intelligence community. For example, the terrorizing impact of the anthrax letters was vastly increased by their synchronization with the immediate aftermath of 9/11. Was this a mere coincidence, or did the authors of the anthrax operation have advance knowledge that 9/11 was coming? How could Hatfill have been able to coordinate his supposed actions with 9/11? Once again, the rogue networks of the invisible government, and not any disgruntled loner, emerge as the prime suspects.

And there were other disinformation operations. Former CIA Director James Woolsey, a neocon who worked for a law firm representing Ahmed Chalabi's Iraqi National Congress, began a vigorous campaign to blame the anthrax attacks on Iraq. In addition, an anonymous letter was sent to police, apparently in September, accusing an Egyptian-born American scientist who had been laid off by USAMRIID of being a terrorist. The FBI questioned him and said that he was innocent. Details of the letter have not been released. Rosenberg thought it likely that this letter had been sent by the perpetrator.

According to Rosenberg's January 2002 statement,

> The FBI has surely known for several months that the anthrax attack was an inside job. A government estimate for the number of scientists involved in the US anthrax program over the last five years is 200 people. According to a former defense scientist the number of defense scientists with hands-on anthrax experience and the necessary access is smaller, under 50. The FBI has received short lists of specific suspects with credible motives from a number of knowledgeable inside sources, and has found or been given clues (beyond those presented below) that could lead to incriminating evidence. By now the FBI must have a good

idea of who the perpetrator is. There may be two factors accounting for the lack of public acknowledgement and the paucity of information being released: a fear that embarrassing details might become public, and a need for secrecy in order to acquire sufficient hard evidence to convict the perpetrator.

As for the anthrax, Rosenberg agreed that there was no doubt that the spores came from a US government lab:

> All letter samples contain the same strain of anthrax, corresponding to the AMES strain in the Northern Arizona University database (which has been used for identification).....Contrary to early speculation, there are no more than about 20 laboratories known to have the Ames strain. The names of 15 of these have been found in the open literature. Of these, probably only about four in the US might possibly have the capability for weaponizing anthrax. Those four include both US military laboratories and a government contractor.

Rosenberg based these conclusions on a technical analysis of the anthrax spores:

> The extraordinary concentration (one trillion spores per gram) and purity of the letter anthrax is believed to be characteristic of material made by the optimal US process.....The optimal US weaponization process is secret – Bill Patrick, its inventor, holds five secret patents on the process and says it involves a combination of chemicals. There is no evidence that any other country possesses the formula. Under the microscope, the letter anthrax appears to be unmilled. Milled anthrax spores are identifiable because they contain debris. The optimal US process does not use milling. The Daschle sample contains a special form of silica used in the US process. It does not contain bentonite (used by the Iraqis). A "coating" on the spores in the letter sample, indicative of the secret US process, has been observed.

Rosenberg's thesis was that the sender of the anthrax letters had been familiar with a study about using a scenario of this type for a terror attack which had been conducted by anthrax weaponization expert Bill Patrick of USAMRID a couple of years earlier:

> A classified report dated February, 1999 discusses responses to an anthrax attack through the mail. The report, precipitated by a series of false anthrax mailings, was written by William Patrick, inventor of the US weaponization process, under a CIA contract to SAIC. The report describes what the US military could do and what a terrorist might be able to achieve.....the report predicted about 2.5g of anthrax per envelope (the Daschle letter contained 2g) and assumed a poorer quality of anthrax than that found in the Daschle letter. If the perpetrator had access to the materials and information necessary for the attack, he must have had security clearance or other means for accessing classified

information, and may therefore have seen the report and used it as a model for the attack.

Rosenberg offered the following portrait of the anthrax killer: "Insider in US biodefense, doctoral degree in a relevant branch of biology; Middle-aged American; Experienced and skilled in working with hazardous pathogens, including anthrax, and avoiding contamination; Works for a CIA contractor in Washington, DC area; Has up-to-date vaccination with anthrax vaccine; Has clearance for access to classified information; Worked in USAMRIID laboratory in the past, in some capacity, and has access now; Knows Bill Patrick and has probably learned a thing or two about weaponization from him, informally; Has had training or experience in covering evidence; May have had an UNSCOM connection; Has had a dispute with a government agency; Has a private location where the materials for the attack were accumulated and prepared; Worked on the letters alone or with peripheral encouragement and assistance; Fits FBI profile; Has the necessary expertise, access and a past history indicating appropriate capabilities and temperament; Has been questioned by FBI." (Barbara Hatch Rosenberg, "Analysis of the Source of the Anthrax Attacks," January 17-31, 2002)

During the autumn of 2001, the FBI blanketed central New Jersey with leaflets showing a sample of the anthrax killer's handwriting. The FBI also sent questionnaires to 32,000 US microbiologists, most of whom worked in fields that had nothing to do with the government's anthrax labs. This was clearly busy work designed to avoid making the government the prime suspects in the attacks. George Monbiot of *The Guardian* mocked this farce as "kind of 'investigation' which might have been appropriate for the unwitnessed hit and run killing of a person with no known enemies. Rather than homing in on the likely suspects, in other words, it appears to have cast a net full of holes over the entire population." Monbiot reported that he had telephoned an FBI spokesman about this issue. "Why, I asked, when the evidence was so abundant, did the trail appear to have gone cold? 'The investigation is continuing,' the spokesman replied. 'Has it gone cold because it has led you to a government office?' I asked. He put down the phone." Monbiot speculated that the reticence had to do with covering up US violations of international bio-warfare treaties, since "the army's development of weaponized anthrax, for example, directly contravenes both the biological weapons convention and domestic law. So does its plan to test live microbes in 'aerosol chambers' at the Edgewood Chemical Biological Center, also in Maryland. So does its development of a genetically modified fungus for attacking coca crops in Colombia, and GM bacteria for destroying materials belonging to enemy forces. These, as the research group Project Sunshine has discovered, appear to be just a tiny sample of the illegal offensive biological research programmes which the US government has secretly funded. Several prominent scientists have suggested that the FBI's investigation is being pursued with less than the rigour we might have expected because the federal authorities have something to hide. The FBI has dismissed them as conspiracy theorists. But there is surely a point after which incompetence becomes an insufficient explanation for failure." (*The Guardian*, May 21, 2002)

This would appear to have been Barbara Hatch Rosenberg's line as well. In a sympathetic profile in the March 18, 2002 *New Yorker*, Nicholas Lemann reported that Rosenberg believes that the American bioweapons program, which won't allow itself to be monitored, may be in violation of the 1972 Biological Weapons convention. If the anthrax attacks were the work of a lone, disgruntled, mad scientist, the case for strengthening international safeguards would be enhanced. Rosenberg's basic demand was that this program be monitored. Fair enough, but not the whole story.

Towards the end of June, 2002 the FBI obtained a search warrant to examine the Maryland home of Dr. Steven J. Hatfill, 48, a bio-defence researcher who had worked at Fort Detrick, Maryland. Hatfill said at once that he was the victim of a witch-hunt. When he lived in Rhodesia, Hatfill once studied close to a school which bears the same name as the bogus address on the envelopes containing the fatal doses of anthrax. (*The Guardian*, June 28, 2002)

On July 2, *New York Times* columnist Nicholas D. Kristof referred to Hatfill as "Mr. Z" and strongly suggested that the FBI should jail him as the anthrax terrorist. "If Mr. Z were an Arab national, he would have been imprisoned long ago. It's time for the FBI to make a move: Either it should go after him more aggressively, sifting thoroughly through his past and picking up loose threads, or it should seek to exculpate him and remove this cloud of suspicion." In essence, the FBI did neither.

Kristof and the other journalists hostile to Hatfill claimed that in the late 1970s, Rhodesian special forces attacked black-owned farms with anthrax, and they sought to link Hatfill to these attacks. Hatfill held a press conference on August 12, 2002 in which he once again denied everything. In late August 2002, a paid two-page advertisement in the *Washington Times* argued that the anthrax killer had to be a member of the US military, probably someone with access to the US off-budget, secret biological-warfare laboratories, or else someone with access to the Science Applications International Corp. (SAIC) report on anthrax-mailing. The author of the ad was a certain Pete Velis. Velis asserted that Steven Hatfill was not the perpetrator. Velis maintained that the evidence indicated that the mailings were probably prepared beginning two years earlier, and that the purpose was political – to scare the US into a domestic security/wartime response – and not to kill a lot of people. He noted that the targets were among the strongest potential opponents of "Executive Branch/Homeland Security Wartime Powers expansions," citing, for example, the mailing to Senate Judiciary Committee Chairman Patrick Leahy (D-VT.). The SAIC report, which Velis says contained "the exact specifications of the anthrax mailed" would suggest that the mailers came from a group of military officers with access to the SAIC report. (*Washington Times*, August 26, 2002) A day earlier Hatfill and his lawyer held a second press conference, which received exceptionally broad media coverage, denouncing the FBI and Attorney General John Ashcroft for the tactics used in their investigation.

Barbara Hatch Rosenberg, after having been interviewed by the FBI, said that the agents had asked repeatedly whether a team of government scientists could be trying to frame Hatfill. "They kept asking me did I think there might be a group in the biodefense community that was trying to land the blame on Hatfill," she told the press. (*Washington Times*, August 3, 2002)

Whatever the gyrations of the FBI, it was clear that the anthrax came from the US government, and that the FBI had deliberately flubbed the investigation. The pond draining of 2003 changed nothing in this picture. By the summer of 2004, it was evident that the FBI would never solve the anthrax case because it did not want to awaken the US population to the reality that terrorism can come, and indeed does come, not out of a distant cave, but out of a US government lab on a military base. As for Hatfill, he was most probably a fall guy. If the FBI was incompetent before 9/11, and incompetent in its first major test thereafter, what then is the likely truth value of the statements made by the FBI about 9/11 itself?

THE WASHINGTON DC AREA SNIPER

In the fall of 2002, a series of sniper murders once again immersed the Washington DC area in fear and terror. These started in Montgomery County, Maryland, and soon spread south into Virginia. Here again the suspect pool was defined as snipers, and snipers are trained by the military services and certain police units. Any competent investigation would have started with lists of snipers trained by the government, especially recently retired or disgruntled ones. But this would once again have made the government into the prime suspect, and again the FBI refused to do this. The investigation was supposedly placed under the control of Montgomery County police chief Charles Moose, who ignored the imperative of sifting through the sniper pool, and instead acted as if the shooters could have been any casual passerby. Moose announced that telephone tip lines were being set up, and that he would rely on information from the citizenry to catch the felons. Weeks went by. After every sniper attack, road blocks were set up to encircle the entire surrounding area, but nothing was ever found. Local radio stations featured interviews with trained snipers who argued that real snipers were humanitarians who would never fire on unarmed civilians.

Finally information arrived which permitted the identification of the vehicle used by two suspects, who were caught while sleeping at a rest stop on I-270. Sure enough, the older of the two had been trained as a sharpshooter by the US Army. He and his younger partner were quickly categorized as lone itinerant psychopaths. This affair served to terrorize the national capital area, including Congress, the Supreme Court, and the executive departments, for the best part of two months. It refreshed and revived the horror generated by 9/11, and provided the immediate backdrop for the November 2002 election. That time around, al Qaeda and its mythical apparatus were not needed.

XI
INSIDER TRADING, CELL PHONES, MI-6 AND MOSSAD

A week after 9/11, the Institute for Counter Terrorism (ICT, also cited in some reports as the International Policy Institute for Counter Terrorism), located in Herzliya, Israel, called attention to very suspicious patterns of insider trading in put options (options to sell stock) in the shares of United Airlines and American Airlines, two companies whose planes were involved in the 9/11 attacks. Entitled "Black Tuesday: World's Largest Insider Trading Scam," the article was written by Don Radlauer. According to Radlauer's research, there was a 9,000% increase in United Airlines (UAL) put options between September 6 and September 10. Put options trading in UAL stock went up to 285 times the normal daily average on the Thursday before 9/11. American Airlines witnessed a 6,000% increase in put options in comparison to the usual average. In addition, there was a sharp rise in short interest in the shares of brokerage houses that had offices in the World Trade Center. Put options on Morgan Stanley went up to 27 times the usual level, and shorts of Merrill Lynch jumped to 12 times normal. This was accompanied by unusual buying of 5-year US Treasury notes, US government securities which are considered among the safest instruments for asset protection in case of some large world catastrophe.

Put options are long-shot bets that a given stock will decline in value in a specific time frame. If the stock goes down, the trader who buys these rights to sell shares racks up a profit many times in excess of the amount invested. Selling the stock of a company short is another way to try to profit from expected price falls. CBS' *60 Minutes* commented on September 19 that "the afternoon before the attack, alarm bells were sounding over unusual trading in the US stock options market." Bloomberg Business News remarked on September 20 that "this could very well be insider trading at the worst, most horrific, most evil use you've ever seen in your life…this would be one of the most extraordinary coincidences in the history of mankind if it were a coincidence."

It is widely assumed that the CIA tracks all important stock transactions, including the sensitive area of put options, in real time, as part of its Echelon and Promis software surveillance. The San Francisco Chronicle soon reported that a "source familiar with the United trades identified Deutsche Bank Alex. Brown, the American investment banking arm of the German giant Deutsche Bank, as the investment bank used to purchase at least some of these options." (Marrs 90) Alex. Brown (A.B. Brown), supposedly the oldest investment bank in the US., had been swallowed up by Bankers Trust in 1997. Alex. Brown had numerous CIA connections. Until 1998, the chairman was A. B. "Buzzy" Krongard, who left in that year to become counselor to CIA Director George Tenet. On March 26, 2001, Krongard received an important promotion within the CIA. (Marrs 90)

The US Securities and Exchange Commission pledged to get to the bottom of this question, as did the Bundesbank, Germany's central bank. But all references to 9/11 insider trading soon disappeared from the press. The finance oligarchs were not interested in pursuing this investigation, which appeared by its very nature to undercut the official version of 9/11. The 9/11 commission was eager to liquidate the entire matter in a few mendacious lines:

> Highly publicized allegations of insider trading in advance of 9/11 generally rest on reports of unusual pre-9/11 trading activity in companies whose stock plummeted after the 9/11 attacks. Some unusual trading did in fact occur, but each such trade proved to have an innocuous explanation. For example, the volume of put options – investments that pay off only when a stock drops in price – surged in the parent companies of United Airlines on September 6 and American Airlines on September 10 – highly suspicious trading on its face. Yet, further investigation has revealed that the trading had no connection with 9/11. A single US-based institutional investor with no conceivable ties to al Qaeda purchased 95 percent of the UAL puts on September 6 as part of a trading strategy that also included *buying* 115,000 shares of American on September 10. Similarly, much of the seemingly suspicious trading in American on September 10 was traced to a specific US-based options trading newsletter, faxed to its subscribers on Sunday, September 9, which recommended these trades. These examples typify the evidence examined by the investigation. The SEC and the FBI, aided by other agencies and the securities industry, devoted enormous resources to investigating this issue, including securing the cooperation of many foreign governments. These investigators have found that the apparently suspicious consistently proved innocuous. (9/11 commission 498 note 130)

Here is yet another example of the 9/11 commission begging the question. The issue is not whether the 9/11 commission's alleged "single US-based institutional investor" had "no conceivable ties to al Qaeda." It is rather whether such an investor had inside foreknowledge of the 9/11 attacks. Al Qaeda, after all, is an organization of patsies whose primary role in the entire affair is to distract attention from the underlying realities of the case. We must conclude once again that the 9/11 commission is lying.

The commission certainly ignored another huge attempted financial crime, which has generally received far less publicity than the put options. An abnormal spike of over $100 million in credit card charges was processed on 9/11 through computer disks in the WTC; of course, the computers were destroyed. However, the data was eventually recovered at a cost of about $25,000 per hard disk drive unit. No criminal investigation or prosecution followed in the attempted embezzlement, instead, the data retrieval company Convar was sold to Kroll Security, a CIA-linked firm.

Moreover, hard disks are damaged by temperatures over 70 C. Steel melts at 1535 C, or 22 times hotter. This is another resounding implosion of the wild theories purporting to explain how structural steel could collapse, essentially from the smoky heat of burning carpets, since the jet fuel had burned off in the first few minutes.

CELL-PHONE CALLS?

In the first days and weeks after 9/11, phone calls made by passengers of the hijacked jetliners to persons on the ground played a central role in the fabrication of the official version of 9/11. If the 9/11 commission had been serious, it would have published a complete compendium of the phone calls made by 9/11 victims, with complete transcripts and complete recordings where available. The phone calls should have been thoroughly investigated to determine their authenticity. This is one of the many obvious things which it was the plain duty of the 9/11 commission to do, but which it refused to do. Instead, the 9/11 commission has relied on fragmentary hearsay evidence for the contents of the calls, which it has then used without any process of evidentiary evaluation to shore up its 9/11 story.

The assembling, collating, and evaluation of the entire canon of alleged 9/11 phone calls is a task which goes beyond the scope of the present study, and which needs to be tackled in a separate and comprehensive effort. The alleged Barbara Olson telephone call, which loomed so large during the first week after 9/11, presents many contradictions; these have been discussed by Gerhard Wisnewski. The main difficulty with the reported Barbara Olson phone calls is that the sole source is Theodore Olson, the Solicitor General of the United States and a central figure in an aggressive and reactionary clique which played a key role in the Clinton impeachment and other destabilization operations against the legal government. This was again the same Olson who had instructed the US Supreme Court that "it is easy to imagine an infinite number of situations...where government officials might quite legitimately have reasons to give false information out." (Yahoo News, March 22, 2001) Without attempting to set forth the numerous internal problems presented by the available version of the Barbara Olson phone calls, we can safely disregard this material as very dubious hearsay evidence from an entirely unreliable source. Ms. Olson's renommée as martyr of terrorism made her book, *The Final Days: The Last, Desperate Abuses of Power by the Clinton White House,* a best-seller upon its publication in October 2001.

Other phone calls present mutual contradictions. As Woody Box has pointed out, the two American Flight 11 attendants Betty Ong and Amy Sweeney allegedly each made a separate phone call to report the ongoing hijacking. Ms. Ong talked about hijackers spraying mace, but Ms. Sweeney did not. Ms. Sweeney reported seeing a bomb with yellow wires, which Ms. Ong did not mention. Are the two flight attendants reporting events as seen in different parts of the plane, or are the calls fakes, simulated by well-trained imposters working for intelligence agencies as part of the general orchestration of 9/11? These are important questions, but too much questions of opinion to be considered here.

In conformity with the methodology employed in this study, we rather need to ask if there is anything about the reported 9/11 victims' phone calls which takes us beyond the realm of opinion and into that of physical-technical impossibility. The answer to this is at least a provisional and partial yes: there is persuasive evidence that cell-phone calls from planes flying above about 8,000 feet would have been intermittent at certain times, and totally unfeasible at others.

The 9/11 commission report never inquired as to whether cell-phone calls can be made from planes at any altitude. It therefore conveys the notion that cell phones would work fine at 10,000 feet, at 20,000 feet, or 30,000 feet, and would allow conversations of several minutes or more in length. Some of the 9/11 phone calls may have been made with GTE Airfones, the telephones typically installed in the seat back in front of each passenger. These required credit cards for activation, and would have been reasonably reliable at most altitudes and in most locations. Other 9/11 phone calls were almost certainly made with cellular wireless telephones. Whether these cell phones could have been used or not on 9/11 in some of the ways described is subject to serious question.

CELL-PHONE CALLS NOT FEASIBLE OVER 8,000 FEET

Airlines banned the use of cell phones a number of years ago because the cell-phone signals interfered with the navigation systems of their aircraft. For this reason, many people have never tried to use cell phones while traveling in planes. If they did, they might be surprised to find that their cell phones do not work very well, or do not work at all. Professor Michel Chossudovsky contends that " given the prevailing technology in September 2001, it was extremely difficult, if not impossible, to place a wireless cell call from an aircraft traveling at high speed above 8,000 feet.

One expert quoted by Chossudovsky comments: "Wireless communications networks weren't designed for ground-to-air communication. Cellular experts privately admit that they're surprised the calls were able to be placed from the hijacked planes, and that they lasted as long as they did. They speculate that the only reason that the calls went through in the first place is that the aircraft were flying so close to the ground."
(http://www.elliott.org/technology/2001/cellpermit.htm)

Just after 9/11, Alexa Graf, a spokeswoman for AT&T, told a reporter: "It was almost a fluke that the [9/11] calls reached their destinations... From high altitudes, the call quality is not very good, and most callers will experience drops. Although calls are not reliable, callers can pick up and hold calls for a little while below a certain altitude" (http://wirelessreview.com/ar/wireless_final_contact/)

Further doubts were raised about the slovenly and duplicitous methods of the 9/11 commission just a few days after its final report was released in late July 2004. This occurred when American Airlines and Qualcomm announced that they would, in the near future, be able to offer consumers a new wireless technology that would permit airline passengers to use their cell phones while aloft in a commercial airliner. The very fact that this event was placed in the future as of July 2004 was irrefutable real-world evidence that it had not generally been possible in the past, for example in September 2001. (http://www.qualcomm.com/press/releases/2004/040715_aa_testflight.html)

This innovation was notable enough to attract the attention of the press. One paper commented: "Travelers could be talking on their personal cell phones as early as 2006. Earlier this month [July 2004], American Airlines conducted a trial run on a modified aircraft that permitted cell phone calls." (*Washington Post*, July 27, 2004) *Aviation Week* described the new technology as follows:

> Qualcomm and American Airlines are exploring ways for passengers to use commercial cell phones in-flight for air-to-ground communication. In a recent 2-hour proof-of-concept flight, representatives from government and the media used commercial Code Division Multiple Access (CDMA) third-generation cell phones to place and receive calls and text messages from friends on the ground.

For the test flight, which took off from Dallas-Fort Worth, an airliner was fitted out with antennas in the front and rear of the cabin to transmit cell-phone calls to a small in-cabin CDMA cellular base station. This "pico cell" transmitted cell-phone calls from the aircraft via a Globalstar satellite to the world-wide terrestrial phone network. (*Aviation Week,* July 20, 2004) Needless to say, neither this service, nor the associated third-generation hardware, nor the pico cell CDMA base station inside the cabin (which functions like a moving cell-phone communication tower inside the plane) was operational in September 2001.

According to aviation communications experts, the crucial consideration in determining whether the cell-phone calls could have been made is the altitude of the aircraft at the time. Once a plane reaches 8,000 feet, which often occurs just a few minutes after takeoff, cell-phone calls are in general not feasible. The only way passengers could have gotten through to family, friends, and authorities using their cell phones is if the planes were flying below 8,000 feet. And even at low altitudes of below 8,000 feet, cell-phone communication is of poor quality. The crucial question is therefore: at what altitude were the planes traveling, when the calls were placed?

The details provided by the 9/11 commission on the altitude of the airplanes are fragmentary, but there is no blanket contention that the planes were consistently traveling at low altitude. On the contrary, the 9/11 commission report seems to indicate that a considerable number of the cell-phone calls were placed while the planes were traveling at altitudes above 8,000 feet, which is generally the maximum altitude for cell-phone transmission. (Michel Chossudovsky, "More Holes in the Official Story: The 9/11 Cell Phone Calls," (http://globalresearch.ca/articles/CHO408B.html) Professor Dewdney has arrived at similar conclusions. Here is yet another area where the 9/11 myth and the 9/11 commission report collide with the boundaries of physical reality and possibility.[6]

MI-6 AND MOSSAD

9/11 was carried out primarily by a US-centered rogue network or invisible government faction, but it was not carried out alone. The foreign intelligence service which contributed the most indirect support to 9/11 was unquestionably the British MI-6. The cooperation and interpenetration of the Anglo-American intelligence agencies is so overwhelming and so thoroughly institutionalized that it is hardly noticed by US commentators. The CIA and MI-6 are virtually Siamese twins sharing a number of vital organs. This fact is much deplored by those of us who believe that the British Crown, the City of London, the UK Foreign and Commonwealth Office, and Oxford Circus (the London home of MI-6) are among the most baneful factors influencing American national life, but it is by now a well-established and entrenched fact. Whatever is known to the US National Security Agency at Fort Meade, Maryland, is known simultaneously to the British GCHQ at Cheltenham, by virtue of bilateral intelligence-sharing agreements. Some light has been thrown on this phenomenon by Claire Short, when she reported that the red boxes sent to her by the UK intelligence service contained texts of private conversations of Kofi Annan which had been bugged by the Anglo-Americans. GCHQ also had a recent whistleblower who fleshed out other parts of this picture.

Many of these arrangements go back to World War II, and they have never been abrogated. The British functioned as the junior partners of the US invisible government during the Iran-Contra affair, and they continue to do so today. Although the British may be the junior partners in terms of military assets and disposable resources, they are often very much the senior partner when it comes to developing strategies and plans. Who could know the Arab and Muslim worlds better than the British orientalists? The overall Anglo-American plan for the balkanization of the Middle East, the Bernard Lewis plan, is really a distillation

---

[6] "Cells" are zones of transmission. Airplanes traverse cells quickly, forcing the cell-phone link to switch zones frequently, causing fading or loss of the connection. Yet there seem to be no reports that any of the alleged cell-phone conversations ever mentioned the subject of poor connections, which would be odd – unless the calls were fakes, and their script-writers thought it wiser not to bring up this topic. As for the origin of the alleged phone calls, versatile software reportedly exists that will mimic anyone, requiring only a brief recording of their voice to register its characteristics. It can then dub the new voice in real time over an actor's speech, effectively reproducing the words of A with the voice of B. This hypothesis seems difficult to accept for many people, perhaps due to the unfamiliarity of the technical application, which might not be commercialized due to security concerns. A similar hesitance obtains with regard to remote-control hijacking, although neither scenario is as high-tech as it appears. Voice dubbing and radio remote control technologies go back many decades; cheap remote-controlled toys have been on the market for years.

of two centuries of historical experience by the British Arab Bureau and the British India Office.

The extraordinarily close US-UK alliance lets the British side do what it wants within institutional channels, discreetly and silently. If we were to detail the extent of British participation in the history of NATO state-sponsored terrorism, in the Afghan guerrilla movement against the Soviets, in the foundation of al Qaeda, in the development of the figure of bin Laden (who once reportedly kept a pied-à-terre in the London suburb of Wembley), in the role of London as the premier world center of Islamic fundamentalism and of other terrorism, and a host of other subjects, we would essentially have to re-write almost this entire book from a slightly different point of view. In short, there can be no doubt that the main supporting role in 9/11 was played by British intelligence and British assets generally.

CIA and MI-5/MI-6 have also practiced a certain division of labor. Although congressional and parliamentary oversight is usually derisory, there is always the chance that an investigation may reveal embarrassing secrets. Therefore it has sometimes seemed advantageous to have the CIA undertake certain tasks in the UK, and to have MI-6 do certain jobs in the US – precisely to avoid the problem of legislative oversight in the country whose territory was being violated. During World War I and World II, the British were happy to run operations designed to get the US embroiled in war – operations which were welcomed by the Wall Street finance oligarchy. In 1976, by contrast, CIA Director George Bush was implicated in a campaign to overthrow the Labour Party government of Britain by helping to orchestrate a series of scandals. (Tarpley 1992 Internet edition) This campaign was part of a transatlantic effort to install the unspeakable Margaret Thatcher as British Prime Minister.

The Israelis, by contrast, have never wanted to accept the reciprocity of intelligence sharing which the British have more or less instituted. Israel is far less willing to share its state secrets than the British have been. The result has been that the Israelis have had to work hard to purloin the kind of US secrets which the British have obtained as a matter of course. The archetypal British deployment in this regard occurred when they staffed their Washington Embassy with Kim Philby, Donald MacLean, and Guy Burgess. The British got the information they wanted, and some of it even ended up in Moscow and Beijing – thanks to these three dedicated triple agents of the British Crown. This trio had some close scrapes, but they never saw the inside of jail. The Israelis, by contrast, had to rely on US Navy civilian employee Jonathan Pollard, who was found out in the mid-1980s and sentenced to life in prison, where he still remains despite pleas on his behalf by Netanyahu. British espionage can use the existing channels set up by treaties and agreements; the Israelis have to improvise networks informally as they go along, which can often be more risky.

Perhaps this is why the more picaresque stories of foreign intelligence involvement in the US during 2001 tend to focus on the Israelis. One such episode involved five Israeli moving men who were arrested on 9/11 after cavorting on a New Jersey rooftop while they were filming, with evident jubilation, the collapse of the World Trade Center towers. According to *Ha'aretz*, they "were arrested after they went up on the roof of a building and posed grinning for photographs with the burning towers in the background. Police found a large amount of cash in their car and suspected them of being members of a terrorist group." They were later charged with living and working in the US without permits and were ordered deported. The five were held for more than two months in a Brooklyn prison. Israeli Ambassador David Ivry, Richard Clarke's friend, claimed they were being held under poor conditions. Deputy Secretary of State Richard Armitage and two New York Congressmen worked to secure their release. When the men were arrested, they all had two sets of passports, one Israeli and one European, prompting the law enforcement authorities to consider them Mossad agents and apparently suspects in the 9/11 attacks. In addition, an Israeli drug gang was rounded up shortly after the 9/11 attacks. One of the gang leaders, whose apartment was two blocks from the WTC, was arrested when he refused to evacuate his apartment in the emergency. Drugs, cash, and guns were discovered in his apartment, and he was arrested, as were his accomplices. (*Ha'aretz*, October 29, 2001)

The five moving men were finally deported, according to the *New York Times*. According to this report, "The five were asked to take polygraph tests before being allowed to leave. But Paul Kurzberg refused on principle to divulge much about his role in the Israeli Army or subsequent work for people who may have had ties to Israeli intelligence." Kurzberg's attorney, Steven Noah Gordon, said that his client and the others had all finally agreed to the polygraph exams. One of Kurzberg's interrogations lasted seven hours. The other four Israelis were Oded Ellner, Omer Gavriel Marmari, Sivan Kurzberg, and Yaron Shmuel. Two additional Israelis were detained in Cleveland, both of whom had just completed their service in the Israeli Defense Forces. At least 50 Israelis were detained after 9/11, with arrests reported in San Diego, Houston, Kansas City, St. Louis, New York, and Cleveland. (*New York Times*, November 21, 2001)

On October 10, two Israeli men were arrested as they attempted to enter the Legislative Palace in Mexico City. They were armed with 9-mm pistols, nine grenades, explosives, three detonators, and 58 bullets. The two men, Salvador Gersson Smike and Sar Ben Zui, were wrestled to the ground by a group of Mexican workers, and were then detained by the Mexican Attorney General's office. (*Crónica de Hoy*, October 13, 2001)

Anton Chaitkin reports that Menachem Atzmon, a convicted criminal crony of Israeli PM Ehud Olmert, controlled security at Logan airport (EIR, Jan. 2003).

MEGA

In January 1997, the National Security Agency (NSA) intercepted a phone conversation between an Israeli official at the embassy in Washington, and

Danny Yatom, the head of the Mossad, Israel's foreign intelligence service. The official wanted permission from the spy boss to "go to Mega" in order to procure a copy of a confidential letter that had been sent by then-US Secretary of State Warren Christopher to Palestinian Authority President Yasser Arafat, containing US assurances about a recently negotiated agreement for an Israeli military withdrawal from the Hebron area in the West Bank. Yatom, according to the NSA intercept, rejected the request, admonishing his agent, "This is not something we use Mega for." (*Washington Post*, May 7, 1997)

A name mentioned in relation to the Mega scandal was that of Leon Fuerth, Vice President Albert Gore's national security adviser, and a fanatical supporter of the Likud. The *Washington Post*, in a 1998 profile of Fuerth, reported that he had been under suspicion by US intelligence officials of delivering sensitive US policy information to Israeli Prime Minister Benjamin Netanyahu of the Likud. Why was the Mega issue dropped? In March 1999, British author Gordon Thomas asserted in his book entitled *Gideon's Spies* that Israel had blackmailed the Clinton Administration with a threat to release tapped telephone conversations between the President and Monica Lewinsky. In her testimony before independent counsel Kenneth Starr, Lewinsky had reported that the President had warned her, on March 29, 1997, at the height of the Mega hunt, that he suspected the White House telephones were being tapped by agents of an unnamed foreign country.

THE CARL CAMERON REPORTS, DECEMBER 2001

US public attention was focused on Israeli intelligence activities by a series of three news features by Carl Cameron in mid-December 2001. Cameron had received detailed information from Washington sources. At the time of this report, Cameron said that 60 Israelis were still being held by US authorities. As many of 140 Israelis had been arrested, including many before the 9/11 attacks. According to Cameron, many of the Israelis "stated they served in military intelligence, electronic surveillance intercept and/or explosive ordnance units." The Israelis, some of whom were "described as active Israeli military or intelligence operatives, have been detained on immigration charges or under the new Patriot Anti-Terrorism Law," Cameron reported. According to this report, there was "no indication the Israelis were involved in the Sept. 11 attacks, but investigators suspect that they may have gathered intelligence about the attacks in advance and not shared it." On this sensitive issue, a highly placed investigative source told Fox News there were "tie-ins," but refused further details. "Evidence linking these Israelis to 9/11 is classified, cannot tell you about evidence that has been gathered. It is classified information," the source said. An Israeli Embassy spokesman offered categorical denials, and said any suggestion of Israelis spying on or in the United States is simply not true.

Another group of Israelis in North Carolina was suspected of keeping an apartment in California to spy on a group of Arabs whom the US authorities were investigating for links to terrorism. It was further reported that numerous US government agencies were part of a working group that had been compiling evidence in the case since the mid-1990s. The probe had documented hundreds of incidents in cities and towns across the country; the investigators had concluded that this extensive pattern might "well be an organized intelligence-gathering activity."

Many Israelis detained claimed that they were art students from the University of Jerusalem or Bezalel Academy. These self-styled Israeli art students often sought to make contact with US government personnel by saying they wanted to sell cheap art or handiwork. Cameron's documents indicated that these art students had "targeted" and penetrated military bases, the Drug Enforcement Administration, the Federal Bureau of Investigations, and dozens of other government facilities – including even secret offices and unlisted private homes of law enforcement and intelligence personnel.

Another phase of the investigation, said Cameron, had resulted in the detention and arrest of dozens of Israelis working at kiosks and pushcarts in American malls, where they had been selling toys called "Puzzlecar" and "Zoomcopter." These vendors had ceased their operations when press reports surfaced about Israelis being arrested for immigration violations.

A report obtained by Cameron from the General Accounting Office investigation which referred to Israel under the euphemism of "Country A" reported: "According to a US intelligence agency, the government of country A conducts the most aggressive espionage operation against the US of any US ally." A Defense Intelligence Agency report specified that Israel had a "voracious appetite for information....The Israelis are motivated by strong survival instincts which dictate every fact of their political and economic policies." "[Israel] aggressively collects military and industrial technology and the US is a high priority target." "Israel possesses the resources and technical capability to achieve its collection objectives," the DIA document concluded. (Carl Cameron, "Suspected Israeli Spies Held by US" Fox News, Dec. 11-14, 2001)

AMDOCS

Another of Cameron's installments dealt with the role of the Israeli-controlled company AMDOCS in the installation of the new White House communications system during the mid-1990s. This issue had surfaced earlier. According to a May 2000 story in *Insight* magazine, the employees of an Israeli company had enjoyed almost unsupervised access to White House telephone lines and other extremely sensitive communications equipment. The *Insight* article, entitled "FBI Probes Espionage at Clinton White House," reported that FBI counterintelligence investigators were probing an Israeli operation to spy on top US officials by hacking into secure telephone networks. "More than two dozen US intelligence, counterintelligence, law-enforcement and other officials have told *Insight* that the FBI believes Israel has intercepted telephone and modem communications on some of the most sensitive lines of the US government on an ongoing basis," the story said, specifying that the investigation involved eavesdropping on calls to and from the White House, the National Security Council, the Pentagon, and the State Department.

According to *Insight*, the FBI was tracking an Israeli businessman working for a local phone company, whose wife was suspected of being a Mossad officer working out of the Israeli Embassy in Washington. Federal agents searched his office, and found a list of the FBI's most sensitive phone numbers, including "black" lines used for wiretapping. "Some of the listed numbers were lines that the FBI used to keep track of the suspected Israeli spy operation," said *Insight*. Authorities were alerted to this operation by a phone manager who became suspicious about the activities of a subcontractor working on phone-billing software and hardware designs for the CIA; the subcontractor was employed by an Israeli-based company. *Insight* reported that the means of spying involved a private company which provides record-keeping software and support services for major phone companies in the United States. Insight quoted an anonymous US government source as saying, "It is a politically sensitive matter. I can't comment on it beyond telling you that anything involving Israel on this particular matter is off-limits. It's that hot." *Insight* did not name this firm as AMDOCS, but Cameron later supplied the name.

Cameron reported that, over the previous year and a half, the FBI had been investigating Bell Atlantic and the telecommunications billing company AMDOCS of Chesterfield, Missouri. According to Cameron's sources, a senior-level employee of AMDOCS had a separate T1 data phone line running directly from his St. Louis offices to Tel Aviv. Cameron noted that AMDOCS had the contracts with the 25 largest telephone companies in the United States to handle their directory assistance, calling record and billing work, which in effect gave AMDOCS real-time access to every telephone in the US, including records of all phone calls. According to Cameron, AMDOCS had been investigated on several occasions by the FBI and other law enforcement agencies, for suspected ties to the Israeli Mafia, as well as to espionage.

In 1999, the National Security Agency issued a TOP SECRET/Sensitive Compartmentalized Information report, warning that US phone records were getting into the hands of foreign governments – specifically the Israeli government. US authorities were especially concerned about the possibility that the Israeli Mafia was monitoring their communications traffic. One reason for this concern was a 1997 incident in which FBI, Secret Service, DEA and LAPD telecommunications were "completely compromised by Israeli organized crime," using precisely the data streams supervised by AMDOCS. In this instance, a major Federal and local investigation of an Israeli-linked organized-crime ring, trafficking in cocaine and ecstasy, had been thwarted, because "the bad guys had the cops' beepers, cell phones, and even home phones under surveillance." Investigators concluded that AMDOCS may have been the source of the leak.

And AMDOCS was not the only Israeli company with access to White House communications. The London *Sunday Times* had reported in the spring of 2001 that Israeli intelligence agents had used Telrad, a company subcontracted by Nortel to develop a communications system for the White House, to tap data flowing from the White House. These data were copied into a secret Israeli computer in Washington and then transferred to Tel Aviv two to three times a week. According to this report, Israel had intercepted e-mails from President Clinton as a result of this operation. Telrad was Israel's leading telecommunications company, which began by supplying phones to the Israeli Ministry of Communications in 1951. In 2001, Telrad provided "secure communications systems for the Israeli Defense Forces," according to the website of its major parent company, Koor Industries. Koor owned 80% of Telrad; the other 20% was owned by Nortel. Nortel itself was reported to be in a marketing partnership with Comverse. (London *Sunday Times*, May 21, 2000)

Comverse was Comverse Infosys, an Israeli-controlled company which provided "wire tapping equipment for law enforcement." Using Comverse software, law enforcement agencies employ computers to tap into the elaborate nationwide system of telephone switchers and routers, routing the targeted phone conversations into the computers of investigators authorized to do the wiretaps. Comverse managed and maintained the computers and the software, giving Comverse potential access to all of the data. Fox reported that "Attorney General John Ashcroft and FBI Director Robert Mueller were both warned October 18th in a hand-delivered letter from 15 local, state, and federal law enforcement officials," who complained that "law enforcement's current electronic surveillance capabilities are less effective today" than they were before Comverse was brought in under new US federal legislation.

In Israel, Fox reported, Comverse worked so closely with the government that the Ministry of Industry and Trade (formerly headed by Ariel Sharon) paid 50% of the firm's research and development costs. Fox added: "But investigators within the DEA, INS and FBI have all told Fox News that to pursue, or even suggest Israeli spying through Comverse, is considered career suicide." Fox reported that the FBI center at Quantico, VA handled the government contracting and purchasing of the wiretap equipment and "for years they have thrown much of the business to Comverse. A handful of former US law enforcement officials involved in awarding Comverse government contracts over the years were then hired to work for the company. Numerous sources say some of those individuals were asked to leave government service under troubling circumstances. What troubles investigators most is that in some cases in New York, certain suspects altered their behavior dramatically right after supposedly secret wire taps had begun, and this caused grave concern that they were tipped in advance." (Fox News, Dec. 13, 2001)

COMVERSE INFOSYS

Fox linked the Israeli spy operation to September 11, saying that "US investigators digging into the 9/11 terrorist attacks fear that suspects may have been tipped off to what they were doing by information leaking out of AMDOCS." This segment dealt with another Israeli high-tech company, Comverse Infosys, which furnished wiretapping equipment for US law enforcement. Under a 1994 law, private telecommunications and computer companies were required to make their network of switchers and routers available to law enforcement for wiretapping. Some investigators believed that Comverse electronic eavesdropping equipment had a "back door" through which wiretaps could be intercepted by unauthorized parties. One source said that the standing joke among US law-enforcement agents was that their wiretaps were going directly to Tel Aviv.

Secretary of State Colin Powell commented on the Israeli arrests at a State Department briefing held on December 13:

> Reporter: There were 60 Israeli citizens who have been picked up in the post-September 11 sweep, many of whom, if not all of whom, are connected to Israeli intelligence.... Are you concerned about such intelligence operations on US soil, and have you taken up this issue with your counterpart in Israel?

> Powell: I'm aware that some Israeli citizens have been detained, and I've been in touch with the Israeli government as to the fact that they have been detained in making sure that they have rights of access to Israeli diplomatic personnel here in the United States. With respect to why they are being detained, and the other aspects of your question, whether it's because they are in intelligence services or what they were doing, I will defer to the Department of Justice and the FBI to answer that, because, frankly, I deal with the consular parts of that problem, not the intelligence or law-enforcement parts of that problem.

The Israeli Embassy in Washington offered its usual blanket denial of any Israeli espionage in the US. Pro-Israeli pressure groups mobilized in the wake of the Carl Cameron broadcasts in an effort to suppress this highly embarrassing and suspicious news. Among the most active was a group called CAMERA ("Committee for Accurate Middle East Reporting in America"), which launched an e-mail, fax, and phone call campaign, to force Fox TV to drop its probe of the Israeli espionage scandal. Fox soon caved in, and no more reports were broadcast. Fox had also removed the transcripts of Cameron's reports from its website by the end of December 2001.

In fall 2002, the German liberal weekly *Die Zeit* of Hamburg returned to the question of Israeli espionage in the US before 9/11. This paper concluded that "between December 2000 and April 2001 a whole horde of Israeli counter-terror investigators, posing as students, followed the trails of Arab terrorists and their cells in the United States. In their secret investigations, the Israelis came very close to the later perpetrators of September 11. In the town of Hollywood, FL they identified the two former Hamburg students and later accused terror pilots Mohammed Atta and Marwan al Shehhi as possible terrorists. Agents lived in the vicinity of the apartment of the two seemingly normal flight school students, observing them around the clock... the Israelis provided a list including the names of at least four of the 19 hijackers of September 11, but this was apparently not treated as sufficiently urgent by the CIA and therefore not passed on to the FBI." According to this account, the US agencies dawdled and temporized, and then reacted with annoyance when the massive presence of Israeli espionage was discovered. Two who were on the alleged Israeli list were Khalid Al-Mihdhar and Nawaf Al-Hazmi, both supposedly on American 77, the plane the government claims hit the Pentagon. (*Die Zeit*, October 1, 2002) The Israelis doubtless knew a great deal in advance, but they can always point to their *pro forma* warning to the US government that an attack was imminent.

Adding up these reports, we can conclude that Israel maintained a massive and illegal espionage operation in the US, spying on all phases of American life, from the White House and the federal agencies through the business world to the foot traffic in shopping malls. Israel minutely observed the Atta-Shehhi-Jarrah-Hanjour patsy operation, and the Israeli government formally warned the US about it. The central contention coming out of the Carl Cameron reports is once again that "US investigators digging into the 9/11 terrorist attacks fear that suspects [meaning the 19 alleged hijackers] may have been tipped off to what they were doing by information leaking out of AMDOCS."

Naturally, this evaluation presupposes the validity of the official version which is contested and rejected here. If the 19 patsies were working under the direction of a faction of the US invisible government, as is contended here, what could the role of the Israelis have been? Could the Israelis have functioned as a cut-out, allowing certain kinds of communication between the US mole network and the patsies, e.g., by passing as Arabs and bypassing wiretaps? The very serious matter of Israeli agents of influence in the US government attempting to co-determine US policy towards Iran and other countries, urgently raised by the FBI investigation of Larry Franklin as an Israeli mole in the Pentagon in late August 2004, is discussed in the closing chapter.

The Israeli newspaper *Ha'aretz* later reported that, about two hours before American 11 hit the North Tower, two employees of the Israeli company Odigo who worked in Herzliya, Israel, had received an email message warning that terror attacks in New York City were imminent. Odigo was an Internet instant messaging service. The message had been sent through Odigo's instant messaging. Odigo had offices in New York City about two blocks from the World Trade Center. The full text was never made public. (*Ha'aretz*, September 26, 2001) The FBI was informed of this message, but, true to form, did nothing. The last press references to the Odigo warnings came in late November 2001. The 9/11 commission ignored this matter.

XII
CONSPIRACY THEORY:
THE GREAT AMERICAN TRADITION

The neocons, who are themselves a conspiracy, do not like conspiracy theories. But if we look at actual American history, we find conspiracy theories everywhere, even in the most exalted places. The neocon hysteria about conspiracy theories is therefore radically anti-historical, like so much else about this ideological and fanatical faction.

As the Harvard historian Bernard Bailyn convincingly argues in his prize-winning study, *The Ideological Origins of the American Revolution* (1967), the American Revolution was based on a conspiracy theory which saw the individual actions of George III as all being governed by a singly unifying design, which was to impose tyranny on the UK's North American colonies. This theory had been learned by some among the founding fathers from such British political figures as Edmund Burke, who made similar allegations themselves in a slightly different context. As Bailyn points out, the notion of a conspiracy centered on George III and his court was shared by the broadest spectrum of the founding fathers, from firebrand revolutionaries to cautious right-wingers like Dickinson.

Before the United States ever existed, there was a conspiracy theory. According to Bailyn, the Americans of the eighteenth century

> ...saw about them, with increasingly clarity, not merely mistaken, or even evil, policies violating the principles upon which freedom rested, but what appeared to be evidence of nothing less than a deliberate assault launched surreptitiously by plotters against liberty both in England and in America. The danger in America, it was believed, was in fact only the small, immediately visible part of the greater whole whose ultimate manifestation would be the destruction of the English constitution, with all the rights and privileges embedded in it. This belief transformed the meaning of the colonists' struggle, and it added an inner accelerator to the movement of opposition. For, once assumed, it could not easily be dispelled: denial only confirmed it, since what conspirators profess is not what they believe; the ostensible is not the real; and the real is deliberately malign. It was this – the overwhelming evidence, as they saw it, that they were faced with conspirators against liberty determined at all costs to gain ends which their words dissembled – that was signaled to the colonists after 1763; and it was this above all else that in the end propelled them into Revolution. (Bailyn 95)

This conception was endorsed by George Washington in the Fairfax Resolution of 1774, written in collaboration with George Mason. Here Washington asserted the existence of a "regular, systematic plan" of oppression.

In conformity with this plan, the British government was "endeavoring by every piece of art and despotism to fix the shackles of slavery upon us." Washington wrote in a letter of this time that "beyond the smallest doubt…these measures are the result of deliberation…I am as fully convinced as I am of my own existence that there has been a regular, systematic plan formed to enforce them." (Bailyn 120)

Thomas Jefferson agreed; he wrote in a pamphlet of 1774 that although "single acts of tyranny may be ascribed to the accidental opinion of a day… a series of oppressions, begun at a distinguished period and pursued unalterably through every change of ministers, too plainly prove a deliberate and system-atical plan of reducing us to slavery." (Bailyn 120) This language prefigures the final text of the Declaration of Independence.

John Adams estimated in 1774 that "the conspiracy was first regularly formed and begun to be executed in 1763 or 4." At other times Adams traced the conspiracy back to the 1750s and the 1740s, mentioning in this context Governor Shirley of Massachusetts. According to Adams, the proponents of the conspiracy were exchanging letters that were "profoundly secret, dark, and deep;" this was a part of what Adams called a "junto conspiracy." (Bailyn 122) According to the Boston Committee of Correspondence, one of the most important pre-Revolutionary institutions, awareness of the conspiracy was a gift of divine providence, practically a revelation. They thanked God who had "wonderfully interposed to bring to light the plot that has been laid for us by our malicious and invidious enemies." (Bailyn 122) For these colonists, God was a conspiracy theorist.

Even the Tories, the pro-British faction among the colonists, believed in a conspiracy theory of their own. In 1760 the royalist Governor Bernard of Massachusetts alleged that a "faction" had organized a conspiracy against the customs administration; he saw this group as a secret, power-hungry cabal. (Bailyn 151)

As Bailyn sums up his exhaustive reading of the pamphlet literature and political writings of the time, "the conviction on the part of the Revolutionary leaders that they were faced with a deliberate conspiracy to destroy the balance of the constitution and eliminate their freedom had deep and widespread roots – roots deeply embedded in Anglo-American political culture…. The configuration of attitudes and ideas that would constitute the Revolutionary ideology was present a half-century before there was an actual Revolution… and among the dominant elements in this pattern were the fear of corruption – of its anti-constitutional destructiveness – and of the menace of a ministerial conspiracy. At the very first signs of conflict between the colonies and the administration in the early 1760s the question of motivation was openly broached and the imputation of secret purposes discussed… The conviction that the colonies, and England itself, were faced with a deliberate, anti-libertarian design grew most quickly where the polarization of politics was most extreme…. But in some degree it was present everywhere; it was almost universally shared by sympathizers of the American cause…. The explosion of long-smoldering fears of ministerial conspiracy was by no means an exclusively American phenomenon. It was experienced in England too…." (Bailyn 144-145)

THE DECLARATION OF INDEPENDENCE: CONSPIRACY THEORY

The US Declaration of Independence signed in Congress in Philadelphia on July 4, 1776, is one of the most celebrated conspiracy theories of all time. Here we read towards the beginning a description of the present situation of the states which notes that

> …when a long train of abuses and usurpations, pursuing invariably the same object, evinces a design to reduce them under absolute despotism, it is their right, it is their duty, to throw off such government and to provide new guards for their future security….

This is followed by a long catalogue of misdeeds and abuses committed by the British monarch, introduced by the refrain: "He has…." At the end of the catalogue, there is a summary paragraph which makes clear that what has been presented should not be thought of as a laundry list of complaints about disparate events, but rather as the implacable and systematic operations of a concerted plot – of a conspiracy. In the words of Thomas Jefferson, as edited by Benjamin Franklin and others:

> The history of the present King of Great Britain is a history of repeated injuries and usurpations, all having, in direct object, the establishment of an absolute tyranny over these States.

The ministers changed, the policies shifted, but the controlling goal of tyranny remained. It is a conspiracy theory of the type which would make many a modern academic or neocon talk show host squirm. It is also one of the greatest political documents of world history. Were Jefferson and Franklin paranoids, mere conspiracy buffs?

It is perfectly correct to say that the United States as a country was founded on conspiracy theory, one which served as a powerful unifying ideology for the entire revolutionary generation. The approach of their analysis, it should be noted, was empirical as well as analytical: they recognized the need to back up their conspiracy theory with an abundant supply of factual material. This point of documentation and intelligibility is a key point, which the analysts and researchers of today need to remember.

Abraham Lincoln often serves as a kind of touchstone of morality and legitimacy in American politics, and he generally deserves this distinction. For progressives as well as traditionalists and conservatives (as distinct from right-wing radicals and neofascist neocons), the notion of getting right with Lincoln has long been a fixture of American political thinking.

What would Lincoln do if he were confronted – as we are today – with the attempt to found an entire system of government upon a set of uncorroborated assertions about a certain violent event which has aroused hysterical passions and which has been seized upon by those in power to set off an unjust and aggressive war of conquest? Instead of speculating as to what Lincoln might have done, let us look at what he actually did. For Lincoln was, in his youth, confronted with a situation very much like our own after 9/11 and the beginning of continuous warfare.

SPOTTY LINCOLN

For the young Lincoln, the question regarded the James K. Polk administration's policy towards Mexico. Polk was a slaveholder and a proto-Confederate who wanted to expand US territory towards the south in such a way as to increase the power and influence of the slave bloc. Polk was willing to make sweeping territorial concessions to the British in regard to the disputed Oregon Territory, where he repudiated the famous "fifty-four forty or fight" slogan in favor of a rotten compromise. By contrast, Polk's entire administration was devoted to tireless efforts to embroil the US in an aggressive war with Mexico. Polk first sent an envoy named Stockton to meet with the leaders of Texas, urging them to start a conflict with Mexico which the US could then portray as a new outrage perpetrated by the dictator Santa Anna. But Sam Houston wisely rejected this proposal, and would not act as Polk's provocateur. The best study of this attempt is Glenn W. Price's *The Origins of the War with Mexico: The Polk-Stockton Intrigue* (1967), and it can be shown to those who assert that conspiracies do not exist. Here was one which tried to provoke war but failed.

Later, Polk ordered General Zachary Taylor to take a military force across the Nueces River to the Rio Grande. The international border between Texas and Mexico was then about half way between the Nueces and the Rio Grande. When Taylor's forces got to the present site of Brownsville, Texas on the northern bank of the Rio Grande, they marched across Mexican farms and into the middle of a Mexican township located there. This inevitably led to fighting in which some of the US troopers were killed. Polk then used this incident as a pretext for extorting a declaration of war from the US Congress, pretending that US troops had been killed by Mexicans on US soil! The Mexican War of 1846-1848 was on. The armed clash provoked by Polk became the 9/11 tocsin for the Mexican War. The pressure on any politician to go along with Polk's orchestrated incident was as great as today's pressure to go along with the 9/11 myth.

In the midst of the war hysteria, some of the better Americans of the age refused to go along. One was Henry David Thoreau, who went to jail rather than pay a special surtax connected with the conflict. Former President John Quincy Adams led a group of antislavery northeastern Whigs called the Immortal

Fourteen who voted against Polk's supplemental budget request to fund the army in the field.

Abraham Lincoln in early 1848 was an obscure Illinois Whig and admirer of Henry Clay who had just arrived in Washington to begin serving his term as a member of the US House of Representatives. We are dealing here not with Lincoln the war president who saved the Union, but rather with Lincoln as a member of the opposition during another war – the Mexican War. Polk's 1848 State of the Union address was a defense of the administration's Mexico policy. This was the first major speech that Lincoln heard after being sworn in as a congressman. Polk was an earlier president who could never admit a mistake:

> ...the great bulk was his justification in detail, page after page, of every one of the actions of the United States, and the Polk administration, in the war with Mexico. The most salient quality of this long presentation was its relentless self-righteousness. Its total defensiveness. Polk and America were always and in every regard in the right; Mexico was *always* and in *every* way in the wrong. Doubly wrong: Mexico was not just the aggressor who started the war; Mexico was also wrong in every point leading up to that beginning, and had been wrong at every point since. And now Mexico was further wrong in not agreeing swiftly to her own dismemberment – to the "liberal" and "generous" terms that we are now offering. (Miller 164)

It was under these circumstances that the young Illinois congressman offered his famous series of Spot Resolutions – demanding to know from Polk exactly where, in what spot it had been on American soil that the bloodshed had taken place – with the obvious overtone that the fighting had not taken place on US territory at all, but in an area long settled by Mexicans and belonging to Mexico. Lincoln made a speech in favor of his Spot Resolutions on December 22, 1847, after just ten days in the House. Lincoln hammered away at these same issues in later speeches on January 12 and again on January 22, 1848.

The January 22 speech portrayed Polk as a provocateur, and demanded that he tell the truth about what had happened:

> Let him answer, fully, fairly, and candidly. Let him answer with facts, and not with arguments. Let him remember he sits where Washington sat, and so remembering, let him answer, as Washington would answer. As a nation should not, and the Almighty will not, be evaded, so let him attempt no evasion – no equivocation. If the president cannot or will not give the desired answers...then I shall be fully convinced, of what I more than suspect already, that he is deeply conscious of being in the wrong – that he feels the blood of this war, like the blood of Abel, is crying to Heaven against him.

Lincoln argued that Polk had been determined all along to find a pretext for war with Mexico; Polk had proceeded

> ...by fixing the public gaze upon the exceeding brightness of military glory – that attractive rainbow, that rises in showers of blood – that serpent's eye, that charms to destroy – he [Polk] plunged into it, and has swept, on and on, till, disappointed in his calculation of the ease with which Mexico might be subdued, he now finds himself, he knows not where.

Lincoln did not hesitate to attack Polk personally, nor to advance doubts about his mental state:

> How like the half insane mumbling of a fever-dream is the whole war part of his late message!...His mind, tasked beyond its power, is running hither and thither, like some tortured creature on a burning surface, finding no position, on which it can settle down, and be at ease... As I have said before, he knows not where he is. He is a bewildered, confounded, and miserably perplexed man. God grant that he may be able to show, there is not something about his conscience, more painful than all his mental perplexity!

Lincoln was convinced that the attempt to assign Polk's plots, lies and provocations such a central role in American public life was destined to have terrible consequences, and in this he was amply justified. The Mexican War and its aftermath, built upon Polk's falsehoods, precipitated the crisis that led directly to the Civil War. But before that Lincoln paid a considerable personal price for his principled stand in favor of truth. For his adversaries, he became "Spotty Lincoln," who had refused to support Polk's rationale for the war. Some Democratic editors referred to Lincoln as a Benedict Arnold.

One who baited Lincoln in such terms was Senator Steven Douglas, the Illinois Democrat who was later one of Lincoln's four opponents in the 1860 presidential election. At the very first of the Lincoln-Douglas debates of 1858, held at Ottawa, Illinois, Douglas spoke of Lincoln in these terms: "Whilst in Congress he distinguished himself by his opposition to the Mexican War, taking the side of the common enemy against his own country [voice from audience: That's true"] and when he returned home he found the indignation of the people followed him everywhere, and he was again submerged or obliged to retire into private life, forgotten by his former friends [voice from audience: "And will be again"]."

Lincoln never gave up his principled position about Polk's method of engineering the war. When Lincoln received the Republican presidential nomination in 1860, he was asked to assemble a short campaign autobiography or autobiographical sketch for use in the campaign. Here it would have been easy to omit all mention of the Spot Resolutions, but Lincoln obviously felt that the question of truth was more important. He stood his ground in the 1860 sketch, arguing that

> ...the act of sending an armed force among the Mexicans was unnecessary inasmuch as Mexico was in no way molesting, or menacing

the US or the people thereof, and… it was unconstitutional, because the power of levying war is vested in the Congress, and not in the President.

On this point, Lincoln never wavered. Many scholars and biographers who otherwise admire Lincoln have been puzzled or even scandalized by his tenacity on this issue. What Lincoln saw, and which the scholars often do not see, was the fatally pernicious consequences of lies in public life. In this sense, as in so many others, Lincoln was the anti-neocon. Lincoln also knew that if provocations were allowed to pass unchallenged, executive rule by provocation and by the threat of provocation would soon be the result. As he wrote to his friend Herndon on February 15, 1848:

> Allow the President to invade a neighboring nation, whenever he shall deem it necessary to repel an invasion, and you allow him to do so, whenever he may choose to say he deems it necessary for such purpose – and you allow him to make war at pleasure….Kings had always been involving and impoverishing their people in wars….(Miller 164-191)

These examples from the life of Abraham Lincoln suggest that, if he were alive today, our greatest president would hardly have accepted the fantastic myth of 9/11 in the way that most current politicians have done. Lincoln would have been at the very least a skeptic in regard to the official version and its many fallacies. He might well have been sympathetic to the 9/11 truth movement, since it is this movement which has stood up for the best of traditional American values against the overbearing oppression of the much-repeated lie. All of the neocon arguments about the need to stifle domestic dissent in time of war fall to the ground when confronted with the example of Lincoln.

THE PARANOID STYLE

Objections to the 9/11 imposture in its official version are often dismissed as conspiracy theories. Supporters of the official version use this a term of contempt, even though it is clear that to label a point of view as a conspiracy theory is in no way to refute it. The charge or insult of conspiracy theory is not only demagogical, but also intellectually dishonest, since the official version, involving as it does bin Laden and al Qaeda acting at a distance from remote caves with the help of laptops, represents a conspiracy theory (or conspiracy hoax) of a peculiarly fantastic type. Implicit in this procedure is the assumption that a conspiracy theory which is endorsed and embraced by the controlled corporate media is no longer a conspiracy theory, but rather respectable, and presumed true. Minority views which are not supported by the controlled corporate media remain conspiracy theories, and cannot be credible, no matter how true they can be shown to be. To these applies the warning issued by the deranged prevaricator in the White House:

> We must speak the truth about terror. Let us never tolerate outrageous conspiracy theories concerning the attacks of September the 11th,

malicious lies that attempt to shift the blame away from the terrorists themselves, away from the guilty. (UN General Assembly, November 10, 2001)

The entire controversy about conspiracy theory is a diversion, and is generally conducted in such a way as to lead away from the facts on the table. Charges of conspiracy theory represent in their own way a form of ideological terrorism, and grow out of the intellectual climate of cold war McCarthyite witch-hunts. Conspiracy itself has a history as long as humanity, since it is one of the primordial forms of political action. Machiavelli writes about conspiracy in a long chapter of his *Discourses*; what he means by conspiracy is a plot to kill a ruler and to seize power in his place, like the conspiracy organized by the Pazzi family against the Medici in the 1480s. Conspiracy is also an active category of the Anglo-Saxon common law.

Conspiracy theory as a term of opprobrium is relatively new. It dates back to the work of Richard Hofstadter of Columbia University. Hofstadter was himself a kind of neocon *ante litteram*, a neocon before there was a word for it, who became a direct beneficiary of McCarthyism: he took over a job vacated by Prof. Philip Foner, who had come under ostracism as a member of the Communist Party USA. In his essay on "The Paranoid Style in American Politics" (1964) and in his other writings Hofstadter took issue with the 1880s-1890s prairie populist critique of international bankers, a critique which today seems prophetic in its foreshadowing of the destructive shenanigans of Lord Montagu Norman of the Bank of England during the interwar period (Norman was part of Brown, Shipley in London, the home office of Prescott Bush's Brown Brothers, Harriman in Wall Street) and of the International Monetary Fund during the entire postwar period. But for Hofstadter, radical critics of Anglo-American finance oligarchy were paranoids. His essay is doubly suspect because it appeared in the wake of the Kennedy assassination, and seemed to suggest that the many critics of the Warren Commission report were also – paranoids. An interesting problem was posed for Hofstadter in that sophisticated western Europe, where populist paranoia was supposedly less strong, was even more critical of the Warren Commission report than was the alleged US citadel of paranoia.

Hofstadter's favorite habit of tarring political forces he did not like, such as the populists, with the brush of paranoia appears illegitimate. The paranoid typically fears that there is a conspiracy afoot specifically against himself. For Hofstadter, this notion becomes impossibly broad: anyone he thinks he sees a conspiracy anywhere is *ipso facto* a paranoid. What is lost here is the necessary reference point in reality: is there a conspiracy going on or not? US Attorneys have been proving the existence of conspiracies to juries for a long time, and they have generally escaped the charge of paranoia.

It is impossible to write political history without admitting from time to time the possibility of confidential agreements for concerted action made in advance. There are of course times when conspiracy plays no role: an absolute tyrant at the

XII: Conspiracy Theory: The Great American Tradition

height of his power has no need of conspiracy; he can act directly by issuing orders. (Yet even figures like Hitler and Stalin turn out to have been less absolute than usually assumed; it is enough to think of Hitler's chronic need to keep an eye on his Gauleiters, or the fact that the USSR functioned as an oligarchy during more years of its history than it did as a tyranny.) Similarly, an absolutely spontaneous mob – a rarity, although a theoretical possibility – is also innocent of conspiratorial planning. Between these two extremes, some form of surreptitious concerted action can frequently be found.

As has been stressed throughout this book, US society today is neither a tyranny nor a democracy; it is organized from top to bottom according to the principle of oligarchy or plutocracy. The characteristic way in which an oligarchy functions is by means of conspiracy, a mode which is necessary because of the polycentric distribution of power in an oligarchical system, and the resulting need to secure the cooperation and approval of several oligarchical centers in order to get things done. Furthermore, the operations of secret intelligence agencies tend to follow conspiratorial models; this is what a covert operation means – coordinated and preplanned actions by a number of agents and groups leading towards a pre-concerted result, with the nature of the operation remaining shielded from public view. So, in an oligarchical society characterized by the preponderant role of secret intelligence agencies – such as the United States at the beginning of the twenty-first century – anyone who rules out conspiracies *a priori* runs the risk of not understanding very much of what is going on. One gathers that the phobia against alleged conspiracy theory in much of postmodern academia is actually a cover story for a distaste for political thinking itself.

"Conspiracy theorist" as an all-purpose term of *ad hominem* argument to dismiss arguments which cannot be refuted thus goes back to the years after the Kennedy assassination, when the public was expected to accept that it was US government policy that this great crime, along with the further assassinations of Martin Luther King and Robert Kennedy in 1968, would remain permanently unsolved, and that those who objected would be vilified.

A more recent hue and cry against so-called conspiracy theory has been raised by the neocon academic Daniel Pipes, doubtless a nepotistic close relative of the Richard Pipes who was a prominent member of Bush 41's exercise in anti-Soviet alarmism, Team B. Pipes is a neo-McCarthyite who harasses academics who show sympathy for the Palestinian cause through his witch-hunting Campus Watch organization. He was also a beneficiary of a recess appointment to the board of the United States Institute of Peace, a procedure to which Bush 43 resorted when it became apparent that the US Senate would never approve Pipes. Pipes' book, *Conspiracy: How the Paranoid Style Flourishes and Where It Comes From* (1997) defines conspiracy theory as "the fear of a nonexistent conspiracy," as well as a form of political pornography.

But what if the conspiracy exists? For Pipes, one's own ignorant prejudice that no conspiracy exists trumps anything that might be determined by empirical research. Pipes relies frequently on his interpretation of Occam's razor, the nominalist proposition that explanations should be kept simple, or more precisely that theoretical entities should not be multiplied beyond necessity (*entia non sunt multiplicanda praeter necessitatem*). In the hands of Pipes, this becomes an infallible all-purpose argument in favor of lone assassins over multi-member plots, since a lone assassin approach is always more economical than a conspiratorial group. But what if necessity, which even Occam mentions, dictates something more complicated to account for the effects observed? Pipes and his friend Gerald Posner, who has written an especially meretricious book supporting the 9/11 myth, have no answer.

There is one conspiracy which Pipes does believe in: he alleges an Islamist conspiracy to take over or destroy the United States. According to Pipes, one of the focal points for this conspiracy is the Committee for American Islamic Relations (CAIR), which he thinks wants to impose Islamic law on this country. In any case, we can be certain that Pipes has learned all about conspiracies from his enthusiastic participation in the neocon mutual admiration and self-promotion society, which has been remarkably successful in making its banal and mediocre members into intellectual and political authorities.

LINCOLN'S HOUSE DIVIDED SPEECH: CONSPIRACY THEORY

Certainly one of the most famous speeches in American political history is the one which students still know as the House Divided Speech of 1858. This is Lincoln's address to the Illinois Republican Convention in the process of his nomination as candidate for the US Senate. Here Lincoln is dealing with a series of events which had greatly increased sectional tensions between North and South, between the slave and free states. These events included Stephen Douglas's sponsorship of the Kansas-Nebraska Act, an attempt to mandate squatter sovereignty on the question of slavery in the territories which had set off a severe round of violence on the part of pro-slavery border ruffians. The forces of slavery had been helped by the policies of President Franklin Pierce, a doughface and an ancestor of Barbara Bush, the mother of the current tenant of the White House. These policies had been continued under President James Buchanan, another doughface or northerner who embraced the slave bloc for political reasons. Finally, there had been the infamous Dred Scott decision, written by the old Jacksonian Democrat Roger Taney, who had asserted that blacks could not be citizens, that they had no rights, and that federal limitations on slavery were illegal. Were these events, carried out over a period of several years by a heterogeneous group of protagonists, mere coincidence and happenstance, or did they possess an internal coherence and interrelation? Lincoln saw it as very likely that the events of the 1850s were the result of conspiracy:

> We cannot absolutely *know* that all these exact adaptations are the result
> of preconcert. But when we see a lot of framed timbers, different

portions of which we know have been gotten out at different times and places and by different workmen – Stephen [Douglas, Senator and Democratic Party leader], Franklin [Pierce, US President, 1854-57], Roger [Taney, Chief Justice of the US Supreme Court, and author of the Dred Scott decision], and James [Buchanan, US President, 1857-1861], for instance – and we see these timbers joined together, and see they exactly make the frame of a house or a mill – ... in *such* a case, we find it impossible not to *believe* that Stephen and Franklin and Roger and James all understood each other from the beginning, and all worked upon a common *plan* or *draft* drawn before the first lick was struck.

Yes, the House Divided speech adumbrates a conspiracy theory. Nor was Lincoln the only founder of the Republican Party with a penchant for this form of analysis: a similar outlook can be found in the speeches of William Seward, the New York governor and senator who went on to serve as Secretary of State under Lincoln and Johnson. Seward was responsible for the 1860 campaign platform and key slogans of the Republicans. Seward needed a way to express distaste for the slavery-based southern society, along with resentment about the insatiable and inordinate power of the southern states over the federal government. He chose to do this while avoiding outright abolitionism. Seward's answer was the theory of the Slave Power Conspiracy, understood as the coordinated actions of the slave bloc designed to consolidate permanent power over the federal government. It was this slogan that helped to put Lincoln in the White House in 1860. Here the reference of conspiracy could not be more explicit. Any Republican of today who objects in principle to conspiracy theory should be reminded of the absurdity of his position, since his party rose on the basis of an overt conspiracy theory, expounded by leaders who were moral and intellectual giants compared to the pygmies of today.

As Eric Foner has shown in his work on the ideology of the early Republican Party, when the GOP prepared to contest the election of 1860, the new party needed a clearer ideological vision than it had possessed in 1856. On the one hand, the slavery issue loomed very large. On the other hand, the Republicans did not wish to make outright abolition their main slogan, for fear of a backlash in various states, even in the North. The central concept of the Republican Party in 1860 thus turned out to be the Slave Power Conspiracy. This theory saw the ruling slaveholder elite of the southern states as preparing to assert total control over the federal government in Washington, and thus threatening the freedom and the livelihood of every person in the north, whether they cared about slavery as an issue or not.

Thus, the United States was founded on a conspiracy theory. Abraham Lincoln's first important speeches in Congress were devoted to exposing a conspiracy by Polk and his friends to unleash the Mexican War. Lincoln's House Divided speech, one of the most celebrated political utterances in the chronicles of the US, adumbrates a conspiracy theory. The Republican Party itself first captured the presidency thanks to the efficacy of a conspiracy theory.

XIII
THE 9/11 MYTH:
COLLECTIVE SCHIZOPHRENIA

The wily Shafts of state, those Juggler's tricks
Which we call deep Design and Politicks
(As in a Theatre the Ignorant Fry,
Because the Cords escape their Eye
Wonder to see the Motions Fly)…
Methinks, when you expose the Scene,
Down the ill-organ'd Engines fall;
Off fly the Vizards and discover all,
How plain I see thro' the Deceit!
How shallow! And how gross the Cheat!…
Look where the Pully's tied above!
Oh what poor Engines move
The Thoughts of Monarchs, and Design of States,
What petty Motives rule their Fates!…
Away the frighted Peasants fly,
Scar'd at th'unheard-of Prodigy…
Lo, it appears!
See, how they tremble! How they quake!"

– Jonathan Swift, "Ode to the Honourable Sir William Temple"
(1689)

Received opinion in the United States has come to regard the official version of the events of 9/11, that is to say the 9/11 myth, as normal. Those who doubt the veracity of the official, mythical account are likely to be accused of being mentally imbalanced, and possibly paranoid. In this chapter, we will seek to turn the tables on the official mythographs and their gullible followers. We have already discussed some of the fantastic, contradictory, and absurd features of the official myth. We now turn our attention to the problem of why this myth has been accepted by so many people, especially in the English-speaking world.

Our conclusion is that readiness to believe in the myth is correlated with a mental outlook which can only be described as schizophrenic and autistic. In other words, there is something more than fear and stress at work. The resulting outlook operates not just at the level of individuals, but also in the Anglo-American culture as a whole. To do justice to this dangerous but fascinating phenomenon, we must venture into the fields of psychology and psychoanalysis to develop a familiarity with some of the main features of schizophrenic and autistic thinking. This will allow us to evaluate the 9/11 myth as a product of troubled and clouded thinking, and will also shed light on the role of the main purveyor of the myth, G.W. Bush.

"The only thing we have to fear is fear itself," said Franklin D. Roosevelt at his inauguration in March, 1933. The advice of the Bush regime to the American people is, by contrast, "Be afraid! Always!" As we have seen, in the aftermath of 9/11 US public life has come to be founded more and more upon an outright fantastic myth which is often invoked, but never demonstrated or proven. US institutions have more and more built their foundations upon a provocation.

The impact of the myth on American life and on the psychology of individual citizens has not been sufficiently studied by psychologists, since most of them also worship at the shrine of the myth. But in a general way, it is possible to see that the prevalence of the myth reflects a mass psychopathology of delusion and false consciousness, a turning away from reality into a politics of myth. The United States is well on its way under the second Bush regime to becoming an autistic power, estranged and alienated from surrounding reality. This poses the question: why does anybody believe the official story of 9/11, with all of its absurdities? What explains the power of the myth?

Countries which have chosen to build their polity upon myth have generally fared poorly. The classical example is of course German Nazism, whose leaders openly rejected reality in favor of a fantastic world of Germanic and Wagnerian heroes and monsters. The politics of modern Serbia, which has seen defeats dating back to the fourteenth century as more real and more relevant than the economic realities of today, are another example. Unless the 9/11 myth can be deconstructed and demystified, we will soon experience many more of the unpleasant effects of mythical politics here in the United States.

The desperate expedient of turning to terrorism to deal with a crisis is like choosing to initiate a heroin habit to get through a rough patch of personal life, as Sanguinetti reminds us. A key aspect to consider, Sanguinetti argues, "in connection with a strategy which is founded upon provocation, is as old as the world: Seneca already remarked – and if I quote him, it is because, being Nero's counselor, he was an expert in state terrorism and provocations – that it is 'easier not to embark upon this path than it is to stop, once embarked upon it.' Like a drug, artificial terrorism needs and requires to be administered in always more massive and *more frequent* doses." (Sanguinetti 19)

The problem, after all, is that terrorism – like all kinds of murder – will out, and open secrets cannot be kept forever. As Sanguinetti stresses, "the fragility of such artificial terrorism resides however in this: once you proceed with such politics, it becomes even more well-known, and therefore judged, and all that had constituted the strength of this politics now constitutes its weakness, whilst the great advantages it assured its strategists now turn into a major inconvenience." (Sanguinetti 40)

PLATO'S CAVE AND LOCKE'S SENSE CERTAINTY

In retrospect, 9/11 emerges as a made-for-television spectacle of death and destruction in which all plausibility is sacrificed for visual effectiveness on the screen. A half century ago, such an operation would have been much more difficult. Movies go back over 100 years. By 2004, the US population had been addicted to the television screen for some 50 years; the younger generations had never known anything else. Computer screens had been around for 30 years. Finally, the vogue of video games had been strong for several decades. The result was that a world of flickering images projected on screens of various sizes and types had displaced experienced reality for many, or rather had become the centerpiece of their experienced reality. The computer enhancement of Hollywood films and other trick effects had further blurred the notion of what was real.

This was an old problem, the problem of sense certainty, appearing in a new form. It had been discussed by Plato in *The Republic*, in the celebrated passage of Book VII devoted to the cave. In the age of 9/11, Plato's cave was even enjoying a new revival of interest because of the way it had been crudely reflected in the movie *The Matrix*. Plato imagined ignorant and unenlightened humanity as confined to an underground cave, illuminated only by faint diffuse sunlight from the cave entrance and the light of a fire. Humanity sat tied and fettered, forced to stare at a blank rock face in front of them; they could not turn their heads. Behind them was a wall, and between the wall and the fire a walkway. Along the walkway came bearers of statues, effigies and other artifacts, holding them up above the wall so that their shadows were cast on the rock face in view of the fettered audience. The bearers supplemented their flickering shadowy show with sound effects as best they could, which echoed from the rock face. The fettered audience of course became convinced that the shadows on the rock face in front of them were the very substance of reality, and prided themselves on their knowledge of the various shadows and the order in which they usually appeared. If any of the fettered victims were brought into the sunlight, he would suffer unspeakable pain and take a long time to become accustomed to the light. If any of them who had been in the sunlight tried to explain the nature of the world above to the cave dwellers, he risked enraging them, and being torn to pieces.

This is Plato's figure for the human predicament, always starting from a naïve epistemology of sense certainty applied to the discrete manifold that is accessible to the senses. Because of the attractive power of sense certainty, most people do not want to advance from opinion, which deals with shadows and reflections, to the higher form of understanding, which deals with mathematical thinking, and to the highest faculty of reason, which seeks to clarify the good and the other Platonic ideas through the exercise of dialectical thought. But this is the path which those who love truth and reason, the philosophers, must attempt to tread.

In modern times, the ruler of the cave has been John Locke, the great codifier of English empiricism, with his doctrine that the mind is a blank slate, and that its entire content derives from the accumulation of sense impressions. Locke's sensationalism, itself borrowed from Paolo Sarpi of Venice, has been the key to the degradation of mental life in the English-speaking world for over three centuries. By comparison, the French Cartesian approach, although deeply flawed, has fared marginally better. The Leibnizian outlook has fared best, even though undercut by the most difficult of circumstances. This may be at least one of the reasons why mass gullibility in regard to 9/11 has been the greatest in the English-speaking world, while France, Germany, Italy, Japan, and other nations have all had either a best-selling book and/or a prime time nationwide television program devoted to a serious critique of 9/11. What we need to remember is that if Plato's cave were to be depicted for the modern world, it would have an endless video tape of the events of 9/11 projected on the rock face in front of the fettered cave inmates.

THE 9/11 MYTH AS MASS SCHIZOPHRENIA

Our thesis here is that the 9/11 myth represents a form of mass schizophrenia. It was designed in this form by the terrorist controllers, far from any Afghan caves, who actually planned and executed this project. The schizophrenia of the 9/11 myth is congenial to the mental outlook of Bush and the neocons, who have been the most energetic propagators of the myth. The mass broadcasting of the myth as a compulsory article of faith by numerous important institutions has clearly induced a schizophrenic shift in the collective psychology of the US population, and may well be generating individual cases of schizophrenia at an accelerated rate. This direction has been suggested by Dr. John Gray, the celebrated author of *Men are From Mars, Women Are From Venus*, in his remarks to the International Inquiry on 9/11 in Toronto at the end of May 2004.

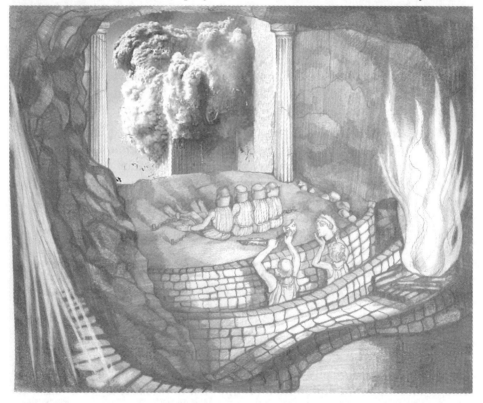

The purpose of terrorism, of course, includes terror – the chilling effect of fear which has already heavily impacted political speech, trade union militancy, and intellectual life. This is so obvious that it hardly needs to be commented upon. As all those who lived through it can remember, the shock of 9/11 was profound, and successfully paralyzed whatever real political life there was in the US for more than two years, certainly until the Democratic primary contest began to heat up towards the end of 2003. The Democratic Party collapsed during 2002, and it is not clear that it has recovered to this day.

According to the distinguished psychoanalyst Dr. Justin A. Frank, MD, Bush functions as a highly effective purveyor of fear and terror because he is gripped by real fear in his own subconscious. One cause of Bush's fear is the disintegration of his own personality, which is never far away. In this regard, Bush's "tightly held belief system shields him from challenges to his ideas – from critics and opponents, but, more importantly, from himself. Just beneath the surface, it's hard not to believe that he suffers from an innate fear of falling apart, a fear too terrifying for him to confront….He's appeared close to falling apart in public repeatedly; after wandering off the track while speaking, his statements disintegrate into often meaningless fragments until he finds his way, ends the discussion, or attacks the questioner." (Frank 64) In Frank's view, Bush also fears retribution, something which the public might associate with his fear of a Nuremberg prosecution for his crimes in the Iraq war, but which at a deeper level certainly involves 9/11 in some form: "the terror of which [Bush] promises to rid the world is in fact a different fear altogether: his intractable dread of his own individual punishment. And now that Bush has, in his grandiose imagination, identified himself with the entire nation, the nation has become the target for the personal retribution he feels is his due." (Frank 100) This would suggest that Bush's internal guilt, anxiety and stress may well have increased sharply in the wake of 9/11, and of Iraq. Dr. Frank's study *Bush on the Couch*, although eminently useful in many respects, does not discuss the evolution of Bush's pathologies over time, as for example in relation to the history of his admin-istration. Frank also avoids the obvious implications of his findings for 9/11, which he seems to find too hot to handle.

At its root, the belief structure of the 9/11 myth is not a factual account of an historical, real-world event. Still less is it an example of euhemerism, in which real events are preserved in more or less distorted mythical form. The 9/11 myth is rather a collective psychosis of a paranoid schizophrenic type. Let us explore for a moment what this might mean. What is now referred to as schizophrenia was formerly known as *dementia praecox*; the change in terminology is due to Eugen Bleuler, who used it to describe not so much a split personality as a lack of coordination among various psychological functions. Bleuler was also the first to speak of the special quality of schizoid thinking, which he called autistic.

Simple schizophrenia is marked by a reduction in external relations and interests; this may include a lack of curiosity. "Emotions are lacking in depth; ideation is simple and refers to concrete things…and a retreat to simpler or stereotyped forms of behavior." Paranoid schizophrenia generally occurs in later life, and "is characterized primarily by unrealistic, illogical thinking, with delusions of persecution or grandeur, and often by hallucinations." In psychoanalysis, the description of schizophrenia emphasizes "regressive symptoms," seen as "a retreat to less mature levels of the ego (the reality-testing portion of the psyche), along with attempts to replace the existing world, from which the patient has retreated, by such phenomena as hallucinations, delusions, fantasies of world reconstruction, and peculiarities of language." (Silvano Arieti, "Schizophrenia," *Encyclopedia Britannica*, 1971) The points of contact with Bush as the chief 9/11 fear-monger, and with the 9/11 myth, are manifold.

In this context, neocon utopian thinking, with its explicit "fantasies of world reconstruction," can be seen as a step towards schizophrenic thinking. One is reminded of the comments of retired Army Colonel Larry Wilkerson, who was serving as Colin Powell's chief of staff in the State Department, apropos of certain leading neocons. "I call them utopians," Wilkerson told a reporter. "I don't care whether utopians are Vladimir Lenin on a sealed train to Moscow or Paul Wolfowitz. Utopians, I don't like. You're never going to bring utopia, and you're going to hurt a lot of people in the process of trying to do it." Wilkerson added that he had "a lot of reservations about people who have never been in the face of battle, so to speak, who are making cavalier decisions about sending men and women out to die. A person who comes to mind in that regard is Richard Perle, who, thank God, tendered his resignation and no longer will be even a semiofficial person in this administration. Richard Perle's cavalier remarks about doing this or doing that with regard to military force always, always troubled me." (*Washington Post*, May 5, 2004)

Thus, it is the mythographers and myth-mongers – those who love to brand critics and skeptics as paranoids – who are really the psychopaths. Chief among these is of course Bush 43 himself, who has functioned as the leading propagandist of the 9/11 myth, from a few days after 9/11 through the 2004 Republican National Convention and his fall re-election campaign. The thesis of this chapter is the existence of a destructive dialectic between the mass psychosis of 9/11 and the personal psychopathologies of Bush as a media presence. In this dialectical relationship, the mass psychosis and the individual pathologies of the (apparent) ruler become each other's simultaneous cause and effect. To make this clearer, let us turn to a discussion of the paranoid personality written twenty-five years before Bush became a fixture on the national scene: "The person most vulnerable to a persecutory paranoid state is the tense, insecure, suspicious person who has little basic trust in other persons, who has always found it difficult to confide in others, tends to be secretive, usually has few close friends, and is addicted to solitary rumination. These characteristics are sometimes hidden behind a façade of superficial sociability and talkativeness. Above all, there is a rigidity about such a person's thinking which becomes most obvious when he is under emotional stress. This may give an impression of certainty and self-assurance, but actually it is based upon profound insecurity, upon a need to be dogmatic because of an inability to tolerate suspended judgment." (Norman Alexander Cameron, "Paranoid Reactions," *Encyclopedia Britannica,* 1971)

FRANK ON BUSH AS MEGALOMANIAC AND SCHIZOPHRENIC

This reads like a psychological profile of George W. Bush, and is coherent with the lucid analysis of Bush's mentality given by Dr. Justin Frank in his recent *Bush on the Couch*. Frank describes Bush as a megalomaniac operating behind the hail-fellow-well-met affability of a small-town philistine booster of the Babbitt type. According to Frank, "a careful consideration of the evidence suggests that behind Bush's affable exterior operates a powerful but obscure delusional system that drives his behavior. The most precise psychiatric term to describe his pathology is most frequently used to identify a particular condition exhibited by schizophrenics that, as we'll see, has broader applications as well: megalomania. The psychological concept of megalomania refers as much to a mental attitude as to actual behavioral manifestations….Freud calls megalomania a protective delusion of power and greatness that serves as a defense against fear, against paranoid anxieties." (Frank 200-201) Bush is thus that type of schizophrenic called a megalomaniac, and the 9/11 myth to which he has devoted his life is entirely coherent with his mentality. The 9/11 myth is in fact a massive attempt to impose schizophrenic and autistic thinking on the entire American and world public. This may explain why those who wish to rebel against the myth often tend to insist that Bush (or Cheney) had to have planned and directed every aspect of 9/11 personally and in advance. Even though Bush's limited mental equipment seems to rule this out, this reaction is humanly understandable, since Bush has been beyond any doubt the main propagandist of the 9/11 myth. So, to destroy the myth, it is often seen as necessary to blame the mythograph. The extent of Bush's actual responsibility is discussed elsewhere in this book, where it is asserted that Bush was probably not informed of the details in advance, but certainly embraced the demands of the perpetrators soon after the fact. In this sense, the insistence on blaming Bush is justified as a matter of political shorthand, if not of precise analysis and historical fact.

Dr. Frank writes about Bush 41's favorite technique of "evacuating" his fear onto the US population, both for his own relief and better to terrorize the electorate. He also discusses Bush 43's penchant for projection. Here is another passage from the earlier discussion of this complex: "The paranoid patient gets rid of his intolerable sense of guilt through unconscious mechanisms of denial and projection. He denies his primitive hostile or erotic impulses and projects them – that is, he ascribes them to other persons. Projection is rarely done at random. Usually the patient unwittingly selects, as the alleged carriers of his own impulses and his own guilt, persons who have correspondingly minimal unconscious trends." (Norman Alexander Cameron, "Paranoid Reactions," *Encyclopedia Britannica,* 1971) This fits well with what Dr. Franks writes about projection in Bush 43: Projection for Frank is "the primitive defense mechanism by which an individual endows others with his own negative attributes." (Frank 152) Applying this to the tenant of the White House, Frank finds that, "incapable of safely confronting the true extent of his own sadism, Bush had to project his sadism onto an enemy of his own creation – one he entered the White House ready to demonize and destroy; one whose annihilation would serve to protect his own fragile, deluded sense of self." (Frank 115) As always, Frank is talking about Iraq, but, like most of his analysis, this applies just as well to bin Laden and al Qaeda as it does to Saddam.

No thinking person can fail to have been impressed by the degree to which Bush, in his attempt to demonize Saddam Hussein, engaged in self-description. Saddam, Bush alleged, was an oppressor, a violator of international law, a leader in contempt of the international community, an aggressor – all accusations which applied just as well or better to Bush himself. Joseph Gabel's comment is highly relevant: "...racist regimes, being generally insensitive to humor...are, by contrast, keen on caricature, mainly in its crude forms....The caricaturist, without realizing it, is really drawing himself....Clearly the caricaturist sees his own essence. In this category of ideas, one could say that the sociocentric and ethnocentric caricature is the deranged perception of false consciousness." (Gabel 123 note) Frank calls attention to Bush's tendency for projection and description in regard to Saddam Hussein, although the same dynamics are at work in the portrayal of bin Laden. According to Franks, "none of this has gone unnoticed by the public. Indeed, the pronounced parallels between Bush and Saddam may well have promoted a wider understanding of Bush's destructive self, rather than hiding it. As suggested by the many circulating photos of Bush's face digitally merged with Saddam's image – a computer trick that reveals a dramatic pictorial understanding of the process of projection – satirists instinctively understand that there is a pot-calling-the-kettle-black aspect to the showdown between Bush and Saddam." (Frank 116) And more to the point, between Bush and the supposed authors of the 9/11 attacks.

Part of Bush's guilt is almost certainly the fact that, while he probably was not aware of the full 9/11 plot before the fact, he became aware of most of it after that fact, most likely during the course of the day on September 11. Bush was the recipient of an ultimatum by the rogue network inside the US government which carried out the attacks, an ultimatum demanding that he go on television and denounce foreign terrorists for the attacks, and then proceed to implicate bin Laden, al Qaeda, Afghanistan, and to wage the war of civilizations against the Arab and Muslim world which the plotters evidently desired. For these reasons, Bush's burden of guilt and dissembling must be very heavy indeed.

So much for preliminaries. When we enter the world of the 9/11 myth, we find ourselves on the terrain of mass psychosis, mass hallucination, mass delusion. The twentieth century has shown how powerful these ideological figments can be. This book proceeds from the standpoint of Platonic idealism; a Marxist might say that with 9/11, we enter the world of radically false con-sciousness, where the superstructure has become completely detached from social and material reality in a way that Marx never contemplated in his writings. A suggestive study that addresses precisely this complex of problems is Joseph Gabel's 1975 *False Consciousness: An Essay on Reification*. Gabel sees reification (hypostatization) as the making of people, ideas, and time into *things*. His point of departure is the gross fact of mass belief in ideological chimeras, specifically Nazi and Stalinist ideology. The 9/11 myth is of a piece with these.

GABEL: THE POLICE CONCEPT OF HISTORY

Gabel elaborates a lengthy definition of the political world view which is correlated with alienated and manipulated political life under the rule of schizophrenic/autistic ideologies which exhibit a low degree of fidelity to reality. Gabel called this the "police concept of history;" if he were writing today, he might well have called it the intelligence community or CIA theory of history. Gabel writes: "The police concept of history is the negation of the historical dialectic, in other words the negation of history. ...History's driving force is not the ensemble of objective forces but good or evil individual action...since the 'event' is no longer understood as the normal substratum of the course of History, but as miracle or catastrophe; it is no longer dependent on scientific explanation but on black or white magic. In the Manichean diptych of this view, the hero (leader) and the traitor represent two poles of the same principle of reificational negation of the autonomy of history. It is therefore a pseudo-history, a non-dialectical result either of success due to the genius of the leader or failure explicable through treason; an authentic 'syndrome of external action' permits the privileged system to evade eventual responsibility.

The police concept of history represents the extreme form of political alienation; it is both a sociocentrism which dichotomizes the world into a privileged system [the US] and a non-privileged remainder [the Arab and Islamic world], and a phenomenon of consciousness of a schizophrenic nature. Since the privileged system is considered as perfect, extra-temporal and extra-dialectical, the event – particularly the unfavorable event – can only be explained by means of external action; it is experienced as an unexpected, 'undeserved' catastrophe, which is no longer integrated into the normal course of events whose succession constitutes the threat of concrete, dialectical temporality. One can compare this ensemble with the two specific elements in the clinical picture of schizophrenia, *the syndrome of external action* and the *deranged experience of the end of the world* (*Weltuntergangserlebnis*, abbreviated as WUE by German authors), the clinical translation of the appearance of the dialectic in a reified world which can accept the event only as a catastrophe." (Gabel 115-116, with my interpolations)

Here we have the principal elements or memes of the 9/11 myth in a clinical description a quarter century before the fact. The event has nothing to do with real historical forces. The realities of world commodity flows and of the world financial system in particular go out the window. Bin Laden and al Qaeda provide a *deus ex machina* of absolute evil and black magic. 9/11 is the undeserved catastrophe or WUE, experienced as a nightmare out of the blue. In order for such notions to gain mass acceptance, the American ideology had to already have traveled a considerable distance down the road towards schizophrenia and autism, and such mass acceptance has in turn further accelerated that descent. For Gabel, schizophrenia is a loss of contact with reality and with history. His definition of schizophrenia depends heavily on the notion that, for the schizophrenic, development over time has become incomprehensible, while relations in space have become all-important. In space we can often choose to move, but time does not permit this. Therefore there is a close relationship between a radically antihistorical view of the world, as for example among the neocons and the Bush regime, and the syndromes of clinical schizophrenia, prominent among whose symptoms Gabel sees morbid rationalism, understood as a weak hold on reality: "In the light of recent work, schizophrenia appears as a loss of the sense of personal history, and psychotherapy therefore consists of a reconstruction of the totality of the person with a reintegration into history. From the viewpoint of the investigator the schizophrenic loss of the historico-dialectical perception of reality can be seen in the form of a preponderance of the spatial factor or as a loss of experienced time: as over-spatialization or as sub-temporalization." (Gabel 116) Gabel's work here dovetails with that of Frank, who points to Bush 43's notorious refusal to discuss the details of his youthful debauchery before the age of about 40. It is as if these episodes were repressed and no longer accessible to memory – at least, in Bush's own propaganda patter. Frank is certainly on firm ground when he points to the fundamentalist belief structure of Bush and of so much of his base as representing a rejection of human history, personal history, and of natural history as well: "Just as fundamentalist creationist teachings deny history, the fundamentalist notion of conversion or rebirth encourages the believer to see himself as disconnected from history. George W. Bush's evasive, self-serving defense of his life before he was born again displays just this tendency....To the believer, the power of spiritual absolution not only erases the sins of the past, but divorces the current self from the historical sinner." (Frank 59-60)

WOE IS *WUE*: CATASTROPHE FROM OUTSIDE A PERFECT SYSTEM

A vital part of the WUE brought about inside the perfect system by evil forces is that these evil forces are axiomatically seen as coming from *outside* of that perfect system. Evil is always external, never home grown, as it was for the racist southern sheriff who thought that all racial tensions were the work of outside agitators. "The result is that when the evidence of the historicity of existence forces itself on the misoneism (hatred of change) of reified consciousness, it appears as an unexpected catastrophe, inexplicable and often attributed therefore to external action....For sociocentrism, the privileged system being perfect, any change (particularly any unfavorable change) is the work of external maleficent powers." (Gabel 288 and note) Gerhard Wisnewski has related this idea most directly to 9/11. As Wisnewski points out, "from outside" is the central slogan of the official version of 9/11. "The impression is produced that the perpetrators came 'from outside': from outside of the building, from outside of America, even from outside civilization. The official version of these events screams 'outside, outside, outside.'" (Wisnewski 143)

In a world axiomatically defined by terrorism, the Manichean outlook seems destined to win out. Sanguinetti saw something similar in Italy at the beginning of the strategy of tension: "In view of terrorism presented as absolute evil, evil in itself and for itself, all the other evils fade in to the background and are even forgotten; since the fight against terrorism coincides with the common interest, it already is the general good, and the State, which magnanimously conducts it, is good in itself and for itself. Without the wickedness of the devil, God's infinite bounty could not appear and be appreciated as is fitting." (Sanguinetti 3)

Gabel insists again and again on the key role played by the loss of the historical dimension, and it is clear that this problem was shared by twentieth-century America with Nazi Germany and with Soviet Russia. Anglo-American propaganda exhibits an overwhelming tendency to demonize enemy leaders: Noriega, Milosevic, bin Laden, and Saddam Hussein are notable examples, but the tendency goes back to Kaiser Wilhelm at the very least. Today the explicit speech of propaganda is conducted on the overtly infantile plane: good guys and bad guys, of bad actors, and most of all terrorists. Gabel writes: " For Gabel, this is another symptom of reification (hypostatization): "As a prisoner of a universe where space takes the place of duration, man in the reified world cannot understand history as the expression of creativity and spontaneity. Consequently the undeniable fact of change forces itself on this 'consciousness of immediacy' as a catastrophe, as a sudden change from the outside that excludes mediation.... Seen in this perspective, history appears as a function of *demiurgic action*. An external force (God, the hero, a party) transcends the efficiency of its auto-nomous dialectic. Reified consciousness is essentially ahistorical: *mens momentanea sive carens recordationem* [a mind in the moment, or lacking memory], said Leibniz on this subject." (Gabel 151) Here is history reduced to a fairy tale, with the cocaine-abusing, alcoholic, mentally-impaired Bush as the hero of the good, and the rich, misfit, raving ideologue bin Laden as champion of evil. How can hundreds of millions of people believe in such a product?

Gabel discusses the stress on biological heredity and race as one of the leading anti-historical features of the Nazi outlook, and there is evidence that Hitler was also well aware of this. Gabel points out that Nazi ideology, with its glorification of race and biology, was marked by "morbid rationalism in its worst form." Gabel argues that "any unfavorable event for this racial pseudo-value is itself extra-historicized and 'understood' in terms of treason or conspiracy: the ideology of national socialism is logically inseparable from the theory of the 'stab in the back.'" (Gabel 117) If fascism comes to the United States, it is now certain that its ideology will prominently feature the 9/11 events as a stab in the back to a benefactor by an ungrateful and treacherous outside world; fascist neocons are already spouting this point of view. Ironically, the German request for an armistice in 1918, which Hitler later condemned as a stab in the back by Social Democratic politicians, was actually the work of Field Marshal Ludendorff and other future backers of Hitler. As for 9/11, which Bush blames on the Arab and Muslim world, it too had some of its main backers inside the US military and intelligence services.

SCHIZOPHRENIA: REJECTION OF HISTORY AND REALITY

Frank sees Bush's paranoid schizophrenic hostility to real historical processes reflected in some well-known aspects of his bureaucratic methods. One is his insistence on absolute, unquestioning loyalty on the part of his underlings: "Like the alcoholic father who is threatened by the independence of his family members, Bush demands absolute loyalty and conformity, trying to freeze his national family in time...." (Frank 46) For Frank, Bush has no use for history in any form; he remarks, "with a president who refuses to view history as anything but an enemy he cannot afford to acknowledge or engage, it's impossible not to wonder what painful lessons of history we may be doomed to repeat." (Frank 161)

One way of denying historical reality is to wipe out the past; another is to insist that the leading delusion of one's own time is destined to last forever. The Nazis did this in one way, Bush in another: "the historical time of national socialism was dominated... by the chimerical hope of an empty eternity" – there was the promise of a thousand year Reich, sometimes escalated to 20,000 years of Nazi world domination. (Gabel 134) For Bush and the neocons, this has become the nightmare vision of a war against terrorism which is literally endless.

Bush's fraudulent "war on terrorism" is of course a war of civilizations directed against the 1 billion Arab and Muslim people in the world; it is more hypocritical than Hitlerism because it assiduously denies its own real content. In reality, the "war on terrorism" is a racist war against Arabs and Muslims today, with China and perhaps Russia as candidates for all-out attack at some later time. From time to time the real essence explodes to the surface, as in Bush's call for a crusade, or in General Boykin's comments on satanic Islam. Neocon radio talk show hosts like Michael Savage are more explicit every day, and it is they who service the belief structure of Bush's hard-core followers. Gabel sees racism as another denial of reality and history: "The racist perception of human reality is schizophrenic in several ways," he observes. Gabel also detects a depersonalization of members of the targeted group, "which is reflected particularly in caricature, the strongest weapon of ethnocentrism." (Gabel 123)

In Bush's fear-mongering oratory, the denial of reality is so great that it often approaches the qualities of hallucination, and sometimes enters into that domain. "It will be admitted that there exists a certain analogy between hallucinatory consciousness which, in its demand for homogeneity, is forced to alienate in a hallucinatory form the tendencies that it no longer manages to organize in a concrete totality, and, on the other hand, reified political consciousness which, in its postulate of political homogeneity – a postulate which the totalitarian state tries to put into practice – attributes to the foreigner (in the widest sense of the term, implying also political heterodoxy) facts for which a simple dialectical consideration of reality would permit a rational explanation to be given." (Gabel 279-280) Frank connects this to the hatred of the lawful character of reality, which we see in Bush – who loves to live outside the law as an individual, from his drunk driving arrests through his National Guard shenanigans to his illegal election – and in the neocons – who hate the very concept of international law: "Wilfred R. Bion points out that the part of the personality that hates internal law – the laws of reality, of time, of responsibility, of loss – hates external reality as well. It attacks links made in the mind, undermining the capacity to think and organize that comes from facing reality and its limitations. Living outside the law of mature responsibility becomes both the midwife of omnipotent fantasy and the mortician of the capacity to think." (Frank 89)

Bush boasts about his own penchant for seeing the world in black and white, as a single Manichean opposition of good and evil, with no nuances or gray areas. As Frank notes, "there are no shades of gray in this fight for civilization …. Either you're with the United States of America, or you're against the United States of America." (Frank 13) Gabel saw the same phenomenon in the Nazis: "By virtue of the implicit Manichean postulate of ideological thought, the enemies of enemies so often enjoy an undeserved favorable prejudice; for the political Manichean one is either" with us or against us, as Bush constantly repeats. (Gabel 97 note)

INFANTILE EGOCENTRISM AND ETHNOCENTRISM

Many have noted the primitive and childish quality of the Bush/neocon analysis, with its mindless parroting about good guys and bad guys. Bush's oratory also shares another key feature of the infantile mind – egocentrism, or the tendency to see large and distant events as having been caused by ones own petty actions. This is exemplified by the suburbanite who thinks that getting the car washed will make the rain come down. After 9/11, Bush notoriously divided the world into terrorist bad guys and pro-American good guys. He insisted, in other words, that the world should be forever organized around this single event. Gabel shows that adult egocentrism and schizophrenia go together: "A zoologist who, having been successively bitten by a dog and a cat, used as a scientific concept 'the animal species which bites zoologists' would be guilty of false egocentric identification….False identification is an important aspect of the anti-dialectical structure of ideologies and, at the same time, a valued technique of economy of effort for propaganda." (Gabel 92) What egocentrism represents in the stunted individual, ethnocentrism accomplishes for the sick society. Think of Bush's post-9/11 axis of evil, composed of Iraq, Iran, and North Korea. Yet, there had been no rogue states' summit to sign a treaty of alliance among these three. Iraq and Iran had been enemies, and North Korea, a true hermit kingdom, lived in its own isolation. Yet, Bush insisted like a small child in defining the three exclusively in relation to himself – within, it should go without saying, a universe of discourse already defined by the 9/11 myth. Once again, Gabel described something similar under the Nazis. Under the Nazi regime, "the non-German world seems to a large extent to have been interpreted in terms of the postulate that the enemy world was homogeneous. This was less because of a working hypothesis about propaganda than ideological convictions of a delirious nature…." (Gabel 120) The Nazis portrayed a world of capitalists, Bolsheviks, and Jews who were all mythically united in their hatred for Germany.

Although often couched in religious terms, the neocon ideology is close not only to that of the Nazi jurist Carl Schmitt, but also to that of the Nazi sociologist Gumplowitz, whose major work was devoted to the conflict of the races. This is also not far from Huntington's clash of civilizations. In each of these cases, history is dominated by mythical entities. We think of the Cambone-Boykin-Geoffrey Miller axis in the Pentagon and US Army; Boykin was responsible for a raving declaration that his Christian God is stronger than the God of Islam, and that Islam is satanic. In reality, Boykin knows nothing of universal Christianity, and the god he worships is between totem and Mammon. Schizophrenic personalities like Boykin and Miller (a member of the sinister religious sect called The Fellowship) were observed to have been over-represented among the personnel of the Nazi concentration camps. The same would appear to be the case among the Bush administration; Cambone, Boykin, and Miller have become the architects of the gulag that stretches from Guantanamo Bay and Abu Ghraib to the system of illegal CIA secret dungeons and illegal ghost prisoners reported to be operating in numerous countries. Frank notes that "the eminent psycho-analyst Vamik Volkan has written that we need an enemy to rally the community around a 'chosen trauma.' Almost immediately after 9/11, Bush began speaking of the war, in grandiose terms, as a kind of epic and eternal struggle....Making the war against terrorism perennial keeps him in power, by keeping the terror externalized." (Frank 98) Although Frank hesitates to say so, 9/11 is obviously the chosen trauma.

BUSH'S DIVINE MISSION
AS SCHIZOPHRENIC SYMPTOM

Bush has spoken of his own role in regard to 9/11 and Iraq as a divine mission assigned to him by God; especially chilling was his remark that he did not consult his own father before the aggression against Iraq, but did consult his "higher father." Here we have the image of the hero who goes forth on a divine quest to hold back the forces of chaos and the WUE. As Frank reminds us, "Bush has always been surprisingly explicit in declaring that he sees himself on a mission from God, and it is his belief in that divine assignment in which we see the most potent combination of politics, psychology, and faith at work." (Frank 71) For Gabel, this notion of a divine mission is an integral part of the schizophrenic mis-perception of historical change in the real world. Gabel links "the syndrome of external action and the deranged experience of the end of the world....Consequently, when the event forces itself into reified consciousness, the latter makes this evident through a double technique of partial obscuration: from the point of view of causal explanation it interprets it as the act of an external power; on the level of lived experience its experiences it either as a catastrophe or, on the contrary, as a sudden significant (and always heteronomic) irruption into the axiological void [vacuum of values] of the world itself: a *divine mission*. In short, like a manic crisis, the WUE is an axiological crisis, a sort of storm of values on the boundaries of two atmospheres of different axiological-dialectical density....Thus a connection is created between morbid rationalism and the phenomenon of the end of the world experience. It is as one aspect of the anti-dialectical mode of being-in-the-world that one can place the WUE in the same ambit as deranged perceptions, hallucinations, and other elements of sub-realist experience." (Gabel 292-293) Heteronomy is the opposite of autonomy; it is the unfree state of being controlled by outside forces, such as manipulation of the traumas of one's own past.

In a striking insight, Gabel shows that the road to a thoroughly schizophrenic foreign policy is paved with ultimata. The Bushes have been prodigal with ultimata: there was one to Saddam Hussein in 1991, one to the Taliban regime in 2001, and another to Saddam in 2003. For Gabel, these come straight from the schizophrenic tool kit of projection; he says that "behavior does exist on a societal level that is phenomenologically close to the psychiatrists' 'mirror symptom' – This is when a State – usually totalitarian – chooses a fictitious interlocutor in order to have an act of violence or a territorial conquest ratified in the form of a supposed negotiation. This is – just like the clinical phenomenon in question – an illusion of encounter with an artificial interlocutor; a behavior of schizophrenic structure." (Gabel 259)

Reagan hailed the "magic of the marketplace," obviously a very white magic. In the grim times of 9/11, Bush 43 has had to deal mostly with black magic, but there have been exceptions. One was in the dreamtime that lasted a week or two for some observers after the fall of Baghdad to the Anglo-American aggressors. Frank is right to comment that "there's no clearer example of magical thinking than the 'Mission Accomplished' banner that served as a backdrop to Bush's flight-suit photo op on the *Abraham Lincoln*." (Frank 86) The essence of magic is action at a distance, which Sir Isaac Newton unfortunately made presentable in the Anglo-American world. The official story of 9/11, with everything directed in the last analysis by bin Laden using his laptop in the distant cave of Afghanistan, represents a thinly veiled version of magical action at a distance. Gabel pointed out more than a quarter of a century earlier that racism too is based on a magical and irrational world outlook which "also admits fairly often the existence of action at a distance of an undeniably magico-schizophrenic nature....this is the very definition of paranoid deranged thought...." (Gabel 123-4)

RESULT: THE 9/11 MYTH AS PSYCHOPATHOLOGY

Because of the capitulation of the Democratic party and the associated liberal intellectual establishment, Bush and the neocons have enjoyed success as mytho-graphers beyond their wildest dreams. The tenant of the White House may have discovered in the powers of myth a stimulant more potent than his beloved Jack Daniels; at one point, according to a reporter, Bush appeared "bedazzled by his administration's own mythmaking." (*New York Times*, July 31, 2003) Out of the preceding considerations, we can gradually come to understand the 9/11 myth in its actual status as a kind of *Ersatz* or substitute religion, or more precisely as an hysterical *Ersatz* civic religion designed to promote social cohesiveness when all other ideologies have failed. What Franks says in his summary of Bush and Iraq applies even better to the American public and the 9/11 myth: "The individual who clings tenaciously to unverified beliefs confuses his beliefs with fact, and often inflicts this confusion on others in his struggle to resolve it in his favor. When many people are persuaded to subscribe to the same pretense, of course, it can gain the aura of objectivity; as British psychoanalyst Ron Britton has observed, 'we can substitute concurrence for reality testing, and so shared phantasy can gain the same or even greater status than knowledge.' The belief doesn't become a fact, but the fact of shared belief lends it the valuable appearance of credibility. The belief is codified, takes hold, and rises above the level where it might be questioned. Shared beliefs can come to define a community; religion is, after all, a communal structure, uniting groups in shared beliefs. In societies where religion is especially powerful, such shared beliefs can actually become law, imposed on others, often restricting their behavior." (Franks 62)

THE 9/11 MYTH AND
THE EPIDEMIC OF AUTISM IN THE US

There remains the question of to what degree the social and intellectual hegemony of the 9/11 myth, especially as purveyed by its mentally impaired poster boy, is generating avoidable schizophrenic disorders in the US population and abroad. One form that such an epidemic might take would be an upsurge of autism among the most vulnerable members of society – among children, who are amazingly adept at absorbing the fears, anxieties, and distortions of the adult world around them. Evidence of just such a phenomenon is not hard to find. About two years after September 11, *Newsweek* devoted an important cover story to "Girls, Boys, and Autism." According to the article, there are now more than a million Americans suffering from this disorder, 80% of them males. The article gives no figures for the growth in the number of cases, but the publication of this article and the attention it received suggests that the number of cases is rising, especially among the most vulnerable – children, but not among them alone. (*Newsweek*, September 8, 2003) In 2002 the *New York Times* reported that "a shocking report from California last week suggested that a large increase in childhood autism in that state over the last 15 years is a true epidemic, not a statistical mirage inflated by artificial factors." (*New York Times*, October 23, 2002) Research by qualified experts will be necessary to determine whether there is in fact a causal link between the 9/11 myth and these disturbing reports.

According to some, the autism epidemic is genetically determined. According to others, it is a by-product of certain ill-advised vaccinations. But there is no reason why it could not be socially, culturally, and politically determined. This is exactly what one would expect in a traumatized country dominated by a compulsory schizophrenic belief system, whose apparent leadership figure demonstrates a whole range of megalomaniac schizophrenic symptoms. One means of fighting the growth of culturally and socially induced autism would surely be to junk the schizophrenic myth of 9/11, and replace it with a true and reasoned account of what took place in the real world.

XIV
NETWORKS OF INTEREST

...no one can be called a good man who, in order to support
himself, takes up a profession that obliges him at all times to
be rapacious, fraudulent, and cruel, as of course must be all
of those – no matter what their rank – who make a trade of war.
– Niccolò Machiavelli, *The Art of War*.

The neocons are an intensely ideological faction, and we are therefore on firm
ground if we examine their ideology as a guide to their conduct. We must only
remember that the neocons make a rigid separation between the "elite truths" that
they tell each other – their esoteric doctrine – and the belief structure they offer
for the edification of the masses – the more diluted exoteric doctrine. The
esoteric doctrine is often transmitted verbally, rather than by published writings.
Still, the published writings allow us to see the basic neocon outlook clearly
enough. What we find is an embrace of war, violence, hatred, coups, martial law,
and, most important for our present purposes, terrorism.

The supreme neocon guru is Leo Strauss (1899-1973), who taught politics for
many years at the University of Chicago, and later at St. John's of Annapolis.
Strauss was a Marburg Kantian of the Herman Cohen school who did his
doctorate with the irrationalist Ernst Cassirer. Strauss studied for two years with
grants of the Rockefeller Foundation, which he procured with the help of the
Nazi legal theorist Carl Schmitt. Among Strauss's students were Alan Bloom, the
author of the *Closing of the American Mind*, and Harvey Mansfield of Harvard.

The Straussian-neocon network is now extensive, and stretches over three
generations. Neocons are famous for helping one another up the career ladder,
and for teaching courses based only on neocon texts. They are narrow-minded,
sectarian, and essentially ignorant of philosophy and history. They are an
ideological faction, often a fanatical faction.

We are talking about Wolfowitz, Feith, Bolton, Luti, Schulsky, Scooter
Libby, Cambone, Hadley and others who run the Bush administration. Neocons
outside of government include Perle, Woolsey (both have held high office),
Irving and William Kristol, Norman and John Podhoretz, Saul and Adam Bellow,
and so forth. The older generation of neocons were often made-over Trotskyist
communists; they have retained Trotskyite theories like the notion of competing
elites; the neocons see a battle between the liberal elite and themselves as central
to the political process.

LEO STRAUSS'S NIHILIST REVOLUTION: AN APOLOGY FOR TERROR

At the heart of Leo Strauss's political thought is an open apology for terrorism. This idea is illuminated in Strauss's exchange of comments with Alexandre Kojève, a neo-Hegelian official of the French finance ministry, in the 1950s. At the heart of this debate is the question of the universal and homogeneous state, and how philosophers should react to its existence. The universal homogeneous state means something like a world where war and underdevelopment have been eliminated, and in which leisure time and well-being are rising. For most people, the universal homogeneous state would look like a world of peace, progress, and prosperity, man-made heaven on earth.

But for Strauss and Kojève, peace, progress, and prosperity mean the end of history because they wipe out the "higher" human values, which depend upon politics, and thus upon war. (Implicit also is the idea that peace, progress, and prosperity are bad for oligarchical domination, a cause dear to Strauss and Kojève.) Strauss sums it up thus: "This end of History would be most exhilarating, but for the fact that, according to Kojève, it is the participation in bloody political struggles as well as in real work or, generally expressed, the negating action, which raises man above the brutes." (Strauss 208)

For Strauss and Kojève, "unlimited technological progress and its accompaniment, which are indispensable conditions of the universal and homogeneous state, are destructive of humanity. It is perhaps possible to say that the universal and homogeneous state is fated to come. But it is certainly impossible to say that man can reasonably be satisfied with it." (Strauss 208) This view of technology is that of the Greek historian called the Old Oligarch (who did not like the long walls and the Athenian navy), and is certainly not that of Plato. For Strauss, Greek philosophy is a screen upon which he projects his own ignorant opinions.

Not caring about what Plato really thought, Strauss advances towards his terrible conclusion: "If the universal and homogeneous state is the goal of History, History is absolutely 'tragic.' Its completion will reveal that the human problem, and hence in particular the problem of the relation of philosophy and politics, is insoluble." (Strauss 208)

In Strauss's view, the imminent coming of the universal homogeneous state means that all progress accomplished by mankind to date has been worthless: "For centuries and centuries men have unconsciously done nothing but work their way through infinite labors and struggles and agonies, yet ever again catching hope, toward the universal and homogeneous state, and as soon as they have arrived at the end of their journey, they realize that through arriving at it they have destroyed their humanity, and thus returned, as in a cycle, to the prehuman beginnings of History." (Strauss 209)

This raises the question of the violent revolt against the universal homogeneous state, which is what Strauss regards as inevitable and desirable: "Yet there is no reason for despair as long as human nature has not been conquered completely, i.e., as long as sun and man still generate man. There will always be men (*andres*) who will revolt against a state which is destructive of humanity or in which there is no longer a possibility of noble action or of great deeds." (Strauss 209)

When the real men revolt against too much peace, progress, and prosperity, what will be their program? Strauss: "They may be forced into a mere negation of the universal and homogeneous state, into a negation not enlightened by any positive goal, into a **nihilistic negation**. While perhaps doomed to failure, that **nihilist revolution** may be the only great and noble deed that is possible once the universal and homogeneous state has become inevitable. But no one can know whether it will fail or succeed." (Strauss 209, emphasis added)

What can be understood by nihilistic negation and nihilist revolution? In the nineteenth century, nihilism was an ideology of terrorism; the crazed bomb-throwers who assassinated statesmen and rulers across Europe and America (including President McKinley) were atheists, anarchists and nihilists. In the twentieth century, the nihilist revolution was synonymous with some of the most extreme factions of fascism and Nazis. "Long live death!" was a slogan of some of them. With these lines, Strauss has opened the door to fascism, murder, mayhem, war, genocide, and most emphatically to terrorism. And he is not shy about spelling this out.

LEO STRAUSS: BACK TO THE STONE AGE

What will the nihilist revolution look like? Strauss writes: "Someone may object that the successful revolt against the universal and homogeneous state could have no other effect than that the identical historical process which led from the **primitive horde** to the final state will be repeated." (Strauss 209, emphasis added) The primitive horde or primal horde refers to the human communities of the Paleolithic hunting and gathering societies, to the foragers and cave people of the Old Stone Age. Strauss is endorsing a nihilistic revolt that will have the effect of destroying as much as 10,000 years of progress in civilization, and in hurling humanity back to its wretched predicament in the Paleolithic. Here Strauss finds a momentary common ground with Rousseau, who also had a liking for the Paleolithic; here we are close to the ideas which animated the reign of terror in the French Revolution.

Strauss comes as a Job's comforter to those who have been thrown back into the Old Stone Age: "But would such a repetition of the process – a new lease on life for man and humanity – not be preferable to the indefinite continuation of the inhuman end? Do we not enjoy every spring although we know the cycle of the seasons, although we know that winter will come again?" (Strauss 209)

Springtime for Leo Strauss has thus acquired the idiosyncratic meaning of a cataclysmic return to the horrors of the Old Stone Age.

Short of turning back the clock to the Paleolithic, Strauss sees one promising possibility latent in Kojève's universal homogeneous state. This concerns the opportunity for political violence, yet another form of terrorism: "Kojève does seem to leave an outlet for action in the universal and homogeneous state. In that state the risk of violent death is still involved in the struggle for political leadership…. But the opportunity for action can exist only for a tiny minority. And besides, is this not a hideous prospect: a state in which the last refuge of man's humanity is political assassination in the particularly sordid form of the palace revolution?" (Strauss 209) Such sporadic and limited violence is not enough for Strauss.

Marx and Engels had written about the realm of freedom which would result from higher stages of economic development in the form of a communist utopia. Strauss transforms their communist slogan into an invective against middle class progress and middle class values in general when he concludes this passage with the call: "Warriors and workers of all countries, unite, while there is still time, to prevent the coming of the 'realm of freedom.' Defend with might and main, if it needs to be defended, the 'realm of necessity.'" (Strauss 209) Putting aside the superficial polemic against communist utopia, Strauss's goal here is to argue that peace, progress, and prosperity are destructive to oligarchy, and anything must be preferred to such an outcome.

Here we have a blanket endorsement of forms of violence and mayhem, including terrorism and war, in doses large enough to send world civilization back to the Stone Age. This implies genocide on a scale far beyond Hitler, Stalin, and Mao. Today's world population is about 6.25 billion, and barely subsists on the basis of realized technological and industrial progress. But under hunting and gathering conditions, the demographic carrying capacity of the earth would be reduced to 25-50 million. If implemented today, Strauss's program for dismantling the universal homogeneous state would mean a genocide of something approaching 6 billion victims, two whole orders of magnitude beyond Hitler and Stalin together.

And even this must be put into perspective. Strauss notoriously feared to write what he really believed; the public could never face the full truth of his doctrines. Therefore, what we find written in *On Tyranny* is very likely a somewhat diluted view of his real views. So if Strauss Lite, the exoteric version that he felt comfortable publishing at the height of his career, spells up to 6 billion victims, God save us from the full fury of Strauss's esoteric version as it may be transmitted among the neocons infesting and controlling the United States government under the Bush regime.

The most urgent anti-terrorist measure of them all would thus appear to be a purge of neocons from all branches of government (including the Carl Schmitt disciples Scalia, Rehnquist, and Thomas on the Supreme Court), and a general quarantine of neocons as what they really are, neo-fascists and neo-Nazis.

NEOCON FAMILY TREE

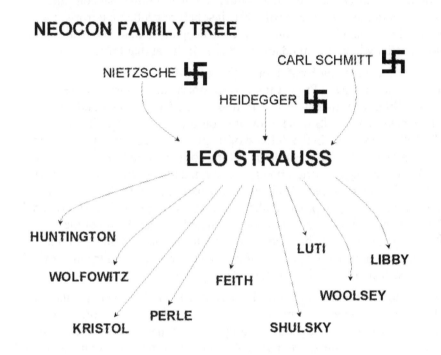

NEOCONS PREFER WAR TO PEACE

When Strauss talks about the universal and homogeneous state, as we have seen, he is referring to something which the ordinary person might identify as peace, progress, and prosperity, with a good measure of equality and international harmony. For most people, such a situation might seem to be almost ideal, but for the self-styled neocon intellectual, it represents the abolition of all human values and of everything that makes life worth living. The US Constitution mandates that the government pursue the General Welfare, but for the neocons this is anathema, since among other things it threatens their most cherished principle – oligarchy. In particular, the neocons were not happy with the subsiding of the Cold War, and viewed the 1993 Oslo peace accords between the Israelis and the Palestinians, as well as the Good Friday agreement regarding Northern Ireland in 1998 – which the world warmly welcomed – with great consternation. These aspects of neocon thought are derived most prominently from the proto-fascist Nietzsche, but also from the card-carrying Nazis Carl Schmitt and Martin Heidegger, and of course from their chief guru, the neo-fascist professor Leo Strauss. Since the neocon rejection of some of the greatest goods of civilization is likely to be incomprehensible to many readers, we need to pause to illustrate it.

In May 2004 the *Washington Post* carried an article by Corey Robin, assistant professor of political science at Brooklyn College in the City University of New York. Robin had carried out interviews with some well-known neocons and fellow travelers in the late summer of 2001, just before synthetic terrorism transformed the scene. Here we can sample the deep discontent and restless desire for conflict which prevailed among these circles at that time.

Robin heard from Irving Kristol, the father of William Kristol, the central figure of the warmongering Project for a New American Century, whose website was vainly calling for full-scale war with Iraq during Clinton's second term. Kristol lamented that the US was too focused on economic prosperity, and was not sufficiently aggressive in the defense of its global hegemony. "It's too bad," complained Kristol. "I think it would be natural for the United States ... to play a far more dominant role in world affairs... to command and give orders as to what is to be done. People need that. There are many parts of the world where an authority willing to use troops can make...a healthy difference." Kristol reserved particular contempt for any concern about the health or well-being of the population in general, which he scorned as a matter for accountants. "I think it's disgusting that ... presidential politics of the most important country in the world should revolve around prescriptions for elderly people."

Robin found that the neocons prized "mystery and vitality over calculation and technology," and even over money and markets. Lewis I. "Scooter" Libby, one of the schemers who brought us the Iraq war, commented that "the cult of peace and prosperity found expression in President Clinton's weak and distracted foreign policy," which had made it easier for bin Laden to run wild. Robin commented further: "Though conservatives reputedly favor wealth and prosperity, law and order, stability and routine, they disdained Clinton for his very pursuit of these virtues. His quest for affluence, they argued, produced a society that lost its depth and political meaning." And again: "Clinton's vision of a benign international order, conservatives argued, betrayed an unwillingness to take on a world of power and violence, of mysterious evil and unfathomable hatred. Coping with such a world requires pagan courage and barbaric *virtù*, qualities many conservatives embrace over the more prosaic goods of peace and prosperity."

The neocons, according to Robin, see 9/11 as an opportunity to exalt their "political virtues such as heroism and struggle" over "the numbing politics of affluence" because of their new-found ability to go to the public with "calls for sacrifice and destiny." The neocons were afflicted by a self-righteous and hypocritical megalomania: they fervently believed that the United States, with its $500 billion yearly trade deficit and its hollow army of ten divisions could "govern events – and determine the outcome of history." Based on this evidence, it is fair to say that at the turn of the millennium, the neocon faction was searching for new opportunities for conflict and violence. When those opportunities arrived, the neocons rejoiced and rushed into their favorite enterprise of sending other people's children into useless wars. (*Washington Post*, May 2, 2004)

NEOCONS: CUCKOLDS OF MARS

Catholic traditionalist Patrick Buchanan showed some awareness of this same restlessness and desire for new conflicts among the neocons during the 1999-2000 presidential campaign, when he commented that he was alarmed by the clique around candidate G.W. Bush – a reference to the neocon group that pretentiously and ignorantly called itself the "Vulcans." In a speech about foreign policy, Buchanan noted that he had worked with some of these neocons in previous administrations, and that he now found them consumed by nostalgia for the Cold War, and therefore very likely to pursue "conflict," "intervention," "confrontation," and "bullying." Buchanan ridiculed the "little magazines" of the neocon cabal, where they had been developing their concept of the US as a "benevolent global hegemon" – a role which many other states could be counted upon to reject. Buchanan added that, while the Clinton crowd had at least been canny enough to pick fights with smaller powers like Serbia, the Bush clique was determined to promote confrontation with larger powers who had the capability of inflicting great harm on the United States. The great exemplar of all these trends, said Buchanan, was Wolfowitz, who at that time thought he was on the way to being secretary of state.

Vulcan, or Hephaestos, was of course the Graeco-Roman god of volcanoes, fire, and the smithy. He was married to Venus, but she betrayed him in favor of Mars, the god of war. So Vulcan was a cuckold of Mars, as our ignorant and pretentious Vulcans seem to have forgotten. But Mars has come back to make them cuckolds too, in Iraq and shortly in Afghanistan as well.

David Brooks had written in *Newsweek* that, during the 1990s, Americans had "renovated our kitchens, refurbished our home entertainment systems, invested in patio furniture, Jacuzzis, and gas grills." Leaving aside the arid banality of Brooks' class-distorted view of the world, we must recall that for most Americans there was no peace dividend worth mentioning at the end of the Cold War. (*Washington Post*, May 2, 2004) And the pre-9/11 world was in reality no idyll, but rather a world of growing financial breakdown and military tension, as we have shown elsewhere in this book.

CARL SCHMITT: POISON GAS ON GERMAN CITIES

Leo Strauss was the product of three main intellectual and political influences. First among these was the proto-Nazi Friedrich Nietzsche, who was designated by Nazi ideologist Alfred Rosenberg as one of the four precursors of Hitlerism (the others were the operatic composer Richard Wagner, the anti-Semitic LaGarde, and the racist Houston Stewart Chamberlain). A second was the card-carrying Nazi Martin Heidegger, who praised Hitler in his inaugural speech as rector of the University of Freiburg. Finally, there is the card-carrying Nazi Carl Schmitt, the main legal theorist of the Third Reich.

Schmitt's ideas have directly contributed to the shattering of the US political consensus under the Bush regime. For Schmitt, politics comes down to the distinction between friend and foe. Starting from this extremely meager reduction of human motivation, he goes on to equate politics with warfare: if there is no warfare or conflict, then politics is dead, and life is no longer worth living. Schmitt therefore wants politics to be the monopoly of a strong state, and he does not like the idea that the state or the government could be influenced by the citizens. Schmitt's thought is thus revealed as authoritarian, dictatorial, fascistic. It is from Schmitt that Samuel Huntington got his idea that an enemy image is absolutely necessary for the cohesion of any society. In reality, however, it is primarily an oligarchical society which requires an enemy image, because that society is based on an irrational principle of domination which cannot stand the scrutiny it would receive in peacetime. George Orwell understood this aspect well when he suggested in *1984* that the endless war among Oceania, Eurasia, and Eastasia was really a war waged by each of these states against its own population, for the purpose of perpetuating a hierarchical society. The key concept dates back at least to Ibn Khaldun, the 13th century father of sociology, who noted that the Arabs only stopped fighting each other when it was necessary to unite against an outside enemy.

The card-carrying Nazi Schmitt was also a bitter opponent, not just of the Treaty of Versailles and the League of Nations, but of international law and international treaties in general. Like his neocon descendants of today, he was an ardent unilateralist. Here are some of Schmitt's typical comments about international law: "We are talking again about basic rights, about the basic rights of peoples and of states, and especially about the basic rights of those states who have, mindful of their own race, gotten themselves into the proper domestic order. Such a state is the national socialist state, which has led the German people back to an awareness of itself and its race. We proceed from the most self-evident of all basic rights, the right to one's own existence. This is an inalienable, eternal basic right, in which the right to self-determination, self-defense, and to the means of self-defense is included....From our solid standpoint we can see through that world of legalistic argumentation and that huge apparatus of treaties and pacts, and assign this tower of Babel to its rightful place in the history of international law."

Schmitt was the author of Article 48 of the 1919 Constitution of the Weimar Republic, which was the clause that allowed the Reich President to declare an emergency or state of siege and thereafter rule by decree. Schmitt's activity during the 1920s was largely devoted to agitating in favor of the dissolution or marginalization of the Reichstag (parliament) and the institution of a dictatorship of the President of the Reich. One of Schmitt's favorite sayings was that sovereignty meant the ability to declare a state of emergency. If you can find what organ of government has the ability to call out the state of siege, suspend the legislature, and impose martial law, Schmitt reasoned, you have found the place where sovereignty is actually located.

For Schmitt, the concept of emergency rule is a totally lawless realm; under it, the ruling authority can do literally anything it wants, without regard to law, separation of powers, constitutional freedoms, equity, or anything else. In one of his essays Schmitt approvingly quotes a speech by the Reich Justice Minister Schiffer to the Reichstag on March 3, 1920, in which Schiffer points out that under Article 48, the Reich President can attack "German cities with poison gas, if that is, in the concrete case, the necessary measure for the re-establishment of law and order." (Schmitt, *Die Diktatur*, 201) Schmitt was adamant that the emergency provisions of the Weimar constitution were theoretically and practically unlimited, and could be used to justify the greatest imaginable atrocities. We see here a tradition of thought, alive in the Schmittian-Straussian neocons of today, which would have no trouble in accommodating a crime on the scope of 9/11.

In July, 1932 the Nazis and their allies carried out a cold coup against the minority Social Democratic caretaker government in Prussia, the largest political subdivision of Germany. The pro-Nazi government in Prussia then became the springboard for Hitler's seizure of power via a legal coup in January 1933. Carl Schmitt was the lawyer for the coup forces in the German supreme court in Leipzig. (The parallels of this action to the Schwarzenegger/Warren Buffet oligarchical coup in California in 2003 are more than suggestive, since California is the largest US political subdivision in the same way that Prussia was in Germany.) Schmitt also provided legal services for Hitler's seizure of power in January, 1933.

Carl Schmitt wrote articles for the gutter-level anti-Semitic tabloid *Der Stürmer*, edited by Julius Streicher. In 1934, when Hitler massacred the brown-shirted SA leader Ernst Röhm and his faction for supporting a second revolution against the financiers, industrialists, and the army, Schmitt quickly emerged as one of Hitler's most shameless apologists. In his scurrilous pamphlet, "Der Führer Schützt das Recht" ("The Führer defends the law"), Schmitt endorsed the Byzantine theory according to which law is a successful act of strength by the stronger party against the weaker. Schmitt wrote that the primary task of the Führer was "to distinguish friend from enemy…The Führer takes the warnings of German history seriously. That gives him the right and the power to found a new state and a new order….The Führer protects the law from the worst abuse, when he – in the moment of danger – through the power of his leadership as supreme judge, directly creates law. His role as supreme judge flows from his role as supreme leader. Anyone who wants to separate one of these from the other is trying to unhinge the state with the help of the justice system….the Führer himself determines the content and scope of a crime." (Schmitt 200) This opens the door to every arbitrary outrage under color of law. While these ideas, so dear to today's ruling neocons, have been applied to Abu Ghraib, it is also clear that they are equally applicable to 9/11.

STRAUSS AND NIETZSCHE

As a young man, Strauss was an enthusiastic devotee of Nietzsche. Strauss wrote: "I can only say that Nietzsche so dominated and bewitched me between my 22nd and 30th years, that I literally believed everything that I understood of him ..." (Strauss to Karl Löwith, 23 June 1935, in Strauss, Leo and Karl Löwith, "Correspondence," *Independent Journal of Philosophy*, vol. 5/6, 1988, pp. 177-192.) For the young Strauss, Nietzsche was an idol, and the main vehicle of his youthful protests: "... the young Strauss, after a day of reading at the Prussian State Library, would go to a café on Unter den Linden and pronounce the name 'Nietzsche' loud enough to be heard at the other tables." (See Leo Strauss, "An Unspoken Prologue to a Public Lecture at St. John's," *Interpretation*, vol. 7, no. 3 1-2; cited by Michael Platt in Deutsch and Soffer, 23.) According to Straussian scholars, "In Nietzsche, Strauss certainly discovered the immoderation of philosophy, but in Nietzsche, especially the late Nietzsche, he also met the love of his life." (ibid.)

As the neocons never tire of reminding us, ideas have consequences. If Strauss is based to such an extraordinary degree on Nietzsche, then we may be permitted to take a minute to see which Nietzsche it was that Strauss admired so much. The indications are that it was Nietzsche as the glorifier of hierarchy, slavery, violence, war, and terrorism. In some of the notes that Nietzsche made during the time he was writing his *Genealogy of Morals*, we read: "Which way? **We need a new terrorism**." ("Das Problem – wohin? Es bedarf einen neuen Terrorismus.") (Nietzsche vol. XIV, p. 334, emphasis added.)

Or, in the section of *Ecce Homo* entitled "Why I am a fate," we find the following: "I know my fate. My name will be linked someday to the memory of something monstrous – to a crisis whose like never existed on earth, to the deepest clash of conscience, to a decision conjured up against everything which had been believed, promoted, held sacred up to then. I am not a man, **I am dynamite**." ("Ich kenne mein Los. Es wird sich einmal an meinem Namen die Erinnerung an etwas Ungeheures Anknüpfen, – an eine Krisis, wie es keine auf Erden gab, an die tiefste Gewissens-Kollision, an eine Entscheidung, heraufbeschworen gegen alles, was bis dahin geglaubt, gefordert, geheiligt worden war. Ich bin kein Mensch, **ich bin Dynamit**.") (Nietzsche vol. VII p. 317, emphasis added.) This passage was a favorite of the German neocon Armin Mohler, the author of the *Conservative Revolution in Germany, 1918-1932*.

Nietzsche was full of contempt and hatred for the middle class, family life, and the quest for economic security, which he always saw in connection with the inferior "last men." Nietzsche is the great glorifier of war, conflict, violence, and cruelty, which he regards not just as unavoidable but also as positive goods: "We think that hardness, forcefulness, slavery, danger in the alley and the heart, life in hiding, stoicism, the art of experiment and deviltry of every kind, that everything evil, terrible, tyrannical in man, everything in him that is kin to beasts of prey and serpents, serves the enhancement of the species 'man' as much as its opposite does." (*Beyond Good and Evil* 54-55) It is from Nietzsche that today's neocons derive their endless fascination with warfare and bloodshed: "You should always be such men as are always looking for an enemy – for *your* enemy. And with some of you there is hate at first sight. You should seek your enemy and wage your war – a war for your opinions….You should love peace as a means to new wars. And the short peace more than the long. I do not exhort you to work but to battle. I do not exhort you to peace, but to victory. May your work be a battle, may your peace be a victory! …You say it is the good cause that hallows even war? I tell you: it is the good war that hallows every cause. War and courage have done more great things than charity…. Are you ugly? Very well, my brothers! Take the sublime about you, the mantle of the ugly." (*Zarathustra* 74)

Bush's supporters among the Christian fundamentalists and Christian Zionists would perhaps be surprised to know what neocons (to whom Bush has turned over the government) think about Christ and Christianity. Nietzsche referred to Christ as an "idiot," (*Twilight of the Idols/The Antichrist* 202). In addition to his famous proposition that God is dead, Nietzsche also proclaimed a special role for himself: "I am… the Anti-Christ" (*Ecce Homo* III 2) Nietzsche, like Strauss after him, was an exponent of European atheist nihilism, and this remains the underlying *esoteric* outlook of the neocons who are ruling the US. At one point Nietzsche asks himself, "What does nihilism mean?" His answer "That the highest values are devalued. The goal is missing: the answer to 'why?' is missing." (Lukacs, *Von Nietzsche zu Hitler* [Frankfurt am Main: Fischer, 1966], 69) If God is dead, all crimes are allowed.

Thus the neocon publicist Robert Kaplan, a veteran of the Israeli Defense Force, wrote in his recent *Warrior Politics* that a pagan ethos of war and cruelty is necessary to face the great crises of this age. For Kaplan, the philosophical and social content of Christianity is a great obstacle to inculcating the proper attitude in the US ruling class. Among other things, Kaplan finds that the Roman Emperor Tiberius (under whose rule the crucifixion of Christ took place) has been treated unfairly by historians, and deserves to be rehabilitated. Similarly, one of neocon Paul Wolfowitz's favorite quips is reportedly the infamous *Oderint dum metuant* – let them hate me, as long as they fear me – a line from the Latin writer Accius later popularized by the infamous Emperor Caligula.

Strauss is well aware that Nietzsche is a genocidalist, but this does not disturb his admiration for the sage of Turin. As Strauss wrote in *What is Political Philosophy* (1959): "Being certain of the tameness of modern western man, [Nietzsche] preached the sacred right of 'merciless extinction' of large masses of men….He used much of his unsurpassable and inexhaustible power of passionate and fascinating speech for making his readers loathe, not only socialism and communism, but conservatism, nationalism, and democracy as well. After having taken upon himself this great political responsibility, he could not show his readers a way to political responsibility. [I. e., he could not seize power, WGT] He left them no choice except that between irresponsible indifference to politics and irresponsible political options. He thus prepared a regime which, as long as it lasted, made discredited democracy look again like a golden age. He tried to articulate his understanding both of the modern situation and of human life as such by his doctrine of the will to power." In other words, Strauss knows very well that Nietzsche was a precursor of Hitler, but supports him anyway as a philosopher for today.

A storm cellar for neocons and failed pols in the Rumsfeld Pentagon has been the Defense Policy Board, chaired by Richard Perle, the virulent neocon war-monger whom British Labour Party Foreign Secretary Dennis Healey dubbed the "prince of darkness" back in the 1980s. On September 19, 2001, Perle used the Defense Policy Board as the springboard for the neocon war drive against Iraq that produced an unprovoked and aggressive war in March 2003. Other members of the Defense Policy Board included: Henry Kissinger, George Shultz, Helmut Sonnenfeldt, Fred Iklé, James Schlesinger, Dan Quayle, Harold Brown, James Woolsey, and Newt Gingrich. Perle was eventually forced to resign, in part because of corruption charges against him stemming from Trireme Corp, and his relation with Hollinger Corp. boss Lord Conrad Black. This board of unelected and unaccountable extremist ideologues, known as the Wolfowitz cabal, needs to be urgently and permanently dissolved.

In a 19-hour meeting on September 19-20, 2001 Perle, Newt Gingrich, James Woolsey, and Wolfowitz pushed hard for an immediate operation against Iraq Wolfowitz's plan was to have the US take over southern Iraq militarily as an opposition beachhead and use the Basra oil revenues to overthrow Saddam Hussein. Perle wanted Saddam Hussein's "regime ... overthrown quickly with military force." This was too much for Powell, at least in that phase. (October 12, 2001)

SAMUEL HUNTINGTON: IT WILL HAPPEN HERE

Samuel Huntington, in his 1981 study entitled *American Politics*, described the periodic explosions of the "American Creed," which he saw as a mixture of liberty, equality, individualism, and democracy. He viewed American history as punctuated by a series of periods of heightened political awareness and activity which he called "creedal passion periods." His forecast was that "if the periodicity of the past prevails, a major sustained creedal passion period will occur in the second and third decades of the twenty-first century." Huntington included the Great Awakening religious movement of the 1740s, the Revolution of 1776, the Great Revival c. 1800, the Jacksonian movement, the abolitionism of the 1850s, the Progressives, the 1968 student and antiwar movements, etc. However, Huntington blurred his attempt to look into the future by excluding from consideration social and economic upheavals like the Populists of the 1890s and the mass strikes of the 1930s. If these are included, what Huntington might call a creedal passion period might occur during the latter part of the first decade of the 21st century, i.e., between 2005 and 2010. The Carl Schmitt disciple Huntington associated this with a coming turn toward an authoritarian or fascist regime. In the next creedal ferment explosion, he wrote, "the oscillations among the responses could intensify in such a way as to threaten to destroy both ideals and institutions" in this country. This might include "the replacement of the weakened and ineffective institutions by more authoritarian structures more effectively designed to meet historical needs."

ARMAGEDDON AND APOCALYPSE IN THE US MILITARY

Although the neocons are an obvious focus of danger in the American society of today, they by no means represent the only threat. We must also pay attention to those self-styled religious factions which cultivate notions of the approaching end of the world and the return of the Messiah. These are the groups which propagate notions of the end of historical time through the apocalypse, and embellish this with the imminence of Armageddon, the mythical last battle before the end of the world. Those who profess these doctrines blatantly disregard the advice of St. Augustine, the greatest father of the Latin church, who warned Christians that it was "ridiculous" to become obsessed with the date and time of the end of the world. The modern irrationalists who camouflage themselves as Christians have left traditional Christianity behind, and have reduced the content of their religion to the cynical support of such figures as Bush and Ariel Sharon, both regarded, and perhaps accurately, as harbingers of the apocalypse.

The presence of a large mass of apocalyptic Armageddon thinkers in American life is a serious problem, since some versions of this belief structure call upon the individual to act in ways which are thought to accelerate the end time towards world catastrophe, thus speeding the return of the Messiah. The popular novels of the "Left Behind" series, which deal with life after the so-called rapture, or in-gathering of the saved elect, have fostered mass delusions on precisely this point.

Apocalyptic and Armageddon thinkers in the high ranks of the military services represent an even more serious problem than they do in the society in general. How can we let a self-styled "evangelical Christian" close to a nuclear button, when that person's demented belief structure may dictate that the launching of a rogue missile attack on Russia, China or some Arab state would bring with it the beneficial by-product of the end of the world and the creation of the kingdom of God on earth? The various fellowships and chaplaincies of evangelical-Pentecostal stamp in the US military, which are often under the influence of British or Israeli intelligence agencies, therefore represent a grave threat to US national security. Is the US officer corps reliable? Under present conditions of pervasive penetration by the apocalypse-Armageddon network, their reliability is open to grave doubt.

In December 2001, a senior European diplomatic source observed that the current situation in the Middle East contained the danger of a world war even before the end of that year. "If this goes much further," said the source, "we in the West will be coming closer to a general conflict with 1.5 billion Muslims in the world. And never forget the 'Armageddon Factor,' the powerful Christian fundamentalist elements in the United States, who are applying massive pressure on the American Administration, to give full backing to the Israelis, so that the fundamentalists can achieve their Armageddon aims." (EIR, December 4, 2001)

To sample the mentality of these networks, let us hear now from General Albion Knight, US Army retired, who was the 1992 vice-presidential candidate for the US Taxpayer Party, and thus the running mate of Howard Philips on that ticket that year. We cite from Gen. Knight's essay, "Old Testament Parallels to Our Times," which was published in early 1990s by the *McAlvany Intelligence Advisor*:

Our current military leadership are a bunch of wimps!...The final – and probably the most important part of my analysis – is following through on the implications of the claim that I (and a growing number of others) make that there is a close similarity between the conditions described in the Old Testament about the two Jewish nations, Israel and Judah, between 750 BC and 586 BC and those we see in America today. They were rotting from within at the same time they faced major external danger. Therefore, the Lord removed His protection from them, allowed them to be defeated, taken in exile and screened out to find the solid remnant of 10% which He used to rebuild. I was drawn into an intensive study of the Old Testament prophets Isaiah, Jeremiah, Ezekiel, Amos, Hosea, Micah, Joel and Habakkuk. It was like reading today's newspaper they were so startlingly descriptive of today's conditions in America. **From this study, I am strongly convinced that God has removed His protection from America and we shall very soon experience a series of sudden and violent crises which will shake us to our roots.** They will drive us to our knees – either in despair or prayer. I am afraid that there will be more of the despair than of the prayer. The solution given to God to those two nations was, "Stop doing the evil that you are doing and turn back to Me and I will heal your land. If not, you will have disaster on your hands." That is our message, too. Now my own attitude: from these analyses, I was put into a mood of deep despair. Yet, the Bible study also reminded me that God uses a few strong men who know who they are, whose they are, and what they ought to do. I must also admit that the words of Winston Churchill, "Never, Never, Never, Never Give up!" rang in my ear. Also the example of Howard Phillips who takes a realistic but optimistic view – We must be prepared in case God finds use for us in His plan. So I am not throwing in the towel. (emphasis added)

Here the General expresses the common contempt for the current political and military leadership of this country, along with the idea that future US catastrophes will present well-deserved punishment for the monstrous excesses of this country. One senses that the sort of outlook would regard such cataclysmic events as 9/11 with a grim satisfaction, as proof of the efficacy of God's will and God's retribution.

In May 2000, we find another fragment, "America Betrayed," which is expressive of General Knight's views towards the close of the Clinton administration. Here we find that the Republican impeachment agitation has indeed resonated deeply among religious irrationalists of this type, and has in effect pushed Gen. Knight and his associates very far down the road of rebellion against the elected government. Gen. Knight writes: "Sex and perjury were the wrong impeachment offenses. It should have been on his [President Clinton's] treachery and failure to live up to his oath of office." Gen. Knight went on to recount that, during the Reagan years, he had been asked to draw up a program of what actions a crypto-communist American president might take if he got into power. "We concluded that a Marxist and/or communist president, if he ever came to power, would focus on the transfer of national sovereignty at every opportunity to international organizations. He or she would also weaken the armed forces physically, mentally and spiritually. The 'dumbing down' of our public school educational system would also accelerate. Furthermore, we decided that a Marxist president would assist all or most of America's enemies – Russia, China, Cuba, radical Islam, North Korea and others. He would disregard the Constitution at every opportunity and rule by decree, meaning executive orders would earmark such an administration. Bogus arms control agreements, buying-off or intimidating Congress by stealing the FBI files of its members, controlling the media and trying to stop all alternative media would also be major goals."

Inevitably, Gen. Knight concluded that Clinton had carried out the crypto-Marxist program in full: "What has Clinton done in this regard? He has hit every one of the above actions and more. ... Clinton has helped Marxists and terrorists and their 'world revolution' at every opportunity. Cultural Marxism is also a key Clinton goal. He has been giving us a bad example that it is all right to lie, cheat, steal, threaten and even rape women if it is done in high office. There is a steady movement toward a Gestapo-like control over the people. There is today in the US a total lack of any sense of nation and its protection as required by his oath-of-office. Furthermore, Clinton has been selling and giving our nuclear and other high technology secrets to communist China and giving Russia the money to re-arm at US taxpayers' expense." (Anthony LoBaido, WorldNetDaily.com, May 6, 2000.)

When. General Edwin Walker gave speeches of this type to his troops in Germany in the early 1960s, he was given the sack, and Senator Fulbright denounced him as a harbinger of a threatened military coup in this country. Now active duty officers are presumably more discreet, but there are obviously many active duty officers of high rank who believe what Gen. Knight feels free to talk about. Here if anywhere was an area for the 9/11 commission to probe, but it did not do so.

These considerations lead us back to the self-styled patriot militias of the 1990s, who were so often led by retired officers with military intelligence connections. In those days, the foreign intelligence agency that was most active in fomenting militia activity was unquestionably Britain's MI-6. Today the media emphasis is on al Qaeda, and the militias are seldom heard of. But in the real world of secret intelligence operations, things move more slowly. The patriot militia networks are still there with their anti-government, right-wing anarchist, and white supremacist-xenophobic programs.

After Oklahoma City, the potential of the right-wing anti-government evangelical fanatics for terrorism and violence was re-affirmed by an armed standoff between police and "Republic of Texas" activists demanding the secession of Texas in April 1997. This insurrection was led by Richard Otto, alias "White Eagle," who put out a call inviting members of militias around the country to come to the site, armed for a shootout. The agent provocateur Otto turned out to have been "trained and set into motion by an Air Force officer who toured the world practicing New Age pagan rituals, in consultation with senior British intelligence drug-rock-sex gurus such as Gregory Bateson." Otto finally surrendered on May 3, 1997. (Tony Chaitkin, "The Militias and Pentecostalism," www.larouchepub.com)

Another anti-government agitator with impeccable military credentials was a certain Jim Ammerman. Ammerman was a charismatic Pentecostal who controlled various networks of chaplains in the US armed forces, in federal prisons, and in the FBI. He claimed to possess supernatural prophetic powers, and preached the imminent end of the world. According to Ammerman, the US government was illegal; in his view, Clinton deserved to be executed. During the April 1997 siege, Ammerman was brought in to mediate between the Texas separatist fanatics and the FBI. Ammerman exemplifies one of several apocalyptic networks within the US military.

A videotape popular among militia groups in the 1990s was "The Imminent Military Takeover of the United States," a speech by the Reverend Colonel Ammerman to the Prophecy Club of Topeka, Kansas. Here Ammerman warned that President Clinton, aided by masses of foreign troops he claimed were already on American soil, would soon put the nation under martial law – if God did not end the world before the current President can act. Ammerman proclaimed that President Bill Clinton should long ago have been executed for avoiding the Vietnam draft. Ammerman, who retired in 1977 as a US Army colonel and chaplain, was described by the Prophecy Club as a former Green Beret and "CIA official" with 26 years in the military and a top-secret security clearance. He was the leader of some 200 chaplains serving in the US Armed Forces under the aegis of the Chaplaincy of Full Gospel Churches. He and his chaplains were accustomed to speak in tongues and perform supernatural cures. Ammerman boasted to his audiences in those years that his chaplains were providing him with inside information about military activities ordered by what he claimed was the illegal dictatorship of the US President. ("The Militias and Pentecostalism," www.larouchepub.com)

In an interview granted on May 22, 1997, Colonel Ammerman stated: "**There is a network of colonels and above, throughout the military, who would stand by the Constitution and against the President. They know who they**

are, and they are in close communication with each other. They could control the country if they need to." ("The Militias and Pentecostalism," www.larouchepub.com, emphasis added)

Ammerman spoke frequently in this context of the "multi-jurisdictional task force," a repeated theme in his exhortations to the militias. The military was allegedly combined, under the Federal Emergency Management Agency, with other departments of the Federal government and with local governments. When the President tried to use this overreaching military against the people, Ammerman claimed, the "good" military officers would side with armed citizens against the President. Ammerman's own organization was created at the request of an Army officer, Gen. Ralph E. Haines, Jr. General Haines had been vice chief of staff of the US Army in 1967-68, and at that time was in charge of counter-insurgency preparations in the continental United States. He worked with the full resources of the Army under him, including military intelligence capabilities, to plan to cope with black ghetto riots and civil disturbances during the Vietnam War. Haines deployed combat units to Detroit and Washington, D.C., during rioting after Martin Luther King's assassination. General Haines went public in an April 11, 1968 press conference, describing his "Operation Garden Plot." He had planned and directed the military arrangements for the takeover of every single American city, and arranged the linkages between the military and Justice Department, local police, and state governments. Haines "said that detailed military planning for the summer began in February. The 'garden plot' preparations were national, he said, including 'every city you can think of.' Many officers who were to be assigned to specific cities in a military mobilization visited them in mufti [civilian clothes] to familiarize themselves with the terrain, the social and economic problems of potential riot areas, and the police with whom they would work if called, the general said." (*New York Times*, April 14, 1968) An admirer of the Haines-Ammerman project was the same Gen. Albion Knight, an apocalyptic co-thinker from whom we have already heard.

Militia units under the direction of military intelligence controllers have never hesitated to attack military facilities in the same way the Pentagon was attacked on 9/11. Just one example: during July 1997, a certain Bradley P. Glover and six other persons were rounded up for plotting to bomb US military bases, beginning with Fort Hood, Texas. The FBI said that Glover and an associate were arrested on July 4 near Fort Hood, in possession of various weapons; others in on the alleged plot were charged with possession of pipe bombs and machine guns. The arrests allegedly resulted from Missouri state police infiltration of paramilitary groups. Glover was featured in the *Wichita Eagle* on April 30, 1995, as the pre-eminent Kansas militia leader. He was said to control about 1,000 armed men in the southern half of the state. In a 1995 interview, Glover said that he had initiated the militia movement in Kansas in November 1994. Glover also said he was a former Naval Intelligence officer. ("The Militias and Pentecostalism," www.larouchepub.com)

PRIVATE MILITARY FIRMS

Machiavelli warned the Italian princes of his day in his *Arte della Guerra* that unemployed mercenaries and professional soldiers would inevitably stir up coups and conflicts in order to procure jobs and glory for themselves. This warning became highly relevant at the end of the Cold War. In the Thirty Years War the story of Wallenstein's camp shows that certain kinds of military activities can become self-perpetuating and totally disconnected from their original political purpose.

After Vietnam, the US military exhibited the pathologies of a defeated army. These recalled the sociological developments among the defeated or embittered forces of Germany and Italy after the First World War, when defeated veterans became one of the initial constituencies of fascism. When the Cold War ended, many of these same defeated officers became unemployed or in fear of becoming so. Defeated and unemployed military officers represent a dangerous phenomenon in any society, and today this problem is compounded by the issue of a mercenary (or all-volunteer) force. Machiavelli wrote about precisely this problem in his 1521 *Art of War*, in which he drew on his parallel study of the ancient world and of the events of his own tumultuous times. His conclusion was a warning which we would do well to bear in mind today:

> I say...that ... governments should fear those persons who make war their only business... And if a prince has not enough power over his infantry to make them disband and return cheerfully to their former occupations when a war is over, he is on the road to being ruined. For no infantry can be so dangerous as that which is composed of men who make war their only calling, because a prince either must keep them continually engaged in war, or must constantly keep them paid in peacetime, or must run the risk of their stripping him of his kingdom. But it is impossible to keep them forever engaged in war, or forever paid when war is over; therefore, a prince must run no small risk of losing his kingdom. (Machiavelli 19-20)

Retired US military officers are notoriously venal; they feel that they have missed out on the chance for wealth which civilians have enjoyed. How many such military officers lost their retirement investments or were otherwise financially ruined by the crash of the NASDAQ after the spring of 2000? Probably quite a few, and here is where an acute observer like Machiavelli might start looking for desperate men, ruined by debt, with superb martial skills, who might be recruitable as mercenaries for a desperate enterprise.

Private military firms received a massive round of public attention in relation to the Abu Ghraib prison torture scandal of May 2004. According to press accounts at the time, employees of CACI in Arlington, Virginia as well as those of Titan Corporation of San Diego worked in that infamous Iraqi jail. CACI's website announced that it had taken up the task of helping US intelligence agencies worldwide in gathering information for the war on terrorism, and in analyzing and managing that information. Titan claimed that it only provided interpreters for Abu Ghraib, not torturers. CACI has 7,600 employees and a turnover of $845 million per year. It provided what it called "interrogation specialists" for places as distant as Afghanistan and Kosovo. A CACI instructor was fired at Abu Ghraib for urging military police to carry out interrogations using illegal techniques.

In the spring of 2004, there were 25,000 employees of private military firms in Iraq. In addition to the inevitable Halliburtons and Bechtels, these mercenaries included employees of Vinnell Corporation, who received the task of training the new Iraqi army. Dyncorp, a competitor of Vinnell, received the contract for training the new Iraqi police. Olive Security of the UK protected television camera crews during the war, and later turned to providing security for the construction projects of Bechtel. The leader of this security detachment was Harry Legge-Bourke, who had gone skiing with Prince Charles. Also active in Iraq was the American security firm Kroll Associates. The security firm Blackwater provided snipers who flew over Baghdad, killing Iraqis without benefit of judicial process. It was the killing of some Blackwater employees in Fallujah which provoked the epic April-May 2004 battle for that town which ended in a US defeat. The firm Custer Battles provided security along the road leading to the Baghdad Airport, a shooting gallery for passing occupation vehicles. There were other private military firms: Centurion, Global Risk, and the Stone Foundation, to name just a few. Northrop Grumman, Halliburton, and other companies developed or acquired private military firms as their corporate subsidiaries.

According to the German news magazine *Der Spiegel*, private military firms claim competence in all departments of warfare, including "nuclear planning." Most of the employees of the private military firms come from the retirees of the US Navy Seals, the US Army Delta Force and Rangers, and the British SAS. The vogue of the private military firm began in grand style in 1992, when then-Pentagon boss Dick Cheney awarded a contract to Brown & Root, a pillar of the US establishment and today Kellogg, Brown and Root, a Halliburton company, to determine which military jobs could best be outsourced to private firms. (*Der Spiegel*, "Die Folterer von Baghdad," May 3, 2004)

US and British intelligence operations have been in the process of privatization since the 1970s. This process was more advanced in Britain, and was given an additional impetus in the US by Reagan's Executive Order 12333, which opened the door to the privatization of virtually everything. One of the mothers of British private defense firms is the Special Air Services (SAS), the commando operation long commanded by Colonel David Stirling. The SAS are traditionally heavily Scottish, and one of their traditions is that they allegedly take no prisoners. In other words, they execute prisoners in flagrant violation of the laws of war. One is reminded of the *Private Eye* cover of a few years back, which appeared after a particularly blatant SAS assassination of a suspect. One

SAS trooper asks the other: "Why did you shoot him 43 times?" The answer: "I ran out of bullets."

The privatized SAS system illustrates the many advantages of the private military or security firm for maintaining plausible denial in covert operations, while at the same time reducing or eliminating the oversight powers of government. The SAS has over the years spun off a series of private security and mercenary recruitment firms led by its retired or reserve-status officers. Among the first and most infamous of these was Keenie Meenie Services (KMS), whose name was taken from the Swahili term for the motion of a snake in the grass. During its heyday in the 1980s, KMS shared offices with Saladin Security, another SAS firm, next door to the 22nd SAS Regimental HQ in London. The firms were run by Maj. David Walker, an SAS South American specialist; Maj. Andrew Nightingale of SAS Group Intelligence; and Detective Ray Tucker, a former Arab affairs specialist at Scotland Yard.

Other SAS spin-off firms have included Kilo Alpha Services (KAS), directed by former SAS Counter-Terrorism Warfare team leader Lt. Col. Ian Crooke; Control Risks, run by former SAS squadron leader Maj. Arish Turtle; and J. Donne Holdings, run by SAS counterespionage specialist H.M.P.D. Harclerode, whose firm later provided bodyguards and commando training for Libyan leader Muammar Qaddafi.

SAS operations under the KMS label were important during Iran-Contra: in 1983, Lt. Col. Oliver North hired KMS to train the Afghan mujahideen, to mine Managua harbor in Nicaragua, and to train the Nicaraguan Contras. At the same time, KMS provided personal security for the Saudi ambassador to Washington, Prince Bandar, a close associate of Bush 41 and Bush 43. KMS has a long history in the Arab and Muslim world. One of its first known assignments in the 1970s was to aid Oman in repressing a revolt in its province of Dhofar. Oman remains a de facto British colony; its officer corps is dominated by retired British officers. KMS has also worked in Kuwait, Bahrain, Saudi Arabia, and Qatar, all of which include numerous former SAS officers in their security apparatus. The security chief in Bahrain, Ian Henderson, for example, was an SAS officer in Kenya during the Mau Mau period. The Omani chief of security was a former SAS officer, as was the case in Dubai, the home of KMS official Fiona Fraser, a Stirling relative.

The relations of these SAS firms with the Iran-Contra narcotics trafficking emerged dramatically in August 1989, when reports surfaced in the British and Italian press that the Colombian Cali Cartel, historically most closely tied to the George Bush machine, had hired SAS veterans to assassinate Pablo Escobar of the rival Medellín Cartel. On Aug. 16, 1989, three days after the story broke, Colombian presidential candidate Luis Carlos Galán, an opponent of the drug trade, was assassinated. Some in the Colombian government said British mercenaries were involved. Among those reportedly working for the Cali Cartel were Col. Peter McAleese, a former SAS officer in Malaysia; Alex Lenox, a former member of the SAS Counter-Terrorism Warfare task force; and David

Tomkins, a veteran of Afghanistan. Among other British private military firms are also the London-based Defence Systems Ltd. and Executive Outcomes, both of which were active over a number of years in destabilizing the peace process in Angola. (Joe Brewda, "The SAS: Prince Philip's Manager of Terrorism," *EIR*, October 13, 1995)

Another private military firm is Aegis Defense Services Ltd., which in the summer of 2004 was awarded a $293 million contract to provide security for the US Project and Contracting Office in Iraq, the entity which is tasked with distributing $18.4 billion of US largesse there. The chief executive of Aegis is Tim Spicer, a former lieutenant colonel in the Scots Guards who has a past history of involvement in British colonial atrocities in Northern Ireland. Two soldiers under Spicer's command were convicted of murder in the 1992 shooting death of Belfast teenager Peter McBride. Spicer stubbornly defended the two murderers, despite their conviction which was confirmed on appeal in the British courts. Irish-American civil rights groups protested the awarding of the lucrative Iraq contract to Spicer. Paul O'Connor of the Pat Finucane Centre (named after the victim of an MI-5 terrorist provocateur) pointed out that Spicer evidently believed that his troops were above the law. Rev. Sean McManus of the Irish National Caucus told a reporter, "President Bush should tear up this contract immediately out of decency and respect." During the 1990s, Spicer worked for Sandline International in Papua New Guinea and Sierra Leone. In 1999 a British parliamentary inquiry found that Sandline had shipped arms into Sierra Leone in violation of a UN arms embargo. Sandline also fought a dirty war against rebels in Papua New Guinea in 1997. (*Washington Post*, August 9, 2004)

RAND CORPORATION NUCLEAR PLANNERS

The imagination which produced 9/11 was evidently an imagination that did not hesitate to sacrifice thousands of lives. But intellectuals ready to sacrifice not thousands but tens or even hundreds of millions of lives to the imperatives of imperial hegemony have been influential in and around the United States govern–ment for more than half a century. These are the "defense intellectuals," the nuclear planners of the RAND Corporation. These are the Strangeloves who have been studying charts marked "World Targets in Megadeaths" for many years.

One of the most influential of these was Albert Wohlstetter, who died in January, 1997 at the age of 83. According to his admirers, Wohlstetter was more influential in national affairs than Henry Kissinger, even though the latter is more bombastic and more infamous. From 1960 to 1990, Wohlstetter was the premier US strategic thinker. Among his disciples, he counted leading neocons like Richard Perle and Paul Wolfowitz. At his death, Wohlstetter was lionized by Robert L. Bartley, the editor of the *Wall Street Journal* and, as a participant in the Olson salon, one of the prime movers in the impeachment of Clinton. Every editorial on America's geopolitical strategy that appeared in *The Wall Street Journal* during the previous 25 years was said to have been the product of

Wohlstetter. Neocons saw Henry Kissinger as the leader of the "dove team" in foreign policy over much of this period, stressing diplomatic stratagems, while in this perspective Wohlstetter was the undisputed leader of the "hawk team," which stressed military moves of breathtaking creativity and imagination.

One of Wohlstetter's best-known and most typical works was his article, "The Delicate Balance of Terror," which appeared in *Foreign Affairs* in January 1959. The main thesis here was that the US was very vulnerable to a Soviet first strike; an adequate US retaliation to a surprise attack was not at all assured. Wohlstetter urged his readers to support "maintaining the delicate balance of terror" with measures involving sacrifice, and to develop "a new image of ourselves in a world of persistent danger." Wohlstetter's pessimistic finale: "It is by no means certain that we shall meet the task." (Kaplan 171) This is the eternal neocon refrain, from Wohlstetter to the bomber gap/missile gap to Team B and the window of vulnerability to the terrorism experts of today.

Early exponents of this school were Bernard Brodie, author of *The Absolute Weapon* (1946), who advocated US nuclear first use against the Soviets, and John von Neumann, the game theorist. In the intelligence unit of Curtis LeMay's Strategic Air Command there were Stefan Possony, a right-wing extremist from Hungary, and General George Keegan. Another Hungarian was Leo Szilard, an early theoretician of mutually assured destruction, or deterrence theory. Then there was Herman Kahn, the author of *On Thermonuclear War* (1960), who advocated nuclear first strike capabilities, limited nuclear war, fallout shelters, and generally thinking the unthinkable. The review of this book in *Scientific American* read: "This is a moral tract on mass murder: how to plan it, how to commit it, how to get away with it, how to justify it." (Kaplan 228)

RAND nuclear war scenarios from around 1960 called for – depending on the kind of strategy used – 150 million Americans dead and 60% of US industry destroyed, with 40 million Soviets dead and 40% of Soviet industry destroyed; or else 110 million Americans dead and 50% of US industry destroyed, with 75 million Soviets dead and 50% of Soviet industry gone. (Kaplan 228) A mind that could imagine this would have no trouble imagining 9/11. Fortunately, the RAND Strangeloves never got the chance to test their crackpot theories in a confrontation with the USSR. The Cuban missile crisis, the world's greatest thermonuclear confrontation, was conducted by President Kennedy in complete disregard of RAND, and of aggressive leaders like Dean Acheson and generals like Curtis LeMay and Lyman Lemnitzer, the Northwoods terrorist planner who chaired the US Joint Chiefs of Staff. The one place where RAND ideas were used was Vietnam, where a conventional version of the RAND counterforce doctrine was attempted in the form of Operation Rolling Thunder, a shock and awe exercise involving massive B-52 carpet bombing. But the utopian strategy of the RAND crackpots proved a complete failure. As Fred Kaplan wrote, "Vietnam brought out the dark side of nearly everyone inside America's national security machine. And it exposed something seamy and disturbing about the very enterprise of the defense intellectuals. It revealed that the concept of force underlying all their formulations was an abstraction, practically useless as a guide to action." (Kaplan 336) This mood of military defeat and intellectual bankruptcy is the starting point for today's neocon cabal, since this is the world the Wohlstetter protégés Wolfowitz and Perle gravitated toward in precisely those years.

The RAND Corporation remains a sinister threat, but it also provided a rollicking farce in the run-up to the Iraq war. A special briefing on the nefarious nature of Saudi Arabia before the Defense Policy Board was ordered up by Perle, who could find no better orator than an undistinguished former member of my own staff in the EIR bureau in Wiesbaden, Germany during the 1980s. Despite the fact that he was by no stretch of the imagination an area specialist, he was tapped in the summer of 2002 by Perle to give a delirious PowerPoint presentation on Saudi Arabia as "the focus of evil" in the modern world. Even the Bush administration was embarrassed.

YODA: ANDREW MARSHALL, RUMSFELD'S FUTUROLOGIST

Andrew Marshall was one of Albert Wohlstetter's whiz kids at the RAND Corporation back in the 1950s. He has worked for the Defense Department for more than forty years, and is one of the last survivors of the original RAND kindergarten run by Wohlstetter. Born in 1921, the octogenarian heads up Rumsfeld's Office of Net Assessment in the Pentagon. Marshall is able to count among his protégés such figures as Cheney, Rumsfeld, and Wolfowitz. He was a strong backer of Bush 41's Team B alternative estimates group in 1976, which prepared Wolfowitz and other neocons for their leading roles in the Reagan Administration. Marshall was also close to the ultra-right Committee on the Present Danger, where General Lyman Lemnitzer, the author of Operation Northwoods, was also an activist. Lemnitzer had been encouraged to work with CPD by President Gerald Ford. Here is an important element of continuity between the Operation Northwoods clique and today's Pentagon. Marshall is no conservative; his profile is rather that of a radical right-wing reformer and Utopian thinker. He is one of many bureaucrats who have never been called to account over 9/11.

An exchange from a recent interview is typical: "Q: What's the next radical change the US will reveal on the battlefield? Marshall: One future intelligence problem: knowing what drugs the other side is on....People who are connected with neural pharmacology say that new classes of drugs will be available relatively certainly within the decade. These drugs are just like chemicals inside people, only with behavior-modifying, performance-enhancing characteristics. [This leads to] jokes that a future intelligence problem is going to be knowing what drugs the other guys are on."

Marshall is an apostle of shock and awe: "There are ways of psychologically influencing the leadership of another state. I don't mean information warfare, but some demonstration of awesome effects, like being able to set off impressive explosions in the sky. Like, let us show you what we could do to you. Just visually impressing the person." Are we safer? Marshall opines: "A friend of mine, Yale economist Martin Shubik, says an important way to think about the world is a curve of the number of people 10 determined men can kill before they are put down themselves. That has varied over time. His claim is that it wasn't very many for a long time, and now it's going up. It's not just the US. All the world is getting less safe."

A very revealing question is this one: "Q: Did 9/11 change your mind about anything? Marshall: Not much. It was obvious that we were wide open to attack." (Douglas McGray, "The Marshall Plan," *Wired Magazine*, November 2002) A rather cavalier statement, since Marshall's job was supposed to be using his imagination to devise possible futuristic modes of attack against this country, and recommending timely measures to ward off such peril. If the 9/11 catastrophe was due to a failure of imagination, Marshall's Office of Net Assessment comes as close as anything to being the US government's imagination bureau. But Marshall wants no part of the responsibility for 9/11, despite having been an influential leader in the Pentagon for more than four decades.

Marshall is also associated with the view of China as a bellicose and hegemony-seeking power destined to clash with the US during the 21st century. Marshall is not surprisingly the darling of many neocon think tanks like Frank Gaffney's Center for Security Policy, one of the nerve centers of the neocon warmonger elite in Washington. "He's as Delphic as they come – days may go by before he utters a word," says a former member of Marshall's Office of Net Assessment. Says another: "He's hard to draw a bead on because he spends his time coming up with every conceivable future scenario that could threaten the US." Every one except 9/11, it would seem. According to Jonathan Pollack of the Naval War College in Newport, Rhode Island, Marshall "is not very interested in the here and now, but is primarily interested in hypothesizing futures that cut against the grain, and you can argue that we really do need someone like that. His interest is to take events as they are understood and find a way to turn them on their head, to conflate understanding, and look for patterns or possibilities that could be studied. And he often comes up with quirk results. It's like he thinks of the world as a bell curve and is only interested in the tails of distribution. [He is] a worrywart." But not overly worried about 9/11, as we have seen. (Jason Vest, "The Dubious Genius of Andrew Marshall," *The American Prospect Online*, February 15, 2001)

The official version of 9/11 says that the attacks came out of a distant cave in Afghanistan. But it makes more sense to explore networks and agencies which have means, motive, and opportunity, as well as a track record of advocating and promoting large-scale violence. Who knows what capabilities are being prepared even now in an isolated branch office of some private military firm, Armageddon network, public relations firm, or Utopian-reactionary think tank?

XV
ISLAMIC FUNDAMENTALISM: FOSTERED BY US FOREIGN POLICY

We must stress again that international terrorism should never be seen as a spontaneous sociological phenomenon arising directly out of oppression and misery. International terrorism and national liberation struggles are always mediated through a level of clandestine organization in which the efforts of intelligence agencies come decisively into play. Many international terrorist groups are false-flag operations from the very beginning. Others assume false-flag status as the result of coordinated arrests, assassinations, and takeovers by intelligence agencies. Even where there is an authentic national liberation organization, intelligence agencies will create false-flag operations under their own control to mimic it, perpetrating atrocities in its name in an effort to isolate and discredit it. Here again, deception and dissembling are the rule.

Again and again, terrorist groups with US-UK backing have intervened against progressive nationalists in the Arab world, and in favor of their Islamic fundamentalist competition.

Recruiting for terrorist groups once they exist is another matter. The ability to recruit is profoundly influenced by the prevalence of misery, poverty, and oppression. Here we must account for the relative economic and political distress of the Arab world, and of parts of the broader economic world as well. What we find are the fruits of imperialism, colonialism, and neo-colonialism. The political climate in the Arab world today cannot be understood as the outcome of autochthonous factors, as thinkers in the Oswald Spengler *Kultur* tradition like Samuel Huntington and Bernard Lewis would have us believe. These experts prefer to forget that the Arab world they see before them has been occupied, trampled, and manipulated by two centuries of European intervention, going back to Napoleon's invasion of Egypt. Neocons such as Lewis and Huntington also prefer a radically anti-historical approach, according to which anti-western Islamic fundamentalism, especially in its terrorist emanations, is simply a self-evident fact. But it is not a self-evident fact, as we now will seek to show.

What needs to be grasped is the fact that US policy, like that of the British Empire earlier, objectively favors the growth of Islamic fundamentalism. Islamic fundamentalism can mean many things, but here it is taken to mean an anti-western theocratic regime in which the Islamic clergy, mullahs, imams, and ayatollahs as they may be, play the leading role. We must recall that, until the Ottoman Empire was destroyed by the British and the French during the First World War, most of the countries of the Middle East had been subject to the Ottoman Sultan in Constantinople, who was simultaneously the Caliph of Islam. The Ottoman Empire claimed to operate according to the Islamic law, or sharia.

For centuries, the British had cultivated the smaller ethnic groups of the Ottoman Empire with a view to inciting them to rebel against the Ottoman Sultan: thus, the British began working with the Serbs around the time of the American Revolution; they helped the Greeks to become independent after the Napoleonic wars. Under Lord Palmerston in the 1830s and 1840s, the British introduced the ideas of a homeland for the Jews in Palestine. At first, British Jews were not interested: Lord Rothschild, it was said at that time, wanted a seat in the House of Lords, not a seat under a palm tree in Palestine. Later, the British developed a presence among the Copts, the Armenians, and others. The French posed as protectors of Christians in the Levant, and became the backers of the Lebanese Maronite Christians.

During these years the British Arab Bureau and the British Indian Office carefully profiled the Arab psychology and ideology. Their starting point was that the Arabs would inevitably become hostile to British colonialism, and that nothing could be done to prevent this. However, these British orientalists also concluded that it might well be possible to provide synthetic ideologies for the inevitable Arab revolt which would help to make it self-isolating, abortive, and impotent. An obvious way to do this was to make the revolt not specifically anti-British, but anti-western and anti-European in general, lest the Arabs be able to ally with Russia or Germany to eject the UK. The Islamic tradition offered the raw material for the fabrication of a synthetic ideology of Arab rejection of the west to which today's more fantastic ideologues of the Arab and Islamic worlds are much indebted.

When the Ottoman Empire took the German side during the First World War, British Col. T.E. Lawrence was able to incite the Arabs of the Hijaz (today's Saudi Arabia) to rebel against the Ottoman sultan. The British in effect promised that all Arab lands occupied by the Ottoman Turks would be turned over to the Arabs when the war had been won. However, with the Balfour Declaration of 1917, the British also promised part of this same territory to the Jews for their homeland. To make matters worse, the British and the French also promised most of these same lands to each other in the secret Sykes-Picot agreement.

Precisely because it was imperial, Ottoman imperial rule had not been conducive to intellectual or material progress – as had been understood by Aeneas Silvius Piccolomini and Nicholas Cusanus in the latter half of the fifteenth century when the Ottoman domination was beginning. The Ottoman peoples did not participate in the European Reformation and the wars of religion, notably the Thirty Years War, which had convinced Europeans that political solutions and war-avoidance were better than hecatombs of slaughter waged by doctrinaire religious factions. Ottoman economic development also lagged behind that of Europe. Because of these conditions, there are basically four types of regimes which are currently possible in the ex-Ottoman territories. These are:

1. **Reactionary monarchies** – This was the variant at first favored by the British when they occupied various Arab states under the League of

Nations mandates after 1918. Working with the House of Saud and the Hashemite family, the British promoted monarchy in Egypt, Saudi Arabia, Iraq, Syria, and Jordan. These regimes, like that of King Farouk in Egypt, were widely viewed as corrupt puppets of the imperialists who were not interested in national progress, but rather in amassing private wealth. In Saudi Arabia, for example, human chattel slavery remained legal until 1965, and was widely practiced after that, especially in households. Household slavery also remains common in the Gulf emirates, and explodes onto the local pages of the Washington papers every now and then when a visiting diplomat from the Gulf brings a personal slave or two on a diplomatic mission. Ironically, chattel slavery was abolished in Kuwait thanks to the Iraqi invasion of 1990, but was then re-established with the help of Bush's Operation Desert Storm in 1991. (Tarpley 1996) Most of the Arab monarchs were overthrown, although monarchy still hangs on in Morocco, Saudi Arabia, Jordan, and among the petty princelings of the Gulf. Iran, although not an Arab country, was ruled by an emperor until 1979. Clearly, these regimes are not suitable for the task of economic development and general progress in their countries.

2. **Modernizing nationalist regimes** – These may be democratic republics, but they are more likely to be military governments possibly evolving into plebiscitary forms of democracy. They may call themselves Arab socialists, as Nasser did. The best hope the Arabs had of sharing in the level of scientific and technological progress attained in the most advanced parts of the world was offered by nationalist regimes whose program was one of economic development and modernization. The prime example was that of Mustafa Kemal **Ataturk**, who created the first permanent republic in Asia, the **Turkish Republic** of 1923. Rejecting the sultanate and the caliphate in favor of the Turkish nation, Ataturk implemented the separation of mosque and state, making Turkey a modern, secular republic. He introduced the Roman alphabet in place of Arabic script, outlawed the veil for women and the fez for men, and promoted the European hat as the "headgear of civilization." Harems were discouraged, while women were given the right to vote and held public office. Ataturk introduced the Gregorian calendar, the metric system, and family names. A dirigist five-year plan for economic development was introduced in 1933. Public law was based on modern European criminal and civil codes, rather than the sharia. Ataturk saw religion as a matter of purely personal and private belief and preference, and all religions were tolerated. Ataturk would have to rank at or near the top of any list of the nation-builders and modernizers of the twentieth century. Among his other achievements, he helped Turkey to be the only defeated power of World War I which escaped fascist rule. In retrospect, if there was one experiment in the Muslim world which the US should

have supported, it was that of Ataturk. If his ideas had prevailed more generally, there could be no talk of the clash of civilizations today. Given this impressive record, how did the Allies of World War I, including the United States treat Ataturk? They tried with every means possible to overthrow him, to isolate him, and to carve Turkey into a series of petty states. In the Peace of Paris in 1919, the Treaty of Versailles with Germany was bad, but the Treaty of Sèvres which was imposed upon Turkey was an act of grotesque lunacy. It was clearly the peace to end all peace. Turkey was supposed to be divided into French, Italian, and Greek zones of occupation, while the Bosporus and the Dardanelles were occupied by the British and French. There was an attempt to create an independent Armenia in eastern Anatolia. The British and French even attempted to lure the US into taking over a piece of Turkey, but in those days the US was smart enough to decline. That was fortunate, since Ataturk was able to defeat the armies the Allies threw at him; he was able to guarantee the national independence and territorial integrity of Turkey. His brutal treatment of Greeks and Armenians, who were fighting for the Allies, must be seen in this context. Ataturk was not the first of his type; that honor may go to the Albanian Mohamed Ali Pasha of Egypt, a general with an ambitious program of industrialization and reforms who also annexed Syria in 1839, foreshadowing Nasser's United Arab Republic.

3. **Hereditary dictatorships** – These hereditary dictatorships have emerged after the fall of monarchies, and sometimes occur as a degenerate form of the nationalist-modernizing state. Key examples are the regime of Hafez Assad and his son in Syria after 1963, and indeed that of Saddam Hussein in Iraq, with the first being far more odious. Hafez Assad ruled a murderous, pervasive police state in which the minority Allawites ruled over a resentful majority. Yet, Assad was always the darling of New York and London: Kissinger once said that he hoped God would forgive him, but that there would always be a soft spot in his heart for Hafez Assad. The regimes of Hosni Mubarak in Egypt and of the mercurial Colonel Qaddafi in Libya can be assimilated to this group.

4. **Fundamentalist theocracies** – The leading example is Iran, which is enough to show that this form cannot be effective for national development in the hostile climate of globalization. In 1978, President Carter's National Security Director Zbigniew Brzezinski, anxious to avenge Soviet support for North Vietnam against the US in the recent Vietnam War, was convinced by British Arabists and orientalists that Islamic fundamentalism could be used to destabilize the five large Muslim-majority republics of Soviet central Asia – Kazakhstan, Uzbekistan, Tajikistan, Khirgizia, and Turkmenistan. This outlook could also be employed to disrupt the ethnic labyrinth of the Caucasus and Trans-Caucasus – notably in Chechnya. In this way, Brzezinski argued, Islamic fundamentalism could become the definitive "bulwark against

communism." In order to provide a powerful center from which this new ideology could radiate, Brzezinski and Carter connived to foment a typical CIA "people power" pseudo-revolution, this time with Islamic fundamentalist overtones, in order to overthrow the Shah of Iran in 1979. The Shah was personally in many respects a monster, and his Savak secret police were as murderous as any in the world. However, the Shah was bringing in European construction firms to create infrastructure and whole new cities; a good example was the immense building operation at Bandar Abbas (today Bandar Khomeini) by the Italian civil engineering firm Condotte d'Acqua under Loris Corbi. But since the Shah could not tolerate free political activity, he had no effective mass political party to support him. The chosen instrument for the Shah's ouster was the benighted Ayatollah Khomeini, a figure of ineffable darkness, worse than Savonarola. Let there be no mistake: Brzezinski did everything to overthrow the Shah, and then to make sure that no secular politician like Shapour Baktiar took power in his stead: US Air Force Gen. Robert Huyser from Al Haig's NATO staff was sent to Iran with the message that only Khomeini would be acceptable to the United States. (Dreyfus and La Levée 50-53) The rise of Khomeini represented a novelty in the recent history of the Middle East: it was a theocracy of the Islamic clerics or mullahs, bankrolled by wealthy bazaar merchants and related interests. The ascendancy of Khomeini meant that Iran's economic and cultural development was frozen – or in reverse – for most of two decades. But Khomeini's Iran did become a center of propagation of Islamic fundamentalist ideology, just as Brzezinski had intended, although the Soviets were not the only ones to pay the price. Soon the US-UK intelligence agencies were able to play Iraq against Iran in the 8-year long Gulf War of the 1980s, which wrecked and bankrupted both societies even further. The Israelis were so pleased with this war that they wanted it to go on forever, while the Iranian mullahs organized suicidal human wave assaults by little children against prepared and fortified Iraqi positions.

Despite neocon blathering about democracy, and Bush's so-called Middle East initiative, the US never had any serious plans for democracy in Iraq. To begin with, the US itself cannot seriously be described as a democracy; the US is currently an oligarchy in Plato's precise definition of a "constitution teeming with many evils...based on a property qualification...wherein the rich hold office and the poor man is excluded," a system favoring "the member of a ruling class – oligarchy." (*Republic* 544c, 550c, 545a) Sure enough, the regime created by the US in Iraq in the spring of 2003 was an ... oligarchy, composed of twenty-five handpicked puppet oligarchs with a weak revolving presidency. Such arrangements have been perpetuated after the alleged restoration of Iraqi sovereignty. US interference in post-communist Russia favored oligarchical domination through the Yeltsin coterie in a similar way. As of right now, there is probably not a sufficient material-economic basis for western-style democracy in Iraq, although after several years of economic reconstruction there might well be. But in any case, it is clear that the US as presently constituted is no longer a progressive force on the world scene – which was not always the case in the past.

The open secret of the post-1945 world is that the US and the other NATO states have systematically and implacably opposed the reasonable alternative of modernizing secular nationalism among the Arab and Islamic states, while favoring the fundamentalist alternative, the more benighted the better. Modernizing secular nationalists are by far the most effective adversaries of the imperialists – they have the potential to score real political, diplomatic and cultural gains for their countries. Theocratic reactionaries are easier to isolate, since their appeal is more circumscribed. In practice, Washington and London have always fostered the rise of fundamentalists, while attempting to eliminate modernizing nationalists.

It must be added that while fundamentalist figures like Ayatollah Khomeini of Iran were baneful from every point of view, there are today perfectly reasonable figures who identify themselves as Islamists – people like Adel Hussein of Egypt and Hassan Turabi of Sudan. These figures seem to represent something of the progressive impulses of the 1950s-1960s, expressed today within the dominant Islamic idiom. Significantly, these figures are incessantly vilified and targeted by imperialists of all stripes. If reasonable policies were ever to re-emerge in the west, reasonable Islamists would have no trouble in finding modes of cooperation.

Despite US-UK hostility, Arab leaders of the Nasser type had some margin of maneuver as long as the Soviets offered some kind of an alternative to Washington and London. But as the USSR weakened and finally disintegrated, this margin grew narrower and finally disappeared in 1991, when the Soviets could do nothing for their former ally, Iraq.

Iran – After World War II, the first attempt to renew the progressive nationalism of Ataturk came with the rise of Prime Minister **Mossadeq** in Iran. Mossadeq's program centered on the 1951 nationalization of the Anglo-Iranian Oil Company, known today as BP. With the breaking of the British protectorate in Iran, the fledgling CIA of Allen Dulles and Kermit Roosevelt organized a military coup against Mossadeq, which was followed by a restoration of imperialist control over Iran's oil, and an era of political reaction under the Shah.

Egypt – In 1952, a group of nationalist army officers ousted the notoriously corrupt and inept King Farouk. A coup by junior officers brought Colonel Gamal abd el **Nasser** to power. Nasser's progressive nationalist program was based on the expulsion of the British occupation forces, followed by the nationalization of the Suez Canal, with the canal tolls being used to finance the building of the Aswan High Dam on the Upper Nile. The Aswan project was key for flood control and hydroelectric energy, on the model of FDR's Tennessee Valley Authority. After the British were gone, Nasser seized the canal with great fanfare, becoming an Egyptian national hero. Nasser was quickly opposed by British Prime Minister Sir Anthony Eden and the Dulles brothers, and soon became the target of a British-French-Israeli intrigue: Israel would launch a surprise attack across the Sinai, and an Anglo-French task force would seize the canal under the guise of restoring order. This crude conspiracy led to the Suez crisis of October-November 1956, and was seen as a personal affront by US President Eisenhower. After the USSR issued a unique nuclear ultimatum to the British and French, threatening London and Paris with nuclear destruction, the US and the USSR joined in the UN Security Council to vote against the old-style Anglo-French imperialists and their Israeli auxiliaries. The US position in the post-1956 Middle East was founded on the broad sympathy won when Washington torpedoed the adventurous plans of the British and French imperialists. Sadly, those gains were totally squandered during the subsequent decades, as the US itself assumed the role of the chief imperial oppressor of the Arab states. But in 1956, Nasser's Egypt had clearly emerged as the leading Arab state. Egypt became the nucleus of an attempted re-unification of the Arab world in the form of a secular United Arab Republic, which Syria and Yemen joined, and towards which Iraq gravitated for a time. Nasser used his radio, the Voice of the Arabs, to condemn the Saudi monarchy for its practice of chattel slavery, especially of black Africans. Egypt became the target of another Israeli pre-emptive attack in the June 1967 Six-Day War, and was unable fully to recover in the 1973 Yom Kippur War, which was orchestrated by Kissinger. As for Nasser, he was hounded mercilessly until he died in 1970. He was replaced by Sadat, who ousted the Soviet advisers Nasser had brought in. But even Sadat was too much of a nationalist for the Anglo-Americans: he was assassinated in 1980 by a group which included al-Zawahiri, today alleged to be bin Laden's right-hand man and personal physician. Despite his role in the Sadat assassination, Zawahiri was able to live openly in London for years. This suggests that Zawahiri is indeed an asset of MI-6.

Iraq – When the British seized control of Iraq in 1919, they installed a reactionary monarchy of the Hashemites. In 1958, the puppet monarch King Faisal was assassinated. General **Kassem** became prime minister and instituted a program of modernizing reforms, including the progressive constitution of 1959. The 1959 Iraqi constitution and other Kassem-era legislation made literacy compulsory, abolished slavery, and guaranteed equal rights for women. The impact of these reforms was permanent. To cite only one example, during the mid-1970s the Iraqi Ambassador to Rome was a highly intelligent woman, Selima Bakir. As any Iraqi nationalist would, Kassem assumed the position that Kuwait was an integral part of Iraq. In this he was correct since Kuwait had been illegally detached from the Ottoman Empire by the British in 1899 to prevent the German-sponsored Berlin to Baghdad railway from ever reaching the head of the Gulf. In 1962 the British fomented a revolt of the Kurds under the Barzani clan, and Kassem was assassinated in 1963. After Kassem was assassinated by the CIA and replaced by then CIA asset Saddam Hussein, the chance for successful development in Iraq was severely limited. The positive features of Iraq during the Saddam Hussein years were largely inherited from the Kassem era.

Pakistan – The great opportunity for modernization in Pakistan came under **Ali Bhutto** in the mid-1970s. Bhutto was determined to advance his country to the leading edge of modern technology with a peaceful nuclear energy program in the Eisenhower Atoms for Peace tradition. He was soon confronted by Kissinger, who threatened to make a terrible example of him unless he desisted from his ambitious development plans. Shortly thereafter, Bhutto was overthrown by the US-supported coup of General Zia ul Haq. Bhutto was framed up on various charges and hanged by the new regime in accordance with Kissinger's earlier threats. Bhutto's wife and children later took refuge in West Germany. Fundamentalist tendencies have grown in the era following the death of Bhutto.

Kosovo – When the Federal Republic of Yugoslavia began to break up in 1991, the ethnic Albanian Muslim population of the province of Kosovo under the leadership of the secular nationalist LDK party responded by a highly effective non-violent self-organizing process, which allowed them to defy the Serb occupiers for most of the rest of the 1990s. Using the tools of passive resistance, the Kosovars created their own parallel government, including their own school system, their own separate elections, their own public health system, and their own parallel system of economic enterprises. The leader of this magnificent effort was Ibrahim **Rugova**, who made pilgrimage after pilgrimage to Washington during the 1990s, always sporting the Parisian red silk scarf which was his trademark. But the US was never willing to lift a finger for Rugova and the eminently reasonable LDK. When Slovenia, Croatia and Bosnia declared independence from Serb-dominated Yugoslavia, Rugova hesitated: the Kosovars, unlike the others, had no guns, and the US had never provided them. In 1997, the neighboring state of Albania, with which the Kosovars wished to be united, disintegrated as the result of the collapse of a series of Ponzi-scheme financial speculations. As the Albanian state collapsed, its weapons depots were looted, and many of these weapons soon found their way across the border into Kosovo. This engendered the Kosovo Liberation Army (KLA), a very dubious outfit composed of narcotics smugglers, Islamic fundamentalists from Kosovo and abroad, and out-and-out terrorists. As the KLA's clashes with the Serbian police and army increased, the Serbs responded as any occupier would, and atrocities on both sides became the order of the day. This time the US, in the person of Madeleine Albright, became the direct sponsor of the terrorist KLA. Starting in March, 1999, the US and NATO waged a criminal 78-day bombing campaign against Serbia, one of the great acts of international vandalism in then late twentieth century – all in support of KLA-related demands. As for Rugova and the LDK, they were trampled, and the US depended more and more on the KLA.

Afghanistan – This country was able to manage some slow modernization during the 1950s under the king Mohammed Zahir Shah, who had assumed the throne in 1933. Afghan development has always hinged on a large hydroelectric and water project in the center of the country, which has never been fully carried out. The King was deposed in 1973, and by 1978 there emerged the progressive regime of **Noor Mohammed Taraki,** a pro-Marxist poet and novelist with very special talents. Taraki legalized trade unions, instituted a minimum wage, and promoted housing, health care, and public sanitation. He favored improvements in the status of women. Taraki tried to eradicate the cultivation of the opium poppy, which had made his country the world's leading producer of heroin. Taraki also cancelled all debts owed by farmers, including tenant farmers, and began a land reform program to break up the holdings of absentee landlords and latifundists. Taraki thus offended the feudal interest, which was strong in the country. Brzezinski regarded Taraki as a Soviet asset, and later boasted to the *Nouvel Observateur* that US destabilization teams launched a clandestine operation against Taraki in early 1979, prominently playing the Islamic fundamentalist card. In September 1979 there followed a US-backed coup by the CIA asset Hafizulla Amin, who executed Taraki and rolled back his reforms in the name of setting up a fundamentalist Islamic state in the service of the feudal landowners. Amin's reactionary measures resulted in a backlash against him, and he was himself toppled within two months. In the face of renewed assaults by Brzezinski's opium-poppy mujahideen, the Soviets invaded Afghanistan at Christmas, 1979. During the various phases of the Afghan war that followed, the CIA always supported the most benighted, the most reactionary, the most opium-mongering factions – especially their favorite, Gulbuddin Hekmatyar.

The CIA was looking for forces of absolute self-isolating negativity, incapable of getting along with Iran or anyone else. In the decade of war that followed (December 1979- February 1989), Afghanistan was economically and demographically destroyed. The second generation of Brzezinski's mujahideen, the Islamic fundamentalist students or Taliban, assumed power in 1994. Like Pol Pot in Cambodia in the wake of Kissinger's bombing destruction of that country in the 1970s, the Taliban represented an unspeakable retrogression towards barbarity. But, just as Kissinger and G. H. W. Bush had supported Pol Pot, the Bush 41 administration found many ways to support the Taliban, who were viewed as ideal because of their inability to ally with Iran or any of the ex-Soviet central Asian republics. As Michael Parenti has pointed out, the US taxpayers paid the salaries of the entire Taliban government in 1999. (Parenti 65) And under Bush 43, this support became even more explicit, as Unocal lobbyists sought a deal with the Taliban to build their oil pipeline to central Asia. During this phase, Kissinger, neocon Zalmay Khalilzad, retired State Department anti-terror official Robert Oakley and Leila Helms (daughter of the former CIA director) were successfully lobbying on behalf of Unocal.

The goal was to keep the Taliban regime off the State Department terrorist state list, since that would have blocked any pipeline deal. In his first spring in office, Bush offered a large grant to the Taliban. This caused columnist Robert Scheer to comment: "Enslave your girls and women, harbor anti-US terrorists, destroy every vestige of civilization in your homeland, and the Bush administration will embrace you. That's the message sent with the recent gift of

$43 million to the Taliban rulers of Afghanistan. The gift…makes the US the main sponsor of the Taliban." ("Bush's Faustian Deal with the Taliban," *Los Angeles Times*, May 22, 2001)

Palestine – After Israel had occupied the West Bank of the Jordan River, the Gaza Strip and the Sinai Peninsula in June 1967, the Israelis found themselves ruling over some two million Palestinians. Under the United Nations system it is illegal to annex territory acquired through armed conflict without the approval of the United Nations Security Council, which in this case was not forthcoming. Rather, the UNSC passed resolution 242, calling on Israel to withdraw to the internationally recognized borders from June 1967. (In the run-up to the Iraq war, Bush spokesmen accused Iraq of having violated some 17 United Nations Security Council resolutions; they conveniently forgot that Israel was the all-time champion in that department, since Israel is currently in violation of some 30 UNSC resolutions regarded the territories it has occupied since 1967. But the US never proposed war to enforce compliance with those resolutions.) The Israeli occupation of conquered Palestine was oppressive and humiliating, and a national resistance soon emerged in the form of the Palestinian Liberation Organization (PLO). Its leader was **Yasser Arafat**, a secular nationalist more or less in the Nasser mold. Since the PLO had few weapons, and since the Israeli army was a dominant presence, the PLO began doing what the Jews had done between 1945 and 1948 against the British occupation of the same territory: they launched guerrilla warfare, which the occupiers quickly labeled terrorism. The official Israeli line was that there was no Palestinian people, but this was soon disproved.

From the beginning, the Israeli Mossad was active in conducting provocations which it sought to attribute to the PLO and its peripheries: attacks on airliners and on the 1972 Olympic games in Munich are therefore of uncertain paternity. The more horrendous the atrocity, the greater the backlash of world public opinion against the PLO. There is no doubt that the Mossad controlled a part of the central committee of the organization known as Abu Nidal, after the *nom de guerre* of its leader, Sabri al Banna. In 1987-88, just as the first Palestinian intifada uprising was getting under way, there emerged in the occupied territories the organization known as Hamas. Hamas combined a strong commitment to neighborhood social services with the rejection of negotiations with Israel and the demand for a military solution which was sure to be labeled terrorism. Interestingly enough, one of the leading sponsors of Hamas was Ariel Sharon, a former general who was then a cabinet minister.

These facts are widely recognized: US Ambassador to Israel Daniel Kurzer, an observant Jew, stated late in 2001 that Hamas had emerged "with the tacit support of Israel" because in the late 1980s "Israel perceived it would be better to have people turning toward religion, rather then toward a nationalistic cause." (*Ha'aretz*, Dec. 21, 2001) In an acrimonious Israeli cabinet debate around the same time, Israeli extremist Knesset member Silva Shalom stated: "between Hamas and Arafat, I prefer Hamas…Arafat is a terrorist in a diplomat's suit, while the Hamas can be hit unmercifully." (*Ha'aretz*, Dec. 4, 2001) This tirade provoked a walkout by Shimon Peres and the other Labor Party ministers. Arafat added his own view, which was that "Hamas is a creature of Israel which, at the time of Prime Minister Shamir, gave them money and more than 700 institutions, among them schools, universities, and mosques. Even [Israeli Prime Minister] Rabin ended up admitting it, when I charged him with it, in the presence of Mubarak." (*Corriere della Sera*, Dec. 11, 2001) With incredible arrogance, the Bush administration has pronounced Arafat as unfit to be a negotiating partner. In effect, they are choosing Hamas – or worse, an act of incalculable folly for Israel and for the United States as well.

This list could go on and on. In Bangladesh, Kissinger persecuted Sheikh Mujibur Rahman of the Awami League, the leading nationalist force on the scene after independence in the early 1970s. In Lebanon, Kissinger did everything possible to destroy the 1943 multi-sectarian constitution and set off a civil war. Later, when Gen. Aoun, a Maronite Christian but much more a Lebanese nationalist, attempted to save the country's independence, he was sabotaged by the United States.

The flip side of this pattern is the brutal treatment meted out to those in Europe who have wanted to make development deals with the Arab states on the obvious basis of mutual advantage. A celebrated case is that of the elimination of Enrico Mattei, the president of the Italian state oil company, ENI, as we saw in Ch. II. The German banker Juergen Ponto was interested in financing development projects in the Arab world and in Africa; he was eliminated by the Baader-Meinhof gang in 1977. It is evident that the Baader-Meinhof was acting as a false-flag operation for CIA and MI-6. There were some thirty attempts to assassinate French President Charles de Gaulle. There were many motivations for this, but a prominent one was the pro-Arab diplomacy of the French government.

Given the implacable US and NATO persecution of progressive Arab nationalist leaders, this breed has tended to disappear entirely from the scene. With the remaining choices narrowed to reactionary monarchies, such as the Saudis, repressive dictatorships, such as that typified by Hafez Assad, or experiments with Islamic fundamentalism, it is not surprising that many young Arabs regard the fundamentalists as the viable option. If the western powers do not like this, they must be reminded that it is they who have, with their mindless imperialist arrogance, rendered the progressive nationalists almost extinct.

As I stated in 1994 in my address to the Inter-Religious Conference in Khartoum, Sudan, the basis of Christianity comes down to the two great commandments: love God, and love your neighbor as yourself. Love of God is a matter of faith, about the details of which it may prove impossible to agree. But where agreement is eminently possible is the second sphere: love your neighbor, the Golden Rule. In today's world, love your neighbor means good works in the form of large-scale economic and infrastructural development projects to tackle the still-unfinished business of the post-1945 world: the integral scientific, technological, and economic advancement of the former colonial sector, of the third world. Here Christian charity converges with Muslim social solidarity, with Confucian benevolence, with the similar imperatives in Buddhism and Hinduism, and with the imperatives readily embraced by secularists of good will.

Not so long ago, the world witnessed United Nations Development Decades, oil for technology conferences, and related international efforts to promote world economic development. Today such efforts have disappeared. All that remains is globalization, which is destroying the Arab and Islamic worlds in the same way it is destroying every other part of the planet. Deranged thinkers like Huntington, Brzezinski, and Kissinger imagine that their crude geopolitics is a clever, even cunning pursuit of US imperial self-interest. In reality, their policies are suicidal. If we wish to identify some policies which have actually worked well for the United States in past years, the census looks as follows:

The Monroe Doctrine, for establishing the United States as a supporter of the rights of small nations to the freedom of the seas, and as an opponent of European colonialism.

The Atlantic Charter of 1941, for proposing the Four Freedoms – freedom of speech, freedom of religion, freedom from fear, freedom from want – as the basis for the postwar world.

The Bretton Woods system of 1944-1971, for using New Deal methods to foster the greatest economic expansion the world has ever seen.

The Marshall Plan of 1947, for providing a model of economic reconstruction for war-ravaged Europe, and for preventing a resurgence of economic depression in the US.

The US response to the 1956 Suez crisis, for repudiating imperial domination of the Middle East, and advocating fair treatment for the Arabs.

The strong world position of the US in the third quarter of the twentieth century was largely due to these policies. Today's neocons and their fellow travelers are structurally and temperamentally incapable of advocating anything so effective. New leadership in the wake of the expected US party re-alignment is required. These policies must of course be supplemented by the creation of an independent and sovereign Palestinian state in the west bank and Gaza, made viable by a comprehensive economic development program from which all states in the region, including Israel, should benefit.

In the meantime, the US must drop its double standard on terrorism: Israel's policy of targeted assassination of its opponents without benefit of judicial process is the essence of state-sponsored terrorism, no matter how many times it is endorsed by Cheney. The US has armed Israel with $70 billion worth of weapons, including the F-16s and missiles which are used to kill Palestinian civilians in direct violation of US law. All such US aid should be used as a lever to secure Israeli acceptance of the two-state solution. These steps would go far towards inhibiting terrorist recruitment.

XVI
ELECTION 2004: IN THE SHADOW
OF SYNTHETIC TERRORISM AND WAR

It will happen here.
– Bush administration official, Spring 2004.

By the end of May 2004, an intelligence pattern pointed conclusively to the grave and open-ended threat of a new round of synthetic ABC (atomic-bacteriological-chemical) terror attacks in the United States, Great Britain, Canada, and possibly other nations. This threat included nuclear detonations, radiological dirty bombs, poison gas and other chemical weapons, or biological agents, to be unleashed in such urban settings as New York City, Los Angeles, Chicago, Washington DC, Vancouver BC, or London. The putative goal of these operations was to produce a worldwide shock several orders of magnitude greater than the original 9/11, with a view to stopping the collapse of the Bush administration, the Wall Street-centered financial structures, and the US-UK strategic position generally.

US/UK intelligence was prepared to attribute responsibility to controlled patsy terrorist groups, which in turn the media would link to countries like Iran, Syria, Cuba, North Korea, or Saudi Arabia, thus setting these states up for attack. Behind the threat was substantially the same secret command cell in the United States which set up the 9/11 events, which had been able to continue in operation because of the abject failure of all 9/11 investigations to identify them. These forces were in a desperate flight forward to escape from their increasingly grim position. Their goal was to establish a neocon fascist dictatorship in the United States, complete with martial law, special tribunals, press and media censorship, and the full pervasive apparatus of the modern police state.

The chatter in Washington in late spring 2004 pointed to state-sponsored terrorism on a grand scale, with the desperados of the neocon faction calling the shots. The rogues were once again inclined to score an "own goal" of the Americans. Given the prominence of the Congress, it could also have been called Operation Guy Fawkes, recalling the state plot to blow up the Houses of Parliament on November 5, 1605.

Reliance on synthetic terrorism as a matter of *raison d'état* (the right of the state above the law; ends justifying means) was like a heroin habit: as each dose wore off, another and more powerful injection was required. In May 2002, some 300 government, military and business executives met in a seminar entitled "Homeland Security 2005: Charting the Course Ahead," which was conducted by the ANSER Institute for Homeland Security. ANSER ("Advancing National Strategy and Enabling Results") was created in 1958 by RAND and the Air Force

as a contract advisory agency on national security. The seminar participants
were already lamenting that the government had not "managed to engage the
American people" in supporting the urgency of changes in national security
organization. UPI reported that "several participants" – who asked to remain
anonymous – said "they felt that without another terrorist incident, keeping
public attention to the gaps in security and support for the expenditures was
growing more difficult." Conference speakers included Lawrence Castro, NSA
Coordinator for Homeland Security Support; Rear Admiral Richard Cobbold,
Director of Britain's Royal United Services Institute for Defense Studies; Leon
Fuerth; Frank Gaffney; several officials of the Office of Homeland Security; and
numerous former Defense Department and CIA officials. (ANSER website, May
6, 2002)

The new phase in the campaign for martial law and a state of emergency
began during the closing months of 2003, when it was clear to insiders that the
Iraq adventure was headed for defeat. In his year-end column of December 31,
2003, *New York Times* neocon and Nixon emeritus William Safire cynically
predicted that the "October surprise" for the 2004 election would come in the
form of "a major terror attack in the US." The United States was, in short, once
more threatened by a coup d'état – not a coup against the existing government,
but an operation aimed at shocking, disciplining and dragooning the entire
political process for escalated foreign aggression, with the homeland secured by
emergency rule. It went without saying that those associated with such a coup
were felons, war criminals, and traitors to their country.

On May 26, 2004 Attorney General Ashcroft and FBI Director Robert
Mueller announced a coming summer "perfect storm" of terrorism. According to
advance wire service reports, US officials had "obtained new intelligence
deemed highly credible indicating Al-Qaeda or other terrorists are in the United
States and preparing to launch a major attack this summer….(AP, May 25, 2004)
This was accompanied by an unprecedented propaganda barrage. A few samples
will suffice.

THE BUSH REGIME TALKS TERROR

Bush and Cheney had made the demagogy of terror their stock in trade and
daily bread since 9/11. But April 2004 marked a watershed, a qualitative
escalation. On April 21, Bush delivered two speeches which represented a
palpable escalation of his usual tone of fear. In the afternoon, he assured the
Newspaper Association of America, composed of newspaper editors, that Iran
"will be dealt with" if they pursue a nuclear development program. Bush went on
to characterize the United States as "a battlefield in the war on terror." He was at
pains to build up the stature of Al Qaeda, whose members he emphatically
characterized as "smart…tough…and sophisticated." Because the terrorists were
so formidable, Bush said the United States "is a hard country to defend. Our
intelligence is good. It's just never perfect, is the problem. We are disrupting

some cells here in America. We're chasing people down. But it is – we've got a big country."

Later, Bush spoke to the same themes at a closed-door gathering at the White House: "...On Tuesday evening, Bush told Republican congressional leaders during a meeting at the White House that it was all but certain that terrorists would attempt a major attack on the United States before the election, according to a congressional aide. The leaders were struck by Bush's definitiveness and gravity, the aide said..." (*Washington Post*, April 22, 2004)

It must be remembered that synthetic terrorism depends on many people doing things that make sense to them within their own limited purviews, but which are in fact dictated by the needs of the operation of which they are a part. Bush might think he was just practicing smart politics by inculcating fear in the US citizenry. The reality behind the statements was an insurrectionary network of moles inside the federal government who would stop at nothing. They marched to the tune of a private command center outside of the government which also deployed patsies and expert professionals. Not every official who parroted the terror line was aware of what might be coming, although his speechwriter or other handlers might. When we come to figures like Cheney, the likelihood that he was a witting participant rises substantially.

Vice President Cheney had been predicting imminent terrorist attacks on the US in many of his speeches since no later than May 20, 2002. On that day, Cheney went on Fox News Sunday to announce that "In my opinion, the prospects of a future attack against the United States are almost certain." For Cheney, the question of a new terrorist assault on the US is "not a matter of if, but when."

Several weeks later, an account published under the title "White House Nightmare Scenario" in the "Washington Whispers" column of *US News and World Report* reflected the thinking of top Bush officials about the relation between terrorism and the coming US presidential elections. According to this article, 'White House officials say they've got a "working premise" about terrorism and the presidential election: It's going to happen. "We assume," says a top administration official, "an attack will happen leading up to the election." And, he added, "it will happen here." There are two worst-case scenarios, the official says. The first posits an attack on Washington, possibly the Capitol, which was believed to be the target of the 9/11 jet that crashed in Pennsylvania. Theory 2: smaller but more frequent attacks in Washington and other major cities leading up to the election. To prepare, the administration has been holding secret anti-terrorism drills to make sure top officials know what to do. "There was a sense," says one official involved in the drills, "of mass confusion on 9/11. Now we have a sense of order." Unclear is the political impact, though most Bushies think the nation would rally around the president. "I can tell you one thing," adds the official sternly, "we won't be like Spain," which tossed its government days after the Madrid train bombings.' (*US News and World Report*, 17 May 2004)

National Security Adviser Condoleezza Rice told Fox News on Sunday, April 19, that the government was bracing for possible terrorist attacks before November's Presidential election. Referencing March's Madrid bombings, she said the opportunity for terrorists to influence the election might "be too good to pass up for them," and that "the terrorists might have learned, we hope, the wrong lesson from Spain." [sic] Rice expatiated on this theme: "I think we also have to take seriously that [terrorists] might try during the cycle leading up to the election to do something…. In some ways, it seems like it would be too good to pass up for them, and so we are actively looking at that possibility, actively trying to make certain that we are responding appropriately." Hinting that preparations to defend against a terror attack might not be successful, she added, "The hard thing about terrorism is that they only have to be right once, and we have to be right 100 percent of the time. And nobody can be certain there won't be another attack."

AZNAR'S ATTEMPTED TERROR-ASSISTED COUP

Condoleezza Rice's remarks came in the context of a lengthy US tour by José María Aznar, the defeated Spanish Prime Minister. Aznar was ousted in Spain's March 13 elections, partly because 90% of Spaniards rejected Aznar's subservience to Bush in joining the US invasion coalition in Iraq, and partly because Spanish voters were convinced that Aznar was lying about the March 11 terrorist attacks on commuter trains in the Madrid region. Aznar was defeated by the magnificent mobilization of Spanish trade unions and left parties against terrorism; this recalled the actions of the German unions, who had stopped the Kapp-Luttwitz putsch of 1920 with a general strike.

Aznar was counted as a neocon, and his party contained the remnants of Francisco Franco's falangist-fascist apparatus. Aznar promoted the thesis that the March 11 terrorist attacks decided the Spanish elections in favor of the PSOE (socialist) challenger, Zapatero, and that his own defeat was a victory for terrorism, since the newly elected Zapatero, acting in conformity with the will of the Spanish people, withdrew the Spanish troop contingent from Iraq soon after taking office.

The Spanish elections were viewed with hysteria by Washington elites, first because of the Spanish quitting the coalition, but also because the terrorist attacks had failed to produce the expected effects. The Washington consensus had previously been that terrorism would infallibly stampede the voters of any country into voting for the incumbent, but this time the anti-Bush challenger was the beneficiary. Aznar was known to have attempted to call off the Spanish vote and to continue to rule by decree, but his efforts were blocked. Aznar's briefing would seem to have included the notion that if there was going to be pre-election terrorism, it needed to be of sufficient magnitude to provide a pretext for calling off all scheduled elections.

In mid-April, Aznar began issuing warnings of election-related terrorism, directed most immediately to Tony Blair and George Bush. Aznar said, "I told George Bush, and Tony Blair and other political leaders to be extremely careful before elections ... and to be very vigilant." (*Once Noticias*, Once-TV, Mexico, April 19, 2004; EIR, May 22, 2004) During his visit to California, Aznar referred more than once to a terrorist attack to take place in the United States in June, 2004, which would lead to a Federal Emergency Management Agency takeover of the country. (*International Herald Tribune*, May 15, 16, 17, *Los Angeles Times*, May 15, 2004)

On May 18, *El Pais* reported that Aznar had visited Los Angeles and then went on to Washington, where he met Defense Secretary Rumsfeld. Present at the meeting were various Democratic and Republican Congressmen. After the meeting, during an appearance at the Heritage Foundation, Rumsfeld spoke about Aznar's briefing: "In Spain, in Madrid, the terrorists changed the result of the elections, without any doubt. In a premeditated way, as a consequence of the intentions of the terrorists, the election results were changed. I had dinner with Prime Minister Aznar, and he is convinced that this is how it happened." In California, Aznar told the press on Monday that Islamic terrorism has as objective to influence elections in democratic countries. "If they could do it in Spain, why would they not intend to do it in another place?" he said and added, "It's important to understand that the terrorists will do everything to change the next elections in the USA. They will do everything possible to make the US fail."

He furthermore said in Los Angeles that he thought that the government of Zapatero sent an "inappropriate message to the terrorists by withdrawing the troops." Aznar also had a 40-minute meeting with President Bush in the White House. Present at the meeting were: Vice President Dick Cheney, Condoleezza Rice, Colin Powell, and White House Chief of Staff Andrew Card. The White House press spokesman identified the meeting as "private" – "a meeting with a good friend of the President."

An important sidelight on these statements by Aznar was the revelation that the group accused of carrying out the Madrid bombings was thoroughly penetrated by informants working for the Spanish police, according to *El Mundo* of May 6, 2004. The Madrid bombings were synthetic terrorism. *El Mundo* reported that among the people arrested for the Madrid bombing were two police informants. This paper published an exclusive report given by Rafa Zhueri, who was among those arrested after the bombings. Zhueri revealed that he had worked for years as a police informant for a unit of the Spanish Civil Guard (UCO – Unidad Central Operativa). The article was headlined "I informed the Civil Guard that an Asturian offered me dynamite." The US controlled corporate media ignored these astounding revelations.

More information on the extremely suspicious nature of the Madrid bombing was reported by the Swiss daily *Neue Zürcher Zeitung* on May 27, 2004 in an article entitled "Crime Under the Eyes of the Police." This lengthy piece expressed amazement that the alleged perpetrators of these terrorist acts were not sophisticated sleeper-cell agents, but notorious criminals well-known over many years to European intelligence agencies, including the Spanish ones.

Jamal Zougham, one of the main suspects, was arrested after March 11. He had also been rounded up after September 11, 2001. Although well known to police and intelligence services of Spain and France and under continuous investigation, he was nevertheless allowed to travel to France, Germany, Britain, and Norway, where he met with others also under surveillance as terrorists. Furthermore, at least two of those arrested in Madrid had been previously identified as active in drug-trafficking. In addition, the mine worker who was accused of procuring the explosives for the March 11 attacks was also a known drug dealer. There were reliable reports that he and another of those arrested had worked as police informants.

The mystery was therefore why such people were able to prepare a bomb attack of such dimensions under the noses of the police, the *NZZ* wrote. The article suggested that the real operation was perpetrated not by these suspects, but by others. In reality, those now under arrest most probably represented a collection of patsies. The real prime suspects in the Madrid attacks were neither ETA nor Al Qaeda, but rather Spanish and Italian neofascists of the Stefano delle Chiaie school, whose modus operandi has always been attacks on trains, as seen in the 1974 Italicus bombing, and the 1980 Bologna railroad station explosion which killed upwards of 80 persons.

The 9/11 commission was an investigative failure and a blatant cover-up, but it did serve as an excellent propaganda soapbox for figures such as the former Navy Secretary and establishment operative John Lehman. In the Spring 2004 New York sessions of the commission, Lehman stressed repeatedly that the overwhelming consensus among US officials was that new terror attacks were coming soon. This view was shared by former New York City mayor Rudolph Giuliani. It was repeated by Kean and Hamilton when the 9/11 commission's report was delivered.

KERRY EMBRACES THE TERROR MYTH

Democratic presidential nominee John Kerry did not offer an alternative to the Bush demagogy of terror. Instead, the Skull & Bones Boston Brahmin oligarch Kerry enthusiastically embraced the Bush-Cheney nightmare vision of the United States as a nuclear terrorist battlefield. While Kerry might have believed that he was merely pandering to the demands of certain pro-Likud pressure groups, he was in fact providing precious credibility and cover to the most sinister plot yet directed against the United States. On May 27, Kerry began a series of speeches billed as his 11-day foreign policy tour. "The single greatest threat we face in the world today [is] a terrorist armed with nuclear weapons," Kerry said in Palm Beach on June 1. "Take away politics, strip away the labels: since that dark day in September, have we done everything we could to secure these dangerous weapons and bomb making materials? No! ... There was a time when the possibility of nuclear war was the most important responsibility entrusted to every American President. The phrase 'having your finger on the nuclear button' meant something very real.... The proposal I am laying out today: to ask that America launch a new mission... to prevent the world's deadliest weapons from falling into the world's most dangerous hands. If we secure all bomb-making materials, ensure that no new materials are produced for nuclear weapons, and end nuclear weapons programs in hostile states like North Korea and Iran, we can and will dramatically reduce the possibility of nuclear terrorism.... Here's what we must do: The first step is to safeguard all bomb-making material worldwide. That means making sure we know where they are, and then locking them up and securing them wherever they are. Our approach should treat all nuclear materials needed for bombs as if they were bombs."

Kerry was also ready to go Bush one better by adding Saudi Arabia to the target list for economic warfare and possible invasion, a notion long dear to Likudniks which has been gaining ground among some US pseudo-leftists lately. Kerry's prescription was for energy independence in order to obtain a free hand to settle with the Saudis: "If we are serious about energy independence, then we can finally be serious about confronting the role of Saudi Arabia in financing and providing ideological support of Al-Qaeda and other terrorist groups," Kerry said in Seattle on May 27. "We cannot continue this Administration's kid-glove approach to the supply and laundering of terrorist money.... I will launch a 'name and shame' campaign against those that are financing terror. And if they do not respond, they will be shut out of the US financial system. The same goes for Saudi sponsorship of clerics who promote the ideology of Islamic terror. To put it simply, we will not do business as usual with Saudi Arabia." (www.johnkerry.com)

Nor did Kerry stop with Saudi Arabia, or the usual targets like Iran and North Korea (see his *New York Times* interview of May 28). His foreign policy speeches, all built around the danger of nuclear terrorism, were replete with threats against India, Pakistan, China and Russia – some very formidable powers which even the Bush neocons had shied away from. Kerry was blunt about US pretensions to exercise custody over Russia's nuclear deterrent: "More than a decade has passed since the Berlin Wall came down. But Russia still has nearly 20,000 nuclear weapons, and enough nuclear material to produce 50,000 more Hiroshima-sized bombs. For most of these weapons and materials, cooperative security upgrades have not been completed. . . And at the current pace, it will take 13 years to secure potential bomb material in the former Soviet Union. We cannot wait that long. I will ensure that we remove this material entirely from sites that can't be adequately secured during my first term. . . It is hard to believe that we actually secured less bomb making material in the two years after 9/11 than we had in the two years before. At my first summit with the Russian President, I will seek an agreement to sweep aside the key obstacles slowing our efforts to secure Russia's nuclear stockpiles."

The North Korean crisis, with its alleged nuclear proliferation dangers, was largely manufactured by the US as a means of dragooning South Korean and Japanese support during the preparations for the US invasion of Iraq. Here Kerry again offered a more strident version of the Bush-Cheney line: "In East Asia, North Korea poses a genuine nuclear threat, while we have begun to strip American troops to relieve the overburdened forces in Iraq," he said in Seattle on May 27. "This Administration has been fixated on Iraq while the nuclear dangers from North Korea have multiplied," Kerry said in Palm Beach on June 1. "We know that North Korea has sold ballistic missiles and technology in the past. And according to published reports, North Korean uranium ended up in Libyan hands. The North Koreans have made it clear to the world – and to the terrorists – that they are open for business and will sell to the highest bidder. We should have no illusions about Kim Jong-Il, so any agreement must have rigorous verification and lead to complete and irreversible elimination of North Korea's nuclear weapons program. For eighteen months, we've negotiated over the shape of the table while the North Koreans allegedly have made enough new fuel to make six to nine nuclear bombs." On June 1, Kerry also attacked China, India, Pakistan, and Iran as places which must show greater cooperation with international controls over all nuclear materials.

In the midst of his relentless evocation of the looming threat of nuclear terrorism, Kerry also embraced the Bush-Cheney preventive war doctrine: "This strategy focuses not only on what we must do, but on what we must prevent," Kerry said on May 27 in Seattle. "We must ensure that lawless states and terrorists will not be armed with weapons of mass destruction. This is the single gravest threat to our security. Any potential adversary should know that we will defend ourselves against the possibility of attack by unconventional arms. If such a strike does occur, as commander-in-chief, I will respond with overwhelming and devastating force. If such an attack appears imminent, as commander-in-chief, I will do whatever is necessary to stop it. And, as commander-in-chief, I will never cede our security to anyone." (www.johnkerry.com) Many Democrats opposed this trigger-happy approach, and these remarks by Kerry took "him close to Mr. Bush's preemption doctrine," as a *Washington Post* editorial pointed out on May 30.

The key proposal of Kerry's nightmarish foreign policy tour also involved nuclear terrorism. Kerry announced on June 1 in affluent Palm Beach that he would appoint a national "nuclear terror" czar if elected. "So let it be clear: finally and fundamentally, preventing nuclear terrorism is our most urgent priority to provide for America's long-term security," he said. "That is why I will appoint a National Coordinator for Nuclear Terrorism and Counterproliferation who will work with me in the White House to marshal every effort and every ally, to combat an incalculable danger. We have to do everything we can to stop a nuclear weapon from ever reaching our shore – and that mission begins far away. We have to secure nuclear weapons and materials at the source so that searching the containers here at the Port of Palm Beach isn't our only line of defense – it is our last line of defense." (www.johnkerry.com)

No matter how far Kerry might go in attempting to outflank Bush on the right, he could not change the fact that, as long as there are elections, the Democratic Party will always have to ask for some meager concessions for the blacks, women, trade unionists, teachers, environmentalists, and lawyers who are important components of its base. But these groups were all slated for marginalization in the post-coup environment, and the Bush regime was a more attractive vehicle for administering martial law than the Democratic Party ever could ever be.

PREPARATION FOR EMERGENCY RULE

On May 11-12, the US Federal Emergency Management Agency (FEMA) ran a large-scale exercise involving more than 2,500 federal employees to determine how the federal government could continue operating in the face of a massive terrorist attack or other catastrophe. The government employees went to more than 100 secret sites, as part of a training exercise to prepare them to operate under catastrophic conditions. The exercise, called "Forward Challenge '04," was in preparation for over a year, according to Homeland Security Secretary Tom Ridge, who spoke to reporters from an undisclosed location. (*Washington Post*, May 14, 2004) Ridge had been hyping the "perfect storm" of coming terror in his own way for many weeks. Speaking at an event in Las Vegas in mid-April, Ridge said the government must "ratchet up" security from now through the 2005 inauguration, not based on "specific or credible intelligence" but rather on suspicion that high-profile political, economic and athletic events were good targets. (*USA Today*, 20 April 2004)

There was also an intensive pattern of incidents pointing in the direction of a terrorist attack on rail systems, on the Madrid model. This pattern included suspicious activity in the Northeast rail corridor between Washington and Boston. A Philadelphia television station reported the discovery of a wireless transmitter carefully hidden in the gravel along the SEPTA (Southeast Pennsylvania Transit Authority) rail tracks in Philadelphia. An infrared sensor, painted black and buried in the trackside ballast, was found along the SEPTA tracks, which could be used as a triggering device. It sent a signal when a moving object crossed its infrared beam. (WPVI News, Philadelphia, May 20, 2004)

On May 6, British Prime Minister Tony Blair announced that the new head of the British intelligenceservice MI-6 would be John Scarlett. The choice immediately caused protests from British political opposition leaders. Scarlett was the author and stubborn defender of the now discredited and artificially sexed-up Iraqi WMD report issued by the Blair government in support of the US-UK war drive. Dr. David Kelly lost his life in the scandal that developed around the manipulations in this report, but the role of the government was whitewashed in the inquiry conducted by Lord Hutton of the Law Lords. This appointment meant that MI-6 would lack the leadership of a competent and independent professional who might act to prevent the coming terrorism, and would instead be under the domination of a political hack of dubious judgment and loyalty. (AP, May 6, 2004)

This problem was compounded by Bush's nomination of the blueblood Porter Goss to replace Tenet as head of the CIA. Goss had most recently been a member of Congress for Florida, but he was also a former CIA agent. In 1961, as a new CIA recruit, Goss had joined the staff of JM/WAVE, the CIA's Miami station. At one time the station chief was Theodore G. Shackley, an ally of the Bush machine and a kingpin of the CIA old-boy networks. In those days, this was the command center for the anti-Castro Cubans who took part in the abortive Bay of Pigs invasion. It was also the center of Operation Mongoose, which was officially an operation to assassinate Castro, but which was used as a cover for aspects of the Kennedy assassination. The JM/WAVE milieu produced a number of the Watergate burglars, and was later a center for Iran-Contra drug-running and gun-running. Finally, as we have seen, the JM/WAVE Iran-Contra era infrastructure provided the vivarium for Atta, Shehhi, and Jarrah, the three accused 9/11 pilots.

In addition, the US government appeared to have imposed an embargo on the sharing of critical anti-terror intelligence with European authorities. Whatever the intent, the net effect of this blackout was to screen certain activities in the US from scrutiny by the allies. In an article published May 6 the German economic paper *Handelsblatt* reported, in reference to a similar article which appeared in the *Wall Street Journal*, that Spanish investigators, like many of their colleagues in Europe, were finding it very difficult to obtain information from US circles which are engaged in the fight against terrorism. Mentioned was the case of Spanish Judge Balthazar Garzón who reportedly was unable to proceed with certain investigations on Al Qaeda after Sept 11th, like the case of Al Qaeda member Ramzi Binalshibh, who was imprisoned in an unknown location. The problem was compounded by the fact that the alleged anti-terrorism fight in the US was being conducted by non-public military courts and military intelligence, which were not sharing testimony and evidence with their European colleagues. (*Handelsblatt*, May 6, 2004)

AN ORGY OF TERROR PROPAGANDA

The scenario of portable nuclear weapons being used against US cities was prepared by a lengthy campaign of movies and news reports. In early 2004 the Arabic-language newspaper *al-Hayat* reported that Osama bin Laden and al Qaeda had acquired Soviet-built tactical nuclear weapons from Ukraine, and had stored them in safe places for future use. According to a February 8, 2004 Reuters account, "after the Soviet Union broke up in 1991, a former Russian National Security adviser, Gen. Alexander Lebed, said that up to 100 portable suitcase-sized bombs were unaccounted for. Moscow has denied such weapons existed." But Lebed "said each one was equivalent to 1,000 tons of TNT and could kill as many as 100,000 people." The bombs were allegedly sold to Al Qaeda when Ukrainian scientists visited the Afghan city of Kandahar in 1998, during the time of the Taliban regime, which the US says harbored Al Qaeda. Another variant involved the activities of Dr. A. Q. Khan, father of the Pakistani nuclear program, who allegedly sold nuclear weapons technology, know-how, and equipment to all comers until his activities were exposed. Yet this could scarcely have occurred without the knowledge and connivance of the ISI, whose director is said to be appointed by the CIA.

Yet another variation involved Iran, a country against which the neocons, notably Michael Ledeen of the American Enterprise Institute, have never stopped inveighing. During the recent Hamburg, Germany trial of Abdel-Ghani Mzoudi (subsequently acquitted on charges of complicity in the 9/11 attacks), a statement was introduced into evidence by an unidentified informer of the Bundeskriminalamt, the German equivalent of the FBI, who alleged that Iranian intelligence was the actual initiator of the 9/11 attacks. The statement came from an alleged Iranian defector who had supposedly fled from Iran in July 2001. According to this source, "Department 43" of Iranian intelligence was created to plan and conduct terror attacks, and mounted joint operations with Al-Qaeda. Osama bin Laden's son, Saad bin Laden, had made repeated consultative visits to Iran." (DPA, January 22, 2004).

Lurid accounts of coming ABC terrorist attacks proliferated in the US media. Whatever the subjective intentions or motivations of the authors, these accounts objectively served as propaganda preparation for terror attacks, specifically by introducing to the US public the alien notions of emergency rule, martial law, and the state of siege, all of which were favorite themes of neocon writers going back to the Nazi Carl Schmitt. A particularly fulsome example was the article by Michael Ignatieff which appeared on May 2, 2004 in the *New York Times Magazine*. Ignatieff raved:

> Consider the consequences of a second major attack on the mainland United States – the detonation of a radiological or dirty bomb, perhaps, or a low-yield nuclear device or a chemical strike in a subway. Any of these events could cause death, devastation and panic on a scale that would make 9/11 seem like a pale prelude. After such an attack, a pall of mourning, melancholy, anger and fear would hang over our public life for a generation.
>
> An attack of this sort is already in the realm of possibility. The recipes for making ultimate weapons are on the Internet, and the materiel required is available for the right price. Democracies live by free markets, but a free market in everything – enriched uranium, ricin, anthrax – will mean the death of democracy. Armageddon is being privatized, and unless we shut down these markets, doomsday will be

for sale. Sept. 11, for all its horror, was a conventional attack. We have the best of reasons to fear the fire next time.

A democracy can allow its leaders one fatal mistake – and that's what 9/11 looks like to many observers – but Americans will not forgive a second one. A succession of large-scale attacks would pull at the already-fragile tissue of trust that binds us to our leadership and destroy the trust we have in one another. Once the zones of devastation were cordoned off and the bodies buried, we might find ourselves, in short order, living in a national-security state on continuous alert, with sealed borders, constant identity checks and permanent detention camps for dissidents and aliens. Our constitutional rights might disappear from our courts, while torture might reappear in our interrogation cells. **The worst of it is that government would not have to impose tyranny on a cowed populace. We would demand it for our own protection.** And if the institutions of our democracy were unable to protect us from our enemies, we might go even further, taking the law into our own hands. We have a history of lynching in this country, and by the time fear and paranoia settled deep in our bones, we might repeat the worst episodes from our past, killing our former neighbors, our onetime friends. (emphasis added)

This hype was debunked by expert opinions on *The Power of Nightmares* documentary on BBC 2, which revealed that the expected casualties from a dirty bomb would be *zero*.

The coming of martial law to the US in the wake of a new large-scale terror attack was also the theme of Ted Koppel's *Nightline* broadcast of April 7, 2004. Here Koppel was joined by former terror czar Richard Clarke and the Reagan White House chief of staff Kenneth Duberstein. The broadcast was titled "The Armageddon Plan," and featured questions of continuity of government (COG) after an attack that had decimated the US Congress. Koppel asked Duberstein: "Aren't we left for at least the foreseeable future with some sort of martial law anyway?" Duberstein eagerly replied: "You have to suspend rights." Koppel elaborated: "And during that period, then, and given the sense of panic that is inevitable under circumstances like this, the executive branch of government takes on extraordinary power, doesn't it?" Clarke chimed in: "I think in any war where Washington were destroyed, inevitably, there would be a period of, for lack of a better term, something like martial law." (*Nightline*, April 7, 2004)

No terrorist attack would be complete without the advance airing of a scenario docudrama to provide the population with a conceptual scheme to help them understand the coming events in the sense intended by the oligarchy. For any and all future attacks, this detail was attended to on Sunday June 6, 2004 at 8 PM EDT, when FX cable network broadcast *Meltdown: The Threat is Real*, a 2004 docudrama produced by Craig Anderson Productions and Apolloscreen. This two-hour scenario drama starred Bruce Greenwood and Arnold Vosloo. The plot summary: "Government agencies and civilians respond to a terrorist attack on an American nuclear reactor." Subtext: "Terrorists didn't have to build a nuclear weapon…we built it for them." The blurb also showed dark figures with rocket-propelled grenades advancing towards two nuclear cooling towers, while other terrorists parachuted in from above."

Other commentators cynically discussed the coming terror assault in direct relation to the November presidential elections. A May 2 article by *New York Times* correspondent David Sanger entitled "Calculating the Politics of Catastrophe" summarized the pattern of "obsessive" discussion in Washington circles about the electoral impact of another terror attack on the US. According to Sanger, both the Bush and Kerry campaigns were weighing the impact of a "nightmarish, unpredictable event" that could shift the election. Bush, he noted, had begun to talk more openly about such an event, "perhaps to brace the country for the worst, perhaps to begin the political inoculation if domestic defenses fail." Bush insiders were reportedly most concerned, not about the lives of the innocent victims, but rather about the possibility that a new terror attack might boomerang against the current tenant of the White House. Their cynical calculations were compared to "a kind of macabre game theory in which security experts and political operatives – two classes of people who typically do not interact much in Washington – are calculating what the political fallout of an attack might be." Sanger quoted a senior administration official as saying, "The message the terrorists learned in Madrid is that attacks can change elections and change policy. It's a very dangerous precedent to have out there." Noting the standard US neocon line of denouncing the Spanish population for learning the "wrong lesson" from the terrorist attacks and for "appeasing" terrorism, Sanger went on to point out that the Bush administration was busy preparing scenarios on the ways a terrorist attack could "change elections" in the US in Bush's favor. Sanger wrote: "Mr. Bush's political aides – speaking only on background, because no one dissects terror on the record – argue that the crazier the world gets, the more it plays to the theme of the campaign: Now more than ever, the country needs a president who has proved to be strong on terror."

The main issue, the Bush backers agreed, was not prevention, but timing: if the terror attacks came too far in advance of the elections, the initial impulse to rally around the President might dissipate, "because the shock value would be gone, and because this time American defenses are supposed to be up. So within a month or so, the thinking goes, horror could give way to analysis about whether the billions spent on security were well spent – and if Mr. Bush focused on the right threats." Thus, a terror attack in June or July might backfire on Bush. "One reason the administration is so obsessed with security for the conventions," wrote Sanger, "is that those gatherings attract large concentrations of the American elite in two major cities. But they also may be sufficiently far ahead of the election to allow time for predictable finger-pointing. Terrorists, some believe, might try to undertake an attack that could be credibly portrayed as a result of the Iraq war, rather than as a 9/11 replay." Sanger did not mention the scenario that built on the lessons of Aznar's fall: martial law, emergency rule, and no elections at all.

In a May 20, 2004 op-ed entitled "Beware of any Stretch-Run Surprises," the *Wall Street Journal*'s Al Hunt forecast that the presidential contest could be determined by "unanticipated events." Chief among these was a terrorist attack. Hunt noted the hypocrisy of the Bush line on terror: "The Bush administration and outside terrorist experts repeatedly have cautioned that another attack on the homeland is likely. The White House, politically, had it both ways: taking credit for avoiding any assault since 9/11, while at the same time warning that another was likely, even inevitable." GOP leaders are betting that a new terror wave will play in to their hands; Hunt cited veteran Republican operative Charles Black as stating that "my instinct is there likely will be a rally around the incumbent effect" in the event of a new round of terror. From here it was not far to the conclusion that some really serious terror might also allow Bush to dispense with the election formalities altogether, and enjoy enhanced public support while doing so.

The scurrilous television personality Sean Hannity blurted out the entire scenario when he blabbered: "If we are attacked before our election like Spain was, I am not so sure that we should go ahead with the election…we had better make plans now because it's going to happen." Hannity was close to advocating the violent overthrow of the US Constitution.

The Washington Post used the release of the latest set of Nixon administration tapes to issue what can only be interpreted as a threat to the Congress in the form of a signal piece bearing the headline "Haig Said Nixon Joked of Nuking Hill." The content involved a telephone conversation between Nixon's then Chief of Staff, Gen. Alexander Haig, and Secretary of State Henry Kissinger, in March 1974 – months before Nixon was forced out of office. "I was told to get the football," reported Haig to Kissinger, a reference to the codes used by the president to order nuclear attacks. In response to a question from Kissinger, Haig specified that the request is for "His nuclear black bag. He is going to drop it on the Hill." The context is Nixon's growing fear of his own looming impeachment. This item could not have been reassuring to members of Congress. (*Washington Post*, May 27, 2004)

THE ANGLO-AMERICAN EMPIRE IN BREAKDOWN CRISIS

The grounds for the wave of terror propaganda were to be found in the stunning reverses suffered by the Bush regime over the first half of 2004. During April, Iraqi resistance forces initiated a national uprising against the invasion of their country. The failure of the vaunted US military machine before Fallujah and Najaf ended the myth of US superpower invincibility, and set off uncontrollable processes of disintegration throughout the global system. During May, the war crimes and atrocities carried out by US, UK and other coalition forces in Iraq wrecked the moral credibility of the United States and its allies, making these aggressive powers into an object of absolute execration around the world. This situation was encapsulated in the stern condemnation of Bush's policies delivered during his June 4 visit to the Vatican by Pope John Paul II. The ad hoc "Coalition of the Willing" assembled by the Bush regime had begun to disintegrate, with Spain, Honduras, the Dominican Republic, Kazakhstan, Norway, and the Philippines either leaving Iraq or announcing their departure. Governments subservient to Bush in Great Britain, Italy, Poland, Denmark, and other countries were facing a grim electoral future. The entire alliance system created by the US at the end of World War II was increasingly a dead letter. The three principal leaders of world aggression, Bush, Blair, and Sharon, were engulfed by domestic political crises threatening them with ouster over the short term, with increased danger of prosecution and the wrecking of their political machines amidst recrimination for Iraq and other disasters. Concomitantly with these events, the New York-London financial system began to exhibit symptoms of severe instability leading to systemic crisis.

The US was running a merchandise trade deficit of over $500 billion, and a federal budget deficit which actually approaches $750 billion. The US was a bankrupt state. Greenspan's policies had solved the dot.com bubble by creating a housing bubble and a bond bubble. Because of the manifest bankruptcy of the United States, the Anglo-American finance oligarchs feared the termination of the US dollar as a reserve currency. This would take the form of a dumping of the dollar as the currency in which the posted price of oil is expressed by Saudi Arabia, Iran, Indonesia, and other OPEC states. The far stronger and more stable euro would be the beneficiary of these moves, and it is the euro which would prove to be far more attractive to most countries in a world divided into currency blocks. The European Union had been pressing Russia to accept payment for oil in euros, which, if accomplished, would place the EU out of reach of Anglo-American and Israeli blackmail threats of oil shortages.

Russia and Germany in particular were actively discussing this measure, which harks back to the post-World War I Russo-German Apollo agreements, a nightmare for the Anglo-Americans. Taken together, these developments suggested the collapse of the entire US imperialist system. The protagonists of the coming terror were determined to disrupt these processes, imposing on the world a regime of unilateral US *diktat* and military intervention, with a domestic police state to make sure that no opposition emerged on the home front.

THE NEOCONS UNDER ATTACK

The neocons were deeply concerned about their own personal fate. During their ascent, this exceptionally ideological and close-knit faction had by its arrogance and incompetence made many enemies. During May, there were repeated editorial calls for the firing of not just Rumsfeld, but also of Wolfowitz and the other neocons who had made such a mess of the Pentagon. The demand to oust Rumsfeld and Wolfowitz was raised by the veteran Republican Senators who exercised great authority within that party. Right-wing columnist Robert Novak, in a *Washington Post* op-ed on the Chalabi scandal, commented: "Republican Senators, who do not yet want to be quoted by name, feel there must be some accountability for this massive blunder, as there must be for the prisoner abuse scandal. They want the President at least to consider" firing Rumsfeld, Wolfowitz, and perhaps others of the neo-con gang. The senior Republican Congressional leaders were backed in this, by high US military brass. (*Time*, May 25; *New York Times* May 24, 2004) According to press accounts, Senators Warner and McCain led a group of about a dozen senior GOP leaders who called on Bush to demand the sacking of Rumsfeld and Wolfowitz as a matter of urgent political expediency. Bush reportedly sat stony-faced and said nothing.

The May 20 US military/mercenary raid against the Baghdad offices of Ahmed Chalabi pointed to a new and grave danger for many top Bush administration and neocon figures. Chalabi was of course the darling of the neocons, who had channeled upwards of $40 million in official US government funding to him. He was a source of fantastic reports of Iraqi weapons of mass destruction, and of the eagerness of the Iraqi masses to rise up in revolt against Saddam Hussein. It now turned out that Chalabi had betrayed a vital US state secret to his patrons in Iran by telling the Iranians that the US had broken the secret code used by Iranian diplomats and agents. This revelation alerted the Iranians to their vulnerability, and cut off a key means of US espionage against Iran and its partners. The question thus arose as to who in the US government could have given Chalabi such highly classified information, thus committing a very serious federal crime. Chalabi's closest contacts were known to have been Cheney, Rumsfeld, Wolfowitz, and a few others. This issue became the subject of an FBI investigation of these and other top Bushmen.

The information that Chalabi and his intelligence chief Aras Karim Habit were alleged to have passed to the government of Iran "was highly classified, and known only to a few in the US government," wrote *Time*'s Romesh Ratnesar. "The probe will examine whether US officials illegally transmitted state secrets to Chalabi's "Iraqi National Congress," the INC. The investigation could ultimately reach high-ranking civilian officials at the Pentagon and the Defense Intelligence Agency who had dealings with Chalabi and his organization." Ratnesar cited "a senior US official" as his source. *New York Times* reporters David Johnston and Richard Oppel, Jr. also citing "government officials," called the information "so highly classified that federal investigators have intensified their inquiry to find out whether anyone in the American government gave the material to Mr. Chalabi." They also cited "intelligence officials" saying that the probe, by the FBI, centered on the handful of US officials with regular contact with Chalabi in Washington, and an even smaller number who had access to the intelligence. "Most of them were at the Pentagon," they wrote; however, Chalabi himself, on *Meet the Press* on May 23, acknowledged three personal meetings with Vice President Cheney. Leading neocons not currently serving in government, such as Michael Ledeen, Richard Perle, Kenneth Timmerman, and Laurie Mylroie, vociferously defended Chalabi. (*Time*, May 25; *New York Times* May 24, 2004)

There was also the special prosecutor investigating the leaking to Robert Novak of the fact that Valerie Plame, the wife of Bush critic Ambassador Joseph Wilson (who exposed the fraud of the Bush 2002 State of the Union charges that Iraq had sought uranium yellowcake in Niger) was working for the CIA. Prime suspects were Bush's political strategist Karl Rove, and White House Chief of Staff Andrew Card. Revealing the identity of a CIA agent is a serious felony under federal law.

Allegedly in regard to the outing of Valerie Plame, Bush retained his own private attorney, Jim Sharp. Sharp had represented Gen. Richard Secord, yet another Iran-Contra figure, who was accused of taking part in the illegal arms shipments of the mid-1980s. Cheney already had a private lawyer, Terrence O'Donnell of the Washington DC law firm Williams & Connelly. According to *Capitol Hill Blue* of June 3, sources familiar with the Federal investigation say that Bush knew about the Plame leak, and that he took no action to stop the release of Plame's name. This would make him accessory to a serious federal crime.

At the root of the Valerie Plume affair was the role of her husband, Ambassador Joseph Wilson, in refuting the baseless claim that Iraq had sought to purchase uranium yellowcake from Niger. This fake story was buttressed by documents which turned out to be forged. Of interest in this regard was the neocon ideologue Ledeen, because the faked documents first surfaced in Rome, where Ledeen possessed extensive contacts. A federal grand jury was formed to investigate this matter. Ledeen, like so many Bush officials, was an alumnus of the 1980s George H. W. Bush-Poindexter-Abrams-Oliver North Iran-Contra gun-running and drug-running scandal, and mobilized these networks as part of the post 9/11 assault on Iraq. In December 2001, Ledeen moved to revive the Iran connection, setting up a meeting between two Pentagon civilian neo-cons and Manucher Ghorbanifar, an Iranian arms dealer whom the CIA called a criminal and liar. Three days of meetings in Rome involved Harold Rhode, Larry Franklin, Ghorbanifar, and two unnamed officials of the Iranian regime. After the conquest of Iraq, Rhode was sent to Baghdad as the contact point between the Office of Special Plans and Chalabi. Ghorbanifar, in a Dec. 22, 2003 interview with *Newsweek*'s Mark Hosenball, reported that he maintained contact with Rhode and Franklin "five or six times a week" through June 2003, when he had a second meeting with Rhode in Paris. This back channel to the Iranians came under intense scrutiny.

Richard Perle was the target of a huge civil suit growing out of his alleged involvement in the fraudulent conveyances and embezzlement carried out by the neocon press baron and moneybags Lord Conrad Black, who may have taken money from Hollinger to help fund neocon think tanks like the American Enterprise Institute. Perle had worked closely with the purloining Lord in recent years, and might also face criminal charges in this case. A report prepared for the Hollinger board by Richard C. Breeden, a former head of the Securities and Exchange Commission, called on Perle to give back $5.4 million to Hollinger. (*Washington Post*, September 1, 2004)

Retired CIA analyst Ray McGovern warned that the allegedly "credible intelligence" cited by Ashcroft in his warning that Al Qaeda is preparing to "hit the United States" was most likely yet another fabrication. "'Intelligence' is being conjured up once again to serve the political purposes of the Bush administration," McGovern wrote. According to McGovern, "the President, Ashcroft, Defense Secretary Donald Rumsfeld, et al. have a deeply personal incentive to make four more years for Bush a sure thing." McGovern noted that according to a memo issued by White House Counsel Alberto Gonzales on January 25, administration officials might be prosecuted for "war crimes" because of the treatment of prisoners in Afghanistan. Gonzales stressed that "grave breaches" of the Geneva Conventions are war crimes under US law, and added: "It is difficult to predict the motives of prosecutors and independent counsels who may in the future decide to pursue unwarranted charges" based on the War Crimes Act passed by Congress in 1996. Gonzales urged Bush to declare that the Geneva Convention regarding prisoners of war does not apply to Taliban or Al-Qaeda detainees, and that such a determination "would provide a solid defense to any future prosecution." And all that, McGovern notes, was before the Abu Ghraib revelations. McGovern continued:

> For the Bush administration, the nightmare is losing the November election – a prospect believed to be unlikely until just recently. For many of us citizens, the nightmare is the President and his associates resorting to extra-legal measures to ensure that there is no regime change in Washington for four more years....Yes, this could mean a constitutional crisis without parallel in the history of our country....But was there not a good warm-up in the fall of 2002? Did we not then experience a constitutional crisis when Congress was duped into ceding to the President its constitutional power to declare war? And it was all accomplished by spreading the myth that Saddam Hussein was close to exploding a mushroom cloud over us – a myth based on a known forgery alleging that Iraq was acquiring uranium from Africa. Could an elevated threat level be used as a means of "justifying" martial law and postponement of the election? No doubt such suggestions will seem too alarmist to those trusting that there is a moral line, somewhere, that the President and his senior advisers would not cross. I regret very much to say that their behavior over the past three years leaves me doubtful that there is such a line....If my doubts are justified, the sooner we all come

to grips with this parlous situation the better. (Ray McGovern syndicated column, *Common Dreams*, June 2, 2004)

In an interview on Amy Goodman's *Democracy Now!* radio program, McGovern commented on the significance of Bush's retaining an attorney. Among the things on Bush's mind, McGovern repeated, is that he might be facing a war crimes prosecution if voted out of office. Another issue for Bush, according to McGovern, is that "four more years becomes even more important to me [Bush] and Ashcroft and Rumsfeld," because of the war crimes indictments hanging over their heads. McGovern: "I say this, because I am more frightened now than at any time over the last three and a half years, that this administration will resort to extra-legal methods, to do something to ensure that there are four more years for George Bush." (*Democracy Now!* June 4, 2004)

On June 3, CIA Director George Tenet announced his resignation, and was quickly joined by the CIA Deputy Director of Operations, James L. Pavitt, the spymaster of clandestine services. Tenet was evidently forced out by Bush and Cheney, but was willing to portray his own dismissal as a resignation for family reasons, mainly his desire to spend more time with his adolescent son. Tenet, as a Clinton holdover, was not a doctrinaire Straussian or Skull & Bones member, and thus was not and could never be a member of the Bush/neocon core group. For many weeks, neocons like Richard Perle, Frank Gaffney, James Woolsey, Newt Gingrich and others had been attempting to scapegoat Tenet for the US disasters in Iraq and elsewhere. Tenet did of course preside over 9/11 and the Iraq invasion, which established a prima facie case of his incompetence (or complicity). His departure allowed Bush to claim that there was some account-ability in the current administration. More germane to the issue of the coming terrorism, Tenet was so discredited as to have become a controversial symbol of the failure of the Bush administration to defend the US. In a speech the previous week, even Tenet's friend Al Gore had demanded his resignation. With Tenet still in office, a coming terror event might have given rise to a wave of accusation and resentment against a CIA Director who by that time would have failed in warding off not only 9/11, but also whatever the second wave had to offer.

In the immediate aftermath of the Tenet ouster, the neocon gang appeared to have gained a momentary respite. Douglas Jehl of *The New York Times* reported on June 5 that the simultaneous departure of Tenet and Pavitt shifted the balance of power within the US intelligence community in favor of the Pentagon neocons. Jehl wrote that "Without Mr. Tenet in place, the power balance in a rivalry between the CIA and the Defense Department may tilt more toward Stephen Cambone." Jehl attributed this view to "Congressional officials." (*NYT*, 5 June 2004)

In the wake of the Tenet resignation, indications began to surface that the mental disintegration of "dry drunk" Bush had gone farther than usually surmised. Doug Thompson of *Capitol Hill Blue* wrote: "President George W. Bush's increasingly erratic behavior and wide mood swings has the halls of the

West Wing buzzing lately as aides privately express growing concern over their leader's state of mind. In meetings with top aides and administration officials, the President goes from quoting the Bible in one breath to obscene tantrums against the media, Democrats and others that he classifies as "enemies of the state…" The President's abrupt dismissal of CIA Directory George Tenet Wednesday night is, aides say, an example of how he works. "Tenet wanted to quit last year but the President got his back up and wouldn't hear of it," says an aide. "That would have been the opportune time to make a change, not in the middle of an election campaign but when the director challenged the President during the meeting Wednesday, the President cut him off by saying 'That's it, George. I cannot abide disloyalty. I want your resignation and I want it now.'" Tenet was allowed to resign "voluntarily" and Bush informed his shocked staff of the decision Thursday morning. One aide says the President actually described the decision as "God's will." (*Capitol Hill Blue*, 4 June 2004) Perhaps the tenant of the White House needed to get his thyroid checked.

COUNTERVAILING TENDENCIES?

By summer 2004, the situation of the party of terrorism inside the United States was uncertain. The political leaders who would be the beneficiaries of new terror attacks were figures like Bush, Cheney, Rumsfeld, Wolfowitz, Ashcroft, Ridge, and the neocon *Gestapo* (as Colin Powell calls it) in general. The main agencies for their dictatorship would be FEMA (Federal Emergency Management Agency), Ridge's Department of Homeland Security, the Department of Justice, and the FBI. The US military, especially the US Army, had become profoundly disillusioned with the Bush-Cheney preventive war policy. They also resented being scapegoated for the Abu Ghraib atrocities, which were ordered by CIA, DIA, and Cheney's mercenary contractors.

Some generals realized that a successful terror coup, by cementing the current gang in power for the foreseeable future – without benefit of checks and balances – would guarantee that US forces would be fed into meatgrinders far worse than Iraq. In addition to Syria, Iran, North Korea, and Cuba, a post-coup US regime could not avoid collision with China and/or Russia. It remained to be seen whether this awareness would be enough to motivate the US military to do something to stop such a coup. Similar considerations apply to the State Department, which had virtually no place in the post-coup world eagerly planned by the neocons. Incredibly, the Congress was conniving in its own liquidation with a bill ordering instant elections to replace deceased Congressmen, which passed the House.

Sidney Blumenthal, a former advisor to the Clinton Administration working with Salon.com, wrote a piece in the *Guardian* on how the US officer corps had turned against Secretary of Defense Donald Rumsfeld. The piece, was headlined "America's Military Coup." Retired General William Odom, who was the head of the National Security Agency, the main US electronic spying center, and who had moved to the Hudson Institute, was quoted saying: "It was never in our interest to go into Iraq. It is a diversion from the war on terrorism; the rationale for the Iraq war (finding WMD) is phony; the US army is over-stretched and being driven into the ground; and the prospect of building a democracy is zero. In Iraqi politics legitimacy is going to be tied to expelling us. Wisdom in military affairs dictates withdrawal in this situation. We can't afford to fail – that's mindless. The issue is how we stop failing more. I am arguing a strategic decision." Another military figure told Blumenthal that Rumsfeld was "detested" and that "if there's a sentiment in the army it is: support our troops, impeach Rumsfeld." Blumenthal then referenced an essay by Lt. Col. Charles Dunlap which had received a prize in 1992 from then General Colin Powell. The title of the piece was "The Origins of the American Military Coup of 2012," which was a cautionary tale of how the US military launched a coup because of the failures of the civilian government. (*Guardian*, May 13, 2004) Former CENTCOM commanders Zinni and Hoar also published attacks on the Rumsfeld-Wolfowitz policies. One account suggested that, given the degree of military hatred against the administration, any other country would have already witnessed a military coup.

Ashcroft had claimed that just after the Madrid bombing, an Al Qaeda spokesman had announced that "90 percent of the arrangements for an attack in the United States were complete." But *Newsweek* terrorism writers Michael Isikoff and Mark Hosenball pointed out that the only known basis for Ashcroft's claim was a note sent to a London Arabic newspaper immediately after the Madrid bombing, which said that a major attack against the United States was "90 percent ready." The authenticity of this report was questioned at the time by some US officials. (*Newsweek web exclusive*, May 26, 2004)

TERRORIZING THE CONGRESS

On June 9, the US Capitol, including Congress and the Supreme Court, was evacuated in panic because of a report that an airplane without a transponder was approaching Washington DC. The plane turned out to belong to Governor Ernie Fletcher of Kentucky, who was coming to attend the funeral of former President Reagan, but authorities appear to have used this incident to terrorize the Congress in an unprecedented manner. Photographers, Secret Service agents and members of a military choir were finishing preparations for the Rotunda ceremony when Capitol Police suddenly burst in, shouting: "Evacuate the building now! Now! Move! Move!" Congressmen, senators, and staff members ran like rabbits as police officers shouted, "This is not a drill!" Some jettisoned briefcases and laptops, and women flung off high heels. Amy Call, a spokeswoman for Senate Majority Leader Bill Frist, reported that police had told people to "run, get out of the Capitol," because of the "imminent" approach of an airplane. Nearby, on the Mall, US Park Police and Capitol Police also ordered people to flee. "Do not stop," officers yelled. "Keep moving." "Ladies and gentlemen, let's move like our lives depend on it. I mean it!" a DC police officer shouted. F-16 fighter jets and Black Hawk helicopters were sent to intercept the errant twin-engine turboprop plane. The plane's transponder, which signals its identifying information to ground controllers, was broken, Brian Roehrkasse, a spokesman for the Department of Homeland Security, told the press later. (*Washington Post*, June 10, 2004)

The July 4 Independence Day holiday was marked by a pattern of hysterical terror propaganda in the US mass media. Part of this was the publicity campaign around the new book *Imperial Hubris*, about to be published by Brassey's, which was attributed to Anonymous, a currently serving officer of the CIA whose real name was allegedly Michael Scheuer. Anonymous was said to have been the first leader of the CIA's Osama bin Laden station during the mid-1990s, which did not inspire confidence. At the center of the hype over this book, pushed by CNN's David Ensor and others, was the assurance that an ABC terror attack on the US was imminent. The *New York Times* of June 23 quoted Anonymous as having "a pressing certainty that Al Qaeda will attack the continental United States again, that its next strike will be more damaging than that of 11 September 2001, and could include use of weapons of mass destruction." Anonymous open-ly lionized bin Laden, saying that bin Laden's vast accomplishments were due to the fact that he actually believed deeply in something. Anonymous, following the line of Richard Clarke, was highly critical of the Bush regime for having deviated from the true existential world struggle against al Qaeda: "There is nothing that bin Laden could have hoped for more than the American invasion of Iraq," wrote Anonymous, who described Bush as al Qaeda's ideal American president.

What emerged from the Clarke and Anonymous volumes taken together was a growing recognition in US ruling circles that the Iraq adventure had long since crossed the line into irrevocable disaster. Their concern was therefore to safe-guard oligarchical rule post-Iraq. To obtain this, they were more than willing to jettison the pathetically incompetent Bush regime and its phalanx of discredited neocon ideologues. But Clarke and Anonymous were both the type of bureaucrat who could expect to enjoy vastly increased power under martial law. The Clarke-Anonymous attempt was therefore to preserve false-flag terrorism in the guise of al Qaeda as the indispensable means of social control for the indefinite future. In this regard they appeared more than willing to tolerate a new round of ABC/WMD terrorism to make sure that the terror card remained available, since they evidently could see no other way of maintaining the current system.

Even more explicit was the book *Osama's Revenge*, whose author, the "former FBI consultant" Paul L. Williams, was publicized by Fox News on June 28, 2004. According to Williams, Osama bin Laden already had 20 Soviet-made suitcase bombs, and these weapons were already in the United States! Williams estimated al Qaeda's strength in this country at about 5,000 sleeper agents ready for action. He also cited a warning that New York City was a nuclear target, which was allegedly given by Tenet to Bush in October 2001, but never communicated to Mayor Giuliani.

To organize the terror drumbeat more effectively, the Bush White House was known to fax inflammatory and apocalyptic talking points on terrorism to its phalanx of reactionary talk show hosts. On June 24 at 2:25 PM on Fox News, the "terrorist and security expert" Harvey Kushner opined that al Qaeda is certain to attack the United States during the summer. On June 30 at 4:55 PM, Col. Oliver North (sitting in for the vacationing neofascist syndicated radio talk show host Rush Limbaugh) announced that the lesson of Madrid was that there was sure to be a large-scale terror attack in the US before the November elections.

CALLING OFF THE ELECTIONS

At this time, the Bush regime also openly broached the question of calling off the November presidential election, something that had not been done in the midst of real shooting wars in 1864 and 1944. According to *Newsweek*, DeForest Soaries, the chairman of the US Election Assistance Commission, had asked Ridge to urge Congress to pass legislation giving the government power to cancel or reschedule a federal election. Soaries noted that New York City had suspended its primary elections on the day of the Sept. 11 attacks, but the federal government did not possess that authority. Ironically, the US Election Assistance Commission was a new agency which had been created in the wake of the 2000 election fiasco. Left liberals were disturbed; *The Nation* published a parody of a future Bush speech announcing there would be no vote.

This first wave of Bush-inspired election cancellation propaganda peaked in mid-July 2004. At this point neocon ideologue Norman Ornstein of the American Enterprise Institute proposed the creation of a kind of committee of public safety of top-level oligarchs who would have the function of calling off elections. According to Ornstein,

> Congress should pass a law creating a blue-ribbon commission to which it would delegate the authority to make decisions about postponement of presidential and congressional elections in the aftermath of a terrorist attack or major natural disaster. The commission should consist of people with high profiles and impeccable reputations for integrity, and include some people with experience in election administration. From the public sector, the kinds of people to consider would include former senators such as Warren Rudman and Alan Simpson; former representatives such as Tom Foley, Lee Hamilton, Bob Walker and John Brademas; former Cabinet members such as Lynn Martin and Donna Shalala; and leaders of business, labor and higher education who have comparable reputations and public profiles....The commission would function only if a disaster triggered the need for a decision, and it would operate under a specific set of directives that would make a decision to postpone any election, in whole or in part, the last recourse. Such a decision should be made only through broad consensus, requiring a two-thirds vote by the commission. (*Washington Post*, July 16, 2004)

With all the arid banality of the true neocon, Ornstein did not face the fact that his new oligarchical commission would in effect have become the supreme governing authority of the United States, although he is probably aware of this. Ornstein's proposal amounted to subverting the Constitution while granting dictatorial power to the discredited hacks who bore much of the responsibility for the country's predicament, be it through their sins of omission or of commission.

As the presidential campaign unfolded, the Bush campaign showed a cynical willingness to use terror threats and terror demagogy as a kind of political auxiliary to their efforts. During the days just after Kerry had announced his choice of Senator Edwards as his vice presidential candidate, the lugubrious and plodding Tom Ridge of the Department of Homeland Security called a press conference to announce that there was a new, but wholly undefined, threat on the horizon. Ridge had obviously taken over the Ministry of Fear portfolio from Ashcroft, who was too widely hated and too discredited to be effective. Ridge's remarks were clearly aimed at chopping off the Edwards bounce for the Democrats. Some Democrats grumbled.

The Democratic National Convention ended in Boston on Thursday, July 29. Here again, a modest five-point pop in the polls for Kerry was observable. But on the afternoon of Sunday, August 1, it was Ridge's turn once again, this time with a litany of threats against the IMF and World Bank in Washington DC, against Prudential in Newark, and against the New York Stock Exchange and Citibank in Manhattan. It was Howard Dean who spoke up with refreshing candor, pointing to the obvious political motivation and political timing of the new wave of Bush terror demagogy. Speaking on CNN Late Edition, Dean said that he was "concerned that every time that something happens that's not good for President Bush, he plays his trump card, which is terrorism. His whole campaign is based on the notion that 'I can keep you safe, therefore, in times of difficulty in America, stick with me.'"

With that, Dean had confirmed his historical merit of being the only national politician willing to challenge the sanctimonious shibboleths of the new terror state. He was immediately taken to task by neocon Democrat Joe Lieberman, less a monotheist than a zealous adept of the cult of Deimos and Phobos, the gods of fear and terror. "That's outrageous," said Lieberman of what was merely obvious. GOP Senator Mitch McConnell of Kentucky, the Senate majority whip and apostle of venal election practice also criticized Dean. "I think that's the most cynical view," whined McConnell. "The president, after all, is the president, even if he's running for re-election." Dean courageously rejected the idea that he, Dean, was responsible for politicizing the terror threat, pointing out that it was Bush who had done this. "When you're going to run on inspiring fear in the American people, that's politics," Dean countered. "The president himself made the choice to inject politics into the campaign on terrorism. That was his choice. He's now going to have to live with the consequences." CNN later conducted a poll among its viewers to see how many thought that the new terror alert was a political stunt.

It soon became known that the allegedly urgent information upon which this orange alert was based was about four years old, and had just serendipitously turned up in a computer captured in Pakistan. One thinks of Tony Blair's use of old term papers, *Readers Digest* articles, and messages found in hollow trees for his various imaginative and opportunistic dossiers. A senior law enforcement official told a reporter: "There is nothing right now that is new. Why did we go to this level? ...I still don't know that." (*Washington Post*, August 3, 2004) Worse still, it turned out that the computer actually belonged to a Pakistani anti-terrorism expert, Muhammad Naeem Noor Khan. When the US outed him, a fair number of ongoing investigations in London had to be rolled up, to the chagrin of the police. But this side of the story was suppressed, so the rogue network were likely able to save some of their assets while scoring a lasting public relations victory.

On August 12, Kerry ventured to attack Bush for having dawdled with the second graders at the Booker School, listening to "My Pet Goat" while thousands of innocents died. Responding to Kerry's attacks a day or two later, Bush claimed that he had been collecting his thoughts while he remained with the children, and even suggested that what he did in the first minutes was not important. "What is relevant," according to Bush, "is whether or not I understand and understood then the stakes....And I made a determination that we would do everything we could to bring those killers to justice and to protect the American people." Bush told Larry King of CNN that "it's easy to second-guess a moment," said Bush; the important thing was that he quickly "recognized we were at war" and mobilized the nation for his series of wars. (*Washington Post*, August 13, 2004) Bush clearly wasted more than 15 minutes after the North Tower impact, and wasted another 7 minutes after the South Tower impact. In that time, he should have been issuing crisp orders to mobilize air defenses, deploy combat air patrols over the Capitol and Pentagon, cut through layers of bureaucracy, and generally administer a bureaucratic blow-torch to a corrupt and somnolent bureaucracy that was honeycombed with subversive moles. But Bush, who had been on vacation for much of his time in office before September 11, did none of these things. Bush nevertheless made his own supposed prowess on 9/11 the theme of the Republican National Convention at the end of August and the beginning of September.

LARRY FRANKLIN, MOSSAD, AND IRAN

As July turned into August, the visible emphasis shifted from terror and martial law towards a new war, this time with Iran. Naturally, war and terror were linked, as they always had been On August 27, 2004 CBS News broke the story of an alleged Israeli mole in the Pentagon who had been passing US secrets to the Israeli Embassy by way of AIPAC, the American Israeli Public Affairs Council, a powerful arm of the Zionist lobby. Under investigation was Larry Franklin, a middle-level functionary working for the Wolfowitz-Feith-Luti-

Shulsky clique in the Pentagon. The FBI was asking questions about the neocon clan of Wolfowitz, Feith, Perle, and David Wurmser, an Iran specialist working for Cheney. The general line of questioning about these figures was: "Do you believe certain people would spy for Israel and pass secret information?" (*Washington Post*, September 4, 2004)

This same Larry Franklin had been named in my June 6 news release, "Rogue Bush Backers Prepare Super 9/11 False Flag Terror Attacks." Franklin was indicated as one of the vulnerable links in the neocon network which found itself in a hysterical flight forward to try to salvage the debacle of their Iraq war by expanding that war to neighboring countries, notably Iran. The threat of a new round of "own goal" synthetic terrorism, quite possibly in the ABC dimension, was linked to the preparation of that wider war. The logic at work was that of an "October surprise," this time on the scale adequate to shock the post-9/11 world.

The best working hypothesis to understand the Israeli mole investigation was that neocon networks in the Pentagon were very close to embroiling the United States in a war with Iran. This would likely come as an Israeli and/or US pre-emptive bombing attack on Iran's nuclear facilities, possibly combined with a terrorist attack inside the US using weapons of mass destruction, which the corporate controlled media would immediately blame on Iran.

Whatever forces were behind the naming of Franklin, it was logical to assume that their main aim was to break up neocon preparations for a surprise attack on Iran, which the neocons had been boasting about in the media with special emphasis for some weeks. Backing the Franklin probe were in all probability military factions who had no desire to be fed into the Iranian meatgrinder, and who did not fancy a neocon fascist dictatorship. The immediate goal was to knock Rumsfeld, Wolfowitz, Feith, Bolton, Rice, Abrams and their cheering section in the media and think-tanks onto the defensive. While the exposure of Franklin was a positive step, it was far from decisive, and the neocons were still in a position to unleash the dogs of war, especially with the help of Sharon. The US was therefore not far from the brink of war with Iran, and at the same time was entering a period of steadily increasing danger of synthetic terrorism designed to steal or cancel the November elections, and thus freeze the current neocon clique in power for the foreseeable future.

IRAN: OCTOBER SURPRISE IN SEPTEMBER?

On August 19, Martin Sieff of UPI warned: "Forget an October Surprise, a much worse one could come in September: Full-scale war between the United States and Iran may be far closer than the American public might imagine." Sieff quoted remarks made by Iranian Defense Minister Ali Shamkhani on August 18 which bluntly warned that if Iranian military commanders believed the United States were serious about attacking Iran to destroy its nuclear power facility at Bushehr, or to topple its Islamic theocratic form of government, the Iranian military would not sit back passively and wait for the US armed forces to strike the first blow, as President Saddam Hussein in neighboring Iraq did in March 2003. They would strike first. "We will not sit to wait for what others will do to us," Shamkhani told al-Jazeera. "Some military commanders in Iran are convinced that preventive operations which the Americans talk about are not their monopoly," he added. With this, the Iran-Iraq border became a flash point of hair-trigger confrontation in the restless war agitation of the neocons. Iranian General Yahya Rahim Safavi, commander of the Iranian Revolutionary Guards, said earlier in August: "If Israel should dare to strike our nuclear installations, we will come down on its head like a heavy hammer crushing its skull." This was in response to repeated threats by Israeli Defense Minister Shaul Mofaz that his forces were ready to take the "necessary steps" to eliminate the Iranian capability, an oblique reference to Israel's 1981 destruction of Iraq's Osirak reactor. (*Washington Post*, August 30, 2004)

One day earlier, neocon Undersecretary of State for Arms Control and International Security John Bolton had told an audience at the Hudson Institute in Washington that it was imperative that the Iranian nuclear program be brought before the UN Security Council. "To fail to do so would risk sending a signal to would-be proliferators that there are no serious consequences for pursuing secret nuclear weapons programs," said Bolton. "We cannot let Iran, a leading sponsor of international terrorism, acquire nuclear weapons and the means to deliver them to Europe, most of central Asia and the Middle East, or beyond," Bolton added. "Without serious, concerted, immediate intervention by the international community, Iran will be well on the road to doing so."

Similar threatening noises came from Condoleezza Rice at the Bush National Security Council. According to well-informed sources, Rice was directed by Cheney to call Sharon during the last week of August 2004; she advised the Israeli leader that the US was considering an attack on Iran, and suggested that Sharon put his withdrawal from the Gaza Strip on hold for the time being, and focus rather on dealing with the "Iranian menace." On August 19, William Luti of the Pentagon neocon cabal told a conference call of Congressional aides from both parties that there were at least five or six countries in the world with traits which "no responsible leader can allow." Luti appeared to be hinting that Bush's axis of evil needed to be expanded to more countries which would be eligible for pre-emptive attack. (*Time*, September 13, 2004)

Iranian public opinion had been shocked by a raving, psychotic column by Charles Krauthammer in the July 23 *Washington Post*: "The long awaited revolution [in Iran] is not happening. Which [makes] the question of pre-emptive attack all the more urgent. If nothing is done, a fanatical terrorist regime openly dedicated to the destruction of 'the Great Satan' will have both nuclear weapons and missiles to deliver them. All that stands between us and that is either revolution or pre-emptive attack." Iranian observers compared this to the US propaganda campaign which had preceded the attack on Iraq.

Anxious to return the compliment, the Iranians responded to the publication of the 9/11 commission report by attacking the 9/11 myth, always a sensitive point for the US regime. The *Teheran Times* described the report as a "whitewash," because it assumed that the CIA, FBI, and US military all "acted in good faith." The paper said the commission report excluded "a priori the most important question raised by the events of September 11, 2001: did US government agencies deliberately permit – or actively assist – the carrying out of this terrorist atrocity, in order to provide the Bush administration with the necessary pretext to carry out its program of war in central Asia and the Middle East and a huge buildup of the forces of state repression at home?" The *Times* scored the report's refusal to name names, and specifically asked, "were any of the Al Qaeda operatives, especially the ringleaders and organizers of the suicide hijackings, at some point assets or agents of the US intelligence services?" In this context, the *Teheran Times* recalled the origins of al Qaeda in the guerrilla war against the Soviets in Afghanistan, where the central role of the US intelligence agencies was well documented. The article noted: "Khalid Sheikh Mohammed, the reported mastermind of the 9/11 attacks, was a longtime associate of Abdul Rasul Sayyaf, a leader of the Afghan Northern Alliance and current ally of the US-backed Afghan president, Hamid Karzai." (*Teheran Times*, July 27, 2004)

US FORCES IN IRAQ AS HOSTAGES TO IRAN – OR TO SHARON?

Competent US military commanders dread the prospect of war with Iran. Iran is four times the area of Iraq, and has three times the population. Its infrastructure was not destroyed during the Kuwait war in the way that Iraq's was, and Iran has not been subjected to 13 years of crippling UN sanctions on everything, including food and medicine. The Iranian military forces are intact. In case of war, Iran could be expected to use all means ranging from ballistic missile attacks on US and Israeli bases to asymmetrical warfare. The situation of the US forces already in Iraq could quickly become extraordinarily critical. Shamkhani alluded to this prospect when he said that "The US military presence will not become an element of strength at our expense. The opposite is true because their forces would turn into a hostage." In reality, the US forces in Iraq were already hostages – to Sharon, who could involve them in war with Iran at any time of his choosing.

For purposes of analogy, the Iraq war so far could be compared to the first months of the Korean War, from June to November 1950. By provoking Iran to go beyond logistical support for guerrillas and the sending of volunteers, and come into the war with both feet, the neocons would be inviting a repeat of the Chinese intervention and the disastrous US retreat south from the Yalu to south of Seoul, which still stands as the longest retreat in US military history. Just as Chinese entry into the Korean conflict in late November 1950 created a wholly new and wider war, Iranian entry into the US-Iraq war would have similarly incalculable consequences. The choices might quickly narrow to the large-scale use of nuclear weapons or defeat for the current US hollow army of just 10 divisions. War with Iran meant a military draft, just for starters. If Iran could close the Straits of Hormuz with its new anti-ship missiles, it would mean rationing of food and fuel. Bloated speculative financial structures could hardly survive.

ANOTHER STEP TOWARDS WORLD WAR III

The use of nuclear weapons by the US against Iran would have a dangerous complication: Iran is an important neighbor and trading partner of the Russian Federation, which is helping with Iran's nuclear power reactor program. The threatened US/Israeli raid on Iran might kill Russian citizens as well. Such a US attack on Iran might prod the Russian government into drawing its own line in the sand, rather than sitting idle as the tide of US aggression swept closer and closer to Russia's borders, as one country after another in central Asia was occupied. In other words, a US attack on Iran bids fair to be the opening of World War III, making explicit what was already implicit in the invasion of Iraq. The Iran war project of the neocons was the very midsummer of madness, and it underlined once more that the neocons had to go.

RUSSIANS EXPOSE US-UK TERROR ROLE AFTER SCHOOL MASSACRE

In early September, 2004, terrorists attacked a school in Beslan, North Ossetia, in the Russian Federation. Before this hostage crisis was over, more than 300 people, over half of them children, were killed. On Monday, September 6, Russian President Vladimir Putin made remarks to the western press which exposed the key role of the US and British governments in backing Chechen terrorism. Whatever Putin's previous role in events regarding Chechnya, his post-Beslan political posture tended to undercut the legitimacy of the supposed Anglo-American "war on terror," and pointed up the hypocrisy of the Bush regime's pledge that it would make no distinction between the terrorists and those who harbor them – since Washington and London were currently harboring Chechens implicated in terrorism. All in all, Putin's response to Chechen events, on the eve of the third anniversary of 9/11, brought the collapse of the official 9/11 myth measurably closer. The hypocritical terror demagogy of Bush and Blair was now undercut by the head of state of another permanent member of the UN Security Council.

On Monday, September 6, Putin spoke for three and one half hours with a group of some 30 western correspondents and Russia experts at his dacha near Novo Ogarevo outside Moscow. Most of the US press ignored these remarks. Putin, a KGB veteran who knew whereof he spoke, told the gathering that the school massacre showed that "certain western political circles would like to weaken Russia, just as the Romans wanted to destroy Carthage." He thus suggested that the US and UK, not content with having bested Russia in the Cold War, now wanted to proceed to the dismemberment and total destruction of Russia – a Carthaginian peace like the one the Romans finally imposed at the end of the Punic Wars in 146 BC, when they poured salt into the earth at Carthage so nothing would every grow there again. (*Le Monde*, September 8, 2004) There was no link between Russian policy in Chechnya and the hostage-taking in Beslan, said Putin, meaning that the terrorists were using the Chechen situation as a pretext to attack Russia. According to a paraphrase in *Le Monde*: "The aim of this international terrorism, supported more or less openly by foreign states, whose names the Russian president does not want to name, is to weaken Russia from the inside, by criminalizing its economy, by provoking its disintegration through propagating separatism in the Caucasus and the transformation of the region into a *place d'armes*, a military staging ground for actions directed against the Russian Federation."

"Mr. Putin," continued *Le Monde*, "restated the accusation he had launched in a veiled form against western countries which appear to him to use double-talk. On the one side, their leaders assure the Russian President of their solidarity in the fight against terrorism. On the other hand, the intelligence services and the military – 'who have not abandoned their Cold War prejudices,' in Putin's words – maintain contacts with those the international press calls the 'rebels.' 'Why are those who emulate Bin Laden called terrorists and the people who kill children, rebels? Where is the logic?' asked Vladimir Putin, and then gave the answer: 'Because certain political circles in the West want to weaken Russia just like the Romans wanted to destroy Carthage.' 'But, continued Putin, "we will not allow this scenario to come to pass."' *Le Monde* went on: "This is, according to [Putin] a bad calculation, because Russia is a factor of stability. By weakening it, the Cold War nostalgics are clearly acting against the interests of their own country." In Putin's words: "We are the sincere champions of this cooperation [against terrorism], we are open and loyal partners. But if foreign services have contacts with the 'rebels,' they cannot be treated as reliable allies, as Russia is for them." (Daniel Vernet, "*M. Poutine accuse et s'explique sur sa 'guerre totale' au terrorisme*," *Le Monde*, September 8, 2004)

In *Guardian* correspondent Jonathan Steele's account of the meeting with Putin, the Russian President gave this response to the US and UK on the question of negotiating with the Chechen guerrillas of Aslan Maskhadov: "Why don't you meet Osama bin Laden, invite him to Brussels or to the White House and engage in talks, ask him what he wants and give it to him so he leaves you in peace? You find it possible to set some limitations in your dealings with these bastards, so why should we talk to people who are child-killers?" (*Guardian*, September 7, 2004)

On Saturday, September 4, Putin had delivered a national television address to the Russian people on the Beslan tragedy, which had left more than 300 dead, over half of them children. The main thrust was that terrorism constitutes international proxy warfare against Russia. Among other things Putin said: "In general, we need to admit that we did not fully understand the complexity and the dangers of the processes at work in our own country and in the world. In any case, we proved unable to react adequately. We showed ourselves to be weak, and the weak get beaten." "Some people would like to tear from us a tasty morsel. Others are helping them. They are helping, reasoning that Russia still remains one of the world's major nuclear powers, and as such still represents a threat to them. And so they reason that this threat should be removed. Terrorism, of course, is just an instrument to achieve these gains." "What we are dealing with, are not isolated acts intended to frighten us, not isolated terrorist attacks. What we are facing is direct intervention of international terror directed against Russia. This is a total, cruel and full-scale war that again and again is taking the lives of our fellow citizens." (Kremlin.ru, September 6, 2004; EIR, September 7, 2004)

Around the time of 9/11, Putin had pointed to open recruitment of Chechen terrorists going on in London, telling a German interviewer: "In London, there is a recruitment station for people wanting to join combat in Chechnya. Today – not officially, but effectively in the open – they are talking there about recruiting volunteers to go to Afghanistan." (*Focus* – German weekly news magazine, September 2001) In addition, it is generally known in well-informed European circles that the leaders of the Chechen rebels were trained by the CIA, and that the Chechens were backed by US-sponsored anti-Russian fighters from Afghanistan. In the summer of 2004, US-UK backed Chechens destroyed two Russian airliners and attacked a Moscow subway station, in addition to the school atrocity.

Some aspects of Putin's thinking were further explained by a press interview given by Aslambek Aslakhanov, the Chechen politician who was one of Putin's official advisors. A dispatch from RIA Novosti reported Aslakhanov's comments as follows: "The terrorists who seized the school in Beslan, North Ossetia, took their orders from abroad. 'They were talking with people not from Russia, but from abroad. They were being directed,' said Aslambek Aslakhanov, advisor to the President of the Russian Federation. 'It is the desire of our "friends" – in quotation marks – who have probably for more than a decade been carrying out enormous, titanic work, aimed at dismembering Russia. These people have worked very hard, and the fact that the financing comes from there and that they are the puppet masters, is also clear.'" Aslakhanov, who was named by the terrorists as one of the people they were going to hold talks with, also told RIA Novosti that the bid for such "talks" was completely phony. He said that the hostage-takers were not Chechens. When he talked to them, by phone, in Chechen, they demanded that he talk Russian, and the ones he spoke with had the accents of other North Caucasus ethnic groups. (RIA Novosti, September 6, 2004; EIR, September 7, 2004)

On September 7, RIA Novosti reported on the demand of the Russian Foreign Ministry that two leading Chechen figures be extradited from London and

Washington to stand trial in Russia. A statement from the Russia Foreign Ministry's Department of Information and Press indicated that Russia would put the United States and Britain on the spot about extraditing two top Chechen separatist officials who had been given asylum in Washington and London, respectively. They were Akhmad Zakayev, known as a "special representative" of Aslan Maskhadov (currently enjoying asylum in London), and Ilyas Akhmadov, the "Foreign Minister" of the unrecognized "Chechen Republic-Ichkeria" (then residing in the USA). (RIA Novosti, September 7, 2004; EIR, September 8, 2004)

"SCHOOL SEIZURE WAS PLANNED IN WASHINGTON AND LONDON"

This was the headline of an even more explicit unsigned commentary by the Russian news agency KMNews.ru. This analysis blamed the Beslan school massacre squarely on the US and British intelligence agencies. The point of departure here was that Shamil Basayev, the brutal Chechen field commander, had been linked to the attack (something that Putin advisor Aslambek Aslakhanov had said was known to the Russian FSB, successor of the KGB). The article highlighted the recent rapprochement of London and Washington with key representatives of Aslan Maskhadov: Britain's grant of asylum to Akhmad Zakayev (December 2003) and the USA's welcome for Ilyas Akhmadov (August 2004). Basayev, viewed in European circles as a straight-out CIA agent, openly claimed responsibility for the school massacre almost two weeks after the fact.

KMNews: CHECHEN TERROR BOSS ON US STATE DEPARTMENT PAYROLL

The Russian news agency KMNews wrote: "In early August, ... 'Minister of Foreign Affairs of the Chechen Republic-Ichkeria' Ilyas Akhmadov received political asylum in the USA. And for his 'outstanding services,' Akhmadov received a Reagan-Fascell grant," including a monthly stipend, medical insurance, and a well-equipped office with all necessary support services, including the possibility of meetings with political circles and leading US media...."What about our partners in the 'anti-terrorist coalition,' who provided asylum, offices and money to Maskhadov's representatives?" asked the Russian press agency. Citing the official expressions of sympathy and offers of help from President Bush, National Security Adviser Condoleezza Rice, and State Department spokesman Richard Boucher, KMNews warned: "But let's not shed tears of gratitude just yet. First we should ask: were 'Special Representative of the President of CRI' Zakayev or 'Minister of Foreign Affairs of the CRI' Akhmadov, located in Great Britain and the USA, aware of the terrorist acts that were in preparation? Beyond a doubt.... And let's also find out, how Akhmadov is spending the money provided by the Reagan-Fascell Foundation. We note: this

Foundation is financed by the US Congress through the budget of the State Department!

Thus, the conclusion is obvious. Willingly or not, Downing Street and the White House provoked the guerrillas to these latest attacks. Willingly or not, Great Britain and the USA have nurtured the separatists with material, information and diplomatic resources. Willingly or not, the policy of London and Washington fostered the current terrorist acts... As the ancients said, *cui bono*? Perhaps we are too hasty with such sweeping accusations against our 'friends' and 'partners'? Is there a motive for the Anglo-American 'anti-terrorist coalition' to fan the fires of terror in the North Caucasus?... Alas, there is a motive. It is no secret, that the West is vitally interested in maintaining instability in the Caucasus. That makes it easier to pump out the fossil fuel extracted in the Caspian region, and it makes it easier to control Georgia and Azerbaijan, and to exert influence on Armenia. Finally, it makes it easier to drive Russia out of the Caspian and the Caucasus. *Divide et impera!* [divide and conquer] – the leaders of the Roman Empire already introduced this simple formula for subjugation."

KMNews: TERROR SUPPORTERS "ON THE BANKS OF THE THAMES AND THE POTOMAC"

KMNews continued: "Alas, it must be recognized that the co-authors of the current tragic events are to be found not in the Arab countries of the Middle East, but on the banks of the Thames and the Potomac. Will the leadership of Russia be able to make decisions, in this situation?" "Yes – if there is the political will. The first thing is that black must be called black, and white, white. It is time to admit that no "antiterrorist coalition" exists, that the West is pursuing its egotistical interests (spreading its political influence, seizing fossil fuels deposits, etc.). Our own coalition needs to be formed, with nations that are genuinely interested in eliminating terror in the North Caucasus. Finally, it is time to change the entire tactics and strategy of counter-terrorism measures. It is obvious that catching female suicide bombers on the streets of Moscow or carrying out operations to free children who are taken hostage, are, so to speak, the 'last line of defense.' It is time to learn to make preemptive strikes against the enemy, and it's time to carry combat onto the territory of the enemy. Otherwise, we shall be defeated." (Source: KMNews.ru, September 7, 2004; EIR, September 8, 2004)

Izvestia stressed the probable ethnic composition of the terrorist death squad, and its likely role in exacerbating tensions in the ethnic labyrinth of the Caucasus. *Izvestia* found the targeting of North Ossetia in the Beslan incident "not accidental," pointing to the danger of "irreversible consequences" for interethnic relations between Ossetians, Ingushis and Chechens. "Russia is now facing multi-vectored threats along the entire Caucasus," the paper wrote. (*Izvestia*, September 3, 2004)

In the wake of Putin's speech, prominent Russian commentators discussed the recent terror campaign against Russia in terms of a possible *casus belli* for a new East-West conflict. Several commentaries reaffirmed Putin's key statement that international terrorism has no independent existence, but functions only as "an instrument," wielded by powerful international circles committed (in part) to the early destruction of Russia as a nuclear-armed power. A commentary in the widely read Russian business news service RosBusinessConsult (RBC) was entitled "The West is unleashing Jihads against Russia." In language reminiscent of the Cold War, RBC charged that the recent wave of terror attacks against Russia, beginning with the sabotage of two airplanes and a terror bombing at a Moscow subway station, and culminating so far in the Beslan attack, was immediately preceded by what RBC calls "an ultimatum from the West," for Russia to turn over the Caucasus region to "Anglo-Saxon control."

ANGLO-AMERICAN TERROR ULTIMATUM TO RUSSIA FROM THE LONDON *ECONOMIST*

"Some days prior to the onset of the series of acts of terrorism in Russia, which has cost hundreds of lives, a number of extremely influential Western mass-media, expressing establishment positions, issued a personal warning to Vladimir Putin, that Russia should get out of the Caucasus, or else his political career would come to an end. Therefore, when the President on Saturday spoke of a declaration of war having been made against Russia, this was not just a matter of so-called 'international terrorism'... One week prior to the first acts of terrorism, the authoritative British magazine, the *Economist*, which expresses the positions of Great Britain's establishment, formulated the Western position concerning the Caucasus, and above all the policy of the Anglo-Saxon elite, in a very precise manner," RBC wrote.

CZECH NGO BLOWS UP RUSSIAN TANK; BRITISH EXPERTS TRAIN CHECHEN GANGS

The RBC commentary went on to cite the *Economist* of August 19, 2004, which contained what RBC characterized as the virtual ultimatum to Russia. RBC noted that "the carrying out of such a series of coordinated, highly professional terrorist attacks, would be impossible without the help of qualified 'specialists.'" RBC noted that at the end of August one such "specialist," working for an NGO based in the Czech republic, was arrested for blowing up a Russian armed personnel carrier. Also, British "experts" were found instructing Chechen gangs in how to lay mines. "It cannot be excluded, that also in Beslan, the logistics of the operation were provided by just such 'specialists'," noted RBC.

The RBC editorial concluded: "Apparently, by having recourse to large-scale terrorist actions, the forces behind that terrorism have now acted directly to force a 'change' in the political situation in the Caucasus, propagating interethnic wars into Russia... The only way to resist this would be for Moscow to make it known that we are ready to fight a new war, according to new rules and new methods – not with mythical 'international terrorists', who do not and never existed, but with the controllers of the 'insurgents and freedom fighters'; a war against the geopolitical puppet-masters who are ready to destroy thousands of Russians for the sake of achieving their new division of the world." (RBC, September 7, 2004; EIR, September 7, 2004)

In a related comment, the Chairman of the Duma Foreign Affairs Committee, Dmitri Rogozin, declared in an interview on Sunday, September 5: "I think [those behind the terrorism] are those who would like to see Russia totally discredited as a power.... I think that the aim is to destabilize the political situation in the country and plunge Russia into total chaos." (Ekho Moskvy, September 6, 2004) Western press organs responded to the school massacre with a campaign to blame, not the terrorists, but the Putin regime and Russian society. This disingenuous policy further stoked Russian resentment. On September 6, Strana.ru headlined, "Western Press: The Tragedy Is Russia's Own Fault," commenting that "unlike official politicians, journalists do not want to admit that the bombings and hostage-takings in our country are acts of international terrorism." (EIR, September 7, 2004) Another example of this Putin-bashing was the article by Masha Lippman in the *Washington Post* of September 9, 2004. This was quickly followed by a campaign against Putin for being undemocratic, including, with indescribable hypocrisy, the complaint that Putin had not purged his intelligence officers after the school massacre – this from the US, where no one had been held accountable for 9/11.

A basic reason for the US-UK surrogate warfare against Russia was the great Anglo-Saxon fear of a continental bloc of the type which emerged during the run-up to Bush's Iraq aggression. The centerpiece of the continental bloc would be the German-Russian relationship. Washington and London feared that Russia would soon agree to accept euros in payment for its oil deliveries. This would not just prevent the Anglo-Americans from further skimming off oil transactions between Russia and Europe. It would represent the beginning of the end of the dollar as the reserve currency of the world, a role which the battered greenback, weakened by Bush's $500 billion yearly trade deficit and $750 billion budget deficit, can no longer fulfill. If Russia were to adopt the euro, it was expected that the Eurasian giant would quickly be followed by Iran, Indonesia, Venezuela, and other countries. This would put an end to the ability of the US to run astro-nomical foreign trade deficits, and would place the question of a US return to a production-based economy on the agenda.

The 9/11 myth was still a menace to mankind.

AFTERWORD

> The Bush operation in Iowa had all the smell of a CIA covert operation....Strange aspects of the Iowa operation [included] a long, slow count and then the computers broke down at a very convenient point, with Bush having a six point bulge....
> *Manchester Union Leader*, February 24, 1980. (Tarpley and Chaitkin, *George Bush: The Unauthorized Biography*, p. 343.)

> Do you think that the electoral system in the United States is without flaws? Need I remind you of how their elections were held in the United States?
> – Vladimir Putin, December 23, 2004.

The November 2004 election was the first presidential contest to be held in the US after 9/11. The rogue networks of the US invisible government, whose power had been enormously enhanced by their successful execution of the 9/11 crimes, were not inclined to tolerate any changes in the White House which might dilute their power, however minimally. Those who had presided over 9/11 and the subsequent cover-up had to remain in power, partly as a guarantee that no September criminals would be thrown to the wolves, and partly to ensure that the neocon attempt to organize the world through a war of civilizations would not be de-emphasized, but escalated.

Other countries expressed their consternation over the cold coup that gave Bush a second term not so much by protesting the blatant vote suppression and vote fraud, but rather by dumping the US dollar, provoking a dollar crisis which made it clear to all that it was the last days of Pompeii for the moribund US currency. As the dollar reached 1.35 to the euro, the handwriting on the wall presaged the jettisoning of the greenback as the residual reserve currency of the world. This 1.35 figure was also a powerful argument that the entire neocon effort to shore up the US imperial position after 9/11 had been a failure. Since the dollar (including the London eurodollar and the various xenodollars) was the nerve and fist of Anglo-American world domination, the response of the US-UK finance oligarchs and of the intelligence agencies which they control was a sudden frenzy to increase the looting rate of the world economy in a bid to give the US currency some hope for survival.

One feature of this financier frenzy was the attempt to inflict yet another strategic humiliation on the Russian Federation, this time by orchestrating a pro-NATO "people power" coup on the streets of Kiev in the Ukraine. This effort to extend the claws of NATO so far into the Russian defensive *glacis* revealed US intentions as openly hostile, with blunt warnings and inflammatory propaganda campaigns on both sides. (Glacis: a smooth slope or apron of a fortification.)

After their attacks on Afghanistan and Iraq, and after blustering their war threats all through 2004 against Iran and Syria, the neocon fascist madmen were evidently contemplating the absolute zenith of suicidal folly: a confrontation with the Russian Federation, a thermonuclear power which, as Wolfowitz, Brzezinski, and their cliques were well aware, was the only one which retained the unquestioned ability to annihilate the United States and most of its people within a few hours. Every previous case of neocon lunacy was eclipsed by this new outburst of insanity. These events were indicative of what life would henceforth be like in the US under the rule of the 9/11 invisible government networks.

NOT AN ELECTION, BUT A CIA COVERT OPERATION

By all indications, if an honest vote count had occurred, Bush would have lost the Electoral College and very likely the popular vote as well. Every device of vote suppression, voter intimidation, vote fraud, ballot-box stuffing, e-tampering, electronic hacking, and vote stealing was cynically thrown into action by the CIA-Bush machine. Kerry had repeatedly promised his supporters that he would fight to guarantee that every vote be counted. In the hours after the polls had closed, Edwards was sent out with a short speech saying that Kerry would not capitulate, and that "every vote would be counted." But the Kerry campaign crassly reneged on this promise by conceding the election on Wednesday, November 3.

A serious candidate would have announced comprehensive legal actions to seize and impound the electronic, punch card, and optical scan voting machines which had so obviously been rigged in favor of Bush with a view to proving in court that they had been tampered with. Instead, Kerry rushed to surrender, and it was left up to the Green Party and the Libertarian Party to demand an Ohio recount and pay for it with $125,000 of their own money. Kerry, in spite of his war record, proved to be a coward. He had won the election, but he would not fight to save the country from four more years of the Bush gang.

On the Thursday after the vote, Greg Palast contributed a useful article entitled "Kerry Won," which published at TomPaine.com. Here Palast argued that Kerry was the rightful winner in Ohio and New Mexico, among other states. The limitation of Palast's argument was his preponderant stress on "spoilage," the factor which causes about 3% of all votes cast in the US to be thrown out or otherwise invalidated. Spoilage is of course concentrated in low-income, black, and Hispanic polling places which usually vote heavily Democratic. All of this is of course true as far as it goes, although Palast too exclusively focused on these traditional, structural, forms of vote fraud, which have been typical over the past 40 years since William Rehnquist got his start harassing Hispanic voters. But 2004 was not your father's vote fraud. It was a very modern, hi-tech version which could not have been carried out without the full involvement of secret intelligence agencies. In other words, the 2004 vote was stolen by a conspiracy involving the Bush machine and the intelligence community, and it is this question of a grand offensive conspiracy involving spooks which appears to be, as usual, the sticking point for Palast.

During the afternoon of election day, anti-Bush sentiment was buoyed by leaks of exit polls showing that Bush was losing. Exit polling was conducted by Edison Media Research in cooperation with Mitofsky International on behalf of the National Election Pool, the name currently given to the consortium of television networks and the Associated Press which in the past has been called News Election Service, Voter News Service, etc. According to one press report, "the major networks and the

Associated Press began receiving exit-poll data in the early afternoon but pledged in advance not to use it until all the polls had closed in a particular state – even though such information, which is hardly conclusive, routinely leaks out on the Internet. Slate.com and the Drudge Report touted in mid-afternoon early exit polls showing Kerry with a one-percentage point lead in Florida and Ohio as well as significant leads in Pennsylvania, Wisconsin, Minnesota, and Michigan….NBC's Tim Russert noted that Kerry was winning six in 10 independent voters in Ohio. CBS's Ed Bradley noted that Kerry 'won women, he won men, he won first-time voters and he won the independents in New Jersey." (*Washington Post*, November 3, 2004)

As these reports were transmitted through the blogosphere, the impression grew that Bush was on his way to defeat. In an article written in the late evening after the polls closed we read that "according to National Election Poll interviews of voters leaving the polls, Bush appeared to be in a real fight to hold his presidency and avoid joining his father in being swept out of office after a single term. President George H. W. Bush lost his reelection bid in 1992 to Bill Clinton, and the current president systematically sought to avoid the mistakes he believed cost his father that election. But judging from exit polls yesterday, he had not expanded his coalition in any significant ways from four years ago, leading to the fight that was unfolding last night." (*Washington Post*, November 3, 2004)

This is also what Bush and his entourage were thinking. Bush started his day in Crawford, Texas, where he voted. He then proceeded to a rally in Ohio. Here, according to some reports, he met personally with J. Kenneth Blackwell, the Secretary of State of Ohio, the rabidly partisan black Republican who was on the one hand the head of Bush's re-election drive in that state, and at the same time the state official overseeing the voting. Bush then flew to Washington. According to one version, "It was on the plane that strategist Karl Rove started calling around to get the results of early exit polls. But the line kept breaking down. The only information that came through as the plane descended was a BlackBerry message from an aide that simply read: "**Not good**." Not long afterward, Rove got a more detailed picture and told the President and senior aides the bad news. Florida Governor Jeb Bush had been saying the state was looking good, and the Bush team had expected to be ahead in Ohio. But Kerry was leading everywhere. "**I wanted to throw up**," said an aide onboard. …On the ground in Arlington, Va., that afternoon, chief strategist Matthew Dowd was walking around Bush campaign headquarters looking like a "scientist whose formulas were all wrong," said a top Bush staff member. Dowd had designed the strategy for targeting voters, and the exit polls were undermining his every theory. It would take him six long hours to crack the code. When the actual vote counts started coming in at 8 p.m., Dowd noticed that in South Carolina, Virginia and Florida the numbers were what the Republicans expected them to be; the President was outperforming the exit polls. "We've got to go talk to the press. **The exit polls are wrong**," Dowd said. (*Time*, November 15, 2004, emphasis added)

The gloom had been deep in the Bush camp that afternoon. "Discouraging exit polls had poured into Bush-Cheney campaign headquarters in Arlington, with Bush strategists privately describing the early picture as **cataclysmic**…. When the networks initially decreed that Virginia was too close to call, Bill Kristol of Fox News said: "That can't be good for President Bush… But they started reminding reporters and top supporters that those polls had been wrong in 2000, and they asserted that Bush was doing better than the figures suggested. Bush invited reporters into the White House residence around 9:37 PM in an attempt to steady his troops. 'We are very upbeat, thank you. I believe I will win, thank you very much.' The setting was designed to project confidence after a grim day around the White House." (*Washington Post*, November 3, 2004, emphasis added)

Another account corroborates these events: "I saw this look on [Rove's] face and then the phone died," said White House communications director Dan Bartlett. "He said, 'Not good.' It was, Bartlett added, 'like a punch in the gut.' ....'I was sick,' Rove said in an interview as he talked about those moments on the president's plane. 'But then I got angry when I started seeing the numbers. None of them made any sense.' Those exit polls, of course, turned out to be wrong, as many inside the Bush headquarters believed once they began to examine them in detail, and today Rove is celebrated by none other than the president as 'the architect' of the reelection victory." (*Washington Post*, November 7, 2004) But the exit polls were not wrong. The exit polls were by every indication an accurate barometer of the votes the citizens thought they had cast. The difference between the exit polls and the final reported results represents the margin of vote fraud.

Electronic-cybernetic vote fraud of the type practiced by the CIA-Bush machine habitually includes a computer breakdown in the thick of the action, as the 1980 comment from William Loeb reminds us. In 2002, "a computer meltdown resulted in no release of data on Election Day. On Tuesday [November 2, 2004], new problems surfaced: a 2.5 hour data blackout and samples that at one point or another included too many women, too few Westerners, not enough Republicans and a lead for Democratic presidential nominee John F. Kerry in the national survey that persisted until late in the evening. In two instances on election night – the results for Virginia and South Carolina – the networks held off projecting a winner when voting ended because exit polls showed the races were too close to call, only to see President Bush win easily in both states," wrote one journalist. "Successive waves of the national exit poll in the afternoon and evening reported that Kerry had had a two- or three-percentage point lead over Bush nationally and in several key states, including Ohio. Preliminary exit poll results had leaked throughout the day and were posted on a number of websites, including the widely viewed Drudge Report site, which added to the confusion and fanned the media frenzy."

Then came the indispensable computer breakdown, which is generally used as a cover to cook the existing data: "To compound the problem further, a server at Edison/Mitofsky malfunctioned shortly before 11 p.m. The glitch prevented access to any exit poll results until the technicians got a backup system operational at 1:33 AM yesterday. The crash occurred barely minutes before the consortium was to update its exit polling with the results of later interviewing that found Bush with a one-point lead. Instead, journalists were left relying on preliminary exit poll results released at 8:15 PM, which still showed Kerry ahead by three percentage points." (*Washington Post*, November 4, 2004) Bush was officially awarded Iowa on the Friday after the election. It had been too close to call, "but with Bush holding a 12,000-vote advantage, Iowa officials determined yesterday that there were not enough absentee votes for Kerry to overcome Bush's lead." (*Washington Post*, November 6, 2004)

OHIO OUTRAGES

Bush was saved by a "red shift" of about 3% to 5% in a number of key states between the exit polls and the reported results. These discrepancies, it should be noted, were always in favor of Bush, and never to his detriment. The red shift was attributable to vote fraud. A full analysis of vote fraud in the 2004 elections goes beyond the scope of this book. Suffice it to say that Bush's forces used every known device to falsify the results of the elections. The mechanisms of vote fraud in the key battleground state of Ohio have been documented by Robert Fitrakis and his friends at www.freepress.org, and need not be repeated in detail here. A typical case of electronic vote fraud was the following:

> The vote counting was marred in several places by computer glitches. The most serious appears to be in Ohio, which provided Bush with his decisive margin. Election officials in Franklin County, in the Columbus area, said yesterday that a computer error gave Bush 3,893 extra votes in one precinct. Bush actually received 365 votes in the precinct out of 638 votes cast, Matthew Damschroder, director of the Franklin County Board of Elections, told the Columbus Dispatch. It was not clear whether Ohio experienced any other problems with electronic ballots. About 30 percent of the voters in the state voted electronically. (*Washington Post*, November 6, 2004)

In Ohio, vote suppression had been meticulously prepared. Blackwell had seen to it that lists of registered voters had been purged of numerous Democratic voters just before the election, using the favorite GOP pretext that these black, Hispanic, and poor people were actually convicted felons. By the time many of those purged realized what had happened, it was too late for them to be reinstated. Blackwell outdid himself in inventing technical pretexts for rejecting new registrations, and for denying and disallowing absentee ballots for voters suspected of being Democrats. Newly registered Democratic voters received threatening letters informing them that their registrations were being challenged by the Republican Party. They could bring a lawyer and witnesses to their hearings, these letters ominously added. Phantom leaflets alleged that voting had been extended through Wednesday. Other leaflets announced that would-be voters who had unpaid parking tickets, unpaid child support payments, or overdue library books would be dragged from the polls and put in prison.

Imposters placed telephone calls to likely Democratic voters telling them that their polling places had been changed – a fraud which was revealed in many cases only after would-be voters had waited for several hours in the rain to cast their ballots, and were told to start from scratch at their original polling places. Many polling places in black, Hispanic, and low-income areas opened late. When they did open, many of them had no pencils for paper ballots, and above all far fewer electronic voting machines than in previous years, since the Blackwell machine had arranged to transfer these voting machines to affluent Republican suburbs. The lack of voting machines resulted in long lines on a rainy day, and many of the frailer voters simply gave up. Many Republican employers threatened their hourly and other workers with firing if they tarried too long at the polls, and not a few were actually fired. Innumerable votes were lost in this way.

In the days before the election, Blackwell had demanded for the Republican Party the right to place "challengers" inside each polling place. These anti-voter vigilantes were in effect racist and fascist goons whose function was to intimidate and eject likely Democratic voters, whose names were recorded on "caging lists." These challengers had been ruled illegal by the federal district court, but this decision had been overturned by the federal circuit court in the wee hours of election day morning. The US Supreme Court had refused to hear an appeal to this outrageous decision. The knowledge that GOP goons would be running wild in the polling places doubtless convinced many other citizens to stay home. In many polling places, black voters were automatically challenged by the GOP goons and therefore given a provisional paper ballot. The provisional ballot became a new form of second class citizenship, a new Jim Crow system for the 21st century.

There were reports of boxes of provisional ballots being loaded onto mysterious privately owned trucks without any official supervision and disappearing into the night. Hispanic voters were challenged to produce proof of citizenship, including forms of identification that were not prescribed by Ohio law. This made it much harder for Hispanics to cast a ballot. Those who did get to vote had to deal with touch-screen voting machines which did not generate a voter-verifiable paper trail. Many machines persistently registered votes for Bush despite repeated efforts to vote for Kerry or others. All across the US, electronic voting machines manufactured by Diebold, Election Systems and Software, and Sequoia did yeoman service for the Bush campaign, falsifying countless votes. Bush was alleged to have won Ohio by 136,000 votes. When Kerry capitulated, over 155,000 provisional ballots and over 92,000 "spoiled" ballots, most of them from heavily Democratic polling places, had not been counted. All in all, it was a blatant violation of the Voting Rights Act, and a colossal constitutional crisis. But had not the neocon judge Scalia in December 2000 denied that US citizens had any constitutional right to vote?

The grim result of the Bush-Rove vote fraud and the capitulation of the Kerry campaign was yet another step towards domestic anarchy in the United States. The rogue networks of the invisible government were for the moment the masters of the situation. Bush was no president, but an illegitimate ruler – a lawless usurper leading a rogue state, a bandit regime. The "political capital" which Bush claimed he had earned in his post-election press conference was counterfeit. His alleged mandate was as worthless as a rubber check.

After more or less successful coups in 1998 (impeachment), 1999 (bombing Serbia), 2000 (the stolen election), 2001 (the 9/11 attacks), 2002 (the illegal grant of war powers to Bush), 2003 (the Iraq war), and 2004 (another stolen presidential election), the invisible government was already planning its inevitable successor coup for 2005. One form which this may take is a further radical reduction in the powers of the Congress. Senator Frist of Tennessee, the Republican Majority Leader in the Senate, announced that the Democrats' practice of using the filibuster to prevent the confirmation of a handful of right-wing extremists to the federal appellate bench was intolerable, and must come to an end.

Frist's "nuclear option" was unilaterally to re-write the Senate rules by a *coup de main*, a power grab making a filibuster against judicial nominations impossible. Such a measure would reduce the Senate to a one-party fiefdom along the lines of the current House of Representatives, and weaken the Constitutional system of checks and balances by making it far more difficult for the Senate to check a president determined to put racists and fascists into the federal judiciary. The few Republican traditionalists were uneasy over this extremist proposal, and Democratic leaders threatened to paralyze the Senate with parliamentary obstructionism, but whether these forces could stop the Frist coup was not clear.

Naturally, the November 2004 coup could not have gone as smoothly as it did without the willingness of Senator Kerry to capitulate. For some, Kerry's refusal to contest manifest vote fraud was simply the consequence of his Skull & Bones pedigree. These observers imagine that Kerry received a call from Skull & Bones headquarters instructing him to throw in the towel, which he promptly did. The view here is rather that Kerry (and his wife) was an oligarchical specimen, somewhat above the average in intelligence for those circles, but unable to imagine anything other than oligarchical rule and oligarchical methods. The world of the foundations inhabited by Mrs. Kerry is in particular one of the decisive centers of oligarchical influence on American life, and there is every indication that the candidate felt at home here. It is thus Kerry's oligarchical mentality which predisposed him to surrender. Concerning the specific dynamics of the hoisting of the white flag on the day after the elections, Kerry appears to have been convinced to capitulate by Bob Shrum, who had wrecked the early phases of his campaign, and by Mary Beth Cahill, that the provisional ballots plus the absentee ballots in Ohio were not enough to surmount Bush's alleged lead.

Did Kerry have an alternative? He did: from the defeat of the Kapp putsch in Berlin in March 1920 to the defeat of the Aznar putsch in Madrid in March 2004, the successful model for resistance to an attempted coup d'état by a clique of reactionaries has been an open-ended general strike by the labor movement, progressive political parties, students and youth, women's organizations, and their allies. This is what prevented Aznar from setting up a dictatorship in the wake of the Spanish train bombings.

In the United States in November 2004, this would have taken the form of a general strike in favor of constitutional government called out by the Democratic Party, the AFL-CIO, environmentalists, women, progressives, students, and the like. The goal would have been to shut the country down until an accurate vote count had been carried out, which would unquestionably result in the defeat of Bush. Jesse Jackson proposed something along these lines to Gore in 2000, but the idea was refused. It is a rare oligarch who is willing to detonate mass action in the streets, and Kerry too proved no exception. As for the Democratic Party, it feared alienating its plutocratic financial backers far more than the loss of any single election, and was therefore structurally incapable of mass action. If Nader contributed nothing else, he contributed an apt characterization of the Democratic Party as gutless, spineless, feckless, and clueless.

The Democrats were even afraid of taking their stand on the US Constitution. Article XIV, passed by Congress on June 13, 1866 and ratified on July 9, 1868 in response to post-Confederate election chicanery against freedmen, included provisions precisely tailored to activities of the Bush machine in Ohio, Florida, and several other states. Here we read in Section 2:

> But when the right to vote at any election for the choice of electors for President and Vice President of the United States, representatives in Congress, the executive and judicial officers of a State, or the members of the legislature thereof, is denied to any of the male inhabitants of such State, being twenty-one years of age, and citizens of the United States, or in any way abridged, except for participation in rebellion, or other crime, the basis of representation therein shall be reduced in the proportion which the number of such male citizens shall bear to the whole number of male citizens twenty-one years of age in such State.

References to male voters in this amendment would of course be expanded to include all voters in the light of the XIX Amendment. Here was at least a minimal response to Bush's vote fraud coup: cut the basis of representation in the House and Senate in the vote fraud states, thereby diminishing the number of their electors in the Electoral College as well as in the two chambers.

THE 9/11 ISSUE WAS INDEED DECISIVE

Starting in November 2003, I had argued that the 9/11 issue would be the dominant one in the 2004 elections. This thesis recognized first of all that a party re-alignment was due in 2004 in which some new pattern of dominance in the Electoral College was likely to replace the post-1968 pattern of Republican hegemony based on the racist Southern Strategy developed by Kevin Phillips for Nixon. Such a party re-alignment would continue the pattern which has held true since the inception of the current US federal Constitution in 1788, and which has included similar re-alignments in 1828, 1860, 1896, and 1932, as well as 1968. My point was that, if the 9/11 myth had been dismantled, the 2004 election would probably lead to a progressive party re-alignment. If, however, the 9/11 myth were to survive intact, there was an acute danger that the party realignment would produce some form of fascist rule. Unfortunately, this second variant may now be on its way to fulfillment, although it may still be too early to say.

For those seriously committed to defeating the 9/11 myth, the most promising approach was represented by the Independent International Truth Commission, modeled more or less on the Russell-Sartre Vietnam War Crimes Tribunal of 1966-67. The failure of the 9/11 truth movement to convene the IITC prior to November 2004 constituted the single most important defeat of the 9/11 truth movement – a defeat which all the other successes of this movement were not sufficient to counterbalance. The IITC was the adequate forum to demolish the 9/11 myth among intellectuals and opinion leaders internationally as well as to erode it nationally in the US. Instead, the initiatives which were carried out succeeded only in the regional attrition of the myth within the US, which unfortunately turned out not to be enough.

The Bush campaign presented the 9/11 myth as a new compulsory pagan civic mystery cult of which their candidate was the high priest. Bush unwaveringly built his entire campaign on the demagogic ethos of 9/11 and its related chauvinistic and racist themes. 9/11 was evoked in the majority of the most widely used Bush-Cheney television ads. The entire Republican National Convention was organized around the 9/11 motif. 9/11 was conjured up by Bush, Cheney, and their surrogates in every speech. Bush spoke about 9/11 in the televised debates, and returned to stress 9/11 in his campaign crescendo at the end of October. 9/11 was Bush's chief alibi, his pretext, his escape clause; when Bush found that his back was to the wall, he invariably reached for 9/11. The weak and vacillating Kerry allowed Bush to use the 9/11 fiasco, in reality the moment of his greatest malfeasance, as a positive credential.

The veteran Democratic Party consultant (and habitual loser) Bob Shrum argued that, after 9/11, the American people would not tolerate divisive campaigning, and would only reward a positive and upbeat campaigner. Shrum therefore prohibited the obvious attack line against Bush – that he was the Nero of 9/11, the man who fiddled or otherwise dithered while New York burned. This, Shrum held, would represent sacrilege to the 9/11 myth and the oligarchical consensus that stood behind it. Kerry allowed himself to be dominated by Shrum until after the Republican convention, when it was already too late. These events presaged Kerry's final surrender.

Even so, the 9/11 myth came under significant attack. Howard Dean noted in December 2003 that many thought the Bush administration knew about 9/11 in advance, and objected to the phony terror alert designed to step on Kerry's convention bounce. However, Kerry and Edwards failed to hold Bush systematically accountable for his passivity before 9/11, and for freezing that day.

Former Senator Bob Kerrey, himself a 9/11 commission member, announced some days after the vote that he no longer felt bound by the non-partisan pledge sworn by all the commissioners, and outlined how the 9/11 issue could in his opinion have been turned against Bush. In Kerrey's view, this could have been done by stressing Bush's inertia, passivity, and failure to act in any way in response to the many warnings the White House was receiving about the imminence of major attacks – the Nero of 9/11 argument. This would have amounted to an attempt to spin the 9/11 story against Bush from within the confines of the myth, and it can be debated whether such a strategy would have proven effective, but Democratic candidate Kerry was not even capable of this. This approach was also illustrated in the cover story by Benjamin DeMott in the October 2004 issue of *Harper's Magazine*; here the 9/11 commission report a "whitewash," a "cheat and a fraud."

> There's little mystery about why the Commission is tongue-tied. It can't call a liar a liar. The most momentous subject before the 9/11 commission was: What did President Bush know about the Al Qaida threat to the United States, when did he know it, and if he knew little, why so?... Facing his questioners in April 2004, the President said he had not been informed that terrorists were in this country. Conceivably it was at or near the moment when Bush took this position that the members of the Commission who heard him grasped that casting useful light on the relation between official conduct and national unpreparedness would be impossible. The reason? The President's claim was untrue. It was a lie, and the Commissioners realized that they couldn't allow it to be seen as a lie. Numberless officials

had…provided circumstantial detail about their attempts… to educate Bush as candidate, then as president-elect, then as commander in chief, about the threat from terrorists on our shores. The news these officials brought was spelled out in pithy papers both short and long; the documentation supplied was in every respect impressive. Nevertheless, the chief executive, seated before the Commission, declared: *Nobody told me*. And challenging the chief executive as a liar entailed an unthinkable cost – the possible rending of the nation's social and political fabric. (*Harper's*, October 2004)

DeMott reviewed the much-touted Presidential Daily Briefing of August 6, 2001, the gambit employed by Richard Clarke, which was declassified in April 2004 as a result of the fracas generated by the 9/11 commission hearings. This document, it will be remembered, was entitled "Bin Laden Determined to Strike in US," and contained the notation that "the FBI is conducting approximately 70 full field investigations throughout the US that it considers Bin Ladin-related." This is juxtaposed by DeMott with the 9/11 commission's summary of Bush's private testimony on this issue: "*The President told us the August 6 report was historical in nature.*"

DeMott's article should have been used as a briefing paper for a series of attacks by Kerry which would have focused on Bush's evident failure as a leader during the days and weeks leading up to 9/11, when no extraordinary meetings were held, no cabinet officers tasked, no agency heads instructed, no inter-agency process established, and in short nothing done to respond to so many urgent warnings from "clandestine, foreign government, and media reports" about imminent terrorism. This could have been done without challenging the central features of the 9/11 myth itself; it would have relied on what the non-witting part of the government, in other words the various Colleen Rowleys, was reporting about the invisible government rogue networks.

In April 2004, the *Washington Post* had carried a cartoon (repeated in "The Year in Cartoons" on December 19, 2004) which shows a tin man Cheney, a cowardly lion FBI, a scarecrow CIA, and a "Dorothy" Bush watching while a witch flies across the sky, tracing this message: "Surrender Dorothy! Or I'll fly planes into buildings. – Osama." The FBI lion comments: "What's it mean?" 'It's too vague!" complains the CIA scarecrow. "Yeah… and who is this 'Dorothy' character?" adds Bush. Seconded by the ever-scowling Miss Rice, Bush acted as if measures to foil the 9/11 plot were some kind of debutante cotillion which he would never dream of attending unless he had received an engraved invitation with his name calligraphically embossed upon it. That Kerry was incapable of even addressing this mass of empirical evidence of Bush's unfitness for office is a damning commentary on the Democratic challenger's lack of intellectual courage; granted, he owed his candidacy to Dean's immolation by the media on the 9/11 issue.

There would have been an adequate demographic base for an attack on the 9/11 myth. A Zogby International poll commissioned by Jimmy Walter in late August showed that just under 50% of New York City residents did not believe the official version, and thought the US had foreknowledge of the attacks; slightly fewer in New York state agreed.

A Pentagon flash animation on the Internet debunking the government contention that a Boeing 757-200 hit the Defense Department headquarters attracted a mass audience, forcing an article on this subject in the *Washington Post*. For the highbrow, BBC-2 television in October broadcast "The Power of Nightmares," a documentary which contended that al Qaeda simply does not exist, except as a "myth" and "dark illusion." This myth had been created by failed politicians whose slogans no longer work, and who were desperate to keep their power, this program argued. For the lowbrow, Howard Stern hosted spokesmen for the 9/11 truth movement and told his 13 million listeners that he did not believe a commercial airliner hit the Pentagon; a cruise missile, he said, was a far more plausible explanation.

To this must be added the collective impact of scores of websites, plus conferences in Berlin, Lucerne, San Francisco, and Toronto, – all multiplied through innumerable Internet radios, alternative television, videocassettes, DVDs, books, blogs and streaming web postings. The September 11 rally at Manhattan Center in New York City was advertised in the main newspapers of the metropolitan area, and was attended by some 1,300 people. The Los Angeles Citizens' Grand Jury, which met at the Bob Hope Patriotic Hall on October 24, was a people's initiative in which ordinary citizens went far beyond the unanswered questions to roundly condemn several key features of the official myth as physically impossible, while specifying that a rogue network inside the US government were the prime suspects in the case.

Towards the end of October, one hundred left liberal notables and 9/11 researchers including Noam Chomsky, Michael Parenti, Ralph Nader, and Howard Zinn demanded the re-opening of the 9/11 investigation and petitioned New York State Attorney General Eliot Spitzer to undertake this task. But, like all purely legal tactics, the Spitzer complaint ceded the initiative and the timetable to the lawyers, rather than keeping politics in command. Whatever chances this tactic may have had were sharply diminished when Spitzer announced that he was running for governor of New York State; Spitzer was hardly likely to compromise his gubernatorial prospects by becoming the Jim Garrison of the 9/11 cover-up scandal. It is also worth noting that Ralph Nader, in the several C-SPAN press conferences this writer was able to monitor, never brought up 9/11 as one of his core issues, and in fact almost never mentioned 9/11 at all.

The 9/11 truth movement was hobbled by those who persisted in making the "unanswered questions" theme their central issue. One could imagine that, come judgment day, when Gabriel sounds his horn to announce the resurrection, some misguided activists will jump out of their graves to repeat their still unanswered questions. Three years and more after 9/11, it was time to develop some answers.

Another weakness of the 9/11 truth movement was the tendency of some to rely on bereaved family members for their moral and political authority. The 9/11 families represented a broad spectrum; some were models of irenic humanitarianism in the quest for world peace and atonement. Others appeared to be xenophobes and even racists. Some supported Kerry, some supported Bush. One group, obsessed with what it called "intelligence reform," agitated above all to enact the recommendations of the 9/11 commission, some of which amounted to Patriot Act II on the installment plan, and all of which left the actual September criminals untouched. It was in any case a tragic waste to devote the two or three hours the 9/11 truth movement had on C-SPAN to pointless testimonials by family members. For those seriously committed to defeating the 9/11 myth, the only road remained the Independent International Truth Commission.

For the moment, the CIA-Bush machine may appear to have jammed a crowbar into the wheels of history. But it is also worth recalling that the 36-year cycles are only approximations which have held true since the aftermath of the Civil War; in earlier years we can observe a 40-year cycle (1788-1828) and a 32-year cycle (1828-1860). This means that while some profound change in the ruling regime is now unquestionably overdue, this cannot be calculated with chronometric precision. The 1788-1828 cycle almost ended in 1824, when a disputed election thrown into the House of Representatives ended with the victory of John Quincy Adams, with the backing of Henry Clay, over Andrew Jackson. This outcome had the positive effect of prolonging the first 36-year cycle for four more years under Adams, before the disasters of the Jackson presidency. Something of this sort may have happened in 2004 to produce Bush's second term, but in a disastrous and negative key.

There is of course also the more sinister possibility that the long-running era of US constitutional government is simply coming to its natural or unnatural end, and that the Bush cold coup of 2004 is a harbinger of that grim fact. And indeed, the general tendency of the recent machinations of the US shadow government appears as the incessant weakening of the US power base of empire – as a result of foolhardy actions which are supposed to be shoring it up.

Of course, it is only in the world of cable television schizophrenic make-believe that George Bush has been re-elected as president of the United States. Bush is a legitimate president only in the eyes of those well-paid commentators who spent the days after the election inventing fantastic stories about the triumph of moral values (in the person of the alcohol and cocaine-ravaged George W. Bush!) as the true key to the 2004 election. In the real world Bush was defeated by virtue of majority opposition in the country to his misrule, and that majority opposition, although demoralized and disoriented by Kerry's craven capitulation, can only remain and grow.

Normally a failed politician like Bush would have departed after one term, as his notorious father did, taking with him all the hatred, resentment, scandals, and vendettas of a wretched first term. In particular, the rustication of Bush to Crawford, Texas, would have tended to defuse such latent scandals as the exposure of Valerie Plame, the traducing of US state secrets to neocon darling Ahmed Chalabi, the counterfeiting of the Niger yellowcake documents, and the Israeli mole in the Pentagon. As it is, all these scandals, like the Watergate break-in of 1972, remain to haunt the second Bush term. And to these must be added the far greater scandals first of the 9/11 attacks themselves, and now of the massive vote fraud of 2004. Here is a mass of scandal material more than sufficient to blow Bush II into interplanetary space.

But now G.W. Bush wants to prolong his hold on the White House for four more years. The conflicts which were suppressed by voter intimidation and vote fraud are still boiling in the cauldron of a US society tormented by war and depression, and these conflicts will necessarily find ways to explode in Bush's face. One way that this may happen is through conflict inside the Republican Party. In the weeks before the election I had argued that the Republicans might not survive relegation to the opposition. This was true enough, but it now would appear that they may not be able to survive their current monopoly of the entire US federal government either. Since the GOP dominates the executive, the legislative, and the judicial branches, we can expect that conflicts in the broader society will also take the form of conflicts within the Republican Party. The rush to the exits of Powell, Ashcroft, Ridge, and other cabinet secretaries in the weeks after the election was not a good omen for Bush. Then Bush attempted to nominate former New York City Police Commissioner Bernard Kerik, a stooge and creature of Rudolph Giuliani, to be the new Secretary of Homeland Security. The result was an avalanche of derogatory revelations about Kerik which speedily terminated his candidacy.

Then, in the wake of a question from a soldier about the failure of the Pentagon to provide armored vehicles for the troops in Iraq, there followed a wave of vehement attacks against Rumsfeld. This time the glib rhetoric of the Pentagon boss was not effective. Republican senators like McCain, Hagel, and others proclaimed they had no confidence in the Defense Secretary. William Kristol joined the yelping pack to call for Rumsfeld's ouster, showing that there is no loyalty among neocons (or at least no loyalty to one who is not a professed disciple of Leo Strauss).

All of this took place before Bush's second term had even begun. Eisenhower's second term was marred by the scandal of White House chief of staff Sherman Adams and his vicuña coats. Nixon's second term was cut short by the Watergate affair. Reagan could easily have been impeached over the Iran-Contra affair of his second term, had Lee Hamilton not been on the scene to protect the invisible government. Clinton was of course impeached in his second term, although over trifles in comparison to what is hanging around Bush's neck. There is therefore good reason to see Bush as vulnerable to second-term problems of much greater magnitude.

This will no doubt be exacerbated by Bush's characteristic megalomania; his announced determination is to privatize the Social Security system. Wall Street financiers know that, in addition to the problems generated by the weakness of the dollar, they also face a demographic problem: by about 2007, the first cohorts of the postwar baby boom generation will begin to retire. At this point they will stop being net buyers of stocks and mutual funds, and will become net sellers of those instruments. This means that the current updraft in the stock market will be replaced by a powerful downdraft, potentially leading to a crash. The finance oligarchs have therefore been concerned to find a way to pump US government funds directly into the stock market, in the hopes of maintaining the bloated speculative prices that still prevail. Their preferred solution is to batten on to the Social Security payroll tax for that purpose. This amounts to the destruction of the last surviving component of the Franklin D. Roosevelt New Deal. Bush may well find that his efforts to loot Social Security for the benefit of the Wall Street financiers will unleash forms of social and political resistance which it will be difficult for him to withstand.

IRAQ AND PALESTINE:
THE FUTILITY OF IMPERIALISM

Soon after Bush's vote fraud operation, the US moved with sickening predictability to crush the Iraqi resistance in Fallujah. After an immense slaughter of civilians, the US command announced that it had "broken the back" of the Iraqi resistance. The US propaganda machine had been at great pains to build up a certain Zarqawi as the leader of the Iraqi resistance, and there was every reason to believe that Zarqawi, to the extent that he exists at all, was run by the US as a counter-gang to the coalition forces. Notably, during the same week in October when BBC 2 was broadcasting its documentary entitled "The Power of Nightmares," which advanced philosophical doubts about the existence of bin Laden and his band in the real world, Zarqawi felt moved to rush to the defense of bin Laden's credibility by proclaiming his own eternal loyalty to the erratic Saudi sheikh – which only confirmed that both bin Laden and the phantomatic Zarqawi, around whom the strangest rumors swirl, are CIA/MI-6 projects from beginning to end.

In reality, the US forces had only succeeded in shifting the main theater of resistance combat northward to Mosul. The death of Arafat during the same period underlined that the US occupation of Iraq was now just as bankrupt as the Israeli occupation of the Palestinian territories. In both cases, the foreign occupation of sovereign Arab territory is the cause of the resistance; the only way to end hostilities is to end the foreign occupation, which becomes more odious to the victim population with each successive month.

In the case of the Palestinian territories, the general outlines for peace are doubtless those of the Yasser Abed Rabbo-Yossi Beilin Geneva accord of November 2003: all Israeli settlements must be removed from the occupied territories, and a Palestinian state must be erected in the West Bank and Gaza as a sovereign state, not a glorified Bantustan. The Israeli wall might be legitimate, but only on Israeli land, if it follows the internationally recognized line of demarcation. The Palestinian right of return must apply only to the new Palestinian state, and not to Israel. Israeli settlers and Palestinian refugees ought of course to be indemnified, and here is one area where the United States and the European Union could contribute. The Palestinian state must extend security guarantees to Israel, and to be effective, these must not be undermined by false-flag synthetic terror. One Italian philosopher, Enrico Nuzzo of Salerno, has suggested that both Israel and Palestine could become members of the European Union, a proposal which would facilitate economic reconstruction and development. In one way or another, a comprehensive Marshall Plan for the underdeveloped and war-torn states of the entire Middle East should be provided, under non-monetarist auspices.

The mindless Bush regime never tires of repeating the mantra of "finish the job" and "a democratic Iraq." Here again, it is the US occupation which is radicalizing the situation by eliciting a national resistance. Peace can come only after the occupation is ended. The situation of the hapless US forces in the country could soon become extraordinarily critical, leading to their concentration in a few enclaves in the desert supplied from the air. Iraq would appear to be converging on something like the famous Sicilian vespers of 1282, when a spontaneous general mass uprising, triggered by an insult to a Sicilian lady leaving a church service, suddenly drove the French occupying forces of Charles of Anjou out of that Mediterranean island.

THE DEATH AGONY OF THE DOLLAR SYSTEM

In November 2004, the US dollar collapsed to a level of $1.35 to the euro. Exchange bureaus in Europe were selling euros for $1.45, as American tourists howled. It looked like the beginning of a new world monetary crisis, for the first time since 1973. The immediate trigger was a comment from Greenspan, attending a finance conference, to the effect that the US current account deficit was unsustainable because foreigners could not be counted on to keep buying dollar-denominated assets. Soon the Russian and Indonesian central banks signaled that they were continuing to diversify out of the dollar, and it became clear that the Chinese central bank was doing the same thing.

Although the euro had been gaining ground fast of late, two thirds of world central bank reserves were still kept in dollars, for a value of $2.3 trillion. At stake was the absurd and obsolete role of the dollar as the sole reserve currency of the world, a role which has become increasingly untenable since the emergence of a solvent rival currency in the form of the euro. The US was by far the world's largest debtor nation, with almost $3.3 trillion in net foreign liabilities.

The inherent instability in the dollar system was that the dollar was the reserve currency while the US was also the biggest debtor on the planet, and things were getting worse fast. According to the OECD *Economic Outlook*, the US current account deficit was on track to rise to $825 billion per year (or 6.4% of GDP) by 2006, approximately the mid-point in Bush's second term.

By 2008, when Bush is getting ready to head for the last roundup, the US current account deficit would likely rise to 8% of GDP per year. But, as the gnomes of the City of London pointed out, the breaking point will be reached well before that. The dollar, in their view, was headed for a $1.80 to the euro exchange rate in the near future. That would then pose a problem for the holders of some $11 trillion in dollar-denominated assets, the largest single category of the world's "wealth." If the dollar were to begin an even more dramatic slide, they would be motivated to run for the exits, dumping their dollar assets and sinking the greenback. That would blow out the US housing bubble causing a "deep recession," the polite term for a world economic breakdown crisis. Fear of this is mainly what is keeping many central bankers from selling off their dollars right now; this is what Larry Summers, Clinton's Treasury Secretary (now president of Harvard) has called "the balance of financial terror." (*London Economist*, December 4, 2004) In other words, a dollar devaluation of the most serious type is now inevitable, and may bring down what passes for a world monetary system. How much of that $11 trillion in dollar-denominated paper will survive? Will it be 40%? Or 25%? Or less? In any case, the amount of wealth in the world is going to turn out to be much less than is currently thought, because so much of that $11 trillion will shortly be exposed as purely fictitious capital.

The dollar's reserve currency status is the true heart of US international arrogance. As Simon Nixon commented, the privileged status of the dollar gives the US "the freedom to keep printing dollars without sparking inflation, enabling it to fund wars, giant trade deficits, government spending programs and tax cuts." The US is thus bereft of an economic reality principle. The really decisive issue is when a major oil producer will stop accepting dollars. Nixon notes that the British pound's half-life as a reserve currency after World War II ended when Saudi Arabia stopped taking pounds. Today, when it comes to the dollar, "even the Saudis are wavering… If the oil producers turn their back on the dollar, the ramifications for the global economy will be immense.…[B]oth oil exporters and importers would switch a significant proportion of their reserves into euros, thus triggering a stampede out of the dollar into euros." Another "danger is that if Asian central banks do stop buying dollars, the result will be a devastating collapse of the US currency." The US therefore faces "a challenge to their economic hegemony." (London *Spectator*, October 18, 2003; *Philadelphia Trumpet*, February 2004) During 2004, there has already been a net outflow from the US of long-term foreign investment.

Perhaps the neocons will goad Saudi Arabia or Russia into taking the plunge. Putin and Schröder discussed how the EU could buy oil from Russia with euros in early October, 2003. That news "set off a chain reaction in the private sector, leading to a fourfold increase in euro deposits in Russian banks this year and sending Russian citizens scrambling to change their stashes of greenbacks into euro notes." (*Daily Telegraph*, October 10, 2003; *Philadelphia Trumpet*, February 2004) The solution to the world monetary crisis was a new Bretton Woods system among euro, yen, and dollar, with fixed parities set by participating governments, the comprehensive re-regulation of financial markets, and a mechanism for international clearing and gold settlement to prevent any participant from running chronic deficits in the way the Anglo-Americans customarily had. Most important, the new Bretton Woods had to be a monetary system explicitly geared to the fullest scientific, technological, and economic development of the third world, with rising living standards, longevity, and energy throughput for humanity as a whole.

THE NEW COLD WAR WITH RUSSIA

This book differs from all studies of 9/11 which have been examined so far in the importance it gives to the US-Russian nuclear forces relation as the framework in which the 9/11 criminal attacks must be understood. This book proceeds from an intelligence and counterintelligence picture of explosive US-Russian military, political, and terrorist tensions which have been masked to some extent by the charade of friendship which Bush and Putin have practiced in public. The view here is that on 9/11 Putin, seeing the hegemony of the invisible government lunatics in Washington and London, decided to adopt a policy of war avoidance through broad concessions to the US at many levels, including central Asia.

Putin could see that the neocon war plans for the Middle East would exhaust, weaken, and disperse US forces, while Russia might become stronger over the same months and years. In the service of this policy, Putin was prepared silently to swallow many a bitter affront and injury. To this extent, the relation between Bush and Putin may be seen in the light of the Hitler-Stalin relationship of September 1939-June 1941. This analogy is suggestive, but we should not follow it into every detail. We must also remember, as General Suvorov's "icebreaker" thesis specifies, that Stalin was preparing his own attack on Hitler, Operation Thunder, for early July 1941. Hitler, with his smaller forces, was able to strike first, in effect beating Stalin to the draw. This is the kind of unstable relation that now obtains between the world's two great nuclear powers. And there should be no doubt that, if Russia can destroy the US superpower, as it most assuredly can, then it is a sophistry to deny that Russia emphatically qualifies as a superpower too. Scenarios have suddenly become plausible which lead to general thermonuclear war.

The future being prepared for Russia by the neocons became clear shortly after Putin assumed power. Shortly before 9/11 Jeffrey Tayler wrote a cover story for the *Atlantic Monthly* ("Russia is Finished") in which he developed an apocalyptic perspective for the Eurasian giant:

> Internal contradictions in Russia's thousand-year history have destined it to shrink demographically, weaken economically, and possibly disintegrate territorially. The drama is coming to a close, and within a few decades Russia will concern the rest of the world no more than any Third World country with abundant resources, an impoverished people, and a corrupt government. In short, as a Great Power, Russia is finished. (*Atlantic*, May 2001)

Note well: "*internal* contradictions." Cultural determinism, and not the IMF, not the great criminal revolution of shock therapy, not Jeffrey Sachs, not Anders Aslund, not the US-UK oil cartel's campaign to loot the oil of Siberia, not US-UK support for Chechen and other terrorists.

In this contest, Putin has the decisive merit of simply wanting to defend his country from the Anglo-Americans. As the Beslan school massacre showed, Putin was also the victim of Anglo-American terrorism. Putin has shown great restraint in not reacting to US-UK provocations, like the *Kursk* incident and others. Putin has also been right: the neocons have substantially weakened the US military position in the world. Putin has also been correct in thinking that a few years might give Russia some important strategic trump cards useful for facing down the self-styled Anglo-American neocon supermen. This was illustrated on November 18, 2004, when Putin announced that Russia possessed a new and advanced strategic nuclear missile unlike any held by any other country.

Some speculated that this was a mobile third generation version of the Topol-M missile, known to NATO as the SS-27. Others thought Putin was referring to the Bulava submarine launched long-range ballistic missile. Whichever it was, it appeared that this new Russian missile had capabilities which would allow it to defeat any US strategic anti-missile defense over the relevant historical future. Putin stressed that foreign countries would not be able to match his new missile for a very long time. Russia appeared to be ahead of the US in a number of key strategic departments; it appeared that Putin had chosen to generously support certain key areas of weapons development which might give him a critical advantage over the Anglo-Saxons if confrontation were to loom.

Another example of this was the SS-N-22 Sunburn, called Moskit in Russian, a supersonic cruise missile which could fly as fast as Mach 3 and as low as nine feet above the surface of the water. This formidable weapon had clearly been conceived for the purpose of destroying US aircraft carriers, and it was said to have been sold to China (and to Iran, according to some unconfirmed reports). Russia's nuclear deterrent was not just alive and well, it was extremely robust.

Why Putin had chosen November 18 to make this momentous announcement became clearer on Sunday, November 21, when the CIA and the National Endowment for Democracy (NED) attempted a "people power" coup in Ukraine. The cynical propaganda technicians of Connecticut Avenue had orchestrated a mass movement of street mobs around the presidential candidacy of former prime minister Yushchenko, whose main attraction for them was his pledge to lead Ukraine into full membership in NATO. The candidacy of current Prime Minister Yanukovych had received explicit support from Putin.

The Yushchenko supporters were using the playbook developed by the NED in toppling Milosevic in Serbia in 2000; the same methods had also been successful in ousting the pro-Moscow Eduard Shevardnadze in the "revolution of roses" in Georgia in the first days of 2004. (In Belarus, a similar attempt had been beaten back.) The Yushchenko forces styled themselves as the orange revolution, and blocked the streets of Kiev, claiming that the apparent election victory by Yanukovych represented vote fraud. Many were sincerely interested in democratic reform, but this did not make them any less dupes of the perception-mongers from Washington. The street mobs were able to secure the rejection of the election results by the supreme court, and the calling of a new election for several weeks later.

Much of the operation had been conduited through Poland by the Brzezinski family clique; in addition to Zbigniew, the prophet of 9/11 and the man responsible for the 1979-1988 Afghan War and thus for the emergence of bin Laden & Co., there was now also his nepotistic son Mark, a veteran of the Clinton NSC. Zbigniew was notorious as a hysterical Russophobe and nostalgic of the petty Polish nobility, or *szlachta*. Both Brzezinskis were giving media interviews around the clock during the first days of the Ukraine crisis, and it may have been in their service that Lech Walesa, the former president of Poland, made bold to offer his services in Ukraine as a mediator.

Support for Yanukovych was strong in the industrialized cities in the eastern Ukraine, where much of the population were ethnic Russians. Yushchenko's own political fiefdom was an economic wasteland. Fascist skinheads could be seen among Yushchenko's orange legions, but western commentators were willing to count them as democratic because they were anti-Russian. When Yanukovych's victory was abrogated in the courts, officials in the eastern Ukraine began to talk about home rule, and then about secession. If secession were tried, would anyone try to prevent it by force? Would Russia intervene on the side of the secessionists? Would Poland, now a NATO power, intervene against Russia? Would the US and the rest of NATO then be drawn into the worst of all insane adventures? Putin had some sharp exchanges with EU foreign affairs spokesmen, since many Europeans had foolishly allowed themselves to be taken in by the orange carnival. However, German

Chancellor Schröder seemed to have some understanding of the farce in Kiev, and his planned summit with Putin was successfully held in Schleswig just before Christmas, although the crucial step of adopting the euro for paying the EU's oil bills was apparently not taken.

Needless to say, Ukraine is the royal road taken by every invader of Russia, from Napoleon to Hitler. Tampering with Ukraine is a recipe for triggering the instinctive defense of Russia, which is still a powerful instinct in most Russians. What possible American interest could be served by extending NATO all the way to the Crimea? In the meantime, this book's view of the world strategic context had been decisively validated. Putin underlined this with his wry Christmas present to the Anglo-Americans, which was the nationalization of the huge Yukos oil company, whose former boss, the oligarch Khodorkovsky, remained in jail. Putin's move was seen as a prelude to the large-scale roll-back of the widespread illegal *nomenklatura* privatizations of Soviet state property under Yeltsin's pro-IMF regime in the early 1990s.

The Bush regime won yet another Oscar for international hypocrisy in regard to the Ukrainian situation. Bush had just stolen another term in office thanks to a vote fraud of pharaonic proportions. But while he savored vote fraud in Ohio and Florida, he claimed to find it intolerable in Kiev. The same was true of the farcical European Union election observers, who had been invited in by the US State Department under the auspice of the Helsinki accords and the OSCE. They were blind to vote fraud in Columbus, but eagle-eyed in Kiev. (The same crew proposed to validate the bloody *grand guignol* of US-backed elections in Iraq – but only from the safety of Jordan!)

US strategy had been concerned with isolating, impoverishing, and destabilizing the Union of Soviet Socialist Republics, its successor states, and its alliances for a long time. In 1989-90, the NATO coalition had succeeded in dismantling its long-time adversary, the Warsaw Pact. With the fall of the communist regimes in eastern Europe, the Soviet-led economic bloc, the Comecon or CMEA (Council for Mutual Economic Assistance), also fell apart. The Soviet Union itself had needlessly been driven into extinction in December 1991. In 2004, it became increasingly evident that Anglo-American policy aimed at breaking up the Russian Federation, the old RSFSR, itself. The overarching goal here was absolute and uncontested Anglo-American world domination, to be obtained by completing the Balkanization of Russia as a great power. The Russian strategic arsenal would be removed or at least divided somewhere along the way. An included feature of this geopolitical quest was of course Russia's status as the world's second largest oil exporter.

The great development of 2003 was the re-emergence, after a century of futile and fratricidal conflict, of the continental bloc of France, Germany, and Russia, the main alternative to bankrupt Anglo-American world domination. In 2002 Germany had provided leadership for this bloc with Schröder's steadfast rejection of the neocon Iraq aggression. In 2003 Chirac and Villepin had taken over the lead, also with regard to Iraq. In 2004, Putin had challenged the Anglo-Americans over their sponsorship of terrorism and hostile intent.

The last days of 2004 were a somber time. There was much consternation across the world because of the prospect of four more years of Bush. There is a considerable body of evidence that the modern territorial national state is becoming obsolete and may need to be replaced. But it may not yet be conclusive.

If we recall Machiavelli's three moments of monarchy, oligarchy, and democracy (corresponding to the ontological categories of the one, the few, and the many, which will always be with us), then we must note that all attempts to go beyond the national state (the United Nations, the European Union) have been conducted on an oligarchical basis, and thus contain strong tendencies which are antithetical to human progress and to the overcoming of the current world crisis. The main problem of oligarchy is its mediocrity and inertia, the latter being especially stubborn because change requires convincing so many different oligarchs to cooperate. The prevalent oligarchy needs to be balanced by a strong executive, in effect a world president. This was the genius of the new monarchy of early modern Europe, in which kings like Louis XI of France and Henry VII of England allied with their respective bourgeoisies to terminate the abuses of the feudal aristocracy.

Given the profoundly oligarchical nature of the current world, it is much to be feared that any world government institutions which might be created in the foreseeable future would be even more vitiated by oligarchy than the existing ones. The problem facing advocates of world government is to chart a course for arriving at a unified world executive, an extremely touchy matter for many obvious reasons. If it could be done peacefully, a future world federal state might supercede the current United Nations in the same way the US federal Constitution replaced the Articles of Confederation, which had an oligarchical congress but no executive to check them. But, given the power of the neocon warmonger clique in today's world, it appears dilatory and utopian to even speculate on such possibilities. It is unfortunately more likely that world government will be attained, if it ever is, as a result of a new and cataclysmic world war in which entire national states, weakened by the globalization depression, will disappear as readily as royal dynasties did at the end of World War I.

We are living in the twilight of the Anglo-American world order, a system of planetary domination by the Whig financier faction since just after 1700. This system had certain positive features, but it has now become a barrier to human progress, and it is past time for it to exit the world scene:

> The old order changeth, yielding place to the new,
> And God fulfills himself in many ways,
> Lest one good custom should corrupt the world.
>
> Tennyson

By some reckonings, we now stand at the beginning of a new fascist era. If that night must come, let it at least have the vivid clarity and sharpness of a polar night, not clouded by the fog of myth and lies.

W.G.T.
December 23, 2004

Addendum to the Fourth Edition
Prescription for American 9/11 Truth Movement:
Diversity and Civility in Discussion, Unity in Action.

Webster Tarpley broadcasting with 9/11 Truth authors Gerhard Wisnewski and Andreas von Buelow (Germany) and Thomas Meyer (Switzerland), on his World Crisis Radio Show on RBN Live on Sept. 9, 2006, from Kandern-Holzen, Germany, near the point where France, Germany, and Switzerland come together.

Tarpley: Since we have the 5th anniversary I'd like to make a few comments of my own about the state of the movement in the US.

We've got a round table here going of the leading experts in Central Europe. You might think to yourself it might not be possible to assemble the leading experts in the United States around the same table because of the unfortunate atmosphere that has broken out in our movement....

I wanted to propose from my point of view the following formula for how we can cooperate, because I think this is obviously what we need to do. Don't be scandalized by the word cooperation.

We have to recognize that on the one side there is a sphere of theoretical discussion. In this any serious scientific hypothesis, historical, philosophical hypothesis can be discussed, should not be banned, should not be censored.

We don't want people coming talking about men from Mars or the intervention of the Holy Ghost or the equivalents in other religions, but a theoretical discussion should always go on. At the same time though, we also have now a mass organizing dimension which simply was not there in past years, when people thought that the 9/11 movement amounted to a series of list serves...

In our movement there has to be a sphere of theoretical discussion, which has to be done in a business-like and respectful manner, without slander, without defamation, without *ad hominem* attacks on every page.

And then in addition to that we've got the sphere of mass organizing. Certain tasks simply have to be done, and in order to do them you've got to join with other people, who may not have exactly your views on this or that theoretical question.

And if you make the theoretical question a reason not to join in, in united front cooperation, then your motives are perhaps not what you might think they are.

We've got to organize websites, we've got to organize large conferences, we've got to support 9/11 truth candidates, like Bob Bowman, like Carol Brouillet, and Craig Hill in Vermont.

We've got to go for the impeachment of Bush-Cheney with the 9/11 crimes as the first item on the agenda. We've got to carry out drill monitoring, we've got to expose, denounce and shut down those weapons of mass destruction drills that threaten to go live. We've also got to think about what to do if the war is widened, if there is an attempt to call off the elections, to impose some kind of dictatorship. We've got to begin bringing the American people to the point that we saw in Spain in March 2005, when that legendary general strike shut down the country and forced the neo-fascist Aznar to back down from his plan for a dictatorship.

So in other words, we have a political movement.

Now we have a movement where one guy says, I see a dot. The next guy says, No dot. I see a bulge, or a pod. No bulge or pod, says the other side. One says, I see planes. The other side says, I see no plane. One guy says, It's an atomic bomb. No, a hydrogen bomb, says the next. These are of course important questions. But again, the mystery novel is a whodunit, not how-done-it, and the question of the technical means used has to take second place to the overarching political question: Who did it? Who carried this out? And there of course, the touchstone, the basis of the movement, now I think it's fair to say, 5 years into the discussion, is MIHOP, made it happen on purpose. That the US government or parts thereof as we wish to define it – and this can be done in many ways – executed, brought out and conducted these actions, in my view through drills, maneuvers, exercises and so forth.

This is the political basis of cooperation, and once we have the political basis, the technical questions can also be handled, but within that context of broad cooperation.

Let me ask Gerhard Wisnewski: You and I were together in Berlin, with 12 or 13 people from the German movement, and it was a very business-like discussion basically among friends, and at the end, this was the foundation of *Das Netzwerk*, the German 9/11 network, including a new website, and including what warmed my heart in particular, a strong endorsement of the idea of the independent international truth commission, which is obviously one of the main mass-organizing tasks that we have – an Independent International Truth Commission modeled on the Russell-Sartre tribunal, that could provide a forum not only to amplify the work of the research community that we represent, but also to have an airing, an impartial airing, of theoretical issues inside the movement. Maybe you could say something about that meeting in Berlin, a little bit of who was there, and what came out of it.

Gerhard Wisnewski: Yes, thank you Webster. We had about 13 people here from Germany: the leading people of the German 9/11 movement, including Andreas von Bülow, Matthias Broeckers, and other people who are well-known here in Germany. We tried to establish a network, a research network about 9/11, because before we were single people, individuals who wrote their books, articles, their websites, and now we try to come together in this network. I'm very sad to hear these things about the US, and these detailed discussions, this detail war on several issues. I think it's impossible that two people are 100% of the same opinion on what happened on 9/11. There is so much information and details, and I think we should not start a war on these details because this would be exactly the thing the opposite side wants us to do now, and I totally agree with Webster that this is the second step, the technical aspects and details, and first of all, we have to do a lot of research together: Who did, and who performed this operation on 9/11? And I would be very happy if the American movement would come back also to this method of work.

Tarpley: One other person I've talked to in Europe about this, Simon Aronowitz in London, was telling me about a week ago: You have shop talk, you have a research discussion, which is your shop talk. But you've also got things like stopping the Third World War, getting the truth out to the largest possible number of people, and somehow you've got to make these things coexist.

BIBLIOGRAPHY

Adler, Alexandre. *J'ai vu finir le monde ancien*. Paris: Grasset, 2002.

Ahmed, Nafeez Mosaddeq Ahmed, John Leonard. *The War on Freedom: How and Why America was Attacked September 11, 2001*. Joshua Tree CA: Tree of Life Publications, 2002.

Anonymous. [Michael Scheuer] *Imperial Hubris: Why the West Is Losing the War on Terror*. Washington DC: Brassey's, 2004.

Archick, Kristin, and Paul Gallis. *Europe and Counter-terrorism*. New York: Nova Science, 2003.

Baer, Robert. *Sleeping with the Devil: How Washington Sold Our Soul for Saudi Crude*. New York: Crown, 2003.

Bailyn, Bernard. *The Ideological Origins of the American Revolution*. Cambridge MA: Belknap Press, 1967.

Bamford, James. *Body of Secrets: Anatomy of the Ultra-Secret National Security Agency from the Cold War through the Dawn of a New Century*. New York: Doubleday, 2001.

Bamford, James. *A Pretext for War: 9/11, Iraq, and the Abuse of America's Intelligence Agencies*. New York: Doubleday, 2004.

Barbash, Tom. *On Top of the World: Cantor Fitzgerald, Howard Lutnick, and 9/11: A Story of Loss and Renewal*. New York: Harper Collins, 2003.

Baylis, John, and John Garnett, eds. *Makers of Nuclear Strategy*. New York: St. Martin's Press, 1991.

Beamer, Lisa, with Ken Abraham. *Let's Roll: Ordinary People, Extraordinary Courage*. Wheaton IL: Tyndale House, 2002.

Benjamin, Daniel and Steven Simon. *The Age of Sacred Terror*. New York: Random House, 2002.

Bernstein, Richard and the Staff of the *New York Times*. *Out of the Blue: The Story of September 11, 2001, From Jihad to Ground Zero*. New York: Times Books/Henry Holt, 2002.

Bishop, John. *The Package*. Digital video transfer. Metro-Goldwyn Mayer Home Entertainment, 1989.

Blondet, Maurizio. *11 settembre: colpo di stato in USA*. Milan: Effedieffe, 2003.

Blondet, Maurizio. *Chi comanda in America*. Milan: Effedieffe, 2002.

Blondet, Maurizio. *Cronache dell'anticristo*. Milan: Effedieffe, 2001.

Blondet, Maurizio. *Osama Bin Mossad*. Milan: Effedieffe, 2003.

Blondet, Maurizio. *La strage dei genetisti*. Milan: Effedieffe, 2004.

Bodansky, Yossef. *The High Cost of Peace: How Washington's Middle East Policy Left America Vulnerable to Terrorism*. New York: Forum, 2002.

Borradori, Giovanna ed. *Philosophy in a Time of Terror: Dialogues with Jürgen Habermas and Jacques Derrida*. Chicago: University of Chicago Press, 2003.

Brisard, Jean-Charles and Guillaume Dasquié. *Bin Laden: La verité interdite.* Paris: DeNoël, 2001.

Broder, Henryk M. *Kein Krieg, Nirgends: Die Deutschen und der Terror.* Berlin: Berlin Verlag, 2002.

Bröckers, Mathias. *Verschwörungen, Verschwörungstheorien, und die Geheimnisse des 11.9.* Frankfurt am Main: Zweitausendeins, 2002.

Brown, Cynthia ed. *Lost Liberties: Ashcroft and the Assault on Personal Freedom.* New York: New Press, 2003.

Brzezinski, Zbigniew. *The Grand Chessboard: American Primacy and its Geostrategic Imperatives.* New York: Basic Books, 1997.

Von Bülow, Andreas. *Die CIA und der 11. September: Internationaler Terror und die Rolle der Geheimdienste.* Munich: Piper, 2003.

Bunel, Pierre-Henri. *Menaces Islamistes: ces terroristes qui dévoient l'Islam.* Paris: Carnot, 2002.

Bush, George W. *Our Mission and Our Moment: Speeches Since the Attacks of September 11.* Washington DC: The White House, 2001.

Chaliand, Gérard. *L'arme du terrorisme.* Paris: Louis Audibert, 2002.

Chesler, Phyllis. *The New Anti-Semitism: The Current Crisis and What We Must Do About It.* San Francisco: Jossey-Bass, 2003.

Cipriani, Antonio, and Gianni Cipriani. *Sovranità limitata: storia della eversion atlantica in Italia.* Roma: Edizion Associate, 1991.

Clarke, Richard. *Against All Enemies.* New York: The Free Press, 2004.

Cohen-Tanugi, Laurent. *An Alliance at Risk: The United States and Europe since September 11.* Transl. George A. Holoch Jr. Baltimore: Johns Hopkins University Press, 2003.

Cole, David. *Enemy Aliens: Double Standards and Constitutional Freedoms in the War on Terrorism.* New York: New Press, 2003.

Coll, Steve. *Ghost Wars: The Secret History of the CIA, Afghanistan, and Bin Laden, from the Soviet Invasion to September 10, 2001.* New York: Penguin, 2004.

Chomsky, Noam. *9-11.* New York: Seven Stories Press, 2001.

Chossudovsky, Michel. *The Globalization of Poverty and the New World Order.* Second edition. Shanty Bay, Ontario, Canada: Global Outlook, 2003.

Cooley, John K. *Unholy Wars: Afghanistan, America, and International Terrorism.* Sterling VA: Pluto Press, 2002.

Crotty, William ed. *The Politics of Terror: The US Response to 9/11.* Boston: Northeastern University Press, 2004.

Démaret, Pierre. *Target de Gaulle: The True Story of the 31 Attempts on the Life of the President of France.* New York: Dial Press, 1971.

DeMasi, Nicholas. *Ground Zero: Behind the Scenes.* New York: TRAC Team (Trauma Recovery Assistance for Children), 2004.

Deutsch, Kenneth L. and Walter Soffer eds., *The Crisis of Liberal Democracy: A Straussian Perspective* [Albany NY: State University of New York Press, 1987

Dreyfus, Bob and Thierry La Lavée. *Hostage to Khomeini*. New York: New Benjamin Franklin House, 1981.

Elliston, John. *PsyWar on Cuba: The Declassified History of US Anti-Castro Propaganda*. Australia: Ocean Press, 1999.

Falk, Richard. *The Great Terror War*. Northampton MA: Olive Branch Press, 2003.

Fallaci, Oriana. *La rabbia e l'orgoglio*. Milan: Rizzoli, 2001.

Federal Emergency Management Agency. *World Trade Center Building Performance Study: Data Collection, Preliminary Observations, and Recommendations*. FEMA Region II, New York, NY, May 2002.

Flamigni, Sergio. *Convergenze parallele: le Brigate rosse, i servizi segreti, e il delitto Moro*. Milano: KAOS, 1998.

Fouda, Yosri, and Nick Fielding. *Masterminds of Terror: The Truth Behind the Most Devastating Terrorist Attack The World Has Ever Seen*. New York: Arcade, 2003.

Frank, Justin A. *Bush on the Couch: Inside the Mind of the President*. New York: Regan Books, 2004.

Friedman, Thomas L. *Longitudes and Attitudes*. New York: Farrar, Strauss, Giroux, 2002.

Gabel, Joseph. *False Consciousness: An Essay on Reification*. New York: Harper and Row, 1975.

Gates, Robert M. *From the Shadows: The Ultimate Insider's Story of Five Presidents and How They Won the Cold War*. New York: Simon and Schuster, 1996.

Gerard, John, S. J. *What Was the Gunpowder Plot? The Traditional Story Tested by Original Evidence*. London: Osgood and McIlvaine, 1897.

Gökay, Bülent and R.B.J. Walker. *11 September 2001: War, Terror, and Judgement*. London: Frank Cass, 2003.

Griffin, David Ray. *The New Pearl Harbor: Disturbing Questions about the Bush Administration and 9/11*. Northampton MA: Olive Branch Press, 2004.

Giuliani, Rudolph W., with Ken Kurson. *Leadership*. New York: Hyperion, 2002.

Govier, Trudy. *A Delicate Balance: What Philosophy Can Tell Us About Terrorism*. Boulder CO: Westview Press, 2002.

Guerrilla News Network. *Aftermath: Unanswered Questions from 9/11*. Videocassette. 2002 ff.

Hauerwas, Stanley and Frank Lentricchia. *Dissent From the Homeland: Essays After September 11*. Durham NC: Duke University Press, 2003.

Hay, Malcolm V. *The Jesuits and the Popish Plot*. London: Kegan, Paul, Trench, Trubner, 1934.

Hershberg, Eric and Kevin W. Moore. *Critical Views of September 11: Analyses From Around the World*. New York: New Press, 2002.

Judah, Tim. *Kosovo: War and Revenge*. New Haven CT: Yale University Press, 2000.

Hilder, Anthony J. *Illuminazi 9-11*. Videocassette. Free World Films, 2001.

Hoffman, Jim and Don Paul. *"9/11" Great Crimes/ A Greater Cover-Up*. San Francisco CA: Irresistible/Revolutionary, 2003.

Hoffman, Jim and Don Paul. *Waking up from Our Nightmare: The 9/11/01 Crimes in New York City*. San Francisco CA: Irresistible/Revolutionary, 2004.

Hopsicker, Daniel. *Welcome to Terrorland: Mohammed Atta and the 9-11 Cover-Up in Florida*. Eugene OR: Mad Cow Press, 2004.

Hudson, Rex A., and Marilyn Majeska, ed. *The Sociology and Psychology of Terrorism: Who Becomes a Terrorist and Why?* Report Prepared under an Interagency Agreement by the Federal Research Division. Washington DC: Library of Congress, 1999.

Hufschmid, Eric. *Painful Questions: An Analysis of the September 11th Attack*. Santa Barbara CA: HugeQuestions.com, 2002.

Icke, David. *Alice in Wonderland and the World Trade Center Disaster: Why the Official Story of 9/11 is a Monumental Lie*. Wildwood MO: Bridge of Love, 2000.

Kaplan, Fred. *The Wizards of Armageddon*. New York: Simon and Schuster, 1983.

Kick, Russ. *Fifty Things You're Not Supposed to Know*. New York: The Disinformation Company, 2003.

Kolko, Gabriel. *Another Century of War?* New York: New Press, 2002.

Langewiesche, William. *American Ground: Unbuilding the World Trade Center*. New York: North Point Press/Farrar Strauss Giroux, 2002.

Liss, Helene, with the Loizeaux Family. *Demolition: the Art of Demolishing, Dismantling, Imploding, Toppling and Razing*. New York: Black Dog & Leventhal, 2000.

Longman, Jere. *Among the Heroes: United Flight 93 and the Passengers and Crew Who Fought Back*. New York: Harper Collins, 2002.

De La Maisonneuve, Eric, and Jean Guellec. *Un monde à repenser, 11 septembre 2001*. Paris: Economica, 2002.

Machiavelli, Niccolò. *The Art of War*. Ed. Neal Wood. Indianapolis: Bobbs-Merrill, 1965.

Mann, James. *The Rise of the Vulcans: The History of Bush's War Cabinet*. New York: Viking, 2004.

Marrs, Jim. *Inside Job: Unmasking the 9/11 Conspiracies*. San Rafael CA: Origin Press, 2004.

Meyer, Thomas. *Der 11. September, das Böse und die Wahrheit: Fakten, Fragen, Perspektiven*. Basel, Swizterland: Perseus Verlag, 2004.

Meyerowitz, Joanne. *History and September 11*. Philadelphia: Temple University Press, 2003.

Meyssan, Thierry. *9/11: The Big Lie*. London: Carnot, 2002.

Meyssan, Thierry. *Pentagate*. London: Carnot, 2002.

Millegan, Kris, ed. *Fleshing Out Skull and Bones: Investigations into America's Most Powerful Secret Society*. Walterville OR: Trine Day, 2003.

Miller, John and Michael Stone with Chris Mitchell. *The Cell: Inside the 9/11 Plot, and Why the FBI and CIA Failed to Stop It*. New York: Hyperion, 2002.

Miller, William Lee. *Lincoln's Virtues: An Ethical Biography*. New York: Knopf, 2002.

Mueller, Leo A. *Gladio – das Erbe des kalten Krieges*. Hamburg: Rohwolt, 1991.

Mylroie, Laurie. *Study of Revenge: Saddam Hussein's Unfinished War Against the United States*. Washington DC: AEI Press, 2000.

National Commission on Terrorist Attacks Upon the United States. *The 9/11 commission Report*. New York: Norton, 2004.

Newhouse, John. *Imperial America: The Bush Assault on the World Order*. New York: Knopf, 2003.

Nietzsche, Friedrich. *Werke: Taschenausgabe*. Leipzig, Kröner, 1905 ff.

Paine, Thomas. *The Complete Writings of Thomas Paine*. Ed. Philip S. Foner. New York: Citadel Press, 1945. 2 vols.

Parenti, Michael. *The Terrorism Trap: September 11 and Beyond*. San Francisco: City Lights Books, 2002.

Picciotto, Richard, with Daniel Paisner. *Last Man Down: A Firefighter's Story of Survival and Escape from the World Trade Center*. New York: Berkley, 2002.

Posner, Gerald. *Why America Slept: The Failure to Prevent 9-11*. New York: Random House, 2003.

Pororti, David. *September 11th Families For Peaceful Tomorrows: Turning Our Grief into Action for Peace*. New York: RVD Books, 2003.

Price, Glenn W. *The Origins of the War with Mexico: the Polk-Stockton Intrigue*. Austin TX: University of Texas Press, 1967.

Prouty, L. Fletcher. *JFK: The CIA, Vietnam, and the Plot to Assassinate John F. Kennedy*. New York: Citadel Press, 1996.

Prouty, L. Fletcher. *The Secret Team: The CIA and its Allies in Control of the United States and the World*. Englewood Cliffs NJ: Prentice Hall, 1973.

Pyszczynski, Tom, Sheldon Solomon, and Jeff Greenberg. *In the Wake of 9/11: The Psychology of Terror*. Washington DC: American Psychological Association, 2003.

Raimondo, Justin. *The Terror Enigma: 9/11 and the Israeli Connection*. New York: iUniverse, 2003.

Ruppert, Michael. *Crossing the Rubicon: The Decline of the American Empire at the End of the Age of Oil*. Gabriola Island, BC: New Society Publishers, 2004.

Record, Jeffrey. *Hollow Victory: A Contrary View of the Gulf War*. Washington DC: Brassey's US, 1993.

Rieff, David. *Slaughterhouse: Bosnia and the Failure of the West*. New York: Simon and Schuster, 1995.

Riesman, David. *The Lonely Crowd: A Study of the Changing American Character*. New Haven CT: Yale University Press, 1950.

Rosen, Jeffrey. *The Naked Crowd: Reclaiming Security and Freedom in an Anxious Age.* New York: Random House, 2004.

Sammon, Bill. *Fighting Back: The War on Terrorism – From Inside the Bush White House.* Washington DC: Regency, 2002.

Sanguinetti, Gianfranco. *On Terrorism and the State: The Theory and Practice of Terrorism Divulged for the First Time.* London: Chronos Press, 1982. Online at www.notbored.org/on-terrorism.html.

Schami, Rafik. *Mit Fremden Augen: Tagebuch über den 11. September, den Palästinakonflikt, und die Arabische Welt.* Heidelberg: Palmyra, 2002.

Schmitt, Carl. *Positionen und Begriffe.* Hamburg, 1940.

Sheehy, Gail. *Middletown, America: One Town's Passage from Trauma to Hope.* New York: Random House, 2003.

Der Spiegel. Inside 9-11: What Really Happened. New York, St. Martin's Press, 2001.

Sell, Louis. *Slobodan Milosevic and the Destruction of Yugoslavia.* Durham NC: Duke University Press, 2000.

Stevens, Sir John. *Stevens Inquiry III: Overview and Recommendations, 17th April 2003.* London, 2004.

Strauss, Leo and Alexandre Kojève. *On Tyranny.* New York: The Free Press, 1959. Revised and expanded edition.

La strage di stato: controinchiesta. Milano: Samonà and Savelli, 1970.

Suskind, Ron. *The Price of Loyalty. George W. Bush, the White House, and the Education of Paul O'Neill.* New York: Simon and Schuster, 2004.

Swift, Jonathan. "The Conduct of the Allies, Nov. 1711," in *Political Tracts, 1711-1713.* ed. Herbert Davis. Princeton: Princeton University Press, 1951.

Tarpley, Webster Griffin. *Against Oligarchy; Essays and Speeches* 1970-1996. Washington Grove MD: Washington Grove Books, 1996. www.tarpley.net.

Tarpley, Webster Griffin, et al. *American Leviathan: Administrative Fascism under the Bush Regime.* Washington DC: EIR, 1991.

Tarpley, Webster. "The Brits Bash Bubba," in *The Conspiracy Reader* ed. Al Hidell and Joan d'Arc. Secaucus NJ: Citadel Press, 1999.

Tarpley, Webster Griffin, et al. *Chi ha ucciso Aldo Moro?* Rome: Partito Operaio Europeo, 1978.

Tarpley, Webster Griffin and Anton Chaitkin. *George Bush: The Unauthorized Biography.* Washington DC: EIR, 1992. Reprinted, Joshua Tree CA: Progressive Press, 2004. www.progressivepress.com.

Tarpley, Webster Griffin. "Project Democracy's Program: The Fascist Corporate State." *Project Democracy: The Parallel Government Behind the Iran-Contra Affair.* Washington DC: EIR, 1987.

Tarpley, Webster Griffin. *Surviving the Cataclysm: Your Guide Through the Greatest Financial Breakdown in Human History.* Washington Grove MD: Washington Grove Books, 1999. (www.tarpley.net)

Thomas, Gordon. *Gideon's Spies: The Secret History of the Mossad*. New York: St. Martin's Press, 1999

Trinkhaus, George. *NBC Spins 9/11*

TV-Asahi. *JFK Assassination: Truth After 40 Years*. Videocassette of television broadcast. Tokyo 2003.

Unger, Craig. *House of Bush, House of Saud: The Secret Relationship Between the World's Two Most Powerful Dynasties*. New York: Scribner, 2004.

US Congress, Joint Inquiry into Intelligence Activities Before and After the Terrorist Attacks of September 11, 2001. *Report of the US Senate Select Committee on Intelligence and US House Permanent Select Committee on Intelligence*. December 2002. Cited as JICI.

US House of Representatives, Committee on Science. *Learning From 9/11 – Understanding the Collapse of the World Trade Center*. March 6, 2002. Serial No. 107-46A. Washington DC: Government Printing Office, 2003.

US House of Representatives, Committee on Science. *The Investigation of the World Trade Center Collapse: Findings, Recommendations, and Next Steps*. May 1, 2002. Serial No. 107-61

US House of Representatives, Permanent Select Committee on Intelligence, Subcommittee on Terrorism and Homeland Security. *Counterintelligence Capabilities and Performance Prior to 9-11*. July 2002.

Von Essen, Thomas, with Matt Murray. *Strong of Heart: Life and Death in the Fire Department of New York*. New York: Regan/Harper Collins, 2002.

Vanden Heuvel, Katrina. *A Just Response:* The Nation *on Terrorism, Democracy, and September 11, 2001*. New York: Thunder's Mouth Press/Nation Books, 2002.

Webb, Gary. *Dark Alliance: The CIA, the Contras, and the Crack Cocaine Explosion*. New York: Seven Stories Press, 1998.

Willan, Philip. Puppet Masters: The Political Use of Terrorism in Italy. London: Constable, 1991.

Williams, Paul L. Osama's *Revenge: The Next 9/11*. Amherst NY: Prometheus Books, 2004.

Wisnewski, G.; Landgraeber, W.; Sieker, E.: *Das RAF-Phantom – Wozu Politik und Wirtschaft Terroristen brauchen*. Knaur Verlag, München, 1992, 1997

Wisnewski, G.; Landgraeber, W.; Sieker, E.: *Operation RAF – Was geschah wirklich in Bad Kleinen?* Knaur Verlag, München, 1994

Wisnewski, Gerhard: *Operation 9/11. Angriff auf den Globus*. Knaur Verlag, München 2003

Wood, Allan and Paul Thompson. "An Interesting Day: President Bush's Movements and Actions on 9/11." Center for Cooperative Research, May 2003.

Woodward, Bob. *Bush at War*. New York: Simon and Schuster, 2002.

Wright, Jeremy. *9/11 Citizens Inquiry*. Videocassette. Toronto, 2004.

APPENDIX:
THE LONDON EXPLOSIONS,
THE ROGUE NETWORK, BUSH, AND IRAN

By Webster G. Tarpley

Originally published in *Global Outlook* magazine.

Washington DC, July 11 – Last week's London explosions carry the characteristic features of a state-sponsored, false flag, synthetic terror provocation by
networks within the British intelligence services MI-5, MI-6, the Home Office,
and the Metropolitan Police Special Branch who are favorable to a wider Anglo-
American aggressive war in the Middle East, featuring especially an early pre-
emptive attack on Iran, with a separate option on North Korea also included.
With the London attacks, the Anglo-American invisible government adds another
horrendous crime to its own dossier. But this time, their operations appear
imperfect, especially in regard to the lack (so far) of a credible patsy group
which, by virtue of its ethnicity, could direct popular anger against one of the
invisible government's targets. So far, the entire attribution of the London crimes
depends on what amounts to an anonymous posting in an obscure, hitherto
unknown, secular Arabic-language chatroom in the state of Maryland, USA. But,
based on this wretched shred of pseudo-evidence, British Prime Minister Tony
Blair – who has surely heard of a group called the Irish Republican Army, which
bombed London for more than a decade – has not hesitated to ascribe the
murders to "Islam," and seems to be flirting with total martial law under the Civil
Contingencies Act. We are reminded once again of how he earned his nickname
of Tony Bliar.

SCOTLAND YARD KNEW IN ADVANCE

That the British Government knew in advance that blasts would occur is not open
to rational doubt. Within hours of the explosions, Israeli Army Radio was
reporting that "Scotland Yard [London police headquarters] had intelligence
warnings of the attacks a short time before they occurred." This report, repeated
by IsraelNN.com, added that "the Israeli Embassy in London was notified in
advance, resulting in Foreign Minister Binyamin Netanyahu remaining in his
hotel room rather than make his way to the hotel adjacent to the site of the first
explosion, a Liverpool Street train station, where he was to address an economic
summit." This report is attributed to "unconfirmed reliable sources." At around
the same time, the Associated Press issued a wire asserting that "British police
told the Israeli Embassy in London minutes before Thursday's explosions that

they had received warnings of possible terror attacks in the city," according to "a senior Israeli official." This wire specifies that "just before the blasts, Scotland Yard called the security officer at the Israeli Embassy to say that they had received warnings of possible attacks...."

According to eyewitness reports from London, BBC claimed between 8:45 and some minutes after 10 AM that the incidents in the Underground were the result of an electrical power surge, or alternatively of a collision. Foreign bigwigs, presumably not just Netanyahu, were warned, while London working people continued to stream into the subway. These reports have been denied, repudiated, sanitized, and expunged from news media websites by the modern Orwellian Thought Police, but they have been archived by analysts who learned on 9/11 and other occasions that key evidence in state-sponsored terror crimes tends to filter out during the first minutes and hours, during the critical interval when the controlled media are assimilating the cover story peddled by complicit moles within the ministries. These reports are not at all damaging to Israel, but are devastating for British domestic security organs. An alternative version peddled by Stratfor.com, namely that the Israelis warned Scotland Yard, is most probably spurious but still leaves the British authorities on the hook. Which Scotland Yard official made the calls? Identify that official, and you have bagged a real live rogue network mole.

Another more general element of foreknowledge can be seen in the fact reported by Isikoff and Hosenball of Newsweek that, since about November 2004, the US FBI, but not other US agencies, has been refusing to use the London Underground.

Operations like these are generally conduited through the government bureaucracies under the cover of a drill or exercise which closely resembles the terror operation itself. So it was with Amalgam Virgo and the multiple exercises held on 9/11, as I show in my 9/11 Synthetic Terror: Made in USA (Joshua Tree CA: Progressive Press, 2005). So it was with the Hinckley attempt to assassinate Ronald Reagan, when a presidential succession exercise was scheduled for the next day, as I showed in my George Bush: The Unauthorized Biography (1992; reprint by Progressive Press, 2004). An uncannily similar maneuver allows the necessary work to be done on official computers and on company time, while warding off the inquisitive glances and questions of curious co-workers at adjoining computer consoles.

THE COVER STORY TERROR DRILL

Such a parallel drill was not lacking in the London case. On the evening of July 7, BBC Five, a news and sports radio program, carried an interview with a certain former Scotland Yard official named Peter Power who related that his firm, Visor Consulting, had been doing an anti-terror-bombing drill in precisely the Underground stations and at the precise times when the real explosions went off. Peter Power and Visor had been subcontractors for the drill; Power declined to name the prime contractors. Small wonder that Blair, in his first official report to the Commons on July 11, went out of his way to rule out a board of inquiry to probe these tragic events.

Tony Blair may be eyeing the advantages of emergency rule for a discredited lame duck like himself, but the British people may have a different view. The alternative is clear: on the one hand is the American response after 9/11, marked by submissive and credulous gullibility in regard to the fantastic official story of what had happened. On the other hand is the militant and intelligent Spanish response after March 11, 2004, marked by powerful mass mobilization and righteous anger against politicians who sought to manipulate the people and sell a distorted account of events. Which way will the British people go? Straws in the wind suggest that the British response may be closer to the Spanish, although it may develop more slowly because of the lack of mass organization and related factors. If this is the case, Tony Blair, Jack Straw, and the rest of the malodorous "New Labor" crypto-Thatcherites will be out the window.

My thesis is that the London explosions represent a form of communication on the part of the transatlantic Anglo-American financier faction with Bush, Blair, and the heads of state and government assembled at Gleneagles, Scotland for the G-8 meeting on the day of the blast. The London deaths were designed to deliver an ultimatum in favor of early war with Iran. Here a word of clarification may be necessary. The demonization of Bush by his many enemies, while understand-able, risks blurring the basic realities of power in the US and UK. Since the Bay of Pigs and the Kennedy assassination (to go back no further than that), we have been aware of a secret team. During the Iran-contra era, the same phenomenon was referred to as an invisible, secret or parallel government. This is still the matrix of most large-scale terrorism. The question arises for some: do Bush and Cheney tell the invisible government what to do, or does the invisible govern-ment treat the visible office holders as puppets and expendable assets? To ask the question is to answer it: Bush, Cheney & Co. are the expendable puppets. The explanation of terror is not Bush "makes it happen on purpose," or "MIHOP," as some seem to argue, but rather invisible government MIHOP, an altogether more dire proposition.

How then does the invisible faction communicate with the public mouthpieces? Given the violence of the power relations involved, we can be sure that it is not a matter of sending out engraved invitations announcing that the honor of Bush's presence is requested at the launching of an attack on Iran. Rather, the invisible and violent rogue network communicates with Bush, Blair, and others by means coherent with their aggressive nature – as they did on 9/11. Bush, of course, is a weak and passive tenant of the White House whose instinct is to do virtually nothing beyond the day-to-day routine.

We therefore need to note that the London blasts come after two months of vigorous and impatient prodding of Bush by the invisible government. On May 11, a small plane almost reached the White House before it was turned away, while the Congress, the Supreme Court, and the White House (but not the Pentagon, the Treasury, etc.) were evacuated amid scenes of panic. The White House went to red alert, but Bush was not informed until it was all over, and was riding his bicycle in the woods near Greenbelt, Maryland. Flares were dropped over the Brookland district and Takoma Park, MD. The resemblance of all this to a classic coup scenario was evident. On May 18, a live hand grenade, which turned out to be a dud, landed near Bush as he spoke at a rally in Tbilisi, Georgia.

On June 29, the approach of another small plane led to an evacuation of the Congress and the Capitol, again with scenes of panic. On the afternoon of July 2, no fewer than three small planes came close to Bush's Camp David retreat in the Catoctin Mountains of Maryland; this story was suspiciously relegated to the local news page of the Washington Post. The details of these incidents are of little interest; what counts is the objective reality of a pattern. These incidents also provide background for Bush's unbalanced behavior on July 5 at Gleneagles, when he crashed into a policeman while riding on his bicycle. Then came the London blasts on July 7.

What is it that the invisible government wants Bush and Blair to do? Scott Ritter announced last January that Bush had issued an order to prepare an attack on Iran for the month of June. According to a well-informed retired CIA analyst I spoke with on July 3, this order actually told US commanders to be ready to attack Iran by the end of June. This project of war with Iran is coherent with most of what we know about the intentions of the US-UK rogue faction, and thus provides the immediate background for the London explosions. The Bush administration and the Blair cabinet have failed to deliver decisive military action, and the invisible government is exceedingly impatient.

One way to increase the pressure on Iran would be to implicate a group of Iranian fanatic patsies in the London bombings. This would not be difficult; in fact, as I show in 9/11 Synthetic Terror, the British capital, referred to during the 1990s as Londonistan, is home to the largest concentration of Arab and Islamic patsy groups in the entire world, in such infamous locations as Finsbury mosque and Brixton mosque; these groups are known to have enjoyed de facto recruiting privileges in Her Majesty's Prisons. But perhaps an Iranian patsy group would be too obvious at this time. More likely may be the sinking of a US warship in the Gulf by a third country, duly attributed to Iran.

In a recent speech, Dr. Ephraim Asculai of Tel Aviv University made two main points: first, that there is no military solution to the Iranian nuclear issue, and second, that there is no such thing as a point of no return in nuclear weapons development. Dr. Asculai showed that South Africa, Sweden, and other nations had turned away from deploying A- bombs well after having acquired the ability to produce them. Dr. Asculai is evidently arguing against widespread tendencies in the US-UK-Israeli strategic community who are whipping up hysteria around the notion that Iran is now indeed approaching exactly such a point of no return.

For her part, Miss Rice of the State Department has now declared that it will no longer be sufficient for Iran to turn away from nuclear weapons production; the entire Iranian program for nuclear energy production will also have to be dismantled, in her view. Such maximalism makes a negotiated solution impossible as long as the current Washington group holds power.

SCO: US GET OUT OF CENTRAL ASIA

The US, UK and Israel have been on the brink of war with Iran for at least a year, and the rogue network is generally aware that time is not on its side. There is also an important new development which threatens the ability of the Anglo-Americans to wage war. On July 5, the summit of the Shanghai Cooperation Organization (SCO), which brings together China, Russia, Uzbekistan, Krygyzia, Kazakhstan, and Tajikistan plus new members India, Pakistan, and Iran, issued a call for the United States to vacate the bases seized in the autumn of 2001 under the cover of the 9/11 emergency and the looming invasion of Afghanistan. The parties to this call represent about half of the world's population. This demand was immediately rejected by the State Department, but veteran Russian Eurasian expert Yevgeny Primakov crowed that for the first time a formula had been agreed to by which the US would be ejected from this region. The US presence goes back to the Bush-Putin emergency hotwire talks of September 11, 2001, when Putin, seeing that the madmen had seized control in Washington, dropped Russian objections to a US intrusion into the former Soviet republics of central Asia. The US-UK can attack Iran from Iraq in the west, from Afghanistan in the east, and from Qatar in the south, but without the Uzbek and Kyrgyz bases, the Anglo-American ability to attack from the north as well will be severely limited.

The SCO states are also concerned about US-backed "designer color revolutions" on the recent Georgian (rose) and Ukrainian (orange) models, traditionally known as CIA "people power" revolutions, being used to destabilize their governments. To make matters worse for Washington and London, Kazakhstan is a few months away from opening an oil pipeline to China, which will diminish the US-UK ability to use their Gulf presence to blackmail Beijing. Washington and London are also dismayed by the pro-Iranian overtures in various fields being made by their Shiite puppets in Baghdad.

And what of the report in the Washington Post of July 11, which claims that US and UK planners are now contemplating a sharp reduction in the US forces in Iraq? The most plausible explanation is that this is pure disinformation, similar to news blips issued by both Hitler and Stalin in May and June of 1941. It should also be noted that the British plan explicitly provides for most of the forces now at Basra to go to Afghanistan, where they would be positioned for operations against Iran, or into central Asia.

Generally, the invisible government appears dismayed by its loss of momentum and the constant erosion of the political position of its asset, Bush. 110,000 US factory workers lost their jobs in June, the worst total in a year and a half: autos and textiles are collapsing. The housing bubble may also be nearing its end, with the bankruptcy of Fannie Mae on the near-term agenda. World derivatives have officially reached $300 trillion, with JP Morgan Chase holding the largest single portfolio. The one virtuoso performance of July 7 was that of the Federal Reserve, Bank of England, and European Central Bank, which flooded equity and capital markets with liquidity through such vehicles as the Plunge Protection Team (PPT), turning a big Wall Street loss into a small gain.

During the recent Reopen 9/11 tour of eight European cities, Jimmy Walter repeatedly forecast that the general predicament of the Bush regime and the US financier faction would lead to another large-scale terror attack before the end of 2005; this has now occurred, and there is no end in sight. The tide of US public opinion has now definitively turned against the Iraq war and to some degree against Bush, as all major polls demonstrate. Notable is the 42% affirmative response to the Zogby International question as to whether, if it could be proved that Bush lied to launch the Iraq war, he should be impeached. Larry Franklin of the Wolfowitz-Feith neocon apparatus has been indicted for divulging US secrets, and the American-Israeli Public Affairs Council has been raided twice; further indictments are expected. Karl Rove has now been revealed as the source of the Valerie Plame leak, making Rove and perhaps other White House officials fair game for federal indictment. The Niger yellowcake forgeries and the Chalabi state secrets cases are still pending – to say nothing of two stolen elections and the 9/11 Septembergate itself. All these factors incline the rogue network to seek an improvement in their situation through a flight forward to a wider war in Iran. Those who stand to lose most by such an Iranian adventure must now mobilize to make Mr. Bush's second term as eventful as Nixon's second term turned out to be in 1974.

THE PHONY WAR ON TERROR: TIME TO QUARANTINE THE REAL AGGRESSORS

Speech to the Axis of Peace Conference or Axe de la Paix, *held in Brussels, Belgium, November 17th and 18th, 2005. The conference gathered political and intellectual personalities from more than thirty nations, who are committed against the logic of war, with a view to establishing a permanent structure that will make the voice of peace be heard.*

Text of speech to the conference by Webster G. Tarpley:

400 years ago this month, the English King James' first minister Robert Cecil unveiled his masterpiece, the Gunpowder Plot to blow up King and Parliament. The attempt was blamed on Guy Fawkes and other plotters, who were tortured and executed. The Catholics, the Pope, the Jesuits and the Spanish were blamed too, setting up centuries of conflict and imperial expansion. But the plot was a synthetic provocation staged by Cecil. Terrorism was a birth pang of the Anglo-American financier faction, and terrorism accompanies that faction in its moribund senility today.

According to today's neocon Bush regime in Washington, the central event of world history is the attacks of September 11, 2001. The neocons demand that world affairs be organized around what they call the war on terrorism, supposedly waged by the United States, Great Britain, and the other English-speaking powers against the dark powers of radical Islam. This phony war on terrorism comes complete with preventive nuclear sneak attacks on any country the Bush regime chooses. These can be supplemented by conventional aggression, and by the so-called color revolutions, the new name for the traditional CIA "people power" coups.

The main premise of the war on terror is the myth of September 11 – 3,000 people allegedly killed by a group of 19 hijackers including Mohammed Atta, all members of al Qaeda, led by Osama bin Laden operating from a cave in Afghanistan with a laptop computer, etc. My main point today is that this premise is a big lie, as I argue in my book, *9/11 Synthetic Terror: Made in USA* (Joshua Tree CA: Progressive Press, 2005). The 9/11 events were a deliberate provocation carried out from within the US military, security, and intelligence apparatus by a deeply entrenched faction variously called the invisible government, the secret government, the parallel government, the rogue network, the secret team. This faction cuts across the CIA, the Pentagon, the NSA, the FBI, the Treasury, the Federal Reserve, and other key parts of government. It is a faction which has been operating for more than a century. It meshes with the British MI-6 and Defence Ministry.

9/11 was a successful coup d'état designed to shift the Bush White House into the War of Civilizations mode described by Samuel Huntington. The Arab and Islamic worlds were the first targets, to be followed by China, and also Russia, as per the Wolfowitz doctrine. 9/11 thus joins the tradition of self-inflicted or imaginary attacks going back to the explosion of the USS *Maine* in Havana harbor in 1898, which launched the Spanish-American War, and with it US Imperialism. The secret government tried to stage a fascist march on Washington against President Franklin D. Roosevelt, and tried to assassinate him. They have brought us the Bay of Pigs, the Kennedy assassination, the fake Gulf of Tonkin incident (partly admitted in recent weeks by the NSA), the Vietnam War, the attempted assassination of Reagan, the gun-running and drug-running of the Iran-contra affair, the bombing of Serbia, the sinking of the Russian submarine *Kursk*, and, their crowning achievement, 9/11, followed by the invasions of Afghanistan and Iraq. US presidents are generally puppets of this rogue network, which responds to the needs of Wall Street and the City of London.

It was this rogue network which sent Bush an ultimatum on 9/11 with the words: "Angel is next." The meaning was: launch the war on civilizations, or be liquidated. Bush speedily complied, turning the US government over to them.

In the terminology of intelligence work, Bin Laden, Atta, and the rest are patsies. They are double agents, fanatics, dupes, *agents provocateurs*. They operate under the umbrella of al Qaeda, a group which can only be described as the Arab Legion of CIA and MI-6, a classic counter-gang or pseudo-gang against Arab nationalism. Their ethnic and religious background allows the Arab and Islamic world to be blamed for terrorist acts. They receive support from the CIA, as typified by Bin Laden's famous kidney dialysis. These figures have criminal intent, but what they do not have is the physical and technical ability to produce the effects observed – just as Lee Harvey Oswald, no matter how evil he was, could not have fired the requisite number of shots at President Kennedy in Dallas.

The terrorist controllers and case officers for Atta and the others were evidently Able Danger, a joint project of the Defense Intelligence Agency and the Special Forces Command. Since Able Danger came to light, we have learned that Able Danger destroyed 2.5 terabytes of its own records, equal to about a quarter of the Library of Congress, the largest library in the world. Rumsfeld has forbidden Able Danger officers to testify to Congress.

The patsies could operate freely and openly, without being arrested, because of the network of moles inside the US government. These moles are loyal to the invisible government, not to the constitution and the laws. They make sure the patsies are available to be scapegoated, and they destroy the evidence and organize the cover-up after the fact. The moles are responsible for paralyzing US air defenses for one hour and forty-five minutes on 9/11, in comparison with average intercept times of 15-20 minutes at most both before and after. No outside force could have obtained this result.

The trained professionals, the technocrats of death, are the third group. They do possess the physical-technical ability to crash planes and other flying objects into buildings, and to destroy the World Trade Center with controlled demolition. Some of these professionals operate from inside government bureaucracies, and others from private offices. They seek anonymity, not publicity.

Recent progress in 9/11 research has focused on the role of war games, military exercises, and terror drills in hiding and facilitating the terror actions of 9/11. So far we know of 14 separate exercises on or related to 9/11. Some were used to suppress air defenses by moving fighter planes to northern Canada and Alaska, far from the 9/11 targets. Others paralyzed air defense by inserting false radar blips onto the radar screens of defense personnel, and with commercial and military aircraft which reported themselves as hijacked.

But there is another dimension. A drill staged at the National Reconnaissance Office in Chantilly, Virginia that morning was based on the idea of flying commercial airlines into office buildings. There is every reason to believe that the kamikaze aircraft were controlled from here, the US spy satellite headquarters. Amalgam Virgo, another drill associated with 9/11, involved firing a cruise missile against a land target from a rogue freighter in the Gulf of Mexico. This likely prepared what was done to the Pentagon, since it is clear that no commercial airliner ever hit that building.

Most ominous of all was Global Guardian, a 9/11 drill simulating all-out thermonuclear war with bombers, missiles, and submarines. This drill included an attempt at outside penetration of the nuclear command structure by a "bad" outsider with access to a key command and control system. Here was the secret portal through which the rogue network was ready to launch nuclear war on 9/11. On 9/11, Bush called Putin with an ultimatum: the US would seize Afghanistan, plus bases in ex-Soviet central Asia. If Putin had rejected this, the US rogue network had the capability to set off World War III by ordering nuclear escalation.

When state terrorists attack, they often do it under the cover of an announced, seemingly legal drill that closely resembles or mimics the terror operation. This helps camouflage the criminal intent of the coup plotters inside their own bureaucracy. The drill is just a drill, until it goes live. During the Cold War, Hilex 75 and Able Archer 83 were drills that could have led to real confrontation and war.

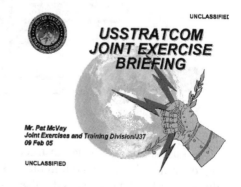

UNCLASSIFIED

USSTRATCOM JOINT EXERCISE BRIEFING

Mr. Pat McVay
Joint Exercises and Training Division/J37
09 Feb 05

UNCLASSIFIED

When President Reagan was shot in 1981, a presidential succession exercise (Nine Lives) was scheduled for the next day, as a cover for operations. The London July 7 bombings of this year were prepared by exercises named Atlantic Blue by the UK, Topoff III by the US, and Triple Play by Canada, which simulated an attack on the London Underground while an international conference was going on in the UK. On July 7 itself, Peter Power's Visor Associates were simulating explosions in the same stations at the same times that bombs exploded, as BBC 5 reported.

Peter Power, ex-Scotland Yard, heads a private security firm which was running terror drills in the London Underground on July 7, 2005, as he told the BBC:
Power: At half past nine this morning we were actually running an exercise for a company of over a thousand people in London based on simultaneous bombs going off precisely at the railway stations where it happened this morning, so I still have the hairs on the back of my neck standing up right now.
Host: To get this quite straight, you were running an exercise to see how you would cope with this and it happened while you were running the exercise?
Power: Precisely.

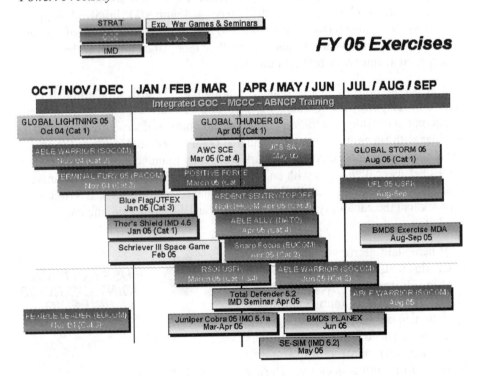

Last summer, Cheney instructed the Pentagon to prepare the atomic bombing of Iran, to be carried out in the wake of a new, larger-scale 9/11. It is clear this was to be state sponsored, false flag synthetic terrorism, designed to give a pretext for the attack.

In the US and other NATO states, a citizens' watch for these dangerous rogue drills has been established to meet the threat. In August, Sudden Response 05 was to simulate a 10-kiloton nuclear explosion in Charleston, South Carolina. A mobilization of concerned citizens protested this drill and, we believe, shut it down. Then came a gas dispersion drill in New York City, and Granite Shadow / Power Geyser, involving weapons of mass destruction in Washington DC. These drills were denounced and protested.

Right now, in the month of November, we are in the midst of the densest concentration of drills since 9/11 itself. First there is Vigilant Shield, a radiological dirty bomb going off in the port of Mobile, Alabama. This is to be answered by Global Lightning, an exchange of nuclear missiles between the US and North Korea, with US ABM missile defense engaged. Simultaneously there is Positive Response and Global Storm, the new name for Global Guardian under the regime of first-strike preventive nuclear attack. These involve a confrontation with Russia over the Ukraine.. Any of these drills could be used as a cover to launch real nuclear provocations and nuclear attacks. War planning against Venezuela continues. Worldwide vigilance is needed to prevent the worst.

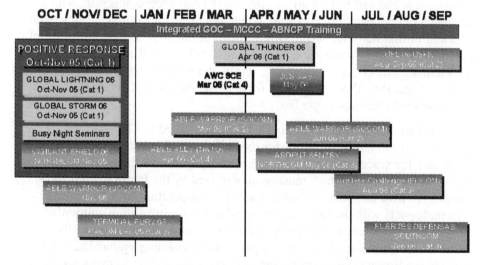

The Bush regime is now in crisis because of the lost war in Iraq, the criminally negligent response to hurricane Katrina, and the highest gasoline prices in history. Libby has been indicted, and Rove, Feith, Wolfowitz and Ledeen may follow. As in the movie *Wag the Dog*, Bush or the neocons are tempted to start a war to escape this crisis. During Watergate, when Nixon declared a nuclear red alert in October 1973, British Prime Minister Edward Heath saw blatant political motives. Whenever Nixon asked for the football, the briefcase containing the secret nuclear launch codes, White House officials Kissinger and Haig watched him closely to keep his finger off the nuclear button. In the summer of 1974, Defense Secretary Schlesinger told US commanders to disregard orders for any military attack coming from Nixon unless they had been confirmed by Schlesinger or Kissinger. Today the situation is similar, and the Democratic Party and the NATO states must demand that the unstable Bush and the desperate neocons be placed under special surveillance during their ouster to prevent new adventures of incalculable dimensions.

But as long as Bush can keep his base of 30-35% of the US population, he can wage war in Iraq indefinitely, and possibly widen that war to Syria and Iran. Bush's hold on his base is due largely to the power of the 9/11 myth over certain parts of the American people. Whenever Bush is held accountable for anything,

his response is to cite 9/11. His arguments for the war in Iraq are not based on Iraq, but rather on 9/11. There is only one way to erode Bush's hard core base, and that is by attacking the 9/11 myth. Destroy the 9/11 myth, and the September criminals may be called to account. Destroy the 9/11 myth, and Bush will be neutralized. Peace-loving governments and institutions around the world must address this task, with a campaign of denunciation, exposure, and political education on the truth about 9/11 and the nature of terrorism. One vehicle for this would be an Independent International Truth Commission on 9/11, modeled on the Russell-Sartre Tribunal for Vietnam. The convocation of such a truth commission for 9/11 is more urgent than ever, and should be top priority for anti-war forces well before the Congressional elections a year from now.

On October 5, 1937, Franklin D. Roosevelt called in Chicago for a quarantine of the fascist dictators, for the isolation and boycott of aggressors. Since then the wheels of history have turned, and it is now the Bush-neocon regime in Washington which must be quarantined by the forces of civilized humanity. There can be no military or security cooperation with the neocons. Free trade pacts with the neocons are suicidal. Bush officials are guilty of international conspiracy to wage aggressive war, a capital crime under the Nuremberg precedents. When the US population is turning against Bush, it is tragic to see Europe and Japan continuing to support him on so many issues. It is time for the world to quarantine the aggressor. In so doing, it will have the support of the American people.

(The contents of the appendix are not included in the index.)

INDEX

Webster Griffin Tarpley's World Crisis News is broadcast Saturdays from 2 to 4 pm ET and available all week on demand at www.GCNLive.com. He is also a regular guest on Alex Jones, Rense, KPFK Midday News, KPFA Guns and Butter, Jack Blood (GCN), Power Hour, Meria Heller, and other talk radio programs. For details see the Authors on the Air *link at www.progressivepress.com. DVD's of Tarpley's slide and lecture presentations are available from Progressive Press: (1) Four events from 2001; (2) L.A, Grand Jury 10/04, NYC: 9/11 Truth, Key to Stop War, 3/05; (3) with Barrie Zwicker, Seattle, 4/06; (4) Arizona, 2/07; (5, 6) Irvine, 3/07, two DVDs; (7) Vancouver, June 2006; (8) San Diego, 7/7/07; (9) Pearl Harbor Lecture, 7/8/07; also Audio CD, Radio CKLN Toronto.*

9/11 Synthetic Terror: Made in USA

The new work by Webster Tarpley, co-author of *George Bush: The Unauthorized Biography*. Named "Bible of the 9/11 Truth Movement" because it provides *answers* as well as questions about 9/11, and *purpose*, invoking the urgency of 9/11 Truth as the only means to stop the mad rush to war on Iran.

9/11 Synthetic Terror has earned an enthusiastic reception as the only working model of the 9/11 plot: a rogue network of moles, patsies, and professional killer cells, operating in privatized paramilitary settings, and covered by corrupt politicians and corporate media.

Life-long intelligence expert Tarpley had already shown in his first book in 1978 that the Red Brigades, supposedly leftist terrorists, were actually patsies of the neo-fascist masonic P2 lodge, which was ensconced in the top drawers of Italian government and society.

STATE-SPONSORED FALSE-FLAG TERROR: THE ROGUE NETWORK
Covered by Controlled CORPORATE MEDIA
PATSIES FOOLS, FANATICS, FAKES, FALL GUYS, DOUBLES, DUPES, OSWALDS...
MOLES: DISINFO AGENTS WHO INFEST GOVERNMENT AND MEDIA, HANDLERS.
HIT MEN: PROS, TECHNICIANS, SAS, MERCENARY KILLERS: *REAL* TERRORISTS.
PRIVATIZED COMMAND CENTER

Thus *9/11 Synthetic Terror* cuts quickly to the chase. After highlighting salient impossibilities in the official "myth of the 21st century," he shows how overwhelming evidence of a covert false-flag or "own-goal" attack on 9/11 also fits the historical template of state-sponsored terrorism.

So the simplistic Big Lie – that "it's paranoid to think 'our own government' could do it" – is exploded. Only state actors have the resources for spectacular terrorism. The subtitle *"Made in USA"* rejects spurious leads to Pakistan or Saudi Arabia, muddled "blowback" theories and fantasies of "heroic" terrorism.

9/11 Synthetic Terror places 9/11 in the context of an ongoing Cold War, with an eye-opening new overview of modern history and geopolitics. A blockbuster of 512 pages, for only $17.95.

"Brilliantly and most sovereignly written; can't stop reading. Webster delivers a devastating judgment. Congratulations! I endorse *9/11 Synthetic Terror* wholeheartedly." – Andreas Von Bülow, former German Minister of Defence, Science and Technology.

"The strongest of the 770+ books I have reviewed here at Amazon… without question, the most important modern reference on state-sponsored terrorism." – Robert Steele, ex-CIA and Marine Intelligence officer, #1 non-fiction reviewer on Amazon.

Listen anytime to Tarpley's weekly talk show World Crisis Radio at http://www.gcnlive.com/On_Demand. He is a regular guest on Rense, Alex Jones, KPFK Midday News, KPFA Guns and Butter, Jack Blood, Power Hour, Meria Heller, and other talk radio programs. For details see the Authors on the Air link at www.progressivepress.com.

DVD's from Progressive Press